Lonely Planet Publications
Melbourne | Oakland | London | Paris

Martin Hughes,
Sarah Johnstone & Tom Masters

London

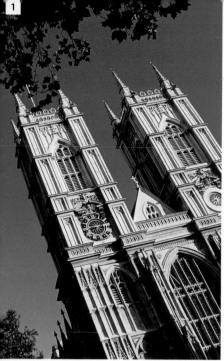

The Top Five

1 Glorious Architecture
Visit Westminster Abbey, one of the finest churches in Christendom (p125)
2 Fascinating Art
Explore Britart at the Saatchi Gallery (p157)
3 Stunning Views
See for miles atop the London Eye (p157)
4 Top Shops
Browse through the famous Harrods department store (p325)
5 Terrific Touring
See the sights on the top deck of a traditional red bus (p88)

Contents

Published by Lonely Planet Publications Pty Ltd
ABN 36 005 607 983

Australia Head Office, Locked Bag 1, Footscray
Victoria 3011, ☎ 03 8379 8000, fax 03 8379 8111
talk2us@lonelyplanet.com.au

USA 150 Linden St, Oakland, CA 94607
☎ 510 893 8555, toll free 800 275 8555
fax 510 893 8572, info@lonelyplanet.com

UK 72–82 Rosebery Ave, Clerkenwell, London,
EC1R 4RW ☎ 020 7841 9000, fax 020 7841 9001
go@lonelyplanet.co.uk

France 1 rue du Dahomey, 75011 Paris
☎ 01 55 25 33 00, fax 01 55 25 33 01
bip@lonelyplanet.fr, www.lonelyplanet.fr

© Lonely Planet 2004
Photographs © Neil Setchfield and as listed (p399), 2004

The Authors

MARTIN HUGHES

Martin was born and bred in Dublin where he dithered for five years in journalism and public relations before shifting to London. After some very odd jobs, he took off on a three-year World Tour, returning to London each summer to raise funds. He eventually settled in Melbourne, where he works as a freelance journalist and travel writer. He returns at least twice a year to London for cultural catch-ups and assignments.

Martin was the coordinating author of this book. He wrote the Introducing London, City Life (with assistance from Sarah Johnstone) and History chapters, and contributed to the Arts, Neighbourhoods, Eating, Drinking, Entertainment and Sleeping chapters.

SARAH JOHNSTONE

Sarah came to London soon after university, and 12 years later she's still there. A freelance journalist, Sarah has worked for *Reuters*, *Business Traveller* magazine and Virgin's in-flight magazine. Her work has also appeared in the *Times*, *Independent on Sunday* and the *Face*.

Sarah wrote the Architecture chapter and contributed to the City Life, Arts, Neighbourhoods, Eating, Drinking, Entertainment, Shopping and Sleeping chapters.

TOM MASTERS

Tom grew up in Buckinghamshire, moving to Bloomsbury at 18 to study Russian literature. He has had 10 London postcodes, although never one beginning with S. Tom has worked abroad in journalism and TV, but London's wonderful public transport system and cheap rent keep him coming back.

Tom wrote the Walking Tours, Excursions and Directory chapters, and contributed to the Neighbourhoods, Eating, Drinking, Entertainment, Shopping and Sleeping chapters.

PHOTOGRAPHER

Welsh-born Neil Setchfield has worked as a full-time travel photographer for the past 15 years. His work has appeared in over 100 newspapers and magazines throughout the world, as well as in food and guide books. In his spare time he drinks beer and laughs a lot – not always at the same time.

Neil is represented by Lonely Planet Images. Many of the images in this guide are available for licensing: www.lonelyplanet images.com.

Introducing London

The sun is shining brighter in London these days, and the English capital is aglow. It has always been a compelling capital but right now it's also one of the most dynamic hubs on earth, leading the vanguard in music, visual arts, fashion, film and, these days, even food. It's not the technicoloured swagger of the swinging '60s but London's back in the spotlight and it _is_ certifiably groovy.

This mammoth metropolis is a world in one city; at once exhilarating, irrepressible, intimidating, stimulating and brimming with spectacle and possibilities. It can be different things to different people, but these qualities are always in abundance, making London the place to be right now.

Not only is it home to magnificent historical architecture and such familiar landmarks as Big Ben, St Paul's Cathedral and Westminster Abbey, it's a cornucopia of cultural wealth that boasts some of the world's greatest museums and art galleries (treasures which, since 2002, are mostly ours for free). The London of Harrods, the Ritz, Buckingham Palace and Mayfair still charms with the decadence of a bygone era but these days London is riding on the crest of the wave and only looking forward.

Propelled by the energy, vitality and aspirations of a population made up of some 40 different ethnic groups, it's a tapestry of different cultures, unparalleled in complexity and colour. Home to between seven and 12 million inhabitants (depending on where you stop counting), London seduces some 30 million of us who tramp through it each year. While it receives all-comers with (usually) open arms, beneath the cosmopolitan veneer its own distinct personality remains intact. Amid the onslaught of globalisation, London struts proudly across the world stage.

Wandering through its rain-sodden streets is a unique experience. We take giddy delight in its icons: the open-backed red buses, black cabs, police bobbies and their hats, pinstriped workers and London Underground signs. We record sounds that ring in our ears long after our gig here is done: accents from around the world, the diesel engines of black cabs,

Lowdown

Population 7.2 million
Time zone Greenwich Mean Time
3-star double room £130
Coffee in the West End £1.75
Cheapest ride on the Tube £2
No-no Reference to 'Cool Britannia' – that was an international thing
Pint of lager £2.25
Best way to annoy a Londoner Stand on the left-hand side of a Tube escalator
Best view From Waterloo Bridge
Latest slang for cocaine 'Celebrity hairdresser' (need a trim?)

5

the disembodied voice of the newspaper vendor, toffs on their mobile phones – and the occasional 'Oi! Out of my facking way you Muppet!'

Luckily, whether you're looking for pubs once frequented by Charles Dickens, the soldiers with the big bearskin hats or the new Stella McCartney fashion store, you won't have to venture far from the core of the behemoth. And those sights that do require legwork are genuinely worth the effort – the Victorian Valhalla of Highgate Cemetery, the home of cricket at Lord's or the splendid Hampton Court Palace that so attracted King Henry VIII. Look hard enough and you'll find hidden gems like the eccentric Sloane's Museum, the gripping Cabinet War Rooms or the cutting-edge Design Museum – these could be highlights of your trip.

The centre is pocked with elegant squares and green expanses, and there are vast parks just a hop, skip and Tube ride away. Primrose Hill, Richmond Park and Hampstead Heath provide vast panoramic views of the city although none compares to the London Eye.

After dark, when Londoners aren't huddled around tables bantering in Victorian boozers, the city fizzes with creative energy, expressed through a bristling music scene, an incomparable club culture and mainstream arts the match of anywhere on the planet. The opportunities for being entertained in London these days are limited only by your spending and staying power.

London is not a place you can ever 'do'; it's evolving too quickly even for its occupants to fully grasp, never mind the time-challenged tourist. It will enthral you, seduce you and, on any given day of the week, probably lead you to a hangover. Experiencing London is not about ticking off the sights – it's about the conviviality and banter of a traditional pub, watching football on the box and spending hours over the Sunday newspapers. It's about a gig in Camden, a club in Brixton and a night at the opera. It's about a visit to the garden where Keats wrote his most famous poem, a glimpse of celebrity and finding respite in an elegant square. It's about the aromas from a stroll through Chinatown, a boat ride on the Thames and being told off for swinging around the pole of a double-decker bus. It's about being stunned by the history, awed by the architecture and amazed by the multiculturalism. It's about the unexpected delight of sunny days and small talk about miserable ones. It's about the choices you make at closing time. But most of all it's about leaving this book in your room now and then, and letting yourself be carried by the ebb, flow and rhythm of a city in perpetual motion.

Just make sure you mind the gap.

MARTIN'S TOP LONDON DAY

It starts sluggishly after Martin's Top London Night Before: scrambled eggs in a not-so-greasy Soho café with the *Guardian* newspaper for company. I wander over to the National Gallery and check out a *section* of its awesome collection, after which I take a moment to marvel at the transformation that is Trafalgar Square. Ambling through sunny St James's Park, I hope to attract the pelican that once trailed me through the garden like a cheeky street performer. I soak in the gravitas of Westminster, synchronise my watch with Big Ben and cross the Thames. Through the rejuvenated South Bank, I head for my own restoration at the juice stand in bustling Borough market where I say 'pukkah' a lot, like the market's most famous customer. At the Tate Modern, I admire the collection, architecture and view from the 7th-floor balcony café. I'll buy a T-shirt in Topman and a shirt at Zara, cheap and funky and not available at home. At the nearest bus stop, I'll wait for one of the open-backed Routemasters to roll along and cruise through the city in the front seat. As my stop approaches, I'll hang off the pole until the conductor tells me off. I settle in to an atmospheric pub for traditional fish and chips and real ales, and watch Arsenal beat United on the box 5-0. I head to a gig and the night becomes a blur.

Essential London
- National Gallery (p95)
- St James's Park (p122)
- South Bank (p155)
- Trafalgar Square (p95)
- Westminster (p125)

– *Martin Hughes*

City Life

City Life

LONDON TODAY

London, far from being the cold, impassive city it is so often lazily portrayed as, is a welcoming, pulsating and contradictory place to find yourself in. Literally and metaphorically. While the city sets international trends in fashion and the arts, the traditional London of Harrods, Buckingham Palace and the Ritz marches on alongside. At the risk of sounding like a pimp, it's this very juxtaposition of styles that gives London its vibrancy and its intensity. It's a city that thrives on its ever-changing elusiveness. But what's it like to live here?

Transport is the biggest bugbear for Londoners and the challenge Mayor Ken Livingstone is most keen to face. In 2003, he slapped a £5 tax on private cars entering the centre of town. The populace was in uproar and then, after a few months, begrudgingly patted the mayor on the back as the traffic jams disappeared and the average speed in the centre rose by 10km an hour. He has set about integrating the whole of London transport and has also brought much improvement in the bus service, but getting the creaking underground system into shape is a much more ambitious project. The Tube is fine, even efficient, until you come to rely on it. When you *need* to get somewhere, the chances are that somebody will have spilled a cup of tea somewhere and the whole line grinds to an infuriating halt. Ken reckons he's up to this challenge as well, although he has his hands full just trying to stop the central government from flogging the system off to the private sector.

Of course the city has its problems, just like any other. One of the most unsightly is the street litter. Some councils are better than others at tidying up – Soho gets a thorough scrubbing down every morning after the night before – but it's the litterbugs that we find most objectionable. It's galling to see people, possibly the majority, casually chuck rubbish out of car windows or toss their litter on the street. Get with it, London!

It's not just tourists who are stung by the expense of the place. Low-rise London can't accommodate all the people who want to live here and we're currently seeing the biggest migration of people *out* of London since WWII. Blue-collar workers like nurses and firemen are being forced out, with some having to commute several hours just to get to work. The waiting list for council housing might as well be endless, and most young Londoners struggle to stand still, never mind pull themselves up into the property market.

But it's not all doom and suburban gloom. There is no ghettoisation in London, and the haves live cheek by jowl with the have-nots. The mayor is also being proactive on this front (see Urban Planning & Development p34).

Nor is the exodus sucking the life out of the city; if anything, it's making the centre more of a social destination as well as a place to earn a crust. The push outwards has helped to create clusters that are like self-contained minicities on their own,

Hot Conversation Topics

- 'Who'll get voted out next?' Although *Big Brother*'s popularity has been waning, Britain is barmy about this show: almost twice as many votes were cast in the previous series than in the 2003 local elections. Even the people who don't watch the show hate it so much that they can't help talking about the grip it takes on the nation.

- Londoners love celebrity – even, it seems, if one's only claim to fame is claiming to fame. Why is Elizabeth Hurley an A-list celebrity, apart from the fact that she has large breasts and once dangled them in a dress held together by safety pins?

- 'Will we get the Olympics?' London, having put its millennium mishaps behind it, is making a bold bid to stage the 2012 Olympics. If successful, vast swathes of the East End will be regenerated. Competition is stiff: Paris, New York, Madrid, Moscow and Istanbul will also be waiting for the announcement in July 2005.

- 'How is he getting on at Real Madrid?' Britain is besotted with David Beckham – the gorgeous captain of the England football team, Britain's most talked about man, and 'Adonis' for short.

Liverpool St Station

while the demand for central locations has seen the regeneration of many areas and led to impressive urban renewal. London is looking better than ever: the centre is no longer choked by traffic; buildings have been scrubbed up and new ones erected; previously run-down areas like Clerkenwell, Shoreditch and Hoxton have been funked up; the long-neglected South Bank of the Thames has been transformed into a gallery and playground for the city; and a major development of Trafalgar Square has revealed the magnificent public space that was there all along.

One fairly recent feature of London – and no doubt a measure of its status and appeal – is the number of young Europeans choosing to relocate here (mostly propping up the restaurant and hotel service industry). As well as helping to create a more cosmopolitan European vibe, the arrival of this continental crew increases the chances of getting a decent coffee.

As sophisticated as they are in some regards, Londoners are also terribly undiscerning in others. So many chain pubs, cafés and restaurants have sprung up over the last decade that it's difficult to tell streets apart. Some are distinguished only by their width and depth of litter. The Starbucks chain is the most recent villain, having swamped the city and doing more than any one else to turn London into 'Generica', a place where all the urban landscapes look the same.

The spread of the chains continues because a cash-rich and time-poor populace is too busy staying ahead to think ahead. The economy is booming thanks to being outside the eurozone, making it all the more difficult for Londoners to understand the relative skimping of foreign tourists. Money flows here and there's a new-found confidence in the air. Despite several millennium mishaps – a bridge that wobbled so much it had to be closed down, and the white elephant known as the Millennium Dome – Londoners have surprised even themselves in the zeal with which they forge ahead, confidently tossing their hat in the ring to host the 2012 Olympics.

Londoners also give a damn. Although they'd be more likely to vote somebody out of *Big Brother* than into Parliament, despite a mainstream apathy – or perhaps propelled by it – London still has a sizable, active corps of radicals ready to take to the streets and challenge the status quo. Between one and two million people marched in 2003 to protest against the imminent US/British-led invasion of Iraq. Protests, rallies and assemblies are part of the fabric of life in this city.

What's amazing is that the capital – ancient and modern, sprawling and compact, angry and indifferent, stolidly English and increasingly multicultural – works quite as well as it does. It is a lesson in life for some and a rite of passage for others. The music of the city will resound in your ears long after you've left.

CITY CALENDAR

London's charms don't depend on the weather or time of year, although you'll obviously have a brighter time of it in summer when there are festivals galore and the mood is relentlessly upbeat. Spring and autumn are good times for a peek, with softer showers and thinner crowds. Winter's all cold, wet and dark, although if you're after outdoor pleasures, you'll have them largely to yourself.

For a full list of events in and around London, look out for the LTB's bimonthly *Events in London* and its *Annual Events* pamphlet. You can also check the website at www.londontouristboard.com or call the **London Line** (☎ 09068 663344).

JANUARY

NEW YEAR'S CELEBRATIONS
Countdown to midnight at Trafalgar Square – London's biggest bash. If you can get up the following morning, the mayor of Westminster leads 10,000 musicians and street performers through central London, from Parliament Square to Berkeley Square, in the lively London Parade.

INTERNATIONAL BOAT SHOW
Excel, Docklands; www.bigblue.org.uk
Early January sees this long-running exhibition of all things aquatic.

LONDON ART FAIR
Business Design Centre, Islington;
www.londonartfair.co.uk
Over 100 major galleries participate in this contemporary art fair, now one of the largest in Europe, with thematic exhibitions, special events and the best emerging artists.

CHINESE NEW YEAR
Chinatown; www.chinatown-online.co.uk
In late January/early February, Chinatown fizzes, crackles and pops in this colourful street festival, which includes a Golden Dragon parade and eating and partying aplenty.

FEBRUARY

PANCAKE RACES
Spitalfields Market, Covent Garden and Lincoln's Inn Fields
On Shrove Tuesday, in late February/early March, you can catch pancake races and associated silliness at various venues around town.

MARCH

HEAD OF THE RIVER RACE
Thames, from Mortlake to Putney; www.horr.co.uk
Some 400 crews participate in this colourful annual boat race, held over a 7km course.

APRIL

LONDON MARATHON
Greenwich Park to the Mall; www.london-marathon.co.uk
Some 35,000 masochists cross London in the world's biggest road race.

OXFORD & CAMBRIDGE BOAT RACE
From Putney to Mortlake; www.theboatrace.org
Big crowds line the banks of the Thames for this annual event, where two of the country's most famous universities go oar-to-oar and hope they don't sink (again).

MAY

ROYAL WINDSOR HORSE SHOW
www.royal-windsor-horse-show.co.uk
Prestigious five-day equestrian event attended by royalty, gentry and country folk.

CHELSEA FLOWER SHOW
Royal Hospital Chelsea; www.rhs.org.uk
The world's most renowned horticultural show attracts green fingers from near and far.

JUNE

ROYAL ACADEMY SUMMER EXHIBITION
Royal Academy of Arts; www.royalacademy.org.uk
Beginning in June and running through August, this is an annual showcase of works submitted by artists from all over Britain, gratefully distilled to a thousand or so pieces.

BEATING THE RETREAT
Horse Guards Parade, Whitehall
A warm-up for the Queen's birthday, this pompously patriotic evening event involves military bands and much beating of drums.

TROOPING OF THE COLOUR
Horse Guards Parade, Whitehall
The Queen's birthday (she was born in April but the weather's better in June) is celebrated with much flag-waving, parades, pageantry and noisy flyovers.

Only in London

Hot Cross Bun Ceremony (Widow's Son Pub, 75 Devon St; Good Friday) This nostalgic ceremony commemorates a Good Friday many moons ago when a mother hung a hot cross bun – believed to bring luck – in a basket waiting for her son to return from his first sea voyage. He never returned but every year on the same date she hung another bun in the unwavering hope that someday he would. When she died and her cottage was demolished, the collection of stale buns passed to a pub that was built on the site, where the tradition continues.

Changing of the Quill (St Andrew Undershaft Church, St Mary Axe; 6 April; ☎ 7283 2231) Every three years (next one in 2005) there is a memorial service to John Stow, the first chronicler of London, who is buried here. A learned address is made to his monument and the Lord Mayor replaces the quill in its hand, presenting the old one to the child who has written the best essay on London.

Dogget's Coat & Badge Race (On the Thames from London Bridge to Chelsea; July – dates vary according to tide) Thomas Dogget, an Irish actor and theatre manager, organised this race in 1715 to be contested by novice watermen who, at the time, were the equivalent of modern-day London cabbies. Rowers still compete for Dogget's coat and badge – although cash prizes are also awarded to their clubs – and the winner is feted in a traditional ceremony in the Banqueting Room of the Fishmongers' Hall, led by two mace bearers.

Swan Upping (Third week of July) Held along stretches of the River Thames, this is the annual census of the swan population and dates from the 12th century, when the Crown claimed ownership of all mute swans, a noble delicacy at the time. By tradition, scarlet uniforms are worn by The Queen's Swan Marker and Swan Uppers, and each boat flies appropriate flags and pennants. 'Upping' means turning the birds upside-down to tag them or check whether their beaks are marked or not. In the 15th century, the Crown granted ownership of swans with marked beaks to the Vitners and Dyers companies.

Horseman's Sunday (Hyde Park Crescent; September) A vicar on horseback blesses more than 100 horses outside the Church of St John & St Michael, W2, followed by horse jumping in Kensington Gardens.

Punch & Judy Festival (Covent Garden Piazza; late September/early October) In the twilight of summer, puppet fans gather in the tourist heart of London for much Punching and Judying (not to mention crocodiles and policemen) in the very spot the first performance took place.

Pearly Harvest Festival Service (St Martin-in-the-Fields, Trafalgar Square; www.pearlies.co.uk; early October) Over 100 Pearly Kings and Queens (see p14) attend a service here in their full, sparkly clobber, followed by much slapping of thighs, posing for photographs and a right royal knees up.

ARCHITECTURE WEEK
www.architectureweek.org.uk
Late June is about exploring the city's architecture and urban landscapes with various events across town.

WIMBLEDON LAWN TENNIS CHAMPIONSHIPS
www.wimbledon.com
The world's most splendid tennis event – weather permitting – is as much about strawberries, cream and tradition as smashing balls.

JULY
CITY OF LONDON FESTIVAL
www.colf.org
Two weeks of top-quality music, dance and theatre held in some of the finest buildings, churches and squares in the financial district.

PRIDE PARADE
www.prideparade.org
Gay and lesbians paint the town pink in this annual extravaganza, featuring a parade and a huge evening party in Hyde Park (locations may change).

GREENWICH & DOCKLANDS INTERNATIONAL FESTIVAL
www.festival.org
Every weekend in July, you can catch (mostly) free and outdoor dance, theatre and music performances on either side of the Thames.

SOHO FESTIVAL
www.thesohosociety.org.uk
All sorts of shenanigans from a Waiter's Race to a spaghetti-eating contest and lots of food stalls at this charity fundraiser.

BBC PROMENADE CONCERTS (THE PROMS)
www.bbc.co.uk/proms
Two months of outstanding classical concerts at various prestigious venues. The last night is broadcast from Hyde Park.

RESPECT FESTIVAL
www.respectfestival.org.uk
A free outdoor music and dance festival (at changing venues), dedicated to promoting anti-racism and featuring big-name headline acts.

AUGUST
NOTTING HILL CARNIVAL
www.thecarnival.tv
Europe's biggest – and London's most vibrant – outdoor carnival is a celebration of Caribbean London, featuring music, dancing, costumes and a little street crime over the summer Bank Holiday weekend.

GREAT BRITISH BEER FESTIVAL
www.gbbf.org
If you think there's an oxymoron in the name, have your perceptions merrily overturned by joining tens of thousands in downing a wonderful selection of local and international brews.

SEPTEMBER
THAMES FESTIVAL
www.thamesfestival.org
Celebrating London's greatest natural asset, the River Thames, this cosmopolitan festival provides fun for all the family with fairs, street theatre, music, food stalls, fireworks, river races and a spectacular Lantern Procession.

GREAT RIVER RACE
From Ham House to the Isle of Dogs;
www.greatriverrace.co.uk
Barges, dragon boats and Viking longships race 35km to contest these traditional boat championships.

LONDON OPEN HOUSE
www.londonopenhouse.org
For a weekend in late September, Joe Public is invited in to see over 500 heritage buildings throughout the capital that are normally off-limits.

OCTOBER
DANCE UMBRELLA
www.danceumbrella.co.uk
London's annual festival of contemporary dance features five weeks of performances by British and international dance companies at venues across London.

TRAFALGAR DAY PARADE
Trafalgar Square
Commemorating Nelson's victory over Napoleon, marching bands descend on Trafalgar Square to lay a wreath at Nelson's Column.

LONDON FILM FESTIVAL
National Film Theatre & various venues; www.lff.org.uk
The city's premier film event attracts big overseas names and is an opportunity to see more than 100 British and international films before their cinema release.

NOVEMBER
LONDON TO BRIGHTON VETERAN CAR RUN
Serpentine Road; www.vccofgb.co.uk/lontobri
Pre-1905 vintage cars line up and rev up at dawn in Hyde Park before racing to Brighton.

STATE OPENING OF PARLIAMENT
House of Lords, Westminster; www.parliament.co.uk
The Queen visits Parliament by state coach amid gun salutes to summon MPs back from their long summer recess.

GUY FAWKES NIGHT (BONFIRE NIGHT)
Commemorating Guy Fawkes' attempt to blow up Parliament in 1605, bonfires and fireworks light up on 5 November. Primrose Hill, Alexander Palace, Clapham Common and Crystal Palace Park are the places to aim for.

LORD MAYOR'S SHOW
www.lordmayorsshow.org
In accordance with the Magna Carta of 1215, the newly elected Lord mayor of the City of London travels in a state coach from Mansion House to the Royal Courts of Justice to seek their approval. The floats, bands and fireworks that accompany him were added later.

REMEMBRANCE SUNDAY
Cenotaph, Whitehall
Everyone wears a red poppy and the Queen, prime minister and other notables lay wreaths at the Cenotaph to remember those who died in two world wars.

DECEMBER
LIGHTING OF THE CHRISTMAS TREE & LIGHTS
Some celebrity is carted in to switch on all the festive lights that line Oxford, Regent and Bonds streets, and a huge Norwegian spruce is set up in Trafalgar Square.

CULTURE

IDENTITY

Don't come looking for a typical Londoner because there's no such thing. Although the populace is primarily white and Anglo-Saxon, more than a quarter of locals are from different ethnic backgrounds and 'typical Londoners' in the 21st century are as likely to wear a turban as a bowler hat, a burqa as a pin-stripe suit or an LA Lakers shirt as a Ben Sherman. London is in a constant state of flux, which is why it's such a vigorous place.

Throughout history, refugees and immigrants arrived in dribs and drabs. Pockets of distinction soon emerged as groups of Irish, Greek, Chinese, Turks and Jews set up home. Then in the 1950s, Britain opened the gates and ushered in a huge influx of people from the former colonies of the Empire, particularly from the Indian subcontinent, the West Indies and Africa.

Naturally, the new arrivals clustered together and pretty soon areas took on the colours of their new ethnicity as the settlers sought to preserve the customs and way of life: Sikhs in Southall, Bengalis in Shoreditch, Chinese in Soho, West Indians in Brixton, Africans in Hackney, Irish in Kilburn, Vietnamese in Hackney, Jews in Golders Green and Cypriots, Turks and Kurds in Stoke Newington. The walls came down as successive generations integrated and now the boundaries, where they exist at all, are blurry at best. Londoners these days can be of any colour and follow any creed.

Roughly 12 million people live in Greater London, some 7.2 million of them close to the centre. Population is growing by 1.4% per year and the average age is decreasing (36, compared with 38 nationally). London's nonwhite population is the largest of any European city. With an estimated 33 ethnic communities and a staggering 300 languages being spoken, it's no empty boast when the mayor calls London 'a world in one city.'

It's virtually impossible to generalise about a city so big and diverse, but we'll give it our best shot. The most common preconceptions about Londoners being reserved, inhibited and stiflingly polite are codswallop. Much is made about their silence on the Tube, although we don't know of any metro in the world where the passengers are high-fiving and breaking into song. It's true that they are polite and love a queue, which are two of the best things about them (particularly when you're seeing the sights). London is one of the most crowded places on the planet. What's more, it often feels like it's on the verge of a breakdown so it's only natural that people should modify their behaviour in order to cope.

They are not necessarily reserved, although like most big-city dwellers, they are dashing around in their own little worlds with things to do and people to see. They're 'twenty-four sev...' – too busy to even finish that sentence, never mind notice tourists. At the same time, they'd never refuse a request for help and when you do befriend a Londoner you'll have a couch to sleep on any time you want.

They're a tolerant bunch, unfazed by outrageous dress or behaviour. This tolerance generally means only low levels of chauvinism, racism, sexism or any other 'ism' you can think of. The much-publicised racial tensions of Northern England haven't existed in London for decades. The annual London Pride in late June/early July is a sparkling celebration of gay culture that passes off without incident, and London's

Underground Etiquette

Given the vital role it plays in London life, it's natural that the Tube should have its own code of customs. Not adhering to the code is how we annoy Londoners most. Here's your guide on how to fit in.

Don't stop to get your bearings as soon as you get through the turnstiles. Absolutely under no circumstances should you stand still on the left hand side of the escalator; it's reserved for people far busier than you and others keen to exercise and tone their bottoms. Do move along the platform and don't point at the little furry things running along the lines. When the train pulls in, stand aside until passengers have got off. Under pain of death, do *not* offer your seat to the elderly, disabled, pregnant or faint; instead, you should bury your head in a book and pretend you can't see them. It's fine, even courteous, to leave a newspaper behind in the morning but it's your bloody litter in the evening. Do mind the gap.

London Royalty

The cockney monarchs are the Pearly Kings & Queens, the sparkly spectacles that wear tens of thousands of studded buttons sewn into their clothes. A 19th-century barrow boy by the name of Henry Croft, keen to raise money for the poor, began sewing pearly buttons into his garments to attract attention. Others soon followed pearly suit and a tradition was born. Today's pearlies, often descendants of the originals, work for charities and gather at St Martin-in-the-Fields Church in Trafalgar Square in early October for their annual festival (www.pearlies.co.uk) to sing songs, speak in slang, pose for photographs and slap their thighs a lot.

history of absorbing wave after wave of new immigrants and refugees speaks for itself.

In a city this big, though, you won't have to look far to see the exact opposite of all we've just said. The image of the English football hooligan still rings true, although gangs of lads and lots of beer are recipes for loutish behaviour in any culture. There are pockets of bigotry all over the capital, but you'll encounter few problems in tourist London as long as you don't get 'lippy' with geezers or 'take liberties' (get too familiar). For much of the year, Monday to Friday is about work, drudge, commuting and television – Friday night and Saturday are for partying, and Sunday's about hangovers, newspapers, roast lunches and football on the box. Many Londoners are militant, rail against injustices and join demos, although more again are likely to ponder the same issues quietly over a pint.

The only thing they like more than celebrity is the backlash. It's sport to trumpet someone as the next big thing, wait until he's at the point of greatness and then groan 'he used to be good but now he's shite'. They're constantly in pursuit of what's hip, trying to keep ahead of the pack. Discount airliners have changed their lives and weekend breaks in European capitals are their safety valves. They love their music, arts, literature, television and football.

They're quietly assured right now. They complain a lot, particularly about London, but they wouldn't dream of living anywhere else.

LIFESTYLE

On a good day, Londoners might flatter themselves that because material girl Madonna chose to move here this city must have the best lifestyle on the planet. On a bad day, stuck on yet another crowded tube train and late for work, harsher realities begin to filter through. London is an exhilarating city, but also pricey and congested, and without Madonna's millions, things are sometimes going to get tough.

Making a life for yourself here can feel like running for one of the city's old-fashioned red Routemaster buses. Sometimes you make it to the running board at the back, the traffic suddenly clears and, with a jolt, you're on a wonderful journey. Sometimes you make it, panting, through the open back door, only to find everything's stalled. And occasionally, despite a lung-bursting sprint, the bus takes off without you and you're left coughing on fumes and waving your fist impotently while trying not to fall under the wheels of a black cab.

Even those already on the bus aren't sitting that pretty. Londoners work the longest hours in the European Union and live in its most expensive city. Disposable income doesn't come cheap. While the Office of National Statistics puts the average London salary at £35,000 a year (or £26,000 for those in their late 20s), a recent survey shows first-time home buyers are looking at an average price of £188,000 for a property. That's difficult when banks only want to lend you three times your income. And it's even more difficult to save for the necessary £42,000 deposit when, according to the National Housing Federation, renting a one-bedroom flat takes 44% of an average worker's net income (and a three-bedroom flat, 78%). Only those who work in the City – or those earning an equivalent salary of between £60,00 and £200,000 – don't have to struggle, and the stock-market recession in recent years has unsettled even some of those high earners.

Key workers, like nurses, ambulance drivers and teachers, often earn less than £24,000 a year and sometimes find it so costly to live in the capital, they commute from outside. Middle-class parents suffer guilt about not backing the increasingly chaotic public education system when they send their precious offspring to private schools, and young career-minded singletons spend such long hours in the office that enrolling with dating agencies and speed-dating is now the thing to do. These are the issues gnawing at different sectors of the London populace, so why do any of the 7 million inhabitants live here?

Why indeed? Because they want to live in world-famous London. Because it's Britain's economic motor. Because it's not just the detritus of fast-food wrappers, advertising flyers and garbage bags full of beer bottles at your doorstep, it's the unrivalled outpourings of thousands of years of human culture. This city of London is one of the most vibrant, multi-culturally diverse spots on earth, where you can listen to any style of music or eavesdrop on conversations in nearly 100 languages. 'No city in the world is more internationalised,' mayor Ken Livingstone has said. And he's right.

Even with some 30% of its area given over to parkland, it doesn't come close to making it into Europe's top 10 cities for quality of life. However, if you live in London, you soon get used to being able to see great art any day of the week. You soon get accustomed to being able to order a Peruvian breakfast, before going local with a jacket potato for lunch, then returning to a global menu – Indian, Greek, Russian or Caribbean – for dinner.

Londoners are certainly not immediately friendly and people don't chat to each other in shops or on the street. But they make up for it around the water cooler at work, where gossip might centre around TV shows like *The Sopranos*, whatever is in iconoclastic celebrity magazine *Heat* or who's just got married or pregnant in the office (celebrities you see in *Heat* have made both of those pastimes quite trendy). With such great London pubs and ales to explore, going for an after-hours drink with workmates, as well as friends, is usually a regular event. In fact, Londoners, only slightly less than countryside Britons, have elevated social drinking to an art form. At less poverty-stricken times of the year (ie not January), some of them are liable to spend more time in their local than in the home that's eating up 44% of their budget.

Londoners walk blithely past well-known faces from television, film or the music business, because they see them fairly regularly. Which is why a lot of celebrities love it here, and why you see them more.

The distances across the city, and the poor public transport, mean people tend to find an area that suits them and stick to it. But when it comes to deciding what suits you, you are spoilt for choice. How about indie-music Camden? Fashion-conscious Notting Hill? Literary Hampstead? Cutting-edge Hoxton? Or arty, sleazy, gay Soho? You'll eventually find your niche.

But just because London is one of the most genuinely tolerant cities on earth doesn't mean it's totally devoid of racism or homophobia, and if you live in London, there are undoubtedly other downsides. The crumbling infrastructure has led to poverty and ultimately to crime, although because rich and poor often live side by side, there aren't any real ghettos. Thankfully, too, a marked 38% rise in muggings, mobile-phone theft and other street offences in the 12 months to March 2002 has since been cut back at least 16% by a Metropolitan Police initiative.

Still, no one comes looking for neatly trimmed lanes and white picket fences in London anyway. But you should fit in well if you're prepared to muster all your energy in hot pursuit of that red London bus. Isn't that it pulling into the curb right now?

Kensington (p133)

FOOD

Pardon the pun, but food is hot in London these days, and dining out is suddenly cooler than clubbing. Thanks to a dedicated band of foodies – and a slightly over-excited media with nothing better to do – there's been a revolution in the restaurants of London in the last five or six years; the purveyors of stodge were lined up against the wall, stripped of their pinnies and replaced by a slick and savvy new corps of young chefs. Even the most seasoned gourmet can't fail to be impressed.

Eating out here can be as diverse, stylish and satisfying as anywhere else on the planet these days. It's no exaggeration to call London a foodie destination, as its top restaurants can hold their own with the best in the world. Designer eating is all the rage, with restaurant openings attracting as much glitz and glamour as fashion parades, and sightings of Gordon Ramsay or Jamie Oliver turning normally sensible women into scatterbrains. New restaurants appear almost daily, and you can hardly open a menu without elbowing some celebrity chef or renowned restaurateur.

All this mightn't sound terribly exciting – 'World Capital Offers Reasonable Chance of Enjoyable Meal' is hardly the stuff that sells newspapers – unless you've endured the monumental dreadfulness that *was* British food. London is, after all, the capital of a nation that gave the world beans on toast, mushy peas and chip butties. Whereas before, we visited London *in spite* of the food, these days you might find it's one of the star attractions.

You can still get greasy fries, overcooked vegetables and traditional British stodge (particularly in pubs), but with chefs absorbing the influences of this most cosmopolitan of cultures, you're more likely to get the world on your plate – anything from *agedashi* to *zahtar*. Look hard enough and you'll find some 70 different cuisines, a reflection of London's multicultural wherewithal. A huge variety of ethnic food is now consumed by everyone – tandooris from the Indian subcontinent, kebabs from Turkey and Cyprus, chicken Kievs from Ukraine, borscht from Poland, *injera* from Eritrea, falafel from the Middle East, dim sum from China, sushi from Japan. Pizza and pasta are the staples of every London high street, and curry remains the de facto national dish. And the good news is that Londoner's newfound appreciation of food has permeated every rung of the culinary ladder.

But it's not just dining out that's got Londoners in the mood – food is suddenly interesting, and they're talking about it, being more adventurous in their own kitchens and more discerning when they shop. Farmers' markets have sprung up all over the place, tantalising shoppers with fruit and vegetables that taste remarkably like fruit and vegetables did in the days before supermarkets ran the world. The bad press received by the British cow focussed minds on the joys of organic produce and there's now a plethora of chemical-free producers,

Top 10 Books on London Culture & Society

- *18 Folgate Street* – Dennis Severs
- *Guide to Ethnic London* – Ian McAuley
- *London: A Biography* – Peter Ackroyd
- *London, A Social History* – Roy Porter
- *London in the 20th Century: A City and its People* – Jerry White
- *London Perceived* – VS Pritchett
- *London, The Unique City* – Steen Eiler Rasmussen
- *Pull No More Bines: My East End* – Gilda O'Neill
- *Sin City: London in Pursuit of Pleasure* – Giles Emerson
- *Soft City* – Jonathan Raban

The London café experience (p225)

grocers, markets, cafés and restaurants. Suspicion also swelled the ranks of the meat-free brigade, and there are now several gourmet vegetarian dining options.

The bad news, folks, is that all this comes at a price, and the blossoming of the London food scene does not equate to value for money. Unless you're in the know or have a good guide (nudge, nudge) you generally have to dig pretty deep to eat well, although, even then, choosing a restaurant can be a hit-and-miss affair. You could as easily drop £30 on a 'modern European' meal that tastes like it came from a can as spend a fiver on an Indian dish that makes your palate spin and your heart sing (so follow our recommendations in the Eating chapter).

Ask any Londoner what they like most about their city, and the diversity of food will be near the top of every list. It must be said, though, that the gastronomy isn't nearly as good as locals reckon; it's just 10 times better than it used to be. And we don't have the heart to tell them that they were the last to join the revolution.

City Life – Culture

Traditional English Tucker

Although English food has never exactly been welcomed at the world table, it does have its moments, particularly a Sunday lunch of roast beef and Yorkshire pudding or a cornet of fish and chips eaten on the hoof.

The best place to sample London soul food is in the pub, where menus feature the likes of bangers and mash (sausages served with mashed potatoes and gravy), Shepherd's pie (a baked dish of minced lamb and onions topped with mashed potatoes), an assortment of pies and the ploughman's lunch (thick slices of bread served with chutney, pickled onions and Cheddar or Cheshire cheese). Old reliables on the dessert tray include bread-and-butter or steamed puddings, sherry trifle and the alarmingly titled 'spotted dick', a steamed suet pudding with raisins that has now been rechristened 'Spotted Richard' by the supermarket giant Tesco for reasons, it says, of propriety.

The most English of dishes, though, is fish and chips: cod (rare these days), plaice or haddock dipped in batter, deep fried and served with chips doused in vinegar and sprinkled with salt. American chains threaten traditional shops but there are still a few gems around, such as Rock & Sole Plaice in Covent Garden (p227) and the North Sea Fish Restaurant in Bloomsbury (p228).

The staple lunch for many Londoners, from the middle of the 19th century until just after WWII, was a pie filled with spiced eel (then abundant in the Thames) and served with mashed potatoes, liquor and a parsley sauce. Nowadays, the pies are usually meat-filled and the eel served smoked or jellied as a side dish. The best places to try this are Manze's near Bermondsey Market (p333), Castle's in Camden Town (p250) and Goddards Pie House in Greenwich (p246).

The Top Table

The concept of celebrity chefs is relatively new to London but, boy, has it taken off. Here are a few to look out for.

Gordon Ramsay The current bad boy of the crop and possibly the finest chef London has ever seen. He was recently awarded a third Michelin star for his eponymous Chelsea restaurant, but is as famous for his temper, tantrums and denigration of fellow chefs as he is for exquisite creations.

Jamie Oliver The kitchen pin-up boy, Oliver wowed food fans with his TV series, *The Naked Chef*, so-called because the recipes were pared back and made simple. He lays on the cheeky, cockney patois too thick but seems to be an all-round top geezer. In 2003, he opened a new restaurant called Fifteen (p235), where he took 15 underprivileged youngsters and trained them – in theory at least – into professional chefs to work under him.

Nigella Lawson Nobody has done more to get men into in cooking than this self-trained TV chef whose voluptuous curves and finger-licking sensuality attract as much attention as what she can do with a rrrrrrrrrack of lamb.

17

FASHION
Britannia Waives the Rules

The thing about London is its constant evolution, where 'hot' fast becomes 'not' depending on who moves where, wears what, eats what, where, and with whom. Just one wrong move, bad name, wrong chain store or bad frock can kill the vibe, and a once-cool zone on the London Underground is boarded up and abandoned forever.

Take Neale St in Covent Garden, once one of the hottest streets in the city, with door after door of creative and exciting stores, pumping with style and energy; now it's now little more than a street full of shoe and sport chain stores. Saving a shred of its reputation are a few little side streets cutting across it, containing the last remaining traces of past style, with stores like Duffer of St George (p319), Mooks, Slam City Skates or Space NK (p319), a new-age-type concept 'mall' with a few good, small boutique stores like Paul Frank and Hope & Glory.

Currently riding on a high again for its fashion, London has some of the hottest new talent rubbing (padded) shoulders with several old faithfuls. Often born of the prestigious 'St Martins School of Art' – incubators for the likes of John Galliano, Stella McCartney and Alexander McQueen – this 'British Fashion Pack' is creative, original and often controversial. Big fashion houses like Chanel, Givenchy and Chloe snap up the hottest new talent. Young designers are directed into a new future while themselves leading the way and challenging all that is safe. Love it or hate it, they keep the rest of the fashion world on its toes and celebrities like Sadie Frost, Gwyneth Paltrow and Kate Moss well dressed.

St Martins

Most of the stars of the British fashion industry have passed through the rather shabby doors of St Martins on Charing Cross Rd, the world's most famous fashion college. Founded in 1854, Central St Martins School of Art & Design – to give its rather cumbersome and correct title – began life as a place where cultured young people went to learn to draw and paint. In the 1940s, a fashion course was created and within a few decades aspiring designers from around the world were scrambling to get in. Courses are more than one hundred times oversubscribed these days and the college has faced some criticism for admitting names over talent (a famous Beatles daughter, to name just one). St Martins' graduate shows – for which Stella had friends Naomi Campbell and Kate Moss model – are one of the highlights of the fashion calendar and are ALWAYS shocking, making huge statements – be they good, bad or ridiculous.

The less-conspicuous Royal College of Art only takes postgraduates and its fashion course is just as old and almost as successful as St Martins. Its alumni are said to provide the backbone of some of the world's most prestigious fashion houses.

Off the catwalk, London is currently riding on the 'Cool Britannia' vibe it enjoys overseas, all that is vintage, all that is heritage, all that is the 'New Mod'. Carnaby St was the original home of the British 1960s: pop culture, mods, Scooter Boys, Twiggy. It has recently been cleaned up and reborn after decades of tacky tourist gift stores paying homage to the worst elements of London. Now they're mostly gone and have been replaced with concept stores for the likes of Puma, Ben Sherman, Fred Perry and Lambretta, all of which are vintage street/sport brands, supported by ska boys and skinheads of the past, and carried on today with the new mods – bands like Oasis, Blur and Coldplay to name a few.

Also on this British heritage rebirth vibe are labels like Burberry, Pringle and Hacket. Originally classic Hooray Henry/Country Weekend style, they've now been adopted by the new 'Gentry Geezer', a strange hybrid of scooter-riding, lager-swilling, golf-playing,

London shop window (p318)

football-hooligan, cashed-up-wide-boy and Lock, Stock and Two Smoking Barrel types. The epitome of this geezer is Guy Ritchie (Mr Madonna) or Jason Statham, a cheeky, chirpy cockney with an estate in the country and a South Kensington town house. Combining the four-wheel drive Jeep with a mountain bike in the city streets – a bizarre mix of all that's country with all that's concrete.

Sitting alongside these are the traditional 'Savile row' boys, wearing a 'Gieves and Hawkes' high-brake lean-cut suit and stovepipe pants, just a touch too short to reveal an elastic-ankled 'Church' dealer boot. Add a cutaway collar and monogrammed business shirt with a full Windsor knot in a silk tie. It's a slightly dapper old London city look, supported by the cream of British movie celebrities, the Primrose Hill dwellers Jude Law and Johnny Lee Miller, and that rare individual, the footballer-turned-movie-star, Vinnie Jones. This is where you'll see the slick understated statement makers, where labels like Gucci, Prada and Paul Smith fit into place.

The British fashion industry has always been more on the edge of younger, directional stuff, and never really established that very polished 'Gucci Slick'; the London equivalent is the bespoke men's tailoring of Savile Row. London has no history of real couture like Paris or Milan, where tastes in styles and fabrics are much more classic and refined. The market also shapes British fashion to a large extent; customers here are more likely to spend £100 on a few different bargains – hence the boom in outlet malls – while their sisters in Paris and Italy will blow the lot on one piece, which they'll wear regularly and well.

So London fashion has always been about 'wow', with a few old reliables keeping the frame in place and mingling with hot new designers who are often unpolished through lack of experience but bursting with talent and creativity. Many big global names watch the shows of these fledgling stars for influence and direction, then produce their much sharper and slicker variations of the same thing.

The fashion world sometimes makes fun of London because of its slightly amateur approach – take the London Fashion Week (see the boxed text) for example, with the tent, late shows, media hype and champagne for breakfast. It all creates a groovy kind of chaos that feels half-baked and slightly bonkers to the serious players. But this is London's signature, and local designers who try to emulate the slick polish of the Italian shows, or the generic nature of the American ones, can be sure they'll get annihilated in the press.

They will have their own unique style and it sits well on them. But just in case you were beginning to feel inferior or even shy about revealing your wardrobe here, remember that not all Londoners have this great style. Whenever you begin to feel a little intimidated, take heart in these two words: Elton John.

London Fashion Week

Each February and September, London Fashion Week fills the diaries of London's most stylish and well connected, who gather in a big tent to see the latest collections from over 100 local designers. Although the event is only a minor stop on the international fashion tour, it's wild, late, troubled and inspired – and known and loved for all of these qualities. Most of the shows are by invitation-only, but some events are open to the public. Check listings or www.londonfashionweek.co.uk if interested.

SPORT

England proudly gave the world many of its most popular games, including football, rugby, cricket and tennis. It rankles with the English, however, that the world took many of these sports and became better at them than the creators themselves. Having said that, England is a major world sporting power and London hosts a calendar of prestigious sporting events that would be the envy of any other city in the world. Londoners are generally potty about sport and are fiercely passionate about their teams, although they draw the line when it comes to actually participating. There is no one team in any major sport that represents the whole of London.

There is no dedicated sports newspaper, probably because the coverage from the dailies is so good. The *Daily Telegraph*, the *Times* and the *Guardian* all have particularly hefty back pages. The tabloids obviously go for the scandal but they are often the first to break major stories. The *Daily Sport*, by the way, is not a sports paper, unless photographs of glamour models wearing nothing but a pair of Arsenal socks count.

Football

Football was invented in England around the 12th century, when unruly mobs tore each other to shreds in pursuit of some kind of ball. Despite repeated royal bans, the ruffians kept playing until 1863 when the Football Association was founded and the formal rules of the contemporary game were adopted.

You may know this game as 'soccer', but calling it that won't endear you to the natives. (A public school boy coined the term 'soccer' in the 1880s. It was, and still is, common practice for these privileged chaps to abbreviate words while adding 'er' to the end. When asked if he wanted to play rugger – rugby – the student said he'd rather play soccer, a curious abbreviation of 'association'.) Football is by far the most popular sport in London, which is home to 14 teams playing in every division of the Nationwide League.

The season climaxes in May with the FA Cup final, traditionally played at Wembley Stadium, although it has been moved to Cardiff's Millennium Stadium in recent years while Wembley is being refurbished (it's due to reopen in 2005). This is the oldest football competition in the world, where, with a good run, amateur teams could get the opportunity to scalp the likes of Manchester United. Such romantic notions are at the cornerstone of the competition and the game in general, and the reason why football is the most popular game in London and the world.

The most successful clubs are Arsenal (the 'Gunners'), Chelsea (the 'Blues'), Tottenham Hotspur ('Spurs'), Charlton (the 'Addicks') and Fulham (the 'Cottagers'), all of which were in the top league, the Premiership, at the time of writing (West Ham – the 'Hammers' – will be back there soon). The Gunners and the Hammers are so-called because their original teams were drawn from munitions and ironworkers over a century ago, while Charlton got its nickname after its tradition of treating visiting teams to a fish supper after games – haddock became 'addick' in the local vernacular and the name stuck.

Arsenal, by far the biggest and most successful club, has been the only team to challenge Manchester United's dominance in recent years, nabbing the title in 2002. However, Russian billionaire Roman Abramovich bought Chelsea FC in the summer of 2003, and has spent more than £75m buying some of the world's best talent in an audacious bid to win the title.

The biggest rivalry in the city is between them and fellow north Londoners Tottenham Hotspur. Arsenal's fans were traditionally Irish and Greek, while Spurs' supporters were predominantly Jewish – the two have loathed each other since 1913 when Arsenal moved into the neighbourhood. The club will soon be moving from Highbury, the famous stadium it has occupied since then.

The other local derby is between Chelsea and Fulham, although there's not that much needle involved in this one because Fulham has only recently become a threat on the pitch. Local derbies that you *don't* want to go and see are first division Millwall against any other south London team – factions of their 'firm' are nutters and violence is common.

Despite having five or six teams in the top flight at all times, London has always played second fiddle to the north of England, the game's real stronghold. Between them, London clubs have only won 14 titles since the league began in 1863, with Arsenal claiming 11 of

London Dream Team

Goalkeeper
Carlo Cudicini (Chelsea) Italian pretty boy and great keeper.

Defenders
Sol Campbell (Arsenal) The rock in England's defence.

Steve Carr (Tottenham) Exciting Irish winger.

Alain Goma (Fulham) Classy French defender.

Midfielders
Juan Sebastian Veron (Chelsea) Sensational Argentinian, still to reach full potential in England.

Patrick Viera (Arsenal) Awesome powerhouse from France.

Gustavo Poyet (Tottenham) Tough-tackling, goal-scoring Uruguayan.

Robert Pires (Arsenal) Stylish French winger, one of the best in the Premiership.

Damien Duff (Chelsea) Mesmeric Irish midfielder.

Forwards
Thierry Henry (Arsenal) Goal scorer par excellence – in another league.

Robbie Keane (Tottenham) Slightly podgy, totally brilliant Irish striker.

Martin Hughes (Firhouse Celtic) Gifted winger, sadly underrated and tragically overlooked.

Dogs & Gee-Gees

Gambling is something close to the hearts of many Londoners, and even the Queen likes a little flutter every now and again. There's no better way to lose your money than horse racing, traditionally known as 'the sport of kings' and colloquially known as the gee-gees (child-speak for horses). There are several racecourses within a short drive of London if you fancy a day at the track. The flat-racing season lasts from April to September while the National Hunt (over fences) takes place from October to April. The Queen and her entourage turn up for Royal Ascot in June, while Derby Day at Epsom the same month is much more down-to-earth.

Although greyhound racing, the urban cousin of horse racing, was introduced from the US, it seems right at home in London as it combines three local passions: gambling, drinking beer and cheap entertainment. Walthamstow is the most popular place to watch eight dogs chasing a mechanical rabbit, and it's more fun than we'd care to admit.

them. Nevertheless, London is one of *the* greatest cities in Europe if you're a football fan, as some of the world's best players strut their stuff here and there are top games to see every week.

The season runs from mid-August to mid-May, although there are no matches the weekend before international games. However, it's virtually impossible for the casual fan to get a ticket for one of the top matches, and you're better off watching it in the pub, like most ordinary fans that can't afford the outrageous £20 to £60 ticket price. Alternatively, go and see a first division match and sense the atmosphere that many believe has been lost in the slick, new, family-entertainment Premiership.

English football reached its pinnacle in 1966 when Bobby Moore lifted the World Cup trophy for England at Wembley. It sank to its deepest low in the 1980s when fans rampaged across the Continent and all English clubs were banned from European competition. This, combined with two stadium disasters that cost the lives of 140 fans, spoiled the general public's appetite for the game.

Football was revolutionised in the early 1990s thanks to billions of pounds in TV money, slick marketing off the pitch and foreign flair on it. Author Nick Hornby set the ball rolling, so to speak, with his brilliant book *Fever Pitch*, the memoirs of a soccer fanatic. It brought credibility back to football, even made it hip, and pretty soon the stands were packed again. TV coverage improved beyond recognition, which was lucky because many ordinary fans were suddenly priced out of the game, an unfortunate by-product of its modernisation.

At many clubs now, fans can't get to see games unless they cough up for an expensive season ticket in the summer. And so a new pub culture has emerged, where drinking pints and watching big games in the company of charismatic commentator Andy Gray, is a regular Sunday afternoon and Monday night pastime (or mid-week if your liver's up to it). Most games, at least those featuring the less-glamorous teams, are played on the traditional Saturday afternoon.

English club football has underachieved in Europe (the big prize these days) over the last decade. There have been a few decent runs in competitions, but the only major success was Manchester United winning the Champions League in 1999. The England national team has also promised much but failed to deliver.

The big political issue facing football at the moment is the ever-widening gap between the giant clubs and the rest. Smaller clubs are gambling all they've got on reaching – and staying in – the Premiership and then risking bankruptcy when they don't. The runway of the nationwide league is littered with the carcasses of teams who gambled everything to get to the big time and failed. Many say the game is forgetting its roots.

Walthamstow Stadium (p312)

Rugby

Two different codes of rugby are played in Britain: rugby union and rugby league. Union is traditionally the privilege of the middle and upper classes, while league is predominantly played and supported by the workers. Predictably, then, London is the heartland of union and has four big teams: Harlequins, Saracens, London Wasps and London Irish. The main competitions are the Zurich Premiership and the terrifically exciting – and relatively new – Heineken Cup, contested by the top clubs in Europe. The season runs from August to May, and games are played Saturday and Sunday afternoons. Union has a big following among women, which has nothing at all to do with the physique of rugby players or the very social nature of the support.

The most important annual international competition is the Six Nations Tournament, which takes place in February/March and is contested by England, Scotland, Wales, Ireland, France and Italy. Each team plays alternate home and away matches, and plays each of the other teams only once during the competition. This is one sport that the English invented and *are* particularly good at; they've wiped the floor with the opposition in this comp over recent years, although they still trail behind the powerhouses of the southern hemisphere. They play at Twickenham in London, hallowed turf of English rugby. Unfortunately, unless you've got connections, it's nigh on impossible to get tickets to the internationals.

Rugby is believed to have originated in 1823 at Rugby School in Warwickshire, England, when a fellow by the name of William Ellis picked up the ball and ran with it during a football match and was chased by the other players.

Rugby league broke away in the 1890s. The rules are similar to union, although it's a bit more like the traditional sport of British Bulldog, where players barge their way through a wall of opponents to reach the other side. The London Broncos are the only team outside northern England, the heartland of the code.

Cricket

During the days of the Empire, the English brought the game of cricket to the colonies, thrashing the pants off the savages while teaching them how to be gentlemen. The tables have turned, and these days the likes of Australia and India give England a regular thumping.

If you're unfamiliar with the rules and have only seen bits and pieces of the game, you may see cricket as a form of English torture (and if there was ever a case to be made for TV highlights, surely this is it). On the other hand, if you're patient and learn to appreciate the intricacies of the game, you may find it immensely rewarding and think watching every single ball of a five-day test match is a perfectly good use of one's time. What's even more surprising to people who don't know a googly from an Internet search engine is that fans love following the cricket on the radio!

Tests are international matches lasting five days, and are regarded as the purist form of the sport. The one-day game, where each team bats once and faces a limited number of balls, is a fairly recent development – it's TV-friendly, more accessible for the uninitiated, and regarded as totally irrelevant by purists.

The England team tours each year and hosts at least one touring side from the rest of the cricket-playing world (primarily Australia, the Indian subcontinent, South Africa, Zimbabwe and the West Indies). Most keenly contested is the biannual test series against Australia, known as 'the Ashes'. (The name comes from a mock obituary published in the *Times* after a great Australian victory in 1882, which said that the 'body' of English cricket had been cremated and the ashes taken to Australia.)

Although the national team has been poor for much of the last decade, it is perpetually on the brink of a comeback and tickets for the big tests can still be difficult to come by unless you book in advance.

The teams that make up the main domestic competition in England are drawn from counties (or shires), disproportionately from the 'home counties' (southeast of England, around London). This is known as County Cricket and the season lasts from April to September. The world's best cricketers – Warne, McGrath, Gibbs, Muralitharan and Shoaib Akhtar among them – regularly come over and play for stints with the county teams.

Some of the original clubs established in the 18th century still survive today, including the famous Marylebone Cricket Club (MCC) based at Lord's (p188), the sport's spiritual home, in North London. Lord's is also home to Middlesex, one of London's two county cricket clubs. The Oval (p196) is home to the team of the moment, Surrey, and also hosts international fixtures.

Tennis

Wimbledon, that quintessentially English affair – which also happens to be the world's most famous tennis tournament – has been held in SW19 since 1877. In late June/early July, tennis fever grips London as the world's best players congregate for the sport's most prestigious event, and fans descend on Wimbledon for strawberries and cream, perhaps a little bit of sunshine, Cliff Richard singing (if you're particularly unfortunate), and high drama on the grass courts.

England – as you will gather if you're in London at this time – is desperate for a local winner, something it hasn't been able to celebrate since Fred Perry won in 1936 and Virginia Wade in 1977. Each year, the media hype for the great English hopes, Tim Henman and Greg Rusedski, goes into overdrive. (Well, for Tim anyway. Greg's brand of Englishness has a very thick Canadian accent.) Newspapers will go totally over the top when English players win their early round matches, plastering their sports pages with headlines suggesting 'this could be the one', and then quietly slumping back to reality when they're knocked out before the quarter finals.

For the best seats, you have to enter a public ballot (p312) between August and December of the previous year. If you don't plan so far in advance, you *can* get tickets at the venue during the tournament but the queues are exceedingly long, prices exorbitant and conditions cramped – you may end up thinking that Wimbledon is, ahem, a bit of a racket.

You can catch many of the top male players strutting their stuff at an annual warm-up tournament at the Queen's Club in Hammersmith, which takes place two weeks before Wimbledon.

MEDIA

London is in the eye of the British media, an industry comprising some of the best and worst of the world's television, radio and print media.

Newspapers

The only truly and exclusively London newspaper is the right-wing *Evening Standard*, a jingoistic tabloid that comes out in early and late editions throughout the day. Foodies should check out the restaurant reviews of London's most influential critic, Fay Maschler, while style aficionados shouldn't miss Friday's *ES magazine*, an indispensable guide to the city's cutting edge. *Hot Tickets* is a useful listings supplement on Thursday. The *Standard* also publishes an even 'liter' version of its stories in the freebie *Metro*, which is available at tube stations during the week.

Sports Without Strain

The English like their sports so much they even invented games they could play down the pub. The late 1980s was the heyday for darts, when entire arenas were turned into bars for major competitions, TV audiences were huge and the best players were household names. Internal divisions somewhat spoiled the sport but it's still shown on Sky Sports, where incomparable commentator Bill Waddell is famous for tearing the English to shreds and concocting his own language from the bits he could salvage.

Snooker is another sport that used to get massive TV audiences, although, on the face of it, you'd be hard-pressed to think of a duller spectacle. But trust us, close and important games can be as tense and exciting as a penalty shoot-out in the World Cup. The game still gets healthy TV audiences, largely down to entertaining players like rapscallion Londoner Ronnie O'Sullivan, the best player in the world.

National newspapers in England are almost always financially independent of any political party, although their political leanings are easily discerned. Rupert Murdoch is the most influential man in British media and his News Corp owns the *Sun*, the *News of the World*, the *Times* and the *Sunday Times*. As we went to press, there was impassioned debate about proposed new legislation aimed at lifting the restrictions on barons like Rupert investing in British TV; the results will have far-reaching implications. The industry is self-regulating, having set up a Press Complaints Commission in 1991 to handle public complaints.

There are many national daily newspapers, and competition for readers is incredibly stiff; although some papers are printed outside the capital, they are all pretty London-centric. There are two broad categories of newspapers, variously distinguished as quality/popular, broadsheet/tabloid, heavies/red-tops, upmarket/downmarket, high-brow/gutter press or good/bad. Britain has some of the best – and 'best worst' – newspapers in the world. Broadsheets like the *Guardian* and the *Independent* are pillars of the fourth estate, and while tabloids like the *Sun* and the *Mirror* are scurrilous rags, they're the most scurrilous rags in the world and you have to admire – almost – their unstinting willingness to sink to new lows.

At the very bottom end of the market in terms of content – though tops in circulation – are the *Sun*, *Mirror*, *Daily Star* and *Daily Record* tabloids, which are full of salacious gossip, scandal and sex (although they are also often the first to break major sports stories). Over recent years the *Sun* has switched political allegiances to support Labour, although it still manages to do so in a conservative, nationalistic way. The *Sun* and the more independent *Mirror* are mortal enemies and delight in goading and ridiculing each other. Competition between them is fierce, although the *Sun*'s circulation is almost double that of its more independent rival, whose sales have been in freefall. The *Daily Mail* and *Daily Express* reckon they are a cut above their tabloid cousins, although they're both unpalatably 'patriotic'. Most of the above have Sunday editions and the readership is predominantly working class.

Readers of the broadsheets are extremely loyal to their paper and rarely switch from one to another. The *Daily Telegraph* (also known as the 'Torygraph' for its unquestioning support of the Conservative party) far outsells its rivals. It is sometimes considered old-fogeyish, but nonetheless, the writing and world coverage are very good. The *Times* is traditionally the newspaper of the establishment and supports the government of the day; it's particularly good for sports. On the left side of the political spectrum – even if the political spectrum hardly has a left side anymore – is the *Guardian*, read by the so-called chattering classes (middle-class liberals); it features lively writing and supports 'worthy causes', is very strong in its coverage of the arts and has excellent supplements, including a review of the world media called the *Editor*, which comes out as a supplement every Saturday. Politically correct, the *Independent* tries to live up to its name but is struggling to stay afloat. The pink-coloured, business-oriented *Financial Times* has a great travel section on the weekend.

The Sunday papers are as important as Sunday mornings in London. Most dailies have Sunday stablemates and predictably the tabloids have bumper editions of trashy gossip, star-struck adulation, fashion extras and mean-spirited diatribes directed at whoever they've decided to hunt for sport on that particular weekend. The qualities have so many sections and supplements that two hands are required to carry even one from the shop. The *Observer*, established in 1791,

Quick Reference Guide to English Newspapers

- *The Times* is read by the people who run the country.
- *The Mirror* is read by the people who think they run the country.
- *The Guardian* is read by the people who think about running the country.
- *The Mail* is read by wives of the people who run the country.
- *The Daily Telegraph* is read by the people who think the country ought to be run as it used to be.
- *The Express* is read by the people who think it is still run as it used to be.
- *The Sun* is read by people who don't care who runs the country as long as the girl on page three has big knockers.

is the oldest Sunday paper and sister of the *Guardian*; there's a brilliant Sports supplement with the first issue of the month. Even people who normally only buy broadsheets sometimes slip a copy of the best-selling *News of the World* under their arm for some Sunday light relief.

Magazines

There is an astonishing range of magazines published and consumed here, from celebrity gossip to political heavyweights. Lads' monthlies like *FHM*, *Loaded* and *Maxim* powered the growth of consumer magazines in the 1990s, as new readers tucked into a regular diet of babes, irreverence and blokeishness.

London loves celebrity, and *Heat* is the most popular purveyor of the literary equivalent of junk food. US import *Glamour* is the queen of the women's glossies, having toppled traditional favourite *Cosmopolitan*, which is beginning to look a little wrinkled in comparison with its younger, funkier rival – maybe time for a nip and tuck. *Marie Claire*, *Elle* and *Vogue* are regarded as the thinking woman's glossies.

A slew of style magazines are published here – *i-D*, *Dazed and Confused*, *I-Style* – and all maintain a loyal following. The achingly trendy design, décor and fashion magazine *Wallpaper* has made a huge splash in the few years since it has been launched, although its reputation has slipped since its founder and editor split in 2003.

Zwemmer's bookstore (p327)

Political magazines are particularly strong in London and range from the ultraconservative *Spectator* to the left-leaning *New Statesman*, both excellent mags. The satirical *Private Eye* (p26) has no political bias and takes the mickey out of everyone. You can keep in touch with what's happening internationally with the *Week*, an excellent round-up of the British and foreign press.

Time Out is the listings guide *par excellence* and great for taking the city's pulse, while the *Big Issue*, sold on the streets by the homeless, is not just an honourable project but a damned fine read. London is a publishing hub for magazines and produces hundreds of internationally renowned publications specialising in music, visual arts, literature, sport, architecture and so on. There's a comprehensive list of these in the Directory chapter (p375).

New Media

There's a thriving alternative media scene catering to the many who feel marginalised by the mainstream media, much of which still covers global protests by describing the hairstyles of the 'ecowarriors'. Some sites worth checking out include **Indymedia** (http://uk.indymedia.org), the global network of alternative news, the outstanding and original **Urban 75** (www.urban75.com), the weekly activists' newsletter from **SchNews** (www.schnews.org.uk) and the video activists **Undercurrents** (www.schnews.org.uk).

Email magazines have taken off here in a big way, largely because they're so good. **The Friday Thing** (www.thefridaything.co.uk) is a well-written and exceedingly cheeky weekly mag covering news, culture and current affairs. Online gossip sites have also gained notoriety in recent years by knocking spin on its arse and breaking some big stories about celebrities misbehaving. Check out **Popbitch** (www.popbitch.com) and the satirical technology newsletter **Need to Know** (www.ntk.net).

Broadcasting

Radio has been hugely popular in London since Arthur Burrows first read the news in the inaugural broadcast in 1922. The BBC is one of the greatest broadcasting corporations in the world and one of the standard bearers of radio and television journalism and programming (p190). Its independence frequently irks the establishment and it incurred the very significant wrath of the British government in 2003 because of its tenacious probing of the events leading to the US/British/Australian-led invasion of Iraq.

There was a public spat between the BBC's Andrew Gilligan and the government's press secretary Alistair Campbell, who was accused by the BBC of 'sexing up' a dossier of evidence against the Iraqi regime in order to generate public support for going to war. The country's chief weapons expert, Dr David Kelly, committed suicide after being named by the government as the source of the BBC's report; an inquiry into Dr Kelly's death was under way at the time of writing. Blair's government and the BBC have come under enormous public pressure as a result of the tragedy and heads were expected to roll.

New media ownership laws introduced in 2003 paved the way for major newspaper proprietors to own British terrestrial television channels, namely Channel Five. There are fears in some quarters of a cultural colonialism with cheap US TV shows swamping the airwaves, although given the slender popularity of brilliant American shows like *The Sopranos* and *The West Wing* in Britain, you'd think it was unlikely that inferior ones would get much attention.

The BBC broadcasts several stations, including BBC 1, 2, 3, 4 and 5, catering to young, mature, classical, arts and talkback audiences respectively. Londoners are still smarting over the axing of the BBC's Greater London Radio (GLR). It was local, intelligent and played interesting music – precisely what's missing from most of the commercial dross being broadcasted today. XFM is your best chance of hearing interesting music these days.

Britain still turns out some of the world's best TV, padding out the decent home-grown output with American imports, Australian soaps, inept sitcoms and trashy chat and game shows of its own. There are five regular TV channels. BBC1 and BBC2 are publicly funded by a TV licensing system and, like BBC radio stations, don't carry advertising; ITV, Channel 4 and Channel 5 are commercial channels and do. These are now competing with the satellite channels of Rupert Murdoch's BSkyB – which offers a variety of channels with less-than-inspiring programmes – and assorted cable channels.

Digital radio and TV are being touted and hyped – the radio offered 26 stations at the last count – but the uptake has been slow so far. Many listeners and viewers feel that the investment in new technology is damaging to the core channels and that the BBC is spreading itself too thinly, trying to chase ratings and compete with the commercial channels rather than concentrating on its public service responsibilities.

LANGUAGE

English is the country's greatest contribution to the modern world. It is an astonishingly rich language containing an estimated 600,000 uninflected words (compared with, for example, Indonesian's or Malay's 60,000). It's actually a magpie tongue – just as England plundered treasure for its museums, so, too, the English language dipped into the world's vocabulary, even when it already had several words of the same meaning. Dr Johnson, compiler of the first English dictionary, tried to have the language protected from foreign imports (possibly to reduce his own workload) but failed. As far as English goes, all foreigners are welcome.

English-speakers are spoilt for choice when they go looking for descriptive words such as nouns and adjectives, as you'll discover pretty quickly (fast, swiftly, speedily, rapidly, promptly) by looking in a thesaurus. Some 50 years ago, linguists came up with Basic English, a stripped down version with a vocabulary of 850 words, which was all one needed to say just about anything. But where's the fun in that? Shakespeare himself is said to have contributed more than 2000 words, along with hundreds of common idioms such as poisoned chalice, one fell swoop, cold comfort and cruel to be kind.

Be grateful if English is your mother tongue because it's a bitch to learn, and has possibly the most illogical and eccentric approach to spelling and pronunciation of any language. Take the different pronunciation of rough, cough, through, though and bough. Attempts to rationalise English spelling are passionately resisted by people who see themselves as the guardians of proper English and rail against the eminently sensible American decision to drop the 'u' from words such as colour and glamour.

In terms of accent, Standard English or Received Pronunciation (RP) centres on London and, traditionally, was perceived to be that spoken by the upper classes and those educated at public schools. It is by no means the easiest form to understand; in fact, sometimes it's near impossible ('oh, eye nare' apparently means 'yes, I know'). Those 'what talk posh' despair at the perceived butchering of their language by most ordinary Londoners, who speak what's come to be known as 'Estuary English', so called because it's a sort of sub-cockney that spread along the estuary in post-war London. And so a common language divides the city.

London's Languages

These days, you'll encounter a veritable Babel of some 300 languages being spoken in London, and there are pockets of the capital where English is the second language (eg Shoreditch in the East End, Soho's Chinatown, Dalston and Stoke Newington).

The BBC is considered the arbitrator on the issue, and by comparing the contrived – and frankly hilarious – tone of old newsreels from WWII with today's bulletins, it's obvious that Standard English has gone from posh to a more neutral middle register.

Some say that Estuary English – which can now be heard within a hundred-mile radius of the capital – is quickly becoming the standard. Its chief features, according to Stephen Burgen in Lonely Planet's *British Phrasebook*, are: rising inflection; constant use of 'innit'; a glottal 'T', rendering the double 'T' in butter almost silent and making 'alright' sound like 'orwhy'; and, in general, a slack-jawed, floppy-tongued way of speaking that knocks the corners off consonants and lets the vowels whine to themselves. The lack of speech rhythm that can result from blowing away your consonants is made good by the insertion of copious quantities of 'fucks' and 'fucking', whose consonants are always given the full nine yards. In London there are many people whose speech is so dependent on the word 'fuck' they are virtually dumbstruck without it.

But like just about everything in London, the language is constantly changing, absorbing new influences, producing new slang and gradually changing the meaning of words. The city's ethnic communities are only beginning to have an influence and many young Londoners these days are mimicking Caribbean expressions and what they perceive to be hip-hop speak from black urban America.

As England has absorbed wave after wave of immigrants, so too will the insatiable English language continue to take in all comers. Meanwhile, as class distinctions exist, the linguistic battle for London will rage on.

Cockney

The term cockney was originally a derogatory one. Derived from the old English for 'cock's egg', it was used by Shakespeare to describe a fool and later came to be associated with the uneducated working classes of London and the way they spoke. It was a dialect that had remained virtually intact since the 11th century and its typical features were dropped ls (ball/baw), missing consonants (daughter/dau'er), the hard 'th' replaced with a double v (brother/bruvver) and the soft 'th' replaced with a double f (nothing/nuffink). If you're having difficulty hearing the sounds, just think of the quintessential cockney, actor Michael Caine, particularly in the film *Alfie*. This cockney is not all that different from the Estuary English spoken by most Londoners today.

The upper classes, predictably, looked down their noses at the poor and the way they spoke. However, a certain folklore grew up around cockney during the golden era of the music halls at the end of the 19th century. Working class performers like Albert Chevalier created a quaint, folksy version of the East End that middle-class audiences found quaint, unthreatening and entertaining. The image of salt-of-the-earth, cheeky chappies and irrepressible East Enders became widespread. After a while, being and speaking cockney became something to be proud of. Indeed, perhaps inspired by an inverted snobbery, cockney soon came to apply only to those East Enders born within earshot of the church bells of St Mary-le-Bow.

Old Cockney in Common Usage

apples and pears	stairs
artful dodger	lodger
barnet (fair)	hair
boat race	face
borassic (lint)	skint
brown bread	dead
currant bun	son
dicky bird	a word
dog and bone	phone
ginger beer	queer (gay)
jackanory	story
mae west	best
mince pies	eyes
mutt and jeff	deaf
radio rental	mental
rosy (rosy lea)	tea
tea leaf	thief
tin of fruit	suit

However, cockney is best know for its rhyming slang, which entered the vernacular in the first half of the 19th century. Market traders devised it, possibly, so they could talk to each other privately in public, or street villains perhaps developed it as a code.

Cockney slang replaces common nouns and verbs with rhyming phrases, whereby wife becomes 'trouble and strife' and so on. With familiarity, the actual rhyming word in some phrases gets dropped so the wife simply becomes trouble; 'loaf' (of bread) becomes head; 'china' (plate) means mate; 'syrup' (of fig) is a wig; and a butcher's (hook) is a look.

You'll still hear conversations peppered with cockney phrases, although the slang has evolved considerably, and often ridiculously, since its East End origins. You wouldn't Adam and Eve the number of new versions and sometimes even the locals don't have a Danny La Rue what's being said – and that's no word of a porky pie.

ECONOMY & COSTS

London is Europe's richest city and has become a mecca both for those in search of jobs and international corporations drawn by the city's reputation as a financial hub. Its wealth might not be immediately obvious to the visitor passing blocks of high-rise buildings on the way into town, but London beats the likes of Hamburg and Vienna in terms of wealth per head of population. The financial gap between the haves and have-nots is significantly wider in London than in most cities.

The bad news for visitors is that London is by far the most expensive city in the European Union (EU) and one of the most expensive locations on the planet. Accommodation and transport costs are particularly high compared with the rest of the EU. These factors, together with higher duty on items such as alcohol and tobacco, are why visitors' credit cards get a flogging in the capital.

One in eight Britons lives in the capital and they keep pouring in – the population is growing at five times the national average. They're drawn to the big smoke by fatter pay packets as much as the bright lights, as wages are around 20% higher in the capital than elsewhere in Britain. But the extra dough barely covers the increased cost of living according to the Centre for Economics and Business Research, which estimates that Londoners actually have a lower standard of living than their compatriots outside the city. Rents, for example, are as much as 56% more expensive. Going out will set you back more, with drinking at least 5% more costly than elsewhere. On top of that, almost a quarter of all Londoners have to commute 51 minutes or more to get to work each day, more than anywhere else in the country. And people here work hard; the statutory working week is 48 hours against 40 in most of the rest of Europe and 35 hours in France.

Standard Spends

Pint of Lager £2.25
Financial Times newspaper £1
36-exposure colour film £4
City-centre bus ticket £1
Adult football ticket £20 to £40
Three-course meal with wine/beer from £30
Taxi per km 90p
Cinema ticket £9
CD £15
Admission to a big-name club on a Friday £15

Property prices have boomed in recent years, making it nigh impossible for first-time buyers to get a start. The average wage in London is around £26,000 and potential homebuyers can't even get mortgages big enough to let them buy into the *bottom* of the market. No wonder those working in essential services like police, teachers and nurses, on an average wage of £19,000, are leaving the city in droves. Most analysts predict that the price of houses will fall in some of London's ritzier neighbourhoods over the next few years but should keep climbing – albeit at a much slower rate – in most parts of London.

Nevertheless, London is the proverbial economic powerhouse, and its £159 billion Gross Domestic Product (GDP) would make it the ninth largest economy in Europe – larger than those of Sweden, Poland, Norway, Austria or Denmark.

Much of this wealth is generated in the square mile known as the City, the original settlement of London, the financial core, and the reason it has survived and prospered over nearly two millennia. It is the most prosperous area in the EU generating more wealth than any other region in the block. A quarter of Londoners are employed in business services. Every working day, up to 300,000 workers descend on the City, make a million here and there, and then race home in time for tea. At night and weekends, the City is deserted.

Some of London's biggest employers are its airports: Heathrow (the world's busiest commercial airport), Gatwick and Stansted together provide some 35,000 jobs. Pockets of industry and manufacturing still exist on the outskirts of town.

The British economy as a whole is buoyant; growth is just over 2% and twice the eurozone average, while inflation is steady at around 2%. This explains why the British government is in no hurry to join the 11 neighbouring nations in the eurozone. Britain dropped out of the preparations for the European Monetary Union (EMU) in 1998 because its economy was out of shape, but that humiliation has turned to something of a triumph as a recovered and robust Britain has sprinted past its sluggish euro neighbours.

Playing Footsies

London is Europe's most important financial centre in terms of volume of shares traded. The organisation that actually runs the market is the London Stock Exchange, the most international of the world's stock exchanges. If you ever wondered what the 'footsie' (FTSE 100) is, it's an index that tracks the share price movements of the top 100 companies and is calculated every 15 seconds the market is open.

Tony Blair is getting some stick from other European leaders and is said to favour joining the EMU, although his chancellor, Gordon Brown, is most definitely not. The proposal was last considered in a serious way in 2003, during which much of the British media reacted hysterically and misguidedly about the possible 'surrender of Britain's autonomy'. The decision then was, 'we'll join, just not yet'. The City is already set up for the euro, using it in foreign exchange and bond markets, and is indifferent to the political debate.

One thing's for sure, as long as business is good, Britain won't be converting to the euro and bringing its interest rates into line with the rest of Europe, so sterling will continue to rule Brittania's finances for some time to come.

GOVERNMENT & POLITICS

LOCAL GOVERNMENT

When 12th-century King Richard the Lionheart gave London the right to self-government in exchange for a little pocket money, supporters cheered 'Londoners shall have no king but their mayor'. That's been true for the City of London ever since, but Greater London, where the vast majority of the population lives and works, has had a trickier time of it.

Some form of the Greater London Council (GLC) was going about its business quietly for a few centuries, looking after local interests and acquiescently toeing the national government's line. That all changed when Labour man Ken Livingstone took over as boss of the council in the early 1980s, the same time Margaret Thatcher was prime minister. These two couldn't have been more different and a clash was inevitable. Livingstone campaigned for cheaper public transport in the capital and generally became a thorn in Thatcher's side. She got so fed up with him that in 1986 she abolished the GLC altogether, and London became the only major capital in the world without a self-governing authority. Fourteen years later, the Labour government brought back a new version, the Greater London Assembly (GLA), and arranged elections for London's first-ever popularly elected mayor (see below).

Red Ken

London's first ever popularly elected mayor is a colourful, charismatic character who has done much to improve London for tourists. As the leader of the Greater London Council (GLC) during the 1980s, 'Red Ken' – as the socialist is known – went head to head with that most conservative of prime ministers, Margaret Thatcher. He pushed a huge 'Fare's Fair' campaign to reduce the cost of public transport in London, and put a giant counter on the roof of County Hall, which gave updated unemployment figures and was clearly visible from the House of Commons. Thatcher became so infuriated with Livingstone that she scrapped the GLC altogether.

He entered Parliament as an MP and proposed many policies that seemed radical at the time, but which have since been adapted as government policy. His refusal to always toe party line made him popular with Joe Public but earned him the mistrust of the parliamentary party. He was a hate figure for the right-wing tabloids, and the *Sun* once called him 'the most odious man in Britain'.

When Labour decided to reinstate the London council as the Greater London Assembly (GLA), popular Livingstone seemed a shoo-in for the job of mayor. However, Tony Blair was determined to halt Livingstone's election bandwagon and, at the end of a drawn-out saga, gave the party's nomination to somebody else. Crash, bang, wallop...Livingstone resigned from the party and ran as an independent candidate promising to lock horns with the central government whenever it came to London's best interest. He swept to victory on a tide of popular support in May 2000.

Livingstone did little in his first year apart from banning pigeons from Trafalgar Square. With those pesky blighters almost out of the way, and the famous square being given a facelift, he has since made transport his number one priority, fighting tooth and nail against the government-proposed privatisation of the Underground, improving bus services, and introducing the bold, risky and apparently successful congestion tax in 2003. His most important strategy is the £100bn London plan, a planning framework for the city over the next decade, which aims to overhaul London's use of resources and its relationship with the environment. One of its toughest and most contentious challenges is the provision of affordable housing and the mayor's plan to build 15 new skyscrapers by 2013 has been widely derided. Some say the plan will be the capital's biggest makeover since the aftermath of the Great Fire in 1666.

Despite a concerted effort by the *Evening Standard* to embroil him in scandal in 2002, Livingstone continues to enjoy some popularity, which is rare for any elected leader in London. However, Londoners love a backlash and the real test will come when he runs for re-election in 2004.

Whatever the outcome, Livingstone's stint as mayor stands as a remarkable comeback in a political career that most believed had crashed and burned.

The 25-member GLA has limited authority over transport, economic development, strategic planning, the environment, the police, fire brigades, civil defence and cultural matters. It is elected from GLA constituencies and by London as a whole. It is not a conventional opposition, but can reject the mayor's budget, form special investigation committees and hold the mayor to public account. It currently comprises nine Conservatives, nine Labour Party members, four Liberal Democrats and three members of the Green Party. It has its headquarters in the futuristic GLA building in Southwark, beside Tower Bridge.

The City of London has its own government in the form of the Corporation of London, headed by the *Lord* Mayor (note that only the City mayor gets to be Lord) and an assortment of oddly named and peculiarly dressed aldermen, beadles and sheriffs. It sits at the Guildhall. These men – and they usually *are* male – are elected by the City of London's freemen and liverymen. Though its government may appear out of time and obsolete in the third millennium, the Corporation of London still owns roughly a third of the supremely wealthy 'square mile' and has a good record for patronage of the arts.

London is furthered divided into 33 widely differing boroughs (13 of which are in central London), run by democratically elected councils with significant autonomy. These deal with education and matters such as road sweeping and rubbish collecting. The richest borough in terms of per capita income is Richmond in the west; the poorest is Barking in the east.

NATIONAL GOVERNMENT

London is, of course, the seat of the national government. For the record, Britain is a constitutional monarchy with no written constitution and operates under a combination of parliamentary statutes, common law (a body of legal principles based on precedents, often dating back centuries) and convention.

Parliament is made up of the monarch, the House of Commons and the House of Lords. The monarch is essentially a figurehead who brings in the tourists, while the House of Commons is where the real power lies. It comprises a national assembly of 659 constituencies (or seats) directly elected every four to five years. The leader of the biggest party in the House of Commons is the prime minister, who appoints a cabinet of 20 or so ministers to run government departments. Prime Minister Tony Blair's Labour Party holds a massive majority over the Conservative Party, which has been in the doldrums now for a decade. Although Labour's popularity has plummeted during its second term – during which Tony Blair became the longest continuous serving Labour prime minister in history – it's doubtful whether the 'invisible' Conservatives will be able to stop the party reaching a third term at the next general election, due in 2006.

The House of Lords has a little power but these days it's largely limited to delaying legislation – even then, it's only a question of time before it goes to the Queen to be rubber-stamped. For centuries, the House of Lords consisted of some 900 'hereditary peers' (whose titles passed from one generation to the next), 25 Church of England bishops and 12 Law Lords (who also act as Britain's highest court).

Houses of Parliament (p128)

City Life – Government & Politics

Tony Blair has targeted the Lords with the same zeal the mayor went for the Trafalgar Square's pigeons – the similarities possibly end there – and most of the hereditary peers were shuffled out in 1999. Ninety-two of them have been allowed to stay, for the time being. A new system of 'life peerage' was introduced which, critics say, allowed the prime minister to hand out plum jobs to loyal MPs who wouldn't have to go through the bother of getting elected in the future. In the second stage of Lords reform (for which there is no time frame), elected peers will enter the upper house for the first time and hereditary peers will be swept away altogether.

ENVIRONMENT

THE LAND

Greater London comprises 607 sq miles enclosed by the M25 ring road. As well as being essential to the trade upon which London was built, the River Thames divides the city into north and south, a partition that had much more than geographical implications. The Romans designated the south bank as a seedy London of gaming and debauchery, and for almost two millennia thence, respectable and cultured folk settled on the northern side while the outcasts lived in the insalubrious south. The potential of the South Bank has only been realised in the last decade.

Although London grew from the area known as the City, it doesn't have a single focal point. Its expansion was never really planned; rather, the burgeoning city just consumed outlying settlements. Thus – as any reader of Dickens will appreciate – London today is more a patchwork of villages than a single city. Although the city can feel like a never-ending concrete jungle, there are actually huge swathes of green on its outskirts – take Richmond Park and Hampstead Heath – and large parks like Regent's and Hyde in the centre.

GREEN LONDON

The most serious environmental problem concerning the centre of London, the pollution and chronic congestion caused by heavy traffic, has been partially alleviated since 2003 when the Mayor's Congestion Tax was introduced, whereby every car entering the centre had to pay £5 for the privilege. There are now 15% to 20% fewer vehicles on central streets, traffic jams are fewer and average speeds have nearly doubled. What's more, it's possible to inhale the air on many streets without it grating on the back of your throat, and London is a much more enjoyable place to stroll around because of it (see also Urban Planning & Development p34).

Recycling has been available in London for many years but mainly in the form of community bins rather than household ones, and the mainstream haven't really been encouraged to go green. Some boroughs are better than others but the London average for recycling household waste is a miserable 9%.

To look at the Thames' murky waters, you'd assume it was another pollution black spot, but below the surface, its health has improved dramatically in recent years and the river is playing an increasingly important role in recreation. By 1962, the combined impact of untreated sewage and industrial pollution had killed off virtually every sign of life in the river, but it's home to some 115 species of fish, including shad, sea lamprey and even salmon (for which special ladders have been built over the weirs). With them have come 10,000 herons, cormorants and other waterfowl which feed on the fish; even otters have been spotted on the river's upper reaches. The reason it still looks so murky in central London is that it is the brackish centre of marine and freshwater zones.

London boasts more parks and open spaces than any city of its size in the world – from the neatly manicured (Holland Park, St James's Park) to the semi-wild (Richmond Park, Bushy Park). Between them they provide suitable habitats for a wide range of animals and birds.

The mammal you're most likely to spot on land is the grey squirrel, a North American import that has colonised every big park and decimated the indigenous red population.

Hedgehogs also live here, though their numbers are dwindling, perhaps due to the increased use of slug pellets. You probably won't be able to see foxes because of their nocturnal habits but they're here, while Richmond Park hosts badgers as well as herds of red and fallow deer.

Bird-watchers, especially those keen on waterfowl, will love London. There are ducks, pelicans and the Queen's swans in St James's Park, and more ducks and beautiful, chestnut-headed great-crested grebes in Hyde Park's Serpentine. London canals are also happy hunting grounds for spotting waterfowl.

Garden birds, such as long-tailed and great tits, sparrows, robins and blackbirds, roost in all the parks, but some parks attract more interesting migrants. In Holland Park in spring, you might glimpse flocks of tiny goldcrests. Kestrels also nest around the Tower of London. The open stretches of the commons in Barnes and Wimbledon also harbour a rich assortment of birds and mammals.

A Different London Underground

Pressure on space is nothing new to central London – when Victorian engineers were faced with the same problem they decided to build down, digging tunnels, railways and roads, and burying rivers beneath the city. So much activity took place down there that a veritable subterranean city exists beneath your feet.

Although the Thames is the only river associated with London now, the city is criss-crossed by many 'lost' waterways that have come to run underground. Fleet St is named after the most famous of all, the Fleet, which rises in Hampstead and empties into the Thames at Blackfriars Bridge. By the 18th century it had become a reeking sewer and was covered up.

Also, the dozen or so bridges spanning the Thames are far outnumbered by the 30-odd tunnels that zigzag beneath its course. After several failed attempts, the first tunnel was opened in 1840 and it later became the Underground's East London line.

The **London Wildlife Trust** (LWT ☎ 7261 0447; www.wildlondon.org.uk) maintains more than 50 nature reserves in the city, which offer the chance to see a range of birds and occasionally small mammals. Battersea Park Nature Reserve has several nature trails, while the Trent Country Park even boasts a Braille trail through the woodlands. Parts of Hampstead Heath have been designated a Site of Special Scientific Interest for their wealth of natural history. The LWT maintains more than 50 nature reserves in the city, which offer the chance to see a range of birds and occasionally small mammals.

For more information on nature reserves and wildlife habitats contact the LWT at Harling House, 47–51 Great Suffolk St, London SE1 0BS.

Green fingers won't want to miss the exotic plants in the exceedingly lovely Kew Gardens (p200), while London's parks boast a variety of common or garden trees, shrubs and flowers. Many Londoners also take pride in their private gardens, which range from handkerchief-sized back yards to sprawling mini-estates, some of which open for a few days each summer through the National Gardens Scheme (NGS). Admission usually costs £2, which goes to charity. For a pamphlet listing dates and participants, contact the **NGS** (☎ 01483-211535; www.ngs.org.uk) at Hatchlands Park, East Clandon, Guildford GU4 7RT.

Microeconomics

The need for additional homes is one of the most pressing issues impacting on the quality of life in London, and various schemes have been put in place to try to solve this crisis. There are now special government housing grants for key workers, such as nurses, ambulance drivers and so on, and Mayor Ken Livingstone has introduced a requirement that, to gain planning permission for building projects, developers allocate 50% of the scheme to affordable housing (although when it came to agreeing on a deal for the Dome and surrounding area he was reportedly willing to settle for 40%).

One of the most attention-grabbing projects in this area has been the idea by architectural practice Piercy Conner for Microflat developments. These are clipped-together buildings of small but space-saving, prefabricated one-bedroom flats, much in the same vein as Japanese capsules (although at 15 sq metres by 15 sq metres, somewhat larger). The idea was tested in a shop window at Selfridges, complete with one glass wall and 'micronauts' and garnered enormous publicity. Fans say it will make central London living affordable; its detractors believe it's a mere gimmick. Who's right will only be proved when Piercy Conner comes through in negotiations with developers and get the Microflat off the ground.

URBAN PLANNING & DEVELOPMENT

Central London has been considerably smartened up in recent years, and Mayor Ken Livingstone is at the forefront of other bold and imaginative schemes to make the city a more pleasant place to live and visit. Traffic was banished from the north side of Trafalgar Square, now connected by a new pedestrian plaza that stretches to the National Gallery, itself undergoing massive renovations. Plans are afoot to give seedy Leicester Square the same treatment and transform it into a clean and sociable European-style plaza, while the ongoing development of the South Bank continues to impress.

But the biggest challenge facing London is how to house its growing population without encroaching on the green belt surrounding the city. Previously run-down central areas like Hoxton, Clerkenwell and Farringdon were dolled up in the 1990s with young populations moving in and converting warehouses. The repopulation of the Docklands continues, but London is quickly running out of space. The mayor has taken measures to address the problem, and as a precondition to receiving planning permission, developers now have to allocate half their overall plans to providing affordable housing. In his London Plan, he has also built in the protection of green space, although business interests are mobilising to scrap that protection and reduce the 'burden' on developers.

In perhaps what is a sign of things to come, the government is facing an inevitable conflict with environmentalists over the proposed regeneration of the Thames Gateway, the 60km on each side of the Thames from east London to the North Sea. The plan is to build 200,000 homes and provide 300,000 jobs but in an area that contains some of Britain's most valuable wildlife sites and a 25km stretch of shore that is designated as an EU high-priority special protection area. Only time will tell.

We'd Be Lost Without Harry Beck

In 1931 an out-of-work engineering draughtsman, Harry Beck, created the city's most famous icon, the London Underground map (p442). Beck realised existing maps were too impenetrable so he designed one that presented an ordered vision of a chaotic city. Beck was paid five guineas (£5.50) for his revolutionary work, which changed the face of London forever and continues to make the city feel almost navigable for tourists and locals alike.

Arts

Arts

London is the humming cultural capital of Europe, with a scene as dynamic and an audience as adventurous as any in the world. The government and business community help London to cut its creative way, but it's the city's boundlessly creative youth that helps to keep it at the forefront across the artistic spectrum. The arts make a fair contribution to London's economic success, but it's the feel-good factor it gives the population that is perhaps most valuable. Hollywood stars have been queuing up to tread the boards of the city's theatres, while London continues to be the heart of English literature and not just the Harry Potter phenomenon. While the dust is still settling after the storm of Britart, the less shocking artists are re-emerging and the scene is still abuzz.

London continues to churn out brilliant television programmes, particularly in comedy and drama, which are watched and celebrated around the world, while the film industry plods along and produces the occasional gem. Musically, London is enjoying its fifth decade leading the way in popular music. It's also a capital of comedy and its dance companies cut a splendid dash across the world stage.

LITERATURE

OLD LITERARY LONDON

London has an honoured position in the history of English literature. The city has stimulated and inspired a stream of local and international writers down the ages, many of whom used it as the setting for their works. What follows is a small selection of seminal moments from the history of literature in London – you can get a detailed listing in *Waterstone's Guide to London Writing* (£3.99), available at Waterstone's bookshops everywhere.

> ### Grub Street
>
> Grub St was the original name of a street in London (now Milton St) inhabited by impoverished writers and literary hacks. In the 18th century, any inferior book or work of literature was known as 'grubstreet', but these days – and you shouldn't read anything into this – the term seems to be used for the whole London publishing industry.

The first literary reference to the city comes in Chaucer's *Canterbury Tales,* written between 1387 and 1400, where the pilgrims gather for their trip to Canterbury at the Tabard Inn in Southwark.

Perhaps the greatest writer, William Shakespeare spent most of his life as an actor and playwright in London around the turn of the 16th century, when book publishing was beginning to take off here. He trod the boards of several Southwark theatres and wrote his greatest tragedies – among them *Hamlet, Othello, Macbeth* and *King Lear* – for the original Globe theatre on South Bank. Collectors of trivia should know that only one of his plays, *Henry IV: Part II*, includes a London setting: a tavern called the Boar's Head in Eastcheap.

Daniel Defoe wrote *Robinson Crusoe* (1720) and *Moll Flanders* (1722) while living in Church St in Stoke Newington; his *Journal of the Plague Years* is a famous account of the Black Death in London during the summer and autumn of 1665.

Two early-19th-century poets found inspiration here. Keats wrote his *Ode to a Nightingale* while living near Hampstead Heath in 1819 and his *Ode on a Grecian Urn* after inspecting the Portland Vase in the British Museum. Wordsworth visited in 1802 and was inspired to write the poem *On Westminster Bridge*.

Charles Dickens (1812–70) was the definitive London author. When his father and family were imprisoned for not paying their debts, the 12-year-old Charles was forced to fend for himself on the streets of Victorian London. Although his family were released three months later, those grim months were seared into the boy's memory and provided a font of experiences on which the author would later draw. His novels most closely associated with the city are *Oliver Twist,* with its story of a gang of boy thieves organised by Fagin in

Clerkenwell, and *Little Dorrit*, whose heroine was born in the Marshalsea – the same prison where his family were interned. His later *Our Mutual Friend* is a scathing criticism of contemporary London values – both monetary and social – and a spirited attack on the corruption, complacency and superficiality of 'respectable' London.

Sir Arthur Conan Doyle (1858–1930) portrayed a very different London and his pipe-smoking, cocaine-snorting sleuth, Sherlock Holmes, came to exemplify a cool and unflappable Englishness the world over. Letters to the mythical hero still arrive at 221B Baker St.

London at the end of the 19th century is described in a number of books. HG Wells' *The War of the Worlds* captures the sense and mood of the times wonderfully. Somerset Maugham's first novel, *Liza of Lambeth*, was based on his experiences as an intern in the slums of south London while his *Of Human Bondage*, so English and of its time, provides the most engaging portrait of late-Victorian London we know.

Dickens House Museum (p102)

20th-CENTURY WRITING

Of the Americans writing about London at the end of the 19th century, Henry James, who settled and died here, stands supreme with his *Daisy Miller* and *The Europeans*. *The People of the Abyss* by the American socialist writer Jack London is a sensitive portrait of the poverty and despair of life in the East End. And we couldn't forget Mark Twain's *The Innocents Abroad* in which the inimitable humourist skewers both the Old and the New Worlds. St Louis–born TS Eliot settled in London in 1915, where he published his poem *The Love Song of J Alfred Prufrock* almost immediately and moved on to his groundbreaking epic *The Waste Land*.

The End of the Affair, Graham Greene's novel chronicling a passionate and doomed romance, takes place in and around Clapham Common during WWI, while *The Heat of the Day* is Elizabeth Bowen's sensitive, if melodramatic, account of living through the Blitz.

Between the wars, PG Wodehouse (1881–1975), the most quintessentially British writer of the early 20th century – who turned out to be an American – depicted the London high-life with his hilarious lampooning of the English upper classes in the Jeeves stories. Quentin Crisp, the self-proclaimed 'stately homo of England', provided the flipside, recounting what it was like to be openly gay in the sexually repressed London of the 1920s in his ribald and witty memoirs, *The Naked Civil Servant*. George Orwell's experiences of living as a beggar in London's East End coloured his book *Down and Out in Paris and London* (1933).

Colin MacInnes described the bohemian, multicultural world of 1950s Notting Hill in *City of Spades* and *Absolute Beginners*, while Doris Lessing captured the political mood of 1960s London in *The Four-Gated City*, the last of her five-book *Children of Violence* series, and provides some of the funniest and

A Case in Point

Literary London, that nebulous space where publishing, journalism and academe intersect, is a grotesque carnival of gossip and spite. The books pages, apparently so irrelevant and sedate, can often be the most brutal and entertaining feature of any publication because there, in those carefully commissioned reviews, one can often glimpse the manifestation of the envy, paranoia and frustration that is the unhappy lot of most full-time writers and academics.

– *Jason Cowley, Guardian, 2002*

Recommended Reading

- *Absolute Beginners* (1959; Colin MacInnes) This brilliant novel is a must-read for anyone interested in the youth culture of London during the '50s, particularly the mod scene and the mixed-up culture that existed in postwar London. It's the best piece of literature to come out of this period and infinitely more engaging than the film of the same name.

- *The Adventures of Sherlock Holmes* (1892; Arthur Conan Doyle) The first collection of short stories featuring the snobby sleuth and his trusty sidekick Dr Watson, this book is for everyone from 10 years old and up who likes mystery and captivating tales. Conan Doyle once described London as 'that great cesspool into which all the loungers of the Empire are irresistibly drained'.

- *Brick Lane* (2003; Monica Ali) The most hyped book since Zadie Smith's *White Teeth*, this debut novel tells the story of Nazneen, an Islamic Bangladeshi woman who comes to London after an arranged marriage and initially accepts her circumscribed life, before embarking on her own voyage of self-discovery. The author, herself half-Bangladeshi, writes with wit and gentle irony.

- *The Buddha of Suburbia* (1991; Hanif Kureishi) This winner of the 1990 Whitbread prize is a raunchy, heart-warming, funny and insightful trawl into the hopes and fears of a group of Asian suburbanites in 1970s London, from the pre-eminent Anglo-Asian voice of his generation. It may feel a little aged compared with the chronicles of multiculturalism that have been all the rage in more recent years, but this one arguably has more punch.

- *The End of the Affair* (1951; Graham Greene) Set in battle-scarred London at the end of WWII, this intensely emotional classic deals with a three-way collision between love of self, love of another and love of God (coloured by the very real tension felt by the author between his Roman Catholic faith and the compulsion of sexual passion).

- *Grey Area* (1994; Will Self) Piercing wit, narrative virtuosity and incisive social commentary characterise the writing of Will Self, who is considered by Londoners to be either the best writer of his generation or a smug, self-indulgent smartarse. In this collection of nine short stories – or 'comic nightmares' – he lays into contemporary London and evokes the most disturbing failings of society.

- *High Fidelity* (2000; Nick Hornby) This extraordinarily successful novel by one of London's most famous scribes tackles the really big questions, at least those pertaining to the lives of 30-something men. Is it possible to share your life with someone whose record collection is incompatible with your own? Quite sad and very funny.

- *The Jeeves Omnibus* (1931; PG Wodehouse) One of the funniest writers in English, Wodehouse sends up the English upper classes with 31 stories about Bertie Wooster and his butler, Jeeves, who lived in exclusive Mayfair and revelled the London highlife.

- *Journal of the Plague Year* (1772; Daniel Defoe) Among the most gripping accounts of natural disaster in the history of literature, Defoe's classic reconstruction of the Great Plague of 1665 scans the streets and alleyways of stricken London to record the extreme suffering of plague victims. At once grisly and movingly compassionate.

- *Last Orders* (1997; Graham Swift) Four friends getting on in years cast their minds back to the East End of wartime London in this beautifully written, understated and bittersweet tale. It was made into an equally charming film starring the ultimate cockney, Michael Caine.

- *Liza of Lambeth* (1897; Somerset Maugham) Written during Maugham's final year of medical school, this gritty novel draws on the author's experiences of life on the mean streets of Lambeth and is an uncompromising depiction of working-class Edwardian London. The story carries the occasionally blowsy writing.

- *London Fields* (1989; Martin Amis) By using a constantly shifting narrative voice, Amis makes the reader work damn hard for the prize in this middle-class-fear-of-the-mob epic. Dark and postmodern – Dickens plus swearing and sex, minus compassion, wrote one reviewer – it is a gripping study of London lowlife.

- *London Observed* (1992; Doris Lessing) A collection of stories from this hugely successful and much-celebrated Iranian-born author, who observes London and its inhabitants with the shrewd and compassionate eye of an artist in 18 sketches of the city.

- *London: The Biography* (2000; Peter Ackroyd) Regarded by some as the definitive guide to London, this enormous tome provides a fascinating tapestry on the life and history of the capital, arranged by theme rather than chronologically.

- *Mother London* (2000; Michael Moorcock) This engaging, rambling novel follows three mentally disturbed characters who hear voices from the heart of London, which provides for an episodic romp through the history of the capital from the Blitz to the end of the millennium. The city itself becomes a character, along with its outcasts and marginals, all treated with great compassion by a self-assured author.

- *Mrs Dalloway* (1925; Virginia Woolf) Bloomsbury group stalwart Virginia Woolf goes full throttle with her stream-of-consciousness style in this story, which follows a day in the life of various people trying to cope in 1923 London. It is beautifully crafted, and as brief as it is exhilarating.
- *The Naked Civil Servant* (1968; Quentin Crisp) A 1976 television film of this autobiography, starring John Hurt, made Crisp famous and infamous overnight. It's the story of an openly gay man in London in the 1920s, a world of brutality and comedy, told in Crisp's characteristically sarcastic, self-derogatory, bitchy and very funny way.
- *Oliver Twist* (1837; Charles Dickens) Although not necessarily Dickens' best novel – or a good introduction to the author – this moving story of an orphan who runs away to London and falls in with a gang of thieves is beautifully told with rich, unforgettable characters and a vivid portrayal of Victorian London.
- *Sour Sweet* (1982; Timothy Mo) Nominated for the Booker Prize, this tongue-in-cheek novel follows the fortunes of a Chinese family trying to come to terms with life amongst the 'foreign devils' of London and is a fascinating look at the city through the eyes of an immigrant. Sharp writing and black humour.
- *White Teeth* (2000; Zadie Smith) Zadie Smith's hugely hyped novel is a funny, poignant, big-hearted and affectionate book about friendship and cultural differences, as seen through the eyes of three unassimilated families in north London. It's not quite as dazzling as the critics made out, but nothing could be.

most vicious portrayals of 1990s London in *London Observed*. Nick Hornby found himself as the voice of a generation being nostalgic about his days as a young football fan in *Fever Pitch* and obsessive about vinyl in *High Fidelity*.

Before it became fashionable, authors like Hanif Kureishi explored London from the perspective of ethnic minorities, specifically young Pakistanis in Kureishi's most well-known novels *The Black Album* and *The Buddha of Suburbia* – he also wrote the screenplay for the ground-breaking film *My Beautiful Laundrette*. Author and playwright Caryl Phillips won plaudits for his description of the Caribbean immigrant's experience in *The Final Passage*, while Timothy Mo's *Sour Sweet* is a poignant and funny account of a Chinese family in the 1960s trying to adjust to English life.

The astronomical success of Helen Fielding's *Bridget Jones's Diary* effectively concluded the genre known as 'chick lit', a series of hugely successful books that were, depending on your perspective, about finding Mr Right or about independent, brassy young women finding their voice. Will Self – *enfant terrible* and incisive social commentator – has been the toast of London for the last decade. His *Grey Area* is a superb collection of short stories focusing on skewed and surreal aspects of London.

Finally, Peter Ackroyd is regarded as the quintessential London author and names the city as the love of his life. *London – The Biography* is Ackroyd's inexhaustible paean to the capital, while his most recent book, *The Clerkenwell Tales*, brings to life the 14th-century London of Chaucer.

THE CONTEMPORARY SCENE

Thumb forward to the 21st century and the state of the industry, where publishers have become more like music and film executives than traditional publishers. The shape of the industry is best exemplified by the 2000 runaway success, *White Teeth*, a brilliant debut novel by Zadie Smith about multiethnic assimilation in north London. This novel propelled Smith, pretty much overnight, from obscurity to being the poster girl for young, groovy, literary London.

She arrived on the scene already represented by a ruthless literary agent who invited publishers to bid for the book on the strength of – not even a full manuscript – a sample of 100 pages. The feeding frenzy that followed has already passed into local legend. Zadie filled all the current criteria: as well as being a bloody good writer she was young, gorgeous and multicultural (ie eminently marketable). Bling. Bling. Bling. Bling. All the lights lit up and Grub St went into orbit. Penguin finally claimed victory when they paid the *unknown* author £250,000 for the *unknown* book.

Prize Writers

The Booker is the most important literary fiction prize in Britain. Since its foundation in 1969, it has only been open to Commonwealth and Irish authors but new sponsors, the Man Group, insisted that it be opened up to US writers by 2004, drawing uproar from sections of the British media. The Samuel Johnson award is the richest and most prestigious prize for nonfiction.

Arts – Theatre

Top Five Literary Locations

- Dickens House Museum (p102), where the most London of authors wrote *Oliver Twist*.
- 221B Baker St (p181), the address of Sherlock Holmes, although it didn't even exist in Arthur Conan Doyle's day.
- 84 Charing Cross Rd (p326), the bookshop in Helen Hanff's novel and the dream address for a bookshop, now a chain pub.
- Bloomsbury WC1 (p101), where the influential group of writers, artists and intellectuals known as the Bloomsbury Group lived and worked early in the 20th century.
- Hampstead (p184), a leafy hilltop suburb which was home to great writers such as John Keats (p185), HG Wells and DH Lawrence.

As it turned out, Penguin's 'hunch' was spot on; *White Teeth* was fresh, original and generally fabulous, and the publisher made a handsome profit from it and from her equally impressive follow-up, *The Autograph Man*, in 2002. But it's the nature of the first book's publication that characterises London's literary scene right now: dominated by assorted editors, publishers, agents and booksellers desperately sniffing around for 'the next big thing'. Publishers on a quest for the jackpot are shelling out bigger and bigger advances for new books by unknown authors in the hope that they'll uncover 'the next Zadie Smith'. Which they may just have done.

Once every decade, 20 young British writers are named in the prestigious *Granta* list, which sets the literary agenda for a generation. One of the names in the 2003 dream team, Londoner and Anglo-Bangladeshi Monica Ali, hadn't even been published before she was being trumpeted as one of the most significant British novelists of the day. She met all the criteria and her book, *Brick Lane*, is a winner.

Older, less photogenic authors grumble that literary success is now as much about looks as the quality of the books. Whether a new author is young and gorgeous – has the 'gorge factor' – has much to do with what kind of marketing push each book gets, which, these days, has more bearing on success than what the critics say. Publishers are less likely to give an author the luxury of a couple of books to find their readership, and one can only wonder what masterpieces might never have seen the light of day had the same criteria applied in the 20th century.

In the meantime the media and the marketing folk try to come up with new and marketable trends where none really exist. Some cling anxiously to 'chick lit' although that label is nearly a decade out of date, while one hopeful faction was trying to flog 'granny lit' because there had been a slight increase in the number of books published by over 50s.

As a reaction to the industry's obsession with hip, a couple of editors got together to form a literary movement known as the New Puritans, with a manifesto not dissimilar to the Danish filmmakers' Dogme 95. Their aim was to produce fiction in 'its purest and most immediate form'. The New Puritans banned poetic license, and the New Puritans were widely rubbished.

Whatever the arguments about chasing trends it has, at least, reinvigorated the book publishing industry. Only a few years ago, British newspapers and literary magazines were lamenting the demise of fiction and drafting its obituary. As one of the *Granta* list judges said in 2003, 'There is evidence that this lean spell is drawing to a close…new British fiction is alive and well and in excellent health.'

THEATRE

The spotlight has been on the many Hollywood names appearing on the London stage in recent years, but even behind the scenes, theatre in the English capital has rarely borne such a sense of excitement as now, during the first act of the 21st century.

The stars all came for the kudos of making it in the home of serious English drama – it's certainly not for the money as they generally only take home £250 to £300 a week. Gwyneth Paltrow, Woody Harrelson and Kyle MacLachlan passed muster with the fans and critics, Gillian Anderson, Glenn Close and Madonna didn't. Nicole Kidman shone, shimmying out of her clothes like 'theatrical Viagra' in director Sam Mendes' production of *The Blue Room* at the Donmar Warehouse. Matthew Perry got the thumbs down, in essence because he reprised the role of Chandler in *Friends* in his London stage debut in *Sexual Perversity in Chicago*. Could he *be* any more predictable?

However, while it would be unfair to dismiss these appearances as mere stage dressing, the stars are only half the story. The rest is a tale of inspiring artistic directors taking up new roles, a fresh injection of £25 million of Arts Council funding into theatre nationally, a wealth and depth of local talent and the West End's learning from the experimentation of the fringe.

Writer Lyn Gardner, in a *Guardian* article from 6 July 2002, enthuses about attending performance-style happenings under the railway arches in Bethnal Green or walking into the Lyric Hammersmith and discovering that, instead of sitting in the auditorium, 'your place is on the stage. British theatre has never had quite so much variety and multiformity,' she opines.

In many ways, however, British theatre has always had periods of being revolutionary. At the end of the Civil War in the 1640s, the Puritans decided to shut down Southwark's trademark theatres, believing them to represent a threat, as dens of iniquity. (And certainly, the disorderly behaviour of medieval audiences would shock modern spectators.)

In the 1950s and 1960s too – an era that theatre critic Michael Billington calls the most important in English theatre since the time of Shakespeare – drama managed to perfectly encapsulate the social upheaval of the post-WWII period. John Osborne's *Look Back in Anger* at the Royal Court in 1956 has gone down as generation-defining. However, it wasn't a lone cry in the wilder-

Arts – Theatre

Gilbert & Sullivan

We don't know where they fit in but we thought you'd like to know that these prolific 18th-century Londoners were responsible for the comic operettas *The Pirates of Penzance* and *The Mikado*. William Gilbert (1836–1911) wrote the words and Arthur Sullivan (1842–1900) the music.

ness, and in the following decade a rash of new writing appeared, from Harold Pinter's *Homecoming* to Joe Orton's *Loot*, Tom Stoppard's *Rosencrantz and Guildenstern are Dead* and Alan Ayckbourn's *How the Other Half Loves*. During the same period many of today's leading theatre companies were formed, including the National Theatre, under the director-ship of actor Laurence Olivier, in 1963.

Whether today's trends represent such a seismic shift is a matter for history to decide. However, there certainly is a lot going on. After a period in the West End, the Royal Court has returned to the newly renovated Jerwood Theatre in Sloane Square. Once described by the *New York Times* as 'the most important theatre in Europe', it focuses exclusively on new writing, and in the last decade has nurtured such talented playwrights as Jez Butterworth *(Mojo, The Night Heron)*, Ayub Khan-Din *(East Is East)* and Conor McPherson *(The Weir)*. More work of that ilk, as well as new plays by established writers such as David Hare *(My Zinc Bed)*, will always be found here.

Shakespeare in Limbo

'Ladies and gentlemen, the Royal Shakespeare Company (RSC) has left the building.' Of course, the RSC's departure from the Barbican Centre was never announced with such Las Vegas panache, but in May 2002 that's exactly what the company did. And that decision to quit its long-term London home has had negative consequences for the UK's leading theatre company, from which it might take years to recover.

To appreciate the seriousness of the matter, one has to understand the esteem in which the RSC is held. It was formed in 1960 by respected director Sir Peter Hall, on the back of the then 80-year-old Shakespeare Memorial Theatre in Stratford-upon-Avon (Shakespeare's birthplace, and the site of the RSC's other permanent home). Since, it has introduced many spectators to the wonders of the Bard and played alma mater to such recognised actors as Kenneth Branagh and Judi Dench.

The unpopular instruction to 'exit, stage left' from the Barbican was given by controversial artistic director Adrian Noble. The RSC had staged plays virtually all year round in the complex's two theatres since 1982, but when the lease came up for renewal Noble decided to launch a revamp of the company, including a total reconstruction of its playhouse in Stratford.

To cut a long story short, this large company was forced to act like a party of itinerant troubadours, looking for a new theatre for each separate production in London, ticket sales plummeted and the company had a terrible financial year. Before the ill-planned move even went through, however, Noble announced he was leaving.

More than a year later, the RSC had a new artistic director, Michael Boyd, but it still hadn't found a permanent London base. Whether it decides to resettle or not at some point, it will take considerable time before this major UK troupe can put the ramifications of such a long period of uncertainty (a £1.3 million deficit, lost personnel, lost talent) behind it. There's a Shakespeare quote for every occasion and with the RSC and the Barbican it's been a case of 'parting is such sweet sorrow'.

Over at the National Theatre, on London's South Bank, Nicholas Hynter has assumed the role of director and immediately begun working on one of the perennial problems of London theatre – how to attract younger, more demographically representative audiences. One of his first productions was *Elmina's Kitchen*, about 'yardie' gangster violence in Hackney, which totally subverted the tradition of audiences being mostly white, middle-class and middle-aged. While programming more traditional fare such as *Henry V* and the *Duchess of Malfi*, Hynter also oversaw the transfer of the genre-bending *Jerry Springer – the Opera* to the National.

Another hot topic recently is the news that Kevin Spacey has taken over as artistic director at the Old Vic. The first priority must be the millions of pounds worth of repairs needed on the 180-year-old building. However, Spacey has also promised to appear at least twice a year on the Old Vic's stage – something he's already done during a much-acclaimed performance in *The Ice Man Cometh*. His presence should certainly inject some energy.

Meanwhile, there's a real buzz about the reconstructed Globe, with its mix of traditional Shakespearean staging and radical modern twists. This open-air theatre has mimicked the Elizabethan era with audiences standing scarily close to actors, heckling and ribaldry since it opened in 1997. Now director Mark Rylance has harked back hundreds of years with all-male casts for some productions, while introducing the novel concept of using only female performers in others.

Even off–West End companies in London produce amazing theatre. The Donmar's fame was sealed while Sam Mendes was artistic director, before he became better known for the movie *American Beauty* and for marrying Kate Winslet. Now it's in the capable hands of Michael Grandage, formerly of Sheffield Theatres, where he worked with Joseph Fiennes and Kenneth Branagh. Grandage's first season showed the way, spicing up some standards, for example casting a black actor in Noel Coward's *The Vortex*. It also included European theatre, such as Albert Camus' *Caligula* and *Accidental Death of an Anarchist* by Italian Dario Fo.

Like the Donmar, the tiny Almeida in Islington has long been a byword for engaging theatre. Now it's back in its renovated home, with newly appointed Michael Attenborough launching back into the likes of Ibsen's *The Lady from the Sea*.

Two other small venues always worth checking out are the Young Vic and the Southwark Playhouse. Both places have promising young directors and an intimacy that really brings works to life. In a city where the likes of Judi Dench, Ralph Fiennes, Ian McKellen and Kristen Scott Thomas still appear on stage, perhaps it's unsurprising that Simon Callow (of *Four Weddings and a Funeral* fame) would perform at the 70-seat Southwark Playhouse.

Shakespeare's Globe, Southwark (p161)

Undoubtedly, the West End has experienced financial difficulties since fewer visitors started coming to London after 2001. However, it never suffered the drop-off in sales that hit New York's Broadway, due in part to the West End's willingness to experiment with new theatre. It's certainly not all 19th-century classics like Oscar Wilde's *An Ideal Husband*, George Bernard Shaw's *Pygmalion* or JB Priestley's *An Inspector Calls* in commercial theatres these days – although the last two plays are never far away in some form (*Pygmalion* usually as the musical adaptation *My Fair Lady*). Rather, venues like the New Ambassadors, in particular, have experimented with plays from fringe companies like Shared Experience (*Jane Eyre*) and even explored hip-hop Shakespeare in an unlikely critical success called *The Bomb-itty of Errors*.

Showtime!

Cats might have used up all of its nine lives and been cancelled after 21 years, but musical theatre sings on in London, albeit rather less certainly as ticket sales have fallen. If you're a fan, however, there's still plenty to see, from long runners *Chicago, Phantom of the Opera* and *Les Misérables* to the likes of the newer, Bollywood-themed *Bombay Dreams.*

Some of the offerings have been little more than a 'greatest hits' collection strung together with a threadbare plot. The Abba musical *Mamma Mia!* and the Queen-fest *We Will Rock You*, for example, will really only appeal to those bands' dedicated followers. Other musicals, however, are spared the disapprobation of theatre critics; these include *Chitty Chitty Bang Bang* (for children only), *The Lion King* and Willy Russell's Liverpool melodrama *Blood Brothers.*

Musicals first became popular in London in the 1980s when the Thatcher government cut funding to theatres, which then decided to programme overtly populist shows. The doyen then, as now, was Andrew Lloyd Webber *(Cats, Phantom of the Opera, Joseph and the Amazing Technicolor Dreamcoat)* who has since acquired the title Sir. It's been said by some wags that Conservative supporter Lloyd Webber's 1997 threat to leave England permanently in the event of a Labour victory helped propel Tony Blair to power. In the end, however, he relented and stayed on to give Ben Elton a taste for scripting musicals in their joint venture *The Beautiful Game.* Once a respected writer of the '80s TV show *The Young Ones* and comic novels, the left-wing Elton's now added the rather woeful script of *We Will Rock You* to his CV.

It's true that some of the best theatre in London doesn't even have a permanent home. That's not referring to the Royal Shakespeare Company's rather unfortunate circumstances (p41), but to the smaller touring troupes who thrive on itinerancy. Improbable Theatre had a hit with the 'junk opera' *Shockheaded Peter.* Then it helped create *Sticky*, an extravaganza of sticky tape and fireworks, which is built as tall as a crane, while the audience watches, and then made to change form. Improbable Theatre doesn't always work in London, but keep an eye out, because when it does, it always draws a crowd. For listings, p313.

MUSIC

Whatever your musical inclination, something in London will strike the right chord. Popular music is perhaps the city's greatest contribution to the world of arts, and after more than four decades at the top, it is still a creative hotbed and a magnet for bands and hopefuls from all over. Complementing the home-grown talent is a continuous influx of styles and cultures that keeps the music scene here so fresh. Per head, Britons buy more music than any other nationality – the range is enormous, and we reckon London's still the best place in the world to go and see live bands. For a list of venues, p305.

London's prolific output began with the Kinks and their north London songwriter Ray Davies, whose lyrics read like a guide to the city. 'You Really Got Me', 'All Day and All of the Night' and 'Dedicated Follower of Fashion' capture the anti-establishment mood of the '60s brilliantly, while 'Waterloo Sunset' is the ultimate feel-good London song.

Another London band, the Rolling Stones, got their first paying gig at the old Bull & Bush in Richmond in 1963. Originally an R'n'B outfit, they went on to define rock and roll, and success and teen mayhem came to them quickly. Their second single 'I Wanna Be Your Man' came to them via a chance encounter on the street with John Lennon and Paul McCartney, two blokes down from Liverpool, recording in Abbey Rd and on their way to making their band, the Beatles, the biggest the world has ever known. The Stones, no slouches in the fame stakes themselves, released 'Not Fade Away' in 1964 and they're doggedly sticking to their word after 40 years of swaggering, swilling and swearing.

Classical Connections

Although London's not known for its classical composers, it is closely associated with one of the greatest of all time, George Frederick Handel, who spent most of his life here. Also, JS Bach's youngest son, Johann Christian, spent his last 20 years here and is sometimes called 'the English Bach'.

A Musical Journey Through London

- Zebra crossing on Abbey Rd – the Beatles
- 23 Brook St – former home to composers Handel and Hendrix
- St Martin's College – first Sex Pistols gig
- Tree on Queen's Ride, Barnes – where Marc Bolan died in his mini in 1977
- 6 Denmark Terrace, Muswell Hill – the family home of Ray Davies of the Kinks
- Regent Sound Studios – where many of the '60s best artists recorded, including the Rolling Stones, the Beatles and David Bowie
- Good Mixer, 30 Inverness St, Camden – famous Blur haunt

Struggling to be heard above the din was inspirational mod band, the Small Faces, formed in 1965 and remembered long after. The Who, from West London, got attention by thrashing guitars on stage and chucking televisions out of hotel windows. The band is remembered for rock operas and hanging around far too long flogging their back catalogue. Jimi Hendrix came to London and took guitar playing to levels not seen before or since. In some ways, the swinging '60s ended in July 1969 when the Stones played a free concert in Hyde Park in front of more than a quarter of a million liberated fans.

A local band called Tyrannosaurus Rex had enjoyed moderate success up to then. In 1970, they changed their name to T. Rex, frontman Marc Bolan donned a bit of glitter and the world's first 'glam' band had arrived. Glam encouraged the youth of uptight Britain to come out of the closet and be whatever they wanted to be. Brixton boy and self-proclaimed 'chameleon of pop', David Bowie, began to steal the limelight, sealing his international fame with *The Rise and Fall of Ziggy Stardust and the Spiders from Mars* in 1972, one of the best albums of the decade. Roxy Music, incorporating art rock and synth pop, sang 'Love Is the Drug' in 1975.

Meanwhile, a little band called Led Zeppelin formed in London in 1968 and created the roots of heavy metal. Seventeen-year-old Farok Bulsara came to London from India (via Zanzibar) in the '60s and, in 1970, changed his name to Freddie Mercury; the consummate showman formed the band Queen with a few local lads and went on to become one of the greatest rock and roll stars of all time. Fleetwood Mac stormed the US as much as Britain; their *Rumours* became the fifth-highest-selling album in history (one behind Cambridge boys Pink Floyd). Bob Marley recorded his *Live* album at the Lyceum Theatre in 1975.

While glam opened the door for British youth, punk came along and kicked the fucking thing down, setting about turning the whole British establishment on its head. The Sex Pistols were the most outrageous of a wave of bands, including the Clash and the Damned, which started playing around London in 1976. The Pistols' first single was, appropriately enough, 'Anarchy in the UK.' 'God Save the Queen' and 'Pretty Vacant' followed and were brilliant. The album, *Never Mind the Bollocks Here's the Sex Pistols,* was released a year later to critical acclaim. Punk could have imploded the following year when Johnny Rotten left the band on stage in the US after teasing the audience, 'Ever get the feeling you've been cheated?'

Fortunately, fellow Londoners the Clash had harnessed the raw anger of the time and worked it into a collar-grabbing brand of political protest that would see them outlast all of their peers. They tread the fine line between being pissed-off punks and great songwriters. The Clash were protesters who raged against racism, social injustice, police

Underworld venue, Camden (p307)

brutality and disenfranchisement. The disillusioned generation finally had a plan, and a leader; *London Calling* is a spirited call to arms.

The ranting and raving John Lydon (formerly Johnny Rotten) became an embarrassment to a generation weaned on punk but the reaction to the death of Clash frontman, Joe Strummer, in late 2002 showed that there was still lots to be proud of.

Cockney boy Ian Dury was knocking around in the late '70s, winning fans with his stage charisma (despite being handicapped from childhood polio) and his unusual blend of music-hall/punk rock. He is best remembered for inviting people to hit him with their rhythm sticks in 1977. That same year the Jam, punk pioneers *and* mod revivalists, went on tour opening for the Clash (what days!). Lead singer and bristling live performer, Paul Weller, followed up with a hugely successful solo career. As far away from punk as you could get in the late '70s, the pop frivolity of South London's Squeeze was a sign of things to come.

Out of the ashes of punk came, God knows how, the new wave and new romantics. Guitars were chucked away and replaced with keyboard synthesizers and drum machines. Fashion and image became as important as the music, and it's the seriousness with which the new romantics took themselves that gives the '80s such a bad rap. Overpriced, oversexed and way overdone, '80s London produced such unforgettables as Spandau Ballet, Boy George, Bananarama, Wham! and Howard Jones' haircut. Wham!'s Georgios Panayiotou shaved his back, changed his name to George Michael and went on to a hugely successful solo career.

Local lads the Pet Shop Boys managed to avoid the '80s pop-path to oblivion, redeeming themselves with synth innovation later on. Two bands to start in London in the late '70s were the Police and Dire Straits, who'd shine brilliantly for much of the '80s and become exceedingly annoying later (through Mark Knopfler's overplayed riffs and Sting's wishy-washiness). Depeche Mode broke new ground in neo-synth pop

Top 10 CDs by London Artists

- *Something Else* – The Kinks
- *London Calling* – The Clash
- *Sound Affects* – The Jam
- *The Rise and Fall of Ziggy Stardust and the Spiders from Mars* – David Bowie
- *Exile on Main Street* – The Rolling Stones
- *Violator* – Depeche Mode
- *Head Music* – Suede
- *Modern Life Is Rubbish* – Blur
- *Rafi's Revenge* – Asian Dub Foundation
- *OK* – Talvin Singh

while London adoptee Chrissie Hynde formed the Pretenders and became the first bad-ass rock and roll chick; Neneh Cherry started rapping and Madness came up with a winning ska-pop combo and featured London in many of their hits and video clips. Shane McGowan led London-Irish posse, the Pogues, on a glorious punk rampage through traditional Irish music, capturing the mood of the city with 'The Dark Streets of London' and the achingly beautiful 'A Rainy Night in Soho'.

But it was all to no avail because blonde boy band Bros emerged from south London to top the charts and confirm that the local music scene was really in deep shit. Relief was already coming from up north with the Smiths, and at the end of the decade the Stone Roses and the Happy Mondays broke through with a new sound that had grown out of the recent acid-house raves, with jangly guitars, psychedelic twists and a beat you just couldn't resist. Dance exploded onto the scene, with dilated pupils and Chupa Chups, in 1988's summer of love. A generation was gripped by dance music and a new lexicon had to be learned: techno, electronica, hip hop, garage, house, trance and so on. Although the E generation that launched the rave/dance culture has grown up and the scene is, well, stagnant at best, London still reigns among the best club cities in the world.

The '90s were all about Britpop, a genre broadly defined as back to (Beatles') basics, familiar old-fashioned three chords and all that jazz, with loads of slang and in-references which, frankly, made it so 'British'. There was a very public battle between two of the biggest bands, Blur from London and Oasis from Manchester, and the public loved the tit-for-tat between the cocky geezers from the capital and the swaggering, belligerent Mancs. For the record, Oasis won the popularity contest but the more dynamic Blur are ageing better. Weighing in for the London side were the brilliant and erratic Suede (check out *Head Music*) and Elastica, fronted by the punky, poppy Justine Frischmann.

Skirting around the edges, doing their own thing without the hullabaloo, were Radiohead (from Oxford, close enough to London), in our opinion the best group in the world. As the Britpop bands and fans became more sophisticated, the genre died around 1997. Groups like Coldplay – who released two superb albums in 2000 and 2002 – are in the same mould but several times better than the over-hyped Britpop stars.

The scene is still as vibrant as ever – it's just that the good stuff is lost under an avalanche of commercial crap. A handful of artists seem to be in perpetual rotation at the top of the charts, headed, invariably, by Spice Boy Robbie Williams.

The Cross, Kings Cross (p298)

At the beginning of the 21st century, it's multicultural London pushing things forward, to bend the words of Mike Skinner (aka The Streets), whose debut album, *Original Pirate Material,* took London by storm in 2002 with everyday tales from the life of a modern 'geeza'. It's a genre-straddling classic from a young white rapper originally from Birmingham and now living in Brixton, a cross-cultural gem that lights the way for London's music scene in the 21st century.

The other revelation of recent years has been Ms Dynamite (aka Niomi McLean-Daley), a young rapper from north London who won the prestigious Mercury Award in 2002 for her outstanding debut album, *A Little Deeper.* Her hard-hitting, finger-wagging lyrics are political and challenging. So Solid Crew are the archetypal Brixton rap band, while teenage MC Dizzee Rascal from Bow in East London combines confronting lyrics with an aggressive sound and is one to watch.

London's Asian community has also made a big splash in recent years with Talvin Singh and Nitin Sawhney fusing dance with traditional Indian music to stunning effect, and Asian Dub Foundation bringing their unique brand of jungle techno and political comment to an ever-widening audience, despite being dropped by the major British record labels.

VISUAL ARTS

After a couple of millennia, the sum total of Britain's contribution to the higher echelons of visual art was the romantic landscape painter, JMW Turner (1775–1851). Despite its incredibly rich collections, Britain had never led, dominated or even really participated in a particular epoch or style. That all changed in the twilight of the 20th century when Britart burst onto the scene with its sliced cows, elephant dung and piles of bricks. It's questionable whether the movement will leave a lasting impression but one thing's for sure, for the length of the 1990s London was the beating heart of the art world.

Britart sprang from a show called Freeze that was staged in a Docklands warehouse in 1988. It was organized by showman Damien Hirst and largely featured his fellow graduates from Goldsmiths College. Influenced by pop culture and punk, this loose movement was soon catapulted to notoriety by the advertising guru Charles Saatchi, who came to dominate the scene like a puppeteer. Indeed, you could almost say he created the genre with his free spending and commissioning. From 1992 he held a series of seven exhibitions entitled Young British Artists (YBAs), which featured the vanguard of modern British art. The work was brash, decadent, ironic, easy to grasp and eminently marketable.

To shock seemed the impulse, and the artists did just that: Hirst chipped in with a cow sliced into sections and preserved in formaldehyde, flies buzzing around another cow's head being zapped in his early work, *A Thousand Years;* Chris Ofili provoked with the *Holy Virgin Mary,* a black Madonna made partly with elephant poo; Marc Quinn's macabre sculpture of *A Head* was made with nine pints of his own blood; and Marcus Harvey created a portrait of notorious child-killer Myra Hindley, made entirely with children's hand-prints.

The areas of Shoreditch, Hoxton and Whitechapel – where many artists lived, worked and hung out – became the epicentre of the movement and a rash of galleries moved in. Among these was White Cube, owned by one of the most important patrons of early Britart, Jay Jopling.

The exhibitions sent shockwaves around the world, as sections of society took it in turns to be outraged. Liberals were drawn into defending the works, the media went positively gaga promoting some of the artists like pop stars and Britart became the talk of the world. For the 10 years or so that it rode the wave of this publicity, its defining characteristics were celebrity and shock value. Damien Hirst and Tracey Emin became the inevitable celebrities; people the media knew they could sell to the mainstream.

Tracey Emin Inspires 'Stuckism' – In More Ways than One

Stuckism is a radical art movement devoted to advancing the cause of painting as the most vital means of addressing contemporary issues Stuckism is a direct rebuttal of the 20th-century development of modernism and particularly Britart, which, according to the website (www.stuckism.com), exists 'not by virtue of the work but institutional and financial power, (and is) flattered by critical acquiescence'. The name Stuckism was derived, in the best art historical tradition, from an insult, in this case from Britart poster girl Tracey Emin, who chided ex-boyfriend Billy Childish, 'Your paintings are stuck, you're stuck! Stuck! Stuck! Stuck!'

One of their number, Sean Hall, has a bet with William Hill bookmakers that Charles Saatchi will buy Hall'ss latest work – an ordinary betting slip – for £1000 or more; at the time of research, it was on sale for £10,000 at the Stuckism Centre, 3 Charlotte Rd, Hoxton EC2.

One critic said the hugely hyped movement was the product of a 'cultural vacuum' and had become like the emperor's new clothes, which everyone was afraid to criticise for fear they'd look stupid. 'Cold, mechanical, conceptual bullshit', was how the culture minister described the nominations for the Turner Prize one year.

Tracey Emin went on to become the most famous artist-behaving-badly. She was shortlisted for the Turner Prize with an installation called *My Bed,* her unmade messy bed, strewn with blood-stained underwear and used condoms. For another installation, called *Everyone I Have Ever Slept with 1963–1995,* she sewed the names of all the relevant people on a tent. She was perfect for Britart because she pandered to the public's darkest levels of voyeurism *and* their love of celebrity. When her cat went missing people tore down the notices she put up as *objets d'art*.

But while the world was focusing on the stars, there were a lot of great artists hammering away on the fringes. A highlight of the era has to be Richard Wilson's iconic installation, *20: 50* (1987), which is now a former council chamber in the Saatchi Gallery (p157) filled waist-high with recycled oil. Walking into the room makes you feel like you've just been shot out into space. Martin Creed won 2001's Turner Prize with his brilliant *The Lights Going On and Off.* In his most famous work, *24 Hour Psycho,* Scottish video artist Douglas Gordon slowed Alfred Hitchcock's masterpiece down so much it was stripped of its narrative and viewed more like a moving sculpture, while Gary Hume quietly went about his work, the less-fashionable painting. Hume first came to prominence with his *Doors* series of full-size painting of hospital doors, powerful allegorical descriptions of despair – or just perfect reproductions of doors.

Rachel Whiteread won the Turner Prize in 1993 for *House,* a concrete cast of an East End terrace dwelling that the council

Top Five Galleries

- Tate Modern (p160)
- National Gallery (p95)
- Saatchi Gallery (p157)
- Tate Britain (p129)
- Courtauld Gallery (p99)

controversially knocked down shortly afterwards. In the same week she won £40,000 in the doubly lucrative prize for Worst British Artist of the year, an award set up by former disco funsters KLF, who out-shocked the Britartists by burning £1 million in cash in front of assembled journalists.

That London had embraced modern art was confirmed with the immediate and resounding success of Tate Modern when it opened in 2000, and again when the Saatchi Gallery relocated to the centre of town in 2003.

But Londoners – weaned on a diet of pickled animals, mutilated Barbie dolls and unmade beds – are no longer for shocking. At the 2000 Turner Prize, the most colourful chapter in British art history came to a close as Britart was pronounced dead. The

Taking It to the Streets

As you wander around central London, look out for the works of Banksy, Britain's most celebrated graffiti artist, who uses the streets as the canvas for his beautifully subversive, politically potent stencils and slogans. Straddling street and commercial art, the Bristolian has published two books, staged a gallery show (albeit in a scruffy warehouse in Hackney) and designed the cover of Blur's *Think Tank* album in 2003 – although he remains totally anonymous. He might be the world's most famous stencil artist, but his parents still think he's a humble painter and decorator. It's a thrill just happening upon Banksy's stuff on the streets but visit www.banksy.co.uk first so you'll recognise his signature.

so-called young British artists have grown up and are mostly doing their own thing, and no longer constitute a movement. Meanwhile, it's conceded that new centres of creative energy have replaced London. Some are still trying to flog Britart as the vital creative force it was, partly because nothing has emerged to replace it and partly because museums and collectors invested too much in the genre to just let it die.

BEFORE BRITART

In comparison, the history of British art before the wild ones of the 1990s looks decidedly pedestrian and conformist.

It wasn't until the rule of the Tudors that art took off in London at all. The German Hans Holbein the Younger (1497–1543) was court painter to Henry VIII, and one of his finest works, *The Ambassadors* (1533), hangs in the National Gallery. The English miniaturist Nicholas Hilliard (1547–1619) did portraits of Sir Francis Drake and Sir Walter Raleigh. A batch of great portrait artists worked at court during the 17th century. Best of them was Anthony Van Dyck (1599–1641), a Belgian who spent the last nine years of his life in London and painted some hauntingly beautiful portraits of Charles I, including *Charles I on Horseback* (1638), now in the National Gallery. Charles I was a keen collector and it was during his reign that the Raphael Cartoons, now in the Victoria & Albert Museum, came to London. Dutchman Peter Lely (1618–80) and German-born Godfrey Kneller (1646–1723) succeeded Van Dyck as court painters, and you can see many of their portraits in Hampton Court Palace and the National Portrait Gallery respectively.

Local artists began to emerge in the 18th century. Thomas Gainsborough (1727–88) extended portraiture to include the gentry and is regarded as the first great British landscapist even though most of his landscapes are actually backgrounds. William Hogarth (1697–1764), in contrast, is best known for his moralising serial prints of London lowlife (p82). Thomas Rowlandson (1756–1827) went for gentler cartooning that nonetheless packed a punch; some of his works are on display in the Courtauld Gallery.

England has a fine tradition of watercolourists, beginning with the poet and engraver William Blake (1757–1827), some of whose romantic paintings and illustrations (he illustrated Milton's *Paradise Lost*, for example) hang in the Tate Britain. In contrast, John Constable (1776–1837) studied the clouds and skyscapes above Hampstead Heath, sketching hundreds of scenes that he'd later match with subjects in his landscapes. He was a big influence on French Impressionists.

JMW Turner (1775–1851) represented the very pinnacle of 19th-century British art. Equally at home with oils as watercolours, through innovative use of colour and gradations of light he created a new atmosphere that seemed to capture the wonder, sublimity and terror of nature. His later works – including *Snow Storm – Steam-boat off a Harbour's Mouth*

(1842), *Peace – Burial at Sea* (1842) and *Rain, Steam, Speed* (1844), now in Tate Britain and the National Gallery – were increasingly abstract, and although widely vilified at the time, later inspired the likes of Claude Monet.

The Pre-Raphaelite Brotherhood (1848–54), founded in London, burst briefly onto the scene, rejecting what they saw as the shallow conventionalism of academic painting in favour of 'objective truthfulness'. They took their inspiration from the paintings before Raphael and the works of the Romantic poets. They ditched the pastel-coloured rusticity of the day in favour of big, bright and bold depictions of medieval legends and female beauty.

In the 20th century the abstract, rounded sculptures of Henry Moore (1898–1986) drew international plaudits, eventually. Irish-born Francis Bacon caused a stir when he exhibited his *Three Studies for Figures at the Base of a Crucifixion* (1945) – now on display at Tate Britain – and carried on unsettling the world with his distorted, repulsive and fascinating forms. Around the same time Lucian Freud (1922–) had his first exhibition. The renowned Australian art critic, Robert Hughes, has described him as 'the greatest living realist painter'.

The seminal work of Londoner Richard Hamilton (1922–), *Just What Is It that Makes Today's Home so Different, so Appealing?* (1956), with its references to popular culture and consumerism, is considered by many to be the first piece of pop art, a term coined by an English critic in 1958. Pop art tied in perfectly with the image of London in the swinging '60s. The brilliant David Hockney (1937–) gained a reputation as one of the leading pop artists through his early use of magazine-style images (although he rejected the label). After a move to California, his stuff became increasingly naturalistic as he took inspiration from the sea, sun, swimmers and swimming pools. Two of his most famous works, *Mr and Mrs Clark and Percy* (1971) and *A Bigger Splash* (1974) are displayed at Tate Britain.

Gilbert & George were the quintessential English conceptual artists of the 1960s. They, at the very least, paved the way for the shock and celebrity of Britart and *were* the art as much as the work itself.

New British sculpture emerged in the '80s, dazzling with its original use of materials and techniques. Its most talented artist was Tony Cragg, whose work can also be seen in Tate Britain. But he, like the movement he was part of, faded way into the background when Britart emerged.

CINEMA & TELEVISION

London, and in particular Soho, is the heart of the UK's film, TV and advertising industries. But it's not New York and it certainly isn't Los Angeles. It doesn't have a resident Woody Allen who's lovingly and repeatedly framed its landscape for the big screen and, as much as it aspires to it, it isn't a major force in global cinema.

The English capital is the home of the world's first public broadcaster, the British Broadcasting Corporation (BBC), and it can still turn out world-beating television. When it comes to movies, however, its enormous pool of talent seems to have found a better outlet in the Hollywood studio system than in any indigenous industry. Certainly, there have been some individual movie gems, including most famously *Four Weddings and a Funeral* and *Trainspotting*. However, the renaissance in UK film each gem is supposed to herald always fails to materialise.

Fans often nostalgically refer back to the golden – but honestly rather brief – era of Ealing comedies, when the London-based

National Film Theatre, South Bank (p294)

49

Pilgrim's Progress

Many film locations are obvious, such as Westminster Bridge and Big Ben. Here are a few less obvious places where you can chase the footsteps of your movie heroes. More details are provided in Colin Sorensen's 'London on Film: 100 Years of Filmmaking in London', in *The Worldwide Guide to Movie Locations Presents: London* by Tony Reeves (www.movie-locations.com) or by contacting the London film commission, called Film London, at info@filmlondon.org.uk.

Borough Market (p243) *Bridget Jones's Diary* was filmed in and around the market, particularly along Bedale St (although the last scene is at the Royal Exchange in Threadneedle St). Park St, in Borough, should also look familiar to fans of *Lock, Stock and Two Smoking Barrels*.

King's Cross Station Platform 4 in King's Cross station now has a plaque commemorating its use as Platform 9 and 3/4, from where the Hogwarts Express leaves in *Harry Potter and the Philosopher's Stone* (2001, known as *Harry Potter and the Sorcerer's Stone* in the US).

Leadenhall Market (p111) Also known as Diagon Alley, where aspiring witches and wizards buy their school supplies in *Harry Potter and the Philosopher's Stone*. Harry and Hagrid are seen walking along here and Harry buys a wand.

London Zoo/Regent's Park (p181) Not only where Harry Potter learned that he can communicate with snakes, but also where David wakes up one morning in *An American Werewolf in London* (1981) and where Richard E Grant delivers Hamlet's soliloquy to a family of wolves in the final scene of cult classic *Withnail and I* (1987) – although the wolf enclosure has now been moved.

Maryon Park, Woolwich According to Film London, this is one of the most popular movie tourism sites in London, as fans come to see where the tennis match with the invisible ball took place in the cult movie *Blow Up* (1966).

Tavy Bridge Shopping Centre, Thamesmead The subway behind this shopping centre served as the location for a particularly brutal beating of a tramp by Alex and his droogs in Stanley Kubrick's cult movie *A Clockwork Orange* (1971).

Travel Bookshop, Notting Hill (p327) In truth, the bookshop at 13 Blenheim Cres is not the shop that appears in *Notting Hill* (1999), as that was mocked up behind 142 Portobello Rd especially for the film. However, the owners have long been happy to oblige anyone who wants to take a photograph. Wander along Portobello Rd, Westbourne Park Rd and around Elgin Square Garden and Hempel Garden Square for more movie memories.

Ealing Studios turned out a steady stream of hits. Between 1947 and 1955, when the studios were sold to the BBC, they produced enduring classics from *Passport to Pimlico, Kind Hearts and Coronets, Whisky Galore* and *The Man in the White Suit* to *The Lavender Hill Mob* and *The Ladykillers*. This was also the time of legendary film-makers Michael Powell and Emeric Pressburger, the men behind *The Life and Death of Colonel Blimp* and *The Red Shoes*.

Today, such halcyon days seem far distant, as the industry seems stuck in a rut of romantic comedies, costume dramas and gangster pics, and continues to go through frequent cycles of bust and boom. Producers, directors and actors complain about a lack of adventurousness in those who hold the purse strings, while film investors claim there are not enough scripts worth backing. And each side has a point. For every *Young Adam* (a critically acclaimed Ewan McGregor vehicle) that nearly doesn't get made, there's a *Velvet Goldmine* (a widely panned McGregor movie) that does.

A system of public funding through the UK Film Council exists alongside private investment, and although in 2002 it only accounted for a minority of the £570 million spent on film in the UK, some critics object to the scheme. The *Evening Standard*'s late, lamented former film critic Alexander Walker was one of those who suggested that it led to poor projects being made, simply because the money is there.

Meanwhile, well-known English actors such as McGregor, Ian McKellen, Ralph Fiennes, Jude Law, Liam Neeson, Hugh Grant, Rhys Ifans, Kristen Scott Thomas and Emily Watson spend time working abroad, as do many British directors, like Tony Scott, *(Top Gun, True Romance)* and Ridley Scott *(Bladerunner, Alien, Thelma & Louise, Gladiator)*, Anthony Minghella *(The English Patient, Cold Mountain)*, Michael Winterbottom *(The Claim)* and Sam Mendes *(American Beauty, The Road to Perdition)*.

Although it's not as photogenic as New York, London does appear as a cinematic backdrop more times than you might initially guess. That's been particularly true in recent years. Naturally, the eponymous west London neighbourhood pops up in 1999's *Notting Hill*, but who would have thought that the Dickensian back streets of Borough should feature in such polar opposites as chick-flick *Bridget Jones's Diary* and Guy Ritchie's street-cred gangster romp *Lock, Stock and Two Smoking Barrels.*

The city's combination of historic and ultramodern architecture certainly works to its advantage in this respect. Ang Lee's *Sense and Sensibility,* for example, could retreat to historic Greenwich for its wonderful parkland and neoclassical architecture. Inigo Jones' Queen's House, in particular, features in interior scenes. Merchant Ivory's costume drama *Howard's End* and the biopic *Chaplin* feature the neo-Gothic St Pancras Chambers, while the early 1980s film *The Elephant Man* took advantage of the moody atmosphere around the then-undeveloped Shad Thames (the site of today's Butler's Wharf).

By contrast, the 1999 James Bond movie *The World Is Not Enough* opens with a boat chase down the River Thames, culminating in Pierce Brosnan as Bond jumping into a hot-air balloon at the Millennium Dome.

There are some films that Londoners find heart-warming just because they feature ordinary shots of the contemporary city. The parallel storylines in *Sliding Doors,* where Gwyneth Paltrow's love life hinges on whether she catches a train, had mixed reviews. However, it's quite fun to watch it for the shots of the Underground, west London and Primrose Hill. Similarly 2002's *28 Days Later* from *Trainspotting* director Danny Boyle was criticised, but the opening scenes of central London and Docklands lying abandoned after a biological attack were considered the highlight. Popcorn blockbuster *Mission Impossible* features Liverpool St railway station, John Landis' irrepressibly entertaining *An American Werewolf in London* finishes with a mad chase in Piccadilly Circus, and Finnish director Aki Kaurismäki gave west London a unique patina in his downbeat (and woodenly acted) comedy *I Hired a Contract Killer.*

On the other hand, many of the movies filmed in London show no evidence of it in the final cut. That's because the local industry's backbone consists of two jointly run production studios, Pinewood and Shepperton. Here scenes can be shot indoors on sound and stage sets, as was done with *Star Wars* (Part 1), *Tomb Raider* (I and II), *The Trojan War* (starring Brad Pitt) and *Love, Actually,* the directorial debut from *Four Weddings* and *Notting Hill* writer Richard Curtis. (Unfortunately, unlike in Hollywood, these London studios do not offer public tours.)

In one curious case, however, the use of outdoors London as a setting was deliberately disguised. Stanley Kubrick had the area around the abandoned Beckton Gasworks in Newham mocked up as Vietnam for his tour of duty in *Full Metal Jacket.* The destruction wreaked during filming meant the area had to be closed to the public, and a music video for Oasis was the last thing to be filmed there, before the whole lot was pulled down.

When it comes to televisual output, London plays with a somewhat stronger hand than in film: some 13% of programmes shown during peak viewing times throughout the world still originate in Britain. Typically for the age we live in, it has been accused of dumbing down, and some of its biggest smash hits globally – *Who Wants to Be A Millionaire, The Weakest Link* and *Teletubbies* – do lend some weight to those allegations. However, ever since John Logie Baird demonstrated the world's first broadcast of moving images to London's Royal Institute in 1926 – and the BBC began broadcasts in 1932 (regularly from 1936) – there's been a public service ethic driving British TV.

John Reith, the first director-general of the BBC, took quite a paternalistic view of the audience, seeing the role of TV as being to inform and educate, as much as to entertain, and insisted on quality. There's still a hangover of all this today, although commercial TV stations now outnumber public BBC channels. There are five free-to-air stations: BBC1, BBC2 (established 1964), ITV (1955), Channel 4 (1982) and Channel 5 (1997). Even though cable is now available and digital services were introduced in 1998, the BBC derives funding from a system of TV licences paid for by viewers.

A complete history of English television is obviously not possible here, but anyone familiar with the subject will be aware of an enormously long roll call of classic series from comedies such as *Fawlty Towers* and *Rising Damp* and cop shows such as *The Sweeney* and *The Professionals* to cult series such as *The Prisoner, The Avengers* or *Minder,* from 1970s comedies *(The Good Life)* to heritage offerings in the 1980s *(Brideshead Revisited),* from

Top 10 London Films

Bridget Jones's Diary (2001) Skinny Texan Renee Zellweger piled on the pounds and polished the English accent to play Bridget Jones, the archetypal 30-something London career gal who just can't find a man – until she has to choose between two.

Four Weddings and a Funeral (1994) The first outing from the *Notting Hill* team has Charles (Hugh Grant) and friends dashing all over London and the English countryside (always late) to those four matrimonial engagements and one wake – enduring pain and finding love along the way.

The Ipcress File (1965) More London-centric than any of Michael Caine's other 1960s films (including *Get Carter* and the original *The Italian Job*), this moody spy thriller shows off Blackfriars Bridge, the Royal Albert Hall, Marylebone Station, Trafalgar Square and the Victoria & Albert Museum as they were 40 years ago. A brilliant period piece.

The Krays (1990) Gary and Martin Kemp (from 1980s new romantic band Spandau Ballet) star in this biopic of the notorious Kray brothers, Ronnie and Reggie Kray, whose gang controlled the East End underworld in the 1950s and '60s. Not on the level of *GoodFellas*, by any means, but decent enough to have you wanting to learn more.

The Ladykillers (1955) In the last great Ealing comedy, Alec Guinness is a criminal mastermind planning a heist. He and his gang, including Peter Sellers and Herbert Lom, rent rooms in King's Cross from a little old lady, who unwittingly foils their scheme. Such a classic that maybe even the Coen Brothers' forthcoming remake is a mistake.

Lock, Stock and Two Smoking Barrels (1998) Four silly Jack-the-lads (including Nick Moran and Jason Statham) find themselves £500,000 in debt to a scary East End 'ard man when a rigged card game goes wrong. And then they really get out of their depth, in this anarchic, sassy gangster flick by Guy Ritchie (now Mr Madonna).

My Beautiful Laundrette (1985) An interesting vignette from the Thatcher years, *My Beautiful Laundrette* follows outsider Omar (Gordon Warnecke) and his sometime lover Johnny (Daniel Day-Lewis) in their small-time quest to make it big by opening a fabulous neon-lit, music-filled coin-operated laundry. Of course, Hanif Kureishi's script goes further than that, exploring themes of racism, sexuality, adultery, greed and dignity.

Notting Hill (1999) The title made the eponymous west London suburb world famous, and features lots of local scenes, but the plot of this romantic comedy could have taken place nearly anywhere. It revolves around a US superstar (Julia Roberts) falling in love with a humble bookshop owner (Hugh Grant).

Secrets & Lies (1996) The most popular of Mike Leigh's bleak but funny examinations of the minutiae of working-class British lives, this has Hortense, a successful black optician, go in search of her natural mother. That mother turns out to be Cynthia (Brenda Blethyn in an award-winning role), a rather unbalanced white woman with a troublesome family.

Snatch (2000) More of the same London gangsta attitude from Mr Ritchie in this *Lock, Stock* follow-up. Turkish and Tommy get their fingers burnt trying to rig a boxing match, and then a diamond heist intrudes and things descend into chaos. Most memorable for Brad Pitt's (deliberately) indecipherable Oirish accent.

thrillers *(Edge of Darkness)* to dramas *(The Singing Detective)*: the list could go on endlessly. However, undoubtedly, the two most famous TV serials associated with London itself are the long-running soap opera *Eastenders* and police drama *The Bill*. Ironically, the first of those is actually filmed at the BBC studios in Elstree, Hertfordshire, although Albert Square is said to be modelled on Fassett Square in Dalston. *The Bill* is shot around the East End.

In recent years, Britain, like elsewhere, has been in the grip of reality TV fever. *Big Brother* has made a huge splash, while wannabe pop stars were given the chance to be discovered and moulded in *Pop Idols*. But late at night, you might still find a few typically subversive comedies, from *The Kumars at Number 42* to *The Mark Thomas Product*, hosted by Britain's answer to renegade film-maker Michael Moore. One such hidden gem is *Black Books*, where Dylan Moran plays a London-based Irish misanthrope who's been described as the Basil Fawlty of booksellers.

Anyone wishing to learn more could try Lez Cooke's *British Television Drama: A History*, published in 2003, or Tony Currie's *A Concise History of British Television 1930–2000*. For those wishing to see the inner workings of the Television Centre in White City (in west London), there are regular **BBC tours** (☎ 0870 603 0304; adult/child under 10 and student/senior £7.95/5.95/6.95).

DANCE

Some thank Matthew Bourne and his all-male version of *Swan Lake*, others point to a *Billy Elliot* effect. Whatever the reason, dance in London is thriving. Says an Arts Council spokesperson when interviewed for this update, 'We have a very healthy, extremely vibrant scene'.

It's been roughly a decade since Bourne took classical ballet and mixed it with old-fashioned musical and contemporary dance. However, critics still hark back to the moment his bare-chested dancers appeared at Sadler's Wells, thighs clad in white feathers, as pivotal – a watershed that catapulted dance from the back of the arts pages into the popular mainstream.

Even today, his *Swan Lake* still tours the world, while Bourne's also produced newer pieces, from the Scottish-influenced *Highland Fling* to *The Car Man* (a *West Side Story*–style reworking of Bizet's opera *Carmen*). Having presented his own take on Tchaikovsky in *Nutcracker!*, Bourne should be unveiling a version of *Edward Scissorhands* at Sadler's Wells in late 2005.

Such enormous success has inspired more classically trained dancers to cross over into contemporary forms of dance. Take former Royal Ballet dancers Michael Nunn and William Levitt as an example. After a laddish, Channel 4 television documentary made them famous as the *Ballet Boyz*, their George Piper Dances troupe started pulling in youthful audiences with its combination of modern dance and video diary.

Even the Royal Ballet itself, while still focusing on classical works, has started commissioning younger choreographers such as Christopher Wheeldon. His abstract piece *Tryst,* performed by Darcey Bussell and Jonathan Cope, was widely touted as best new ballet of the year.

Since the late 1990s, audiences' huge appetite for dance has seen an extraordinary development of new spaces. The Place, the birthplace of contemporary dance in London, has undergone a major refurbishment. A major new building has been opened in Deptford for the Laban Centre for Movement and Dance.

Perhaps the most important shot in the gracefully positioned arm, however, has been the reopening of Sadler's Wells. With its new 15-sq-metre stage and modern backstage facilities, it's been able to woo the cream of international troupes, including the likes of the legendary Pina Bausch, Twyla Tharp, Dance Theatre of Harlem and Alvin Ailey.

'London has always been one of the main dance places to be, along with Paris and New York, but this has upped the stakes,' said a spokesperson from Sadler's Wells when interviewed for this update.

The city's multicultural diversity has also been a boon. There's a strong strand of South Asian dance here, exemplified by the work of Shobana Jeyasingh or Akram Khan. Trained in traditional Kathak dance, Khan has been described as 'almost levitating' when he starts to move.

One good bet for seeing Asian performances is usually the **Summer on the South Bank** festival in August (p155). The other main London dance festival is **Dance Umbrella** (☎ 8741 5881; www.danceumbrella.co.uk). Running for six weeks from late September, it's one of the world's leading dance festivals of its kind. Otherwise, for the latest on what's on check www.londondance.com. For more information on specific venues and companies, see p302.

Arts – Dance

Get into the Groove

If what you see on stage inspires you, London offers everything from belly-dancing to tango lessons. Apart from serious professional training at The Place (p302) or the Laban Centre (p302), there are the following schools, or check weekly listings in *Time Out*.

Cecil Sharp House (☎ 7485 2206; www.efdss.org; 2 Regent's Park Rd NW1) For Morris and other English folk dances.

Danceworks (☎ 7629 6183; www.dance works.co.uk; 16 Balderton St W1) Bollywood grooves, flamenco, break-dancing and much more.

Drill Hall (☎ 7307 5060; www.drillhall.co.uk; 16 Chenies St WC1) Salsa, tango, jive and classical Indian dance.

Pineapple Dance Studios (☎ 7836 4004; www.pineapple.uk.com; 7 Langley St WC2) From ballet to jazz, salsa to hip hop and more.

SCIENCE & PHILOSOPHY

The contributions made by Londoners – or those with a strong London link – to diverse fields of science and technology have been innumerable. Isaac Newton (1642–1727), who legend tells us promulgated the law of gravity after an apple conked him on the noggin, moved from Cambridge to London in 1701 and was president of the Royal Society of London from 1703. He is buried in Westminster Abbey. Edmund Halley (1656–1742), the scientist who first observed the comet that now bears his name, and James Bradley (1693–1762), who provided direct evidence that the earth revolves around the sun, were the second and third Astronomers Royal at Greenwich between 1720 and 1762.

The evolutionary theorist Charles Darwin (1809–82) lived for more than four decades at Down House in southeast London. Here he wrote the slightly controversial *On the Origin of Species* (1859), in which he used his experiences during a five-year voyage to South America and the Galapagos Islands to develop a theory of evolution by natural selection. The chemist and physicist Michael Faraday (1791–1867), a pioneer in electromagnetism and inventor of the electric battery (1812), spent much of his adult life in Islington and is buried in Highgate Cemetery.

Twentieth-century London residents who made a great impact on science include the Scot Alexander Fleming (1881–1955), who discovered penicillin while working as a research immunologist at St Mary's Hospital, Paddington, and John Logie Baird (1888–1946), who invented TV and gave the first public demonstration of the newfangled medium in a room above a Greek St restaurant in Soho in 1925.

In the field of philosophy, London can claim a link to Thomas Hobbes (1588–1679), author of *The Leviathan* and the first thinker since Aristotle to develop a comprehensive theory of nature including human behaviour. He was tutor to the exiled Prince Charles and a great favourite at court when the latter assumed the throne as Charles II in 1660. Karl Marx (1818–83), Friedrich Engels (1820–95), George Bernard Shaw (1856–1950) and Mahatma Gandhi (1869–1948) all studied, thought and wrote in the British Museum Reading Room. The influential thinker, pacifist and Nobel Prize–winner Bertrand Russell (1872–1970) was a lecturer at the London School of Economics at the end of the 19th century and was elected to the Royal Society of London in 1908.

Architecture

Architecture

Congratulations on the timing of your journey: the London you're visiting, or planning to visit, is, according to *Observer* newspaper architecture critic Deyan Sudjic, 'in the grip of a once-in-century transformation'. Sudjic's not a fan of all the changes (of which more later), but his view of a fundamental makeover is shared by the president of the Royal Institute of British Architects (RIBA), George Ferguson. 'London is discovering itself,' Ferguson told us enthusiastically when interviewed for this update.

That's not to ignore the fact that a chronic housing shortage, decaying public transport infrastructure and the need for more inner-city regeneration all remain major problems for those who live here. However, recent public architecture has at least generated a sense of energy and adventure about the city.

So what's new? It's not just landmarks such as the Swiss Re Tower to which architects will point, although there are plenty of those as one scans the horizon, from the magnificent Tate Modern and the Millennium Bridge to the London Eye and City Hall. On a much more fundamental level, London has stopped grumpily turning its back on the Thames and begun a new love affair with its river.

At the same time, in this most commercially minded city, there's even a reawakening sense of connectivity and public space – walkways along the South Bank now connect public areas from Butler's Wharf to County Hall. 'It's opened up new vistas,' says RIBA's Ferguson. 'It's now one of the great world city experiences to walk over the new Millennium Bridge, going from Tate Modern straight to St Paul's. It's given people a new understanding of St Paul's and the City.'

Tate Britain, Millbank (p129)

Unlike some great metropolises such as Paris, London was never methodically planned. And compared with other major cities such as New York, it's historically been low-rise. That latter characteristic is now up for grabs, as mayor Ken Livingstone promotes the construction of clusters of tall buildings as a show of economic strength. However, the legacy of London's successive waves of organic growth will always be with it, including a constantly simmering tension between the traditional and the new.

LAYING THE FOUNDATIONS

The roots of the city lie in the walled Roman settlement of Londinium, first established in AD 43 on the northern banks of the Thames. The Saxons who moved into the area after the decline of the Roman Empire are thought to have found that settlement (roughly on the site of today's City or Square Mile) too small. Instead, they built their communities further up the River Thames. In the 7th century an abbey was built on Thorney Island (Westminster Abbey; p125) and the royal palace established at Aldwych. It was only under threat from marauding Danes that the Saxons moved back into the walled city in the 9th century.

Two centuries later the Normans invaded, and soon after William the Conqueror arrived in 1066 the country got its first example of Norman architecture in the shape of the White Tower, now at the heart of the larger Tower of London (p112). The next five centuries saw a gradual move through Gothic to Tudor styles, during which the long-term refurbishment of Westminster Abbey from the 13th to 14th centuries and the construction of Hampton Court Palace (p202) were of the most outstanding architectural interest.

KEEPING UP WITH INIGO JONES

The English were latecomers to the Renaissance, and even then it was one man who was largely responsible for bringing home the artistic ideas that had revolutionised the Continent a hundred years earlier. Take a bow, Inigo Jones (1573–1652). The architect had already been appointed surveyor to Henry, Prince of Wales, in 1610, when he spent a year and a half in Italy. There he became a convert to Palladian Renaissance architecture, a style promoted by the late Andrea Palladio (1508–80), but based on classical Roman style and its notions of mathematically calculated, geometric proportions.

Although Jones is nowadays regarded as one of London's most important designers, at the time his work was often misunderstood. After he returned to England in 1615 and was promoted to the post of surveyor general to King James I, his new-found obsession with Italianate design soon brought him into conflict with traditionalists. At a time when the public purse strings were very tight, he made a start on the landmark Queen's House in Greenwich (p174) and successfully completed the Banqueting House at Whitehall in 1622 (p130), before moving on to a piazza at Covent Garden (since rebuilt).

However, by the time Jones began a similar public space in Lincoln's Inn Fields in 1642, the Civil War had broken out. With the seizure of the king's houses by the Puritan-controlled Parliament the following year, he found himself out of a job and, as a loyal monarchist, was forced to flee London. He was rescued from the siege of Basing House in 1645 and died in 1652 without completing any more buildings.

LONDON'S BURNING

In September 1666, as London was still recovering from the plague, a fire broke out in a bakery on Pudding Lane. Four days later, 80% of the city had been burnt to the ground. It was a national disaster, of course, but one in which few lives were lost. Furthermore, it had a few unexpected benefits: it finally cleansed London of the plague, and it created a blank canvas on which Christopher Wren (1632–1723) would build.

Naturally, Wren wasn't the only architect to get the city back on its feet. The priority was to reconstruct as much of the housing stock as possible as quickly as one could, and that was left to property developers. However, Wren was responsible in whole or in part for 51 churches over a period of nearly 50 years. The most influential architect in London of all time began as a brilliant physicist and astronomer who merely dabbled in architecture. But in the aftermath of the Great Fire, his childhood friend King Charles II appointed him as a member of the commission to rebuild London.

Open Wide, Come Inside

It's human nature to be interested in seeing how the other half lives – especially when the other half lives in a quirky white block of modernist flats or works in the Swiss Re Tower. Our curiosity is even more piqued by what goes on behind closed doors of buildings that have been closed for years, such as the St Pancras Chambers.

Well, thanks to Open House, Londoners and visitors alike can give total vent to their inquisitiveness once a year. One weekend, usually in September, the charity organises for owners of about 500 private buildings to throw open their front doors and let in the public free of charge.

Sometimes major buildings participate. City Hall was first opened to the public during Open House 2002 (although it now also opens at intermittent times during the year), the Lloyd's building, the Foreign Office and Portcullis House have also been made accessible this way and the Swiss Re Tower might be on the schedule in the next few years. Sometimes even more is thrown in: when the St Pancras Chambers were opened, its spaces were lit by 12 artists, among them Tracey Emin.

For more details contact **Open House Architecture** (☎ 09001 600 061, 60p per min; www.londonopenhouse.org). The charity also runs three-hour, architect-led tours (☎ 7267 7644; adult/ student £18.50/13) every Saturday. There's a rolling programme visiting the Square Mile, Bankside, the West End or Docklands.

Another annual event worth keeping an eye out for is **Architecture Week** (☎ 7973 6469; www.architectureweek .org.uk) in June, which has an enticing mix of talks by leading architects, designers and well-known TV design critics, plus events involving actors and bands. It's run as a joint venture between the Royal Institute of British Architects and the Arts Council.

St Paul's Cathedral, the City (p106)

In fact Wren, like the much-besieged Inigo Jones, was a fan of classicism although he combined it with Baroque. He immediately drew up a Utopian plan to reconstruct the entire city along classical lines, replacing the former warren of twisting streets and alleyways with broad tree-lined avenues radiating from piazzas or major public buildings. The scheme was shelved, however, partly for being too radical and partly because the compulsory purchase of land necessary wasn't achievable.

Wren's first two plans for St Paul's Cathedral (p106), his magnum opus, were similarly thrown back in his face. The main objection both times was that the dome atop it was too Roman Catholic and too little like a Protestant steeple. Wren plugged away with substitute proposals, toning down the dome and incorporating a spire. However, the necessary warrant of royal approval signed allowed for 'ornamental' variations. Craftily, during construction Wren gradually slipped many of his previous ideas in through this loophole. By the time this ruse was uncovered, the dome was too far advanced to change.

St Paul's took 35 years to build and Wren turned 66 before it was completed, but in a full and long life he managed to squeeze in a couple of other enduring London landmarks, too. His signature is writ large all over the Royal Exchange in the City, the Royal Hospital Chelsea, the Royal Naval College (p173) and the Drury Lane Theatre. When Wren died in 1723 he was the first person to be buried in St Paul's Cathedral.

With Wren gone, his protégés Nicholas Hawksmoor and James Gibb stepped out of his shadow. Both had worked with the great man while he was alive, especially since parliament passed an act in 1711 to build 50 new churches, but now they moved on to their own masterpieces, such as Christ Church, Spitalfields (Hawksmoor, 1729; p117) and St Martin-in-the-Fields (Gibb, 1726; p97). These two architects' buildings are usually termed English Baroque.

Meanwhile, commercial developers had helped rebuild homes that were lost to the Great Fire. Their exploits are noteworthy for three things. Firstly, many of these developers gave their names to contemporary London streets, such as Storey, Bond and Frith. Secondly, they invented the formula of leasehold when they divided their land into plots and leased them with the proviso that the properties on those plots all be built in a certain style. (Thomas Wriotheseley was the first to do this at Bloomsbury Square.) Thirdly, they set a precedent in London in which commercial concerns drove London's architecture. This is a phenomenon that the city has seen a lot of since.

GEORGIAN MANNERS

By the time the 18th century rolls around, you begin to feel sympathy for Inigo Jones. Whereas he was treated with suspicion for his introduction of classicism to Britain, it seems that now the time was ripe for a revival. Neo-Palladianism is still much in evidence in surviving Georgian town houses. Among the greatest exponents of this revived style were Robert Adam and his brothers. Much of their work was demolished by the Victorians, but an excellent example that endures is Kenwood House (1773; p185) on Hampstead Heath.

The Adam brothers' fame has been eclipsed by that of the 'Regency' architects John Nash (1752–1835) and John Soane (1753–1837). 'Once and only once, has a great plan for London, affecting the development of the capital as a whole, been projected and carried to completion,' wrote John Summerson in his book *Georgian London* (Penguin, 1978). The plan to which Summerson refers is that by John Nash to give London a 'spine' by creating Regent St (p92) as a straight north–south axis from St James's Park in the south to the new Regent's Park in the north. This grand scheme also involved the formation of Trafalgar Square, the development of the Mall and the western end of the Strand, as well as the cutting of Regent's Canal to serve Regent's Park.

Although completed, the plan did involve compromise, as many landowners lining Nash's proposed route refused to sell and he was forced to opt for a sweeping curve of a street. However, that curve was initially a great success. The Victorians (p60) later ripped down some of his buildings, but his legacy remains. Nash worked on Buckingham Palace and left some lovely crescents full of 'Nash terraces' at the entrance to Regent's Park (Park Cres, for example).

Nash's contemporary John Soane was arguably a better architect. However, he lacked the royal patronage that Nash enjoyed and is best remembered today not for a building but for the jaw-dropping collection of *objets d'art* that's assembled in the Sir John Soane's Museum (p98). All that's left of his Bank of England on Threadneedle St is a bastardised version of his exterior wall. The Dulwich Picture Gallery (p178) is a better example of his work.

'GOTHICK' CITY

The 1830s saw a sea change in architectural fashions. One man in particular, August Welby Northmore Pugin (1812–52), lobbied for change. Sick of classicism and Protestantism, Pugin called in his 1836 pamphlet *Contrasts* for 'a revival of Catholic art'. Two years earlier the Palace of Westminster, or the Houses of Parliament (p128), had burnt down and by the time he published *Contrasts*, Pugin was already

Top 10 Exteriors

Any list of buildings of this sort will, by nature, be subjective, but here are a few starting points:

City Hall (Foster & Partners, 2002; p165) Stand across the river from this after nightfall and you can see the spiral ramp within.

Lloyd's of London (Rogers, 1986; p111) Inside-out, with ducts, lifts and stainless steel features on its façade, Lloyd's makes a great sci-fi backdrop.

Oxo Tower Wharf (Lifschutz & Davidson,1996; p159) The neon-lit windows of this Art Deco tower spell out O-X-O vertically; it's a graphic designer's dream.

Palace of Westminster (Barry & Pugin, 1847; p128) This neo-Gothic masterpiece is an elegant symbol of British democracy.

Portcullis House (Michael Hopkins, 2000; Map pp426-7) The politicians inside don't like it much, but many architects think highly of this new Parliamentary building.

St Pancras Chambers at St Pancras Station (George Gilbert Scott, 1874; p182) This giant curving, red-brick edifice looks more like a medieval palace than the railway hotel it is.

St Paul's Cathedral (Wren, 1697; p106) He had to be sneaky to get it built, but Sir Christopher Wren's dome still lords it over London.

Swiss Re Tower (Foster & Partners, 2003; p112) The gherkin-shaped tower with its black winding stripes isn't to everyone's taste, but it's undeniably striking.

Tate Modern (Herzog & de Meuron, 2000; p160) It's the two-storey glass box that's been added to the roof and is lit up at night that creates the extra genius.

Vauxhall Cross (Farrell, 1993; Map pp440-1) This modern ziggurat looks the part as MI6 spy headquarters to perfection.

putting his words into action, by acting as assistant and interior designer to architect Charles Barry during the building's reconstruction. The result, which is what you see today, is typical Victorian High Gothic (often spelled 'Gothick'), with perpendicular towers, pointed arches and ornate turrets and interiors. However, it's a very romantic interpretation of medieval architecture, an outpouring of nostalgia for allegedly more innocent times during a fast-gathering industrial age.

Another leading proponent of the Gothic Revival was George Gilbert Scott, who was responsible for the anachronistic Albert Memorial (p138) in Kensington Gardens, the Foreign Office building in Whitehall and St Pancras Chambers (1874; p182), the hotel at the eponymous railway station. One's admiration for this gingerbread-style masterpiece is tempered somewhat by learning that Gilbert Scott himself once declared it 'possibly too good for its purpose'. Alfred Waterhouse, the creator of the wonderful neo-Gothic building that houses the Natural History Museum (p135), was never recorded making such a claim, although his architecture is equally exquisite.

The emphasis on the artisanship and materials necessary to create these elaborate neo-Gothic buildings led to what has become known as the Arts and Crafts movement, of which William Morris (1834–96) was a leading exponent. Pugin himself was more than simply a designer of buildings, and also worked in furniture, stained glass, metal, textiles, tiles and wallpaper. These were the same media in which Morris worked his famously ornate designs. Morris' work can be best enjoyed in the Green Dining Room of the Victoria & Albert Museum (p134) or the William Morris Gallery (p169).

THE SOUND OF THE SUBURBS

Gothic architecture was only one aspect of the Victorian anticlassical backlash, which in general had a fundamental, lasting impact on London's landscape. Donald Olsen in his book *The Growth of Victorian London* (Penguin, 1976) talks about 'the ambivalent love-hate relationship the Victorians sustained with the London their Georgian parents had bequeathed them'. Essentially romantics and lovers of art, they took exception to the utilitarianism of Georgian and Regency buildings. As students of the classics, they detected a certain inaccuracy in Nash's handling of Roman details in his terraces and were offended by it. Even worse, they considered that Nash's grand plan for London had celebrated London, and as they grappled with the metropolis' congestion, crime and lack of sanitation this was an accolade that they didn't think it deserved.

So, down came large chunks of Georgian Whitehall, down came John Soane's old criminal law courts and eventually down came many of the original buildings lining Regent St. Not even the work of Christopher Wren was considered sacred, and many of his churches were demolished, while others had incongruous stained-glass windows added.

'If the Regency prized smooth stucco,' writes Olsen, 'the Victorians produced the roughest stone surfaces possible; if the Georgians preferred unobtrusive grey bricks, the

Top 10 Interiors

British Library (Colin St John Wilson, 1998; p182) This building's fine, vaguely Scandinavian-influenced interior detailing brings out one's inner bookworm.

British Museum Great Court (Foster, 2000; p101) Oops, the colour of the stone doesn't quite match the older walls, but the spectacular glass and steel roof infuses the new court with life-affirming light.

Courtauld House, Eltham Palace (1937; p178) The domed, circular entrance hall with its woven carpet and sturdy armchairs is one of London's most memorable interior spaces.

Imagination Building (Herron Associates, 1989; Map pp426-7) The unassuming façade of an Edwardian school hides a dazzling, multipurpose interior.

Painted Hall (James Thornhill interior, 1725; p173) The rich ornateness of James Thornhill's mural-covered ceiling and walls will win over even those with modern tastes.

Peterborough Court/Former Daily Express building (Robert Atkinson interior, 1931; Map pp426-7) One of the few examples of 'full-blooded' Art Deco in London, the entrance hall has wiggly black and blue flooring, a silver ceiling rose and metal snake handrails refurbished in 2001; peer through the glass curtain wall.

St Bartholomew-the-Great (p106) This gloomy Norman interior is just right for reflection and contemplation, and parts of *Shakespeare in Love* were shot here.

St Paul's Cathedral (Wren, 1697; p106) Even partly under wraps during renovation Sir Christopher Wren's interior is awe-inspiring.

Sir John Soane's Museum (p98) It's not just the collection of Egyptiana that's quirky, the building also has a glass dome bringing light to the basement.

Tate Modern (Herzog & de Meuron, 1999; p160) It's the huge Turbine Hall entrance space to this art gallery that has most visitors rapt.

Victorians produced the brightest red bricks they could manage; if the Georgians sought restrained, uniform monochrome façades, the Victorians revelled in glazed, polychrome tiles; if the Georgians admired flat cornices topping their buildings, the Victorians sought jagged skylines… for symmetry they substituted asymmetry; for the two-dimensional, the three-dimensional; for the unadorned, the enriched.'

It wasn't only in their architecture that the Victorians rejected 18th-century values, but in the very layout of the city. Rather than planned growth, they were happy to allow the organic growth of the city to reflect their way of living. True, the division of London into various neighbourhoods can be said to have begun in the 17th century, with the creation of St James's, Covent Garden and Bloomsbury. Suburban villas had existed in the 18th century, particularly in Clapham on the south side or Islington, Hackney and Highgate to the north. However, it was when the railway and the omnibus made commut-

Temple Church, Holborn (p100)

ing possible in the 19th century that the dormitory suburb really took hold. Suburbanisation started closer in, in places like Kensington, Chelsea and Notting Hill, before spreading to areas such as Wimbledon, Richmond and Highgate.

Ribbon development – rows of houses, side by side sharing party walls – lined the roads out of central London. Contemporary notions of privacy and individualism meant that the house was very much favoured over Continental-style apartments. However, a few did make an appearance in the 1850s.

DICKENSIAN SLUMS

Property developers such as Thomas Cubitt were instrumental in erecting new middle-class housing in Belgravia and Pimlico. However, the 19th century was also the first age during which homes were purpose-built for the working classes. Before that, poorer city dwellers had tended to inhabit the cast-off homes of the rich. Now with London's population going through a boom – from just under one million at the start of the 19th century to 4.5 million at its end – private property speculators began erecting buildings designed to be affordable for the underprivileged even when new.

The effect this had on building quality is encapsulated in one landlord's instruction to a builder working on 20 hectares of his land in Camden Town to erect 500 third-rate houses, 'or a lesser number of superior rate, so as to be of the same value in 15 years'. This kind of slapdash approach reached its apogee in the East End, where crowded tenements soon turned into crime-ridden slums, or 'rookeries' as they were known.

In the 1860s, philanthropic efforts were begun to ease the suffering of the Victorian poor. The philanthropist William Booth founded the Salvation Army in the East End and Dr Joseph Barnardo established schools for the underprivileged. Meanwhile, on his death in 1869 the businessman George Peabody left half a million pounds for the construction of decent but affordable housing. The Peabody Trust survives today.

Some decades later, architect Ebenezer Howard (1850–1928) also addressed himself to the quality of life in London, deciding the simplest answer was to get out. His plans for green, planned cities outside the capital came to fruition in 'new towns' like Welwyn Garden City and Milton Keynes. The great 'traditionalist' architect Edwin Lutyens (1869–1944) also demonstrated a penchant for the rustic. Although Lutyens, from Sussex, mostly built outside London, he did contribute to the countryside-within-a-city development of Hampstead Garden Suburb. He also designed the Cenotaph in Whitehall, the Reuters Headquarters in Fleet St and Britannic House in Finsbury Square.

FLIRTING WITH MODERNISM

With so much happening during the 19th century, perhaps it's unsurprising the 20th century began so quietly. Not many public buildings of note were built during the first decade and a half, apart from Admiralty Arch (Aston Webb, 1910; p122) and County Hall (Ralph Knott, 1922; p157). In the period between the two world wars English architecture was hardly more creative. Indeed, it was left to visiting architects to inject a bit of life into an otherwise pretty flat scene. Those from Europe, in particular, brought with them the modernist style of architecture, but the monuments they left are on a small scale.

The Russian Berthold Lubetkin (1901–90) is perhaps the best remembered, principally because of the penguin pool, with its concrete spiral ramp, at London Zoo (p181). One of London's earliest modernist structures when it was built in 1934, the pool is still the object of much affection today – and the penguins the envy of many a child.

However, there were also émigrés from Germany, who spent several years in London before moving on to the United States. Among these was the director of the Bauhaus school Walter Gropius (1883–1969). He lived in No. 15 of the flat, geometric-shaped Isokon apartments in Lawn Rd, Hampstead (Map p415), themselves a famous modernist landmark by the Canadian architect Wells Coates (1893–1958). The Grade I–listed flats, whose other tenants included crime writer Agatha Christie, have been undergoing refurbishment and should be reopened after the middle of 2004.

RECONSTRUCTION AFTER THE BLITZ

Hitler's bombs during WWII wrought the worst destruction on London since the Great Fire of 1666, and the immediate problem was a chronic shortage of housing. Developers soon rushed to fill the void, erecting tower blocks to provide as many family homes in as short a time as possible. Unsurprisingly, given the haste, many of the resulting building's were of poor quality, not to mention lacking in aesthetic appeal. Many of those blocks still contribute to London's urban blight today.

Obscure Objects of Desire

Buckingham Palace Ticket Office (Hopkins, 1994; p120) This prefabricated red wooden cabin is erected each year for the crowds that come during August and September; it has a striking, acrylic flyaway roof.

Hammersmith Health Centre (Guy Greenfield, 2000) This curved sliver of a building turns a defensive back to the road, while gazing out onto an internal Japanese garden; it's almost worth getting mildly sick to see it.

London Ark (Ralph Erskine, 1991; Map pp416-17) From the outside of this Hammersmith office building (now occupied by Seagram), everything looks perfectly ship-shape; inside the nine storeys of offices are open plan.

Lord's Cricket Ground Media Centre (Future Systems, 1999; p188) This aluminium-and-glass pod on stilts has been called a spaceship, a bar of soap and a gigantic alien eye peering down on the cricket field.

Peckham Library (Will Alsop, 1999; p196) Obscure mainly in the sense of its location, this playful, colourful building saw off stiff competition to Britain's most prestigious architectural prize, the Stirling.

Penguin Pool, London Zoo (Berthold Lubetkin, 1934; p181) Getting to play every day on a spiral concrete ramp that's a modernist icon, the penguins at London Zoo have things better than most captive breeds.

Public Lavatory (CZWG Architects, 1993) On the corner of Westbourne Grove and Colville Rd, Piers Gough and his firm have created their best-known work: a little Art Deco–style masterpiece.

Red Phone Box (Giles Gilbert Scott, 1924) This once-familiar landmark is found only in tourist areas today (eg around St Paul's); its shape and glass-paned sides were inspired by John Soane's tomb for his wife in St Pancras churchyard.

Sainsbury's, Camden Town (Nicholas Grimshaw, 1988) The supermarket chain now has several innovative-looking stores; this early example has an industrial façade vaguely reminiscent of the Pompidou Centre.

Serpentine Gallery Summer Pavilion (p137) Every summer an architect is invited to erect a temporary pavilion next to the gallery: recent takers include Daniel Libeskind and Brazilian colossus Oscar Niemeyer.

In 1951, the government decided to throw a party to cheer up a populace it believed was suffering a kind of collective post-traumatic stress from WWII. The Festival of Britain was a celebration of the modern nation, and of the centenary of 1851's Great Exhibition in Crystal Palace. All that remains of that patriotic carnival is the Royal Festival Hall (1951, Robert Matthew and Leslie Martin; p159) on the South Bank Centre, the first major public building in London in the modernist style. With its curved roof and Portland stone façade (slightly less grimy than concrete), the hall has traditionally been more loved than the buildings that shot up around it, including Denys Lasdun's National Theatre (1976). However, with the entire South Bank Centre undergoing renovation today, there's been renewed interest in its concrete brutalist style. Across town, at the junction of Charing Cross Rd and Oxford St, even the once-vilified modernist Centre Point Tower (Richard Seifert, 1967) has been listed by English Heritage. The BT Tower (formerly the Post Office Tower, Ministry of Public Building and Works, 1964) always enjoyed far more public affection than Centre Point as one of London's most famous landmarks (and also because of the revolving restaurant at its summit that was once open to all). It, too, has now been granted listed status.

POSTMODERNISM & DOCKLANDS

Modernism held sway until the end of the 1970s. Its Utopian ideal of providing housing for the masses in large-scale, conformist redevelopment schemes and its frequent reliance on public sector funding was very much in keeping with the postwar welfare state. However, as Britain itself experienced a political U-turn with the election of Margaret Thatcher's mould-breaking Conservative Party in 1979, modernist architecture no longer seemed appropriate. In the freewheeling 1980s and early 1990s, a more commercially driven international architecture, postmodernist and high tech, began to take hold.

Whatever the criticisms of postwar publicly funded buildings, however, one could never, looking back at the 1980s and 90s, argue that commercial concerns provided a universally better guarantee of architectural quality. Its record is equally patchy. The utterly unappealing NatWest Tower (Richard Seifert, 1981), for example, still reproachfully skulks over the city skyline as cast-in-concrete proof of that.

Still, there were several successes, including Embankment Place (Terry Farrell, 1990) and most notably Richard Rogers' Lloyds of London building (1986; p111). Rogers was already famous for his collaboration with Italian architect Renzo Piano on the low-level Pompidou Centre in Paris (1977), where the building's exterior consists of a steel skeleton and service elements such as air-conditioning ducts and pipes. Similarly, the high-tech Lloyds tower takes many constructional elements that would normally be found inside the building, from ducts and pipes to lifts and concrete-and-stainless-steel winding fire stairs, and places them on the exterior.

No mention of this era would be complete without discussing the reconstruction of Docklands. The Thatcher-approved plan to transform the unused and neglected docks east of Tower Bridge into London's second financial hub was always a controversial one. The stated intent was to alleviate the congestion of the City. However, people still lived in the area entrusted to the London Docklands Development Corporation (working in tandem first with developers Travelstead and then with Olympia and York), and the social upheaval created by building skyscrapers and offices was enormous.

The terms offered for the acquisition of land for commercial development were often criticised. That was only part of the controversy, though. For all the pain involved, the new Docklands initially didn't seem to work

Canary Wharf Tower, Docklands (p171)

very well. The main transport link, the Docklands Light Railway, proved unreliable for years and, on the central Isle of Dogs, Canadian architect Cesar Pelli's obelisk-shaped Canary Wharf Tower (officially known as One Canada Square, 1991; p171) was so hard-hit by the recession of the early 1990s it had to be saved from bankruptcy. The Museum in Docklands (p172) chronicles much of this ill-fated history.

Only now, in the early years of the 21st century, is Docklands starting to realise the aspirations its planners had for it. Transport has improved beyond belief, especially with the extension of the Jubilee Underground line into the area (see the boxed text below). Meanwhile, the 244m-high Canary Wharf Tower has reached near total occupancy and no longer stands in less than splendid isolation. London's tallest skyscraper is already flanked by the twin-tower HSBC Holdings building and the Citigroup headquarters, while a handful of other towers have begun heading skywards.

THE ROYAL SEAL OF DISAPPROVAL

Even before the riot of multicoloured, Lego-shaped developments began to spread across the Isle of Dogs and Docklands like a postmodern rash, Prince Charles, of all people, proved that the age-old battle between architectural traditionalists and modernisers had not gone away. In 1984 at a speech to RIBA this self-proclaimed architecture expert launched a full-frontal attack on contemporary buildings.

He immediately targeted his sights on a proposed extension to the National Gallery (p95), which he described as 'a monstrous carbuncle on the face of an elegant and much-loved friend'. However, while he had the stage, he took the opportunity to argue for a more 'humane' architecture and eulogise about city churches, Georgian terraces and green parks.

The effect of the Prince's speech was quite remarkable. Indeed, he seems to have caught the public mood and succeeded in getting the firm Arhends Burton & Koralek fired from the National Gallery project, in favour of the partly classical designs of Americans Venturi, Scott Brown and Associates. Another criticised project at Mansion Square House was dropped and a wave of traditionalist buildings was begun.

However, the reaction from many architects was furious. 'Modern architecture is in danger of being obliterated by an indiscriminate wave of nostalgia,' Richard Rogers fumed. And according to Kenneth Powell in his book *New London Architecture*, the Prince's crusade against it ultimately gave postmodernism an unintentioned boost, with architects like James Stirling (responsible for the 1985 Clore Gallery extension to the Tate Britain; p129), Terry Farrell and a whole range of others willing to champion its cause by building it.

Celebrating the Jubilee

No, that title's not harking back to Liz's surprisingly fab party to celebrate 50 years of being Queen in 2002, but talking about the wonderful latest addition to London's ageing Underground. Yes, we know, eulogising about the Tube: it sounds clearly mad. However, while parts of the network look like they haven't had much done to them since the turn of the 20th century, these 11 stations are all roomy and 100 years younger. In Moscow, it's quite common to get on the Underground (ironically modelled on London's) and simply travel round, hopping off to gawp at the sumptuous stations. The new Jubilee Line stations, each designed by a different architect, invite you to do the same – and make you wish the rest could look like this. The stand-out stars, west to east, are:

Westminster (Michael Hopkins; Map pp426-7) Big chunky concrete columns and steel beams make this dramatic station feel like being in Fritz Lang's silent movie *Metropolis*.

Southwark (Richard MacCormac; Map pp426-7) Serving Tate Modern, this sleek station has one curved wall covered in 660 pieces of blue cut glass and lights shaped like elegant ships.

Canary Wharf (Norman Foster; Map p435) At the end of a 265m-long concourse, the escalators head upwards under a curved glass canopy. Monumental in every sense.

North Greenwich (Will Alsop and John Lyall; Map p414) Colourful, flamboyant and popular, this station's blue tiles recall Greenwich's maritime past and throw up interesting physical reflections.

Stratford (Chris Wilkinson; Map p414) With an elegant, curving roof on what looks like a regional air terminal building, the end of the line never before looked this good.

Millennium Dome, Greenwich (p176)

MILLENNIAL CHANGE

The Thatcher years (1979–91) were not kind to London's public schools or hospitals and saw much of the city's low-rent, council-owned housing stock sold off to private owners. Worse, in 1986 the Tories abolished the Greater London Council, which it saw as a power base from which GLC leader Ken Livingstone (now London's mayor) could challenge the government. That left one of the world's largest conurbations without a planning and co-ordinating authority – which was a disaster for public transport.

In 1992, the Major government took a more positive step, with the introduction of the National Lottery, funds from which would be put towards public buildings. Throughout its history, London had never really been a city of *grand projets* on a Parisian-scale, but as the new millennium loomed, that was about to change. Among the scores of projects underwritten by the lottery-funded Millennium Commission were several of the landmarks that would define London in the 20th century: Tate Modern, the Millennium Bridge and the Millennium Dome.

Tate Modern (Herzog & de Meuron, 2000; p160) was a success beyond perhaps even the architects' wildest dreams. From the disused Bankside Power Station (originally by Sir Giles Gilbert Scott), they fashioned an art gallery that went straight to No 2 in the Top 10 London tourist attractions, and then walked away with international architecture's most prestigious prize, the Pritzker.

The Millennium Bridge (Foster, 2000; p160) infamously had a case of the wobbles when it was first opened, but is now generally considered to be a boon to the city. Even the Millennium Dome (Rogers; p176), the dunce of the class of 2000, probably through no fault of its Teflon exterior, looks like having a second lease of life as a sporting stadium – especially as London pursues its dream to host the 2012 Olympics.

While not a publicly funded millennium project, British Airways London Eye (Marks & Barfield; p157) also appeared on the South Bank in 2000, enjoying immense popularity ever since.

COMMON GROUND

All of which brings us back to where we started, in the London of today. The Swiss Re Tower (p112) and the new City Hall (p165) have joined the millennium landmarks. Work has started on the regeneration of the Paddington Basin – a sort of Canary Wharf around a reconstructed Paddington station – and around King's Cross station to bring the Channel Tunnel link into town. Meanwhile, Wembley football stadium has been demolished, to make way for a new stadium by Norman Foster.

Surprisingly, in the face of the recent success of contemporary architecture, traditionalist critics have been more silent than usual. For example, Daniel Libeskind's plan for a spiral-shaped extension of the V&A, the National Museum of Art and Design, gained the backing of the usually conservative English Heritage, although Renzo Piano's project for a 390m 'shard of glass' tower near London Bridge has proved more controversial.

However, concerns about commercially driven development still remain. Deyan Sudjic has written in the *Observer* (18 May 2003) that he worries that the city, having rediscovered its river, is now loving the Thames to death. While the Tate Modern and London Eye have created new areas of the city, bustling with life, he argues 'a lot of the new Thames is not like that. Large stretches are dominated by a continuous wall of riverside apartment blocks that have driven out everything else.'

Community groups have often fought battles against greedy developers. The fact that the Oxo Tower Wharf (p159), for example, has residential apartments as well as shops and restaurants – rather than being solely devoted to offices – represents a success for the Coin St community. Similarly, vociferous opposition to a redevelopment of the area around Spitalfields at the start of the 21st century helped keep things as they were, and at the time of writing, there was an ongoing battle to prevent the construction of a new residential tower that would loom large over Tate Modern.

Yet there are some genuine top-down development efforts to keep the city alive and open to all. Norman Foster's 'World Squares for All' refurbishment of Trafalgar Square (p95) aims to make this a truly personable hub. Terry Farrell is also working on a project to provide easy pedestrian links between several of the so-called 'royal' (but public) parks, from Richmond and Greenwich, through Hyde and St James's to Regent's Park.

For Londoners themselves, the greatest problems are the cost of housing and public transport, the latter needing to be addressed immediately. After the extension of the Jubilee Line of the Underground, there are plans to extend the Docklands Light Railway to London City Airport and the East London Line of the Tube to Hackney.

With these already mooted, RIBA's George Ferguson remains upbeat about London's architectural renaissance. 'There's a hell of a lot more to be done, but people are really having their eyes opened to London's possibilities.'

1

2

1 Saatchi Gallery, South Bank (p157) *2* Barbican centre, the City (pp104-5) *3* Tate Modern, Bankside (p160)

3

THE SAATCHI GALLERY

THE SAATCHI GALLERY

1 *Royal Academy of Arts, Piccadilly (p124)* 2 *St Paul's Cathedral, the City (p106)* 3 *Natural History Museum, South Kensington (p135)* 4 *Tate Modern, Bankside (p160)* 5 *Royal Albert Hall, South Kensington (p138)* 6 *Lassco St Michael's, Shoreditch (p324)* 7 *Royal Academy of Arts*

1 *Big Ben, Houses of Parliament (p128)* 2 *Kensington Palace (p136)* 3 *Westminster Abbey (p125)* 4 *Saatchi Gallery, South Bank (p157)* 5 *Somerset House, the Strand (p98)* 6 *British Museum, Bloomsbury (p101)*

VICTORIA AND ALBERT MUSEUM

SANDERSON

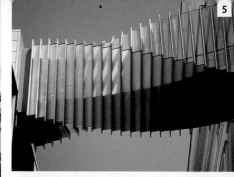

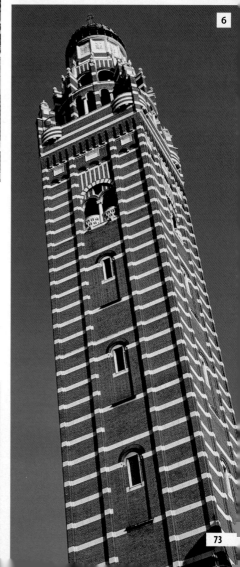

1 *St Paul's Cathedral, the City (p106)* 2 *Victoria & Albert Museum, Kensington (p134)* 3 *Sanderson hotel, Soho (p339)* 4 *Christ Church, Spitalfields (p117)* 5 *Royal Opera House, Covent Garden (p94)* 6 *Westminster Cathedral (p131)* 7 *Kenwood House, Hampstead Heath (p185)* 8 *BT Tower, Fitzrovia (p101)*

1 *City Hall (p165)* 2 *Tower of London (p112)* 3 *Liberty store, Soho (p325)* 4 *Canary Wharf Tower development (p171)*

History

History

21st-CENTURY LONDON

London got off to a stuttering start to the new millennium with many dedicated projects turning out to be damp squibs: 'the largest fireworks display the city has ever seen' was cancelled, the Millennium Dome gobbled up almost £1 billion of public funds before being sold off for a penny and the Millennium Bridge wobbled so much that it had to be closed.

But despite these mishaps and humiliating failures, London is headier and more confident than it has been at any time since the 1960s, partly due to feisty Ken Livingstone, who became London's first directly elected mayor in 2000. For some of his achievements and goals, p30.

FROM THE BEGINNING

THE CELTS & THE ROMANS

There is evidence of life along the Thames valley dating back half a million years and scattered tribes of Celts were probably the first to pitch their tents here. But the conurbation we know as London didn't really take shape until the arrival of the Romans. They first visited in the 1st century BC, traded with the Celts and had a browse around. In AD 43, they arrived with an army led by Emperor Claudius and decided to stay, establishing the port of Londinium. They built a wooden bridge across the Thames (near the site of today's London Bridge) and used the settlement as a base from which to capture other tribal centres, which at the time provided much bigger prizes. The bridge became the focal point for a network of roads fanning out around the region and for a few years the settlement prospered from trade.

This growth was nipped in the metaphorical bud around AD 60 when an army led by Boudicca, queen of the nearby Iceni tribe, took violent retribution on the Roman soldiers, who had abused her family and seized their land. The Iceni overran Camulodunum (Colchester) – which had become capital of Roman Britannia – and then turned on Londinium, massacring its inhabitants and razing the settlement.

Because of the Thames' deep anchorage for their fleet and the relative ease of defending the area, the Romans rebuilt the city around Cornhill, the highest elevation north of the bridge, between AD 80 and 90. A century later, they built a 1.8 mile (3km) long defensive wall around the city, fragments of which still survive today. The original gates – Aldgate, Ludgate, Newgate, Bishopsgate – are remembered as place names in contemporary London. Excavations in the City suggest Londinium, a centre for business and trade although not a fully fledged *colonia* (settlement), was an imposing metropolis whose massive buildings included a basilica, an amphitheatre, a forum and the governor's palace.

By the middle of the 3rd century AD Londinium was home to some 30,000 people of various ethnic groups and there were temples dedicated to a large number of cults. When Emperor Constantine converted to Christianity in 312, it became the official religion of the entire empire. Christ's main rival, the pagan god Mithras, was given the boot.

Overstretched and being worn down by ever-increasing Barbarian invasions, the Roman Empire fell into decline, as did the city of Londinium. When the embattled Emperor Honorius withdrew the last soldiers in 410, the remaining Romans scarpered and the settlement was reduced to a sparsely populated backwater.

TIMELINE	AD 43	80-90	200
	The Romans invade and Londinium is founded.	The Romans rebuild.	Romans build defensive wall around the city.

THE SAXONS & THE DANES

Saxon settlers began crossing the North Sea and establishing farmsteads and small villages in the south of England. For 200 years at least, they appear to have shown little interest in what remained of Londinium.

'Lundenwic' (London port) gradually grew in importance as trade flourished. When Ethelbert, the Saxon King of Kent, converted to Christianity in the late 6th century, Rome designated Lundenwic as a diocese. Its first bishop, Mellitus, built the original St Paul's Cathedral.

Saxon settlement was predominantly outside the city walls to the west, towards what is now Aldwych and as far as Charing Cross, but the settlement became the victim of its own success when it attracted the Vikings of Denmark, who raided the city in 842 and burned it to the ground 10 years later. Under the leadership of King Alfred the Great of Wessex, the Saxon population fought back, drove the Danes out in 886 and re-established what soon became Lundunburg as the major centre of trade.

Saxon London grew into a prosperous and well-organised town divided into 20 wards, each with its own alderman and resident colonies of German merchants and French vintners. But the Danes wouldn't let it lie and Viking raids finally broke the weakening Saxon leadership, which was forced to accept the Danish leader Canute as King of England in 1016. His reign lasted until 1040, during which London took over from Winchester as capital of England.

With the death of Canute's son Harold in 1042, the throne passed to the Saxon Edward the Confessor, who went on to found an abbey and palace at Westminster on what was then an island at the mouth of the River Tyburn (which now flows underground). When Edward moved his court to Westminster, he established divisions that would – geographically, at least – dominate the future of London. The port became the trading and mercantile centre, what we know as the City, while Westminster became the seat of justice and administration.

Historical Reads

- *London: A Biography* – Peter Ackroyd
- *London at War* – Philip Ziegler
- *The Newgate Calender* – Clive Emsley
- *Restoration London, Elizabethan London* and *Dr Johnson's London* – Liza Picard
- *Rodinsky's Room* – Rachel Lichtenstein and Iain Sinclair

THE NORMANS

By the turn of the first millennium, the Vikings – who by this time had trimmed their beards, spoke French and preferred to be known as Normans – controlled much of the north and west of today's France. After the death of Edward the Confessor there was a succession dispute over the English throne. William, the duke of Normandy, mounted a massive invasion of England. In 1066, he defeated his rival, Harold, at the watershed Battle of Hastings, before marching on to London to claim his prize. William the Conqueror – 'Harold the Conqueror' just wouldn't have sounded right – was crowned king of England in Westminster Abbey, ensuring the Norman Conquest was complete. William subsequently found himself in control of what was by then the richest and largest city in the kingdom.

He distrusted 'the fierce populace' of London and built several strongholds, including the White Tower, the core of the Tower of London. Cleverly, he kept the prosperous merchants sweet by confirming the City's independence in exchange for taxes.

410	842	852	886
The Romans pull out of Britain.	Vikings raid London.	Vikings settle in London.	King Alfred reclaims London for the Saxons.

MEDIEVAL LONDON

In 1154, Stephen, the last of the Norman kings, died and the throne passed to Henry II of the powerful House of Plantagenet, which would rule England for the next 2½ centuries (royal power has been concentrated in London ever since). For the next several centuries, London was gripped in a three-way custody battle between the church, the City and the king.

Henry's successors were happy to let the City of London keep its independence so long as its merchants continued to finance their wars and building projects. When Richard I (known as 'the Lionheart') needed funds for his crusade, he recognised the City as a self-governing commune, and the appreciative merchants duly coughed up. The City's first mayor, Henry Fitz Aylwin, was elected sometime around 1190.

In 1215, Richard's successor, John (nicknamed 'John Lackland' because he'd lost Normandy and almost all the other English possessions in France), was forced to cede to the powerful barons, and to curb his excessive demands for pay-offs from the City. Among those pressing him to seal the Magna Carta of 1215 (which effectively diluted royal power) was the by then powerful mayor of the City of London.

Trade and commerce boomed, and the noblemen, barons and bishops built lavish houses for themselves along the prime real estate of the Strand, which connected the City with the Palace of Westminster, the new seat of royal power. The first stone London Bridge was built in 1176, although it was frequently clogged and most people crossed the river with waterboatmen (who plied their trade up until the 18th century). Their touting shouts of 'Oars? Oars?' are said to have confused many a country visitor tempted by more carnal services.

A Boy, A Puss & City Hall

London's current mayor, Ken Livingstone, may be popular but he's unlikely to ever earn the respect and affection Londoners have for his 15th-century predecessor, one Dick Whittington.

Legend has it that Dick, with his faithful feline in tow, was quitting town when he heard the bells of St Mary-le-Bow ringing out the message, 'Turn again, Whittington, thrice mayor of London'. Never one to ignore the advice of a talking bell – and with a steep hill in front of him – Dick returned to the city where he found fame and fortune as *four*-time mayor. A 19th-century plaque on Highgate Hill marks the spot where his fortunes turned.

Though fire was a constant threat in the cramped and narrow houses and lanes of 14th-century London, disease caused by unsanitary living conditions and impure drinking water from the Thames was the greatest threat to the burgeoning city. In 1348, rats on ships from Europe brought the Black Death, a bubonic plague that wiped out almost two-thirds of the population (of 100,000) on regular visits over the following decades.

With their numbers subsequently down, there was unrest among labourers, for whom violence became a way of life and rioting was commonplace. In 1381, miscalculating – or just disregarding – the mood of the nation, the king tried to impose a poll tax on everyone in the realm. Tens of thousands of peasants, led by the soldier Wat Tyler and the priest Jack Straw, marched on London to make their feelings known. The archbishop of Canterbury was dragged from the Tower and beheaded, several ministers were murdered and many buildings were razed before the Peasants' Revolt ran its course. Tyler died at the end of the mayor's blade while Straw and the other ringleaders were executed at Smithfield. However, there was no more mention of poll tax again (until Margaret Thatcher, not heeding the lessons of history, shot herself in the foot by trying to introduce it in the 1980s).

London gained wealth and stature under the Houses of Lancaster and York in the 15th century, also the era of the charitable mayor Dick Whittington (see the boxed text above). William Caxton set up the first printing press at Westminster in 1476, just in time for the century's greatest episode of political intrigue.

1016	1066	1154	c1190
The Danes take London back and Canute is crowned king of England.	William I is crowned in Westminster Abbey.	Henry II of the House of Plantagenet crowned king.	London's first mayor is elected.

In 1483, 12-year-old Edward V of the House of York reigned for only two months before vanishing with his younger brother into the Tower of London, never to be seen again. Whether or not their uncle Richard III – who just happened to become the next king – murdered the boys has been the subject of much conjecture over the centuries. (In 1674 workers found a chest containing the skeletons of two children near the White Tower, which were assumed to be the princes' remains and were reburied in Innocents' Corner in Westminster Abbey.) Richard III didn't have long to enjoy the hot seat, however, as he was deposed within a couple of years by Henry Tudor, first of the dynasty of that name.

Tower of London, Tower Hill (p112)

TUDOR LONDON

London became one of the largest and most important cities in Europe during the reign of the Tudors, which coincided with the discovery of the Americas and thriving world trade.

Henry's son and successor, Henry VIII, was the most ostentatious of the clan. Terribly fond of palaces, he had new ones built at Whitehall and St James's and bullied his lord chancellor, Cardinal Thomas Wolsey, into gifting him Hampton Court.

His most significant contribution, however, was the split with the Catholic Church in 1534 after it refused to annul his marriage to the non-heir-producing Catherine of Aragon. Thumbing his nose at Rome, he made himself the head, no, *supreme* head, of the Church of England and married Anne Boleyn (the second of his six wives). He 'dissolved' London's monasteries and seized the church's vast wealth and property. The face of the medieval city was transformed; much of the land requisitioned for hunting later became Hyde, Regent's and Richmond Parks while many of the religious houses disappeared leaving only their names in particular areas, like Whitefriars and Blackfriars (after the colour of their habits).

Despite his penchant for settling differences with the axe (two of his six wives and Wolsey's replacement as lord chancellor, Thomas More, were beheaded) and his persecution of both Catholics and fellow Protestants that didn't toe the line, Henry VIII remained a popular monarch until his death in 1547.

The reign of Mary I, his daughter by Catherine of Aragon, saw a brief return to Catholicism, during which the queen sanctioned the burning to death of hundreds of Protestants at Smithfield and earned herself the nickname 'Bloody Mary'.

ELIZABETHAN LONDON

By the time Elizabeth I, Henry VIII's daughter by Anne Boleyn, began her 45-year reign, Catholicism was well on the outer, and hundreds of people who dared to suggest otherwise were carted off to the gallows at Tyburn (p81).

London was blooming economically and physically; in the second half of the 16th century the population doubled to 200,000 while the city established itself as the premier world trade market with the opening of the Royal Exchange in 1572. The first recorded map of London was published in 1558, and John Stow produced *A Survey of London*, the first history of the city, in 1598.

1348	1397	1534	1558
Black Death arrives in London.	Dick Whittington first elected mayor.	Henry VIII splits with Catholic Church.	First map of London created.

This was also the golden era of English drama, and the works of William Shakespeare, Christopher Marlowe and Ben Jonson packed them in at new playhouses such as the Rose (built in 1587) and the Globe (1599). Both of these were built in Southwark, a notoriously 'naughty place' at the time, teeming with brothels, bawdy taverns and illicit sports such as bear-baiting. Most importantly, they were outside the jurisdiction of the City, which frowned upon and even banned theatre as a waste of time.

When Elizabeth died without an heir in 1603, she was succeeded by her second cousin, who was crowned James I. Although the son of Catholic Mary Queen of Scots he was slow to improve conditions for England's Catholics and drew their wrath. He narrowly escaped death when Guy Fawkes' plot to blow up the Houses of Parliament on 5 November 1605 was uncovered. The audacious plan is, rather peculiarly, commemorated on this date each year with bonfires and fireworks throughout Britain.

THE CIVIL WAR

Charles I took to the throne in 1625, and the three-way struggle between the king, the City and Parliament finally came to a head. With the City tiring of increasingly extortionate taxes and Parliament beginning to flex its muscle, the crunch came when Charles tried to arrest five antagonistic MPs who fled to the City, and the country slid into civil war in 1642.

The Puritans, extremist Protestants and the City's expanding merchant class threw their support behind Oliver Cromwell and the Parliamentarians (the Roundheads), who battled against the Royalist troops (the Cavaliers). London was firmly with the Roundheads and Charles I was defeated in 1646. He was beheaded outside Banqueting House in Whitehall three years later, famously wearing two shirts on the cold morning of his execution so he wouldn't shiver and appear cowardly.

Cromwell ruled the country as a republic for the next 11 years, during which he banned theatre, dancing, Christmas and just about anything resembling fun. Soon after his death, Parliament decided that the royals weren't so bad after all and restored the exiled Charles II in 1660. It was decided that death wasn't good enough for Cromwell, whose exhumed body was hung at Tyburn (p81) and rotting head displayed on a spike at Westminster Hall for two decades.

Cheerier displays from the era were the buildings of self-taught architect Inigo Jones, who designed the Banqueting Hall in Whitehall in 1622 and the Covent Garden piazza in 1631 (p57).

PLAGUE & FIRE

For all the aristocratic and political goings-on, it's easy to forget that London was still a crowded and filthy place where most of the population lived below the poverty line. The city had suffered from recurrent outbreaks of bubonic plague since the 14th century, but they were only minor inconveniences compared with the Great Plague of 1665. As the 'sweating sickness' spread, the panicked population retreated behind closed doors, only venturing out for supplies and to dispose of their dead. The nincompoop mayor thought that dogs and cats were the culprits and ordered them all killed, thus in one stroke ridding the disease-carrying rats of their natural predators. By the time the winter cold arrested the epidemic, 100,000 people had perished.

Just as Londoners breathed a sigh of relief, another disaster struck. Their city had for centuries been prone to fire but the mother of all blazes broke out on 2 September 1666 in a bakery in Pudding Lane in the City. It didn't seem like much to begin with – the mayor himself dismissed it as 'something a woman might pisse out' before going back to bed – but rising winds fanned the flames and it raged out of control for four days, razing some 80% of London. Only eight people died but most of London's medieval, Tudor and Jacobean architecture was destroyed.

1599	1605	1642	1665
The Globe Theatre opens.	Guy Fawkes fails to blow up Parliament.	Start of Civil War.	The Great Plague.

History of the Gallows

Hanging was the principal form of execution from Anglo-Saxon times up to abolition of the death penalty in 1964, and London was the capital of crime *and* punishment. More than 50,000 people were hanged, principally from the 'Triple Tree' at Tyburn (near what is now Marble Arch), from the 13th to 18th centuries, and thereafter outside Newgate Prison where the Old Bailey now stands. Huge crowds attended these spectacles, more for entertainment than the deterrent authorities had in mind. After 1868, executions were carried out in private, a move prompted by the increasingly depraved and unruly crowds who frequently fought with the deceased's family over the body.

At the beginning of the 19th century there were an amazing 222 capital crimes, including such terrible offences as impersonating a Chelsea pensioner and damaging London Bridge. However, most of these resulted in transportation to Australia rather than execution. The idea of imprisonment as punishment only really came in after 1840.

RESTORATION

One positive to come out of the inferno was that it created a blank canvas upon which the master architect, Christopher Wren, could build his magnificent churches. His plan for rebuilding the entire city was unfortunately deemed too expensive and the familiar pattern of streets quickly reappeared with brick designs replacing the old timber-frame, overhanging Tudor houses. At the same time, Charles II moved to St James's Palace and the surrounding area was taken over by the gentry who built grand squares and town houses.

By way of memorialising the blaze – and symbolising the restoration and resurgence of the subsequent years – the Monument was erected in 1677.

In 1685, some 1500 Huguenot refugees arrived in London fleeing persecution in Catholic Europe. Many turned their hands to the manufacture of luxury goods like silks and silverware in and around Spitalfields and Clerkenwell, which were already populated with Irish, Jewish and Italian immigrants and artisans.

The Glorious (ie bloodless) Revolution in 1688 brought the Dutch king William of Orange to the English throne. He relocated from Whitehall Palace to a new palace in Kensington Gardens, and the surrounding area smartened itself up accordingly. In order to raise finances for his war with France – and as a result of the City's transformation to a centre of finance rather than manufacture – William III established the Bank of England in 1694.

Despite the setbacks of the preceding decades, London's growth continued unabated and by 1700 it was Europe's largest city with 600,000 people. The influx of foreign workers brought expansion to the east and south, while those who could afford it headed to the more salubrious environs of the north and west. London today is still, more or less, divided along these lines.

The crowning glory of the 'Great Rebuilding', Christopher Wren's St Paul's Cathedral, opened in 1710 (p57).

GEORGIAN LONDON

When Queen Anne died without an heir in 1714, the search went out for a Protestant relative (the 1701 Act of Settlement forbade a Roman Catholic from the throne). Eventually they found one, George of Hanover, the great-grandson of James I. He arrived from Germany, was crowned king of England and never even learned to speak English. Meanwhile, the increasingly literate population got their first newspapers, which began to cluster around Fleet St.

Robert Walpole's Whig Party controlled Parliament during much of George I's reign and Walpole effectively became Britain's first prime minister. He was presented with 10 Downing St, which has been the official residence of (nearly) every prime minister since.

1666	1710	1837	1837
The Great Fire.	St Paul's Cathedral opened.	Coronation of Queen Victoria.	Charles Dickens publishes *Oliver Twist*.

London grew at a phenomenal pace during this time, and measures were taken to make the city more accessible. When Westminster Bridge opened in 1750, it was only the second spanning of the Thames after London Bridge, first built by the Romans. The old crossing itself was cleared of many of its buildings and the Roman wall surrounding the City was torn down.

Georgian London saw a great surge in creativity in music, art and architecture. Court composer George Frederick Handel wrote his *Water Music* (1717) and *Messiah* (1741) while living here, and in 1755 Dr Johnson produced the first English dictionary. Hogarth, Gainsborough and Reynolds were producing some of their finest engravings and paintings, and many of London's most elegant buildings, streets and squares were being erected or laid out by the likes of John Soane and the incomparable John Nash (p58).

All the while though, London was becoming ever more segregated and lawless. George II himself was relieved of 'purse, watch and buckles' during a stroll through Kensington Gardens. This was the London of artist William Hogarth (see the boxed text below), in which the wealthy built fine new mansions in attractive squares and gathered in fashionable new coffee houses while the poor huddled together in appalling slums and drowned their sorrows with cheap gin.

To curb rising crime, two magistrates established the 'Bow Street Runners' in 1751. This voluntary group – effectively a forerunner to the Metropolitan Police Force (set up in 1829) – was established to challenge the official marshals ('thief-takers') who were suspected of colluding with the crims themselves.

Of Rakes & Harlots: Hogarth's World

William Hogarth (1697–1764) was an artist and engraver who specialised in satire and what these days might be considered heavy-handed moralising on the wages of sin. His plates were so popular in his day that they were actually pirated, leading Parliament to pass the Hogarth Act of 1735 to protect copyright. They provide invaluable insights into the life – particularly the low variety – of Georgian London. Hogarth's works can be seen in Sir John Soane's Museum in Holborn (p98), Hogarth's House in Chiswick (p198), Tate Britain (p129) and the National Gallery (p95).

In 1780, Parliament proposed lifting the law preventing Catholics from buying or inheriting property. One demented MP, Lord George Gordon, led a 'No Popery' demonstration that turned into the Gordon Riots. A mob of 30,000 went on a rampage, attacking Irish labourers and burning prisons, 'Papishe dens' (chapels) and several law courts. At least 300 people died during the riots, including some who drank themselves to death after breaking into a Holborn distillery. As the century drew to a close, London's population had mushroomed to almost a million.

VICTORIAN LONDON

While the growth and achievements of the previous century were impressive, they paled in comparison with the Victorian era, which began when the 18-year-old Victoria was crowned in 1837. Propelled by the Industrial Revolution, London became the nerve centre of the largest and richest empire the world has ever known, which covered a quarter of the world's surface area and ruled more than 500 million people.

New docks were built to facilitate the booming trade with the colonies and railways began to fan out from London. The world's first underground railway opened between Paddington and Farringdon Rd in 1863 and was such a success that other lines quickly followed. Many of London's most famous buildings and landmarks were also built at this time: the Clock Tower at the Houses of Parliament known as Big Ben (1859), the Royal Albert Hall (1871) and Tower Bridge (1894).

1884	1901	1915	1922
Greenwich Mean Time established.	Queen Victoria dies.	First WWI Zeppelin bombs fall on London.	BBC's first radio broadcast.

Crystal Palace & the Great Exhibition

Queen Victoria's husband, the German-born Prince Albert, organised a huge celebration of global technology in Hyde Park in 1851. The Great Exhibition was held in a 7.5-hectare revolutionary iron-and-glass hothouse, a 'Crystal Palace' designed by gardener and architect Joseph Paxton. So successful was the exhibition – in excess of two million people flocked to see its more than 100,000 exhibits – that Albert arranged for the profits to be ploughed into building two permanent exhibitions, which today house the Science Museum and the Victoria & Albert Museum. The Crystal Palace itself was moved to Sydenham, where it burned down in 1936.

Exactly 10 years after the exhibition the 42-year-old prince died of typhoid and the queen was so prostrate with grief that she wore mourning clothes until her death in 1901 (largely why she is remembered as a dour curmudgeon).

One relatively unsung hero of the era was Joseph Bazalgette. In 1855, he began building more than 1250 miles (2000km) of drains to divert sewage outside the city and make the massive metropolis liveable. The system still forms the basis of London's drainage today.

Though the Victorian age is chiefly seen as one of great Imperial power founded on industry, trade and commerce, intellectual achievement in the arts and sciences was enormous. The greatest chronicler of the times was Charles Dickens, whose *Oliver Twist* (1837) and other works took on the themes of poverty, hopelessness and squalor among the working classes. In 1859, Charles Darwin published the immensely controversial *On the Origin of Species* here.

It was also the era of some of Britain's most capable and progressive prime ministers, most notably William Gladstone (four terms between 1868 and 1894) and Benjamin Disraeli (who served in 1868 and again from 1874 to 1880).

Waves of immigrants, from Chinese to Eastern European, arrived in London during the 19th century, when the population mushroomed from one to six million people. Inner-city slums housed the poor while the affluent expanded out to leafy suburbs. The suburbs of London are still predominantly made up of Victorian terrace housing today.

Queen Victoria – of 'We are not amused' notoriety – lived to celebrate her Diamond Jubilee in 1897, but died four years later aged 81 and was laid to rest in Windsor. Her reign is seen as the climax of Britain's world supremacy, when London was the de facto capital of the world.

Jack the Ripper

The world's most infamous criminal, Jack the Ripper, emerged from the Victorian fog and slayed five prostitutes in 1888, before disappearing again without a trace. The story represents the classic whodunnit and continues to inspire streams of books and films today.

EDWARDIAN LONDON & WWI

Victoria's self-indulgent son Edward, the Prince of Wales, was already 60 by the time he was crowned Edward VII in 1901. London's *belle époque* was marked with the introduction of the first motorised buses, which replaced the horse-drawn versions that had plodded their trade since 1829, and a touch of glamour came in the form of luxury hotels like the Ritz in 1906 and department stores such as Selfridges in 1909. The Olympics were held at White City in 1908.

What became known as the Great War broke out in August 1914 and the first Zeppelin bombs fell near the Guildhall a year later, killing 39 people. Planes were soon dropping bombs on the capital, killing in all some 650 people (half the national total of civilian casualties). Tragic as these deaths were, however, they were but a drop in the ocean compared with the carnage that the next generation would endure during WWII.

1926	1936	1936	1940–41
General strike.	BBC's first television broadcast.	Edward VIII abdicates, and George IV made king.	London devastated by the Blitz.

BETWEEN THE WARS

While the young, moneyed set kicked up their heels after the relative hardships of the war, the 'Roaring 20s' brought only more hardship for most Londoners with an economic slump increasing the cost of living.

The population continued to rise, reaching nearly 7.5 million in 1921. The London County Council (LCC) busied itself clearing slums and building new housing estates, while the suburbs encroached ever deeper into the countryside.

Unemployment rose steadily as the world descended into recession. In May 1926 a wage dispute in the coal industry escalated into a nine-day general strike, in which so many workers downed tools that London virtually ground to a halt. The army was called in to maintain order and to keep the city functioning, and the stage was set for more than half a century of industrial strife.

Despite the economic woes, the era brought a wealth of intellectual success. The 1920s were the heyday of the Bloomsbury Group, which counted the writer Virginia Woolf and economist John Maynard Keynes in its ranks. The spotlight shifted westwards to Fitzrovia in the following decade when George Orwell and Dylan Thomas clinked glasses with contemporaries at the Fitzroy Tavern in Charlotte St.

Cinema, television and radio arrived to change the world, and the British Broadcasting Corporation (BBC) aired its first radio broadcast from the roof of Marconi House in the Strand in 1922, and the first television programme from Alexandra Palace 14 years later.

The royal family took a knock when Edward VIII abdicated in 1936 to marry a woman who was not only twice divorced but, heaven save us, an American. The same year Oswald Mosley attempted to lead the British Union of Fascists on an anti-Jewish march through the East End but was repelled by a mob of around half a million.

WWII & THE BLITZ

Prime Minister Neville Chamberlain's policy of appeasing Hitler during the 1930s eventually proved misguided, and when Germany invaded Poland in September 1939, Britain declared war.

The first year of WWII was one of anxious waiting for the city; although over 600,000 women and children had been evacuated no bombs fell to disturb the blackout. On 7 September 1940 this 'phoney war' came to a swift and brutal end when German planes, the Luftwaffe, dropped hundreds of bombs on the East End, killing 430 people.

The Blitz (from the German 'blitzkrieg' for 'lightning war') lasted for 57 nights, and then continued intermittently until May 1941. The Underground was turned into a giant bomb-shelter, although one bomb arrived at Bank station via the escalator and exploded on the platform, killing more than 100 people. Londoners responded with legendary resilience and stoicism throughout. Their spirit was tested again in January 1944 when Germany launched pilotless V-1 bombers (known as doodlebugs) over the city. By the time Nazi Germany capitulated in May 1945, up to a third of the East End and the City had been flattened, 32,000 Londoners had been killed and a further 50,000 seriously wounded.

Winston Churchill, prime minister from 1940, orchestrated much of the nation's war strategy from the Cabinet War Rooms deep below Whitehall, and it was from here that he made his stirring wartime speeches.

POSTWAR LONDON

Once the celebrations of VE (Victory in Europe) day had died down, the nation faced the huge toll that the war had taken. In response to the critical housing shortage, the government threw up ugly high-rise residences on bombsites in Pimlico and the East

1948	1952	1953	1956
Olympics held in London.	The Great Smog.	Coronation of Queen Elizabeth II.	Red double-decker buses hit the streets.

End. Hosting the 1948 Olympics and the Festival of Britain in 1951 boosted morale. The festival recalled the Great Exhibition of a century earlier but left only the unsightly concrete complex of arts buildings, the South Bank Centre, as its legacy (p62).

The gloom returned, quite literally, on 6 December 1952 in the form of the Great Smog, the latest disaster to beset the city. A lethal combination of fog, smoke and pollution descended and some 4000 people died of smog-related illnesses.

Immigrants from around the world – particularly the former British colonies – flocked to postwar London, where a dwindling population had led to labour shortages. The city's character changed forever. However, as the Notting Hill race riots of 1958 attest, despite being officially encouraged to come, new immigrants weren't always welcomed on the streets.

Rationing of most goods ended in 1953, the year Elizabeth II (yes, the current queen) ascended to the throne, and three years before the first red double-deckers appeared on London's streets.

SWINGING LONDON

Some economic prosperity returned in the late 1950s and Prime Minister Harold Macmillan told Britons they'd 'never had it so good'. London was the place to be during the '60s when the creative energy that had been bottled up in the postwar era was suddenly and spectacularly uncorked. London became the epicentre of cool in fashion and music, and the streets were awash with colour and paved with vitality. Two seminal events were the Beatles recording at Abbey Rd and the Rolling Stones performing free in front of half a million people in Hyde Park.

In 1965, London's local government was reformed as the Greater London Council (GLC), whose jurisdiction covered a much wider area than the LCC's.

The party didn't last long, however, and London returned to the doldrums in the harsh economic climate of the 1970s, a decade marked by punk excess and IRA bombs.

THE THATCHER YEARS

Recovery began – at least for the business community – under the iron fist of Margaret Thatcher, the leader of the Conservative Party, who was elected Britain's first female prime minister in 1979. Her monetarist policy created a canyon between rich and poor while her determination to crush socialism sent unemployment skyrocketing. Her term was marked by rioting and unrest, most famously in Brixton in 1981 and Tottenham in 1985.

The GLC, under the leadership of Ken Livingstone, proved to be a thorn in Thatcher's side and fought a spirited campaign to bring down the price of public transport in London. Thatcher responded in 1986 by abolishing the GLC, leaving London as the only European capital without a local government. The GLC wouldn't resurface again for another 14 years.

'The Firm'

While the world's media descended on Carnaby and King Sts to record 1960s London, two identical twins from the East End were organising an underworld empire that would propel them to notoriety as London's most famous gangsters. Ronnie and Reggie Kray organised a gang called 'the Firm' and soon graduated from protection rackets to gambling clubs in the West End, where they courted publicity and hung with celebrities. Their reign of violence came to an end when they were arrested in 1967 for murdering two other gangsters. Ronnie shot a bloke in the Blind Beggar public house in Whitechapel after he called Ronnie a 'fat poof' (he took exception to the jibe about his weight).

The Krays' profile scarcely waned during their decades in prison – and their fortunes grew from movie rights and autobiographies. Reggie died in jail in 1995, while Ronnie died in 2000, 35 days after being granted compassionate parole.

1958	1966	1969	1979
Notting Hill race riots.	England win World Cup at Wembley.	Rolling Stones play free concert at Hyde Park.	Margaret Thatcher elected prime minister.

While poorer Londoners suffered under Thatcher's assault on socialism, things had rarely looked better for the suits. Riding on a wave of confidence partly engendered by the deregulation of the Stock Exchange in 1986 (called the Big Bang), London underwent explosive economic growth. New property developers proved to be only marginally more discriminating than the Luftwaffe, though some outstanding modern structures, including the Lloyd's of London building (p111), went up amid all the other rubbish.

Like previous booms, the one of the late 1980s proved unsustainable. As unemployment started to rise again and people found themselves living in houses worth much less than what they had paid for them, Thatcher introduced a flat-rate poll tax. Protests all around the country culminated in a march on Trafalgar Square, ending in a fully fledged riot in 1990, which helped to finally see her off.

THE 1990s

In 1992 the Conservatives were elected for a fourth successive term in government. Unfortunately for them, the economy went into a tailspin shortly thereafter, and Britain was forced to withdraw from the European Exchange Rate Mechanism (ERM), a humiliation from which it was impossible for the government to recover.

To add to the government's troubles, the IRA exploded two huge bombs, one in the City in 1992 and another in the Docklands four years later, killing several people and damaging millions of pounds' worth of property.

The May 1997 general election returned a Labour government to power for the first time in 18 years, but it was a much changed 'New Labour' Party, one that had shed most of its socialist credo and supported a market economy, privatisation and integration with Europe. Although Tony Blair and his government come under much criticism for their 'spin without substance', Labour swept to a second term in the general election of 2001 and although issues of public mistrust continue to dog the party, a thriving economy and a virtually invisible Conservative opposition mean it'll probably get a third term.

1986	1990	1997	2000
Greater London Council (GLC) abolished.	Poll tax riots in Trafalgar Square.	Labour sweeps to victory.	Ken Livingstone elected mayor of the re-established GLC.

Neighbourhoods

Neighbourhoods

London can feel like the densest and most impenetrable of cities, a vast and sprawling megalopolis made up of myriad neighbourhoods and lacking any real focus. To make it a little more navigable, we've clumped all its little bits into 13 hefty portions. Get your bearing downtown at the frothy and frivolous **West End**, which is chaotic, colourful and never standing still. It's propelled by a torrent of locals and visitors searching for a good time and is packed with pubs, restaurants, clubs, cinemas and some of the best shopping in the world. At its centre are the neighbourhoods of Soho and Covent Garden, but it also includes the perfectly tousled intellectual pockets of Bloomsbury and Fitzrovia, as well as Holborn, the traditional home to London's fourth estate, and the fading grandeur of the Strand. **South Central** is east of the West End and centres on and around the traditional seats of parliamentary and royal power, at Westminster and the area around St James's. You can add glitzy Mayfair, chichi Chelsea, haughty Hyde Park and the museumlands of Kensington to this exclusive mix. On the other side of the West End is **East Central**, which incorporates the commercial heart, simply known as the

Top Five Old-Fashioned London

- Buckingham Palace (p120)
- Fortnum & Mason (p325)
- Ritz (p344)
- Inns of Court (p100)
- Wallace Collection (p180)

City, along with perpetually trendy Islington. We've christened it after the areas of Clerkenwell, Hoxton and Shoreditch, London's new centres of cool. The area around the **South Bank** is another neighbourhood on the up, and takes in the most central areas south of the river. It has become home to several of London's top attractions in recent years, including the London Eye, Tate Modern, the Saatchi Gallery and the Globe Theatre.

River Thames

From here, the neighbourhood names are geographically self-explanatory. **North Central** refers to irrepressible Camden, charismatic Marylebone and the well-mannered Regent's Park. Overlooking these – often beyond reach of the Tube – the **Northern Heights** are renowned for fashionable villages, heathlands and history. Many of London's showbiz personalities live around Crouch End, Muswell Hill, Highgate and Hampstead (the last has been luring artistic types since the year dot). Notting Hill is the pick of **Northwest London**, a label largely referring to affluent residential areas, including mellifluous Maida Vale and petite Little Venice. The underdeveloped **East End** is immediately associated with cockney geezers, but these days it's buzzy and multicultural. Further east, we cadge a lift from old Father Thames and head **Down River** to witness the Docklands' dramatic revival and the fascinating history of Greenwich. Earl's Court will probably be the most familiar name from **West London**, an area extending to Hammersmith and the BBC's Shepherd's Bush. Little-known areas in **Southwest London** include Fulham and Putney, which offer many a pastoral delight by the river. **South London** takes us into the heart of black and ballsy Brixton and upwardly mobile Battersea, which has much more than a power station and dog's home to recommend it. Finally, we head **Up River**, swimming against the current to Richmond Park, Kew Gardens, Hampton Court Palace and the heart of suburbia.

SUGGESTED ITINERARIES

ONE DAY

Most of us see London in a hurry, but one day would be pushing it a bit. Start your express tour with a (brisk) walk around Westminster and admire Big Ben, Westminster Abbey and the Houses of Parliament. Just soak up its atmosphere; you don't need to visit the sights (pop into the Cabinet War Rooms if you're really keen). Head to grandiose Trafalgar Square, and nip into the National Gallery for a squizz at its sensational collection. Catch a Routemaster open-backed bus up Charing Cross Road into the heart of the West End and lunch in Chinatown. Reinvigorated, go for a wander around Soho and then to Covent Garden (take side streets if you're confident you won't get lost). On your way to St Paul's Cathedral, pop in and have a look at Somerset House and perhaps stop for a cup of tea on its back terrace. If you have time and the inclination, the Courtauld Gallery here is exceptional. After exploring the cathedral, pull into the first traditional-looking pub you come across. Peruse the weekly listings over your beverage of choice, then go and see a band.

THREE DAYS

Visit the British Museum, undergo some retail therapy, go to a football match and sleep. Next morning, head 'sarf' of the river, and start by booking yourself a ticket for the London Eye. Visit Charles Saatchi's 'Trophy Room' of contemporary Britart at the imaginatively named Saatchi Gallery, and compare his collection with the fabulous Tate Modern. Visit the Globe theatre and picture the throngs listening to Shakespeare's words for the first time. Get a big dollop of old London atmosphere at Borough market before heading to the hulking Tower of London for a history lesson. A riverside pub would be nice around now.

ONE WEEK

If you've got the luxury of a week, you won't have to follow the very subjective recommendations above. In whatever order you fancy, fill your week with any of these. South Kensington has three world-class attractions in the Victoria & Albert Museum, the Natural History Museum and the Science Museum (don't forget to visit Harrods). The Victorian Valhalla of Highgate Cemetery is in north London but worth the trip. Don't miss Portobello market on the weekend. A day out in Greenwich – at the National Maritime Museum and on board *Cutty Sark* – will be a day well spent. You don't have to pay the exorbitant admission prices at the palaces and sights of Royal London to get a feel for it. Go for a wander over to Buckingham and Kensington Palaces, and around St James's Park and Kensington Gardens. Don't, like most people, forget smaller sights like Sir John Soane's Museum and the Wallace Collection, two outstanding highlights of any trip to this big smoke.

ORGANISED TOURS

While many people would rather shoot themselves than submit to the traditional coach-tour option, organised tours can nevertheless provide a decent means of seeing the main sights of the city while allowing you to return to certain areas for more in-depth exploration under your own steam. Similarly, for anyone with very limited time, it is (just about) possible to see the major landmarks of the British capital in one day. A huge variety of companies have capitalised on the popularity of tours, and with countless wacky options, and the very good 'jump-on, jump-off' services that allow you to combine group tours with individual exploration, you shouldn't necessarily run a mile at the suggestion, although do proceed with caution.

Air

Adventure Balloons (☎ 01252 844222; www.adventure balloons.co.uk; Winchfield Park, Hartley Wintney, Hampshire) There are flights, weather permitting, every weekday morning shortly after dawn from May to August. London fly-overs cost £165. The flight lasts around one hour, but allow four hours, including take off, landing and recovery.

Aeromega Helicopters (☎ 01708 688361; www.aero mega.co.uk; tube Debden, then taxi to Stapleford Aerodrome, Essex) Thirty-minute flights over London on the first and third Sundays of each month for £115 per person. Hire a whole six-seater helicopter for £450.

Cabair Helicopters (☎ 8953 4411; www.cabair.com; Elstree Aerodrome, Borehamwood, Hertfordshire) Offers the same service at £129 every Sunday.

Boat

For Boat options, p379.

Bus

The following three companies offer commentary and the chance to get off at each sight and rejoin the tour on a later bus. Tickets range from £13 to £16 per adult and £6 to £8 per child. Discounts often apply for those booking online, and tickets are usefully valid for 24 hours.

Big Bus Tours (☎ 0800 1691345; www.bigbus.co.uk)

London Pride (☎ 01708 631122; www.londonpride .co.uk)

Original London Sightseeing Tour (☎ 8877 1722; www.theoriginaltour.com)

Specialist

London Duck Tours (☎ 7928 3132; www.london ducktours.com; departs from outside County Hall; tube Westminster) Uses remarkable amphibious craft based on the design first used in the D-Day landings. The tour cruises the streets of central London before making a dramatic descent into the Thames at Vauxhall.

London Open House (☎ 7267 7644; www.london openhouse.org; 39-51 Highgate Rd, NW5) Sees London as a 'living architectural exhibition'. Tours range from the annual weekend event, some time in September, when over 500 buildings open up especially for the public, to architectural tours and tours for school groups.

Black Taxi Tours of London (☎ 7935 9363; www.black taxitours.co.uk) Hire a black cab with a trained tour guide at the wheel (although you are likely to hear equally amusing tales from any other cabbie in the city). This is not a cheap option, but split between five passengers it seems a good deal more reasonable. You get to choose your route over two hours at £70.

Walking

Association of Professional Tourist Guides (APTG; ☎ 7403 2962; www.touristguides.co.uk) Hire a prestigious blue-badge guide – these guides have studied for two years and passed written exams to do their job.

Citisights (☎ 8806 4325; www.chr.org.uk/cswalks.htm) Organises an impressive number of original walking tours. See the Walking Tours chapter on p205 for do-it-yourself options.

Haunted London Tours (adult/concession £5/4; meet outside St Paul's tube, exit 2, 8pm Thu) Includes London execution sites, and (allegedly) haunted churches and graveyards.

Historical Tours (☎ 8668 4019; www.historicalwalks oflondon.com) Offers many original walking tours of historical interest.

Mystery Tours (☎ 8558 9446; mysterywalks@hotmail .com; adult/concession £5/4; meet outside Aldgate tube station on Wed and Sat at 8pm and Fri at 7pm) Tour Jack the Ripper's old haunts with a Ripper expert.

Original London Walks (☎ 7624 3978; www.walks .com; adult/senior £5/4) Their website lists a huge array of walks.

Sherlock Holmes tours (£5; meet outside Holborn tube station at 7pm Tue) Take in all the major Sherlock Holmes sights, terminating at the house itself on Baker Street. The tours lasts two hours.

THE WEST END

Eating p223; Sleeping p338; Shopping p320

No two Londoners ever agree on the exact borders of the West End (often more a cultural term than a geographical one) but let's just say it takes in the area bounded, broadly, by the Tube stations of Piccadilly Circus, Oxford Circus, Warren Street, King's Cross-St Pancras and Blackfriars. A heady mixture of consumerism and culture, the West End is where great museums and galleries rub shoulders with tacky tourist traps, and instantly identifiable buildings and monuments share the streets with leading fashion houses and entertainment venues of world renown. This is the London of postcard and T-shirt stands and folk memory. Steer clear of the main traffic-congested thoroughfares because it's only through exploring the side streets of the West End that you'll uncover its treasures.

SOHO

London's equivalent to the Left Bank or Greenwich Village, Soho is a vibrant and vivacious quarter, its own star attraction and an unmissable London experience. With its many pedestrianised streets, distinctive shops, quaint buildings, atmospheric laneways, fashion credentials, gay magnetism, exuberant cafés, lively boozers and late-night action you'd be forgiven for thinking the place is maintained for the benefit of the tourists (à la Covent Garden). But its irrepressible spirit is largely down to the 5000-strong community that lives here, the thousands of media sorts who work here by day and the multitudes that come for fun and games after dark – in fact, you get the distinct impression that they couldn't give two figs about the tourists, although they're more than welcome to join in.

The area is well defined as the area penned in by Regent St, Oxford St, Shaftesbury Ave and Charing Cross Rd. Wardour St divides it neatly in two halves; high Soho on the east, and low or West Soho opposite. Old Compton Rd is the de facto main high street and the pinkest precinct. The West End's only fruit 'n' veg market is on atmospheric Berwick St. Carnaby St, the epicentre of 1960s grooviness, is gradually getting its dignity back after decades of tourist tack.

This area was used as one of King Henry VIII's hunting grounds from the 16th century when he dissolved the monasteries and pinched their land. Its former function gave the area its name, 'so-ho' being the rallying call of hunters after they'd spotted their prey. In the early 17th century, after the Great Fire had levelled much of the city, residential development began with an influx of Greek and Huguenot refugees.

Top Five – The West End

- National Gallery (p95)
- Trafalgar Square (p95)
- Somerset House (p98)
- British Museum (p101)
- Transport Museum (p93)

In the 18th century when the well-to-do moved to Mayfair, they were replaced by more foreign immigrants, artisans and radicals. Writers and artists were soon drawn to the cosmopolitan vibe, and the overcrowded area became a centre for entertainment with restaurants, taverns and coffeehouses springing up.

It got even livelier in the 20th century when another new wave of European immigrants settled in, and Soho was a bona fide bohemian enclave for two decades after WWII. Ronnie Scott's famous club on Gerrard St provided Soho's jazz soundtrack from the 1950s while the likes of Jimi Hendrix, the Rolling Stones and Pink Floyd did their early gigs at the legendary Marquee club, which used to be on Wardour St. Soho had long been known for its seediness but when the hundreds of prostitutes who served the square mile were forced off the streets and into shop windows, it became the city's red-light district and a centre for porn, strip joints and bawdy drinking clubs. The scene was only cleaned up in the '80s when the sex shops were regulated. By then, Soho had already been established as a media hub and pleasure den for hard-drinking celebrities and slumming uptowners. In more recent times it has become the heart of gay London.

Covent Garden Market (p333)

DEAN STREET Map pp426-7 & 428

Karl Marx and his family lived hand to mouth at 28 Dean St, above Quo Vadis restaurant (which has its own colourful history – p224) from 1851 to 1856. The founder of modern communism spent his days in the British Library reading room and didn't seem all that interested in earning any money to help his wife raise their family. Three of their children died of pneumonia, and they were eventually saved from the poorhouse by a huge inheritance left to them by Mrs Marx's family, after which they upped sticks and moved to the more salubrious surroundings of Primrose Hill. Today, it's a lively street lined with shops, bars and many other consumer outlets that no doubt would have given Marx indigestion.

LONDON TROCADERO Map p428

☎ 09068 881100; www.troc.co.uk; 1 Piccadilly Circus W1; admission free; ☺ 10am-1am; tube Piccadilly Circus

This huge and soulless indoor amusement arcade has six levels of high-tech, high-cost fun for youngsters, along with cinemas, US-themed restaurants and bars for anyone else with nothing better to do (or nowhere else to take shelter from the rain).

PICCADILLY CIRCUS Map pp426-7 & 428

Although this traffic-snarled junction is not the most pleasant place to linger, it's been a popular meeting spot for centuries, and for some reason, its giant neon-lit signs always make our hearts go giddy with the excitement of being back in London. The hub was named after the stiff collars ('picadils') that were the sartorial staple of the early 17th century (and were the making of a nearby tailor's fortune).

Today, it's best known for a lousy statue, the *Angel of Christian Charity*. Dedicated to the philanthropist and social reformer Lord Shaftesbury, it was derided when unveiled in 1893 and the sculptor skulked into early retirement. Down the years, the angel has been mistaken for Eros, the God of Love, and the misnomer has stuck. It's a handy meeting place for tourists, although most Londoners cringe at that notion. The charging *Horses of Helios* statue at the edge of Piccadilly and Haymarket is a much cooler place to convene, apparently.

Running off the circus, Coventry St leads to the even less attractive Leicester Square, Shaftesbury Ave to the heart of the West End's theatreland, and Piccadilly itself to the sanctuary of Green Park. Regent St runs north to Oxford St and south to the Britain Visitor Centre, parallel to Haymarket which passes New Zealand House, the former Carlton Hotel where the Vietnamese revolutionary leader Ho Chi Minh (1890–1969) worked as a waiter in 1913. Have a look down Lower Regent St for a glimpse of glorious Westminster.

REGENT ST Map pp426-7 & 428

Regent St is the border separating the hoi polloi of Soho and the high-society residents of Mayfair. It was originally designed by John Nash as a ceremonial route, linking the Prince Regent's long-demolished city dwelling with the 'wilds' of Regent's Park, and was conceived by the architect as a grand thoroughfare that would be the centrepiece of a new grid for this part of town. Alas, it was never to be – too many toes were being stepped on and Nash had to downscale his plan. There are some elegant shop fronts that look older than their 1920s origins (when the street was remodelled) but, like in the rest of London, the chain stores are gradually taking over. Two distinguished retail outlets are Hamleys, London's premier toy and game store (p322), and the upmarket department store Liberty (p325).

Top Five Green Spaces

- Hampstead Heath (p185)
- Hyde Park (p137)
- Kew Gardens (p200)
- Regents' Park (p180)
- St James's Park (p122)

COVENT GARDEN & LEICESTER SQUARE

Covent Garden, the heart of tourist London, was developed about 30 years ago as a respectable alternative to Soho. It is dominated by the piazza that gives the area its name, an elegant and easy-going tourist Mecca with boutiques, stalls, pubs and buskers. Sure, it's a tourist trap – Londoners go out of their way to avoid it – but it's a pleasant place to walk around all the same and one of the few parts of London where pedestrians rule over cars. Be aware though, it can get hopelessly overcrowded in summer.

The area around the piazza also features hot spots for street fashion and hip homewares with lots of creative and exciting stores. Neale St is no longer the grooviest strip although the little roads cutting across it maintain its legendary style. Neale's Yard is a strange and charming little courtyard featuring overpriced vegetarian eateries. Floral St is where swanky designers the likes of Paul Smith have stores while a block north on Long Acre you'll find St Martins College of Fashion, the incubator for some of the world's best designers (p18).

The area took shape in the 17th century when Inigo Jones was asked to convert a vegetable field into a piazza, and it soon became a focal point for London society. Writers such as Pepys, Fielding and Boswell used to saunter down in an evening looking for some action. By Victorian times, a bustling fruit and veg market – immortalised in *My Fair Lady* (1964) – dominated the piazza. Whether it was the market, the porters or the general hullabaloo, the tone of the neighbourhood was soon lowered. Coffee houses gave way to brothels, and lawlessness became commonplace, leading to the formation of a volunteer police force known as the Bow Street Runners (p82). In 1897, Oscar Wilde was charged with gross indecency in Bow Street magistrate's court. The market was relocated in 1974 when the piazza was transformed into what you see today.

The area of St Giles – a little pocket around St Giles High St – had perhaps the worst reputation of any London quarter. It was first known as the site of the leprosy hospital, established here in 1101, and later had another dubious distinction of being the place were the condemned stopped for a last drink on their way to be executed at Tyburn

(see St Giles-in-the-Fields p94). As if its association with lepers, prisoners and social outcasts wasn't enough, it was within the boundaries of St Giles that the Great Plague of 1665 took hold. In Victorian times it was London's worst slum, oft name-checked by Dickens. Forbidding streets and smacked-out drug users make at least parts of the area feel like things haven't changed much.

COVENT GARDEN Map p430

London's first planned square is now the exclusive reserve of tourists who flock here to shop in the quaint old arcades, be entertained by buskers, pay through the nose at outdoor cafés and bars, and occasionally have their pockets picked. On its western flank is **St Paul's Church** (☎ 7836 5221; Bedford St WC2; admission free; ⏰ 9am-4.30pm Mon-Fri, 9am-12.30pm Sun). The Earl of Bedford, the man who had commissioned Inigo Jones to design the piazza, asked for the simplest possible church, basically no more than a barn. The architect responded by producing 'the handsomest barn in England'. It has long been regarded as the actors' church for its associations with the theatre, and contains memorials to the likes of Charlie Chaplin and Vivian Leigh. The first Punch and Judy show took place in front of it in 1662.

LONDON'S TRANSPORT MUSEUM Map p430

☎ 7379 6344; www.ltmuseum.co.uk; Covent Garden Piazza WC2; adult/child /concession £5.95/2.50/4.59; ⏰ 10am-6pm Sat-Thu; 11am-6pm Fri; tube Covent Garden

Tucked into a corner of Covent Garden, this unexpected delight explores how London made the transition from streets choked with horse-drawn carriages to streets choked with

Top Five – Multiethnic London

- Dancing at the Notting Hill Carnival
- Having a curry in Whitechapel
- Hanging in Brixton
- Gigging in Hackney
- Walking through Chinatown

horse-powered cars. It conserves and explains the city's transport heritage and is full of displays from the oldest surviving horse-drawn tram to Tube simulators and the original London Underground map (p442). Its hands-on, jump-on and full-on exhibits are popular with all ages, there's an interactive trail specifically for the kiddies and there are often imaginative temporary exhibitions. The **Museum Depot** at Acton Town contains the 370,000 items that can't be displayed in the museum proper, and can be visited by **guided tour** (once a month; £10/8.50) and on occasional **open days** (£6.95/4.95; check website for details of both). You can get your Mind the Gap boxer shorts and knickers at the shop.

THEATRE MUSEUM Map p430
☎ 7943 4700; www.theatremuseum.org; Russell St WC2; admission free; ☼ 10am-6pm Tue-Sun; tube Covent Garden
Conveniently located in the heart of theatreland, this museum is dedicated to British drama from Tudor times to the late 20th century, and also has increasingly impressive exhibitions on opera and ballet. There's a vast collection of costumes, antique masks, wigs, stage sets, painting, posters and assorted memorabilia in the mostly underground space, and the overall effect can be quite disorientating unless you've got a special interest in things thespian. If you don't, focus on a few specific displays – like the Wind in the Willows From Page to Stage exhibition, or profiles of famous actors – and you'll probably get more from your visit. Kids, however, won't have any problems getting into it, as there are lots of activities like theatre make-up demonstrations and craft workshops.

ROYAL OPERA HOUSE Map p430
☎ 7304 4000, 7304 4000; www.royaloperahouse.org; Bow St WC2; adult/concession £8/7; ☼ tours 10.30am, 12.30pm & 2.30pm Mon-Sat; tube Covent Garden)
On the northeastern flank of the piazza is the gleaming, redeveloped – and practically new – Royal Opera House. Unique 'Behind the Scenes' tours take you through the venue, and let you experience the planning, excitement and hissy fits that take place before a performance at one of the world's busiest opera houses. As it's a working theatre, plans can change so you'd best call ahead.

LEICESTER SQUARE Map pp426-7, 428 & 430
Enormous cinemas, nightclubs and a colossal comedy venue dominate this cheerless, disagreeable square, which is badly in need of mayor-driven makeover (reported to be on the cards). Although it is central, pedestrianised and stacked with options for entertainment (Britain's glitzy film premieres take place here) it still feels very much like a place to pass through, quickly, rather than a destination.

It's obviously a bit of a comedown since the 19th century when the square was so fashionable that artists Joshua Reynolds and William Hogarth chose to hang their hats here. There's a small statue of Charlie Chaplin to one side, and plaques in the ground (not that you'd ever be able to see them for the crowds) list the distances from central London to the capitals of various Commonwealth countries.

CHINATOWN Map p428 & p430
Immediately north of Leicester Square – but a world away in atmosphere – are Lisle and Gerrard Sts, the focal point for London's Chinese community and the nearest thing London has to a 24-hour zone. Although not as big as Chinatowns in many other cities – it's just two streets really – this is a lively quarter with Chinese street signs, red lanterns, dragon-adorned moon gates and more restaurants than you could shake a chop stick at. To see it at its effervescent best, time your visit with Chinese New Year in late January/early February (p10).

ST GILES-IN-THE-FIELDS Map p430
☎ 7240 2532; 60 St Giles High St; ☼ 9am-4pm Mon-Fri; tube Tottenham Court Road
Another church that was built in what used to be countryside between the City and Westminster, St Giles isn't much to look at but has an interesting history. The current structure is the third to stand on the site of an original chapel built in the 12th century to serve the Leprosy Hospital here. Until 1547, when the hospital closed, prisoners on their way to be executed at Tyburn stopped at the church gate and quaffed from St Giles's Bowl, a large cup of soporific ale and their last refreshment.

From 1650, they were also brought back here to be buried in the church grounds. An interesting relic in the church is the pulpit that was used for 40 years by John Wesley, the founder of Methodism.

TRAFALGAR SQUARE Map p430

In many ways this is the centre of London, where many great rallies and marches take place, where the new year is ushered in by tens of thousands of revellers, and where locals congregate to celebrate anything from a football victory over Germany to the ousting of the Tories (the Conservative Party). The great square has been neglected over the years, ringed with gnarling traffic and given over to flocks of pigeons that would dive-bomb anyone with a morsel of food on their person. But not any more, oh no.

One of the first things Mayor Ken Livingstone did when he got his gown, comically, was take aim at the pesky pigeons and ban people from feeding them. Once he had reclaimed the square on behalf of the people of London, he embarked on a bold and imaginative scheme to transform it into the kind of space John Nash had intended when he designed it in the early 19th century. Traffic was banished from the northern flank in front of the National Gallery, and a new pedestrian plaza built. The front of the National Gallery itself is being dollied up, with a new façade and entrance hall due to be in place by 2004. The results are already superb and Trafalgar Square can now take its place among the grandest public spaces in the world. Now that the square's looking the part, there are plans to expand the summer programme of cultural events to showcase the city's multiculturalism.

It's now easier to appreciate not only the square but also the splendid buildings flanking it; the National Gallery, the National Portrait Gallery and the eye-catching church of St Martin-in-the-Fields. The ceremonial **Pall Mall** runs southwest from the top of the square. To the southwest stands **Admiralty Arch**, erected in honour of Queen Victoria in 1910, with the Mall leading to Buckingham Palace beyond it. To the west is **Canada House** (1827), designed by Robert Smirke. The 43.5m-high **Nelson's Column** (upon which the admiral surveys his fleet of ships to the southwest) has stood in the centre of the square since 1843 and commemorates the admiral's victory over Napoleon off Cape Trafalgar in Spain in 1805.

Three of the square's four plinths are occupied by notables, including King George

Trafalgar Square (left)

IV on horseback; one, originally intended for a statue of William IV, has remained vacant for more than 150 years. Local contemporary artists were invited to use it as a showcase for their works in recent years, but that plan seems to have been scrapped following very mixed reaction from Joe Public. The debate over how it should be used goes on (a wax model of England football captain, David Beckham, was cheekily erected there during the last World Cup). In a separate issue, the Mayor had tried to erect a statue of Nelson Mandela on the north terrace but a Westminster committee decided, controversially, that it was inappropriate. It seems much more appropriate than another statue that stands in the centre of the square – and the centre of the erstwhile British Empire – that of George Washington, the man who denied England its colonies in the New World.

NATIONAL GALLERY Map p430

☎ 7747 2885; www.nationalgallery.org.uk; Trafalgar Sq WC2; admission free; ⏱ 10am-6pm Thu-Tue, 10am-9pm Wed; tube Charing Cross

With more than 2000 Western European paintings on display, the National Gallery is one of the largest galleries in the world. But it's the quality of the works, and not the quantity, that impress most. Almost five million people visit each year, keen to see seminal paintings from every important epoch in the history of art,

National Gallery Highlights

- *Pentecost* – Giotto
- *Virgin & Child with St Anne & St John the Baptist* – Leonardo da Vinci
- *Arnolfini Wedding* – Van Eyck
- *Venus & Mars* – Botticelli
- *The Ansidei Madonna* – Raphael
- *Le Chapeau de Paille* – Rubens
- *Charles I* – Van Dyck
- *Bacchus and Ariadne* – Titian
- *The Entombment* – Michelangelo
- *Rokeby Venus* – Velásquez
- *The Supper at Emmaus* – Caravaggio
- *Bathers* – Cézanne
- *Sunflowers* – Van Gogh
- *The Water Lily Pond* – Monet
- *Miss La La* – Degas
- *The Hay-Wain* – Constable
- *The Fighting Temeraire* – Turner

including works by Giotto, Leonardo da Vinci, Michelangelo, Titian, Velazquez, Van Gogh and Renoir, just to name a few. Although it can get ridiculously busy in here, the galleries are spacious, sometimes even sedate, and it's never so bad that you can't appreciate the works (like at the big museums in continental Europe). If you have the time to make multiple visits, focus on one section at a time to fully appreciate the astonishing collection.

To see the art in chronological order, start with the relatively modern Sainsbury Wing on the gallery's western side, which houses paintings from 1260 to 1510. This is where you'll also find the Micro gallery, a dozen computer terminals on which you can explore the pictorial database, find the location of your favourite works or create your own personalised tour. In the 16 rooms of the Sainsbury Wing, you can explore the Renaissance through paintings by Giotto, Leonardo da Vinci, Botticelli, Raphael and Titian among others.

The High Renaissance (1510–1600) is covered in the West Wing where Michelangelo, Titian, Correggio, El Greco and Bronzino hold court, while Rubens, Rembrandt and Caravaggio can be found in the North Wing (1600–1700). The most crowded part of the gallery – and for good reason – is likely to be the East Wing (1700–1900) and particularly the many works of the impressionists and post-impressionists, including Van Gogh, Gauguin, Cézanne, Monet, Degas and Renoir. Although it hardly stands out in such exalted

company, the impressive display featuring 18th-century British landscape artists Gainsborough, Constable and Turner is also well worth checking out.

Temporary exhibitions – for which you normally have to pay – go on show in the basement of the Sainsbury Wing and are often outstanding. The highlights listed in the boxed text include many of the most important works, but if you want to immerse yourself in this pool of riches rather than just skim across the surface, borrow a themed or comprehensive audioguide (£4 donation recommended) from the Central Hall. Free one-hour introductory **guided tours** leave from the information desk in the Sainsbury Wing daily at 11.30am and 2.30pm, with an extra tour at 6.30pm on Wednesday. There are also special trails and activity sheets for children.

Spurred on by the transformation of the square, the gallery is sprucing up its elegant 19th-century William Wilkins façade and a new entrance hall is due to be completed by 2004. The handy Gallery Café is in the basement of the West Wing and the fine restaurant Crivelli's Garden is on the 1st floor of the Sainsbury Wing.

NATIONAL PORTRAIT GALLERY
Map p430
☎ 7306 0055; www.npg.org.uk; St Martin's Place WC2; admission free, prices vary for temporary exhibitions; 🕙 10am-6pm Mon-Wed, Sat & Sun, 10am-9pm Thu & Fri; tube Charing Cross/Leicester Square

This spiffy, recently renovated gallery is unusual in that the subjects of the paintings are more important than the artists. It's more about history than art, and provides a great opportunity to put faces to the famous and infamous names of Britain's past and present.

Founded in 1856, the gallery houses a primary collection of some 10,000 works which are regularly rotated. The pictures are displayed in chronological order from top to bottom. An elevator whizzes you up from the entrance hall to the top floor, where the early Tudors line the walls of an Elizabethan-style Long Room. Among them is the only portrait of Shakespeare believed to have been made while the bard was alive. Further along are the Stuarts, and it's around here you realise that it's rather boring looking at obscure royals who appear to be looking down their noses at you, and the only people around are rather posh old ladies who regard each subject like they are ancestors.

The cravat-wearing Duke of Monmouth, the 14th illegitimate son of Charles II, might provide some relief if he's there. Soon after the Catholic James II beheaded the duke in 1685, somebody remembered that, as a royal personage, the duke should have had a portrait. The Royal Surgeon was summoned to stitch the duke's head back on and he was propped up in front of a painter who had 24 hours to capture the essence of his subject before it 'went off'.

Moving along, the self-portraits of Hogarth and Reynolds are interesting, as are the renditions of two of Britain's greatest prime ministers, Gladstone and Disraeli. On the 1st floor you'll find portraits of the current royal family, many of which, particularly the more recent ones, are laughably bad. However, you might be lucky and see one of the two portraits of the Queen made by Andy Warhol.

The ground floor will be of most interest to tourists, focusing as it does on contemporary figures we're more likely to be familiar with, and using a variety of media, including sculpture and photography. The only problem down here is that the artists seem to be getting ideas above their station, and some of the works say more about them than the subject. No court in the land would charge fashion designer Zandra Rhodes if she took a sledgehammer to the bust that some chancer made of her.

Audioguides (a £3 donation is suggested) highlight some 200 portraits and allow you to hear the voices of some of the people portrayed. The Portrait Café and bookshop are in the basement and the Portrait Restaurant is on the top floor.

ST MARTIN-IN-THE-FIELDS Map p430
☎ 7766 1199, 7930 9306 for brass-rubbing or 7839 8362 for concert box office; www.stmartin-in-the-fields.org; Trafalgar Sq WC2; admission free; ☽ 8am-6.30pm; brass-rubbing centre 10am-6pm Mon-Sat, noon-6pm Sun (pay for materials); tube Charing Cross/ Leicester Square

The 'royal parish church' is a delightful fusion of classical and Baroque styles that was completed by James Gibbs (1682–1754) in 1726. Its wedding-cake spire is enchantingly floodlit at night and looks particularly fetching since the redevelopment of the square. The churchyard, now home to a fairly tacky souvenir stall, contains the graves of 18th-century artists Reynolds and Hogarth.

The pleasant, if unremarkable interior has been the site of many royal baptisms, while the crypt is famous for its café (p229) and the curious activity of 'brass-rubbing' (see boxed text

Brass-rubbing

In medieval times, brass monuments portraying stylised figures of knights, nobility and dragons were set into the burial vaults of notable figures. The engravers themselves took rubbings of the monuments (with paper and charcoal) to record their work, and the Victorians made it into a hobby. Nowadays, casts of the brasses are used to protect the originals, along with special crayons, but the effect is still the same. After up to an hour of rubbing, a piece of medieval heritage slowly reveals itself. The perfect impression of the brass makes for a unique souvenir, which the centre will roll up and place in a protective mailing tube for you.

above). But perhaps the biggest draw at this acoustically gifted church, where Handel and Mozart once jammed, is the calendar of classical concerts. There are free lunchtime recitals by students held every Monday, Tuesday and Friday at 1.05pm and candlelit performance at 7.30pm throughout the year (£6-20).

EDITH CAVELL MEMORIAL Map p430
On a traffic island outside the entrance to the National Portrait Gallery is a statue of Edith Cavell (1865–1915), a British nurse who helped Allied soldiers escape from Brussels during WWI and was consequently executed by the Germans. The work is by George Frampton, who also designed the *Peter Pan* statue in Hyde Park.

HOLBORN & THE STRAND
This area – compacted here for convenience's sake – comprises the rough square wedged between the City to the east, Covent Garden to the west, High Holborn to the north and the Thames to the south. Past glory and prominence are its key characteristics: Fleet St was the former home of British journalism while the Strand, connecting Westminster with the City, used to be one of the most important streets in London and was lined with fabulous town houses built by local luminaries and aristocrats. This rich history is only vaguely evident today but while much of this pocket is soulless and commercial, it is saved by some architectural gems, a few splendid galleries and the calm, green recesses of the Inns of Court, the cradle of English law. Behind the Strand run the Victoria Embankment Gardens, a lovely place for

a picnic, a stroll and splendid views across the Thames to the recharged South Bank.

Fleet Street was named after the River Fleet, which in the 17th and 18th centuries was a virtual sewer filled with entrails and other grisly bits from Smithfield Market upriver (p334). Holborn was named after one of its tributaries and both were filled in the late 18th century. The area was a notorious slum in Victorian times and although efforts were made to smarten it up in the early 20th century, it was probably no great loss when the Germans flattened much of it during WWII, after which the current business moved in.

THE STRAND Map pp426-7

At the end of the 12th century, nobles built sturdy stone houses with gardens stretching down to the 'beach' (ie strand) of the Thames, which connected the City and Westminster, the two centres of power. It was one of the most prestigious places in London in which to live; indeed, the 19th-century prime minister Benjamin Disraeli pronounced it 'the finest street in Europe'.

Well it certainly isn't now; these days the Strand is much less than the sum of its parts. Although it contains hallowed hostelries like The Savoy and Simpson's-in-the-Strand, and the wonderful Somerset House with all its riches, the street still feels like a bleak, cheerless and none-too-salubrious place. But concentrating

---

Mission Museum

Warm-up exercises, half-hour breathers, a portable seat, bottled water and an energy-providing snack – it might sound like the preparation for an assault on Everest but these are the experts' recommendations for tackling London's museums. The British Museum alone has more than 2½ miles of corridors, over seven million exhibits and around six million visitors all elbowing each other to see what they can before mental meltdown.

To avoid museum fatigue, wear comfortable shoes, make use of the cloakrooms and free guided tours, and be aware that standing still and strolling promote tiredness – you're much better off walking briskly and sitting down whenever possible. In larger museums your best bet is to choose the section that most interests you and forget the rest even exists. Finally, consult the previews on the **24-Hour Museum website** (www.24hourmuseum.org.uk), which will help you come up with your own plan.

---

on the good things, check out **Twinings** at 216, a teashop opened by Thomas Twining in 1706 and believed to be the oldest company in the capital still trading on the same site and owned by the same family. The **Wig & Pen Club** at 229–30 – note the symbolic wigs and pens in the plasterwork – is the only original Strand building that survived the Great Fire of 1666.

SIR JOHN SOANE'S MUSEUM Map p430
☎ 7405 2107; www.soane.org; 13 Lincoln's Inn Fields WC2; ☻ 10am-5pm Tue-Fri, 6-9pm 1st Tue of month, museum tours 2.30pm Sat (admission £3, tickets sold from 2pm); admission free; tube Holborn

One of the standout sights of London, Sir John Soane's Museum is partly a beautiful, bewitching house and partly a small museum brimming with surprising effects and curiosities, representing the taste of celebrated architect and hoarder extraordinaire, Sir John Soane (1753–1837).

Soane, the son of a country bricklayer, is most famous for designing the Bank of England. In his work and life, he drew on ideas picked up while on an 18th-century grand tour of Italy. He married into money, which he then poured into building this house and the one next door, which the museum recently acquired and plans to expand into by 2004.

The heritage-listed house is largely as it was when Sir John was carted out in a box, and is a main part of the attraction itself. It has a glass dome which brings light right down to the basement, a lantern room filled with statuary, rooms within rooms, and a picture gallery where each painting folds away when pressed to reveal another one behind. It contains Soane's choice paintings, including Canalettos and Turners, drawings by Christopher Wren and Robert Adam, and the original Rake's Progress, William Hogarth's set of cartoon caricatures of late-18th-century London lowlife, for which a specific gallery was built. Among his more unusual acquisitions are an Egyptian hieroglyphic sarcophagus, an imitation monk's parlour, ancient vases and countless objets d'art.

SOMERSET HOUSE Map p430
☎ 7845 4600; www.somerset-house.org.uk; ☻ The House 10am-6pm, Great Court 7.30-11pm; 45-min tours at 1.30pm & 3.45pm Sat (£2.75); tube Temple/Covent Garden

Passing beneath the arch towards this splendid Palladian masterpiece, it's hard to believe that the magnificent courtyard in front of you, with its 55 dancing fountains, was a car park for tax collectors up until a spectacular refurbishment in 2000! William Chambers designed the house in 1775 for royal societies and it now contains the three fabulous museums described below. The courtyard is transformed into a lively ice rink in winter and used for a mixed programme of concerts in summer. Behind the house, there's a lovely sunny terrace and café overlooking the embankment.

The following three sights are actually part of Somerset House, although each is worth a visit on its own.

COURTAULD INSTITUTE OF ART
Map pp426-7

☎ 7848 2526; www.courtauld.ac.uk; Somerset House; adult/concession £5/4; free 10am-2pm Mon; ☼ 10am-6pm

Immediately to your right as you enter the grounds of Somerset House from the Strand, this superb gallery is connected to the Courtauld Institute of Arts, Britain's foremost academy of art history. If you can't face the crowds at the National Gallery (and even if you can) treat yourself to an unhampered stroll between the walls of this wonderful place, lined with works from the most important old masters, impressionists and post-impressionists. The collection was recently augmented with a series of long-term loans, and now counts Rubens, Botticelli, Cranach, Cézanne, Degas, Renoir, Manet, Monet, Matisse, Gauguin, Van Gogh, Toulouse-Lautrec and Moore – we could go on! – among its contributors. There are **lunchtime talks** on specific works or themes from the collection at 1.15pm every Tuesday and a delightful little café provides sustenance.

GILBERT COLLECTION OF DECORATIVE ARTS Map pp426-7

☎ 7420 9400; www.gilbert-collection.org.uk; Somerset House; adult/concession £5/4, free 4.30-5.30pm; ☼ 10am-6pm

The vaults beneath the South Terrace, boasting one of the finest Thames views, are home to this collection of decorative arts, including European silver, gold snuffboxes, Italian mosaics and portrait miniatures bequeathed to Britain in 1996 by Anglo-American businessman and 'magpie' extraordinaire, Arthur Gilbert. The part-dazzling, part-gaudy display has been described as the most generous gift ever made to the nation. There are one-hour **guided tours** (£6.50/6 including admission) each Saturday. Visit two collections on the same day and you can save a quid; see all three and save £2.

Savoy Hotel, the Strand (p341)

HERMITAGE ROOMS Map pp426-7

☎ 7845 4630; www.hermitagerooms.com; Somerset House; adult/concession £6/4; ☼ 10am-6pm

This gallery is an outpost of the State Hermitage Museum in St Petersburg (which holds some three million pieces that make up one of the finest art collections in the world). The galleries are modelled on those in the Imperial Winter Palace, and there's a live feed to St Petersburg and a short video on the State Hermitage Museum itself to get you in the mood. Collections change twice a year, and the Rooms often close between exhibitions so you should telephone first for details.

ROYAL COURTS OF JUSTICE Map pp426-7

☎ 7936 6000; 460 the Strand; admission free; ☼ 9am-4.30pm Mon-Fri; tube Temple

Where the Strand joins Fleet St, you'll see the entrance to this gargantuan melange of Gothic spires, pinnacles and burnished Portland stone, designed by aspiring cathedral builder GE Street in 1874. (It took so much out of the architect that he died of a stroke shortly before its completion.) Inside the Great Hall, there's an exhibition of legal costumes, as well as a list of cases to be heard in court that day. If you like to watch, leave your camera behind and expect airport-like security.

HOLBORN VIADUCT Map pp426-7
tube St Paul's

This fine iron bridge was built in 1869 in an effort to smarten up the area, as well as to link Holborn and Newgate St above what had been a valley created by the River Fleet. The four bronze statues represent Commerce and Agriculture (on the northern side) and Science and Fine Arts (on the south).

Inns of Court

Clustered around Holborn to the south of Fleet St are the Inns of Court whose alleys, open spaces and atmosphere provide an urban oasis. All London barristers work from within one of the four inns, and a roll call of former members would include the likes of Oliver Cromwell and Charles Dickens to Mahatma Gandhi and Margaret Thatcher. It would take a lifetime working here to grasp the intricacies of the arcane protocols of the inns – they're similar to the Freemasons, and both are 13th-century creations – and it's best to just soak in the dreamy atmosphere, relax, and thank your lucky stars you're not one of the bewigged and deadly serious barristers scurrying about you.

Lincoln's Inn (Map pp426-7; ☎ 7405 1393; Lincoln's Inn Fields WC2; ☼ grounds 9am-6pm Mon-Fri, chapel 12.30-2.30pm Mon-Fri; tube Holborn) Lincoln's Inn is the most attractive of the four inns and has a chapel, pleasant square and picturesque gardens that invite a stroll, especially early or late in the day when the legal eagles aren't flapping about. The court itself, although closed to the public, is visible through the gates and is relatively intact, with original 15th-century buildings, including the Tudor Lincoln's Inn Gatehouse on Chancery Lane. Inigo Jones helped plan the chapel, built in 1623 and pretty well preserved.

Gray's Inn (Map pp426-7; ☎ 7458 7800; Gray's Inn Rd WC1; ☼ grounds 10am-4pm Mon-Fri, chapel 10am-6pm Mon-Fri; tube Holborn/Chancery Lane) This inn – destroyed during WWII, rebuilt and expanded – is less interesting than Lincoln's Inn although the peaceful gardens are still something of a treat. The walls of the original hall absorbed the first ever performance of Shakespeare's *Comedy of Errors*.

Temple Church (Map pp426-7; ☎ 7353 8559; Inner Temple; King's Bench Walk EC4; ☼ 11am-6pm Wed-Fri, 11am-2.30pm Sat, 12.45-2.45pm Sun; tube Temple/Blackfriars) Duck under the archway next to Prince Henry's Room and you'll find yourself in the Inner Temple. The church was originally planned and built by the secretive Knights Templar between 1161 and 1185, who modelled it on the Church of the Holy Sepulchre in Jerusalem. The core of the building is the only round church left in London. In 1240 the more conventional, if elongated, Early English chancel was added. The Knights Templar eventually got too powerful and had to be suppressed by the Crown. Their lands were leased to the lawyers who set up the Inns of Court. Stone effigies of 13th-century knights still adorn the floors of the circular nave. Look out, too, for the grotesque faces peeping down from the circular wall just above eye level – some of the figures are having their ears nibbled by monsters. The western door is a Norman original, and is set into a dip that indicates how much ground level has risen over the centuries. The church, badly damaged during WWII, was beautifully restored in the 1960s and now serves as the private chapel of the Middle and Inner Temples, whose gardens are open from 10am-11.30am & 3-4pm Mon-Fri, and 10am-4pm Mon-Fri, respectively. In case you're wondering, there was no 'Outer' temple.

Staple Inn (Map pp426-7; Holborn; tube Chancery Lane) The 16th-century shop front façade is the main interest at Staple Inn (1589), the last of eight Inns of Chancery whose functions were superseded by the Inns of Court in the 18th century. The buildings, mostly postwar reconstructions, are now occupied by the Institute of Actuaries and aren't actually open to the public, although nobody seems to mind a discreet and considerate look around. On the same side of Holborn but closer to Fetter Lane stood **Barnard's Inn**, redeveloped in 1991. Pip lived here with Herbert Pocket in Dickens' *Great Expectations*.

ST ANDREW HOLBORN Map pp426-7

☎ 7353 3544; Holborn Viaduct EC4; ☼ 9am-4.30pm Mon-Fri; tube Chancery Lane

This church on the southeastern corner of Holborn Circus, first mentioned in the 10th century, was rebuilt by Wren in 1686 and was the largest of his parish churches. Even though the interior was bombed to smithereens during WWII, much of what you see inside today is original as it was brought from other churches.

ST CLEMENT DANES Map pp426-7

☎ 7242 8282; Strand WC2; ☼ 8.30am-4.30pm Mon-Fri, 9am-3.30pm Sat, 9am-12.30pm Sun; tube Temple

'Oranges & Lemons, say the bells of St Clements.' Remember the nursery rhyme that incorporated the names of London churches and ended with the sleep-inducing line, 'Here comes a chopper to chop off your head'? Well this *isn't* the St Clements referred to in the first line of that 18th-century verse, although historical fact needn't get in the way of a (feel) good story, and the bells of this church chime the old tune every day at 9am, noon and 3pm. Wren designed the original building in 1682 but only the walls and a steeple added by James Gibbs in 1719 survived the Luftwaffe, and the church was rebuilt after the war as a memorial to allied airmen. Today it is the chapel of the RAF, and there are some 800 slate badges of different squadrons set into the pavement of the nave.

The statue in front of the church quietly and contentiously commemorates the RAF's Sir Arthur 'Bomber' Harris, who led the bombing raids that obliterated Dresden and killed some 10,000 civilians during WWII.

BLOOMSBURY & FITZROVIA

Immediately north of Soho, slightly bedraggled Bloomsbury is the traditional academic and intellectual heart of London, dominated by its university and many faculties, and home to a sight that is, quite frankly, too big and too great for any mere tourist, the British Museum. To its north run pleasant Georgian and Victorian streets, which meet at beautiful squares once colonised by the group of artists and intellectuals of the so-called Bloomsbury Group, which included Virginia Woolf and EM Forster. They were merely carrying on a tradition, of sorts, begun by the likes of Charles Dickens, Charles Darwin, William Butler Yeats and George Bernard Shaw who all lived here or hereabouts. The many blue plaques dotted around are testament to the area's former prominence.

After the war, Fitzrovia to the west was a forerunner to Soho as a bohemian enclave populated by struggling artists and writers who frequented its many pubs, particularly the Fitzroy Tavern. It's a bit of a tourist blind spot these days, its one main sight, the 1960s BT Tower – once the highest structure in London – having closed years ago as a result of terrorist threats.

BRITISH MUSEUM Map pp426–7 & p430

☎ 7323 8000, tours 7323 8181; www.thebritish museum.ac.uk; Great Russell St WC1; admission free, £2 donation suggested; ⏰ galleries 10am-5.30pm Sat-Wed & 10am-8.30pm Thu & Fri, Great Court 9am-6pm Sun-Wed & 9am-11pm Thu-Sat; tube Tottenham Court Road/Russell Square

One of the world's oldest and finest museums, the British Museum started in 1749 in the form of royal physician Hans Sloane's 'cabinet of curiosities', which he later bequeathed to the country. The collection now comprises some seven million items, augmented over the years through judicious acquisition and the controversial plundering of empire.

It is London's most visited attraction, drawing an average of five million punters each year. Before launching into the collection, bear in mind that the back entrance at

Montague Place is usually quieter than the porticoed main one off Great Russell St. The museum's inner courtyard, hidden from the public for almost 150 years, was covered with a spectacular glass and steel roof designed by Norman Foster and opened as the **Great Court** in late 2000; it is the largest covered public square in Europe. The stunning design opens up the labyrinth that is the British Museum and makes its mind-bogglingly vast collection just a tad more accessible, although it's still pretty daunting. If you have the luxury of time, you'd be well advised to make a few visits. Don't try and see too much or you'll end up savouring nothing. Relax, take a few deep breaths, peruse the written guides available at the information desk, consider from the choice of **tours** below and decide which part of the collection you want to focus on.

It's an exhaustive and exhilarating stampede through world cultures with galleries devoted to Egypt, Western Asia, Greece, the Orient, Africa, Italy, the Etruscans, Romans, Prehistoric and Roman Britain and Medieval Antiquities. To help whet your appetite, the following are some highlights that you should definitely try and catch.

The **Rosetta Stone** (Room 4), discovered in 1799, is written in two forms of ancient Egyptian and Greek and was the key to deciphering Egyptian hieroglyphics, which had stymied scholars up to that time. The **Parthenon Marbles** (Room 18, better known – although it's no longer politically correct – as the Elgin Marbles – p102) once adorned the walls of the Parthenon on the Acropolis in Athens, and are thought to show the great procession to the temple that took place during the Panathenaic Festival, on the birthday of Athena, one of the grandest events in the Greek world. Tucked away at the foot of the eastern staircase is the Mexican Gallery (room 27), featuring the 15th-century Aztec **Mosaic Mask of Tezcatlipoca (The Skull of the Smoking Mirror)**, with a turquoise mosaic laid over a human skull. Beyond that, in rooms 33 and 34, the Asian collections contain the wonderful **Amaravati Sculptures** (room 33A), Indian goddesses, dancing Shivas and serene cross-legged Buddhas in copper and stone.

The stunning **Oxus Treasure** (Room 52) is a collection of 7th- to 4th-century BC pieces of Persian gold, which originated in the ancient Persian capital of Persepolis and ended up here after it was rescued from bandits in a Rawalpindi bazaar. The **Sutton Hoo Ship Burial** (Room 41) is an Anglo-Saxon ship burial site dating from 620, which was excavated in Suffolk in 1939. The

Nations Squabble over Marbles

Wonderful as it is, the British Museum can sometimes feel like one vast repository for stolen booty. Much of what's on display wasn't just 'picked up' along the way by Victorian travellers and explorers, but stolen or purchased under dubious circumstances.

Restive foreign governments occasionally pop their heads over the parapet to demand the return of 'their' property. The British Museum says 'no' and the problem goes away until the next time. Not the Greeks, however, who have been kicking up a stink demanding the return of the so-called Elgin Marbles, the ancient marble sculptures that once adorned the Parthenon. The British Museum, and successive British governments, steadfastly refuse to hand over the priceless works that were removed from the Parthenon and shipped to England by the British ambassador to the Ottoman Empire, the Earl of Elgin, in 1806. (When Elgin blew all his dough, he sold the marbles to the government.) All along, the British Museum has sniffed that the marbles were better off under *its* protective care. This arrogance proved tragicomic when it was discovered that earlier in the 20th century the museum had 'cleaned' the marbles using chisels and wire brushes, thereby destroying the finishing applied by the ancient Greeks.

The Greek government has upped the ante in recent years and has almost completed work on an €86 million museum in Athens designed specifically to exhibit the marbles as they were originally displayed in the 5th century BC. With all the media attention that will surround the Olympics in Athens in 2004, the Greeks hope to embarrass the British into returning the priceless artefacts. Only time will tell who blinks first.

Lindow Man (Room 50) is an Iron Age unfortunate who appears to have been smacked on the head with an axe and then garrotted. His remains were preserved in a peat bog until 1984 when a peat-cutting machine sliced him in half.

In the centre of the Great Court – and the heart of the museum – is the world-famous **Reading Room**, which was formerly the British Library and where George Bernard Shaw and Mahatma Gandhi studied, Oscar Wilde and William Butler Yeats mused, and scruffy Karl Marx wrote *The Communist Manifesto*. The northern end of the courtyard's lower level houses the terrific new **Sainsbury African Galleries**, a fascinating romp through the art and cultures of historic and contemporary African societies.

The restored **King's Library**, an 1820 architectural gem that used to contain the library of George III (now relocated to the British Library), will become room number 1 and specialise in the evolution of the museums. It, and at least part of the new **Wellcome Gallery of Ethnography**, which will provide exhibition space for many previously warehoused items, were due to open at the time of writing.

The museum offers nine free 50-minute **eye-Opener tours** of individual galleries throughout the day, and 20-minute **eyeOpener Spotlight talks** daily at 1.15pm focusing on different themes from the collection. Ninety-minute **Highlights tours** (£8/5) leave at 10.30am, 1pm and 3pm daily. If you want to go it alone there is a series of **audio tours** (£3.50) available at the information desk, including a family-oriented one narrated by comedian, writer and all-round top bloke

Stephen Fry. One specific to the Parthenon Marbles is available in that gallery. You could also check out COMPASS, a multimedia public access system with 50 computer terminals that let you take a virtual tour of the museum, plan your own circuit or get information on specific exhibits.

Despite the kudos, all's not well at the cash-strapped museum. Cost-cutting measures such as wholesale job losses and reduced opening hours at various galleries led to industrial strife which forced the temporary closure – albeit only for a day – of the museum in 2002. The government chipped in to avoid further embarrassment although, without a long-term commitment from the bureaucrats, the museum fears more temporary closures of galleries in the future.

DICKENS HOUSE MUSEUM Map pp420-1
☎ 7405 2127; www.dickensmuseum.com; 49 Doughty St WC1; adults/concession £4/3; ⏱ 10am-5pm Mon-Sat; tube Russell Square

This handsome four-storey house is the sole surviving residence of the many that the great and restless Victorian novelist occupied before moving to Kent (leaving a trail of blue plaques behind him). The two-and-a-half years spent here, from 1837 to 1839, were prolific and Dickens dashed off *The Pickwick Papers*, *Nicholas Nickleby* and *Oliver Twist* between bouts of worry over debts, deaths and his ever-growing family. The house itself was saved from demolition and opened as a museum in 1925, and is one of the most interesting of its kind. The drawing room has been restored to its original condition while the other 10 rooms are stuffed with

British Museum, Bloomsbury (p101)

memorabilia. In the Dressing Room you can see texts Dickens had prepared for his reading tours, which include notes and instructions to himself like 'slapping the desk'. You can also see the very same slapped desk, a velvet-topped bureau he had made for his public reading events.

A one-man show, 'The Sparkler of Albion', is performed at 7.30pm every Wednesday from mid-May to mid-September and costs £12.

ST GEORGE'S BLOOMSBURY Map p430
☎ 7405 3044; Bloomsbury Way WC1; ⏱ 9.30am-5.30pm Mon-Fri, 10.30am-12.30pm Sun; tube Holborn/Tottenham Court Road

Not far from the British Museum, this Nicholas Hawksmoor church (1731) is distinguished by its classical portico of Corinthian capitals and a steeple that was inspired by the Mausoleum of Halicarnassus. It is topped with a statue of George I in Roman dress, and you can imagine how the sight of a bloke in a toga went down in 18th-century London. Unfortunately, the church's other distinctive feature is the passage of time writ all over its blackened, grubby exterior. It seems to be always on the verge of closing for restoration but just can't raise enough money, so if you've got a few bob to spare…

PETRIE MUSEUM OF EGYPTIAN ARCHAEOLOGY Map pp418-9
☎ 7679 2884; www.petrie.ucl.ac.uk; University College London (UCL; entrance through the Science Library), Malet Place WC1; ⏱ 1-5pm Tue-Fri, 10am-1pm Sat; tube Goodge Street

If you've got any interest in things Egyptian, you'll love this quiet and oft-overlooked gem, where some 80,000 objects make up one of the most impressive collections of Egyptian and Sudanese archaeology in the world. Behind glass, and amid an atmosphere of academia,

are exhibits ranging from fragments of pottery to the world's oldest dress (2800 BC). The museum is named after Professor William Flinders Petrie (1853–1942), who uncovered many of the exhibits during his excavations and donated the collection to the university in 1933.

PERCIVAL DAVID FOUNDATION OF CHINESE ART Map pp418-19
☎ 7387 3909; www.pdfmuseum.org.uk; 53 Gordon Sq WC1; ⏱ 10.30am-5pm Mon-Fri; tube Russell Square

Although it feels like a fusty old institution, the friendly staff, lack of crowds and quirky collection here make for a rewarding visit. With some 1700 pieces, it's the largest collection of Chinese ceramics from the 10th to 18th centuries outside China. Sir Percival David donated it to the University of London in 1950 on the condition that every single piece be displayed at all times. Consequently, there are a few very ordinary pieces – of great significance, no doubt, just not very interesting to the casual enthusiast – to sift through before you reach the really exquisite stuff, such as wares that used to belong to Chinese emperors. Among the highlights are the David Vases (1351), the earliest dated and inscribed blue-and-white Chinese porcelain, named after Mr Percival himself.

POLLOCK'S TOY MUSEUM Map pp426-7
☎ 7639 3452; www.pollocksweb.co.uk; 1 Scala St; adult/child £3/1.50; ⏱ 10am-5pm Mon-Sat; tube Goodge Street

Possibly a bit creepy for kids but fascinating for adults, this deceptively large museum has what feels like a dusty collection of thousands of old toys ranging from board games, tin toys, puppets, doll houses, teddy bears, wax dolls, comics and craft toys from around the world. The most impressive collection, however, is of toy theatres, which should be no surprise as Benjamin Pollock was the leading Victorian manufacturer of these popular toys. This really is a magical little place (not least because you go up three flights of stairs, down four and leave by the

---

Top Five Quirky London
- Cabinet War Rooms (p129)
- Dennis Sever's House (p117)
- Old Operating Theatre Museum (p163)
- Pollock's Toy Museum (above)
- Tyburn Convent (p138)

Neighbourhoods – The West End

same door!). Follow a higgledy-piggledy trail up creaking stairs and around a warren of rooms, each dedicated to a different toy theme. For over 30s, it's a poignant prance down memory lane. The shop has a fantastic range of wooden toys you're unlikely to see anywhere else.

THE SQUARES OF
BLOOMSBURY Map pp426-7

At the very heart of Bloomsbury is **Russell Square**, the largest in London. Originally laid out in 1800 by Humphrey Repton, it was given a striking facelift and a new 10m-tall fountain a few years ago.

The centre of literary Bloomsbury was **Gordon Square** where, at various times, Bertrand Russell lived at No 57, Lytton Strachey at No 51 and Vanessa and Clive Bell, Maynard Keynes and the Woolf family at No 46. Strachey, Dora Carrington and Lydia Lopokova (the future wife of Maynard Keynes) all took turns living at No 41. Not all the buildings, many of which now belong to the university, are marked with blue plaques.

Lovely **Bedford Square**, the only completely Georgian square still surviving in Bloomsbury, was home to many London publishing houses up until a few years ago, when they were swallowed up by multinational conglomerates and relocated. They included Jonathan Cape, Chatto and the Bodley Head (set up by Woolf and her husband Leonard), and were largely responsible for perpetuating the legend of the Bloomsbury Group by churning out seemingly endless collections of associated letters, memoirs and biographies.

EAST CENTRAL

Eating p229; Sleeping p341; Shopping p323

Forget the movie *Notting Hill* and whatever west Londoners might say, one of the most vibrant, thriving areas of London in recent times has been eastwards, in and around the financial hub known as the City. Capitalists and developers rebuilt London's commercial heart during the smash-and-grab boom of the Thatcher years, but it was artists and boho types that led the most impressive rejuvenation in the area. The once-forgotten northern fringe of the City – namely the areas of Shoreditch and Hoxton – is now the most vital and dynamic in the capital. Clerkenwell, to the northeast of the City, experienced its own renaissance while neighbouring Islington was an earlier example of gentrification and is today synonymous with New Labour and left-leaning fashionistas.

THE CITY

It's confusing to arrive in London and discover a City within a city. While 'the city' might refer loosely to the entire metropolis of London, 'the City' (with a capital) definitely refers to the 'Square Mile' on the northern bank of the Thames, effectively the birthplace of London where the Romans built a walled community 2000 years ago. Nowadays it's overrun by stockbrokers and other money people carrying on the proud Roman tradition of empire-building (albeit strictly financial these days).

Rebuilt in a rather higgledy-piggledly fashion after the savage bombing of WWII, the City got a makeover from the 1980s when the unloved postwar buildings were tumbled to make way for new office development. The most dramatic changes came in a short, sharp burst brought about by the 'big bang' in financial services that followed deregulation in 1989.

The City is positively clogged during the week with pinstriped workers scurrying hither and thither, and tourists piling into St Paul's Cathedral and the Tower of London. Come the weekend and it's like a ghost town: no workers, no shops, just a few savvy tourists taking the opportunity to explore.

BARBICAN Map pp432-3

☎ information 7638 8891, switchboard 7638 4141; www.barbican.org.uk; Silk St EC2; ☯ 9am-11pm Mon-Sat, 10.30am-11pm Sun; tube Barbican/Moorgate

Occasionally long-lost Londoners emerge, blinking, from the labyrinthine Barbican, having done unspeakable things to feed and water themselves for years and still believing Margaret Thatcher is prime minister of Britain. OK, we made that one up. But the maze of elevated walkways that leads to Europe's largest multi-arts venue and home of the London Symphony Orchestra (LSO) does make it easy to become confused.

The problem lies in the centre's history. Begun in the 1970s on a huge bombsite abandoned since WWII, it was originally planned as just a housing scheme – the theatres, concert halls, cinemas and art gallery that attract most visitors were a last-minute addition. Most of the apartments sit in narrow, six- or seven-storey concrete slab blocks on stilts, which are arranged to form the sides of a staggered rectangle (embellished with three towers, a few stray curves and extra paths). And one has to negotiate one's way around, or through, this citadel to find the arts centre, which opened in 1982.

Yet, what in lacks it orientation, the Barbican certainly makes up for in culture and these days even retro chic. Besides the world-class LSO, you'll also find the City of London Symphonia, the English Chamber Orchestra and the BBC Symphony Orchestra performing in the auditoriums here. The programme of theatre has been slightly uneven since the Royal Shakespeare Company moved out of the Barbican in 2002 (see Shakespeare in Limbo p41), however, dance is a strong part of the Barbican's current repertoire.

The highly regarded **Barbican Gallery** (☎ 7638 8891, Level 3, Barbican Centre, Silk St EC2; adult/senior, student & those aged 12-17 £7/5; 🕙 10am-6pm Mon, Tue & Thu-Sat, 10am-9pm Wed, noon-6pm Sun) stages some of the best photographic exhibits in London.

With a recent £7 million refit and a highly re-garded brasserie, the Barbican is much better loved than London's other modernist colossus, the South Bank Centre (p158). Trendy urban architects are racing to get hold of the back-in-fashion apartments. The *Daily Telegraph* newspaper is less decided, once describing the complex as a cross between utopia and a public loo.

For details of the theatres (p313), cinemas (p293) and concert halls (p308), see the Entertainment chapter (p291).

MUSEUM OF LONDON Map pp432-3
☎ 7600 0807; www.museumoflondon.org.uk; London Wall EC2; admission free; 🕙 10am-5.50pm Mon-Sat, noon-5.50pm Sun; tube Barbican

Hiding its light under the bushel of the Barbican and surrounding offices is one of London's most engaging museums. It's a relaxed place to while away a few weekend hours, as locals themselves frequently do when the Square Mile is all but deserted. The museum chronicles the city's evolution from the Ice Age to the 20th century, and is the world's largest urban-history museum.

The newest gallery, called London Before London, outlines the development of the Thames Valley from 450 million years ago. Harnessing computer technology to enliven its exhibits and presenting impressive fossils and stone axe heads in shiny new cases, it somehow feels less warm and colourful than the more-established displays. In these, you begin with the city's Roman era, and move anticlockwise through the Saxon, medieval, Tudor and Stuart periods. Continuing down a ramp and past the ornate Lord Mayor's state coach, this history continues progressively until 1914.

Aside from the magnificent state coach, highlights include: the 4th-century lead coffin, skeleton and reconstructed face of a well-to-do young Roman woman whose remains were discovered in Spitalfields in 1999; the Cheapside Hoard, an amazing find of 16th- and 17th-century jewellery; the lo-fi but heartfelt Great Fire of London diorama, narrated from the renowned diary of Samuel Pepys; and a timeline of London's creeping urbanisation during the 18th and 19th centuries. There are two mock-ups of city streets – one represents Roman London, the other is called Victorian Walk and harks back to the 19th century (although Leadenhall Market, p111, creates a slightly less authentic, but more lively Victorian feeling).

You can pause for a breather in the pleasant garden in the building's central courtyard or head for the adjoining **Museum Café**, which serves light meals from 10am to 5.30pm (from 11.30am on Sunday). Alternatively, on a sunny day, pack some sandwiches and lunch in the next door **Barber Surgeon's Herb Garden**.

Barbican, City (opposite)

Top Five – East Central

- Museum of London (p105)
- The Old Bailey (right)
- St Bartholomew-the-Great (below)
- St Paul's Cathedral (right)
- Tower of London (p112)

When arriving, look for the Barbican's gate seven; before leaving, don't forget to have a browse through the well-stocked **bookshop**.

SMITHFIELD MARKET Map pp426-7

☎ 7248 3151; West Smithfield EC1; tube Farringdon

Smithfield is central London's last surviving meat market. For details see the Shopping chapter (p334).

ST BARTHOLOMEW-THE-GREAT
Map pp426-7

☎ 7606 5171; www.greatstbarts.com; West Smithfield EC1; ⏰ 8.30am-5pm Tue-Fri, 10.30am-1.30pm Sat, 8am-8pm Sun; tube Barbican

This church's most obvious selling point for modern audiences is that scenes from the Oscar-winning *Shakespeare in Love* (and parts of *Four Weddings and a Funeral*) were filmed here. But the location managers for those movies knew what they were doing and St Bartholomew-the-Great turns out to be one of the capital's most atmospheric places of worship. The authentic Norman arches, the weathered and blackened stone, the dark wood carvings and the low lighting lend this space an ancient calm – especially as there's sometimes only a handful of visitors. There are historical associations with the painter William Hogarth, who was baptised here, and with politician Benjamin Franklin, who worked on site as an apprentice printer. The church sits on the corner of the grounds of St Bartholomew's Hospital, on the side closest to Smithfield Market.

GREAT FIRE MEMORIAL Map pp426-7

This small statue of a corpulent boy opposite St Bartholomew's Hospital, at the corner of Cock Lane and Giltspur St, has a somewhat odd dedication: 'In memory put up for the fire of London occasioned by the sin of gluttony 1666'. All becomes clear, however, when you realise the Great Fire was started in a busy bakery. On this site, the Fortune of War tavern once stood. This is where 'resurrectionists' (body snatchers) took corpses to be sold to the hospital's surgeons for use when practising surgery.

CENTRAL CRIMINAL COURT
(OLD BAILEY) Map pp426-7

☎ 7248 3277; cnr Newgate St & Old Bailey; admission free; ⏰ 10am-1pm & 2-5pm Mon-Fri; tube St Paul's

Just as fact is often better than fiction, taking in a trial in the Old Bailey leaves watching a TV courtroom drama for dust. Of course, it's too late to see author Jeffrey Archer being found guilty of perjury here, watch the Guildford Four's convictions being quashed after their wrongful imprisonment for IRA terrorist attacks or view the Yorkshire Ripper Peter Sutcliffe being sent down. However, 'the Old Bailey' is a byword for crime and notoriety. So even if you sit in on a fairly run-of-the-mill trial, simply being in the court where such people as the Kray twins and Oscar Wilde (in an earlier building on this site) once appeared is memorable in itself.

Choose from 18 courts, of which the oldest – courts one, two and three – usually have the most interesting cases. As cameras, video equipment, mobile phones, large bags and food or drink are all forbidden inside, and there are no cloakrooms or lockers, it's important not to take these with you. Take a cardigan or something to cushion the hard seats, though, and if you're interested in a high-profile trial, also get there early.

The Central Criminal Court gets its nickname from the street on which it stands: *baillie* was Norman French for 'fortified church'. The current building opened in 1907 on the combined site of a previous Old Bailey and Newgate Prison. Intriguingly, the figure of justice holding a sword and scales in her hands above the building's copper dome is *not* blindfolded (against undue influence, as is traditionally the case). That's a situation that has sparked many a sarcastic comment from those being charged here.

ST PAUL'S CATHEDRAL Map pp432-3

☎ 7236 4128; www.stpauls.co.uk; St Paul's Churchyard; admission adult/child aged 6-16/senior & student £6/3/5; ⏰ 8.30am-4pm (last entry) Mon-Sat; tube St Paul's

One of the most famous buildings in London, proud bearer of the capital's largest church dome, St Paul's Cathedral has seen a lot in its 300-plus years. This architectural gem almost didn't make it off the drawing board, as Sir Christopher Wren's initial designs were rejected. However, since its first service in 1697, it's held funerals for Lord Nelson, the Duke of Wellington and Winston Churchill, miraculously dodged being bombed out of

ST PAUL'S CATHEDRAL

GROUND FLOOR			CRYPT (keyed in italics)
1 Queen Anne Statue	8 Wellington Memorial	21 Tijou Gates	3 Crypt Café
2 Great West Door	11 Holman Hunt's	22 St Paul's in WWII	9 Toilets
(Main Entrance)	The Light of the World	Photos	10 Treasury
4 All Souls' Chapel	12 Dome & Wren's Epitaph	24 John Donne	13 Nelson's Tomb
5 Exterior Entrance to	15 Quire	Memorial	14 Wellington's
Crypt Café & Shop	16 Choir Stalls	25 Entrances to Crypt	Tomb
6 Monument to the	17 Tijou Gates	26 Entrance to Dome &	18 OBE Chapel
People of London	19 High Altar	Whispering Gallery	23 Wren's Tomb
7 Chapel of St Dunstan	20 American Memorial	28 Chapel of St George	27 Cathedral Shop
	Chapel	& St Michael	

existence during WWII and gone on to host Martin Luther King as well as the ill-fated wedding of Prince Charles and Diana.

All that history, plus one of the city's most magnificent interiors, and people are usually most interested in climbing the dome for the view.

Ah yes, that dome. It's actually three domes, one inside the other, but it made the cathedral Wren's *tour de force* and only a handful of others throughout the world (mostly in Italy) outdo it in size. Exactly 530 stairs take you to the top, but it's a three-stage journey. The cathedral is built in the shape of a cross, with the dome at its intersection. So first find the circular paved area between the eight massive columns supporting the dome, then head to the door on the western side of the southern transept (ie at about 'five o'clock' as you face the altar). Some 30m and precisely 259 steps above, you reach the interior walkway around the dome's base. This is the **Whispering Gallery**, so called because if you talk close to the wall it really does carry your words around to the opposite side, 32m away.

Climbing even more steps – 117, 118, pant, 119! – you reach the **Stone Gallery**, which is an exterior viewing platform, with 360-degree views of London, round from the gherkin-shaped Swiss Re Tower to the Houses of Parliament, circling from Tate Modern to Alexander Palace. The further 152 iron steps to the **Golden Gallery** are steeper and narrower than below and you don't really get that much more of a view, but if you'd like to say you made it to the 111m summit, it's worth doing.

Of course, back on the ground floor, St Paul's offers plenty of riches for those who like to keep their feet firmly on its black-and-white tiled floor. Just beneath the dome, for starters, is a compass and an epitaph written for Wren by his son: *Lector, si monumentum requiris, circumspice* (Reader, if you seek his monument, look around you).

Although a major renovation is under way in the cathedral until well into 2004 or 2005, relatively few of its ornate features are likely to be behind scaffolding at any one time.

In the northern aisle, you'll find the **All Souls' Chapel** and the **Chapel of St Dunstan**, dedicated to the 10th-century archbishop of Canterbury, and the grandiose Duke of Wellington Memorial (1875). In the north transept chapel is Holman Hunt's celebrated painting *The Light of the World*, which depicts Christ knocking at an overgrown door that, symbolically, can only be opened from the inside. Beyond, in the

The City's Livery Companies

In the Middle Ages, most craftsworkers belonged to guilds that organised apprenticeships and were the prototypes of today's trade unions. The wealthier guilds built themselves magnificent halls, and their leaders wore suitably fine costumes, or liveries. These same leaders were eligible to stand for a series of offices, with the post of Lord Mayor of the City of London at the pinnacle.

While the old craft guilds may be no more, more than 100 livery companies live on and their leading lights still stand for office at the Court of Common Council, which runs the Corporation – and thus the City – of London. Although most of the original halls were destroyed in the Great Fire or by the Blitz, some have since been rebuilt and they're impressive, if largely inaccessible, places. One of the most interesting is the Merchant Taylors' Hall in Threadneedle St, which still retains its great kitchen, in use since 1425. The wealthy Vintners' Company occupies the surviving hall. It's on Upper Thames St and dates back to the late 17th century.

If you'd like to visit one of the halls you'll have to ask the **Corporation of London Tourist Information Centre** (Map 9; ☎ 7332 1456; www.cityoflondon.gov.uk; St Paul's Churchyard; ✆ 9.30am-5pm Mon-Fri, 9-30am-noon Sat, or 9.30am-5pm Apr-Sep; tube St Paul's). This office can provide information or organise tickets to the City's livery company halls. They receive stocks of tickets for the Goldsmiths', Fishmongers', Ironmongers', Tallow Chandlers', Haberdashers' and Skinners' halls in February each year but they're snapped up pretty quickly. Otherwise, you can visit the Guildhall, where the liverymen meet to choose two sheriffs in June, and again in September to elect the lord mayor.

cathedral's heart, are the particularly spectacular **quire** (or chancel) – its ceilings and arches dazzling with green, blue, red and gold mosaics – and the high altar. The ornately carved **choir stalls** by Grinling Gibbons on either side of the quire are exquisite, as are the **ornamental wrought-iron gates** separating the aisles from the altar by Jean Tijou (both men also worked on Hampton Court Palace). Walk around the altar, with its massive gilded oak canopy, to the **American Memorial Chapel**, a memorial to the 28,000 Americans based in Britain who lost their lives during WWII.

Around the southern side of the ambulatory is the **effigy of John Donne** (1573–1631). The one-time dean of St Paul's, Donne was also a metaphysical poet, most famous for the immortal lines 'No man is an island' and 'Ask not for whom the bell tolls, it tolls for thee' (both in the same poem!). Unfortunately, his statue was obscured by reconstruction work when we visited. So too was a glass case with photographs of St Paul's during WWII. Both may be visible again on your visit.

On the eastern side of both the north and south transepts are stairs leading down to the crypt, treasury and OBE Chapel, where weddings, funerals and other services are held for members of the Order of the British Empire. The **crypt** has memorials to up to 300 military demigods, including Wellington, Florence Nightingale, Kitchener and Nelson, the last of which is directly below the dome in a black sarcophagus. On the surrounding walls are plaques in memory of those from the Commonwealth who died in various conflicts during the 20th century.

Wren's own tomb is in the crypt, while architect Edwin Lutyens and poet William Blake are also remembered here. In a niche, there is also an exhibit of Wren's controversial plans for St Paul's and his actual working model. St Paul's was one of the 50 commissions the great architect was given after the Great Fire of London wiped out most of the city, and his is the fifth cathedral to stand on this site. The first dated from 604.

The **treasury** displays some of the cathedral's plate, along with some spectacular needlework, including Beryl Dean's jubilee cope (bishop's cloak) of 1977, showing spires of the 73 London churches, and its matching mitre. There is a **Crypt Café** and the restaurant **Refectory** (✆ 9am-5.30pm Mon-Sat, 10.30am-5.30pm Sun), in addition to a **shop** (✆ 9am-5pm Mon-Sat, 10.30am-5pm Sun).

Just outside the north transept (that's to the left as you face the cathedral's entrance stairway), there's a simple **monument to the people of London**, honouring the 32,000 civilians killed (and another 50,000 seriously injured) in the defence of the city and the cathedral during WWII.

Audioguide tours lasting 45 minutes cost £3.50 for adults, or £3 for seniors & students; guided tours lasting 1½ to two hours (adult/child aged 6-16/senior & student £2.50/1/2) leave the tour desk at 11am, 11.30am, 1.30pm and 2pm. There are organ recitals (free) at St Paul's at 5pm most Sundays, as well as celebrity recitals (adults/concessions £8/5.50) at 6.30pm on the first Thursday of the month between May and October. Evensong takes place at 5pm most weekdays and at 3.15pm on Sunday.

GUILDHALL Map pp432-3

☎ 7606 3030; www.cityoflondon.gov.uk; Gresham St EC2; admission free; ⏰ 10am-5pm May-Sep, 10am-5pm Mon-Sat Oct-Apr; tube Bank

Bang in the centre of the Square Mile, the Guildhall has been the City's seat of government for nearly 800 years. The present building dates from the early 15th century, in the sense that the walls survived. Other segments suffered severe damage during both the Great Fire of 1666 and the Blitz of 1940. The oak-panelled roof, for example, was restored in the 1950s by Sir Giles Gilbert Scott, the architect responsible for the Bankside Power Station (now the Tate Modern art gallery).

Most visitors' first port of call is the impressive **Great Hall**, where you can see the banners and shields of London's 12 guilds (or principal livery companies), which used to wield absolute power throughout the City. The lord mayor and sherrifs are still elected annually in the vast open hall, with its chunky chandeliers and its church-style monuments. It is often closed for various other formal functions, so it's best to ring ahead. Meetings of the Common Council are held here every third Thursday of each month (except August) at 1pm, and the Guildhall hosts the awards dinner for the Booker Prize, the leading British literary prize.

Among the monuments to look out for if the hall is open are statues of Winston Churchill, Admiral Nelson, the Duke of Wellington and the two prime ministers Pitt the Elder and Younger. In the minstrels' gallery at the western end are statues of the legendary giants Gog and Magog; today's figures replaced similar 18th-century statues destroyed in the Blitz. The Guildhall's stained glass was also blown out during the Blitz but a modern window in the southwestern corner depicts the City's history; look out for a picture of London's first Lord Mayor, Dick Whittington, and his cat.

Beneath the Great Hall is London's largest medieval crypt with 19 stained-glass windows showing the livery companies' coats of arms. The crypt can only be seen on a free **guided tour** (☎ 7606 3030 ext 1463).

The buildings to the west house Corporation of London offices and the **Guildhall Library** (☎ 7606 3030; Aldermanbury EC2; ⏰ 9.30am-4.45pm Mon-Sat), founded in about 1420 under the terms of Richard 'Dick' Whittington's will. It is divided into three sections for research: printed books, manuscripts and prints, maps and drawings. Also here is the **Clockmakers' Company Museum** (☎ 7332 1868; Guildhall Library, Aldermanbury EC2;

admission free; ⏰ 9.30am-4.45pm Mon-Fri), which has a collection of more than 700 clocks and watches dating back some 500 years. The clock museum sometimes closes for an hour or two on Monday to wind the clocks.

GUILDHALL ART GALLERY Map pp432-3

☎ 7332 3700; www.guildhall-art-gallery.org.uk; Guildhall Yard EC2; adult/senior & student/family £2.80/1/5; ⏰ 10am-5pm Mon-Sat, noon-4pm Sun; tube Bank

In the latter half of 2002, this humble gallery made world headlines when its new statue of former Prime Minister Margaret Thatcher was decapitated by an angry punter with a cricket bat (and one of the gallery's own metal stanchions). A repaired or replacement statue may or may not stay, but there's another reason to visit besides tittering or tutting at the marble lady's fate. Deep in the darkened basement lie the archaeological remains of Roman London's amphitheatre, or coliseum. Only a few remnants of the stone walls lining the eastern entrance still stand, but they're imaginatively fleshed out with a black-and-fluorescent-green trompe l'oeil of the missing seating, and computer-meshed outlines of spectators and gladiators. The roar of the crowd goes up as you reach the end of the entrance tunnel and hit the central stage.

It's a great place for those who were enthralled by Maximus Decimus Meridius in the film *Gladiator*, and certainly a greater revelation than the Corporation of London's fairly dull artworks upstairs. The gallery lies east across the courtyard from Guildhall and St Lawrence Jewry.

CHURCH OF ST LAWRENCE JEWRY Map pp432-3

☎ 7600 9478; Gresham St EC2; admission free; ⏰ 7.30am-2.15pm; tube Bank

To look at the Corporation of London's extremely well-preserved official church, you'd barely realise that it was almost completely destroyed during WWII. Instead, it does Sir Christopher Wren, who built it in 1678, and its subsequent restorers proud, with its immaculate alabaster walls and gilt trimmings. The arms of the City of London adorn the organ above the door at the western end. The Commonwealth Chapel is bedecked with the flags of member nations. Free piano recitals are held each Monday at 1pm, organ recitals at the same time on Tuesday.

As the church name suggests, this was once part of the Jewish quarter – the centre being Old Jewry, the street to the southeast. The district was sadly not without its pogroms. After some 500 Jews were killed in 1262 in mob 'retaliation' against a Jewish money-lender, Edward I expelled the entire community from London to Flanders in 1290. They did not return until the late 17th century.

AROUND BANK Map pp432-3

By its very nature, much of the work of the City goes on behind closed doors. However, a short exploration of the streets around Bank tube station will take you to the door of many financial, as well as political and religious, landmarks. Here, at the tube station's main exit, seven bank-filled streets converge. Take Princes St northwestwards to get to the Guildhall or head northeastwards along Threadneedle St for the Bank of England Museum.

The **Royal Exchange** is the imposing, colonnaded building you see at the juncture of Threadneedle St and Cornhill to the east. It's the third building on a site originally chosen in 1564 by Thomas Gresham and the former home of the London International Financial Futures Exchange. Today, however, it's simply an upmarket office complex and shopping mall, where you can take in the fabulous architecture while buying a Prada bag or Paul Smith shirt. There's also a Conran restaurant, **Grand Café & Bar** (p235), in the central courtyard. Alternatively, you can simply stand on the huge steps, enjoying the view of the Bank of England across Threadneedle St. The Futures Exchange has now moved slightly northeast along Threadneedle St to the Stock Exchange and is hence no longer open to the public.

Moving around the intersection at Bank station, and looking north, your view is variously dominated by (left to right) NatWest Bank's Tower 42, the space-aged 'erotic gherkin' that houses insurance giant Swiss Re and the shiny stainless steel of the Lloyd's of London building.

Turning southeast, you enter Lombard St, which takes its name from the Italian bankers who ran London's money markets between the 13th and 16th centuries after Jewish financiers were expelled. The large signs bearing the banks' founding dates – a grasshopper (1563), a running mare for Lloyd's (1677), a cat and a fiddle – were once banned after they started falling in high winds and killing people. Only during Edward VII's 1901 coronation were they reaffixed (securely).

In the angle between Lombard St and King William St further south you'll see the twin towers of Hawksmoor's **St Mary Woolnoth**

(☎ 7626 9701; ⏰ 8am-5pm Mon-Fri), built in 1717. The architect's only City church, its interior Corinthian columns are a foretaste of his Christ Church in Spitalfields.

Between King William St and Walbrook stands the grand, porticoed **Mansion House** (☎ 7626 2500; www.cityoflondon.gov.uk), the official residence of the Lord Mayor of London, which was built in the mid-18th century by George Dance the Elder. It's not open to the public, though group tours are sometimes available when booked in advance.

Along Walbrook, past the City of London Magistrates Court, is **St Stephen Walbrook** (☎ 7283 4444; 39 Walbrook EC3; ⏰ 10am-4pm Mon-Thu, 10am-3pm Fri), built in 1679. Widely considered to be the finest of Wren's City churches and a forerunner to St Paul's Cathedral, this light and airy building is indisputably impressive. Some 16 pillars with Corinthian capitals rise up to support its dome and ceiling, while a large cream-coloured boulder lies at the heart of its roomy central space. This is an altar by sculptor Henry Moore, cheekily dubbed 'the Camembert' by critics.

Queen Victoria St runs southwestwards from Bank. A short way along it on the left, in front of Temple Court at No 11, you'll find the remains of the 3rd-century AD **Temple of Mithras**. Truth be told, however, there's little to see here. If you're interested in this Persian God and the religion worshipping him, you're better off checking out the **Museum of London** (p105), where sculptures and silver incense boxes found in the temple are on display.

Due west of Bank is Poultry. The modern building at the corner, with striped layers of blond and rose stone, is by Stirling Wilford (the Wilford in question is also behind the much-acclaimed Lowry centre in Salford Quays near Manchester). Behind this, Poultry runs into Cheapside, site of a great medieval market. On the left you'll see another of Wren's great churches, **St Mary-le-Bow** (☎ 7248 5139; Cheapside EC2; ⏰ 6.30am-6pm Mon-Thu, 6.30am-4pm Fri), built in 1673. It's famous as the church whose bells dictate who is – and who isn't – a cockney. Its delicate steeple is one of Wren's finest works and the modern stained glass is striking. There's a good café called the **Place Below** (p239).

BANK OF ENGLAND MUSEUM
Map pp432-3

☎ 7601 5545; www.bankofengland.co.uk; Bartholomew Lane EC2; ⏰ 10am-5pm Mon-Fri; tube Bank

When James II declared war against France in the 17th century, he looked over his shoulder and soon realised he didn't have the funds to finance his armed forces. A Scottish merchant by the name of William Paterson came up with the idea of forming a joint-stock bank that could lend the government money and, in 1694, so began the Bank of England and the notion of national debt. The bank rapidly expanded in size and stature and moved to this site in 1734. During a financial crisis at the end of the 18th century, a cartoon appeared depicting the bank as a haggard old woman, and this is probably the origin of its nickname 'the Old Lady of Threadneedle St' which has stuck ever since. The institution is now in charge of maintaining the integrity of sterling and the British financial system. The gifted Sir John Soane built the original structure although the governors saw fit to demolish most of his splendid bank in the early 20th century and replace it with a utilitarian, no-frills model that they would soon regret.

The centrepiece of the museum – which explores the evolution of money and the history of this venerable institution, and which is not *nearly* as dull as it sounds – is a postwar reconstruction of Soane's original stock office complete with mannequins in period dress behind original mahogany counters. A series of rooms leading off the office are packed with exhibits ranging from photographs and coins to gold bars and the muskets once used to defend the bank. There are heaps of interactive exhibits including one that lets you try your hand at being a foreign-exchange dealer. It's a pity the acoustics are so awful – the chap hammering copies of old Viking coins flat to hand out to tourists should be stopped before a nervy visitor flattens *him*.

LEADENHALL MARKET Map pp432-3
Whittington Ave off Gracechurch St EC1; ⏲ 7am-4pm Mon-Fri; tube Bank

Like stepping into a small slice of Victorian London, a visit to this dimly-lit, covered mall is a minor time-travelling experience. There's been a market on this site since the Roman era, but the architecture that survives is all cobblestones and late-19th-century ironwork; even modern restaurants and chain stores decorate their façades in period style here. The market also appears as Diagon Alley in *Harry Potter and the Philosopher's Stone*. For details of what's on sale, p334.

LLOYDS OF LONDON Map pp432-3
☎ 7623 1000; 1 Lime St EC3; tube Aldgate/Bank

While the world's leading insurance brokers are inside underwriting everything from trains, planes and ships to cosmonauts' lives and film stars' legs, people outside still can't stop admiring the stainless steel external ducting and staircases of the Lloyds of London building. French free climber, or 'spiderman', Alain Robert was so enamoured, he scaled the exterior with his bare hands in 2003.

This love affair with the building endures despite the fact that, though it was a watershed for London when it was built in 1986, Lloyds has since been joined by plenty of other stunning architecture throughout the capital. Lloyds is the work of Richard Rogers, one of the architects of the Pompidou Centre in Paris. His decision to illuminate the façade at night with yellow and blue neon was a particular triumph.

Its brave-new-world postmodernism strikes a particular contrast with the olde worlde Leadenhall Market next door. Watch people whizzing up and down the outside of the building in those all-glass lifts and wonder what that must feel like. Sadly, you usually can't experience it yourself, as access to the elevators and the rest of the interior is restricted to employees or professional groups, who must book in advance.

Leadenhall Market (right)

MONUMENT Map pp432-3

☎ 7626 2717; Monument St EC3; adult/child aged 5-15 £2/1; ⏲ 9.30am-5pm; tube Monument

This is a huge memorial to the Great Fire of London of 1666, which, in terms of the physical devastation and horrifying psychological impact it wreaked on the city, must have been the 9/11 of its day. Fortunately, this event lies further back in history and few people died, so it's possible to simply enjoy Sir Christopher Wren's 1677 tower and its panoramic views of London. Slightly southeast of King William St, near London Bridge, the Monument is exactly 60.6m from the bakery in Pudding Lane where the fire started and exactly 60.6m high. To reach the viewing platform, just below a gilded bronze urn of flames that some call a big gold pincushion, you will need to climb 311 narrow, winding steps. On descent, you're given a certificate to say you did it, and if you did go all the way to the top, you'll feel it's justly deserved.

SWISS RE TOWER Map pp432-3

St Mary Axe EC3; tube Aldgate/Bank

Until and unless architect Renzo Piano's 390m 'shard of glass' tower is erected at London Bridge, Swiss Re tower will remain London's most distinctive skyscraper. Yes, that's it on the horizon, the truly 'phat' missile-shaped building with a transparent glass façade ringed with spiralling black stripes. Despite the fact that, at 41 storeys, the Swiss reinsurance giant's office is slightly shorter than the neighbouring NatWest Tower, you just can't miss it.

In some ways, the 'erotic gherkin's' futuristic, sci-fi exterior could be said to do for London what the Pudong Tower does for Shanghai in China. Inside, however, the prime concern has been to make the building eco-friendly. After doing research with the legendary architect Buckminster Fuller, Norman Foster has laid out the offices so they spiral around internal 'sky gardens'. The windows open and the gardens are used to reprocess stale air, so air conditioning is kept to a minimum.

The gherkin is on the site of the former Baltic Exchange, which was bombed by the IRA in 1992. Unfortunately, the rooftop restaurant of the new tower will not be open to the public, but there is a shopping arcade on the lower floor. If you're really keen to get a full-length view, go to Whitechapel, where there's a clear line of vision along Whitechapel Rd.

TOWER OF LONDON Map pp432-3

☎ 7709 0765; www.hrp.org.uk; Tower Hill EC3; adult/child aged 5-15/senior & student/family £12/7.80/9/34; ⏲ 9am-6pm Mon-Sat & 10am-5pm Sun Mar-Oct, 9am-4pm Tue-Sat & 10am-4pm Sun & Mon Nov-Feb; tube Tower Hill

'Uneasy lies the head that wears the crown'; that quote from Shakespeare's Henry IV seems highly appropriate at the Tower of London, where King Henry VIII's wife Anne Boleyn was beheaded in the 16th century and where the British Crown Jewels are still housed. Begun during the reign of William the Conqueror (1066-87) and largely unchanged in external appearance for at least 600 years, this well-preserved medieval castle is a major English landmark and one of those rare attractions that many tourists really do regard as a must-see.

That means more than two million people visit a year, but there are two tips if you don't want to join the usually lengthy queues. Firstly, buy a ticket from any London Underground station (it's printed on the pink cardboard used for transport tickets and can be bought either on the same day or up to a week in advance). Secondly, go well after the morning crowds have departed. At around 3pm, you can usually walk straight in. Good-value joint tickets are also available at the box office for the Tower of London and Hampton Court Palace.

The tower is one of London's four World Heritage Sites (the others are Westminster Abbey, Kew Gardens and Maritime Greenwich), and, of course, it's a complex rather than one building. The **White Tower** at its heart was the original Norman building, around which **two walls**, an inner wall with 13 towers and an outer wall with five, were erected between 1190 and 1285 by Kings Henry III and Edward I. A moat which once encircled the outer wall was drained after sewage problems led to cholera outbreaks in the mid-19th century. Other buildings have been built alongside the White Tower in the courtyard, from a Tudor chapel and houses to 19th- and 20th-century museums. In the early Middle Ages, the Tower of London acted as a royal residence (until the early 17th century at least), and also as a treasury, a mint, an arsenal and a prison, meaning you will find remnants of those various institutions dotted around the grounds. Throughout the ages, murder and political skulduggery have reigned as much as kings and queens, so tales of imprisonment and executions will pepper your trail.

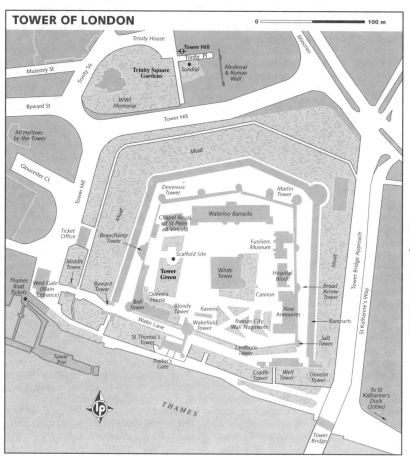

TOWER OF LONDON

0   100 m

Trinity House
Tower Hill
Trinity Pl
Muscovy St
Trinity Sq
Trinity Square Gardens
Sundial
Medieval & Roman Wall
Minories
Byward St
WWI Memorial
Tower Hill
All Hallows-by-the-Tower
Tower Hill
Gloucester Ct
Moat
Tower Hill
Devereux Tower
Martin Tower
Moat
Chapel Royal of St Peter ad Vincula
Waterloo Barracks
Ticket Office
Beauchamp Tower
Fusiliers Museum
Scaffold Site
Middle Tower
Tower Green
White Tower
Hospital Block
Tower Bridge Approach
St Katharine's Way
Moat
Thames Boat Tickets
West Gate (Main Entrance)
Byward Tower
Queen's House
Cannon
Broad Arrow Tower
Bell Tower
Bloody Tower
Ravens
New Armouries
Ramparts
Water Lane
Wakefield Tower
Roman City Wall Fragments
St Thomas's Tower
Salt Tower
Lanthorn Tower
Tower Pier
Traitor's Gate
Cradle Tower
Well Tower
Develin Tower
THAMES
To St Katharine's Dock (200m)
Tower Bridge

Neighbourhoods – East Central

You enter the tower via the West Gate and proceed across the walkway over the dry moat between the **Middle Tower** and **Byward Tower**. Before you stands the **Bell Tower**, housing the tower's curfew bells and one-time home to Thomas More. The politician and author of *Utopia* was imprisoned here in 1534 before his execution for refusing to recognise King Henry VIII as the new head of the Church of England in place of the Pope. To your left are the **casements of the former Royal Mint**, which was moved from this site to new buildings northeast of the castle in 1812.

Continuing past the Bell Tower along **Water Lane** between the walls you come to the famous **Traitors' Gate**, the gateway through which prisoners being brought by river entered the tower. This will look vaguely familiar to anyone

who saw the 1998 film *Elizabeth*, starring Cate Blanchett, because as a princess, Elizabeth I really was brought this way to be imprisoned in the tower (although the movie was filmed elsewhere).

Above the gate, rooms inside **St Thomas's Tower** show what the hall of Edward I (1272–1307) might once have looked like and also how archaeologists peel back the layers of newer buildings to find what went before. Opposite St Thomas's Tower is **Wakefield Tower**, built by Henry III between 1220 and 1240. Its upper floor is actually entered via St Thomas's Tower and has been even more enticingly furnished with a replica throne and a huge candelabra to give an impression of how, as an anteroom in a medieval palace, it might have looked in Edward I's day. During the

15th-century War of the Roses between the Houses of Lancaster and York, Henry VI was almost certainly murdered in this tower.

Below, in the basement of Wakefield Tower, there's a fairly new **Torture at the Tower** exhibition. However, torture wasn't practised as much in England as it was on the Continent, apparently, and the display is pretty perfunctory, limiting itself to a rack, a pair of manacles and an instrument for keeping prisoners doubled up called a Scavenger's Daughter. Frankly, you'd see scarier gear at a modern-day S & M party. To get to this exhibition and the basement level of Wakefield Tower, you enter the tower courtyard through the arch opposite Traitors' Gate.

As you do so, you'll also see at the centre of the courtyard the Norman **White Tower** with a turret on each of its four corners and a golden weather vane spinning atop each. This tower has a couple of remnants of Norman architecture, including a fireplace and garderobe (or lavatory). However, most of its interior is given over to a collection of cannons, guns and suits of armour for men and horses, which come from the Royal Armouries in Leeds. Among the most remarkable exhibits are the 6ft 9in–tall suit of armour made for John of Gaunt (to see that coming towards you on a battlefield must have been terrifying) and alongside it a tiny child's suit of armour designed for James I's young son Henry.

The stretch of green between the Wakefield and White towers is where the Tower's famous **ravens** are found; superstition has it that should these scavengers ever leave the Tower, the monarchy would fall. Since Charles II was told this story, at least six ravens have been kept in residence, with their wings cropped so they may not leave.

Opposite Wakefield Tower and the White Tower is the **Bloody Tower**, with an exhibition on Elizabethan adventurer Sir Walter Raleigh, who was imprisoned here from 1605 to 1616. The Bloody Tower acquired its nickname from the story that the 'princes in the tower', Edward V and his younger brother, were murdered here to annul their claims to the throne. The blame is usually laid at the door of their uncle Richard III, although Henry VII might also have been responsible for the crime.

Beside the Bloody Tower sits a collection of black-and-white half-timbered Tudor houses that are home to Tower of London staff. The **Queen's House**, where Anne Boleyn lived out her final days in 1536, now houses the resident governor and is closed to the public.

North of the Queen's House, across **Tower Green**, is the **scaffold site**, where seven people were executed by beheading in Tudor times. Among them were: two of Henry VIII's eight wives, the alleged adulterers Anne Boleyn and Catherine Howard; the latter's lady-in-waiting, Jane Rochford; Margaret Pole, countess of Salisbury, descended from the House of York; 16-year-old Lady Jane Grey, who fell foul of Henry's daughter Mary I by being her rival for the throne; William, Lord Hastings; and Robert Devereux, earl of Essex, once a favourite of Elizabeth I.

These people were executed within the tower precincts largely to spare the monarch the embarrassment of the usual public execution on Tower Hill, an event which was usually attended by thousands of spectators. In the case of Robert Devereux, the authorities perhaps also feared a popular uprising in his support.

Behind the scaffold site lies the **Chapel Royal of St Peter ad Vincula** (St Peter in Chains), a rare example of ecclesiastical Tudor architecture and the burial place of those beheaded on the scaffold outside or at nearby Tower Hill. Unfortunately, it can only be visited on a group tour or after 4.30pm, so if you aren't already part of a group hang around until one shows up and then tag along. Alternatively, attend a service, which takes place at 9am on Sundays.

Beefy Blokes

While at the Tower of London you're bound to see the Yeoman Warders, better known as the Beefeaters, leading groups of visitors. They sport dark-blue (almost black) and red Tudor costumes for everyday wear, and more elaborate gold and red Victorian ones for ceremonial occasions, that cost £12,000 each. Beefeaters have an interesting history; they've been guarding the tower for more than 900 years.

The more than three dozen Beefeaters employed today have all spent at least 22 years in the armed services and have reached the rank of sergeant major. They can stay in the job until they're 60 and live, with their families, within the tower precincts. As well as conducting joke-filled tours of the Tower, they also enact the age-old Ceremony of the Keys each evening, in which the tower gates are locked and the keys ceremoniously locked away in the Queen's House.

In the 17th century, the Beefeaters received a daily ration of beef and beer and, since beef was a luxury well beyond the reach of the poor at the time, this generated their nickname – as well as much envy from poorer folk.

To the east of the chapel and north of the White Tower is the building visitors most want to see: Waterloo Barracks, the home of the **Crown Jewels**. You file past footage of Queen Elizabeth II's coronation and videos on some of the more prominent pieces before you reach the vault itself, but once inside you'll be confronted with ornate sceptres, cloaks, plates, orbs and, naturally, crowns. A very slow-moving travelator takes you past the dozen or so crowns that are the centrepiece, including the £27.5 million Imperial State Crown, set with diamonds (2868 of them to be exact), sapphires, emeralds, rubies and pearls, and the platinum crown of the late Queen Mother, Elizabeth, which is most famously set with the 105-carat Koh-i-Noor (Mountain of Light) diamond. Surrounded by myth and legend, the 14th-century diamond has been claimed by both India and Afghanistan. It reputedly confers enormous power on its owner, but male owners are destined to die a tormented death.

The **Fusiliers Museum** to the east of Waterloo Barracks is run by the Royal Regiment of Fusiliers who charge a a separate nominal entrance fee. This museum covers the history of the Royal Fusiliers dating back to 1685, and has models of several battles. A 10-minute video gives details of the modern regiment.

The red-brick **New Armouries** in the south-eastern corner of the inner courtyard has an assortment of exhibits. These include pictures of the Royal Menagerie (which was taken from here in 1834 and formed the nucleus of London Zoo) and a list of the tower's famous prisoners, from Ranulf Flambard, bishop of Durham in 1100 to Hitler's henchman Rudolf Hess in 1941.

There are plenty of other attractions, churches, shops, toilets and a restaurant within the tower complex, but before you leave you should also walk along the inner ramparts. This **Wall Walk** begins with the 13th-century **Salt Tower**, probably used to store saltpetre for gunpowder, and ends at the **Martin Tower**, which houses an exhibition about the original coronation regalia. Here you can see some of the older crowns, designed so that the jewels in them could be removed. The oldest surviving crown is that of George I, which is topped with the ball and cross from James II's crown. It was from the Martin Tower that Colonel Thomas Blood attempted to steal the Crown Jewels in 1671, disguised as a clergyman.

The hour-long **guided tours** led by the Yeoman Warders are worth sticking with for at least a bit, as they do bring the various nooks and crannies of the tower to life. These tours leave from the Middle Tower every 30 minutes from 9.30am (on Sunday from 10am) to 3.30pm (2.30pm in winter) daily. The warders also conduct about eight different short talks (35 minutes) and tours (45 minutes) on specific themes. The first is at 9.30am Monday to Saturday (10.15am on Sunday in summer, 11.30am in winter), the last at 5.15pm (3pm in winter). A self-paced audio-guide in five languages is available for £3 from the information point on Water Lane.

AROUND THE TOWER Map pp432-3

Despite the Tower's World Heritage Site status, the area immediately to the north is fairly disappointing, especially as in recent years much of it has been a construction site. Just outside Tower Hill tube station, a giant bronze sundial depicts the history of London from AD 43 to 1982. It stands on a platform offering a view of the neighbouring **Trinity Square Gardens**, once the site of the Tower Hill scaffold and now home to Edwin Lutyens' memorial to the marines and merchant sailors who lost their lives during WWI. A grassy area, off the steps leading to a subway under the main road, lets you inspect a stretch of the **medieval wall** built on Roman foundations, with a modern statue of Emperor Trajan (ruled AD 98 to 117) standing in front of it. At the other end of the tunnel is a postern (or gate) dating from the 13th century.

ALL HALLOWS-BY-THE-TOWER
Map pp432-3

☎ 7481 2928; Byward St EC3; admission free; ☻ 9am-5.45pm Mon-Fri, 10am-5pm Sat & Sun; tube Tower Hill

All-Hallows is where famous diarist Samuel Pepys recorded his observations of the nearby Great Fire of London in 1666. Above ground, it's a pleasant enough church, rebuilt after WWII. There's a a copper spire added in 1957 to make the church stand out more, a pulpit from a Wren church in Cannon St destroyed in the war, a beautiful 17th-century font cover by the master woodcarver Grinling Gibbons and some interesting modern banners.

However, a church by the name All-Hallows (meaning 'All Saints') has stood on this site since AD 675, and the best bit of the building today is undoubtedly its atmospheric Saxon undercroft, or **crypt** (admission £3; ☻ 10am-4pm Mon-Sat, 1-4pm Sun). There you'll find a pavement of reused Roman tiles and walls of the 7th-century Saxon church, as well as coins and bits of local history.

William Penn, founder of Pennsylvania, was baptised here in 1644 and there's a memorial to him in the undercroft. John Quincy Adams, sixth president of the USA, was also married at All-Hallows in 1797.

A 45-minute audioguide tour of the church is available (donation requested). At the **brass-rubbing centre** (⌚ 11am-4pm Mon-Sat, 2-4pm Sun) rubbings cost from £2 to £5.

TOWER BRIDGE Map pp432-3
tube Tower Hill

The sort of iconic symbol of London that schoolchildren recognise the world over, Tower Bridge doesn't disappoint up close. There's something about its neo-Gothic towers and blue suspension struts that catch your eye whenever you're in the vicinity. Built in 1894 as a much-needed crossing point in the east, it was equipped with a then revolutionary bascule (seesaw) mechanism that could clear the way for oncoming ships in three minutes.

Tower Bridge (above)

Though London's days as a thriving port are long over, the bridge still does its stuff, lifting some 500 times a year and as many as 10 times a day in summer. (For information on the next lifting ring ☎ 7940 3984.)

The **Tower Bridge Experience** (☎ 7940 3985; www.towerbridge.org.uk; adult/under 5/senior, student & child aged 5-15/family £4.5/free/3/9.50-19; ⌚ 10am-6pm Apr-Oct, 10.30am-6pm Nov-Mar) explains the nuts and bolts of it all, if you're interested. If you're not particularly technically minded, however, it's still nice to get inside the bridge and look out its windows along the Thames.

HOXTON, SHOREDITCH & SPITALFIELDS

The most celebrated and natural example of urban regeneration took place here from the early 1990s when artists and musicians began taking over abandoned warehouses in this long-neglected corner of central London. Gradually, the number of art galleries and small designer boutiques began to grow. During the dotcom bubble of the late 1990s, as new media companies and financial workers began to join them, bars and restaurants sprang up all over the place, reaching a critical mass where the area's property prices are now seriously upscale.

'Hoxditch', 'Shoho', 'the Hip Square Mile': there are many pretentious diminutives for the crucible of Britart, but the area is still going strong. Long after the legendary Blue Note club opened (on the site of the current bar Bluu; p268), contemporary venues such as the Vibe bar, 93 Feet East and Cargo are carrying on its progressive music policy. Artists Tracey Emin and Gary Hume can still be seen around, and Jay Jopling's edgy White Cube gallery has endured and grown. A few 'tradtional' sightseeing attractions do exist, but you come to this, London's answer to New York's Greenwich Village, mainly to eat, drink, party, shop and generally soak up the atmosphere.

WHITE CUBE GALLERY Map pp420-1
☎ 7930 5373; www.whitecube.com; 48 Hoxton Sq N1; admission free; ⌚ 10am-6pm Tue-Sat; tube Old Street

Alongside Charles Saatchi, owner of the **Saatchi Gallery** (p157), the White Cube's Jay Jopling was the man responsible for bringing Britart to the public's attention (p46 for more on Britart). He worked with a young Damien Hirst before

Saatchi came on the scene, showcased the works of sculptor Antony Gormley (responsible for Gateshead's huge *Angel of the North* sculpture) and married artist Sam Taylor-Wood. Now firmly part of Britain's 'new establishment', Jopling has refurbished his White Cube gallery (the original White Cube in St James has been shut) to include two new floors. The White Cube differs from the Saatchi Gallery in that it's a place where collectors actually come to buy works, but shows by Damien Hirst, Tracey Emin and other less well-known artists also mean it's worth coming simply to view.

GEFFRYE MUSEUM Map pp420-1

☎ 7739 9893; www.geffrye-museum.org.uk; 136 Kingsland Rd E2; admission by donation; ☼ 10am-5pm Tue-Sat, noon-5pm Sun; tube Old Street, then bus No 243, or rail Dalston Kingsland

As in a furniture showroom, this museum is somewhere you wander through row upon row of different household settings, but it's far more engaging than a weekend trip to Habitat or Ikea. Here most of the rooms are in quaint 18th-century almshouses, covered in ivy and looking like something out of a Jane Austen novel from the exterior. Inside, there's a chronological history of domestic interiors; as you walk along one long hallway you can trace how the middle classes lived from Elizabethan times right through to the end of the 19th century.

The 14 almshouses were originally built to provide homes for the elderly poor, with funds bequeathed by Robert Geffrye, a late-16th-century London mayor. However, it was the preponderance of furniture makers and other interior design trades in the neighbourhood that led to the decision to turn these houses into this sort of museum in 1914.

A postmodernist extension (1998) continues the theme, with several 20th-century rooms: a flat from the 1930s, a room in 1950s style, a 1990s converted warehouse. It also houses a gallery for temporary exhibits, a local design centre, shop and restaurant.

More recent still is the exquisite restoration of an **historic almshouse interior** (adult/child under 16 £2/free). It's the absolute attention to detail that impresses, right down to the vintage newspaper left open on the breakfast table (and apparently that contemporary-looking square glass vase really is period). The setting is so delicate, however, that this small almshouse is only open certain weekends of the year and numbers are limited, so check the website or call ahead. Meanwhile, special gardening

events revolve around the museum's lovely herb garden.

DENNIS SEVERS' HOUSE Map pp432-3

☎ 7247 4013; www.dennissevershouse.co.uk; 18 Folgate St; admission Sun/Mon/Mon eve £8/5/12; ☼ noon-2pm 1st & 3rd Sun of the month, noon-2pm Mon following 1st & 3rd Sun of the month, every Mon eve (times vary); tube Liverpool St

This quirky hotchpotch of a cluttered house is named after the late American eccentric who restored it, and long may his name ring. He turned his residence into what he called a 'still-life drama', but could also be described as part opera, part murder mystery. Visitors find they have entered the home of a 'family' of Huguenot silk weavers so common to the Spitalfields area in the 18th century. However, while they see the fabulous restored Georgian interiors with meals and drinks half-abandoned and rumpled sheets, and while they smell cooking and hear creaking floorboards, their 'hosts' always remain tantalisingly just out of reach. It's a unique and intriguing proposition by day, but the 'Silent Night' tours by candlelight every Monday evening are an even more memorable trip (the word is used advisedly). Booking for these evening visits is essential.

SPITALFIELDS MARKET Map pp432-3

Its proximity to Hoxton and Shoreditch means the Sunday market here is still the market of the moment, with young clothes designers and producers of trendy furniture and ornaments selling their wares. Organic produce is on sale Friday and Saturday; p334 for further details.

AROUND SPITALFIELDS Map pp432-3

Dennis Severs' House (see above) is not the only fine Georgian house in Folgate St, north of Spitalfields market; the street is lined with them, and they too were once occupied by the Protestant Huguenots who fled religious persecution in France to settle here in the late 17th century. Bringing with them their skills as silk weavers, their presence is still recalled by such street names as Fleur-de-Lis St and Nantes Passage.

Diagonally opposite the market on the corner of Commercial and Fournier Sts is **Christ Church, Spitalfields** (☎ 7247 7202), where many of the weavers worshipped. The magnificent 'English baroque' structure, with a tall spire sitting on a portico of four great Tuscan columns, was designed by Nicholas Hawksmoor and completed in 1729. Looking up at its haunting

The Satanic Churches?

Heading out to Brick Lane from Liverpool Street station of a night-time, perhaps going for a curry or meeting friends at the Vibe Bar or 93 Feet East, architect Nicholas Hawksmoor's Christ Church, Spitalfields will inevitably loom up in front as you enter Brushfield St. Built in 1714 and considered Hawksmoor's masterpiece, its outsize tower and tall spire make it an impressive sight, but the church is undeniably brooding. It's even more so when you learn that it was built on the site of a Roman cemetery and is, as author Iain Sinclair has evocatively put it, 'floating on a reservoir of memories of the dead'.

It's a funny thing, but a whole conspiracy theory has been built up around Hawksmoor (1661–1736), Christopher Wren's right-hand man in the rebuilding of London's churches several decades after the Great Fire of 1666 ('the year of the beast'!). Rumours have persisted that the strange dimensions of his churches are proof that he was a devil-worshipper, despite no real evidence.

It was Iain Sinclair – once a gardener in Christ Church's grounds – who got the ball rolling when in 1975's *Lud Heat: A Book of Dead Hamlets* he considered the occult pattern formed by the siting of Hawksmoor's churches. A triangle was formed, he contended, between Christ Church, St George-in-the-East and St Anne's, Limehouse. More than that, adding St George's, Bloomsbury and St Alfege in Greenwich made the shape of a pentacle star.

Sinclair also mentioned Christ Church's windows – small portholes above tall, narrow windows below – which he imagined as sexual symbols. Four years later, in his academic text *Hawksmoor*, Professor Kerry Downes also observed that the architect's formal devices 'found recognition only in the present century's exploration of the unconscious'.

After Sinclair and Downes, writer Peter Ackroyd fuelled the Satanic fire with his 1985 novel *Hawksmoor* in which a fictional architect (who's a disciple of Christopher Wren) incorporates human sacrifices into the design of his churches. By 1999 the mythologising had reached the world of comics and graphic novels, when Alan Moore's *From Hell* speculated that Hawksmoor's architectural hero, Vitruvius, was a follower of the pagan god Dionysus.

These diabolical tales are quite fanciful, but once the imagination gets going there's plenty you can read into Hawksmoor's beautiful churches. Why does St Anne's have the pagan symbol of a pyramid in its grounds? Why was it consecrated only six years after completion? And was it divine retribution when Christ Church, Spitalfields was hit by lightning in 1841? Heaven knows.

outline at night, you understand a little how Hawksmoor got his diabolical reputation (see The Satanic Churches? above). While restoration work continues, though, you cannot investigate the matter further by venturing inside.

There are yet more restored Georgian houses along Fournier St, leading to a building that throughout history has demonstrated the sort of religious tolerance that today's world needs. Before the **Great Mosque** here became an Islamic place of worship in 1975, it was a synagogue for Jewish refugees from Russia and central Europe. Before that, it was called the New French Church and echoed to the prayers of Huguenots from 1743 to 1899.

BRICK LANE Map pp432-3

Immortalised in a warm, much-lauded book by Monica Ali (the new Zadie *White Teeth* Smith), Brick Lane is the centrepiece of a thriving Bengali community in an area nicknamed Banglatown. The lane itself is one long procession of curry and balti houses intermingled with sari and fabric shops, Indian cookery stores and outlets selling ethnic knick-knacks. Sadly, the once high standard of cooking in the curry houses is a distant memory, so you're probably better off trying Indian cuisine in Whitechapel (p244) or Tooting (p234). Restaurateurs aside, much

of the Bengali community is, like its Huguenot forerunners, involved in the clothes trade.

Just past Hanbury St is the converted **Old Truman's Brewery**. This was once London's largest brewery and the Director's House on the left harks back to 1740, the old Vat House across the road with its hexagonal bell tower is early 19th century, and the Engineer's House next to it dates from 1830. The brewery stopped producing beer in 1989, and in the 1990s became home to a host of independent businesses such as record label Acid Jazz and music mag *Blues & Soul* (and even home to musician Talvin Singh himself). Now you'll find lots of small shops, as well as a hip café/bar, the **Vibe Bar** (p389) and arts centre.

CLERKENWELL & ISLINGTON

Home to leading London clubs and a hip workaday crowd, Clerkenwell has little hubs of interest around Exmouth Market, Charterhouse St and (the not very) Clerkenwell Green. There aren't too many clerks, now although that's where the area gets its name. Instead, within minutes of 14–16 Farringdon Lane where the Parish Clerks of London performed miracle plays in the 12th century, you'll find the leading liberal newspaper the *Guardian*, dozens of architects' offices, new media firms, jewellers, loft apartments and the usual accompaniment of restaurants, bars and clubs. Islington is a chichi upper-middle-class neighbourhood synonymous with the centre-left 'New Labour' political project. Since Prime Minister Tony Blair and many liberal-minded professionals bought restored Georgian homes here, 'Islington' has virtually become a term of tabloid newspaper abuse. It's also principally a night-time destination and Upper St in particular is lined with ethnic eateries and animated bars. By day, it's worth visiting the Estorick Collection or perhaps tracing the area's literary associations. George Orwell was living at 27 Canonbury Square when he published *Animal Farm* in 1945, while the playwright Joe Orton stayed at 25 Noel Rd for seven years in the 1960s.

ST JOHN'S GATE Map pp426-7
tube Farringdon

What looks like a toy-town medieval gate cutting across St John's Lane turns out to be the real thing. It dates from the early 16th century but was heavily restored 300 years later. The Knights of St John of Jerusalem were soldiers who took on a nursing role during the Crusades, establishing a priory in Clerkenwell that originally covered around four hectares. The gate was built in 1504 as a grand entrance to their church, St John's Clerkenwell in St John's Square. (This had a round nave like the one at Temple Church, and you can still see some of the outline picked out in brick outside.)

Although most of the buildings were destroyed when Henry VIII dissolved every priory in the country between 1536 and 1540, the gate lived on. It had a varied afterlife, not least as a Latin-speaking coffee house run, without much success, by William Hogarth's father during Queen Anne's reign. The restoration dates from the period when it housed the Old Jerusalem Tavern in the 19th century.

ORDER OF ST JOHN MUSEUM
Map pp426-7
☎ 7324 4005; St John's Lane EC1; admission free;
🕙 10am-5pm Mon-Fri, 10am-4pm Sat; tube Farringdon

Inside St John's Gate is the small Order of St John Museum. It recounts the history of the knights and their properties around the world (gently admitting the immorality of the Crusades when seen through modern eyes) and of their successors, the modern British Order of St John and the St John Ambulance brigade.

To get the most out of a visit try to arrive at 11am or 2.30pm on Tuesday, Friday or Saturday for a **guided tour** (adult/senior & student £5/3.50) of the restored church remains. This includes the fine Norman crypt with a sturdy alabaster monument commemorating a Castilian knight (1575), a battered monument showing the last prior, William Weston, as a skeleton in a shroud, and stained-glass windows showing the main figures in the story. You'll also be shown the Chapter Hall where the Chapter General of the Order meets every three months.

CHARTERHOUSE Map pp426-7
☎ 7251 5002; Charterhouse Sq EC1; admission £3;
🕙 guided tours 2.15pm Wed Apr-Jul; tube Barbican/ Farringdon

You need to book nearly a year in advance to see inside this former Carthusian monastery, whose centrepiece is a Tudor hall with a restored hammer-beam roof. Its incredibly popular summer two-hour guided tours begin at the 14th-century gatehouse on Charterhouse Square, before going through to the Preachers' Court (with three original monks' cells in the western wall), the Master's Court, the Great Hall, and the Great Chamber, where Queen Elizabeth I stayed on numerous occasions.

Founded in 1371, the monastery was confiscated by Henry VIII in 1537 and bought by philanthropist Thomas Sutton in 1611, after which it was run as a school for the poor until 1872. Today it's a home to some three dozen pensioners who lead the tours.

KARL MARX MEMORIAL
LIBRARY Map pp426-7
☎ 7253 1485; www.marxmemoriallibrary.sageweb.co .uk; 37a Clerkenwell Green EC1; admission free;
🕙 1-6pm Mon-Thu, 1-8pm Wed, 10am-1pm Sat; tube Farringdon

Clerkenwell has quite a radical history. An area of Victorian-era slums (the so-called Rookery) it was settled by mainly Italian immigrants in the 19th century. Political revolutionary Mazzini joined them and Italy's founding father Garibaldi dropped by in 1836. Memorably, Lenin edited the Bolshevik newspaper *Iskra* (Spark) from this building in 1902–03. Copies of the newspaper have been preserved in today's library, along with a host of other socialist literature. Nonmembers are free to look around between 1pm and 2pm, but you need to become a member (£11 a year) to use the library or borrow its books.

ESTORICK COLLECTION OF MODERN ITALIAN ART Map pp420-1

☎ 7704 9522; www.estorickcollection.com; 39a Canonbury Sq N1, entrance on Canonbury Rd; adult/concessions £3.5/2.50; ⏰ 11am-6pm Wed-Sat, noon-5pm Sun; tube Highbury & Islington

Housed in a listed Georgian town house, the Estorick Collection focuses mainly on 20th-century Italian *futurismo*, with works by such greats as Giacomo Balla, Umberto Boccioni, Gino Severini and Ardengo Soffici. The collection of paintings, drawings, etchings and sculpture, amassed by American writer and art dealer Eric Estorick and his wife Salome, also includes drawings and a painting by the even more famous Amedeo Modigliani. Well-conceived special exhibitions might concentrate on Italian divisionism or a collection of classic Italian film posters. The museum also encompasses an extensive library, café and shop.

SOUTH CENTRAL

Eating p235; Sleeping p343; Shopping p325

MAYFAIR & ST JAMES'S

Technically part of the West End but more like South Central in character, the neighbourhoods of Mayfair and St James are where the fabulously wealthy live and play. St James's is a mixture of exclusive gentlemen's clubs (the Army and Navy sort as opposed to lap-dancing), historic shops and elegant buildings; indeed, there are some 150 historically noteworthy buildings within its 36 hectares. Despite much commercial development, its matter-of-fact elitism remains pretty much intact.

Just south of St James's is the real reason why this area is so exclusive, the seat of royal London and mecca for royalists from around the Commonwealth. Here the grand, processional Pall Mall – named after the croquet-like game played here by Charles II and his court – sweeps alongside attractive St James's Park, up to Buckingham Palace and the Queen's driveway. The district took shape when Charles II moved his court to St James's Palace in the 17th century, and the toffs followed. The great Georgian squares – Berkeley, Hanover and Grosvenor – were built in the next century by which time St James's was largely filled. By 1900, it was the most fashionable part in London, teeming with theatres, restaurants and boutiques. Savile Row is still where gentlemen go for tailoring, Bond Sts (old and new) are where ladies go for jewellery, and Cork St is where they go together for expensive art. Some residents couldn't keep up with the Jones's of St James's and moved out – to be replaced by businesses, offices and embassies. Grosvenor Square is dominated by the US embassy and has a statue of Franklin D Roosevelt at its centre. There's more chance of the stone statue doing a jig than a nightingale singing in Berkeley Square.

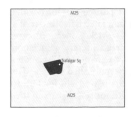

Mayfair is west of Regent St and is where high society gives high-fives to one another; defining features are silver spoons and old-fashioned razzmatazz. As any Monopoly player knows, it's the most expensive place in London, and if you land here you could go bankrupt. In its southeastern corner, nudging Hyde Park, Shepherd's Market is near the site of a rowdy and debauched fair that gave the area its name. The fair was finally banned in 1730, and today 'the old village centre of Mayfair' is a tiny enclave of pubs and bistros.

Glamorous Picadilly bisects Mayfair and St James's, and it's along here where you'll find London icons like Fortnum & Mason, the Ritz and the Royal Academy.

BUCKINGHAM PALACE Map pp426-7

☎ 7839 1377 or 7321 2233 for credit card bookings; www.the-royal-collection.org.uk; SW1; adult/child/concession £12/6/10 (tickets on sale from a kiosk in Green Park); ⏰ 9.30am-4.30pm early Aug-Sep (timed ticket with admission every 15 min); tube St James's Park/Victoria/Green Park

Built in 1705 as Buckingham House for the duke of the same name, this palace has provided the royal family's London lodgings since 1837, when St James's Palace was judged too old-fashioned and insufficiently impressive. It's difficult to miss but if you're having trouble, it stands at the end of The Mall where St James's Park and Green Park converge at a large roundabout dominated by the 25m-high **Queen Victoria Memorial**.

After a series of crises and embarrassing revelations in the early 1990s, the royal spin-doctors cranked up a gear to try and rally public support behind the royals once again. To counter the image of Prince Charles' drooling into the telephone to Camilla about being her tampon – oh please, we'd rather picture our parents having sex – it was decided to swing open the royal doors of the main palace to the public for the first time (well, to 19 of the 661 rooms, anyway). And only during August and September when HRH was holidaying in Scotland. And for a veritable king's ransom, but still, we mustn't quibble – no price is too great for an opportunity to see the Windsor's polaroids plastered all over the fridge door.

The 'working rooms' are stripped down each summer for the arrival of the commoners, and the usual carpet is replaced with industrial-strength rugs, so the rooms don't look all that lavish. The tour starts in the Guard Room, too small for the Ceremonial Guard who are deployed in adjoining quarters; allows a peek inside the State Dining Room (all red damask and Regency furnishings); then moves on to the Blue Drawing Room, with a gorgeous fluted ceiling by John Nash; to the White Drawing Room, where foreign ambassadors are received; and to the Ballroom where official receptions and state banquets are held. The biggest laugh is the Throne Room, which features kitschy his-and-hers pink chairs initialled 'ER' and 'P', sitting smugly under what looks like a theatre arch. It's good to see that they've still got a sense of humour – don't they?

The most interesting part of the tour, for all but the royal sycophants, is the 76.5m-long Picture Gallery, featuring splendid works from the likes of Van Dyck, Rembrandt, Canaletto,

Poussin, Canova and Vermeer, although the likes of these and much more are yours for free at the National Gallery.

CHANGING OF THE GUARD Map pp426-7
Buckingham Palace, SW1; ◷ 11.30am Apr-July & alternate days, weather permitting, Aug-Mar; tube St James's Park/Victoria

This is a London 'must see', although the *idea* of it is much more fun than actually experiencing it. The old guard (Foot Guards of the Household Regiment) comes off duty to be replaced by the new guard on the forecourt of Buckingham Palace, and tourists get to gape – from sometimes as many as 10 people behind – at the bright red uniforms and bearskin hats of shouting and marching soldiers for just over half an hour. The official name for the ceremony is Guard Mounting, which, we dare say, sounds like a more interesting spectacle (p130).

QUEEN'S GALLERY Map pp426-7
☎ 7839 1377, credit-card bookings 7766 7301; www.the-royal-collection.org.uk; southern wing Buckingham Palace, entrance Buckingham Gate; adult/child/concession £6.50/3/5; ◷ 10am-5.30pm; tube St James's Park/Victoria

Works representing more than 500 years of royal taste, from paintings and sculpture to ceramics, furniture and jewellery, go on display in regularly changing exhibitions at this splendid gallery, originally designed by Nash as a conservatory. It was converted into a chapel for Victoria in 1843, destroyed in a 1940 air raid and reopened as a gallery in 1962. A £20 million– renovation for the Golden Jubilee in 2002 enlarged the entrance, added a Greek Doric portico, a multimedia centre and three times as much display space.

ROYAL MEWS Map pp426-7
☎ 7766 7302; www.the-royal-collection.org.uk; Buckingham Palace Rd SW1; adult/child/concession £5/2.50/4; ◷ 11am-4pm Mar-July, 10am-5pm Aug-Sep; tube Victoria

South of the palace, the Royal Mews started life as a falconry but is now a working stable looking after the royals' immaculately groomed horses, along with the opulent vehicles the monarchy uses for getting from A to B. Highlights include the stunning gold coach of 1762, which has been used for every coronation since that of George III, and the Glass Coach of 1910, used for royal weddings. The Mews is closed in June during the four-day racing carnival of Royal Ascot, when the royal heads try and win a few bob on the gee-gees.

Buckingham Palace (p120)

ST JAMES'S PARK Map pp426-7

☎ 7930 1793; The Mall SW1; ☺ 5am-dusk; tube St James's Park

The most pleasant of London's royal parks also has the best vistas, including those of Westminster, St James's Palace, Carlton Terrace and Horse Guards Parade; the view of Buckingham Palace from the footbridge spanning St James's Park Lake is the best you'll find. The flowerbeds are sumptuous and colourful in summer, some of them modelled on John Nash's original 'floriferous' beds of mixed shrubs, flowers and trees. But it's the large lake and waterfowl – including a pod of parading pelicans – that make a stroll or a lounge in this park so special.

ST JAMES'S PALACE & CLARENCE HOUSE Map pp426-7

Cleveland Row SW1; closed to the public; tube Green Park

The striking Tudor gatehouse of this palace, the only surviving part of a building initiated by the palace-mad Henry VIII in 1530, is best approached from St James's St to the north of the park. It is the residence of Prince Charles and his sons, although they were about to shift next door to Clarence House (1828), the former residence of the Queen Mother, in 2004. Still, they might decide to spend more time in his Gloucestershire mansion or perhaps Birkhall, near Balmoral. Arrggh, so many houses, so little time!

This was the official residence of the King and Queen for more than three centuries and foreign ambassadors are still formally accredited to the Court of St James, although the tea-and-biscuits are actually served at Buckingham. Princess Diana, who hated this place, lived here up until her divorce from Charles in 1996 when she moved to Kensington Palace. Ironically, the powers-that-be thought St James's Palace the most suitable place for her body to lie in state after her death in 1997.

When the Queen Mum passed away in 2002, Prince Charles got the tradesmen into **Clarence House** and spent £4.6 million of taxpayers' money reshaping the house to his own design. The 'Royal residences are held in trust for future generations', but the *current* generation will have to pay £5 to have a look at the official rooms between when the decorators move out (around the time this book was published) and Charles moves in a few months later. The house was originally designed by John Nash in the early 19th century, but has been modified much since.

SPENCER HOUSE

☎ 7499 8620; www.spencerhouse.co.uk; 27 St James's Place SW1; adult/concession £6/5; ☺ 10.30am-5.45pm Sun only (except in Jan and Aug); tube Green Park

Just outside the park, Spencer House was built for the first Earl Spencer, an ancestor of Princess Diana, in the Palladian style between 1756 and 1766. The Spencers moved out in 1927 and their grand family home was used as an office, until Lord Rothschild stepped in and returned it to its former glory in 1987 with an £18 million restoration. Visits to the eight lavishly furnished rooms of the house are by guided tour only.

The gardens, returned to their 18th-century design, are open only between 2pm and 5pm a couple of Sundays in June. Tickets cost £3.50.

QUEEN'S CHAPEL Map pp426-7

Marlborough Rd SW1; ☺ only for Sunday services at 8.30am & 11.30am Apr-Jul; tube St James's Park

We're not all that impressed with the royal sights, but this one is quite moving: it's where all the contemporary royals from Princess Diana to the Queen Mother have been laid in the run-up to their funerals. The church was originally built by Inigo Jones in the Palladian style and was the first post-Reformation church in England built for Roman Catholic worship. It was once part of St James's Palace but was separated after a fire. The simple interior has exquisite 17th-century fittings and is atmospherically illuminated by light streaming in through the large windows above the altar.

ADMIRALTY ARCH Map pp426-7

tube Charing Cross

From Trafalgar Square, The Mall passes under this grand Edwardian monument, a triple-arched stone entrance designed by Aston Webb in 1910. The large central gate is opened only for royal processions and state visits.

Top Five – South Central

- Cabinet War Rooms (p129)
- Hyde Park (p137)
- Tate Britain (p129)
- Victoria & Albert Museum (p134)
- Westminster Cathedral (p131)

APSLEY HOUSE
(WELLINGTON MUSEUM) Map pp426-7
☎ 7499 5676; www.vam.ac.uk; 149 Piccadilly W1; adult/concession inc. audio tour £4.50/3; ⏰ 11am-5pm Tue-Sun; tube Hyde Park Corner

This stunning house, one of the finest in the city, used to belong to the first Duke of Wellington and has the distinction of being known as No 1 London, because it used to be the first building one saw when entering town from the west. It was designed by Robert Adam for Baron Apsley in the late 18th century, but later sold to Wellington who lived here for 35 years until his death in 1852. The duke cut Napoleon down to size in the Battle of Waterloo and is well known for lending his name to a sensible, if none too flattering, style of boot.

In 1947 the house was given to the nation, which must have come as a surprise to the duke's descendants who still live here; 10 of its rooms are open to the public today as the Wellington Museum. The house itself is magnificent and retains many of its original furnishings and collections. Wellington memorabilia, including his medals, some entertaining old cartoons and his death mask fill the basement gallery, while there's an astonishing collection of china, including some of the Iron Duke's silverware, on the ground floor. The stairwell is dominated by Antonio Canova's staggering 3.4m-high statue of a naked Napoleon, adjudged by the subject as 'rather too athletic'. The 1st-floor rooms are decorated with paintings by Velasquez, Rubens, Brueghel and Murillo, but perhaps the most interesting is Goya's portrait of the duke, which some years ago was discovered to have the face of Napoleon's brother, Joseph Bonaparte, beneath the duke's. Apparently, the artist had taken a punt on Napoleon winning the Battle of Waterloo and had to do a quick 'about face' when news of Wellington's victory arrived.

BURLINGTON ARCADE Map p428
51 Piccadilly W1; tube Green Park

Flanking Burlington House – home of the Royal Academy of Arts – on its western side is the curious Burlington Arcade, built in 1819 and evocative of a bygone era. Today it is a shopping precinct for the very wealthy and is most famous for the Burlington Berties, uniformed guards who patrol the area keeping an eye out for punishable offences such as running, chewing gum or whatever else might lower the arcade's tone. The fact that the arcade once served as a brothel isn't mentioned.

FARADAY MUSEUM Map p428
☎ 7409 2992; www.rigb.org; 21 Albermarle St W1; £1; ⏰ 10am-5pm Mon-Fri; tube St James's Park

This museum in the Royal Institution (of Science) is dedicated to the celebrated physicist and chemist Michael Faraday, who discovered electro-magnetic, eh stuff, that led to the invention of the dynamo. He also gave his name to the unit of measurement for electricity. This museum – probably only of interest to people who know what 'stuff' means – contains a reconstruction of Faraday's laboratory, where he made many of his discoveries, and which is furnished with many of his original apparatus.

GREEN PARK Map pp426-7
Piccadilly W1; ⏰ 5am-dusk; tube Green Park

Less manicured than the adjoining St James's, this park has trees and open space, sunshine and shade. It was once a duelling ground and served as a vegetable garden during WWII.

No 1 London, Apsley House (above)

GUARDS MUSEUM

☎ 7414 3271; www.army.mod.uk; Wellington Barracks, Birdcage Walk SW1; adult/concession £2/1; ⏱ 10am-4pm Feb-Dec; tube St James's Park

Showing that the royal guards are not a namby-pamby troop employed merely for decoration and to entertain the tourists, this small museum covers the history of the five regiments of foot guards and their role in military campaigns from Waterloo on. It was established in the 17th century during the reign of Charles II and is packed with uniforms, oil paintings, medals, curios and memorabilia that belonged to the soldiers. Perhaps the biggest draw here is the huge collection of toy soldiers in the shop.

HANDEL HOUSE MUSEUM Map pp426-7

☎ 7495 1685; www.handelhouse.org; 25 Brooke St; adult/child/concession £4.50/2/3.50; ⏱ 10am-6pm Tue-Sat (until 8pm Thu) & noon-6pm Sun; tube Bond Street

This 18th-century Mayfair building, where George Frederick Handel lived for 36 years until his death in 1759, opened as a museum in late 2001. It has been restored to how it would have looked when the great German-born composer was in residence, complete with artworks borrowed from several museums. Exhibits include early editions of Handel's operas and oratorios, although being in the hallowed space where he composed and first rehearsed the likes of *Water Music*, *Messiah*, *Zadok the Priest* and *Fireworks Music* is ample attraction for any enthusiast.

In a funny twist of fate, the house at No 23 (now part of the museum) was home to a musician as different from Handel as could be imagined: the American guitarist Jimi Hendrix (1942–69) who lived there from 1968 until his death.

INSTITUTE FOR CONTEMPORARY ARTS Map pp426-7

ICA; ☎ 7930 3647; www.ica.org.uk; The Mall SW1; day membership adult/concession £1.50/1 Mon-Fri, £2.50/1.50 Sat-Sun during exhibitions; ⏱ noon-10.30pm Mon (until 1am Tue-Sat & 11pm Sun); tube Charing Cross/ Piccadilly Circus

Renowned for being at the cutting and controversial edge throughout the arts, the ICA is the place to come any day of the week for all manner of experimental/progressive/radical/obscure films, dance, club nights, photography, art, theatre, music, lectures, multimedia works and book readings. Sure,

much of it might seem like 'craftless tat' (as described by the resigning chairman in 2002), but the fact that Picasso and Henry Moore had their first UK shows here should be sufficient credential. The complex includes a bookshop, gallery, cinema, bar, theatre, and the licensed ICA Café & Restaurant.

The Duke of York Column, up the steps beside the ICA into Waterloo Place, commemorates a son of George III. It was erected in 1834, but never quite caught the public imagination like Nelson's Column in Trafalgar Square, although it's only 6m shorter.

ROYAL ACADEMY OF ARTS

☎ 7300 8000; www.royalacademy.org.uk; Burlington House, Piccadilly W1; adult/under 8/student £7/free/5 during Summer Exhibition, separate charges for temporary shows, other discounts available; ⏱ 10am-6pm Sun, 10am-10pm Fri; tube Green Park

Britain's first art school had to play second fiddle to the Hayward Gallery for a long time, but leapt back into the limelight in recent years with a series of perfectly pitched shows, ranging from the gigantically successful Art of the Aztecs to the Academy's famous – and notoriously patchy – Summer Exhibition from early June to mid-August, which for nearly 250 years has showcased art submitted by the general public. The permanent exhibition in this radically altered Palladian mansion focuses on British art from the 18th century, and features major works from the likes of Reynolds, Gainsborough, Turner, Constable and Hockney.

Taking its lead from Somerset House, in 2002 the Academy transformed its courtyard into a dashing stone-paved piazza with choreographed lights and fountains flanking a statue of founder Joshua Reynolds. Pity they're prone to dollying it up with dodgy art from time to time – less is more, Academy. The Annenberg Courtyard was named after a former US ambassador to London, whose large donation made the development possible. The Burlington Project, a plan to more than double the Academy's space, is slated for completion in 2008.

ST JAMES'S PICCADILLY Map p428

☎ 7734 4511; 197 Piccadilly W1; ⏱ 8am-7pm

The only church Christopher Wren built from scratch and on a new site (most of the others were replacements for ones razed in the Great Fire), this simple building is exceedingly easy on the eye and substitutes what some might call the pompous flourishes of his most famous churches with a warm and elegant user-friendliness. The simple spire, although designed by Wren, was only added in 1968. This is a particularly sociable church: it houses a counselling service, stages lunchtime and evening concerts, provides shelter for an antiques market and an arts and crafts fair (from 10am-6pm on Tuesday, and from Wednesday to Sunday, respectively) as well as, what was the last thing…oh, yeah, teaching the word of God and all that jazz.

WELLINGTON ARCH Map pp426-7

☎ 7973 3539; www.english-heritage.org.uk; Hyde Park Corner W2; adult/student or child/senior £2.50/1.30/1.90; ☺ 10am-6pm Wed-Sun; tube Hyde Park Corner

Opposite Apsley House in the little bit of green space being strangled by the Hyde Park Corner roundabout is England's answer to the Arc de Triomphe, except this one commemorates France's *defeat* (specifically, Napoleon's at the hands of Wellington). The neoclassical arch, erected in 1826, used to be topped by a disproportionately large equestrian statue of Wellington, but this was removed in 1882 and replaced some years later with the biggest bronze sculpture in Britain, *Peace Descending on the Quadriga of War*.

For years the monument served as the capital's smallest police station, but it was restored and opened up to the public as a three-level exhibition space focussing on London's arches. The balcony affords unforgettable views of Hyde Park, Buckingham Palace and the Houses of Parliament.

WESTMINSTER & WHITEHALL

While the City of London has always concerned itself with the business of making money, Westminster's *raison d'être* for almost a millennium has been as the seat of royal and religious authority, and then from the 14th century as the fulcrum of parliamentary power. Predictably then, virtually all of its sights and functions are tied up with the affairs of the nation; its two dominating features are the most important church in England and the most famous parliament in the world. The whole area is a remarkable spectacle of rare architectural cohesion, and an awesome display of power, gravitas and historical import. Westminster is actually the name of the borough that covers much of the West End but in real terms it applies only to the area immediately around Parliament Square. Whitehall, a name synonymous with government and administration, is generally regarded as the area between Westminster and Trafalgar Square. Millbank runs along the river from Westminster to Vauxhall Bridge and is best known as the home of Tate Britain.

London's geography would have been inestimably different had Edward the Confessor not decided to move his royal court near here in the 11th century so he could oversee the construction of Westminster Abbey. Because he did, the royal and commercial centres of London were permanently detached and the shape of the whole of central London was predetermined.

Of course, after you've seen the sights, there's sod all to do on a Westminster evening once the earnest civil servants have scurried off home to watch *Eastenders* after another tough day in the office of the nation.

WESTMINSTER ABBEY Map pp426-7

☎ 7222 5152; www.westminster-abbey.org; Dean's Yard SW1; adult/under 11/concession £6/free/4; ☺ 9.30am-4.45pm & 6-7pm Mon-Fri, 9.30am-2.45pm Sat; tube Westminster

This is one of the most sacred and symbolic sites in England. With the exception of Edward V and Edward VIII, every sovereign has been crowned here since William the Conqueror in 1066, and most of the monarchs from Henry III (died 1272) to George II (died 1760) were also buried here. As well as being the well from which the Anglican Church draws its inspiration, the abbey is also where the nation commemorates its political and artistic idols. It's difficult to imagine its equivalent anywhere else in the world.

The abbey is a magnificent, arresting sight. Though a mixture of architectural styles, it is considered the finest example of Early English Gothic (1180–1280) in existence. The original church was built during the Dark Ages by King (later St) Edward the Confessor in the 11th century, who is buried in the chapel behind the main altar. Henry III (ruled 1216–72) began work on the new building but didn't complete it; the French Gothic nave was finished in 1388. Henry VII's huge and magnificent chapel was added in 1519. Unlike St Paul's, Westminster

Top Five Places of Worship

- St Martin-in-the-Fields (p97)
- St Paul's Cathedral (p106)
- Temple Church (p100)
- Westminster Abbey (p125)
- Westminster Cathedral (p131)

Abbey has never been a cathedral – it is what is called a 'royal peculiar' and is administered directly by the Crown.

Without belittling its architectural achievements, the abbey is probably more impressive from outside than within. The interior is chock-a-block with small chapels, elaborate tombs of monarchy and monuments to various luminaries from down the ages. As you might expect for one of the most visited churches in Christendom, it can get intolerably busy in here and the combination of clutter and crowds can make you wish you were still outside looking in.

Immediately past the barrier through the north door is what's known as **Statesmen's Aisle**, where politicians and eminent public figures are commemorated mostly by staggeringly large marble statues. The Whig and Tory prime ministers who dominated late Victorian politics, Gladstone (who is buried here) and Disraeli (who is not), have their monuments uncomfortably close to one another. Nearby is a monument to Robert Peel who, as home secretary in 1829, created the Metropolitan Police force. They became known as 'Bobby's boys' and later, simply, 'bobbies'. Above them is a rose window, designed by James Thornhill, depicting 11 of the Apostles (Judas is absent).

At the eastern end of the sanctuary, opposite the entrance to the Henry VII Chapel, is the rather ordinary looking **Coronation Chair**, upon which almost every monarch since the late 13th century is said to have been crowned. Below it used to sit the **Stone of Scone** (pronounced 'skoon'), the Scottish coronation stone that Edward I nicked in 1297. Amid much fanfare and nationalistic back-slapping, the stone was returned north of the border in 1996 although the Scots are required to loan it out for future coronations.

Up the steps in front of you and to your left is the narrow **Queen Elizabeth Chapel**, where Elizabeth I and her half-sister 'Bloody Mary' share an elaborate tomb.

The **Henry VII Chapel**, in the easternmost part of the abbey, is an outstanding example of late-perpendicular architecture (a variation of English Gothic), with spectacular circular vaulting on the ceiling. The wooden choir stalls are carved with exotic creatures and adorned with colourful heraldic flags. Behind the chapel's altar is the elaborate sarcophagus of Henry VII and his queen, Elizabeth of York, designed by the Florentine sculptor Pietro Torrigiano.

Beyond the chapel's altar is the **Royal Air Force (RAF) Chapel**, with a stained glass window commemorating the force's finest hour, the Battle of Britain. Next to it, a plaque marks the spot where Oliver Cromwell's body lay for two years until the Restoration, when it was disinterred, hanged and beheaded. The bodies believed to be those of the two child princes (allegedly) murdered in the Tower of London in 1483 are buried here. The chapel's southern aisle contains the **tomb of Mary Queen of Scots**, beheaded on the orders of her cousin Elizabeth and with the acquiescence of her son, the future James I.

The **Chapel of St Edward the Confessor**, the most sacred spot in the abbey, lies just east of the sanctuary and behind the high altar; access may be restricted to protect the 13th-century floor. St Edward was the founder of the abbey and the original building was consecrated a few weeks before his death. His tomb was slightly altered after the original was destroyed during the Reformation.

The south transept contains **Poets' Corner**, where many of England's finest writers are buried and/or commemorated; a memorial here is the highest honour the Queen can bestow. Just north is the **Lantern**, the heart of the abbey, where coronations take place. If you face eastwards while standing in the centre, the sanctuary is in front of you. George Gilbert Scott designed the ornate high altar in 1897. Behind you, Edward Blore's chancel, dating from the mid-19th century, is a breathtaking structure of gold, blue and red Victorian Gothic. Where monks once worshipped, boys from the Choir School and lay vicars now sing the daily services.

The entrance to the **Cloister** is 13th century, while the cloister itself dates from the 14th. Eastwards down a passageway off the Cloister are three museums run by English Heritage. The octagonal **Chapter House** (admission with/ without abbey ticket £1/2.50; ☺ 9.30am-5pm Apr-Sep, 10am-5pm Oct, 10am-4pm Nov-Mar) has one of Europe's best-preserved medieval tile floors and retains traces of religious murals. It was used as a meeting place

WESTMINSTER ABBEY

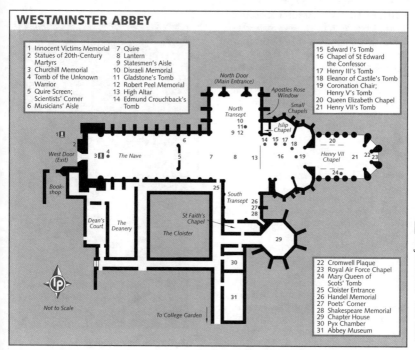

1 Innocent Victims Memorial
2 Statues of 20th-Century Martyrs
3 Churchill Memorial
4 Tomb of the Unknown Warrior
5 Quire Screen; Scientists' Corner
6 Musicians' Aisle
7 Quire
8 Lantern
9 Statesmen's Aisle
10 Disraeli Memorial
11 Gladstone's Tomb
12 Robert Peel Memorial
13 High Altar
14 Edmund Crouchback's Tomb
15 Edward I's Tomb
16 Chapel of St Edward the Confessor
17 Henry III's Tomb
18 Eleanor of Castile's Tomb
19 Coronation Chair; Henry V's Tomb
20 Queen Elizabeth Chapel
21 Henry VII's Tomb
22 Cromwell Plaque
23 Royal Air Force Chapel
24 Mary Queen of Scots' Tomb
25 Cloister Entrance
26 Handel Memorial
27 Poets' Corner
28 Shakespeare Memorial
29 Chapter House
30 Pyx Chamber
31 Abbey Museum

North Door (Main Entrance)

Apostles Rose Window

North Transept

Small Chapels

Islip Chapel

West Door (Exit)

The Nave

Henry VII Chapel

Book-shop

South Transept

Dean's Court

The Deanery

St Faith's Chapel

The Cloister

Not to Scale

To College Garden

by the House of Commons in the second half of the 14th century. The adjacent **Pyx Chamber** (admission with/without abbey ticket £1/2.50; 10am-4.30pm daily) is one of the few remaining relics of the original abbey and contains the abbey's treasures and liturgical objects. The **Abbey Museum** (10.30am-4pm daily) exhibits the death masks of generations of royalty; wax effigies representing Charles II and William III (who is on a stool to make him as tall as his wife Mary), as well as armour and stained glass.

To reach the 900-year-old **College Garden** (10am-6pm Tue-Thu Apr-Sep, 10am-4pm Tue-Thu Oct-Mar), enter Dean's Yard and the Little Cloisters off Great College St.

A walk around the Cloister brings you to the western end of the nave. Set in the floor is the **Tomb of the Unknown Soldier**, surrounded by poppies in memory of those who died on the WWI battlefields.

Straight up the aisle is **Scientists' Corner**, and a section of the northern aisle of the nave is known as **Musicians' Aisle**. Above the screen is a magnificent organ (1730), above which you should check out the beautiful stone vaulted ceiling of the nave and the fan-vaulted aisles.

The two towers above the west door are the ones through which you exit. These were designed by Nicholas Hawksmoor and completed in 1745. Just above the door, perched in 15th-century niches, are the latest sacred addition to the abbey: 10 stone statues of international 20th-century martyrs. These were unveiled in 1998 and they include the likes of Martin Luther King and the Polish priest St Maximilian Kolbe, who was murdered by the Nazis at Auschwitz.

To the right as you exit is a memorial to innocent victims of oppression, violence and war around the world. 'All you who pass by, is it nothing to you?' it asks poignantly. Give it some thought.

There are **guided tours** (7222 7110; Mon-Sat; 1½ hours; £3) that leave several times during the day and limited **audio tours** (£2). One of the best ways to visit the abbey is to attend a service, particularly evensong (5pm weekdays, 3pm at weekends). Sunday Eucharist is at 11am.

There is an extraordinary amount to see here but, unless you enjoy feeling like part of a herd, come very early or very late; last entry is one hour before closing.

HOUSES OF PARLIAMENT Map pp426-7

Visitor's Gallery ☎ 7219 4272; www.parliament.uk; St Stephen's Entrance, St Margaret St SW1; admission free; ⏱ 2.30pm-7.30pm Mon-Wed, 11.30am-7.30pm Thu, 9.30am-3pm Fri; tube Westminster Parliament

The House of Commons and House of Lords are housed here in the Palace of Westminster. Charles Barry and Augustus Pugin built it in 1840 when the neo-Gothic style was all the rage in London, and a good clean has revealed the soft golden brilliance of the original structure. The most famous feature outside the palace is the Clock Tower, commonly known as **Big Ben**. The real Ben, a bell named after Benjamin Hall, who was commissioner of works when the tower was completed in 1858, hangs inside. If you're very keen, you can apply in writing for a free tour of the clock tower (see the website). Thirteen-ton Ben has rung in the New Year since 1924, and gets its hands and face washed by abseiling cleaners once every five years. The best view of the whole complex is from the eastern side of Lambeth Bridge.

At the opposite end of the building is **Victoria Tower**, completed in 1860. The medieval-looking little structure with the colourful tile roof, in triangular Victoria Tower Gardens to the south, is a monument to the emancipation of slaves in the British Empire and was erected in 1834.

The House of Commons is where Members of Parliament (MPs) meet to propose and discuss new legislation, to grill the prime minister and other ministers, and to get their mugs on TV to show their constituents they are actually working.

The layout of the Commons Chamber is based on that of St Stephen's Chapel in the original Palace of Westminster. The current chamber, designed by Giles Gilbert Scott, replaced the earlier one destroyed by a 1941 bomb. Although the Commons is a national assembly of 659 MPs, the chamber has seating for only 437 of them. Government members sit to the right of the Speaker and Opposition members to the left. The Speaker presides over business from a chair given by Australia, while ministers speak from a despatch box donated by New Zealand.

When Parliament is in session, visitors are admitted to the **House of Commons Visitors' Gallery**. Expect to queue for at least an hour if you haven't already organised a ticket through your local British embassy. Parliamentary recesses (ie holidays) last for three months over the summer and a couple of weeks over Easter and Christmas, so it's best to ring in advance

Big Ben, Westminster (left)

to check whether Parliament is in session. To find out what's being debated on a particular day, check the notice board posted beside the entrance or look in the *Daily Telegraph*, or the freebie *Metro* newspaper under 'Today in Parliament'. Bags and cameras must be checked at a cloakroom before you enter the gallery, and no large suitcases or backpacks are allowed through the airport-style security gate. **The House of Lords Visitors' Gallery** (☎ 7219 3107; admission free; ⏱ from 2.30pm Mon-Wed, from 3pm Thu, from 11am Fri) is also open to outsiders and is as good a place for an afternoon nap as any other.

As you're waiting for your bags to go through the X-ray machines, look left at the stunning roof of **Westminster Hall**, originally built in 1099 and today the oldest surviving part of the Palace of Westminster, the seat of the English monarchy from the 11th to the early 16th centuries. Added between 1394 and 1401, it is the earliest known example of a hammer-beam roof and has been described as 'the greatest surviving achievement of medieval English carpentry'. Westminster Hall was used for coronation banquets in medieval times, and also served as a courthouse until the 19th century. The trials of William Wallace (1305), Thomas More (1535), Guy Fawkes (1606) and Charles I (1649) all took place here. In the 20th century, monarchs and Winston Churchill lay in state here.

When Parliament is in recess, there are **guided summer tours** (☎ 7344 9966; 75mins; St Stephen's Entrance, St Margaret St; adult/concession £7/5) of both chambers and other historic buildings. Times change, so telephone or check www.parliament.uk for latest details.

TATE BRITAIN Map pp416-17

☎ 7887 8000 or 7887 8888; www.tate.org.uk; Millbank SW1; admission free, prices vary for temporary exhibitions; ☺ 10am-5.50pm; tube Pimlico (a boat connects the two Tates – p000)

You'd think maybe this gallery would be down in the dumps since its sibling, the Tate Modern, stole half its collection and pretty much all of the limelight when it opened in 2000. On the contrary, the venerable Tate Britain, built in 1897, seems to be revelling in its new second-string status, stretching out splendidly into all its increased space and filling it with the definitive collection of British art from the 16th to the late 20th centuries.

The galleries are broadly chronological in order, and you can expect to see some of the most important works by artists such as Constable and Gainsborough – who have entire galleries dedicated to them – and Hogarth, Reynolds, Stubbs, Blake, Hockney, Bacon and Moore among others. Adjoining the main building is the Clore Gallery, which houses the huge and occasionally superb JMW Turner bequest.

There are several free one-hour **thematic tours** each day, mostly on the hour, along with free 15-minutes talks on paintings, painters and styles at 1.15pm Tuesday-Thursday in the Rotunda. Audio tours for the collection cost £3/2.50 (adult/concession).

The Tate Restaurant is justifiably popular, although the huge mural by Rex Whistler is enough to put some people off their food, in which case you'll find refreshment at the café.

CABINET WAR ROOMS Map pp426-7

☎ 7766 0120; www.iwm.org.uk/cabinet; adult/under 16/concession £7/free/5.50; ☺ Sep-Apr 9.30am-6pm, 10am-6pm Oct-Mar; tube Charing Cross

This magnificently evocative museum occupies the bunkers where Churchill, his cabinet and generals met during WWII, and where the

essential business of government took place while Luftwaffe bombs rained overhead. Protected by 3m of solid concrete, they were able to coordinate their strategy for defeating Hitler, and it was from here that Churchill made the stirring speeches that helped galvanise the British populace. He really let the Fuhrer have it, calling him 'a wicked man'.

Particularly notable are the room where the Cabinet held over 100 meetings during the war; the converted broom cupboard that was Churchill's office; the cramped typing pool where ladies worked feverishly around the clock; the Telegraph Room with a hotline to Roosevelt; and the Map Room with charts showing the movements of troops and ships. In the Chief of Staff's Conference Room, the walls are covered with huge, original maps that were only discovered in 2002. If you squint two-thirds of the way down the right wall, somebody (possibly even Churchill himself) drew a little doodle depicting a cross-eyed and bandy-legged Hitler knocked on his ass. (If you can't see it, as is possible, petition the information desk to have the map moved to the opposite wall.)

The audioguide is very informative and entertaining, when the blasted thing works, and features anecdotes from people who worked here in the nerve centre of Britain's war effort, including petrified trainee typists who took dictation from the cigar-chewing, speech-impeded and short-tempered Churchill.

Beneath the rooms currently on display are some more rooms that were used as a canteen, hospital and shooting range. There are no plans to open these as yet, but next door to the War Rooms, a new museum dedicated to all things Churchillian, the £6 million **Churchill Project**, will open in January 2005 on the 40th anniversary of Churchill's death.

JEWEL TOWER Map pp426-7

☎ 7222 2219; Abingdon St SW1; adult/concession £2/1.20; ☺ 10am-6pm Apr-Sep, 10am-4pm Oct-Mar

Across the road from the Houses of Parliament, the Jewel Tower was built in 1365 to house the treasury of Edward III and is one of the last vestiges of the medieval Palace of Westminster. The moat that originally surrounded the structure was drained in the 17th century. The tower has had various functions over the years, although storing the crown jewels was never one of them. Today, it houses exhibitions describing the history and procedures of Parliament. There is a 25-minute explanatory video, which occasionally works, and this is a useful first stop if you intend visiting the House of Commons. Otherwise, it's a stocky and handsome building with a few interesting exhibits, like a 12th-century Saxon sword.

WHITEHALL Map pp426-7

Whitehall and its extension, Parliament St, is the wide avenue that links Trafalgar and Parliament Squares, and it is lined with many government buildings, statues, monuments and other historical bits and pieces.

BANQUETING HOUSE Map pp426-7

☎ 7930 4179; adult/concession £4/3; ⏱ 10am-5pm Mon-Sat; tube Westminster/Charing Cross

This is the only surviving part of the Tudor Whitehall Palace, which once stretched most of the way down Whitehall and burned down in 1698. It was designed as England's first purely Renaissance building by Inigo Jones after he returned from Italy, and looked like no other structure in the country at the time. Apparently, the English hated it for more than a century.

A bust outside commemorates 30 January 1649 when Charles 1, accused of treason by Cromwell after the Civil War, was executed on a scaffold built against a 1st-floor window here. When the royals were reinstated with Charles II, it inevitably became something of a royalist shrine, although its ceremonial functions faded in time and it was used as the Chapel Royal from the 18th century. It is still occasionally used for state banquets and concerts, but fortunately you don't have to be on the royal A-list to visit. In a huge, virtually unfurnished hall on the first floor there are nine ceiling panels painted by Rubens in 1964. They were commissioned by Charles I and depict the 'divine right' of kings. Maybe he got what he deserved.

CENOTAPH Map pp426-7

Whitehall SW1; tube Westminster/Charing Cross

The Cenotaph (Greek for 'empty tomb') is Britain's main memorial to the Commonwealth citizens who were killed during the two world wars. The Queen and other public figures lay poppies at its base on 11 November.

NO 10 DOWNING STREET Map pp426-7

www.number1-gov.uk; 10 Downing St SW1; tube Westminster/Charing Cross

This has been the site, mostly, of the British PM's official office since 1732, when George II presented No 10 to Robert Walpole, and also of the PM's home since it was substantially refurbished in 1902. It's a deceptively small-looking building on a plain-looking street, and you'll only recognise it from the stoic Bobby standing guard outside. The street has been cordoned off with a rather large iron gate since the final term of Margaret Thatcher, when the IRA launched a concerted campaign to take her out.

Breaking with tradition when he came to power, Tony Blair and his family swapped houses with the then-unmarried Chancellor who traditionally occupied the rather larger flat at No 11. He also commandeered the offices at No 12, traditional base of the chief whip, claiming the need for more workspace.

HORSE GUARDS PARADE Map pp426-7

☎ 0906 866 3344; 11am Mon-Sat & 10am Sun; tube Westminster

In a more accessible version of Buckingham Palace's Changing of the Guard, the mounted troopers of the Household Cavalry change guard here daily, at the official entrance to the royal palaces (opposite the Banqueting House). A lite-pomp version takes place at 4pm when the dismounted guards are changed.

ST JOHN'S SMITH SQUARE Map pp426-7

☎ box office 7222 1061; www.sjss.org.uk; Smith Square, Westminster SW1; tube Westminster

In the heart of Westminster, this eye-catching church was built by Thomas Archer in 1728 under the Fifty New Churches Act (1711), which aimed to stem the spread of nonconformism by swamping the market (so that's where Starbucks got the idea). With its four corner towers and monumental façades, the church was much maligned for the first century of its existence. Queen Anne is said to have likened it to a footstool, although in the version told by the people who run the church, Queen Anne actually requested a church built in the shape of a footstool. Anyway, it's generally agreed now that the church is a masterpiece of English Baroque (although it's no longer a church). After receiving a direct hit during WWII, it was rebuilt in the 1960s as a classical music venue (p309) and, as such, is renowned for its crisp acoustics. The brick-vaulted restaurant in the crypt is called, as you might guess, 'The Footstool', and is open for lunch Monday to Friday, as well as for pre- and post-concert dinner.

VICTORIA & PIMLICO

Clinging to Westminster, Victoria's got all the pizzazz of its neighbour without any of the attractions, which doesn't add up to very much at all. It's best known for coming and going, via its huge train and coach stations. Despite its function as a transport hub, there's not all that much staying unless you're a backpacker availing of its cheap and predominantly cheerless accommodation. The one attraction worth pausing your journey for is the candy-striped Westminster Cathedral a couple of hundred metres from the tube station.

At least Victoria's unattractiveness gives it a smidgen of character; Pimlico, on the other hand, would probably disappear in an X-ray. Thomas Cubitt built most of it in the 19th century, but the developer had obviously done his dash in the creation of swanky Belgravia nearby and was only creating apathetically plain Pimlico for beer money. Its only redeeming feature is the view it affords across the river to the Battersea Power Station.

WESTMINSTER CATHEDRAL Map pp440-1

☎ 7798 9055; www.westminstercathedral.org.uk; Victoria St SW1; cathedral admission free, tower adult/concession £2/1, audioguides £2.50; ☼ cathedral 7am-7pm, tower 9am-5pm Apr-Nov, 9am-5pm Thu-Sun Dec-Mar; tube Victoria

In 1895, work began on this cathedral, the headquarters of the Roman Catholic Church in Britain, and although worshippers began flocking here in 1903, the church ran out of money and the project has never been completed. In some ways, it's London's version of Gaudí's La Sagrada Família in Barcelona – a magnificent work in progress.

John Francis Bentley's design is a superb example of neo-Byzantine architecture: its distinctive candy-striped red-brick and white-stone tower features prominently on the west London skyline. Remarkably few people think to look inside, but the interior is part stunning marble and mosaic and part bare brick, although the stunning bits are slowly climbing up the walls and pillars. The highly regarded stone carvings of the *14 Stations of the Cross* (1918) by Eric Gill and the marvellously sombre atmosphere, especially in early evening when the mosaics glitter in the candlelight, make this a welcome haven from the traffic outside. The views from the 83m-tall **Campanile Bell Tower** are impressive, as is the fact that there's a lift to save you the climb.

Seven Masses are said daily from Monday to Friday, five on Saturday and seven on Sunday. There's a gift shop and a café here, open 10am to 4.30pm daily.

CHELSEA & BELGRAVIA

Chelsea has been one of London's most fashionable precincts ever since the martyr Thomas More moved here in the early 16th century. The 'village of palaces' became one of London's most desirable neighbourhoods in which to live as it was close to the bustle of the City and Westminster yet still relatively remote and concealed behind a big bend in the river. Even when it was well and truly consumed by greater London in the 20th century, it retained its aristocratic angle and even managed to mix it with a Bohemian vibe. Its main artery, the King's Rd, helped propel London into the swinging '60s and Chelsea even managed to get a big slice of punk's cred in the following decade. These days, its residents still have among the highest incomes of any London borough (shops and restaurants presume you do too), the community is as cosmopolitan as the local football team and it's still awash with 'trendy' this and that. And that's the big difference; it feels like the folk of Chelsea are trying to be trendy these days, the area has lost much of its stylish oomph and is now filled with money without much of the magic.

Neighbouring Belgravia, with its white stuccoed squares, has had a reputation for matter-of-fact elitism ever since it was laid out by builder Thomas Cubitt in the 19th century. It's a charming, mainly residential enclave with quaint cobbled mews, numerous embassies, a few wonderful old-fashioned pubs and, these days, nowhere near the affectation of its try-hard neighbour.

ALBERT & BATTERSEA
BRIDGES Map pp436-7 & 440-1

One of London's most striking bridges, the Albert is a cross between a cantilever and a suspension bridge, buttressed to strengthen it as an alternative to closure in the 1960s. It was designed by Roland Mason Ordish in 1873, but later modified by the engineer Joseph Bazalgette (p83). Painted white and pink and with fairy lights adorning its cables, it looks stunning during the day and festive by night. The booths at either end survive from the days when tolls applied.

CARLYLE'S HOUSE Map pp436-7

☎ 7352 7087; 24 Cheyne Row SW3; adult/concession £3.50/1.75; ⏱ 11am-5pm Wed-Sun Apr-early Nov; tube Sloane Square

From 1834 until his death in 1881, the great Victorian essayist and historian Thomas Carlyle lived in this three-storey house, and wrote, in the attic, his famous history of the French Revolution, along with many other works. Legend claims that when the manuscript was complete, a maid accidentally threw it on the fire, whereupon the diligent Thomas patiently wrote it all again. The small, charming terraced house, built in 1798, is purported to be pretty much as it was when Carlyle lived here and the likes of Chopin, Tennyson and Dickens would call around for a natter.

CHELSEA OLD CHURCH Map pp436-7

☎ 7795 1019; Cheyne Walk, Old Church St SW3; ⏱ 1.30pm-5.30pm Tue-Fri & Sun; tube Sloane Square

This church is most well known as a monument to Thomas More (1477–1535), the former chancellor (and current Roman Catholic saint) who lost his head for refusing to go along with Henry VIII's plan to establish himself as supreme head of the Church of England. The church was originally built in the 12th century although it's been modified a few times, most recently after bomb damage during WWII. The interior contains many fine Tudor monuments, most notably the **More Chapel** to the south, which was rebuilt by Sir Thomas in 1528 and retains its wooden ceiling and pillar capitals, examples of the fledgling Renaissance style. At the western end of the southern aisle are the only chained books in a London church (chained, of course, to stop anyone making off with them), including a copy of Foxe's *Book of Martyrs* from 1684.

Outside the church is a gold statue of More, who lived in Chelsea with his family in a property expropriated by Henry VIII after the lord chancellor's execution. Other celebrated former residents of Chelsea, and this street in particular, are *Middlemarch* author George Eliot, who lived and died at No 4, and the painter JMW Turner, who lived at No 119 under the alias 'Booth'.

CHELSEA PHYSIC GARDEN Map pp436-7

☎ 7352 5646; www.chelseaphysicgarden.co.uk; 66 Royal Hospital Rd SW3; adult/concession £5/3; ⏱ noon-5pm Wed & 2-6pm Sun Apr-Oct, noon-5pm during the Chelsea Flower Show, 11am-3pm on Snowdrop Days (1st two Sundays in Feb); tube Sloane Square

Established in 1673 by the Apothecaries' Society to provide a means for students to study medicinal plants and healing, this magical place is one of the oldest botanical gardens in Europe and contains many rare trees, shrubs and plants. Individual corners of the garden are given over to world medicine and plants suitable for dyeing and use in aromatherapy. A number of notable green fingers have worked here over the years, including William Aiton, the first gardener at Kew, and William Forsyth, who gave his name to the forsythia bush.

The statue is of Sir Hans Sloane, the philanthropist who saved the garden from going under in the early 18th century (and whose private collection of antiquities got the British Museum started).

Opening hours for the garden are limited because the grounds are still used for research and education; tours can be organised by appointment.

KING'S ROAD Map pp436-7
tube Sloane Square/ South Kensington

In the 17th century, Charles II set up a Chelsea love nest here for him and his mistress, an orange-seller at the Drury Lane Theatre by the name of Nell Gwyn. Heading back to Hampton Court Palace in an evening, Charles would make use of a farmer's track that inevitably came to be known as the King's Rd. The street was at the forefront of London, nay world, fashion during the technicolour '60s and anarchic '70s, and continues to be trendy now, albeit in a more self-conscious way. The street begins at Sloane Square, to the north of which runs Sloane St, celebrated for its designer boutiques. At 75 Sloane St is the Cadogan Hotel, where Oscar Wilde was arrested (in room No 118, to be precise) in 1895 and later jailed for his 'friendship' (the euphemism of the time) with Lord Alfred Douglas.

MICHELIN HOUSE Map pp436-7
81 Fulham Rd SW3; tube South Kensington

Even if you're not up for dinner at Terence Conran's wonderful restaurant Bibendum (p231) in Michelin House, mosey past and have a look at the superb Art Nouveau architecture. It was built for Michelin between 1905 and 1911 by François Espinasse, and completely restored in 1985. The open-fronted ground floor provides space for upmarket fish and flower stalls, the famous roly-poly Michelin Man appears in the modern stained glass, while the lobby is decorated with tiles showing early-20th-century cars. The Conran Shop is also housed here.

NATIONAL ARMY MUSEUM Map pp440-1

☎ 7730 0717; www.national-army-museum.ac.uk;
Royal Hospital Rd SW3; admission free but donations
requested; 🕓 10am-5.30pm; tube Sloane Square

Next door to the Royal Hospital, appropriately
enough, this old-fashioned museum tells the
history of the British army from the perspective
of the men and women who put their lives
on the line for king and country in eras when
there was honour in doing such. Refreshingly low-tech, it convey the horrors as well
as the glories of war, with exhibits ranging
from the skeleton of Napoleon's horse and
model trenches, through to the usual arsenal
of weapons, artillery and military tactics. Two
of the best exhibitions focus on the life and
times of the 'Redcoat' (the term for the British
soldier from the Battle of Agincourt in 1415
to the American Revolution), and the tactical
battle at Waterloo between Napoleon and the
Duke of Wellington.

ROYAL HOSPITAL CHELSEA
Map pp436-7 & 440-1

☎ 7881 5204; Royal Hospital Rd SW3; admission free;
🕓 10am-noon & 2-4pm Mon-Sat, 2pm-4pm Sun; tube
Sloane Square

Designed by Christopher Wren, this superb
structure was built in 1692 to provide shelter
for ex-servicemen, a function it has carried out
with dignity and aplomb since the reign of
Charles II. Today, it still houses hundreds of war
veterans known as Chelsea Pensioners, who are
fondly regarded as national treasures and can
be seen walking around the grounds in their
dark blue greatcoats (in winter) or scarlet frock-
coats (in summer). At most times, visitors are
free to wander around and visit the hospital's
chapel and museum, which contains a huge
collection of war medals bequeathed by former
residents. From the gardens, there are excellent
framed views across the Thames to Battersea
Power Station. The hospital is off-limits to casual
visitors when it is hosting events, which seems
increasingly common. The Chelsea Flower
Show takes place here in May.

KNIGHTSBRIDGE, SOUTH KENSINGTON & HYDE PARK

Much of west London is high-class territory
and it doesn't get much higher or classier
than 'South Ken', which thanks to Prince
Albert and the 1851 Great Exhibition is
also museum-centric, home to the Natural
History, Science and Victoria & Albert

Michelin House (opposite)

museums all on one road. Albert's memorial,
superbly renovated in recent years, is due
north of this fabulous trio. This is also one of
London's most sophisticated stretches, with
sizeable residents of French, Italian and Far
Eastern communities, all bound together
in prosperity. Kensington High St, a lively
blend of upmarket boutiques and chain
stores, dominates the area of Kensington
itself. North of here is Holland Park, a
residential district of elegant town houses
built around a wooded park. Knightsbridge,
once famous for highwaymen and raucous
drinking is now renowned for its swanky
shopping at Harrods and Harvey Nichols,
and for being a playpen for moneyed and
perpetually-tanned, middle-aged men and
ditzy young rich girls, not necessarily playing together. Screening the denizens of these
well-to-do neighbourhoods from the decidedly more drab Bayswater and Paddington
to the north are the utterly splendid Hyde
Park and Kensington Gardens (think of
them as one big green entity), around which
upmarket hotels and prestigious shops have
long since shooed the hoi polloi away.

VICTORIA & ALBERT MUSEUM

Map pp422-3 & 436-7

☎ 7942 2000; www.vam.ac.uk; Cromwell Rd SW7; admission free, prices vary for temporary exhibitions; 🕑 10am-5.45pm (until 10pm Wed & last Fri of month); tube South Kensington

This vast, rambling and wonderful museum of decorative art and design is part of Prince Albert's legacy to the nation in the aftermath of the successful Great Exhibition of 1851. It's a bit like the nation's attic, comprising four million objects collected over the years from Britain and around the globe. Spread over nearly 150 galleries, it houses the world's greatest collection of decorative arts, including ancient Chinese ceramics, modernist architectural drawings, Korean bronze and Japanese swords, samples from William Morris' 19th-century Arts and Crafts movement, cartoons by Raphael, spellbinding Asian and Islamic art, Rodin sculptures, gowns from the Elizabethan era, dresses straight from this year's Paris fashion shows, ancient jewellery, a 1930s wireless set, an all-wooden Frank Lloyd Wright study, and a pair of Doc Martens. Yes, like the British Museum, this is a place that needs careful planning.

As soon as you enter – if you can take your eyes off the stunning **Chihuly Chandelier** above you – head to the shiny new information and ticket desk, staffed by some of the friendliest and most efficient people of any London attraction. If the main entrance on Cromwell Rd is too busy, go around the corner and enter via Exhibition Rd, where there's another information desk that can provide you with a floor plan. Alternatively, take one of the free **introductory guided tours** that leave from the main reception area every hour from 10.30am to 4.30pm.

Level A is mostly devoted to art and design from India, China, Japan and Korea, as well as European art. There's a quirky gallery dedicated to Fakes & Forgeries, and an equally unusual, fascinating one, the Cast Court, devoted to copies, including a replica of the gigantic Trajan's Column in Rome. Room 40 is all about costume – everything from absurd 18th-century wigs and whalebone corsets to the platform shoes that brought Naomi Campbell crashing to the ground on a Paris catwalk. The collection includes some of Princess Diana's old frocks (which were let out for her sister-in-law Fergie).

The Raphael Gallery (room 48A) is devoted to seven cartoons by Raphael (1483–1520),

paintings commissioned by Pope Leo X as designs for tapestries that now hang in the Vatican Museum.

The Pirelli Garden is a lovely, shaded inner courtyard where you can collect your thoughts over a reasonable latte mid-visit. Beyond the gardens are three original and magnificently ornate refreshment rooms dating from the 1860s. The V&A was the first museum in the world to provide a refreshment room, and these have now become exhibits in themselves. The Canon Photography Gallery (room 38), near here, has excellent rotating exhibits.

On Level B you'll find collections of ironwork (rooms 113 and 114), stained glass (rooms 111 and 116), jewellery (rooms 91 to 93) and a wonderful exhibit of musical instruments (room 40A).

Just off the landing is a famous marble statue, *The Three Graces*, by Antonio Canova. In the 1990s, it was controversially 'saved' for the nation after the public raised £7.6m to buy it from a private owner and prevent it going to the US. When it was privately owned, the statue of the three sisters used to be revolved so guests could admire their fetching posteriors.

The 15 relatively new **British Galleries** feature every aspect of British design from 1500 to 1900, and make for an interesting study into the evolution of British society. Among the exhibits is a decanter and set of glasses that Prince Charles, when he officially opened these galleries in 2001 and was going on the inaugural tour, stopped in front and exclaimed, 'So *that's* where they are'. Apparently a pastry chef at Windsor had 'acquired' them – say no more. Highlights of this floor are the Silver Galleries (rooms 65 to 69) and a wonderful suspended sculpture, *Breathless*, by Cornelia Parker, comprising brass instruments flattened by the weights that open and close Tower Bridge.

The Henry Cole Wing, an add-on at the Exhibition Rd side, contains the largest collection of Constables gathered under one roof. The exhibition focusing on the work of the American architect Frank Lloyd Wright (1869–1959) is worth the climb. Even if you're not going to the restaurant, which is pretty good, there's a changing exhibition featuring the words and drawings of Beatrix Potter on the way there.

The most ridiculous thing, though, is that the V&A's temporary exhibitions are often so compelling that you mightn't get to see anything in the permanent collection – you've been warned.

NATURAL HISTORY MUSEUM

Map pp422-3 & 436-7

☎ 7938 9123; www.nhm.ac.uk; Cromwell Rd SW7; admission free, highlights tours (depending on staff availability) £3, free half-hourly tours of 'wet' zoological exhibits in the Darwin Centre; ⊙ 10am-5.50pm (from 11am Sun); tube South Kensington

Kids – and many adults – will lose their minds at this gem of a museum, a dizzying combination of august artefact and amusement arcade. The museum building itself is gloriously over-the-top. One of London's finest neo-Gothic structures, it was designed by Alfred Waterhouse between 1873 and 1880, and has a grand cathedral-like main entrance. The façade is faced with gleaming blue and sand-coloured brick and terracotta, thin columns and articulated arches, with carvings of plants and animals crawling all over it. Look out for the dinosaur footprints in the forecourt.

Incorporating the old Geological Museum, the collection is now divided between the adjoining Life Galleries (entrance on Cromwell Rd) and Earth Galleries (enter from Exhibition Rd). Where once the former was full of dusty glass cases of butterflies and stick insects, there are now wonderful interactive displays on themes such as Human Biology and Creepy Crawlies, alongside the crowd-pulling exhibition on mammals and dinosaurs, which includes animatronic movers and shakers like the 4m-high Tyrannosaurus Rex. Schoolchildren flock to see these, which leaves more space for the rest of us at the wondrous mammal balcony, the Blue Whale exhibit and in the Ecology gallery, with its replica rainforest.

In some ways, though, it's the Earth Galleries that are the most staggering. As you enter from Exhibition Rd you'll find yourself facing an escalator that slithers up and into a hollowed-out globe. Around its base, single fine samples of different rocks and gems are beautifully displayed. Upstairs there are two main exhibits: Earthquake and the Restless Surface, which explains how wind, water, ice, gravity and life itself impact on the earth. Earthquake is an extraordinary trembling mock-up of what happened to one small grocery shop during the Kobe trembler in Japan in 1995 that killed 6000 people. Excellent exhibitions on the lower floors include Earth Today and Tomorrow, which focuses on ecology; Earth's Treasury, which looks at gems and other precious stones; and From the Beginning, which explores how planets are formed. Touch-screen computer displays and gadgetry abound. To avoid crowds during school term time, it's

Natural History Museum (left)

best to visit early morning or late afternoon, or early on weekend mornings year-round. The Waterhouse Café on the ground floor of the Life Galleries is quite good, with a decent selection of vegetarian dishes.

Phase I of a new state-of-the-art Darwin Centre opened in 2002 and focuses on taxonomy (the study of the natural world). It features some 450,000 jars of pickled specimens, free guided tours every half-hour along the science floors and presentations from museum researchers, although you need to have a special interest in the subject to get much out of it. The even-more-ambitious phase II of the Darwin Centre will showcase some 22 million zoological, botanical and entomological exhibits in 'a giant cocoon', due to open in 2007.

SCIENCE MUSEUM

☎ 0870 870 4868; www.sciencemuseum.org.uk; Exhibition Rd SW7; admission free, IMAX cinema adult/concession £7.10/5.95; ⊙ 10am-6pm; tube South Kensington

This is one of the most cutting-edge, progressive and accessible museums of its kind, and does a terrific job of bringing to lustrous life a subject that is often dull, dense and impenetrable for kids and adults alike. With seven floors of interactive and educational exhibits, it's not only informative but also one of the most entertaining attractions in the city and has something to snag the interest of every age group. Synopsis – an Introduction, inside the door near the Information desk, should be your first stop.

Making the Modern World, on the ground floor, looks back at the history of the Industrial Revolution via examples of its machinery, including vintage cars and the first steam locomotives, Puffing Billy and Stephenson's Rocket from early in the 19th century. In the same exhibition, it looks forward to the exploration of space, complete with rockets and famous recreations. There's also a showcase of everyday technology, products, games and gadgets from throughout the 20th century, guaranteed to make you feel your age.

Go up a floor to find out about the impact of science on food, time, telecommunications and weather, or visit the fascinating Who Am I wing, an interactive exploration of the things that make us all different. Up another level and you're into the world of computers, chemistry and nuclear power. The 3rd floor is the place for old aeroplanes, among them the Vickers Vimy in which Alcock and Brown first flew the Atlantic in 1919, and the Gipsy Moth, in which Amy Johnson flew to Australia in 1930. There's a Flight Lab of interactive exhibits and models exploring aerodynamics, a motion ride stimulator and Health Matters, a jump into the world of modern medicine. On the 4th and 5th floors you'll find exhibits relating to the history of medicine and veterinary science.

Look out for a modern version of Foucault's famous pendulum hanging in the hall. As the day wears on, the pendulum seems to change direction. In fact, because the earth is moving beneath it, it really stays in the same place. This is how Foucault illustrated how the earth rotates on its own axis. The basement has imaginative hands-on galleries for children: the Garden, for three to six-year-olds, Things for seven to 11-year-olds. The Secret Life of the Home, a collection of labour-saving appliances that householders have either embraced or shunned, is for everyone.

The even higher-tech Wellcome Wing, a £50 million extension to the museum that opened in 2000, is filled with hands-on displays focusing on modern science in everyday life. Of special interest are Digitopolis, which focuses on digital technology; On Air, which looks at broadcasting; and Flight Lab, where you can test a model in a wind tunnel or try to get a helicopter off the ground. The 450-seat IMAX cinema (entrance on the ground floor of the Wellcome Wing) has the usual crop of travelogues, space adventures and dinosaur attacks in stunning 3-D.

The Deep Blue Café on the ground floor of the Wellcome Wing opens from 10.30am to 5.30pm daily. There are no guided tours on offer, but you can pick up trail guides for children (lighter covers for younger kids, darker cover for older ones).

Now, with all the scientific know-how at their disposal, we hope the museum can someday resolve the minor problem of having zero natural light.

KENSINGTON PALACE Map pp422-3

☎ 7937 9561; wwwroyalresidences.com; Kensington Gardens W8; adult/child/concession £10.50/7/8, park & gardens free; ⏰ 10am-4.30pm; tube Queensway/Notting Hill Gate/High Street Kensington

This was the main royal residence from 1689, when William of Orange moved here and had Christopher Wren spruce the house up, right until George III became king in 1760 and relocated to Buckingham (perhaps spurred by the ignominy of his predecessor having died of a stroke while squatting on the loo). Queen Victoria was born in a ground-floor room in 1819, but it's most well known in recent times as the home Princess Diana took when she split with Prince Charles.

Self-paced tours of the palace, with audioguide, take you round the surprisingly small, wood-panelled State Apartments dating from the time of William and the much grander, more spacious apartments of the Georgian period. This is still a working palace, housing the London residences and offices of a string of minor royals.

Displayed under low lights you'll see costumes from the Royal Ceremonial Dress Collection, which includes skirts that were so ludicrously wide that they made it impossible for their wearers to sit down, and ensured that rooms of the period were sparsely furnished and designed obstacle-free. The major draw here is a striking collection of Diana's dresses, which you can compare to a load of old frocks donated by the Queen.

Most beautiful of all the quarters is the Cupola Room, where the ceremony of initiating men into the exclusive Order of the Garter took place and where Victoria was baptised; you can see the order's crest painted on the trompe l'œil 'domed' ceiling, which is actually, essentially flat. The room is ringed with marbled columns and niches containing gilded Roman-style statues.

The **King's Long Gallery** displays some of the royal art collection, including the only known painting of a classical subject by Van Dyck. On the ceiling, William Kent painted the story of Odysseus but slipped up by giving the Cyclops two eyes!

The **King's Drawing Room** is dominated by a monumentally ugly painting of **Cupid and Venus**, by Giorgio Vasari (1511–74), an Italian mannerist painter who used to brag about the speed in which he worked and was better known for his historical record of the Renaissance. There are splendid views of the park and gardens from here; you can also see the **Round Pond**, once full of turtles for turtle soup but now popular for sailing model boats.

The **King's Staircase** is decorated with striking murals by William Kent, who painted himself in a turban on the fake dome. Also included is a portrait of Peter, the 'wild child' who had been discovered in the woods of Hanover and brought to England to entertain the jaded court.

The **Sunken Garden** near the palace is at its prettiest in summer; the nearby **Orangery**, designed by Vanbrugh and Hawsmoor as a freestanding conservatory in 1704, is a bright, if rather formal, place for tea.

KENSINGTON GARDENS Map pp422-3
dawn-dusk; tube Queensway/High Street Kensington/Lancaster Gate

Immediately west of Hyde Park, across the Serpentine Lake, these gardens are technically part of Kensington Palace, where Princess Diana lived after her separation from Charles. The Palace and the gardens have become something of a shrine to her memory. A **memorial fountain**, an 80m stone moat with cascading water, is planned to be opened in the summer of 2004 to coincide with the sixth anniversary of her death. It was designed by US landscape designer Kathryn Gustafson and will cost £3m to build. A 12km Diana memorial walk passes here, then loops around the four central royal parks: Kensington, Hyde Park, St James's, and Green Park. If you have kids in tow, visit the **Diana, Princess of Wales Memorial Playground**, in the northwest corner of the gardens.

Art is another character of these gardens – George Frampton's famous statue of Peter Pan is close to the lake, beside an attractive area known as Flower Walk. South of the lake, and near the main road that runs through the park, is the **Serpentine Gallery** (☎ 7402 6075; www.serpentinegallery.org; admission free; 10am-6pm; tube Knightsbridge). There are also sculptures by Henry Moore and Jacob Epstein here.

HYDE PARK Map pp422-3
5.30am-midnight ; tube Hyde Park Corner/Marble Arch/Knightsbridge/Lancaster Gate

London's largest open space weighs in at a whopping 145 hectares, and is an inviting composite of neatly manicured gardens and wild, deserted expanses of overgrown grass. It's a riot of colour in spring and full of milky-white (and soon-to-be-burnt) sunbathers on summer days. It's a magnificent venue for open-air concerts, demonstrations and royal occasions. Gun salutes are fired here and soldiers ride through the park each morning on their way to Horse Guard's Parade in Whitehall. If you fancy a little horse riding in the centre of London yourself, see p199.

Hyde Park is separated from Kensington Gardens by the squiggly L-shaped Serpentine Lake, which was created when the Westbourne River was dammed in the 1730s; it's a good spot for pleasure boating in summer. Henry VIII expropriated the park from the Church in 1536, after which it became a hunting ground for kings and aristocrats; later it became a popular venue for duels, executions and horse racing. It became the first royal park to open to the public in the early 17th century, and famously hosted the Great Exhibition in 1851. During WWII it became an enormous potato bed.

MARBLE ARCH Map pp422-3
tube Marble Arch

John Nash designed this huge arch in 1827. It was moved here, the northeastern corner of Hyde Park, from its original spot in front of Buckingham Palace in 1851, when it was adjudged too small and unimposing to be the entrance to the royal manor. There's a one-room flat inside, London's grandest bedsit. If you're feeling anarchic, walk through the central portal, a privilege reserved for the royal family by law.

SPEAKERS' CORNER Map pp422-3
tube Marble Arch

The northeastern corner of Hyde Park is traditionally the spot for oratorical acrobatics and soapbox ranting. It's the only place in Britain where demonstrators can assemble without police permission, a concession granted in 1872 as a response to serious riots when 150,000 people gathered to demonstrate against the Sunday Trading Bill before Parliament. If you've got something on your chest, you can get rid of it here on Sunday, although it'll be largely loonies and religious fanatics you'll have for company. Nobody else will take much notice.

TYBURN TREE Map pp422-3
tube Marble Arch
A plaque on the traffic island at Marble Arch indicates the spot where the infamous Tyburn Tree, a three-legged gallows, once stood. An estimated 50,000 people were executed here between 1300 and 1783, many having been dragged from the Tower of London.

TYBURN CONVENT Map pp422-3
☎ 7723 7262; www.tyburnconvent.org.uk; 8 Hyde Park Place; admission free; ☼ tours of the crypt 10.30am, 3.30pm & 5.30pm (call beforehand if you can); tube Marble Arch
One of the buildings of this sorrowful and silent place has the distinction of being the smallest house in London, measuring just over a metre in width. A convent was established here in 1903, close to the site of the Tyburn Tree gallows were many Catholics were executed because of their faith during the 19th century, and which later became a place of Catholic pilgrimage. The crypt contains the relics of some 105 martyrs, along with paintings commemorating their lives and recording their deaths. A closed order of Benedictine sisters lives here, as they have for more than a century.

ALBERT MEMORIAL Map pp422-3
☎ 7495 0916 for 40-min guided tours at 2pm & 3pm Sun; www.aptg.org.uk; adult/concession £3.50/3; tube South Kensington/Gloucester Road
On the southern edge of Hyde Park and facing Kensington Gore, this memorial is as over-the-top as the subject, Queen Victoria's German husband Albert (1819–61), was purportedly humble. Albert explicitly said he did not want a monument and 'if (as is very likely) it became an artistic monstrosity like most of our monuments, it would upset my equanimity to be permanently ridiculed and laughed at in effigy'. Ah, he didn't really mean it, they reckoned, and got George Gilbert Scott to build the 52.5m-high, gaudy Gothic monument in 1872, featuring the prince thumbing through a catalogue for his Great Exhibition, and surrounded by 178 figures representing the continents (Asia, Europe, Africa and America), as well as the arts, industry and science. The monument was unveiled again in 1998 after being renovated at huge expense. At the time of writing, the more fitting memorial, Royal Albert Hall, across the road, was being renovated at huge expense. The memorial is certainly eye-catching when it's lit up at night.

ROYAL ALBERT HALL Map pp422-3
☎ 7589 3203; www.royalalberthall.com; Kensington Gore SW7; tube South Kensington
This huge domed, red-brick amphitheatre is adorned with a frieze of Minton tiles and was completed in 1871. Queen Victoria surprised everyone when she turned up to lay the foundation stone for the building and named it after her departed hubbie. It was never intended as a concert venue but rather, and more appropriately, as a hall of arts and sciences. Certainly, whoever designed the acoustics didn't think music would be played here; it is said that the only way a British composer can ever hear his work *twice* is by playing at the Royal Albert Hall, so bad is the echo reverberating around the oval structure. It's best known for hosting the Promenade Concerts (or 'Proms') held here every summer since 1947 (p309).

The only way to see inside is by attending a concert. The venue has been undergoing a massive refurbishment, aimed at restoring it to its original splendour while at the same time upgrading it to modern standards (and fixing the acoustics). This work was due to be completed in 2004.

ROYAL GEOGRAPHICAL SOCIETY (RGS) Map pp422-3
☎ 7591 3000; www.rgs.org; 1 Kensington Gore SW7; admission free; ☼ 10am-5pm Mon-Fri; tube South Kensington
A short distance to the east of the Royal Albert Hall is the headquarters of the Royal Geographical Society, housed in a Queen Anne-style, red-brick edifice (1874) easily identified by the statues of explorers David Livingstone and Ernest Shackleton outside.

The society has a collection of over half a million maps, photographs, artefacts, books and manuscripts, although the Library and Map Room are due to open around Spring 2004 with the completion of its £5 million 'Unlocking the Archives' project, designed to conserve the resources and improve public access to them.

BROMPTON ORATORY Map pp436-7
☎ 7808 0900; 215 Brompton Rd SW7; ☼ 6.30am-8pm; tube South Kensington
Also known as the London Oratory and the Oratory of St Philip Neri, this Roman Catholic church was built in the Italian Baroque style in 1884. It has marble, candles and statues galore, as well as one very important regular in Prime

(Continued on page 155)

1 Coach & Horses pub, Soho (p265) *2* Window shopping, Charing Cross (p326) *3* Royal Academy of Arts, Piccadilly (p124) *4* Trafalgar Square (p95)

139

1 *Courtauld Institute of Art, the Strand (p99)* **2** *Savoy Hotel, the Strand (p341)* **3** *Temple Church, Holborn (p100)* **4** *Royal Opera House, Covent Garden (p94)*

1 Sketch restaurant, Soho (p225)
2 Temple Church, Holborn (p100)
3 National Gallery, Trafalgar Square (p95)

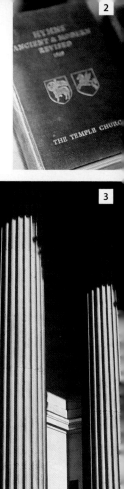

1 Tower Bridge, the City (p116)
2 Spitalfields Market (p117)
3 Lloyds building, the City (p111)
4 St Paul's Cathedral, the City (p106) 5 St Paul's Cathedral (p106)
6 Vibe Bar, Hoxton (p269)
7 St Paul's Cathedral

1 Queen Victoria Memorial,
Buckingham Palace (p120)
2 Tate Britain, Millbank (p129)
3 Natural History Museum,
South Kensington (p135)

1 Harrods department store,
Knightsbridge (p325)
2 Queen Victoria Memorial,
Buckingham Palace (p120)
3 Natural History Museum,
South Kensington (p135)
4 Hyde Park (p137)

1 Globe Theatre, Southwark (p161)
2 Bermondsey Market (p333)
3 Millennium Bridge, Bankside
(p160) 4 Imperial War Museum,
Lambeth (p155) 5 Old Operating
Theatre Museum and Herb Garret,
Borough (p163) 6 National Film
Theatre, South Bank (p294)

1

2

1 *Whitechapel Bell Foundry (p166)*
2 *Walthamstow Stadium (p312)*
3 *National Maritime Museum, Greenwich (p174)* 4 *Canary Wharf Underground station, Docklands (p171)* 5 *Goddards Pie House, Greenwich (p246)* 6 *Nauticalia shop, Greenwich (p331)* 7 *Canary Wharf Tower development, Docklands (p171)*

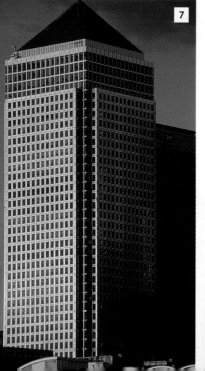

149

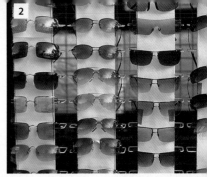

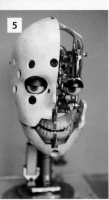

1 *Sherlock Holmes Museum, Marylebone (p181)* 2 *Camden Market (p183)* 3 *Camden Lock Market (p333)* 4 *British Library, Regent's Park (p182)* 5 *Madame Tussaud's, Marylebone (p180)*

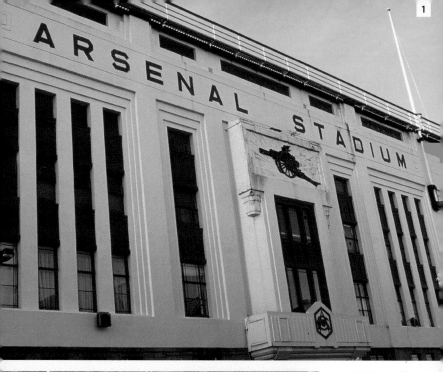

1 *Arsenal Stadium, Highbury (p310)* 2 *Highgate Cemetery (p184)* 3 *Flask pub, Highgate (p275)*

151

1 *Lord's cricket ground, St John's Wood (p188)* **2** *Waitress, Notting Hill (p188)* **3** *Electric Cinema, Notting Hill (p294)* **4** *Advertising brochure, Electric Cinema, Notting Hill (p294)* **5** *Earls Court Exhibition Hall Two (p306)* **6** *Wetland Centre, Barnes (p192)*

1 Battersea Power Station (p194)
2 Kew Gardens (p200) 3 Palm
House, Kew Gardens (p200)
4 Brixton Market (p334)

(Continued from page 138)

Minister Tony Blair. There are six daily Masses on weekdays, one at 6pm on Saturday, and nine between 7am and 7pm on Sunday.

COMMONWEALTH INSTITUTE

Map pp422-3

☎ 7603 4535; www.commonwealth.org.uk; Kensington High St W8; tube High Street Kensington

On the southern side of Holland Park, just off Kensington High St, an open space with fountains and flagpoles fronts the Commonwealth Institute, designed in 1962 to resemble a large tent and created from materials from all over the British Commonwealth. It looks as horrid as it sounds. The rather pedestrian interior has

recently been revamped to extol the virtues of the 54 Commonwealth countries, and it houses temporary exhibits relating to the same.

LINLEY SAMBOURNE HOUSE Map pp422-3

☎ 8994 1019; 18 Stafford Terrace W8; adult/concession £6/4; ☉ tours Sat-Sun; tube High Street Kensington

Tucked away behind Kensington High St, this was the home of *Punch* political cartoonist and amateur photographer, Linley Sambourne, from 1874 to 1910. It's one of those houses whose owners never redecorated or threw anything away: what you see is pretty much the typical home of a well-to-do Victorian family: dark wood, Turkish carpets and rich stained glass. Visits are by 90-minute guided tour only.

ALONG THE SOUTH BANK

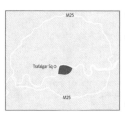

Eating p240; Sleeping p347; Shopping p329

A wall of grand architectural projects since the mid-1990s has turned the Thames's muddy southern bank from a forgotten backwater into one of the capital's most vibrant neighbourhoods. One of these new structures, the replica Globe Theatre, harks back to the area's bawdy history as an Elizabethan pleasure ground, with inns, brothels and bear-baiting pits. Others, like Tate Modern and the Oxo Tower, have refashioned disused icons of the industrial age for the 21st century. Yet more, including the London Eye Ferris wheel, City Hall and the Millennium Bridge, capture the playfulness of late-1990s British culture, mixed with a newfound openness and transparency. The one thing uniting these landmarks is a sense of public space. With the Silver Jubilee Walkway and the Thames Path providing the literal link, there's a virtual conga line of sightseers shimmying along the no-longer-neglected riverbank.

It's hard to get very lost along the South Bank. Since the districts in this chapter line up from west to east – Lambeth, South Bank, Bankside, Southwark, Borough and Bermondsey – you can almost always find the riverbank from which to orientate yourself. The Waterloo tube and mainline railway station (where Eurostar trains arrive from continental Europe) provides easy access to the Royal Festival Hall and all the other buildings of the South Bank Centre. From there, you can also easily reach the London Eye Ferris wheel and the Saatchi Gallery. The nicest way to get to Tate Modern is by crossing the Millennium Bridge from St Paul's. However, it's also reasonably close to London Bridge station, from where you can also reach the London Dungeons, the Fashion and Textile Museum, City Hall and, eventually, Tower Bridge.

LAMBETH

IMPERIAL WAR MUSEUM Map pp416-17

☎ 7416 5320 or 09001 600140; www.iwm.org.uk; Lambeth Rd SE1; admission free; ☉ 10am-6pm; tube Lambeth North/Southwark

Surprisingly, you can be a committed pacifist and still appreciate a visit to the Imperial War Museum. That's because it provides a good lesson in modern history (and because the quote from Plato on one of its walls unfortunately has been proven correct: 'Only the dead have seen the end of war').

So don't be misled by the initial impression of planes, tanks and other military hardware parked in the entrance hall or suspended in the atrium of this huge former hospital. A large percentage of the museum's six levels is given over to exploring the human and social cost of the conflict; and although the focus is supposedly on military action involving British or Commonwealth troops during the 20th century, 'war' is given a wide interpretation here. A couple of floors above popular exhibits like the Trench Experience, where you walk through the grim day-to-day reality of life on

155

Neighbourhoods – Along the South Bank

the Somme front line in WWI, and the Blitz Experience, where you cower inside a mock bomb shelter during a WWII air raid and then emerge through ravaged East End streets (both in the basement), you will find a picture of Nelson Mandela being sworn in as South Africa's first black president after the long war of apartheid. Photographer Kevin Carter's infamous shot of a starving Sudanese child being stalked by a vulture adorns another wall, in an illustration of how often wars have induced famine in sub-Saharan Africa.

Of course, there's still a large military bent in parts, with various exhibits discussing the two World Wars, Korea, Vietnam, the Cold War and other crises since 1945. The Secret War gallery goes behind the James Bond mythology to study the role of spies and Special Forces, while another area is devoted to war paintings, including works by Stanley Spencer and John Singer Sargent.

However, the two most outstanding, and moving, sections are the extensive Holocaust Exhibition (not recommended for under 16s) and a stark new gallery devoted to genocide, featuring a 30-minute film (certificate 12) on crimes against humanity in Cambodia, Yugoslavia and Rwanda.

It's all very well done, but likely to have you racing to the **Tibetan Peace Garden**, in the surrounding grounds, for a bit of quiet contemplation.

LAMBETH PALACE Map pp416-17
Lambeth Palace Rd SE1; tube Lambeth North

The red-brick Tudor gatehouse next door to the church of St Mary-at-Lambeth leads to Lambeth Palace, the London residence of the Archbishop of Canterbury. Although the palace is not usually open to the public, the gardens occasionally are; check with a TIC for details (p395).

MUSEUM OF GARDENING HISTORY Map pp416-17
☎ 7401 8865; www.museumgardenhistory.org; Lambeth Rd SE1; admission free, £3 donation requested; ⏲ 10.30am-5pm Mon-Fri & Sun Feb-mid-Dec; tube Lambeth North

OK, we've had comedy, cooking and even, er, golf; now it's gardening that is the new rock 'n' roll. True? Well, maybe, but in a city holding out the broad attractions of Kew Gardens (p200), the Museum of Gardening History is more of a niche destination for the seriously green-fingered. Established in 1977 in the former church of St Mary-at-Lambeth, essentially to save the building from demolition, it still feels as if it's

Top Five – Along the South Bank
- London Eye (opposite)
- Millennium Bridge (p160)
- Saatchi Gallery (opposite)
- Shakespeare's Globe (p161)
- Tate Modern (p160)

squatting the premises and could pick up and move its collection of hoes, rakes and watering cans within 24 hours. (An appeal is underway to raise money for central heating and other renovations, which might improve matters.)

The museum has one major trump card, however: the charming knot garden in the churchyard. It's a replica of a 17th-century formal garden, with topiary hedges clipped into an intricate design and interspersed with wild daffodils, old roses and herbaceous perennials. Hopefully, by the time you read this, it will have recovered from the unwanted attentions of a now-deceased fox, who found some of its plants as irresistible as catnip and rolled all over them.

Back inside, keen gardeners will enjoy the showcases on the lives and work of the 17th-century Tradescants, the father and son who were gardeners to Charles I and Charles II, respectively (and both enthusiastic collectors of exotic plants from around the globe). Bill and Ben the Flowerpot men (from a classic kids' TV show), plus the garden gnome in the likeness of PM Tony Blair, might also raise wry smiles.

FLORENCE NIGHTINGALE MUSEUM Map pp426-7
☎ 7620 0374; www.florence-nightingale.co.uk; 2 Lambeth Palace Rd SE1; family/senior, student & child/adult £10/3.60/4.80; ⏲ 10am-5pm Mon-Fri, 11.30am-4.30pm Sat & Sun; tube Westminster/Waterloo

A place of pilgrimage for nurses, it's hard not to feel that the Florence Nightingale Museum at St Thomas's Hospital could be edgier and thereby pitch itself to a wider audience more confidently. After all, as the mother of professional nursing, Nightingale (1820-1910) was one of the first modern celebrities – of whom baseball-card type photos were sold – and a good deal more contrary than her public image as a ministering angel admits. Fiercely intellectual and political, she persuaded Secretary of State for War, Sidney Herbert, to let her lead a team of nurses to the Scutari hospital in Turkey during the 1854–56 Crimean War. There, with a little help from the *Times'* first foreign correspondent, William Howard Russell, she established her reputation as 'the Lady of the

Lamp', who improved conditions for ordinary soldier patients. (Although – and this typical Nightingale contradiction goes unmentioned in the exhibition – she failed even to consider that blocked sewers might have contributed to the hospital's lack of hygiene.)

Chronicling this, and the way she subsequently used her fame to establish the first training school for nurses at St Thomas's in 1859, the museum is an important record of a woman who stamped her mark on history. However, it does tend towards hagiography.

SOUTH BANK CENTRE & WATERLOO

BRITISH AIRWAYS LONDON EYE
Map pp426-7
☎ 0870 500 0600; www.ba-londoneye.com; Jubilee Gardens SE1; adult/child 5-15/senior £11/5.50/10; ☽ 9.30am-8pm, to 9pm or 10pm on weekends in May, Jun & Sep, to 10pm Jul & Aug; tube Waterloo

On a clear day from the world's largest Ferris wheel you can see 25 miles in every direction – as far as Windsor to the west and, to the east, nearly out to sea. But it's not just its size and range that make the 135m-tall London Eye, also known as the Millennium Wheel, so immensely appealing. The 32 glass-enclosed gondolas glide slowly and gracefully as the wheel takes 30 minutes to rotate completely, so passengers (up to 25 in each capsule) really get time to take in the experience.

You buy tickets from the office behind the wheel, but the queues get very long, so either arrive very early, or better still, book ahead. You will still need to arrive 30 minutes before your 'flight' to pick up advance tickets.

Original plans were for the wheel to remain on site until 2005 and then be moved. However, for the moment it's staying put, giving the riverside an uplifting, carnival feel.

COUNTY HALL Map pp426-7
tube Westminster/Waterloo

Directly across Westminster Bridge from the Houses of Parliament, this magnificent building with its curved façade and colonnades was once home to the London County Council and then the renamed (1965) Greater London Council, before it was shut by PM Margaret Thatcher in 1986.

There's a vast aquarium in the basement of the Hall, a museum devoted to the work of the artist Salvador Dalí, two hotels and a restaurant (p158).

London Eye, South Bank (left)

SAATCHI GALLERY Map pp426-7
☎ 7823 2363 or 0870 1160 278 for advance tickets; www.saatchi-gallery.co.uk; County Hall, Westminster Bridge Rd SE1; adult/senior & student £8.50/£6.50; ☽ 10am-6pm, 10am-10pm Fri & Sat; tube Westminster/Waterloo

A roll call of the greatest hits of the so-called Young British Art (YBA) movement, the Saatchi Gallery caused a typical minor ruckus on its opening in 2003. Art critics declared that Damien Hirst's *Away from the Flock* (a sheep in formaldehyde in a fish tank) and Tracey Emin's *My Bed* (littered and unmade) were so o-v-e-r, darling, but were proved wrong as the public queued to see the sheep, the bed, Ron Mueck's *Dead Dad* and others.

If you were new to the provocative, in-yer-face oeuvre of YBA (which was first referred to as such in 1992 and probably peaked with 1997's Sensation exhibition) this would be a perfect introduction. Adman and art collector Charles Saatchi has had an uncanny ability to pick the works that would define an era, and acquisitions transferred from storage or from his smaller West London gallery include Chris Ofili's *The Holy Virgin Mary* (paint, paper, glitter and elephant dung), Marcus Harvey's huge *Myra* (the face of Moors child-murderer Myra Hindley replicated from thousands of stencilled child handprints), and Sarah Lucas's *Au*

Top Five Romantic London
- Kissing in the back of a black cab
- A squeeze on top of the London Eye
- Indulging in a champagne picnic on Hampstead Heath on a summer's evening
- Watching fireworks from Primrose Hill on Bonfire Night
- Shopping together for lingerie in Agent Provocateur

Naturel (two melons and a bucket, plus two oranges and a cucumber, arranged side-by-side like a naked couple on a mattress).

The list, with its large concentration on conceptual art, includes Hirst's rather wordily named *The Physical Impossibility of Death in the Mind of Someone Living* (a shark in a fish tank) and *A Thousand Years* (a dead cow's head being eaten by maggots). These sit alongside works by Gavin Turk, Jake & Dinos Chapman and Hiroshi Sugimoto. Other highlights include Ron Mueck's aforementioned translucent sculpture of his father's corpse, in miniature but otherwise spookily hyper-realistic, and Richard Wilson's *20:50*, an overwhelming oil-filled room. (People wander around asking, 'What's that smell?' It's this room.)

Much of this output is world-famous now, but that familiarity needn't breed contempt. So if you've followed the fortunes of Britart closely, or even seen these works before, it's worth coming, because it feels just like visiting old friends. The small percentage of lesser-known pieces doesn't really add much, although the grandiloquent Edwardian surrounds of County Hall, while not strictly an aesthetic match, certainly give the permanent collection and rolling special exhibitions room to breath.

DALÍ UNIVERSE Map pp426-7

☎ 7620 2720; www.daliuniverse.com; County Hall, Westminster Bridge Rd SE1, entrance on Albert Embankment; adult/child aged 3-9/child aged 10-16/senior & student/family £1/4.95/7.50/8.50/24; ☺ 10am-5.30pm; tube Westminster/Waterloo

Just like the Saatchi Gallery's Young British Artists, the Spanish surrealist Dalí was a masterful self-publicist. His impish, moustachioed face frequently crops up in his own works, and as he himself notes in the tunnel of quotes leading to Dalí Universe's main gallery: 'Modesty is not exactly my speciality.' Entering the main room, with its black ceiling and floor, black and mirrored walls and low lighting, is kinda like stepping into the artist's deliciously twisted subconscious. Here, in Europe's largest collection of Dalí's work, his regular leitmotifs, including melted watches, fire, crutches and drawers, appear in themed areas: Sensuality & Femininity, Religion & Mythology, and Dreams & Fantasy. There are more than 500 works displayed, including his famous Mae West Lips Sofa, the backdrop he painted for Hitchcock's film *Spellbound*, and one of his Lobster Telephones, making this the place for serious Dalí fans and the merely curious alike.

LONDON AQUARIUM Map pp426-7

☎ 7967 8000; www.londonaquarium.co.uk; County Hall, Westminster Bridge Rd SE1, entrance on Albert Embankment; adult/child aged 3-14/senior & student/family £8.75/5.25/6.50/25; ☺ 10am- 6pm; tube Westminster/Waterloo

If you prefer to see fish tanks filled with fish, rather than Damien Hirst's pickled cows or sheep, skip the Saatchi Gallery and head for this, one of Europe's largest aquariums. Huge tanks filled with sharks are complemented by fish tanks organised according to different marine environments – you walk between them in long, darkened corridors. But, wait, what's this in the foyer? Looks like the aquarium couldn't resist a little Britart-style fun after all, with a flooded Ford Ka turned into a fish bowl and called…Karp.

SOUTH BANK CENTRE Map pp426-7

A collection of concrete hulks on the southern London landscape, the South Bank Centre is one of those cultural developments that must have seemed like a good idea at the time. That time was from the late 1950s to the late 1970s, when the architectural world was still in thrall to brutalist modernism.

The **Royal Festival Hall** (☎ 7960 4242; www.rfh.org.uk; Belvedere Rd SE1; tube Waterloo) was already on the site, having been erected to cheer up a glum postwar populace as part of the 1951 Festival of Britain. The other temporary Festival of Britain structures around it were demolished, leaving space for the eyesores to come. A venue today for opera, classical, jazz and choral music, the Royal Festival Hall's slightly curved, glass and Portland Stone façade have always won it greater acceptance among Londoners than its contemporary neighbours. A £60 million facelift already underway has seen the opening of new pedestrian walkways and a new outdoor café in Festival Square, which joins its more formal **People's Palace** restaurant (p241) as a place within the RFH to eat. Further renovations mean the Royal Festival Hall will be closed for 18 months from summer 2005.

In the meantime, there are still frequent recitals in the foyer, and every year there, usually in autumn, you can also see the excellent World Press Photo awards – all for free. Another yearly event to watch out for is the eclectic Meltdown Festival of music, dance and performance in June, where a guest curator puts together their fantasy festival. Past curators have included Laurie Anderson, David

Bowie, David Byrne, Nick Cave, Lee 'Scratch' Perry and Robert Wyatt. Admission charges depend on the gig you want to see.

The smaller **Queen Elizabeth Hall**, to the north-east, and the **Purcell Room** host classical and jazz concerts. Their concrete walls are in need of a good clean and there's a real skateboarders' hang-out underneath their elevated floor. However, they are also due to be developed in 2006.

Tucked almost out of sight under the arches of Waterloo Bridge is the **National Film Theatre** (NFT; ☎ 7633 0274 information or 7928 3232 bookings; www.bfi.org.uk/nft; South Bank SE1; tube Waterloo), completed in 1958 and now screening some 2000 films a year. Largely a repertory or arthouse theatre, it runs regular retrospectives and is also one of the venues for the London Film Festival in November. Most excitingly, it also previews some major releases, usually accompanied by a talk with the director or one of the stars. Its list of past guests include Pedro Almodovar, Robert Altman, Steve Buscemi, Ethan Hawke, Ang Lee, Spike Lee, Mike Leigh, Kevin Spacey (unforgettably hilarious), Tim Roth, Ray Winstone, Denzel Washington and many, many more. On a more down-to-earth level, there's a charming café.

Next door to the NFT, the **Museum of the Moving Image** has been closed and will be only reopened (this time as a space for temporary film exhibitions) after the British Film Institute builds a new film centre. This new centre is only in the initial planning stages.

The **Riverside Walk Market**, with prints and second-hand books, takes place immediately in front of the NFT under the arches of the bridge. In summer, this leafy walkway really can feel like parts of Paris's Left Bank (p334 for details).

The **Hayward Gallery** (☎ 7261 0127 information or 7960 4242 bookings; www.sbc.org.uk; Belvedere Rd SW1; adult/concession £8-10/£6-8; ☷ 10am-6pm Mon & Thu-Sun, 10am-8pm Tue & Wed) has always been generally considered an enormously ugly piece of 'brutalist' architecture, but at least now it has a new foyer. If you're not a fan of brutalist buildings, perhaps the best thing to do is to get inside quick, where the fairly bland interior spaces act as an excellent hanging space for modern art and have made it London's leading contemporary and 20th-century art gallery. This is where you'll find major international exhibitions. Admission prices vary according to what's on.

The **Royal National Theatre** (☎ 7452 3000; www.nationaltheatre.org.uk; South Bank SE1; tube Waterloo) is the nation's flagship theatre complex, comprising three auditoria: the Cottesloe, Lyttelton and Olivier. Designed in 1976 by the modernist architect Denys Lasdun, and later dismissed by self-proclaimed architecture critic Prince Charles as resembling a 'disused power station', the reinforced concrete structure underwent a £42 million modernisation in the late 1990s. Backstage tours cost £5 for adult, £4.25 for seniors & students, and depart three times a day Monday to Saturday; for performance details p313.

A short walk eastwards along the South Bank is **Gabriel's Wharf**, a cluster of twee craft shops, snack bars, cafés and restaurants.

The **Jubilee Gardens**, near the London Eye, are also due to be extended towards the South Bank Centre and Hungerford Bridge, adding to a major revamp of the entire area, which hopefully will see the South Bank Centre's reputation massively improved.

LONDON IMAX CINEMA Map pp426-7

☎ 7902 1234; www.bfi.org.uk/imax; 1 Charlie Chaplin Walk SE1; adult/child aged 5-16/senior & student £7.50/£4.95/£6.20, plus £1 advance booking fee, additional films £4.20; ☷ 7 screenings from1-9pm, 2 additional screenings at 10.30am & 11.45am Fri & Sat; tube Waterloo

There's nothing new about the films shown at the London IMAX Cinema; they're the usual mix of 2D and IMAX 3D documentaries about travel, space and wildlife, lasting from 40 minutes to 1½ hours. At this British Film Institute venue, size matters: the 458-seat cinema is the largest in Europe, with a screen 10 storeys high and 26m wide.

OXO TOWER WHARF Map pp426-7

tube Waterloo

Although the Art Deco tower is no longer the headquarters for the stock cube company Oxo, its windows and neon lights are still shaped to spell out this British institution's name across the city. Restored in 1996 after falling into disrepair, the building now houses apartments, a small cluster of designer shops that are great to browse through and a couple of restaurants: the **River Walk Restaurant** on the 2nd floor, and the **Oxo Tower Restaurant** on the 8th (p240). Also on the 8th floor is a **public viewing gallery**, where you can enjoy fabulous views of the Thames and the City.

BANKSIDE

BANKSIDE GALLERY Map pp426-7

☎ 7928 7521; www.banksidegallery.com; 48 Hopton St SE1; admission free; ⏲ 10am-5pm Tue-Fri, 11am-5pm Sat & Sun; tube St Paul's/ Waterloo

In a blind spot to the west of its huge neighbour, this tiny gallery has, comically, had to erect a sign saying 'Tate Modern next door' to prevent repeated cases of mistaken identity. The Bankside Gallery is home to the Royal Watercolour Society and the Royal Society of Painter-Printmakers, and it might be worth making a deliberate detour if you're interested in actually buying some contemporary art. At its constantly changing exhibitions of watercolours, prints and engravings, decent-sized pieces can go for less than £200. Call ahead for the occasional Artists' Perspectives, where artists talk about their work.

TATE MODERN Maps pp426-7 & 432-3

☎ 7401 5120 information or 7887 8008 tickets; www.tate.org.uk; Queen's Walk SE1; admission free, special exhibitions £3-10; ⏲ 10am-6pm Sun-Thu, 10am-10pm Fri & Sat; tube St Paul's/London Bridge

Deservedly the most popular of the Millennium Projects erected in Britain to celebrate the year 2000, Tate Modern is as much about the gallery building as it is about the collection of 20th-century art inside. Leading Swiss architects Herzog & de Meuron created an instant icon with their transformation of the empty Bankside Power Station – leaving the building's central chimney, adding a two-storey glass box to the roof and, perhaps most importantly, utilising the vast Turbine Hall as an unforgettably dramatic entrance space. When the two-storey glass box is lit at night, it makes Tate Modern an aesthetic beacon, but it's also a gallery that celebrates its industrial history. Little wonder it attracted 5.2 million visitors in its first year, becoming the second favourite attraction in London after the long-established British Museum.

From the Turbine Hall, escalators and lifts take art lovers up to the exhibits. Many works,

including Rebecca Horn's *Concert for Anarchy* (a piano hanging upside down from the ceiling) and Picasso's blue-period *Girl in a White Chemise*, are overspills from the Tate (now Tate Britain) gallery at Millbank, which had well and truly reached capacity. Meanwhile, a series of block-colour paintings by Mark Rothko have finally been given the dedicated space that the artist insisted on. These, and other works in the permanent collection – from painters such as Georges Braque, Roy Lichtenstein, Matisse, Pollock, Warhol, sculptors and installations artists like Joseph Beuys, Duchamp, Damien Hirst, Sarah Lucas and Claes Oldenburg, and video artists like Bill Viola (mesmerising) – are arranged according to theme. Two galleries – Landscape, Matter, Environment, and Still Life, Object, Real Life – are on level 3; History, Memory, Society, and Nude, Action, Body, are on level 5.

Special exhibitions, which have included shows by sculptors Louise Bourgeois, Anish Kapoor and Paul McCarthy, take place on the front lawn, in the Turbine Hall and on level 4.

Audioguides, with four different tours, are available for £1. Free **guided highlights tours** depart at 11am, noon, 2pm and 3pm daily.

The **cafés** (⏲ 10am-5.30pm Sun-Thu, 10am-9.30pm Fri-Sat) on levels 2 and 7, plus the espresso bar on level 4, are renowned for their fabulous views over the Thames. There are also tall windows in the galleries where one can gaze out, plus places to relax overlooking the Turbine Hall.

The **Tate-to-Tate** ferry operates between the Bankside Pier at Tate Modern and the new Millennium Pier at sister museum Tate Britain, stopping en route at the London Eye. Services run 10am to 6pm daily, at 40 minute intervals. A three-stop ticket (purchased on board) costs £4.50 (discounts available). One of the ferries is a Damien Hirst dot painting, so you can't miss it.

MILLENNIUM BRIDGE Map pp432-3

Although it nowadays provides a smooth river crossing, the Millennium Bridge will long be known to Londoners as simply the wobbly bridge. Designed by Norman Foster and Anthony Caro, its low-slung frame looks pretty spectacular, particularly when it's lit up at night with fibre-optics – the so-called 'blade of light' effect. But it's still hard to forget this footbridge's abortive opening in June 2000. It was closed after just three days, when it began to sway alarmingly under the weight and movement of pedestrian traffic. A year and a half plus £5 million worth of dampeners later, it reopened and has since conveyed crowds

Top Five London Views

- Buckingham Palace from the footbridge over St James's Park Lake
- From the London Eye
- From Waterloo Bridge (preferably at sunset)
- From the dome of St Paul's Cathedral
- From the top-floor café of Tate Modern

without incident between Peter's Hill (in front of St Paul's) on the Thames' northern bank and Tate Modern and Bankside on the South.

SHAKESPEARE'S GLOBE Map pp432-3

☎ 7902 1500; www.shakespeares-globe.org; 21 New Globe Walk SE; exhibition entrance adult/child under15/senior & student/family £8/5.50/6.50/24 including guided tour; ⏰ 10am-5pm, tours at 9am-noon May-Sep, 10am-5pm Oct-Apr; tube London Bridge

For most of the 20th century, high-school students of English were taught the works of William Shakespeare as high culture, forced to reverentially pore over Macbeth's tragedy or commit to memory Hamlet's soliloquy. However, as has been increasingly recognised in more recent years (Baz Luhrmann's *Romeo + Juliet* and the reduced Shakespeare company being just two examples; p314), the Bard was essentially a popular writer. The world's best-known playwright was always willing to play to the gallery, by peppering his scripts with innuendo.

They know this at the rebuilt **Globe Theatre**, where you can see Shakespeare as he was meant to be performed: with cross-dressing actors and heckling condoned. The circular venue itself is only 200 metres from the original Globe Theatre, which Shakespeare helped found in 1599 and where he worked until 1611. And it's a faithful replica, with a central arena left open to the elements, housing the stage and 500 'groundlings' (standing viewers). That means that artistic director Mark Rylance and his team of actors perform up close and personal with both the standing and seated audience, without stage lighting or sound systems. (There are a few downsides to this set-up, such as the planes flying overhead and the two 'authentic' Corinthian pillars that obstruct much of the view from the seats closest to the stage. However, in the cold of winter performances move to the indoor **Inigo Jones Theatre**, a replica of a Jacobean playhouse connected to the Globe.) For ticket details p314.

If you can't make time to catch *Richard III, The Taming of the Shrew* or any of the other Elizabethan or contemporary plays on the programme, you can walk the boards and learn about the Globe's history with a daytime guided tour of the theatre and the marvellous exhibition below. The original theatre was closed in 1642 after the English Civil War was won by the Puritans, who regarded theatres as dens of iniquity. Its reconstruction became

Shakespeare's Globe (left)

a decades-long labour of love for American actor (later film director) Sam Wanamaker, who helped raise the necessary money, but sadly died three years before the 1997 opening night. The building has been painstakingly constructed with 600 oak pegs (there's not a nail or a screw in the house), specially fired Tudor bricks, and thatching reeds from Norfolk; even the plaster contains goat hair, lime and sand, as it did in Shakespeare's time. The **Globe Café** and **Globe Restaurant** are open for lunch and dinner till 10pm or 11pm.

ROSE THEATRE Map pp432-3

☎ 7593 0026; www.rosetheatre.org.uk; 56 Park St SE1; adult/child aged 5-15/senior & student/family £4/2/3/10; ⏰ 11am-5pm Apr-Sep, 10am-5pm Oct-Mar; tube London Bridge

Though nothing of the original Globe Theatre has ever been found, the foundations of the nearby Rose Theatre, built in 1587, were discovered in 1989 beneath an office building at Southwark Bridge. A 25-minute sound-and-light show at the excavation site takes place every 30 minutes daily.

VINOPOLIS Map pp432-3

☎ 0870 444 4777; www.vinopolis.co uk; 1 Bank End, Park St SE1; adult/under 15/senior £12.50/free/£11.50; ⏰ noon-9pm Mon, noon-6pm Tue-Thu & Sun, noon-9pm Fri & Sat; tube London Bridge

Half trendy wine bar, half rustic vineyard in appearance, Vinopolis provides a slick tour of the world of wine. You really need to follow the audioguide, narrated by British wine expert Oz Clarke, to make sense of the exhibits, so it's not suitable for a flying visit (allow about two hours). However, those with time and patience – who want to know a little more about wine production and regional varieties from France to South Africa and Chile to Spain – will find it interesting. There's the chance to have a little fun sitting on a Vespa for a virtual tour through the Italian hills of Chianti, or 'flying' over Australia's Hunter Valley in the mock-up of an airline cabin – but be warned about the shameless advertorial for Bombay Sapphire gin.

Since it's the kind of place you hang on to one glass as you enjoy five different wine tastings during the tour (thus inevitably mixing wines or mixing wine and water) this is not the best place for wine purists. They would probably be more interested in the dedicated wine-tasting evenings, gourmet food and wine shop and the nearby branch of the wine retailer Majestic. An onsite restaurant, **Cantina Vinopolis**, opens for lunch daily and for dinner Monday to Saturday.

Entry prices for the tour are slightly cheaper (adult £11, senior £10) on Tuesday, Wednesday and Friday. Those under 18 are given fruit juice to sample, as opposed to wine.

CLINK PRISON MUSEUM Map pp432-3
☎ 7378 1558; www.clink.co.uk; 1 Clink St SE1; adult/senior, student & child/family £4/3/£9; ☽ 10am-6pm; tube London Bridge

Having entered the English vernacular through the expression 'in the clink' ('in jail'), this famous prison turns out to be smaller and less of a revelation than its enduring reputation might suggest. It was the private jail from about 1503 of the bishops of Winchester, who had owned vast estates and wielded absolute power on the South Bank of the Thames since the Norman conquest of Britain in 1066. The bishops ran the notorious Bankside brothels and the Clink was often used to jail prostitutes who displeased their masters, alongside debtors, thieves and even actors. It was burned down during the Gordon Riots in 1780, but hadn't been used for a century in any case.

The musty-smelling museum, with its sawdust-covered floors, details the wretched life of the prisoners who were forced to pay for their own food and accommodation and sometimes had to resort to catching and eating mice. But really, there is not much to it.

Guided tours are £1/free (adult/child) but must be booked in advance.

WINCHESTER PALACE Map pp432-3
Just up the road from the Clink, you'll find the remains of the bishops' grand palace. Indeed, there's little more than a 14th-century rose window carved in stone from the Great Hall, high above you, and parts of the flooring, below. The palace was initially built for bishop William Giffard in 1109 and remained home to subsequent bishops for more than 500 years, before being converted into a prison for royalists under Cromwell in 1642. The ruins are visible from the street.

GOLDEN HINDE Map pp432-3
☎ 7403 0123; www.goldenhinde.co.uk; Cathedral St SE1; adult/child/senior & student/family £2.75/2/2.35/8; ☽ 9am-5.30pm; tube London Bridge

Stepping aboard this replica of Sir Francis Drake's famous Tudor ship instantly instils admiration for the admiral and his rather short (generally 5ft 4in) crew. It's a tiny galleon, just 37m long, yet it was home to Drake and company for more than three years, from 1577 to 1580, as they became the first sailors to circumnavigate the globe. Visitors wandering stooped around this reconstruction, which is moored in St Mary Overie Dock, must also marvel at how the taller, modern-day crew managed to take the replica to sea for more than 20 years continuously from its launch in 1973 (and still occasionally do).

Tickets are purchased at the card and souvenir shop just opposite the ship. Theme parties are organised, or you can spend the night aboard for £33 per person, including a supper of stew and bread and a breakfast of bread and cheese. Ring ☎ 0870 011 8700 to book.

SOUTHWARK CATHEDRAL Map pp432-3
☎ 7367 6700; www.dswark.org/cathedral; Montague Close SE1; admission free, £4 donation requested; ☽ 8am-6pm; tube London Bridge

Its fans call it the 'Cinderella of English cathedrals' and complain it's overlooked, but Southwark Cathedral simply *is* smaller and much less impressive than Westminster Abbey and St Paul's. What's nice about it, though, is its seeming willingness to move with the times. So, for example, it has linked events in history by placing a **plaque to actor Sam Wanamaker** (1919–93), the force behind the rebuilding of the nearby Globe Theatre, right next to a green alabaster **memorial to William Shakespeare**, who worked at the original Elizabethan theatre. And just as its northern choir aisle houses the macabre **medieval tomb**, where you can see the ribs of a stone corpse through a shroud, equally the cathedral has made the effort to erect a **Marchioness memorial** near the door, remembering the night in 1989 when a Thames pleasure cruiser hit a dredger and sank with 51 passengers near Southwark Bridge.

Such continuity is possible because there has been a church on this site since at least 1086. The earliest surviving part of the building is the atmospheric retrochoir, which was part of the Priory of St Mary Overie (from 'St Mary over the Water') and dates from the 13th century. However, after the Reformation, the priory was abandoned for use as a bakery and a pigsty. By the 1830s much of the building had fallen into decay, so a lot of it today is Victorian – the nave was rebuilt in 1897. In 1905, the church became an Anglican cathedral.

Audioguides, featuring Prunella Scales, Tommy Steele and Zoë Wanamaker (Sam's actress daughter) and lasting about 40 minutes, are available (adult/child/senior & student £2.50/1.25/£2). Evensong is at 5.30pm weekdays, 4pm Saturday and 3pm on Sunday.

Adjacent to the cathedral is a visitors' centre, containing an exhibition of local history called the **Long View of London** (adult/child/senior & student £3/1.50/2.50; with audioguide adult/child/senior & student/family £5/2.50/4/£12.50; 10am-6pm Mon-Sat, 11am-5pm Sun). Sadly, although it was only completed in 2000, the webcam with views from the tower and several other multimedia displays seem to have been broken when we visited.

A restaurant (10am to 5pm) and shop is open to visitors, but the gardens outside are where you'll find neighbourhood workers lunching in summer.

BOROUGH & BERMONDSEY
BRAMAH MUSEUM OF TEA & COFFEE Map pp432-3
 7403 5650; 40 Southwark St SE1; adult/child/senior & student/family £4/3.50/10; 10am-6pm; tube London Bridge

This is a pleasant, nostalgic place to while away half an hour – provided your visit does not coincide with the arrival of a tour group. Trace the route by which tea conquered the world, making its ways to the sitting rooms of Holland and England and further afield from the eastern seaports of China. Alternatively, simply enjoy the chintzy cornucopia of tea- and coffee-drinking equipment, from floral teacups and silverware to Japanese cans of tea.

After a quality cuppa, served with an egg timer so the tea's brewed just right, you'll realise they just *don't* make them like they used to. Having a rejuvenating mug of coffee here is also a more singular experience than being at Starbucks.

OLD OPERATING THEATRE MUSEUM & HERB GARRET Map pp432-3
 7955 4791; www.thegarret.org.uk; 9a St Thomas St SE1; adult/child/senior & student/family £4/2.50/3/10; 10.30am-5pm; tube London Bridge

In some ways, the old operating theatre of St Thomas's Hospital is more of a toe-curling experience than the London Dungeon (p164), because its allusions to blood and guts are uncontrived. This former Victorian surgical theatre is not for the very squeamish. However, others will be compelled to see the rough-and-ready conditions under which simple 19th-century operations took place – without antiseptic or anaesthetic, and on a wooden table in what looks like a modern lecture hall. Early medical instruments are on display, accompanied by discussions on body-snatching, where the medical profession bought dug-up corpses to practice on. Explanations are also given as to how, without anaesthetic, surgeons had to perform quickly on living patients; one minute to complete an amputation was reckoned about right. Check the museum's website, because sometimes quasi-demonstrations of such 'speed surgery' are held. (Honestly, you'll leave this place praising the heavens for the progress since made in medical techniques.)

There's a nod to alternative therapies in the adjoining herb garret (which, actually, you walk through before the Operating Theatre Museum). The hospital's former apothecary is now hung with bunches of herbs and explanations of their perceived powers. Be warned, though, that there are also human organs kept in jars here.

This small, quirky but highly recommended museum sits at the top of 32 narrow and rickety stairs, so unfortunately there is no disabled access.

ST OLAF HOUSE Map pp432-3
This small office block fronting the Thames on Tooley St (the name of which is actually a corruption of St Olave's St) was built in 1932, and is one of London's finest Art Deco buildings. Note the gold mosaic lettering on the front and the bronze relief sculptures.

LONDON DUNGEON Map pp432-3

☎ 7403 7221 or 09001 600066 recorded information; www.thedungeons.com; 28-34 Tooley St SE1; adult/under 14/student & senior £14.50/£9.75/£12.75; 🕓 10am-6.30pm Apr-Sep, 10am-5.30pm Oct-Mar; tube London Bridge

Blood! Gore! Disease! At the London Dungeon, you'll experience the thrill of disgust at the true horror London can offer. And that's only the length of the queue. Seriously, if you want to join the other screamers at this delightfully camped-up gorefest, it's a good idea to buy tickets online beforehand. Otherwise, you're generally looking at a tortured hour or more standing in line.

The ridiculously popular dungeon is basically a souped-up house of horrors, where you walk and are transported by fairyground-ride boat through a landscape of London's grue-some history. Here you can watch people die of plague or hang on the Tyburn gallows, listen to Anne Boleyn before her head was deftly sepa-rated from her shoulders, and wonder at the assortment of ingenious methods of torture. You'll see a mock French guillotine in action and prostitutes with their entrails hanging out after being mauled by Victorian serial killer Jack the Ripper. By the time Judgement Day arrives, you'll find yourself condemned to death and put aboard the executioner's barge for a 'final trip' through Traitors' Gate. At the Great Fire of London exhibit, you'll run – literally – through a gauntlet of flames.

As a spectator, it's nice to see that you're keeping all those actors in steady jobs.

BRITAIN AT WAR EXPERIENCE Map pp432-3

☎ 7403 3171; www.britainatwar.co.uk; 64-66 Tooley St SE1; adult/under 15/senior & student/family £7.50/4/5/16; 🕓 10am-6pm Apr-Sep, 10am-5pm Oct-Mar; tube London Bridge

Next to the mega-successful London Dun-geon, the Britain at War Experience is much lower key; its old-fashioned mock-ups of bombsites and wartime bars have pathos rather than whiz-bang appeal. From the moment you descend by lift to find man-nequins sheltering from bombs in a London Underground station, you feel like you're in a low-budget, vintage BBC TV set, and indeed later there is a BBC Radio Studio allowing you to hear broadcasts by Churchill and Hitler.

Wartime newspapers sit beside ration books and home front defence posters carrying the now famous warning that 'Careless talk costs lives'. Among these, the highlights are the opportunity to sit in an 'Anderson' domestic air-raid shelter listening to the sounds of an aerial bombardment and a chance to watch colour newsreel footage of the era (always a compelling reminder for postwar generations who tend to think of the past in black and white). The **Imperial War Museum's Blitz Experience** (p155) is a much more professional-looking set. Yet the final display here, in which a voice gives you the all-clear to run past a bombed shop, can unexpectedly raise the hairs on your neck.

HMS BELFAST Map pp432-3

☎ 7940 6300; www.hmsbelfast.org.uk; Morgan's Lane, Tooley St SE1; adult/under 16/senior & student £6/free/4.40; 🕓 10am-6pm Mar-Oct, 10am-5pm Nov-Feb; tube London Bridge

Moored in the middle of the Thames, HMS *Belfast* is a big toy that boys of all ages generally love. Of course, for most of its commissioned life this large, light cruiser had a rather more serious purpose than that. Launched in 1938 from the Belfast shipyard Harland & Wolff, it served in WWII, most noticeably in the Nor-mandy landings, and during the Korean War.

Now, as a branch of the Imperial War Mu-seum, it evokes a genuine sense of naval life, laying out everything from its operations room and bridge (where you can sit in the admiral's chair) to its boiler room and living quarters. You get to inspect the inner workings of the ship, in-cluding the galley, laundry and, more seriously, the onboard operating theatre. There's a video of the Battle of the North Cape, off Norway, in which the ship took part, and, on the open deck, there are 16 six-inch guns, whose sights you can peer through and pretend to aim.

You need to really concentrate on your Visi-tors Guide to find your way successfully around the eight zones on nine decks and platforms, although an alternative is to let your nose lead you and see what you find. Either way, you should be prepared for a lot of scrambling up and down steep ladders and steps.

FASHION & TEXTILE MUSEUM Map pp432-3

☎ 7403 0222; www.ftmlondon.org; 83 Bermondsey St SE1; adult/student/family £16/4/6; 🕓 11am-5.15 pm (last entry) Tue-Sun; tube London Bridge

We're all dedicated followers of fashion these days, it seems, with the clothing industry hav-ing become one of the world's largest. And London – with its cutting-edge street style and designers like Stella McCartney, Alexander McQueen and Vivienne Westwood – is one of its sizzling hot centres. So this museum is particularly well placed and timely.

There are shades of architect Luis Baragan in the impossible-to-miss pink, lemon and orange exterior, actually designed by award-winning fellow Mexican Ricardo Legorreta. Inside, however, things are very cleverly arranged (with black drapings and low lighting, when we visited) so as not to detract from the displays.

It's not only glammed-up fashionistas tottering on their heels around the split-level interior, either. Suburban mums and daughters – and men – come to mooch over the outfits, too. The museum has no permanent collection, but will feature a rolling programme of special exhibitions. At its launch it showcased 20 or so designers' favourite frocks. Check for current shows via their website or phone.

CITY HALL Map pp432-3

☎ 7983 4100; www.london.gov.uk; The Queen's Walk, SE1; admission free; ☾ usually two weekends a month, ring for details; tube Tower Hill/London Bridge

You have to envy Ken Livingstone's luck with offices. In the early 1980s, as the leader of the Greater London Council, left-wing 'Red Ken' was ensconced in the palatial County Hall (home today to the Saatchi Gallery, see page 000). Now as London's Mayor and head of the Greater London Authority, he spends his days in this remarkable creation by Norman Foster and Ken Shuttleworth.

Nicknamed 'the egg' – or, more cheekily, 'the testicle' because of its globular shape – the glass-clad City Hall could also be likened to a spaceman in a helmet. Alternatively, it's the dome of Berlin's Reichstag pushed halfway sideways by a giant hand. The Reichstag was an earlier Foster design and he's transposed some of his ideas there to the egg. Symbolically transparent, especially when lit up at night, City Hall also has an interior spiral ramp ascending above the assembly chamber to the building's roof.

The building opens to the public on certain weekends of the year, during which visitors can tread the halls of power – or a few of them at least. It's possible to follow the ramp (or take a lift) to the 6th-floor meeting room and viewing gallery. Alternatively, one can follow another ramp curving down from the hollowed-out lobby to a basement exhibition hall, committee rooms and a café. From here, you head outside and ascend back to the riverbank via an open-air auditorium reminscent of a Greek assembly.

It's such a memorable experience, and the viewing gallery alone is impressive enough that you have to wonder why the building took a while to win over Mayor Livingstone, who initially disapproved of its design. Real

City Hall (left)

architecture groupies might also want to return to see the building illuminated at night, when the interior ramp is most apparent through the glass façade.

Security to enter the building is understandably tight, but the lines move reasonably quickly.

DESIGN MUSEUM Map pp432-3

☎ 7940 8790; www.designmuseum.org; 28 Shad Thames SE1; family/adult/senior & student £16/£6/£4; ☾ 10am-5.15pm Sat-Thu (last entry), 10am-8.30pm (last entry) Fri; tube Tower Hill/London Bridge

Aesthetic and ascetic in appearance, the 1930s-style white cube that is the Design Museum covers all aspects of contemporary product design. Faced with fairly limited space, director Alice Rawsthorn has decided to abandon the permanent collection of 20th- and 21st-century objects to make more room for special exhibitions over its three floors. However, parts of the museum's own collection of chairs (including ones by Charles and Ray Eames and Ludwig Mies van der Rohe), vacuum cleaners (including Dyson's cyclonic cleaner), record players, telephones and so on will continue to appear in themed displays annually. Recent exhibitions on Manolo Blahnik shoes, the best of European design, and chair design in the past 100 years give a flavour of what the museum does.

As with many museums of its ilk, its shop is a feature, with lavish coffee-table books on design and architecture, lamps, model chairs and scores of other curios. There are also two places to eat: the informal **Riverside Café** (☾ 11am-5.30pm Mon-Fri, 10.30am-5.30pm Sat & Sun), and the more formal **Blue Print Café**, which is actually a restaurant (p242).

165

THE EAST END

Eating p244; Sleeping p348; Shopping p329

Whitechapel, Jack the Ripper's former stomping ground, is now home to one of the city's most exciting contemporary art galleries.

A realm of almshouses and the birthplace of both the Salvation Army and the Barnardo's charity, the Victorian-era East End was the very definition of poverty. This was Jack the Ripper's haunt in the 1880s, when his serial murder of prostitutes had a nation almost paralysed with hysteria. Even in the early 20th century, American author Jack London found he couldn't get a cab willing to take him to Whitechapel and the East End was deliberately omitted from most maps of the time.

Naturally, it's changed a lot in the intervening 100 years – it's in the *A–Z* street map, for a start. And as recent gentrification has swept over Hoxton and the neighbouring City, signs of wealth have also started to trickle over into the areas around Whitechapel and Aldgate East. There's even been a growing focus on ramshackle Hackney, Dalston and Mile End (the subject of a famous song by the band Pulp during the mid-1990s Britpop era).

However, the east of London is still a predominantly working class area, and one particularly impressive legacy of this remains. The waves upon waves of poor immigrants who came here in search of jobs have given the place a brilliantly multicultural feel. While you can still see the houses of the French Huguenot silk weavers in nearby Spitalfields, from Whitechapel eastwards there are plenty of Bangladeshi restaurants, Italian and Jewish businesses and a vibrant Afro-Caribbean population in Hackney and Dalston.

For more about the history and culture of the East End, see London Royalty (p14) and Cockney (p28).

WHITECHAPEL

WHITECHAPEL BELL FOUNDRY Map pp432-3

☎ 7247 2599; www.whitechapelbellfoundry.co.uk; 32-34 Whitechapel Rd; 🕙 shop 9.30am-5pm Mon-Fri, tours 10am Sat; tours £8, children under 14 not allowed; tube Aldgate East

The oldest business in London, established nearby in 1570, this place can be said, literally, to resonate with history. It's the birthplace of the Liberty Bell in Philadelphia and the clock bells of Big Ben and St Paul's Cathedral, among others. After 11 September 2001, the foundry also cast a new bell for New York City's Trinity Church. The 1½-hour guided tours on Saturday offer a revealing insight into a distinguished old trade, but bookings are essential. During office hours, you can view a few small exhibits in the foyer or pick up souvenirs from the shop.

WHITECHAPEL ART GALLERY

Map pp432-3

☎ 7522 7888 or 7572 7878; www.whitechapel.org; 80-82 Whitechapel Rd; admission free; 🕙 11am-6pm Tue-Sun, 11am-9pm Wed; tube Aldgate East

Among the more interesting of London's contemporary art galleries, the Whitechapel hasn't just confined itself to exhibitions by established and emerging artists from Gary Hume and Liam Gillick to Frida Kahlo and Nan Goldin. It also regularly holds debates or talks by musicians and film-makers such as David Byrne and Robert Altman. Behind its Art Noveau façade and entry hall, you'll find revolving exhibitions of photography, painting, sculpture and video art, plus fundraising events, poetry readings and educational programmes. Check the programme online, but remember there's the very pleasant **Whitechapel Art Gallery Café** (p245), regardless of what's on.

ROYAL LONDON HOSPITAL ARCHIVES & MUSEUM Map pp432-3

☎ 7377 7608; www.brlcf.org.uk; St Philip's Church, Newark St E1; admission by donation; 🕙 10am-4.30pm Mon-Fri; tube Aldgate East

The Royal London Hospital was where the Elephant Man, Joseph Merrick, lived as a long-term patient. However, this small museum barely touches on Merrick's tale, perhaps to avoid creating a sideshow out of his tumour- and disease-ridden body. That leaves the existing exhibits – of old surgical instruments, nurses' uniforms and the history of the hospital itself – of more interest to medical professionals than to members of the general public.

AROUND WHITECHAPEL ROAD

Maps pp416-17 & 432-3

Within a few minutes' walk of Whitechapel tube there are a couple of other landmarks that students of modern history might like to see. First find the large **East London Mosque**; Fieldgate St runs parallel behind it, housing not only the decent restaurant **New Tayyab** (p245), but also **Tower House**. This is now a hostel for the homeless, but former residents have included Stalin, Lenin and author Jack London.

You're now also deep in Jack the Ripper territory. In fact, the serial killer's first victim, Mary Ann Nichols, was hacked to death on 31 August 1888 on what is now Durward St behind Whitechapel tube (see Ripping Yarns p168).

Along Whitechapel Rd itself, the criminal connections continue through the centuries. Just before the intersection with Cambridge Heath Rd sits the **Blind Beggar Pub** (☎ 7247 6195; 337 Whitechapel Rd), where the gangster Ronnie Kray notoriously shot dead George Cornell in 1966, in a turf war over control of the East End's organised crime. A barmaid witnessed the murder, and Kray ended up in the Old Bailey – and jail.

After the intersection with Cambridge Heath Rd, this traditionally poor area's history takes a more philanthropic turn, with a bust of **William Booth**, who established the Salvation Army around here in the 1860s, and the **Trinity Green Almshouses**, poor houses built for injured or retired sailors in 1695. The two rows of almshouses run at right angles away from the street, facing a village-type green; but please be considerate when peering through the fence as they are private homes today.

BETHNAL GREEN & HACKNEY

BETHNAL GREEN MUSEUM OF CHILDHOOD Map pp416-7

☎ 8980 2415; www.museumofchildhood.org.uk; Cambridge Heath & Old Ford Rds E2; admission free; 🕙 10am-5.50pm, closed Fri; tube Bethnal Green

The open hall of this Victorian-era building resounds with children's laughter and the clomping of tiny feet, as recent renovations have slightly increased the number of child-friendly, interactive exhibits. Kids can play on oversize dominos boards, dig castles in a sandpit or raid the dressing-up box – all of which costs £1.80. Alternatively, they can join nostalgic older visitors admiring vintage dolls

Top Five – East End

- Bethnal Green Museum of Childhood (below)
- Jack the Ripper trail (p168)
- Ragged School Museum (p168)
- Whitechapel Art Gallery (p166)
- William Morris Gallery (p169)

and rocking horses. ('You mean there were toys before Gameboy, grandma?')

Yes, it's true, and from carved ivory figures to teddy bears, from Meccano to Lego and from peep shows to video games, childhood artefacts from the 17th century to today are on display in this cheery museum. The upstairs gallery, decorated with wrought-iron railings, traces the stages of growing up and showcases toys from Africa, the Caribbean and Eastern Europe, in a reflection of Bethnal Green's multicultural make-up. It doesn't take very long to get around, but there's a café in the middle of the chequerboard ground floor where tuckered-out little tykes and adults can refuel.

HACKNEY MUSEUM Map pp416-7

☎ 8356 3500; www.hackney.gov.uk/hackney museum; Hackney Learning & Technology Centre, 1 Reading Lane E8; admission free; 🕙 9.30am-5.30pm Tue-Fri, 9.30am-8pm Thu, 10am-5pm Sat; rail Hackney Central

Surprisingly appealing, this recently rehoused museum traces the habitation and reflects the multicultural make-up of Hackney – one of the most ethnically diverse neighbourhoods in the UK. It looks like a funky stylist has had a say in the exhibits, as display boards feature translucent squares of the same colour and one case puts single souvenirs and effects from diverse ethnic communities behind square panes of glass – just as you'd expect to find in Elle Deco magazine. Even the ancient Saxon log boat, discovered on the marshes, has been placed in the floor under glass squares, above which sits a replica, which you can pretend to load.

Yet, the design is not so flashy as to interfere with your enjoyment of what's on show, from zoetropes and an early-20th-century locality map to an early pie 'n' mash shop and a hand with painted fingernails, such as you can have done in local, Vietnamese-run salons. There's a copy of the genre-defining London crime novel Yardie, which was published locally. Meanwhile, recorded oral histories can be listened to by

Ripping Yarns

Before the Washington Sniper, the Boston Strangler, Jeffrey Dahmer and Son of Sam came Jack the Ripper. In the terrible pantheon of serial killers, he probably wasn't the first in history. However, the Ripper – whoever he may have been – was the first multiple murderer of the media age, the first to wreak terror across a modern city, and so his legend lives on.

Certainly, 'legend' is the right term, because the actual facts of the Ripper case are often contested, clouded by fabrication or just plain unclear. For convenience's sake, it's generally accepted that he killed and mutilated five prostitutes in the back streets of the East End in 1888 – Mary Anne Nichols in Bucks Row (now Durward St) north of Whitechapel, Annie Chapman in Hanbury St (home to the Truman Brewery), Elizabeth Stride in Berner St (now Henriques St) south of Commercial Rd, Catherine Eddowes in Mitre Square near Aldgate and Mary Kelly in Miller's Court. However, serious scholars and amateur Ripperologists alike admit that the 'Whitechapel Murderer', or 'Leather Apron' as the killer was also known, might have been responsible for as few as four gory deaths or as many as eight.

At the time of the murders, the popular press was just starting to take hold; newspaper editors whipped their readers into a frenzy, sending a *frisson* through Victorian middle-class households with tales of this shadowy sex killer who mutilated and disembowelled his victims. The name 'Jack the Ripper' originates from letters allegedly written by the killer, sent to the police and published in newspapers, although this correspondence might actually have been sent by journalists themselves. Another parcel was sent to the head of a local vigilance committee. Inside was half a human kidney with a letter stating that it was Catherine Eddowes'.

The surgical precision with which the murderer dissected his victims led to the supposition that he might have had medical training. But despite various later theories linking the killings with everyone from Queen Victoria's grandson, the Duke of Clarence, to Polish poisoner Severin Klosowski (aka George Chapman), the killings stopped abruptly in November 1888 and Scotland Yard never got their man. Which, of course, just adds to the mythology.

The police list of serious suspects, before the case was shut in 1892, included Dr Montague John Druitt, a barrister and doctor of law, who killed himself a month after the last official murder. Ultimately, however, it's irrelevant who Jack the Ripper was. While this whodunnit is almost certain to remain unresolved, people still visit the sites of the murders – although there's not that much to see really and you need a good storyteller to bring the tale to life. For one good, two-hour Ripper walk, contact **London Walks** (☎ 7624 3978; www.walks.com; ☯ tours 7.30pm, 3pm Saturday; adult/senior and student £5/4) or just turn up at the main exit of Tower Hill Underground station.

picking up phone handsets, and there are several touchscreens where you can learn more.

It's an attraction that's probably not worth trekking all the way east for, but a must if you're already in the area. Kids will love it. Alternatively, if you prefer not to mingle with over-exuberant school groups, try to make it on a Thursday night or a Saturday.

SUTTON HOUSE Map pp416-7

☎ 8986 2264; suttonhouse@nationaltrust; 2 & 4 Homerton High St E8; adult/child/family £2.20/50p/ 4.90; ☯ 1-5.30pm Fri & Sat, 11.30am-5pm Sun; rail Hackney Central, bus 106, 253 or D6

It's really quite amazing to think of Tudor nobles living in 'ackney, but as East London's oldest surviving house proves, they did, and in some style at that. Abandoned and taken over by squatters in the 1980s (who have left behind an attic wall of graffiti), 16th-century Sutton House could have been tragically lost to history, but it's since been put under the care of the National Trust and magnificently restored.

The first historic room you walk into, the Linenfold Parlour, is the absolute highlight, where the Tudor oak panelling on the walls has been carved to resemble draped cloth. Unfortunately, after that even the ornate Tudor and Edwardian chambers, the Victorian study, the Georgian parlour and the intriguing mock-up of a Tudor kitchen all seem a trifle anti-climatic. The only thing that could top the Linenfold Parlour, we reckon, would be spotting the alleged resident ghost.

There's a café and shop on site, and on the last Sunday of each month you can participate in 'discovery days', when different aspects of mainly Tudor and occasionally more recent history are brought back to life.

MILE END & VICTORIA PARK

RAGGED SCHOOL MUSEUM Map pp416-7

☎ 8980 6405; www.raggedschoolmuseum.org.uk; 46-50 Copperfield Rd E3; admission by donation; ☯ 10am-5pm Wed & Thu, plus 2-5pm 1st Sun of month; tube Mile End

Kids driving you nutty? Want to learn a little more about the East End's past? Then pack your books and head to the Ragged School Museum, a combination of mock Victorian school room and social history museum. Both adults and children are inevitably charmed by the hard wooden benches and desks, with slates, chalk, inkwells and abacuses of the re-created classroom on the 1st floor. During term-time, the museum runs a schools programme, where pupils are taught reading, 'riting and 'rithmetic by a strict schoolma'am in full Victorian regalia; and if you're very good – no talking up the back, there – you can watch and listen to these lessons from the glassed-off gallery. During school holidays, such Victorian role plays are sometimes offered to the general public, so ring ahead.

'Ragged' was a Victorian term used to refer to pupils' usually torn, dirty and dishevelled clothes, and the museum celebrates the legacy of Dr Joseph Barnardo, who founded the first free school for poor East End urchins in this building in the 1860s. So beneath the classroom there's a ground-floor gallery chronicling the area's wider history. The displays manage to touch you with the early poverty of the place and the hardship suffered during and after WWII without ever becoming maudlin – something probably helped by a peppering of colourful anecdotes. Did you know you could once buy lions for £20 from Jamrach's Wild Beast Store in Shadwell?

MILE END PARK Map pp416-7
tube Mile End
The 36-hectare Mile End Park is adjacent to Mile End Rd and the Ragged School Museum. Landscaped to great effect during the millennium year by Tibbalds TM2, it now incorporates a go-kart track, a children's centre for under-10s, areas for public art and an ecology area. The centrepiece, though, is architect Piers Gough's 'green bridge' from the northern edge of the park across Mile End Rd. The bridge itself is actually yellow – confusing until you realise that the 'green' in question refers to the trees that have been planted along its walkway.

VICTORIA PARK Map pp416-7
tube Mile End
If you want a little more green than Mile End Park affords, head north from Mile End tube along Grove Rd, until you reach Victoria Park. This leafy expanse has lakes, fountains, bridges, a bowling green, tennis courts and much more.

WALTHAMSTOW & LEYTONSTONE
WILLIAM MORRIS GALLERY Map p414
☎ 8527 3782; www.lbwf.gov.uk/wmg; Lloyd Park, Forest Rd E17; admission free; ☺ 10am-1pm & 2-5pm Tue-Sat, plus 1st Sun of month; tube Walthamstow Central
The home where Victorian-era designer and socialist William Morris lived as a teenager is now full of his typically ornate floral wallpaper and chintz. The permanent displays also feature woven rugs and carpets, stained glass, painted tiles and furniture, by either Morris himself or by his associates, including Pre-Raphaelite artist Edward Burne-Jones.

Along with Morris' medieval-style helmet and sword, which were made as 'props' for the Pre-Raphaelite murals at the Oxford Union, and the original design for his earliest wallpaper 'Trellis', the downstairs rooms also give an insight into the extremely busy life of a quite fascinating man. The upstairs gallery houses a good selection of Pre-Raphaelite paintings.

From the Underground station, walk northwards along Hoe St for about 15 minutes and turn west (left) on Forest Rd. The gallery is just across the street.

DAVID BECKHAM TRAIL
☎ 8496 3000; www.lbwf.gov.uk/beckham; tube Walthamstow Central, then bus W12 or 257
As if it weren't enough being England's football captain, a global style icon, husband to Posh, friend to Nelson Mandela and the sort of sportsman even a High Court judge would recognise, it seems that Becks is fast on the road to becoming a tourist attraction, too. Waltham Forest Council came up with this little humdinger after receiving calls from fans who wanted to see where David was born in 1975 or kicked his first football, and needed a guiding hand.

You can get all the info on the website, but the tour kicks off five minutes from Walthamstow Central tube station, at Whipps Cross Hospital on Whipps Cross Rd (David's first breath). After this it moves to the Peter May Sports Centre (first free kick) and **Walthamstow Stadium** (David first signed as a used-glass collector for £10 a night). If you make it all the way through to Gilwill Park in Chingford, where a young David went camping with the Cub Scouts, be warned that you will have stared at quite a lot of otherwise unremarkable football pitches and seen lots of sprawling suburbia. As you'll swiftly discover, Becks has come a long way. (More like gone a long way, actually – to Madrid. However, that's another story.)

DOWN RIVER

Eating p245; Sleeping p349; Shopping p330

East of Tower Bridge, London's biggest cluster of skyscrapers in Docklands looks south across the river to the stately parks and buildings of Greenwich. For such close neighbours, these districts are two completely different worlds. Docklands was once London's bustling docks area, where cargo from global trade was landed from the 16th century, but it fell into terminal decline as ships were rerouted to deep-water ports and the

British Empire evaporated after WWII. There are still pockets of history; however, what you see today, especially on the Isle of Dogs and around Canary Wharf, is largely the handiwork of the London Docklands Development Corporation (LDDC), a body established in the free-wheeling 1980s to create a new financial metropolis to take pressure from office space off the City. After a shaky start – thanks to unloved toy-town buildings, initially poor transport and recession – this rather artificial community, still surrounded by some rough neighbourhoods, is only now starting to become the mini-Manhattan envisaged (complete with high winds whipping through its streets).

South of the river, there are some neighbourhoods with mean streets, but not Greenwich (gren-itch) where the only mean thing is the time. Of course, this is home to the Prime Meridian of Longitude, from which global time has been measured since the 19th century, but it has much more to offer than that. It's also the birthplace of Henry VIII and his daughters Mary and Elizabeth, and those regal associations and expansive parklands have left it an air of semi-rural gentility. Now a UNESCO World Heritage Site, it's adorned with marvellous white wedding-cake buildings by Sir Christopher Wren and Inigo Jones.

DOCKLANDS

ST KATHARINE'S DOCK Map pp432-3
tube/DLR Tower Hill

Although it's unashamedly touristy, St Katharine's Dock works, albeit in a very limited sense. With its cafés and one great restaurant, **Lightship Ten** (p245), it makes an ideal spot to pause briefly after a morning's sightseeing at Tower Bridge or the Tower of London. There's a row of twee shops and a hokey pub called the **Dickens Inn**, but it's more entertaining just admiring some of the opulent luxury yachts.

Sadly, the dock's history is rather less appealing than its appearance. More than 1200 houses were razed and 11,000 people made homeless to make way for its creation in 1828. Yet it was never a great success and closed in 1968 – before being resurrected in its current incarnation in the 1980s. Tourists share the space with the financial brokers who work in nearby Commodities Quay.

WAPPING & LIMEHOUSE Map pp432-3 & 435

Author John Stow in his 16th-century *A Survey of London* described Wapping High St as a 'filthy strait passage, with alleys of small tenements or cottages'. It's a far cry from that today, but hardly much more attractive. It was one of the first failed yuppie projects of the 1980s, where luxury flats were built but remained unsold. Although the converted

warehouses and lofts that line the brick road are now mostly occupied, travelling through here is still a fairly unaesthetic experience.

The area was traditionally home to sailors and dockers. One of the historic sites that people like to visit, however, is the **Execution Dock** near the old river police station at Wapping New Stairs. This is where convicted pirates were hanged and their bodies chained to a post at low tide, to be left until three tides had washed over them. A nearby landmark recalls one of the more famous people executed in this way in 1701: the **Captain Kidd Pub**.

Northwards along Wapping Lane and across the Highway, you'll come to **St George-in-the-East**; the shell of the original church you see surrounding the smaller modern building is the remnants of the church erected by Nicholas Hawksmoor in 1726, which was badly damaged by the Blitz in WWII.

Sculptors & Dockers

Once, the painting of ships was the art most practised in docks worldwide. Today in London's Docklands, however, it's sculpture that dominates, with statues and other landmarks commissioned to make the place seem more attractive.

To the southwest of Canary Wharf, for example, is Pierre Vivant's **Traffic Light Tree**. Sitting in the centre of a roundabout, it's composed of 75 sets of red, amber and green lights, flashing manically to reflect the pace of life at Canary Wharf. Guiseppe Lund, the creator of the ornate Queen Mother's gates at Hyde Park, has forged another flower-and-plant-like **entrance gate** from metal at Westferry Circus. Leading furniture designer Ron Arad has erected two sculptures: the **Big Blue** in Canada Park Sq, which looks like a huge, floating sapphire, and **Windwand** at Westferry Circus, a 50m-high red, carbon fibre wand bending gently in the breeze. At Nash Crt, Konstantin Grcic has given us his own take on the iconic Swiss railway clock in **Six Public Clocks**.

For details on other sculptures in the area, see www.canarywharf.co.uk (then go to lifestyle/arts). Even the bridges around here have artistic aspirations. A **footbridge** linking Heron Quays with South Quay has masts and cables evoking a ship at sea, while Future Systems' **green floating bridge** connects West India Quay and Canary Wharf.

Cannon St Rd leads northward to Cable St, where ropes were manufactured in the late 18th century. It was once as long as the standard English measure for cable (180m). Eastwards along Cable St is the former Town Hall building, now a library. On the side wall a large mural commemorates the **Cable St riots** that took place here in October 1936. The British fascist Oswald Mosley led a bunch of his Blackshirt thugs into the area to intimidate the local Jewish population, but were resoundingly repelled.

There isn't much to Limehouse, although it became London's first Chinatown in the late 19th century and was also mentioned in Oscar Wilde's *Picture of Dorian Gray* (1891), when the protagonist passed by this way in search of opium. Today, the most notable attraction is the **St Anne's, Limehouse**, on the corner of Commercial Rd and Three Colt St. This was Nicholas Hawksmoor's earliest church and still boasts the highest church clock in the city. Although built in 1724, it was only consecrated in 1730 (see The Satanic Churches?, p118).

ISLE OF DOGS Map p435

Pundits can't even really agree on whether this is an island, let alone where it got its name from. Stricty speaking it's a peninsula of land on the northern shore of the Thames, although ignoring roads and transport links, it would *almost* be separated from the mainland at West India Docks. Similarly, the origin of 'dogs' remains disputed. Some very reputable organisations suggest it's because the royal kennels were located here during Henry VIII's reign. Other equally reputable sources believe it's a corruption of the word dijks (dikes), referring to the work of Flemish engineers here in the 19th century.

It can be agreed, however, that the centrepiece of the Isle of Dogs is Canary Wharf. If you want to see how the isle once looked, check out **Mudchute Park & Farm** (☎ 7515 5901; Pier St E14; ⏱ 10am-5pm, from 9am in summer; DLR Mudchute), a short distance to the southeast.

Canary Wharf Tower, Docklands (right)

CANARY WHARF Map p435

It's worth visiting Canary Wharf simply because it's so blimmin' surreal. Cesar Pelli's 244m Canary Wharf Tower, built in 1991 at One Canada Square, presides over a toy-town, financial theme park, surrounded by newer towers for HSBC and Citigroup, offices for Bank of America, Barclays, Lehmann Brothers,

Morgan Stanley Dean Witter and more. This thoroughly artificial community is like the set of a sci-fi film. On a good day it's almost utopian, but on a bad day, dark thoughts form about brainwashing and *Bladerunner*-style replicants.

It took a long time for the place to come this far, even. **Canary Wharf Tower**, still the tallest building in London and one of the largest property developments in Europe, had to be saved from bankruptcy before it reached today's levels of occupancy. As home to the *Independent* and *Daily Telegraph* newspapers (among other tenants) it's now nicknamed the 'vertical Fleet St'.

Unfortunately, there's no public access to the tower, but on a sunny day you can head for the open air cafés and bars of increasingly trendy West India Quay.

You can arrive here on the DLR. However, the monumental grandeur of Sir Norman Foster's sleek Canary Wharf Underground station, on the Jubilee line, is a better introduction to this other-worldly region.

MUSEUM IN DOCKLANDS Map p435

☎ 7515 1162; www.museumindocklands.org.uk; Warehouse No 1, West India Quay E14; adult/student with ID & under-16s/senior £5/free/3; ☼ 10am-5.30pm (last entry); DLR West India Quay, tube Canary Wharf

There are some compelling exhibits here, including 'sailor town' (an excellent re-creation of the cobbled streets, bars and lodging houses of a 19th-century dockside community) and a large scale model of the first London Bridge (as it was in the year 1400 on one side and in 1600 on the other). However, don't come to this converted 200-year-old warehouse expecting a simple tale of the docks; the museum has taken a comprehensive overview of the entire history of the Thames since AD 43, which at times is more taxing than engaging.

Ironically, it's at its best when it's dealing with home-turf specifics like the controversial transformation of the decrepit docks into Docklands in the 1980s and the social upheaval and dislocation that accompanied it.

The tour begins on the 3rd floor (take the lift to the top) with the Roman settlement of Londinium and works its way downwards through the ages.

TRINITY BUOY WHARF Map p435

☎ 7515 7153; ☼ 9am-5.30pm; DLR East India

London's only **lighthouse** is located at this brownfield site. The lighthouse was built for Michael Faraday in 1863, and is open the first Friday of each month. Also here is the unusual **Container City,** a community of artists' studios made from shipping containers, stacked side by side and one on top of each other. The web designers, architects and other creative tenants even have their own balconies. The wharf is open to the public every day (follow the signs to the bird sanctuary) and is much loved for film and modelling shoots. There are great views of the Millennium Dome from here, but the wharf is not a place you'd race to immediately in London; rather it's one you visit when you're really getting to know the city.

GREENWICH

For general information on Greenwich, try the **Greenwich TIC** (☎ 0870 608 2000, www.greenwich.gov.uk; Pepys House, 2 Cutty Sark Gardens SE10; ☼ 10am-5pm; DLR Cutty Sark). The attached Greenwich Gateway visitors' centre has a small exhibition of local history. **Greenwich Tour Guides** (☎ 8858 6169, www.greenwichtourguides.co.uk; adult/under-14s/concession £4/free/3) offers tours departing from the TIC at 12.15pm and 2.15pm .

CUTTY SARK Map p435

☎ 8858 3445; Cutty Sark Gardens SE10; adult/child aged 5-16/family £3.95/2.95/9.80; ☼ 10am-5pm; DLR Cutty Sark

Ah, the smell of Lapsang Souchong tea in the morning! So all-pervading is this aroma emanating from the boxes and chests, in fact, that you're never in any doubt as to the *Cutty Sark*'s former cargo, at any time of day. The last of the great tea clippers that sailed between England and China in the 19th century, the ship now sits in dry dock at Cutty Sark Gardens, near the tourist office. Visiting her is a great way to learn about early global trade. Placards explain at length the race to bring home the freshest (and therefore most expensive) tea from China, with short synopses given for children or non-native English speakers.

The *Cutty Sark* (the name is taken from a Robert Burns' poem where it means 'short shirt') was briefly the fastest ship on water when she was launched in 1869, but the introduction of steam soon made her redundant. Still, it's quite pleasant taking a stroll around the decks, examining the teak fittings and maritime souvenirs. With sea shanties playing in the background, and the world's largest collection of colourful ship's figureheads on the lower deck, it almost feels like a fairground attraction, so it's a good diversion for younger kids.

Tunnel Visions

One moment, the Greenwich foot tunnel beneath the Thames is the most claustrophobic place in London, with a spine-chilling aura of fear and mystery. (Will the river burst through before I reach the other side? What's that clunking echo behind?) The next second, it's just a mundane pedestrian underpass between Greenwich and Island Gardens, which has safely withstood the water pressure from above for more than 100 years.

The crime novelist PD James succumbed to the first interpretation with a terrified character in *Original Sin*, and certainly the way the tunnel gradually slopes down towards the middle does initially lend an air of nightmarish infinity. People coming towards you appear first as just feet, before gradually their legs, body and face are revealed.

But then you pass the halfway mark, the exit comes into view and you know you're home and dry, literally. That's the time to reflect on the tunnel's usefulness. Built in 1902 so that workers in Greenwich could reach the docks without having to catch a ferry, it's open 24 hours for those prepared to traverse the 88 or 100 steps at either end. (There's CCTV for security.) Otherwise, the lifts in both dome-shaped entrances will take you up and down from 7am to 7pm Monday to Saturday and 10am to 5.30pm on Sunday.

On a more fanciful note, the tunnel can be seen as an analogy for London's continuing north–south divide. Crossing to the other side is a slightly uncomfortable, but somehow thrilling, rite of passage for the many Londoners – from both north and south – who treat the Thames as if it were the River Styx. Artists haven't missed this mythic potential, either; one art installation here once used red strip-lighting and sound to make it feel like you were pulsing along an artery.

GIPSY MOTH IV Map p435
☎ 8858 3445; Cutty Sark Gardens SE10; DLR Cutty Sark
The question that springs to mind as you stand before this 16m-long craft near the entrance to the Greenwich foot tunnel is whether you would really want to spend 226 days in it on the open sea? Francis Chicester did during 1966 and 1967, making a solo circumnavigation of the globe at 64 years of age. He earned a knighthood for his troubles and inspired a generation of feisty solo yachtsmen and women, including Ellen MacArthur and Emma Richards.

OLD ROYAL NAVAL COLLEGE Map p435
☎ 8269 4747 or 0800 389 3341; King William Walk SE10; admission free; ⏰ 10am-5pm Mon-Sat, 12.30-5pm Sun; DLR Cutty Sark
There are two main rooms open to the public here: the **Painted Hall** and the **Chapel**. They're in separate buildings, because when Christopher Wren was commissioned in 1692 by King William and Queen Mary to build a hospital and retirement home for wounded naval veterans, he decided to split it into two, so as not to obstruct views of the river from the existing **Queen's House** (p174). The hospital was built on the site of the Old Greenwich Palace, Placentia, used by the Tudors, initially for those wounded in the victory over the French at La Hogue in 1692. In 1869, the buiding was converted to a Naval College. Now even the navy has left and the premises are home to the University of Greenwich and Trinity College of Music.

As its name suggests, the **Painted Hall** in the King William Building is almost entirely covered in decorative murals. Even if the ornate 'allegorical Baroque' style of artist James Thornhill is not to your taste, it's hard not to be impressed. The hall was intended as the naval pensioners' dining room but, rather sadly, was declared too magnificent for that once Thornhill got his hands on it.

The artist, who also painted the cupola of St Paul's Cathedral, completed his commission in two stages. The main hall was painted from 1708 to 1712, the upper hall from 1718 to 1725. The ceiling mural of the main hall alone took five years. It celebrates and flatters the monarchy (Thornhill's bosses at the time). King William and Queen Mary, the hospital's founders, sit enthroned amid the Virtues, with Concord and Peace attending – and French King Louis XIV, defeated at La Hogue, grovelling at William's feet. There are mirrors on trolleys throughout the hall, which make it easier to view the ceiling.

The upper hall commemorates the Protestant succession, depicting George I with his family on the western wall. In the bottom right-hand corner Thornhill drew himself into the picture, with his open hand pointing towards his work (or perhaps asking for more than the measly, even for the times, payment of £3 a sq yard for the ceilings and £1 for the walls).

The **chapel** in the Queen Mary Building is decorated in a lighter rococo style. It's certainly a beautiful room, but it's most famous for its organ and acoustics, so if possible come on

173

the first Sunday of the month, when there's a free organ recital at 3pm, or time your visit for eucharist, every Sunday at 11am.

Guided tours of the buildings leave from the Painted Hall every day at 2pm (adult/child under 16 £4/free). These also offer exclusive access to the **Jacobe an undercroft** of the former palace and the hospital's recreational **skittle alley**.

NATIONAL MARITIME MUSEUM Map p435
☎ 8312 6565; www.nmm.ac.uk; Romney Rd SE10; admission free, for special exhibitions charges vary; ☻ 10am-6pm Apr-Sep, 10am-5pm Oct-Mar; DLR Cutty Sark

Everyone, save the most committed landlubber, will appreciate the superlative National Maritime Museum. From the sounds of the sea that wash over the entrance of this magnificent neoclassical building and the glass-roofed Neptune Court on the ground floor to the low-lit 3rd floor with memorabilia of explorers like Captain James Cook and space-age deep-sea diving suits, it's impressive through and through. Some £20 million was spent on its millennial refurbishment: it's not just the money that shows, but also that it was used thoughtfully.

The exhibits are arranged by theme, focusing on trade and empire, Britain's sea power, maritime London, cargoes, the planet's oceans, the future of the sea and much more. Visual highlights include the golden barge built in 1732 for Frederick, prince of Wales, and the huge ship's propeller installed on the ground floor. Here you can also see the uniform Nelson was wearing when he was fatally shot and a replica, used in the Kenneth Branagh film *Shackleton*, of the lifeboat *James Caird* used by explorer Ernest Shackleton and a handful of his men on their epic mission for help. (The real *Caird* is at **Dulwich College**, p178)

The passengers exhibit, about great ocean-going liners and immigration, is enjoyable on many levels, whether you're just eyeing up the classic travel posters, the Art Deco ship's china or the mock cocktail bar, or thinking about the situation and treatment of refugees. The sphere in Neptune's Court, which you enter to see videos on the fragility of the oceans, is one of several exhibits making artful use of technology.

The only downsides are that the maritime paintings aren't as exciting as the rest of the displays, and if you go on a weekday, the place is often overrun with school groups.

QUEEN'S HOUSE Map p435
☎ 8858 4422; Romney Rd SE10; admission free; ☻ 10am-5pm early Sep-May, 10am-6pm Jun-early Sep; DLR Cutty Sark

The Palladian building is the main attraction here, rather than what's in it. Famed architect Inigo Jones started work on it in 1616 for Anne of Denmark, wife of James I, after Jones' return from Italy. However, it wasn't completed until 1635 when it became the home of Charles I and his queen, Henrietta Maria.

The **Great Hall** is the principal room, from which the others radiate. It's a breathtaking cubical space, with a gallery at 1st-floor level. The painting on the ceiling is not the original by Orazio Gentileschi and his daughter Artemisia, but a computer-enhanced photographic stencil. The helix-shaped **Tulip Staircase** leads to the upper rooms, where there are portraits of great seamen and events. However, in the hall, you've already seen the best bit. Film director Ang Lee possibly thought the same when he used it as a backdrop to *Sense and Sensibility* (1995), which starred Kate Winslet and Emma Thompson.

ST ALFEGE CHURCH Map p435
☎ 8858 6828; Church St SE10; admission free; ☻ 10am-4pm Mon-Sat, 1-4pm Sun; DLR Cutty Sark

Not an essential stop, the parish church of Greenwich nevertheless has charm. Designed by Nicholas Hawksmoor in 1714 to replace a 12th-century building, its chancel features a restored mural by James Thornhill (the artist behind the Painted Hall at the Royal Naval College). St Alfege was the archbishop of Canterbury, killed on this site by Vikings in 1012.

FAN MUSEUM Map p435
☎ 8305 1441; 12 Croom's Hill SE10; adult/concession £3.50/2.50; ☻ 11am-5pm Tue-Sat, noon-5pm Sun; DLR Cutty Sark

It sounds twee but this captivating museum proves that good things really do come in small packages, from the 18th-century Georgian townhouse to the fans it houses (an art form of their own). Ivory, tortoiseshell, peacock feather and folded fabric examples are joined in the permanent collection by kitsch battery-powered versions and huge, ornamental Welsh fans. The temporary exhibitions always throw up something special, such as fans used for political advertising.

Behind the house, there's a Japanese-style garden with an **orangery** serving afternoon teas (☻ 3-5pm Tue-Sun; full/half-tea £4.50/3.50).

The Long Road to Longitude

Rarely has a science story proved so sexy. Dava Sobel's remarkable slim volume on the subject, *Longitude*, became an international bestseller; and perhaps the concentrated looks on the faces of Royal Observatory visitors today reveal that 'the true story of a lone genius who solved the greatest scientific problem of his time' (as Sobel's subtitle would have it) is still impossible to resist.

In short, it goes like this. At the start of the 18th century, sailors still had no reliable means to measure a ship's longitude. Working out how far north or south of the equator they were, or their latitude, was easy; they simply needed to measure with a sextant the height of the sun or the Pole Star on the horizon. But they only had complicated astronomical methods – and some other downright kooky formulas – for measuring how far east or west they were from their intended port of call. As a consequence, they all too regularly miscalculated and catastrophically ran aground.

Already by the 16th century, scientists knew that the answer to measuring one's east-west position could lie in comparing local time (measured by the sun) with the reading of a clock set at the time of one's home port. This was based on the knowledge that it takes 24 hours for the earth to complete one revolution of 360 °, so a one-hour difference represents 1/24th of a revolution – or 15° longitude.

However, that meant having a reliable clock on board that would accurately continue to record the time back home. Even two hundred years later, at the start of the 18th century, no such technology had been invented; the often violent pitching of a ship at sea and variable temperatures always caused contemporary watches to lose or gain time.

As a leading sea-going nation in an era of discovery, Britain had perhaps the most to lose. So in 1714 parliament offered an enormous prize of £20,000 to anyone who could discover a method of finding longitude, accurate to within 30 miles.

Some wag suggested a solution involving a wounded dog in London and 'a powder of sympathy' to make a dog on board yelp at certain times, while powerful astronomers, among them Sir Isaac Newton, were convinced the answer would lie in the stars. However, the humble Yorkshire clockmaker John Harrison persevered with different pendulums, springs and metals to develop clocks H1, H2, H3 and finally the implacable watch H4. Eventually, after tests at the Royal Observatory, the sceptical and sometimes plain conniving authorities were forced to relent over H4 and its temperature-resistant bi-metallic strips. They awarded the by-then 79-year-old Harrison the full prize money in 1772.

GREENWICH PARK Map p435

☎ 8858 2608; DLR/rail Cutty Sark/Maze Hill

This is London's largest, and one of its loveliest, parks, with a grand avenue, wide-open spaces, a rose garden and rambling, picturesque walks. It's partly the work of Le Nôtre, who landscaped the palace gardens of Versailles for Louis XIV. It contains several historic sights, a café and a deer park called the **Wilderness**.

If you continue south of the park you come to **Blackheath** (p176).

ROYAL OBSERVATORY Map p435

☎ 8312 6565; www.rog.nmm.ac.uk; Greenwich Park SE19; admission free; ☉ 10am-5pm Oct-May, 10am-6pm Apr-Sep; DLR Cutty Sark

The Royal Observatory allows you to stand with one foot in the world's western hemisphere and the other in the east; it also explains how the **prime meridian** of time you've just straddled came to be located here. The establishment of Greenwich as the point from which all time on the planet is measured harks back to the search for a reliable way to measure longitude in the 17th and 18th centuries (see boxed text above). Charles II, sick of ships foundering because they had no idea of their east–west coordinates, had the Royal Observatory built on the hill here in 1675, intending that astronomy be used to find an accurate means of navigation at sea. The first astronomer royal, John Flamsteed (1646–1719), set up home here, making observations of the skies and stars from the **Octagon Room** – a light, airy, geometrically shaped observatory which is one of the few interiors designed by Sir Christopher Wren to have survived.

Astronomy was a dog's life in those days, as the tales from the excellent observatory make clear. Today, however, that doesn't seem the case. At least, the astronomers who talk you through shows at the adjacent **Greenwich Planetarium** (adult/senior, student & child £4/2; shows 2.30pm Mon-Fri, 1.30pm & 3.30pm Sat, 2pm & 3pm Sun) brim with enthusiasm.

In the end, it was a watchmaker who solved the problem of longitude, but Greenwich was still named as the prime meridian at an 1884 Washington conference, in recognition of all its work. Every day at midday, or 1pm in the summer, the red time ball at the top of the Royal Observatory drops to mark the accuracy and pre-eminence of Greenwich Mean Time (GMT) as standard time.

RANGER'S HOUSE Map p435

☎ 8853 0035; www.english-heritage.org.uk; Greenwich Park SE10; adult/under 5/child 5-15/senior & student £4.50/free/2.50/3.50; ⌚ 10am-4pm Wed-Sun Nov-May, 10am-5pm Oct, 10am-6pm Sep-Apr

Southwest of the observatory is a stately home built for admiral Francis Hosier in 1700 and later used to house the park's ranger. Today, after a refurbishment by English Heritage, it houses the celebrated Wernher collection, a potpourri of jewellery, porcelain, silverware and paintings amassed by a German-born former diamond- and gold-miner who made his riches in South Africa in the 19th century. This truly is an eclectic mix, with things like rare early religious paintings mingled with those by Dutch old masters, Renaissance jewels, medieval ivories, Limoges enamel plate, Meissen pottery figures and huge Beauvais tapestries.

If it all gets too much, you can also ascend to Admiral Hosier's rooftop gazebo to enjoy the view.

AROUND GREENWICH

BLACKHEATH Map p414
rail Blackheath

Looking at a map, you could easily mistake Blackheath for a southern extension of Greenwich Park, but the common and surrounding 'village' have a character very much their own. Known locally as the 'Hampstead of the south', the 110-hectare expanse of open common has played a greater role in the history of London than its much bigger sister to the north. The Danes camped here in the early 11th century after having captured Alfege, the archbishop of Canterbury, as did Wat Tyler before marching on London with tens of thousands of Essex and Kentish men during the Peasants' Revolt in 1381. Henry VII fought off Cornish rebels here in 1497, and the heath was where Henry VIII met his fourth wife, Anne of Cleves, in 1540 (he had agreed to marry her based on a portrait by Holbein, but disliked her immediately in the flesh). Later Blackheath became a highwaymen's haunt, and it was not until the area's development in the late 18th century that the lovely **Paragon**, a crescent of Georgian mansions on the southeastern edge of the heath was built to entice 'the right sort of people' to move to the area, that Blackheath was considered safe. The name of the heath is derived from the colour of the soil, not from its alleged role as a burial

ground during the Black Death, the bubonic plague of the 14th century.

Today the windswept heath is the starting point for the London Marathon in April, a pleasant place for a stroll or somewhere to go fly a kite. It's not uncommon to see artists dabbing away at their easels; apparently these Turner wannabes find the light has a special quality on the heath. There are a couple of historic pubs within reach: the **Hare and Billet** and the **Princess of Wales**.

Along with the Paragon, other notable buildings include the fieldstone **All Saints' Church** (1858), with its needle-sharp spire to the south, and **Morden College**, the Ritz of almshouses, built in 1695 to house 'decayed Turkey Merchants' who had fallen on hard times. The building, now a nursing home and closed to the public, is believed to have been designed by Christopher Wren.

To reach Blackheath from Greenwich Park, walk southwards along Chesterfield Walk and past the Ranger's House (or southwards along Blackheath Ave and through Blackheath Gate) and then cross Shooters Hill Rd.

MILLENNIUM DOME Map p435

When it was opened on the first day of 2000, the huge circus-tent-shaped Millennium Dome was the most ambitious building erected in London since St Paul's Cathedral in 1710; at 380m across, it is Europe's largest single-span covered area, and is supported by 100 masts. Unfortunately, this Richard Rogers creation never really won the public's hearts and minds in the same way as St Paul's.

A large part of the blame for this failure lies with the largely uninspiring exhibits that were used to fill it as a celebration of the millennium year. By the time the £760 million structure closed, it had only attracted 6.5 million visitors, about half the number predicted. Afterwards, the £100,000-a-week cost of maintaining it, even when empty, caused resentment even among those who had initially appreciated its architectural form. All in all, it's now cost more than a £1 billion to build and maintain, and much of this has come from the public purse.

Finally, however, this huge white elephant in North Greenwich looks likely to be transformed. After much wrangling, Mayor Ken Livingstone has given approval to turn the dome and 76 hectares of land surrounding it into a 26,000-seater sports and entertainment venue, surrounded by a Docklands development of 10,000 homes (the environmentally friendly Millennium Village), offices, shopping centres, a school and hotel.

There's still not much to see yet, however, and the area around the dome is locked. If you want to get a good view, you can see it from Docklands or by taking a Thames River cruise (see p379 or Thames Flood Barrier following). Trinity Buoy Wharf (see p172) is also an excellent vantage point.

THAMES FLOOD BARRIER Map p414

tube North Greenwich, rail Charlton, bus 161, 177 & 180
Although it has a very serious purpose, the most striking thing about the Thames Flood Barrier is still its futuristic look. Completed between Greenwich and Woolwich in 1982, it's designed to protect London from floods and surge tides until at least 2030. Its nine concrete piers link 11 movable gates, each as tall as a five-storey building. The silver roofs on the piers house the operating machinery to raise and lower the gates and are like a glittering version of the Sydney Opera House, or Glasgow's Armadillo building.

With water levels rising by as much as 75cm a century, as the river itself narrows, the barrier is increasingly necessary. Some 300 people were drowned in 1953 when the Thames burst its banks, and since the barrier was built it's saved London from another such catastrophe about 70 times. (In January 2003, a record was set when it had to be raised 14 times in the first week alone.)

The best time to see the barrier is when it is raised, and the only guaranteed time this happens is once a month, when the mechanisms are checked. For exact dates and times, ring the **Thames Barrier Visitors Centre** (☎ 8305 4188; www.environment-agency.gov.uk; 1 Unity Way SE18; admission to barrier free, admission to downstairs information centre adult/child/ senior £1/50p/75p; ☺ 11am-3.30pm Oct-Mar, 10.30am-4.30pm Apr-Sep). This tiny centre will also fill you in on the science of daily tides, spring tides and surge tides that threaten the city.

To visit the visitors centre, you need to go by tube, rail (and walk quite a way) or bus. You can get to within 20 minutes' walk of the barrier by taking a train to Charlton station from Charing Cross or London Bridge. To visit the barrier from Greenwich catch bus No 177 or 180 along Romney Rd and get off at the Victoria pub, 757 Woolwich Rd. From

there Westmoor St leads northwards to the visitors' centre.

Boats also travel to and from the barrier, although they don't land. From Westminster it's a three-hour round trip, from Greenwich it takes one hour. From late March to October boats run by **Thames River Services** (☎ 7930 4097; www.westminsterpier.co.uk; from Westminster adult/under 16/senior/family £9/4.50/7.50/24, from Greenwich adult/under 16/senior/family £5.40/2.70/4.40/14.20), leave Westminster Pier on the hour from 10am to 3pm (leaving Greenwich from 11am to 4pm), passing the Dome along the way. From November to March there's a reduced service from Westminster between 10.40am and 3.20pm. See the website for exact times.

FIREPOWER Map p414

☎ 8855 7755; www.firepower.org.uk; Royal Arsenal, Woolwich SE18; adult/child aged 5-15/senior & student £6.50/4.50/5.50; ☺ 10.30am-5pm Wed-Sun; rail Woolwich Arsenal
Not really a place for pacifists or for those of a nervous disposition, Firepower is a whizz-bang, shoot-'em-up display of how artillery has developed throughout the ages. This history proceeds from catapults to nuclear warheads, while the multimedia extravangza Field of Fire tries to convey the experience of artillery gunners from WWI to Bosnia. There's a gunnery hall and a medals gallery, and a Real Weapons gallery where you can even try your hand at shooting a tank or a rifle on a simulator. It's loud and it flashes, but the kids just can't get enough.

CHARLTON HOUSE Map p414

☎ 8856 3951; Charlton Rd SE7; admission free; ☺ 9am-11pm Mon-Fri, 9am-5.30pm Sat; rail Charlton, bus 53, 54, 380 & 442
Lucky Charlton to have this red-brick Jacobean house as a community centre. Fortunately, because community groups use the building day and night during the week, you can also pop in to look at the oak staircase, ornate ceilings and marble fireplaces. On Saturdays, the place is very popular for weddings.

The formal gardens, part of which are thought to have been designed by leading 17th-century architect Inigo Jones, have been recently replanted and landscaped. There are now separate herb and shrub gardens. Elsewhere in the grounds, there's a mulberry tree dating from 1608.

ELTHAM PALACE Map p414

☎ 8294 2548; www.english-heritage.org.uk; Court Rd SE9; adult/under 5/child aged 5-15/concession £6.50/free/3.50/5; ⏰ 10am-4pm Wed-Fri & Sun Nov-Mar, 10am-5pm Oct, 10am-6pm Apr-Sep; rail Eltham

No self-respecting fan of Art Deco should miss a trip to Eltham Palace, not for the scarce remnants of the palace building itself – although that has its own attractions – but for the fabulous Courtauld House in the grounds. If you like 1930s style, you'll be dreaming of moving in (although this is, sadly, not possible).

The house was built during that decade by the well-to-do textile merchant Stephen Courtauld and his wife Virginia; and from the impressive entrance hall with its dome and huge circular geometrically patterend carpet to the marbled bathrooms and advanced electrical fittings it appears the couple had taste as well as money. They also, rather fashionably for the times, had a pet lemur, and the heated cage for the spoiled (and vicious) 'Mah-jongg' is also on view.

Little remains of the 14th- to 16th-century palace where Edward IV entertained and Henry VIII spent his childhood before decamping for Greenwich, apart from the restored Great Medieval Hall. Its hammer-beam roof is generally rated the third best in the country, behind those at Westminster Hall and Hampton Court Palace.

DULWICH & FOREST HILL

DULWICH COLLEGE Map p414

☎ 8693 3601; www.dulwich.org.uk; Dulwich Common SE21; admission free; ⏰ 8.30am-4pm Mon-Fri; rail West Dulwich

In 2001, the world began to rediscover the explorer Ernest Shackleton, and the fantastic tale of his and his men's escape from a failed expedition to the South Pole, in which they all survived more than a year on the Antarctic ice. With the release of photographer Frank Hurley's original footage from the trip, a new IMAX film, an English docudrama and a Hollywood movie, the *Wall Street Journal* has diagnosed a global case of 'Shackletonmania'.

Shackleton was one of Dulwich College's most famous pupils (another was comic writer PG Wodehouse), which is how the school became guardian of one of the most amazing souvenirs of the expedition south. It's the permanent home of the original lifeboat *James Caird* in which Shackleton and a handful

of men sailed some 900 miles (1400km) across the world's most dangerous seas.

The boat is often loaned to museums around the world, so ring ahead to check that is actually here.

DULWICH PICTURE GALLERY Map p414

☎ 8693 5254; www.dulwichpicturegallery.org.uk; Gallery Rd SE21; adult/student & child/senior £4/free/3, Fri admission free; ⏰ 10am-5pm Tue-Fri, 11am-5pm Sat & Sun; rail West Dulwich

The Dulwich is the UK's oldest public art gallery, designed by Sir John Soane in 1811 to 1814 to house Dulwich College's collection of paintings by Raphael, Rembrandt, Rubens, Reynolds, Gainsborough, Lely, Van Dyck and others. Unusually, the collectors, Noel Desenfans and painter Francis Bourgeois, chose to have their mausoleum placed among the pictures.

A new annexe built for the millennium contains space for temporary exhibitions, and there's also now an open-air café.

The museum is a 10-minute walk northwards along Gallery Rd, which starts almost opposite West Dulwich station.

HORNIMAN MUSEUM Map p414

☎ 8699 1872 or 8699 2339; www.horniman.ac.uk; 100 London Rd SE23; admission free; ⏰ 10.30am-5.30pm Mon-Sat, 2-5.30pm Sun; rail Forest Hill

There's little doubt that this extraordinary museum would be a major draw if it weren't so far out of town. Set in an Art Nouveau building with a clock tower and mosaics, the collection of Victorian tea-merchant Frederick John Horniman has a jumble-sale assortment of exhibits that encompasses everything from Africa's largest mask to Emperor Angel fish to a wonderful collection of concertinas. In the ethnographic section, you'll find – among many other things – 'African Worlds', the first permanent gallery of African and Afro-Caribbean art and culture in the UK. The natural history area features a walrus, a stuffed dodo and much more, while the Music Room shows off 3500-year-old Egyptian clappers and early English keyboards.

Besides this, the small Living Waters Aquarium seems a little bit out of place, but its colourful fish do make it a hit with kids.

To get there from Forest Hill station, turn left out of the station along Devonshire Rd and then right along London Rd. The Horniman is on the right.

NORTH CENTRAL

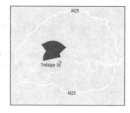

Eating p247; Sleeping p338; Shopping p320

It's hard to believe that merely a hop and a skip from the relentless hubbub of Oxford St is the increasingly hip 'village' of Marylebone with its quintessentially English high street, sedate Georgian squares, smart boutiques, organic shops, exciting restaurants and convivial bars. Until the 18th century, Marylebone was a mostly rural community known after its parish church, which sat on a bank of the River Tyburn: somehow 'St Mary's by the Bourne' morphed into the incomprehensible Marylebone (Marlee-bone).

The neighbourhood has more reasons to be famous than just about any other London quarter, yet it has struggled to be known as anything more than the little residential enclave between the West End and the meticulously manicured Regent's Park. Not only is it home to super sleuth Sherlock Holmes (of Baker St), the world's best and most expensive medical practitioners (on Harley St), the venerable BBC (on Regent St), the spirit of cricket (through the Marylebone Cricket Club, the guardians of the game), it also presents London's greatest conundrum: how come Madame Tussaud's is the city's most popular paying attraction when the wonderful and free Wallace Collection is virtually overlooked? Not even Arthur Conan Doyle's debonair detective could solve that one. As if all this weren't enough, Marylebone recently got another feather in its well-plumed cap when in moved London's real royal couple, Madonna and…some cockney geezer who made a hugely successful film in the last century.

North of the restful Regent's Park, across the canal, is the amiable and affluent village of Primrose Hill, all the more amiable since its residents made a stand against the scourge of Starbucks, and booted globalisation out of Regent's Park Rd. The hill, itself a park, provides wonderful vistas over the centre of London. Further north again is the leafy residential enclave of Belsize Park, where it always feels like Sunday afternoon.

North of Hyde Park, Paddington is best known for its train station (with its splendid mid-19th century iron girder roof) and as the place where a very cute bear arrived after his trip from darkest Peru. It's never had much of a reputation, not least because of its proximity to the notorious gallows at Tyburn. These days, it can be described as scruffy at best and sordid at worst; there's nothing to bring you here although you might pass through on the Heathrow Express. Similarly, Bayswater – named after Bayard's Spring, which supplied the city's drinking water in the Middle Ages – holds little of interest. It's a uniformly bland residential area, bisected by the predominantly naff Queensway. However, given the central location of these areas, their fashionable neighbours, the demand for space and London's fondness for reinventing itself, it can only be a matter of time before Paddington and Bayswater are 'the next big things'.

Despite ongoing efforts to transform the district – including the opening of the fabulous British Library – King's Cross and Euston are still notoriously dodgy and forbidding. Two ugly train stations and one magnificent one dominate the area, while the streets are choked with traffic, lined with ugly grey buildings and paved with general cheerlessness. Street prostitution, crime, racism, drug abuse and drunkenness all feature, and while massive development is taking place in readying St Pancras station to receive the Eurostar by 2007 (the date keeps getting pushed back), the noise and closed-off roads are just adding to the general unpleasantness for now.

Few parts of London can match the breakneck pace with which Camden has been made over and under in the last 50 years. Traditionally home to huge numbers of poor Irish and Greek immigrants, it was run-down and neglected until the early 1970s when all of a sudden it earned the brio of bohemia, and became the place where struggling actors like those of *Withnail & I* hung out and drank hard. When the world-famous market started, Camden became a weekend destination for many Londoners and up sprang many artists' studios and music venues that were the incubators for some of London's finest. It peaked in the early '90s when the market was the home of all things hip and Camden was the epicentre of Britpop. Inevitably, its cool credentials attracted middle-class homebuyers and moneyed wannabes, and the area gradually fell on the sword of its own popularity. It's still savvy and spirited – with the best small music venues in town – but Camden has lost much of the edge that used to set it apart. The drunks – who swigged from their bottles and watched bemused as their locale morphed from one unrecognisable place into another – have partly reclaimed the litter-strewn Camden High St and are raving once again.

Top Five – North Central

- British Library (p182)
- Camden Market (p183)
- Regent's Park (p180)
- St Pancras Station (p182)
- Wallace Collection (below)

WALLACE COLLECTION Map pp426-7

☎ 7935 9500; www.wallacecollection.org; Hertford House, Manchester Sq W1; admission free; ☽ 10am-5pm Mon-Sat, noon-5pm Sun; tube Bond Street

Arguably London's finest small gallery (relatively unknown even to Londoners) the Wallace Collection is an enthralling glimpse into 18th-century aristocratic life. The sumptuously restored Italianate mansion houses a treasure trove of 17th- and 18th-century paintings, porcelain, artefacts and furniture collected by generations of the same family and bequeathed to the nation by the widow of Sir Richard Wallace (1818–90) on condition it should always be on display in the centre of London.

Among the many highlights here – besides the warm and friendly staff – are paintings by the likes of Rembrandt, Hals, Delacroix, Titian, Rubens, Poussin, Van Dyck, Velazquez, Reynolds and Gainsborough in the stunning and aptly named **Great Gallery**. There's a spectacular array of medieval and Renaissance armour (including some to try on), a Minton-tiled smoking room, stunning chandeliers and a sweeping staircase that is reckoned to be one of the best examples of French interior architecture in existence.

Throw in the excellent glass-roofed restaurant, Café Bagatelle, which occupies the central courtyard, and you've got one of the most outstanding attractions in the whole of London.

MADAME TUSSAUD'S Map pp422-3

☎ 0870 400 3000; www.madame-tussauds.com; Marylebone Rd NW1; prices vary, up to £20 (includes London Planetarium); ☽ 9am-5.30pm Mon-Fri, 9.30am-5.30pm Sat-Sun; tube Baker Street

Almost three million people visit London's famous, overpriced and toweringly tedious waxworks each year, so if you want to avoid the queues (particularly in summer) arrive early in the morning, late in the afternoon, or buy your tickets in advance from a ticket agency or over the phone and get a timed entry slot.

Madame Tussaud's dates back more than two centuries when the Swiss model-maker started making death masks of the people killed during the French Revolution. She came to London in

1803 and exhibited around 30 wax models in Baker St, on a site not far from this building, which has housed the waxworks since 1885.

The waxworks were an enormous hit in Victorian times when the models provided the only opportunity for visitors to glimpse the famous and infamous. Just why so many people pay so much money to see the models today is beyond us. We're not total killjoys; if the queues weren't so long and the prices so steep, it could be a laugh but features like the famous **Chamber of Horrors**, which made the waxworks' reputation in the last century, are just plain tasteless today.

Much of the modern waxworks is made up of the **Garden Party** exhibition at the beginning, featuring the celebrities *du jour*, and the **Grand Hall** where world leaders line up. In the Spirit of London 'time taxi', you sit in a mock-up of a London black cab and are whipped through a five-minute historical summary of London, a mercifully short time to endure the god-awful scripts and hackneyed commentary. Among the new models are a blushing Jennifer Lopez that turns pink when you whisper in her ear and a model of Brad Pitt with a silicone and foam buttock that visitors are invited to squeeze.

In case you were wondering what happens to the models of those people whose 15 minutes have passed, their heads are removed and stored in a cupboard just in case they should ever revisit the fickle world of fame.

LONDON PLANETARIUM Map pp422-3

☎ 0870 400 3000; www.london-planetarium.com; Marylebone Rd NW1; entry included in ticket for Madame Tussaud or £2.45/1.50 separately; ☽ usually noon-5pm summer, phone for other times; tube Baker Street

Attached to Madame Tussaud's, the London Planetarium projects a 20-minute star show onto the dome ceiling, which zooms through the cosmos and attempts to explain astronomy and the solar system.

REGENT'S PARK Map pp418-9

☎ 7486 7905; ☽ 5am-dusk; tube Baker Street/ Regent's Park

The most elaborate and ordered of London's parks, Regent's was created around 1820 by John Nash who planned to use it as an estate upon which he could build palaces for the aristocracy. Although the plan never quite came off – like so many at the time – you can get some idea of what Nash might have achieved from the buildings along the Outer Circle and particularly the stuccoed Palladian mansions he built on Cumberland Tce.

Like many of the city's parks, this one was used as a royal hunting ground, and then as farmland, before it was used as a place for fun and leisure during the 18th century. These days, it's a well-organised but relaxed, lively but serene, local but cosmopolitan haven in the heart of the city. Among its many attractions are the London Zoo, the Grand Union Canal along its northern side, an ornamental lake, an **open air theatre** (p316) in Queen Mary's Gardens where Shakespeare is performed during the summer months, ponds and colourful flowerbeds, rose gardens that look spectacular in June, football pitches and summer games of softball.

On the western side of the park is the impressive **London Central Islamic Centre & Mosque** (☎ 7724 3363; 146 Park Rd NW8; tube Marylebone), a huge white edifice with a glistening dome. Provided you take your shoes off and dress modestly you're welcome to go inside, although the interior is fairly stark.

LONDON ZOO Map pp418-9

☎ 7722 3333; www.londonzoo.co.uk; Regent's Park NW1; adult/concession £12/9; ☉ 10am-5.30pm Mar-Oct, 10am-4pm Nov-Jan, 10am-4.30pm Feb-Mar; tube Baker Street/Camden Town

Established in 1828, these zoological gardens are among the oldest in the world and it was actually from here that the word 'zoo' originated. After receiving a lot of flak in recent years, London Zoo has become one of the most progressive in the world. It's in the middle of a long-term modernisation plan and the emphasis is now firmly placed on conservation, education and breeding, with fewer species and more spacious conditions.

A great way to visit the zoo is by canal boat from Little Venice or Camden , but you can also reach it by walking along the canal towpath. There's a delightful **children's zoo**, which is built almost entirely from sustainable materials, and busy programmes of events and attractions (like elephant bathing and penguin feeding) throughout the year.

The **Web of Life**, a glass pavilion containing some 60 live animal exhibits (from termites and jellyfish to the birds and the bees), has interactive displays and, yes, on-show breeding groups to see. It makes a visit to the zoo worthwhile by itself. Elsewhere don't miss the enclosures housing the big cats, the elephants and rhinos, the apes and monkeys, the small mammals and the birds. The elegant and cheerful Penguin Pool, designed by Berthold Lubetkin in 1934, is one of London's foremost modernist structures.

BAKER STREET UNDERGROUND STATION Map pp422-3

One of the original stations of the first underground train line in the world (the Metropolitan Railway) lies underfoot at Baker Street station and can be visited simply by buying an Underground ticket. Baker Street, one of the seven original stations on the line that stretched for all of about 3¾ miles (6km) from Paddington to Farringdon St, opened in 1863. It's on platforms No 5 and 6 (Circle and Hammersmith & City lines) and was restored to its dimly lit former self in 1983.

SHERLOCK HOLMES MUSEUM Map pp422-3

☎ 7935 8866; www.sherlock-holmes.co.uk; 221b Baker St; £6/4; ☉ 9.30am-6pm; tube Baker Street

This museum gives its address as 221b Baker St, but the house in which Sherlock Holmes fictionally resided is actually the Abbey National building a bit further south. Fans of the books will enjoy examining the three floors of reconstructed Victoriana, deerstalkers, burning candles, flickering grates, and maybe even the dodgy waxworks of Professor Moriarty and 'the Man with the Twisted Lip', but might wonder why there isn't more on Arthur Conan Doyle.

ALL SOULS CHURCH Map pp426-7

☎ 7580 3522; Langham Pl W1; ☉ 9.30am-6pm, closed Sat; tube Oxford Circus

A Nash solution for the curving, northern sweep of Regent St was this delightful church, which features a circular columned porch and distinctive needle-like spire, reminiscent of an ancient Greek temple. The church was very unpopular when completed in 1824; a contemporary cartoon by George Cruikshank shows Nash rather painfully impaled on the spire through the bottom with the words 'Nashional Taste!!!' below it. It was bombed extensively during the Blitz and renovated in 1951.

BROADCASTING HOUSE Map pp426-7

☎ 0870 603 0304; www.bbc.co.uk; Portland Pl; ☉ shop 9.30am-6pm Mon-Sat, 10am-5.30pm Sun; tube Oxford Circus

Opposite All Souls is Broadcasting House, from which the BBC began radio broadcasting in 1932. There's a shop stocking any number of products relating to BBC programmes but most activity these days take place in the enormous glassy complex in Shepherd's Bush (hop on the website above if you want to get tickets to a recording).

PADDINGTON, BAYSWATER, KING'S CROSS & EUSTON

ST PANCRAS STATION Map pp420-1

☎ 7304 3921; www.lcrproperties.com; Euston Rd NW1; tours £5 (no booking); 🕑 entrance hall 11am-1.30pm Mon-Fri, tours 11am and 1.30pm Sat-Sun; tube King's Cross

If you use the tube for any length of time, chances are you'll pass through King's Cross-St Pancras station, in which case you should rise to the surface and check out this fabulously imposing Victorian Gothic masterpiece, which was built as a hotel by the renowned architect George Gilbert Scott in 1876. At the back is a dramatic glass-and-iron train shed, engineered by the great Brunel. There are plans to convert the chambers back into a hotel, possibly from some time in 2004, so you should visit this great building while you still can. Bear in mind that there are no lifts and to follow the tour you'll have to climb several flights of stairs.

BRITISH LIBRARY Map pp418-19

☎ switchboard 7412 7000, visitor services 7412 7332; www.bl.uk; 96 Euston Rd NW1; admission free; 🕑 10am-6pm Mon, 9.30am-6pm Tue-Thu, 9.30am-6.30pm Fri-Sat; tube King's Cross

The British Library came in for some stick when it opened in 1998, which was to be expected since it took 15 years to build and, at a cost of £500 million, was Britain's most expensive building. Much of the criticism was levelled at Colin St John Wilson's exterior of straight lines of red brick, which Prince Charles reckoned was akin to a 'secret-police building'. But even people who didn't like the building from the outside – we do – couldn't fault the spectacularly cool and spacious interior.

It is the nation's principal copyright library and stocks one copy of every British publication as well as historical manuscripts, books and maps from the British Museum. The library counts some 186 miles (1300km) of shelving on four basement levels and will have some 12 million volumes when it reaches the limit of its storage capacity.

At the centre of the building is the wonderful **King's Library**, the 65,000-volume collection of the insane George III, given to the nation by his son, George IV, in 1823 and now housed in a six-storey, 17m-high glass-walled tower. To the left as you enter are the library's excellent bookshop and exhibition galleries.

Most of the complex is devoted to storage and scholarly research, but there are also several public displays including the **John Ritblat**

British Library (left)

Gallery: Treasures of the British Library, which spans almost three millennia and every continent. Among the most important documents here are: the Magna Carta (1215); the Codex Sinaiticus, the first complete text of the New Testament, written in Greek in the 4th century; a Gutenberg Bible (1455), the first Western book printed using movable type; Shakespeare's First Folio (1623); manuscripts by some of Britain's best-known authors (eg Lewis Carroll, Jane Austen, George Eliot and Thomas Hardy); and even some of the Beatles' earliest handwritten lyrics.

You can hear historic recordings such as the first one ever, made by Thomas Edison in 1877, James Joyce reading from *Ulysses* and Nelson Mandela's famous speech at the Rivonia trial in 1964, at the **National Sound Archive Jukeboxes**, where the selections are changed regularly. The **Turning the Pages** exhibit allows you a 'virtual browse' through several important texts including the Sforza Book of Hours, the Diamond Sutra and a Leonardo da Vinci notebook.

The **Philatelic Exhibition**, next to the John Ritblat Gallery, is based on collections established in 1891 with the bequest of the Tapling Collection, and now consists of over 80,000 items including postage and revenue stamps, postal stationery and first-day covers from almost every country and from all periods.

The **Workshop of Words, Sounds and Images** documents the development of writing and communicating through the written word by carefully examining the work of early scribes, printers and bookbinders. The sound section compares recordings on different media, from early-20th-century wax cylinders to modern

CDs. The **Pearson Gallery** hosts some sensational special exhibitions, ranging from 'Oscar Wilde: A Life in Six Acts' to 'Chinese Printing Today'.

There are **guided tours** (£6/4.50; 3pm Mon, Wed, Fri, 10.30am & 3pm Sat) of the library's public areas and another that includes a visit to one of the reading rooms (£7/5.50; 11.30am & 3pm Sun). Call the main number to make a booking.

ST PANCRAS NEW CHURCH Map pp418-9
☎ 7388 1461; Cnr Euston Rd & Upper Woburn Pl WC1; 9am-5pm Tue-Fri, 9.15am-11am Sat, 7.45am-noon & 5.30-7.15pm Sun; tube King's Cross

The striking Greek revival St Pancras New Church has a tower designed to imitate the Temple of the Winds in Athens, a portico with six Ionic columns mirroring the Erechtheion on the Acropolis and a wing decorated with caryatids, again like the Erechtheion. When it was completed in 1822 this was the most expensive new church to have been built in London since St Paul's Cathedral. Within the porch you can see a large tablet in memory of the 31 people who lost their lives in the King's Cross tube station fire of November 1987.

LONDON CANAL MUSEUM Map pp420-1
☎ 7713 0836; www.canalmuseum.org.uk; New Wharf Rd N1; adult/child £2.50/1.25; 10am-4.30pm Tue-Sun; tube King's Cross

This quirky and old-fashioned museum is housed in an old ice warehouse (with a deep well where the frozen commodity was stored) and traces the history of Regent's Canal, the ice business and the development of ice cream through models, photographs, exhibits and ar-chive documentaries. The ice trade was huge in late Victorian London, and 35,000 tonnes of it were imported from Norway in 1899.

CAMDEN

CAMDEN MARKET Map pp418-19
cnr Camden High & Buck Sts NW1; 9am-5.30pm Thu-Sun; tube Camden Town/Chalk Farm

Although – or perhaps because – it stopped being cutting-edge several thousand cheap leather jackets ago, Camden market gets a whopping 10 million visitors each year and is London's most popular 'unticketed' tourist attraction. What started out as a collection of attractive craft stalls by Camden Lock on the Grand Union Canal now extends most of the way from Camden Town tube station to Chalk Farm tube station to the north. You'll find a bit of everything but a lot of tourist-oriented

tack (p333 for more information). It's positively mobbed at the weekend, and the spectacle of crowds of people gorging themselves on sausages and chips out of polystyrene boxes ain't pretty.

JEWISH MUSEUM Map pp418-9
☎ 7284 1997; www.jewishmuseum.org.uk; Raymond Burton House, 129-31 Albert St NW1; adult/child/senior £3.50/1.50/2.50; 10am-4pm Mon-Thu, 10am-5pm Sun; tube Camden Town

This branch of the Jewish Museum examines Judaism and Judaic religious practices in the prestigious **Ceremonial Art Gallery**, and the story of the Jewish community in Britain from the time of the Normans to the present day through paintings, photographs and artefacts in the **History Gallery**. There's also a gallery for temporary exhibitions.

The **Jewish Museum, Finchley** (☎ 8349 1143; Sternberg Centre, 80 East End Rd N3; adult/child/concession £2/free/1; 10.30am-5pm Mon-Thu, 10.30am-4.30pm Sun; tube Finchley Central) houses the museum's social-history collections, including the oral history and photographic archives, and hosts changing exhibitions. Its permanent collection includes reconstructions of the tailoring and cabinet-making workshops from the East End, as well as a Holocaust exhibition focusing on the experience of one Jewish Briton who survived Auschwitz.

Barnyard Blitz

So young Londoners don't grow up thinking cows' ud-ders are shaped like milk bottles, a number of farms have been set up across the city where real live farm animals moo, bleat, oink, eat, roll around in shit and do whatever else it is that comes natural to barnyard beings. If you and your kin need a break from urban London, head to:

Coram's Fields (Map pp420-1; ☎ 7837 6138; 93 Guildford St WC1; 9am-7pm Jun-Sep, 9am-6pm Oct-May; tube Russell Square)

Hackney City Farm (Map pp416-7; ☎ 7729 6381; 1a Goldsmith's Row E2; 10am-4.30pm Tue-Sun; tube Bethnal Green, rail Cambridge Heath)

Kentish Town City Farm (Map p415; ☎ 7916 5420; 1 Cressfield Close, Grafton Rd NW5; 9.30am-5.30pm; tube Kentish Town)

Spitalfields Farm (Map pp416-7; ☎ 7247 8762; Weaver St E1; Tue-Sun 10.30am-5.30pm; tube Shoreditch/Liverpool Street)

THE NORTHERN HEIGHTS

Eating p251; Sleeping p349

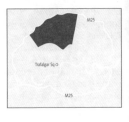

Fashionable north London is made up of villages. In descending order of social status, they begin at Hampstead with its vast, wild and rambling heath, which has been a popular area with writers, artists and the moneyed since the early-19th century when Romantic poet John Keats spent two of his few years knocking about here. The refined and picturesque village of Highgate, perched on top of its own hill, has superb views of London in case the privileged locals get bored with the pleasant parks and verdant woods surrounding them. Muswell Hill and Crouch End, further north and east respectively, also feel like small towns just outside London because the tube reaches neither and they are both self-contained, self-sufficient and somewhat self-satisfied. Edwardian Muswell Hill has a string of exceptional shops, a convivial vibe and the inimitable Alexandra Palace but, curiously, not one good pub. Crouch Enders have it all, just with more celebrities and kids. Stoke Newington isn't part of the chain of hills that make up the Heights, though it may as well be as it can only be reached by bus and is cheerfully detached from the megalopolis. It's dominated by the skinny and hippy-chic Church St, lined with good shops, pubs, restaurants and one of London's best places to be dead, the lovely Abney Park Cemetery.

HAMPSTEAD & HIGHGATE

HIGHGATE CEMETERY Map p415

☎ 8340 1834; www.highgate-cemetery.org; Swain's Lane N6; £2 (plus £1 per camera); ☯ 10am-5pm Mon-Fri & 11am-5pm Sat-Sun Apr-Oct, 10am-4pm Mon-Fri & 11am-4pm Sat-Sun Nov-Mar, tours 2pm Mon-Fri & every hour Sat-Sun Apr-Oct (no bookings); tube Highgate

Most famous as the final resting place of Karl Marx and other notable mortals, Highgate Cemetery is set in 20 wonderfully wild and atmospheric hectares with dramatic and over-decorated Victorian graves and sombre tombs. It's divided into two parts. On the east side you can visit the grave of Marx who, coincidentally, is buried opposite the free-market economist, Herbert Spencer – Marx and Spencer, does it ring a bell? This slightly overgrown and wild part of the cemetery is a very pleasant walk but it's merely the overflow area. It's the wonderfully atmospheric western section of this Victorian Valhalla that is the main draw. To visit it, you'll have to take a tour and deal directly with the brigade of stroppy silver-haired ladies who run the cemetery and act like they are the home guard defending it from the Krauts (eyes straight, shoulders back, chest out, march!). It is a maze of winding paths leading to the Circle of Lebanon, rings of tombs flanking a circular path and topped with a majestic, centuries-old cedar tree. The guides are engaging and gladly point out the various symbols of the age and the eminent dead occupying the tombs, including the scientist Michael Faraday and the dog-show founder Charles Cruft. 'Dissenters' (non–Church of Englanders) were buried way off in the woods. The cemetery still works – the best plots still go to those with the most money – and closes during burials so you might want to call ahead just to be sure it will be open.

Dave Stewart, Crouch End

Until recently, Dave Stewart of the Eurythmics ran a recording studio in a church just off Crouch End Broadway. He once extended an open invitation to his friend, Bob Dylan, to pop by the studio any time he was in London and at a loose end. Sure enough, kicking around town one afternoon, Bob decides to pay Dave a visit, so he hops in a cab and asks the driver to take him to the address on Crouch End Hill. If you've ever been around these parts, you'll know that there are any number of streets featuring the words 'Crouch' and 'End' and 'Hill' so it wasn't that surprising that the poor cabbie dropped him off at the wrong road.

None the wiser, Bob knocks on the door and asks the woman if Dave is in. As luck would have it, her husband was also called Dave (and a big Dylan fan) so she says, 'No, he's just popped out but, please, come in and wait'. Half an hour later, Dave the plumber comes through the door and asks his wife if there are any messages. 'No,' she said, 'but Bob Dylan's in the living room having a cup of tea.'

Dave the plumber eventually told Bob where he could find Dave the rock star, and they all lived happily ever after.

HAMPSTEAD HEATH Map p415

☎ 7485 4491; tube Gospel Oak or Hampstead, rail Hampstead Heath

Sprawling Hampstead Heath, with its rolling woodlands and meadows, is a million miles away – well approximately four – from the city of London. It covers 320 hectares, most of it woods, hills and meadows, and is home to about 100 bird species. It's a wonderful place for a ramble, and you can follow in the footsteps of luminaries such as the poets Coleridge, Keats and Pope as well as painters Hogarth and Constable who all lived around here. Constable studied the clouds and skies above Hampstead Heath, painting more than 100 'skyscapes' that he would later match to subjects in his most famous paintings.

If walking is too pedestrian for you, sections of the heath area are laid out for football and cricket, and there are also several bathing ponds (separate ones for women, men, mixed, dogs). Walk up Parliament Hill or the hill in North Wood, and on a clear day you'll be able to see all the way to Canary Wharf and the Docklands. Those of an artistic bent should make a beeline to **Kenwood House** but stop to admire the sculptures by Henry Moore and Barbara Hepworth on the way.

If you work up a thirst, there's no better place to quench it than at the atmospheric – and possibly haunted – **Spaniard's Inn** (p275), which has a fascinating history and a terrific beer garden.

By night Hampstead Heath is a gay cruising ground, activities that are generally overlooked by the authorities. On South Green, opposite Hampstead Heath station, is one of Britain's oldest lavatories, which was built in 1897 and restored in 2000. This was gay playwright Joe Orton's lavatory of choice for 'cottaging' (cruising for gay sex). George Orwell worked in a bookshop opposite the toilets and doubtless used them now and then for their originally intended purpose.

KENWOOD HOUSE Map p415

☎ 8348 1286; www.english-heritage.org.uk; Hampstead Lane NW3; admission free; ⏱ house 10am-5.30pm Apr-Sep, 10am-5pm Oct, 10am-4pm Nov-Mar (never open before 10.30am Wed & Fri), the Suffolk Collection (upstairs) 11am-4.30pm Thu-Sun; tube Archway/Golders Green, then bus 210

At the northern end of the heath, this magnificent neoclassical mansion stands in a glorious sweep of landscaped gardens leading down to the picturesque lake, around which classical concerts take place in summer (p309). The

Kenwood House, Hampstead (left)

house was remodelled by Robert Adam in the 18th century, and rescued from the clutches of developers by Lord Iveagh Guinness who donated it and the wonderful collection of art it contains to the nation in 1927. The Iveagh Bequest contains paintings by the likes of Gainsborough, Reynolds, Turner, Hals, Vermeer and Van Dyck and is one of the finest small collections in Britain.

Robert Adam's Great Stairs and the library, one of 14 rooms open to the public, are especially fine. The Suffolk Collection has limited opening hours and occupies the 1st floor. It includes Jacobean portraits by William Larkin and royal Stuart portraits by Van Dyck and Lely. The subjects were, pardon the pun, no oil paintings.

The **Brew House Café** has excellent grub, from light snacks to full meals, and plenty of room on the lovely garden terrace.

KEATS HOUSE Map p415

☎ 7435 2062; www.keatshouse.org.uk; Wentworth Place, Keats Grove NW3; adult/child under 16/concession £3/free/1.50; ⏱ noon-5pm Tue-Sun Apr-Oct, noon-4pm Nov-Mar; tube Hampstead, rail Hampstead Heath

A stone's throw from the lower reaches of the heath, this elegant Regency house was home to the golden boy of the Romantic poets from 1818 to 1820. Never short of generous mates, Keats was persuaded to take refuge here by

Charles Armitage Brown, and it was here that he met his fiancé Fanny Brawne, who was literally the girl next door. Keats wrote his most celebrated poem, *Ode to a Nightingale*, whilst sitting under a plum tree in the garden (now replaced) in 1819. Unfortunately, the most valuable mementos – including original manuscripts and love letters – are in need of careful conservation and are no longer on display. That said there is still plenty to see and the house is dripping with atmosphere thanks in part to the collection of Regency furniture amassed here in recent years. Rather than supplying pamphlets or audio guides, the staff here tell stories about Keats and the house as you wander around, perhaps examining the ring he gave Fanny (which she wore for the rest of her life) or the bust of Keats which is set at the poet's exact height: barely 5ft 1in!

American visitors might like to know that the house was saved and opened to the public largely due to the donations of Keats' fans in the US. Staff are playing a kind of US state bingo and need visitors from only two more states to have the full set (so be sure to let them know where you're from). The house will most likely close for a couple of months from Easter 2004; in fact, if you're coming to Hampstead specifically to visit the house at any time, you should probably call ahead just to make sure it's open as ongoing repairs are required.

NO 2 WILLOW ROAD Map p415
☎ 7435 6166; www.nationaltrust.org.uk; 2 Willow Rd; adult/concession £4.50/2.25; ☽ noon-5pm Thu-Sat Apr-Oct, noon-5pm Sat Mar & Nov, guided tours at noon, 1pm and 2pm; tube Hampstead, rail Hampstead Heath

Fans of modern architecture may want to swing past this property, the central house in a block of three, designed by the 'structural rationalist' Ernö Goldfinger in 1939 as his family home. Though the architect was following Georgian principles in creating it, many people think it looks uncannily like the sort of mundane 1950s architecture you see everywhere. They may look similar now, but 2 Willow Rd was in fact a forerunner; the others

were mostly bad imitations. The interior, with its cleverly designed storage space and collection of artworks by Henry Moore, Max Ernst and Bridget Riley, is certainly interesting and accessible to all. A visit is by one-hour guided tour only.

BURGH HOUSE Map p415
☎ 7431 0144; New End Sq NW3; admission free; ☽ noon-5pm Wed-Sun; tube Hampstead

If you happen to be in the neighbourhood, this late-17th-century Queen Anne mansion houses the **Hampstead Museum** of local history, a small art gallery and the delightful Buttery tearoom, where you can get a decent and reasonably priced lunch from Wednesday to Saturday.

FENTON HOUSE Map p415
☎ 7435 3471; www.nationaltrust.org.uk; Windmill Hill, Hampstead Grove NW3; £4.50/2.25; ☽ 2-5pm Wed-Fri & 11am-5pm Sat-Sun Apr-Oct, 2-5pm Sat-Sun Mar; tube Hampstead

One of the oldest houses in Hampstead, this late-17th-century merchant's residence has a charming walled garden with roses and an orchard, fine collections of porcelain and keyboard instruments – including a 1612 harpsichord that was played by Handel – as well as 17th-century needlework pictures and original Georgian furniture.

HIGHGATE WOOD Map p415
☽ dawn-dusk; tube Highgate

With more than 28 hectares of ancient woodland, this park is a wonderful spot for a walk any time of the year. It's also teeming with life, and some 70 different bird species have been recorded here, along with five types of bat, 12 of butterfly, and 80 different kinds of spider. It also has a huge clearing in the centre for sports, a popular playground and nature trail for kids and a range of activities – from falconry to bat-watching – throughout the year. The **Oshobasho Café** (p251) in the centre of the wood has a pretty garden, a tranquil atmosphere and decent vegetarian snacks.

Top Five – Northern Heights
- Hampstead Heath (p185)
- Highgate Cemetery (p184)
- Highgate Wood (right)
- Keats House (p185)
- Kenwood House (p185)

MUSWELL HILL
ALEXANDRA PARK & PALACE
☎ 8365 2121; www.alexandrapalace.com; Alexandra Palace Way N22; rail Alexandra Palace

Built in 1873 as north London's answer to Crystal Palace, Alexandra Palace suffered the ignoble fate of burning to the ground only 16 days after opening. Encouraged by attendance figures, investors decided to rebuild and it reopened just two years later. Though it boasted a theatre, museum, lecture hall, library and Great Hall with one of the world's largest organs, it was no match for Crystal Palace. It housed German POWs during WWI and in 1936 the world's first television transmission – a variety show called *Here's Looking at You* – took place here. The palace burned down again in 1980 but was rebuilt for the third time and opened in 1988. Today 'Ally Pally' (as it is affectionately known, even though locals are paying increased council rates since it was rebuilt) is largely a multipurpose conference and exhibition centre with a number of additional facilities, including an indoor ice-skating rink, the panoramic Phoenix Bar & Beer Garden and funfairs in summer.

The park in which it stands sprawls over some 88 hectares consisting of public gardens, a nature conservation area, a deer park and various sporting facilities including a boating lake, pitch-and-putt golf course and skate park.

STOKE NEWINGTON
ABNEY PARK CEMETERY Map p414
☎ 7275 7557; Stoke Newington Church St N16; admission free; ☾ 8am-dusk; rail Stoke Newington, bus 73

Unfairly dubbed by some as 'the poor man's Highgate', this magical place was bought up and developed by a private firm from 1840 to provide burial grounds for central London's overflow. It was the first cemetery for dissenters and many of the most influential London Presbyterians, Quakers and Baptists are buried here, including the founder of the Salvation Army, William Booth, whose grand tombstone greets you as you enter from Church St. Since the 1950s the cemetery has been left to fend for itself and, these days, is as much a bird and plant sanctuary as a delightfully overgrown ruin. The derelict chapel at the heart of the park could be straight out of a horror film, and the atmosphere of the whole place is nothing short of magical.

NORTHWEST LONDON
Eating p252; Sleeping p351

Upper class St John's Wood, a leafy suburb of genteel houses and overdressed residents, is due west of Regent's Park. Since the Saatchi Gallery relocated to County Hall in 2002, local attractions have been reduced to two prominent addresses and a painted road. The Beatles recorded most of their albums at 3 Abbey Rd, including *Abbey Road* (1969) itself, with the famous shot for the album cover taken on the zebra crossing outside. The other important address is that of world cricket, at Lord's Cricket Ground.

Slightly southwest are Maida Vale and the unexpectedly pretty corner of London known as Little Venice, with its tree-lined streets, handsome locks and colourful boats on Regent's Canal. Little Venice is home to the spectacular pub, **Crocker's Folly**, built by a developer named Crocker after he'd got the inside word that a new rail terminus was going to be built here. The station ended up being built almost a kilometre away and the, er, disappointed Crocker threw himself off the roof.

The status of the famous Notting Hill Carnival (in late August) reflects the multicultural appeal of this part of west London, into which West Indian immigrants moved in the 1950s. After decades of exploitation, strife and the occasional racist riot, the community took off in the 1980s and this is now a thriving, vibrant corner of the city and an emblem for multicultural London. Although there's not a lot to see in Notting Hill – and it's not like it's portrayed in the eponymous and saccharine film – it's a great place to hang out and has lots of highly individual shops, restaurants and pubs. Narrow Portobello Rd is its heart and soul (as opposed to Notting Hill Gate) and most well known these days for hosting London's best market (p334). If you're in the mood for the flicks, you should check out the recently renovated **Edwardian Electric Cinema** (p294), the oldest cinema in the country. Unfailingly fashionable Westbourne Grove, roughly in the northeastern corner, is lined with distinctive shops, pubs, artists' galleries and studios.

Top Five – Northwest London
- Kensal Green Cemetery (p188)
- Leighton House (p188)
- Lord's Cricket Ground (p188)
- Notting Hill Carnival (p12)
- Westbourne Grove (p188)

ST JOHN'S WOOD & MAIDA VALE

LORD'S CRICKET GROUND Map pp418-9

☎ tours office 7616 8585, switchboard 7616 8500; www.lords.org; St John's Wood Rd NW8; tours adult/child/concession £7/4.50/5.50; ⏰ 10am, noon & 2pm Apr-Sep, noon & 2pm Oct-Mar when there's no play; tube St John's Wood

The next best thing to watching a Test at Lord's is the absorbing and anecdotal 90-minute tour of the ground and facilities, which takes in the famous Long Room, where members watch the games surrounded by portraits of cricket's great and good, and a museum featuring evocative memorabilia that will appeal to fans old and new. Australian fans will be keen to pose next to the famous little urn containing the Ashes, which remain in English hands no matter how many times the Aussies beat them. However, it was due to be taken away for restoration at the end of 2003 so you'd better call and make sure it's back. The ground itself is dominated by a striking media centre that looks like a clock radio, but you should also look out for the famous weather vane in the shape of Father Time and the remarkable tent-like modern Mound Stand.

NOTTING HILL & WESTBOURNE GROVE

KENSAL GREEN CEMETERY Map pp416-7

Harrow Rd, Kensal Green W10; tours £5; ⏰ tours 2pm Sun; tube Kensal Green

Thackeray and Trollope are among the eminent dead folk at this huge and handsome Victorian cemetery, which made a name for itself in the 19th century as the place where the celebrities preferred to RIP. Supposedly based on the Cimetière du Père-Lachaise in Paris, the cemetery is distinguished by its Greek revival architecture, arched entrances and the outrageously ornate tombs that bear testimony to 19th-century delusions of grandeur. The two-hour tours start from the Anglican chapel in the centre of the cemetery (wooooooo!).

LEIGHTON HOUSE Map pp436-7

☎ 7602 3316; 12 Holland Park Rd W14; admission by donation; ⏰ 11am-5.30pm Wed-Mon; tube High Street Kensington

Near Holland Park and Kensington – but frequently overlooked – is Leighton House, a gem of a house designed in 1866 by George Aitchison. It was once the home of Lord Leighton (1830–96), who was a painter belonging to the Olympian movement; he decorated parts of the house in Middle Eastern style. The finest of all the rooms is the exquisite Arab Hall, added in 1879 and densely covered with blue and green tiles from Rhodes, Cairo, Damascus and Iznik (Turkey) and with a fountain tinkling away in the centre. Even the wooden lattice work of the windows and gallery was brought from Damascus. The house contains notable Pre-Raphaelite paintings by Burne-Jones, Watts, Millais and Lord Leighton himself. Restoration of the back garden has returned it to its Victorian splendour – as has work on the stairwell and upstairs rooms.

Worth a Trip Further North

FREUD MUSEUM Map pp418-9

☎ 7435 2002; www.freud.org.uk; 20 Maresfield Gardens NW3; ⏰ noon-5pm Wed-Sun; tube Finchley Road

After fleeing from Nazi-occupied Vienna in 1938, Sigmund Freud came to London and to this house where he lived the last 18 months of his life. His daughter – a renowned child psychologist – lived here until she died in 1986, after which, and according to her wishes, it became the Freud Museum. Along with Freud's original couch, the house is crammed with his extensive collection of books and artefacts, while commentary is provided through extracts from his writings. A poignant photograph shows how meticulously Freud tried to re-create his Viennese home in the unfamiliar surroundings of quiet and leafy residential London.

ROYAL AIR FORCE MUSEUM HENDON Map p414

☎ 8205 2266; www.rafmuseum.org.uk; Grahame Park Way NW9; 10am-6pm; tube Colindale (plus easy 10-min walk)

For all things aeronautical, plane spotters should hurry out to Henley and the 'birthplace of British Aviation'. You can trace the history of human flight with the help of more than 70 aircraft, photo exhibitions, flight simulators and a spectacular sound and light show called 'Our Finest Hour' which focuses on the Battle of Britain.

London for Kids

Somewhere along the line Londoners, and Britons in general, got the reputation for being excessively strict with their kids. If it used to be the case, it isn't now. Although the old axiom that children should be seen and not heard in public still has traction, London parents are more likely to pamper their princes and princesses these days. That said, you might not always find nappy-changing facilities or high chairs so it sometimes pays to plan and telephone ahead.

The city is jam-packed with things to keep the little ones amused and there are stacks of fun places for all the family. Central London's many parks never disappoint, while the Science Museum (p135), Natural History Museum (p135), Richmond Museum (p199), Theatre Museum (p94), Bethnal Green Museum of Childhood (p167), Hackney Museum (p167), and Ragged School Museum (p168) are full of engaging gadgets and exhibits. Skip the queues at Madame Tussaud's and the general unpleasantness of the London Dungeon and head instead to the always impressive Tower of London (p112). Check out the London Zoo (p181), the Wetland Centre (p192) and city farms (p159), go for a ride on a canal barge, hop on a Duck Tour (p90) climb aboard the *Cutty Sark* (p172), make loud noises at Firepower (p177) and rub brass at St Martin-in-the-Fields (p97) but don't miss the dizzying heights of the London Eye (p157).

WEST LONDON

Eating p254; Sleeping p353; Shopping p331

As west London fades from the old money of Kensington into the urban sprawl of Hammersmith, the two meet seamlessly in Earl's Court, a hard-to-define no-man's-land. Its '80s nickname 'Kangaroo Valley' attests to the area's popularity with backpackers from down under, which is still the case today. However, Earl's Court is a lot more than just that. Leave the shabby looking Earl's Court Rd with its fast-food bars and busy traffic and you'll be in a quiet world of Victorian mansion blocks and smart restaurants juxtaposed with late-night gay bars. In the 1980s, Earl's Court was the original gay village, later overtaken by Soho, but still not forgotten today. Freddie Mercury lived and died at 1 Garden Place and remains the neighbourhood's most famous resident.

A walk down to West Brompton will reveal the magnificent cemetery and bars spanning all tastes and proclivities. Earl's Court is not a place many would visit for its own merits, but its location and transport links make it a popular area for visitors and a great place for a meal or night out. One of the only notable sights of the area is Brompton Cemetery, the resting place of many west Londoners over the past 200 years, and a pleasant place to explore in good weather.

Despite the unsightliness of Shepherd's Bush Green and the general chaos that rules here, the curiously-named west London hub of Shepherd's Bush is in the process of a very real renaissance and is a great place to hang out and eat. The strange name reputedly comes from the fact that shepherds would graze their flocks on the common here, en route for Smithfield Market in east London, back when Shepherd's Bush was another rural village outside the city. It was here that Miles Syndercombe attempted to assassinate Oliver Cromwell in 1657, failing and being hung, drawn and quartered for his efforts. In the same vein, where children now play on the green, a gallows stood until the 1750s, and this was a popular spot to watch hangings.

Synonymous for many with the sprawling BBC Television Centre in nearby White City that opened in 1960, the area had actually become famous 50 years earlier as the site of the 1908 London Olympics, as well as the Great Exhibition of the same year. The Olympics were held here again in 1948, but the stadium was torn down in 1984, so nothing remains from London's Olympic past today. During the '60s, Shepherd's Bush was used as the setting for the Who's film, *Quadrophenia*, so mods on pilgrimage are not an uncommon sight.

Today Shepherd's Bush is a multi-ethnic place full of quirky cafés, bars and character. It won't disappoint those looking for good venues to eat and drink in, especially since a slew of gastropubs opened in recent years. The world-famous Shepherd's Bush Empire, on the Green, is also one of London's best concert venues, and regularly hosts world-class music acts.

Hammersmith is a different story, a very urban neighbourhood dominated by a huge flyover and roundabout, with little to entice the visitor save some decent restaurants and the famously arty Riverside Studios. With time to spare there's a good set of riverfront pubs on the Chiswick side of Hammersmith Bridge plus a pleasant two-mile (3km) walk along the Thames from the shopping centre beside the bridge to Chiswick itself.

EARL'S COURT & WEST BROMPTON

BROMPTON CEMETERY Map pp436-7

☎ 7351 9936; Old Brompton Rd SW5; ☺ 8am-dusk; tours Sun, £3, meet at 2pm at the South Lodge, Fulham Rd entrance; tube West Brompton

The long main avenue from Brompton Rd leads down to a chapel surrounded by colonnades, modelled after St Peter's in Rome. While the most famous resident is Emmeline Pankhurst, the pioneer of women's suffrage in Britain, the cemetery is most interesting as the inspiration for many of Beatrix Potter's characters. A local resident in her youth before she moved to the North, Potter seems to have taken many names from the deceased of Brompton Cemetery and immortalised them in her world-famous books. Names to be found include Mr Nutkin, Mr McGregor, Jeremiah Fisher, Tommy Brock – and even a Peter Rabbett. Today, Brompton Cemetery serves a second function as a popular gay cruising ground.

SHEPHERD'S BUSH & HAMMERSMITH

BBC TELEVISION CENTRE

☎ 0870 603 0304; Wood Lane, W12; adult/student & child over 10 £7.95/5.95, no children under 10; tour times vary, bookings essential; tube White City

The chance to visit the vast complex of studios and offices that bring the BBC's programmes to the world has now replaced the defunct BBC Experience at Broadcasting House, and anyone interested in TV production should be very glad of it. Guided tours, which change in accordance with broadcasting schedules, take in the BBC News and Weather Centres as well as studios where shows are being made, and it's a fascinating glimpse into the Corporation at shop-floor level. TVC, as it's known to all BBC staff, opened in 1960 and is where TV favourites from *Top of the Pops* to *The Weakest Link* are still filmed each week. Keep your eyes peeled, as part of the fun is the endless TV-star-spotting between locations. Alternatively, if you book in advance online, it is possible to go and watch the recording of certain shows for free at one of the BBC's many London studios. Log on to www.bbc.co.uk/whatson/tickets to see what's available during your stay.

Detail on the Hammersmith bridge

RIVERSIDE STUDIOS Map p414

☎ 8237 1000; Crisp Rd W6; ☺ 9am-11pm Mon-Sat, noon-11pm Sun; tube Hammersmith

This is west London's equivalent of the Institute for Contemporary Arts (ICA), a mixed-media arts centre with two good-sized auditoriums that present films, theatre, modern dance and about a dozen art shows per year. It recently scandalised London by presenting *XXX*, a Spanish production described as 'pornographic' by the *Evening Standard*. It's still the place to be for cutting-edge culture, with a far less stuffy attitude and a better repertory cinema than the ICA. There is also a decent bar, with a fantastic terrace overlooking Hammersmith Bridge, for a drink or meal.

KELMSCOTT HOUSE

☎ 8741 3735; 26 Upper Mall W6; william.morris@care4free.net; admission free; ☺ 2-5pm Thu & Sat; tube Hammersmith

The William Morris Society – established in honour of the designer, craftsman, poet and socialist – is housed in the very building where Morris had his printing press and where he later set up the Socialist League in the coach house. The displays include original interior designs by Morris as well as work by Sir Edward Byrne-Jones and Morris' daughter May. While it has limited opening hours to the public, anyone with a particular interest in Morris is welcome to use the library by arrangement. The society also holds talks and arranges visits to other Morris-connected landmarks in the UK.

SOUTHWEST LONDON

Eating p256; Sleeping p355; Shopping p332

It's the common pursuit of a large proportion of the London populace to find bits of London that aren't like London at all, and much of Southwest London represents such a beacon of bucolic relief. It's here that you escape to the country without leaving the city at all. The best time to visit is on a warm sunny day, when the hours seem to stretch on forever. The area loses some of its shine under grey skies so is best saved for the summer if you have the choice.

During the day Southwest London is a fairly quiet, residential area you'll see lots of young mothers out pushing prams and doing their shopping. This is the best time to enjoy the area's many green spaces – walk along the Thames Path from Putney Bridge to Barnes, lounge by the river in Bishop's Park, play tennis in South Park, sup on a pint by Parson's Green or picnic on Barnes Common.

It's at night that the area comes alive and the resident antipodean and ex-public school populations make themselves known. Fulham is a very popular place to go out in town with a plethora of good pubs, bars and restaurants. Putney and Barnes like to think that they're a little more refined, though a trip to any of the pubs on the High St on a Saturday night will put pay to that opinion.

Although southwest London is a little far out if you're only in London for a long weekend, it's the perfect place to base yourself for a longer stay, which is probably why there are so many Aussies and Kiwis living and working here.

Top Five – Southwest London

- Barnes Common (p192)
- Chelsea Village (right)
- Fulham Palace (below)
- Thames Path (p192)
- Wetland Centre London (p192)

FULHAM & PARSON'S GREEN

Fulham and Parson's Green merge neatly into one neighbourhood that sits comfortably in a curve of the Thames between Chelsea and Hammersmith. While the attractive Victorian terraces and riverside location have drawn a very well-to-do crowd, Fulham's blue-collar roots are still evident in the strong tradition of support for Fulham Football Club. Fulham, though, have been forced out of their home ground at Craven Cottage and their infamous patron, Mohamed Al Fayed, is yet to find them a permanent new home. You can catch a glimpse of the Cottage on Stevenage Rd down by the river or see the team in action at Loftus Rd, Queen's Park Rangers' home ground.

FULHAM PALACE Map pp416-17

☎ 7736 3233; Bishop's Ave SW6; ☾ Mar-Oct Wed-Sun 2-5pm, Nov-Feb Thu-Sun 1-4pm; admission free, children under 16 must be accompanied; tube Putney Bridge

Summer home of the bishops of London from 704 to 1973, Grade One listed Fulham Palace is an interesting mix of architectural styles set in beautiful gardens and once enclosed by the longest moat in England. You can enjoy the small botanic gardens as Catharine of Aragon and Elizabeth I, who both stayed here, once did and learn about the history of the palace and its inhabitants in the museum. Although most of the palace is not open to the public, guided tours can be booked in advance through the museum and cost £4. The surrounding land once totalling 36 acres, but now reduced to 13, forms Bishop's Park with a shady promenade along the river, bowling green, tennis courts, rose garden, café and even a paddling pond with fountain for cooling off in on a hot day.

CHELSEA VILLAGE Map pp436-7

Fulham Rd SW6; www.chelseavillage.com; tube Fulham Broadway

This extensive development surrounds Stamford Bridge stadium, home to **Chelsea Football Club**, with a four-star hotel, restaurants, nightclub and luxury health club. It can be tricky to get hold of tickets for big matches, but try ☾ 7386 7799 – it really depends on how well the team is doing at the time. If you don't get to see an actual game you can book a tour of the ground instead (☾ 0870 603 0005; 11am, 1pm/3pm Mon-Fri, 10am/2pm Sat-Sun; adult/under 5/children/family £8/free/5/26). Or check out **Chelsea World of Sport** (☾ 7915 22222;

10am-4pm Tue-Sun, 10am-one hour before kickoff matchdays; adult/under 5/senior & disabled/child & student/family £10/free/5/7/30). This is Chelsea Football Club's pricey paean to itself, tracing, through multimedia displays, the history and achievements of CFC (not many in recent years), Stamford Bridge Stadium and the ever-expanding Chelsea Village complex. There are stacks of interactive games focusing on other sports like tennis, rowing, volleyball, sprinting and climbing.

PUTNEY & BARNES

Putney, of course, is most famed as the starting point of the Oxford & Cambridge Boat Race (opposite), which is beamed live to millions of people across the globe each spring. There are references to the race in the pubs and restaurants in the area and along the Thames Path. Barnes is less well known and the more villagey in feel. Its former residents include the composer Gustav Holst and author Henry Fielding.

The best way to approach Putney is to follow the signposts from Putney Bridge tube station for the footbridge (which runs parallel to the railtrack), admiring the gorgeous riverside houses, with their gardens fronting the murky waters of the Thames, and thereby avoiding the tatty High St until the last possible minute. If you have the time, walking the Thames Path from Putney to Barnes or meandering across the Common from Putney train station are good ways to reach Barnes. Otherwise, catch the overland train from Vauxhall or Waterloo.

WETLAND CENTRE LONDON

☎ 8409 4400; www.wwt.org.uk; Queen Elizabeth's Walk SW13; adult/concession £6.75/4; ⏱ 9.30am-5pm winter, 9.30am-6pm summer; tube Hammersmith then bus No 283 ('the duck bus'), 33, 72 or 72 or rail Barnes
Europe's largest inland wetland project, the 105-acre Wetland Centre was superbly transformed from four Victorian reservoirs in 2000 and attracts some 140 species of birds and 300 types of moths and butterflies – not to mention 100,000 visitors. From the shop and entrance hall, the outdoor paths divide into two walks around the grounds, both of which take in the habitats of its many residents. While the information cards take in some of the more exotic wetland creatures, you can realistically expect to see ducks, swans, geese and coots, although the odd heron and rarer variation,

such as the mandarin duck, can also be found. When the ducklings are young (in spring and summer) this is a wonderful place to watch the tame birds swim and play – they have no fear of humans, so you can come very close. A great place to bring the kids.

BARNES COMMON & GREEN

Local Nature Reserve Barnes Common consists of rambling, open parkland, scythed by roads but large enough that it's easy to escape the traffic – and to get very lost. This is a great place for an aimless ramble or a picnic (stock up at the delis on Church Rd or Barnes High St). Glam fans may like to hunt out the tree, festooned with tributes, that brought Marc Bolan's life to a premature end in 1977.

The Green, at the western edge of the Common, is in some way responsible for the village feel of Barnes itself and is the highlight for local children, who come armed with bread with which to feed the many ducks bobbing on top of its pond. The village stocks used to stand by the water – parents may like to point this out to misbehaving kids.

THAMES PATH
www.thames-path.co.uk
The section of the Thames Path that runs between Putney and Barnes is a great spot to take in a small part of the 210-mile riverside walk. The initial stretch along the Embankment is always a merry hive of activity, with rowers setting off and returning to their boat clubs and punters from nearby pubs lazing by the water. The majority of the walk, though, is intensely rural – at times the only accompaniment is the call of songbirds and the gentle swish of old Father Thames (yes, we *are* still in London). If you'd rather be on the Thames than along it, you can hire boats from **Chas Newens Marine** (☎ 020 8788 4587; www.chastheboat.com; The Boathouse, Embankment SW15; £65-200 per hour, minimum rental 3 hours; ⏱ 9am-6pm).

BEVERLEY BROOK WALK
www.londonwalking.com or www.tfl.gov.uk/streets/walking/home.shtml
The gentle seven-mile walk from Putney to New Malden station follows a tributary of the Thames and takes in the splendours of Putney Lower Common, Barnes Common, Richmond Park and Wimbledon Common. Much of the walk is rural in nature and offers an ideal opportunity to tramp across parkland and woodland. There are many pubs and cafés on the way for those in need of victual encouragement.

The Boat Race

Even those with absolutely no interest in rowing or in Oxbridge find themselves drawn to the Varsity Boat Race, which takes place along the four-mile stretch of water between Putney and Mortlake at the end of March or beginning of April each year. Maybe it's the tradition, maybe it's the romance of 18 men in the prime of youth pitting their strength and wits against one another, or maybe it's the prospect of the boats sinking and their hoity-toity young contents spilling into the river. If you're heading down to watch (get here early to bag a spot on the bank), here are some facts with which to stun and amaze the 250,000 people with the same idea:

- The 2003 Boat Race was the closest ever – the margin between ecstacy (Oxford) and agony (Cambridge) was just one foot; the biggest margin of victory saw Cambridge win by 20 lengths in 1900
- The boats have sunk six times, most recently in 1978
- The 1877 race ended in a dead heat
- The fastest time of 16 minutes and 19 seconds was achieved by Cambridge in 1998
- Both teams pull an average of 600 strokes to complete the course
- The heaviest oarsmen tipped the scales at 17 stone and 5lbs; the lightest oarsmen came in at 9 stone and 6.5lbs
- Cambridge notched up a record 13 successive victories between 1924 and 1936
- For more details, dip into the official website at www.theboatrace.org

SOUTH LONDON

Eating p258; Shopping p332

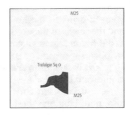

'Sarf' (South) London gets a bad rap. The idea that it's bleaker and offers less to do has been successfully propagated by – guess who? – north Londoners. It is true to say that public transport is worse, because only a small percentage of the Underground network ventures here. However, it really ain't so grim down south. In recent years even north Londoners have discovered there's something rather pleasant about the more affordable property prices and relaxed lifestyle of the river's former B-list side (referring here, of course, to all the place names beginning with that letter, from Battersea to Brixton).

Clapham has long been the flag-bearer for south London style, with plenty of upmarket restaurants and bars lining its high street since the late 1980s. However, in the mid-1990s, anarchic and artistic Brixton started to become gentrified, too.

Attention has started to focus even more recently on Battersea, with the construction of a landmark luxury flats complex, Montevetro, by leading architect Richard Rogers. Firm plans are finally underway for an architectural conversion of the monolithic Battersea Power Station, too.

Kennington already has some lovely streets lined with neo-Georgian terraced houses, so surely it can only be a matter of time before the gentrification of 'Little Portugal' – Stockwell – begins.

BRIXTON

'We gonna rock down to Electric Avenue,' sang Eddy Grant, optimistically, about Brixton's first shopping street blessed with electric lights (just to the left of the Underground station exit). But the Clash's 'Guns of Brixton' took a much darker tone when talking about the riots of the 1980s and community discontent with the police that provoked the street disturbances. Historically, those are just two sides to this edgy, vibrant, multicultural potpourri of a neighbourhood.

There was a settlement here as early as a year after the Norman invasion in 1066.

However, Brixton remained an isolated, far-flung village until the 19th century, when the new Vauxhall Bridge (1816) and the railways (1860) linked it with central London. The years that most shaped contemporary Brixton, however, were the postwar 'Windrush' years, when immigrants arrived from the West Indies in reply to the British government's call for help in solving the labour shortage of the time. (Windrush was the name of one of the leading ships that brought these immigrants to the UK.) A generation later the honeymoon period was over, as economic decline and hostility between the police and blacks (who accounted for only 29% of the population of Brixton at the time) led to the riots in 1981, 1985 and 1995. These centred on Railton Rd and Coldharbour Lane.

Some of the problems still remain. However, the overall mood has been decidedly more upbeat in the last few years. Soaring property prices have sent house-hunters foraging in these parts, and pockets of gentrification sit alongside the more run-down streets. Whatever edge is left from the dark days of the 1980s has only added to the excitement of the area's restaurants (p259) and clubs (p299). Hip hop and reggae still blares from car radios.

Besides coming here to go eating, clubbing, to a gig at the Brixton Academy (p306)or a film at the historic Ritzy (p295), probably the best way to experience the area's Caribbean flavour is to visit Brixton market (p334). Here, you can drink in the heady mix of incense and the smells of the exotic fruits, vegetables and meat on sale. It's a good place to get red snapper, sugar cane or goat's meat for your shopping basket, or to splash out on African clothes and trinkets.

Near Brixton, in Brockwell Park, you'll also find London's best lido, or outdoor swimming pool, Brockwell Park Lido (p304).

BATTERSEA & WANDSWORTH

Southwest along the Thames from Lambeth is Battersea, where dilapidated industrial buildings are fast being replaced by luxury flats. Principal public attractions are a fine riverside park with a children's zoo, and the looming shell of Battersea Power Station.

Poorer, working-class Wandsworth, downriver, was once synonymous with quality headgear. When the Roman Catholic hierarchy in Rome began to order their mitres and birettas from the newly established Huguenot milliners in the 18th century, Wandsworth hats became famous throughout Europe.

Top Five – South London

- Battersea Park (right)
- Brixton Market (p334)
- Brockwell Park Lido (p304)
- Peckham Library (p196)
- Young's Ram Brewery (p195)

BATTERSEA DOGS HOME Map pp440-1
☎ 7622 3626; www.dogshome.org; 4 Battersea Park Rd ⏰ 10.30am-4.15pm Mon-Wed & Fri, 10.30am-3.15pm Sat & Sun; rail Battersea Park

If, like former Spice Girl Geri Halliwell was when she visited, you're in need of a pet and you're a reader who has actually moved to London, you might find yourself a new best friend at this famous shelter for stray dogs. As the RSPCA says, though, a dog is for life, not just for Christmas.

BATTERSEA PARK Maps pp436-7 & 440-1
☎ 8871 7530; ⏰ dawn-dusk; rail Battersea Park

This 50 hectares of greenery stretches between Albert and Chelsea bridges. With its riverside promenade, Henry Moore sculptures and a **Peace Pagoda** (Map p436-7), erected in 1985 by a set of Japanese Buddhists to commemorate Hiroshima Day, its tranquil appearance belies a bloody past. It was once the site of an assassination attempt on King Charles II in 1671 and of a duel in 1829 between the Duke of Wellington and an opponent who accused him of treason.

On weekends, boats can be hired to get around the small lake (£5 per hour); buy your tickets from the booth near the running track (☎ 8871 7537). There's also a small **Children's Zoo** (Map p436-7; ☎ 8871 7540; Battersea Park SW11; adult/senior & child £2.50/1.50; ⏰ 10am-5pm Apr-Sep, 11am-3pm Sat & Sun Oct-Mar). On public holidays there is usually a funfair here, the sound carrying over the river.

BATTERSEA POWER STATION Map pp440-1
rail Battersea Park

Rock fans might recognise it from the cover of Pink Floyd's album *Animals*; film buffs might have seen it in the Ian McKellen version of *Richard III*, others will simply remember it as the building with the four smokestacks that resembles an upside-down table – but all of them are thinking of Battersea Power Station. Another creation by Giles Gilbert Scott, it was generally less loved than the Bankside Power Station (now Tate Modern), but was nevertheless listed as an historic buiding after it ceased operating in 1982. Since then, several proposals to give it a new life – from a Disney theme park, Warner multiplex cinema and Cirque du Soleil theatre to a new train station and shopping and hotel complex – have been mooted but have failed. At the time of writing, owners

Ghetto Fabulous

The West End, west London and Primrose Hill in north London might provide the capital's best star-spotting opportunities, but those born, raised or living in the historically poorer suburb of Brixton have also made a notable contribution to public life. So here's an antidote to all those sarky north London jibes: a list of just a few Brixton alumni you will either certainly have heard of, or are worth getting to know.

- Floella Benjamin – celebrated *Play School* presenter and writer of children's book, BAFTA executive and Brixton resident
- David Bowie – once outrageous, gender-bending rock star (now all grown up); born David Jones at 40 Stansfield Rd
- Linton Kwesi Johnson –'dub poet' and icon for black British artists; has lived in Brixton for more than 40 years
- John Major – often pilloried former British prime minister; born to a circus family and raised here, married in St Matthew's Church
- Magnus Mills – bus driver on the 159 route; became a best-selling novelist with *The Restraint of Beasts*
- Roger Moore – formerly the Saint and James Bond 007; born in Stockwell, where his father was a local policeman
- Chris Morris – bad-boy comedian, resident of Brixton; caused public worry about the new drug 'cake' and announced the 'death' of very healthy Tory MP Michael Heseltine
- Will Self – provocative novelist, perhaps most famous for *My Idea of Fun* (very twisted) and *Great Apes*; Brixton resident
- Paul Simenon – bass player of rock band the Clash was born and raised here (later moved to west London); wrote song 'Guns of Brixton'
- Benjamin Zephaniah – mind-blowingly mellifluous poet, resident in Brixton; fans include Nelson Mandela…and London's Metropolitan Police, who were forced to apologise for nicking a line of his poetry for an ad campaign

Parkview International had asked respected architect Nicholas Grimshaw to come up with a design. His scheme was to transform the building into a huge entertainment auditorium with leisure facilities and shops surrounding it.

WANDSWORTH COMMON Map p414
rail Wandsworth Common/Clapham Junction
Wilder and more overgrown than the nearby common in Clapham, Wandsworth Common is full of couples pushing prams, which has earned it the moniker 'Nappy Valley'.

On the common's eastern side is a pleasant collection of streets known as the **toast rack**, because of their alignment. Baskerville, Dorlcote, Henderson, Nicosia, Patten and Routh Rds are lined with Georgian houses. There's a blue plaque at 3 Routh Rd, home to the former British prime minister David Lloyd George.

Just in the northeast corner of the common, off Trinity Rd, is the amazing **Royal Victoria Patriotic Building**. This listed Gothic colossus has towering steeples and cobblestone courtyards, and was built for orphans of servicemen who had served in the Crimean War of the early 19th century. During WWII it was used as a base by MI5 and MI6 and as a POW camp. Today the building houses a drama school, apartments and a main hall that's very popular as a wedding venue. There's also an atmospheric and romantic restaurant, **Le Gothique** (p259).

YOUNG'S RAM BREWERY Map p414
☎ 8875 7000, 8875 7005; 68 High St SW18; brewery tour adult/child aged 14-17/senior & student £5.50/3/4.50; ☽ visitors centre 10am-6pm Mon-Sat; rail **Wandsworth Town**
The place to go when you want to digest history with a cup of good cheer. Beer (or 'bitter', not lager) has been brewed here since the late 16th century; 1½-hour tours of the brewery leave at noon and 2pm Monday to Thursday and Saturday – call in advance to book. Admission fees include a pint in the old pub attached. Tours of the **stables** (adults/children 5-17/family £3.50/2/9), where a herd of working shires makes their home, need to be booked well in advance. Under-18s must be accompanied by an adult.

To get here from Wandsworth Town station (trains from Waterloo station), walk west on Old York Rd, cross over to Armoury Way and then go south along Ram St to the visitors centre on High St.

CLAPHAM

This area was first settled after the Great Fire of London in 1666, when people, including noted diarist Samuel Pepys, escaped the descrecation of the City to build homes here.

CLAPHAM COMMON Map p414
tube Clapham Common
This large expanse of green is the heart of the Clapham neighbourhood, and mentioned by

Peckham Library (below)

Graham Greene in his novel *The End of the Affair*. The main thoroughfare, Clapham High St, starts at the western edge, and is lined with many of the bars, restaurants and shops that people principally come to Clapham for. However, for a simple stroll it's much more pleasant to explore the more upmarket streets of **Clapham Common North Side** and **Clapham Old Town**, both to the northwest of the tube station.

On the corner of Clapham Park Rd and Clapham Common South Side, you'll find the **Holy Trinity Church**. This was home to the 19th-century Clapham Sect, a group of wealthy Christians that included William Wilberforce, a leading anti-slavery campaigner.

KENNINGTON, OVAL & STOCKWELL

AROUND KENNINGTON Map pp440-1
tube Kennington/Oval

An area of niche interest and home to **Kennington Park**, the remains of the common where preachers used to address large audiences during the 18th and 19th centuries (John Wesley, Methodist Church founder, among them.

Across Camberwell New Rd from the park lies a slice of older religious history. **St Mark's Church** (1824) is really only remarkable for being built on the site of the gallows where Jacobite rebels were wung, before being drawn and quartered.

Off Kennington Lane, just west of its intersection with Kennington Rd, lies a lovely enclave of leafy streets with neo-Georgian houses. Like the toast rack in Wandsworth (p195), it's not really worth travelling south to see Cardigan St, Courtney St and Courtney Square, but if you're in the area anyway, say for the cricket, they provide quite a nice diversion.

OVAL Map pp440-1
☎ 7582 7764; www.surreycricket.com; Kennington Oval SE11; tube Oval

Home to the Surrey County Cricket Club, the Oval is London's second cricketing venue after Lord's. As well as Surrey matches, it also regularly hosts international test matches – where the English team has seen a few defeats in recent years. The season runs from April to September.

AROUND STOCKWELL Map pp440-1
tube Stockwell

Another London neighbourhood that only longer-term visitor, or in this case the connoisseur of Portuguese food (p260), would get to see, Stockwell does harbour **Vincent Van Gogh's home** (Map pp440-1) from 1873 to 1874. The troubled Dutch genius lived at 87 Hackford Rd.

Hitting the Books in Peckham

Anyone who ever went to the cinema in London in the early 1990s will forever remember a ubiquitous (and very naff) ad portraying 'Peckham on a wet, Sunday afternoon' as looking like an idyllic Caribbean island – 'if you're drinking Bacardi.' More recently, this underprivileged neighbourhood was in the national news twice: once for a horrific incident when schoolboy Damilola Taylor was stabbed to death on a housing estate in 2000; the other time when Alsop's **Peckham Library and Media Centre** (Map pp416-17; ☎ 7525 0200; Peckham Sq SE15; admission free; 🕙 9am-8pm Mon-Fri, from 10am Wed, 9am-5pm Sat, noon-4pm Sun; rail Peckham Rye/Queen's Road/Peckham) won the prestigious Stirling Prize for architecture that same year.

When you first see the library – still loved by architects and the public alike – you might feel like you're hallucinating on something a lot stronger than Bacardi. It's a fun, colourful building reminiscent, in shape, of a capital letter F. The outside cladding is green patinated copper, and there's a prominent red 'tongue' above the roof. The upper storey is raised 12m above the ground, cantilevering out well beyond the five-floor vertical block below.

The architectural intention was to create a new focus for community life and thereby help rejuvenate a deprived area. Having the upper storey overlooking Peckham Square opens the library onto a social space. From that level, you can also see the City and the West End, quashing any notion that poverty-stricken Peckham is isolated from the bright lights of London. Visitors are free to enter the library and browse at will.

UP RIVER

Eating p260; Sleeping p356; Shopping p332

Mention Chiswick to most Londoners and they will groan at the sheer bourgeois, golf-playing dullness of the place. Ask how many have actually visited, and perhaps you'll be surprised – Chiswick to many represents an idea rather than a reality, and this quiet west London enclave does not entirely deserve the flak it gets for its well-heeled residents and unfeasibly grand mansions.

With a choice of several District Line tube stations that run the length of Chiswick High Rd, it's best to have an idea of where you are heading before you arrive. Stamford Brook or Turnham Green get you onto the High Rd with ease, and are the best points from which to start exploring. Chiswick High Rd itself is an upmarket yet uninspiring main drag, full of pubs and twee shops with the odd decent restaurant – there will be little to waylay you, so best to head straight down to Hogarth Lane, Church St and the riverfront.

'If I have to choose between Richmond and death, I choose death!' exclaims Nicole Kidman as Virginia Woolf in *The Hours*. The sentiment may seem a bit extreme, but Richmond today remains anathema to Zone One snobs, although it's loved by almost everyone else for its incredible park and lovely walks. Anyone wanting to get out of London for the day without too much trouble or expense should take a trip here, and for people who aren't big city-fans but need to be in London, Richmond is a great place to stay. Centuries of royal history, some stunning Georgian architecture and the graceful curve of the Thames has made this one of London's swankiest locales, home to ageing rock stars and city high-fliers alike.

Richmond itself was historically named Sheen, but Henry VII, having fallen in love with the place, renamed the village after his Yorkshire Earldom. This started many centuries of royal association with the area; the most famous local, Henry VIII, acquired nearby Hampton Court Palace from Cardinal Wolsey after the latter's fall from grace in 1529, while his daughter Elizabeth I died here in 1603 after spending her last years at Richmond Palace.

On exiting the station, you'll find the town itself does not look much different from any other English high street. However, a short walk beyond The Quadrant will reveal the enormous open space of Richmond Green with its mansions and delightful pubs and you'll realise that this is quite a special place.

Crossing the green diagonally will take you to what remains of Richmond Palace, just the main entrance and gatehouse, built in 1501. You can see Henry VII's arms above the main gate: he built the Tudor additions to the edifice, although the palace had been in use as a royal residence since 1125. The green itself was used to feed the village's sheep herds, and hosted jousting matches for the king's pleasure.

The town of Kew is world-famous for its World-Heritage-listed Botanic Gardens, and rightly so – a day at Kew Gardens can be fascinating and appealing even to someone with no knowledge of plants and flowers. This smart west London suburb is a pleasant place for a wander.

Not just synonymous with rugby, Twickenham is also connected with such greats as Alfred Lord Tennyson, Walter de la Mare and Alexander Pope. Marble Hill House and Twickenham Stadium attract visitors in droves to this otherwise quiet and pretty Middlesex town.

Temperate House, Kew Gardens (p200)

Neighbourhoods – Up River

197

For a few weeks each summer the sporting world fixes its glare on the quiet southern suburb of Wimbledon, as it has since 1877; and then the circus leaves town and Wimbledon returns to unremarkable normality. That said, it's a pleasant little place, and the Wimbledon Lawn Tennis Museum will excite any tennis fan, even in December.

Out in London's southwestern outskirts, the wonderful Hampton Court Palace is pressed up against 400-hectare Bushy Park, a semi-wild expanse with herds of red and fallow deer.

Isleworth is a quiet suburb by the Thames without much to draw visitors except for Osterley House and its fine park. Parts of Ealing, once known for its film studios, are reasonably leafy and it has Pitshanger Manor, the country retreat designed by John Soane.

CHISWICK

HOGARTH'S HOUSE Map p414

☎ 8994 6757; Hogarth Lane, Great West Rd W4; admission free; ⏱ 1-5pm Tue-Fri, 1-6pm Sat & Sun Apr-Oct, 1-4pm Tue-Fri, 1-5pm Sat & Sun Nov-Dec & Feb-Mar; tube Turnham Green

This museum, devoted to the life work of artist and social commentator William Hogarth (who live here from 1749 to 1764), is one of the most perfectly sized and presented museums in London. You can see all his most famous works, including the haunting *Gin Lane* and *Marriage à la mode*, in this pretty little house which overlooks a pleasant garden, and enjoy the amusing, dark and caricatured lives of his various protagonists displayed on the walls. More obscurely, there are the private engravings *Before* and *After* (1730), commissioned by the Duke of Montagu and bearing the immortal inscription 'every creature is sad after intercourse'. For those without an interest in London life during the Georgian era, there is little else to see but Hogarth's engravings, as almost no furniture remains. But for those who like Hogarth, this place is a treat. It's also tempting to imagine how Hogarth might respond to the next-door business centre that uses his name!

CHISWICK VILLAGE

Walking around the Hogarth Roundabout (use the subways), take the exit onto Church St where the remains of Chiswick village are incongruously situated not 30 seconds from the monstrous A4 road out of London. You can get a good feel of how Chiswick looked in the 19th century and before from walking down here – some of the buildings date from the 16th century. If you turn right by the church, you will get to **Chiswick Old Cemetery** (open 9am-dusk), where among the many graves you can see Hogarth's and Whistler's. Continuing down Church St you reach **Chiswick Mall**, one of London's most exclusive addresses, where vast mansions overlook the Thames. The walk up the mall towards Hammersmith is delightful on a good day, and there are plenty of riverside

pubs at which to stop for a drink or some lunch. The **Old Ship** (p279) is our top pick.

CHISWICK HOUSE Map p414

☎ 8995 0508; www.english-heritage.org.uk; Chiswick Park, off Burlington Lane W4; adult/child/senior & student £3.30/1.70/2.50; ⏱ 10am-6pm Apr-Sep, 10am-5pm Oct, 10am-4pm Wed-Sun Nov-Mar; rail Chiswick

This is a fine Palladian pavilion with an octagonal dome and colonnaded portico. It was designed by the third Earl of Burlington (1694–1753) when he returned from his grand tour of Italy, fired up with enthusiasm for all things Roman. Lord Burlington used it to entertain friends and to house his library and art collection.

Inside, the ground floor has details of the recent restoration work and also accommodates several statues brought in from the park to protect them. Upstairs, certain rooms have been completely restored to a grandeur some will find overpowering. The dome of the main salon has been left ungilded and the walls are decorated with eight enormous paintings. In the Blue Velvet Room look for the portrait of Inigo Jones, the architect much admired by Lord Burlington, over one of the doors. The ceiling paintings are by William Kent, who also decorated the Kensington Palace State Apartments.

Lord Burlington also planned the house's original gardens, now Chiswick Park, but they have been much altered since his time. The restored Cascade waterfall is bubbling again after being out of action for years. The house, which is about one mile southwest of the tube stations, is opposite the start of Burlington Lane.

SYON HOUSE Map p414

☎ 8560 0883; www.syonpark.co.uk; Syon Park, Brentford; adult/senior, student & child aged 5-15/family £6.25/5.25/15; ⏱ 11am-5pm Wed, Thur & Sun mid-Mar–Oct; tube/rail Gunnersbury, then bus 237 or 267

The home of the dukes of Northumberland since the mid-18th century, Syon House has a fascinating history and is one of the most rewarding visits to make in west London. It started life as a medieval abbey named after Mt Zion, but Henry VIII dissolved the order of Bridgettine nuns who were peacefully established there and had the abbey rebuilt into a handsome residence instead. The understated exterior gives way to a slew of old masters on display and beautiful views towards Kew Gardens. The house's own gardens were modelled by the ubiquitous 'Capability' Brown. Like many stately homes keen to attract the whole family there are some more modern additions not quite in keeping with aristocratic tradition, but the butterfly house should not be missed.

FULLER'S GRIFFIN BREWERY
☎ 8996 2063; Chiswick Lane South W4; tube Turnham Green
Of interest to anyone who enjoys bitter and wants to see it being made, and who wants to take the opportunity to enjoy a comprehensive tasting session, Fuller's Brewery is one of two remaining breweries in London. Tours, which take 1½ hours, need to be booked in advance by telephone and run on Monday and from Wednesday to Friday, at 11am, midday, 1pm and 2pm. Tickets cost £5, or £3.50 for 14 to 18 year olds. No under 14s are admitted.

RICHMOND
RICHMOND PARK Map p414
☎ 8948 3209; ⏰ 7.30am-dusk Aug-Apr, 7.30am-9pm May-Jul; admission free; tube/rail Richmond
The largest urban parkland in Europe, Richmond Park is quite something, offering everything from formal gardens to wild deer and thick woods. Unfortunately it welcomes drivers, which means that several roads cut up the wilderness, and that people-carriers break up views that would otherwise be spectacular. Nonetheless, there is nowhere better in London for a quiet walk, and seeing herds of remarkably docile red deer makes it all the more magical. Coming from Richmond, it's easiest to enter via Richmond Gate or from Petersham Rd. Take a map with you and wander around the grounds – flower lovers should make a special trip to Isabella Plantation in late spring, when the rhododendrons and azaleas are ablaze and the gardens at their most impressive.

Pembroke Lodge, the childhood home of Bertrand Russell, is now a caféteria set in beautiful gardens and affords great views towards central London.

Particularly attractive are the two large lakes at Pen Ponds, in the very centre of the park. There is a deer pen next to White Lodge for those who want to see the red deer up close (they breed so successfully here that there are two annual culls to control their numbers). However, it's far more exciting to see the deer wild in the park, although this involves a degree of luck. It is possible to go horse riding in the park – there are four stables in the immediate vicinity. Call the main park number for more information.

THE THAMES
The stretch of the river bank from Twickenham Bridge down towards Petersham and Ham is one of the prettiest in London. On a sunny day, however, you'd be forgiven for thinking you were at a festival, as the quiet is shattered by hundreds of family groups and drinking parties. The action is concentrated around Richmond Bridge, an original structure from 1777 and London's oldest surviving crossing, only widened for traffic in 1937. The lovely walk upriver to Petersham is often overcrowded in nice weather – best to cut across Petersham Meadows and continue on to Richmond Park if it's peace and quiet you seek.

ST PETER'S CHURCH
Church Lane, Petersham, Surrey; admission free; ⏰ 3-5pm Sun only; tube/rail Richmond
St Peter's is a Norman church that has been a place of worship for 1300 years – the present structure dates from 1266. It's a fascinating place, not least for its curious Georgian box pews, which local landowners would rent while the serving staff and labourers sat in the open seats in the south transept. Against the north wall of the chancel is the unusual Cole Monument, which depicts George Cole, his wife and child, all reclining in Elizabethan dress – an unusual design for an English church.

Of interest to any Canadian, St Peter's is also the burial place of Captain George Vancouver who was laid to rest here in 1798, having contributed a vast amount to the charting of the earth, including, of course, the discovery of Vancouver Island. His unshowy tomb is on the boundary wall of the cemetery.

RICHMOND MUSEUM
☎ 8332 1141; www.museumofrichmond.com; Old Town Hall, Whittaker Ave; admission free; ⏰ 11am-5pm Tue-Sat, 1-4pm Sun (May only); tube/rail Richmond
This small museum offers some interesting perspectives on Richmond and towns in the

surrounding area, all the way back to medieval times. There are lots of things to see, particularly in relation to Richmond's royal history, and the temporary displays are usually very interesting. There is a strong emphasis on educating children, so it's a good place to bring the kids.

KEW

KEW GARDENS Map p414

☎ 8332 5000, 8940 1171; www.rbgkew.org.uk; Kew Rd; adult/under 16/senior, student, over 16 £6.50/free/ 4.50, late entry 45min before hothouses close £4.50; ☼ gardens 9.30am-6.30pm Mon-Fri, 9.30am-7.30pm Sat & Sun late-Mar–Aug; 9.30am-6pm Sep-Oct; 9.30am-4.15pm Nov-Feb; glasshouses 9.30am-5.30pm late-Mar–Oct; 9.30am-3.45pm Nov-Feb; tube/rail Kew Gardens

The Royal Botanical Gardens at Kew are one of the most popular attractions on the London tourist itinerary, which means they can get very crowded during summer, especially at weekends. Spring is probably the best time to visit, but at any time of year this 120-hectare expanse of lawns, formal gardens and greenhouses has delights to offer. As well as being a public garden, Kew is an important research centre, and it maintains its reputation as the most exhaustive botanical collection in the world.

For a good overview of the gardens, take the **Kew Explorer minitrain** (adult/child £2.50/1.50); you can hop on and off at stops along the way. The full circuit takes about half an hour.

Its wonderful plants and trees aside, Kew has several specific sights within its borders. Assuming you come by tube and enter via **Victoria Gate**, you will come almost immediately to a large pond overlooked by the enormous **Palm House**, a hothouse of metal and curved sheets of glass, designed by Decimus Burton and Richard Turner (1848) and housing all sorts of exotic tropical greenery. Just northwest of Palm House is the tiny but irresistible **Water Lily House** (open March to December only), dating from 1852.

If you head northwards, you'll come to the stunning **Princess of Wales Conservatory**, opened in 1987 and with plants in 10 different computer-controlled climatic zones – everything from a desert to a cloud forest. Beyond that is the **Kew Gardens Gallery** bordering Kew Green, which houses exhibitions of paintings and photos, mostly with a horticultural theme.

Heading westwards from the gallery you will arrive at the red-brick **Kew Palace**, a former royal residence once known as Dutch House, dating from 1631. It was very popular with

George III and his family (his wife Charlotte died here in 1818). The gardens surrounding the palace are especially pretty. The palace has been closed for extensive renovations.

If you cut southwards from the palace across the lawns you'll pass a long lake running roughly west to east. To the southwest is **Queen Charlotte's Cottage**, a wooden summerhouse used, again, by George III and his family and surrounded by bluebells in spring. It opens at weekends in summer only. East of the cottage is the **Japanese Gateway** and the celebrated **Great Pagoda**, designed by William Chambers in 1761.

Heading northwards you'll arrive at the 180m-long **Temperate House**, another wonderful iron-and-glass hothouse (although not so hot this time) designed by Burton in 1860 but not completed until 1899.

Due east of Temperate House is the **Marianne North Gallery**. Marianne North was one of those indomitable Victorian female travellers. She roamed the continents from 1871 to 1885, painting their plants and trees along the way. The results of her labour now cover the walls of this small purpose-built gallery.

The Orangery near Kew Palace contains a restaurant, café and shop.

Note that most of the hothouses close at 5.30pm in summer, and earlier in winter.

You can get to Kew Gardens by tube or train. Come out of the station and walk straight (west) along Station Rd, cross Kew Gardens Rd and then continue straight along Lichfield Rd. This will bring you to Victoria Gate. Alternatively, from March to September (with reduced services in October), boats run by the **Westminster Passenger Services Association** (☎ 7930 4721; www.wpsa.co.uk) sail from Westminster Pier to Kew Gardens up to five times a day (p379).

TWICKENHAM

MARBLE HILL HOUSE Map p414

☎ 8892 5115; www.english-heritage.org.uk; Richmond Rd; adult/child aged 5-15/senior & student/ £3.30/1.70/2.50; ☼ 10am-6pm Apr-Oct, 10am-4pm Wed-Sun Nov-Mar; rail St Margaret's

This is an 18th-century Palladian love nest, built originally for George II's mistress Henrietta Howard and later occupied by Mrs Fitzherbert, the secret wife of George IV. The poet Alexander Pope had a hand in designing the park, which stretches down to the Thames. Inside you'll find an exhibition about the life and times of Henrietta, and a collection of early-Georgian furniture.

To get there from St Margaret's station, turn right along St Margarets Rd. Then take the right fork along Crown Rd and turn left along Richmond Rd. Turn right along Beaufort Rd and walk across Marble Hill Park to the house.

MUSEUM OF RUGBY
☎ 8892 8877; www.rfu.com; Gate K, Twickenham Stadium, Rugby Rd; adult/concession £3/2, stadium guided tour & museum £5/3; ☻ 10am-5pm Tue-Sat, 2-5pm Sun; tube Hounslow East, then bus 281 or rail Twickenham

A state-of-the-art museum that will appeal to all rugby lovers, the Museum of Rugby is tucked behind the eastern stand of the stadium. Relive highlights of old matches in the video theatre and then take a tour of the grounds. They depart at 10.30am, noon and 1.30pm (with an additional tour at 3pm on Sunday) but there are no tours on match days.

WIMBLEDON
WIMBLEDON LAWN TENNIS MUSEUM
☎ 8946 6131; www.wimbledon.org; Gate 4, Church Rd SW19; adult/concession £3/4; ☻ 10.30am-5pm, spectators only during championships; tube Southfields/Wimbledon Park

This museum is of specialist interest, dwelling as it does on the minutiae of the history of tennis playing, traced back here to the invention of the all-important lawnmower in 1830 and of the India-rubber ball in the 1850s. It's a state-of-the-art presentation, with plenty of video clips to let fans of the game relive their favourite moments. The museum houses a tearoom and a shop selling all kinds of tennis memorabilia.

WIMBLEDON COMMON
Running on into Putney Heath, Wimbledon Common covers 440 hectares of south London, a wonderful expanse of open space for walking, nature trailing and picnicking. There are a few specific sights on the common, most unexpectedly **Wimbledon Windmill** (☎ 8947 2825; Windmill Rd SW19; adult/child £1/50p; ☻ 2-5pm Sat, 11am-5pm Sun Apr-Oct; tube Wimbledon), a fine smock mill dating from 1817. It was during a stay in the mill in 1908 that Baden-Powell was inspired to write parts of his wonderfully-named *Scouting for Boys*. On the southern side of the common, the misnamed **Caesar's Camp** is a prehistoric earthwork that proves that Wimbledon was settled before Roman times.

BUDDHAPADIPA TEMPLE
☎ 8946 1357; 14 Calonne Rd SW19; admission free; ☻ complex 8am-9.30pm summer, 8am-6pm winter; temple 1-6pm Sat, 8.30-10.30am & 12.30-6pm Sun; tube Wimbledon

Another unexpected sight, this time found in a residential neighbourhood half a mile from Wimbledon Village, is as authentic a Thai temple as ever graced this side of Bangkok. The Buddhapadipa Temple was built by an association of young Buddhists in Britain and opened in 1982. The *wat* (temple compound) boasts a *bot*, or consecrated chapel, decorated with traditional scenes by two leading Thai artists. Remember to take your shoes off before entering the *bot*.

To get to the temple take the tube or train to Wimbledon and then bus No 93 up to Wimbledon Parkside. Calonne Rd leads off it on the right.

Wimbledon Tennis Championships (above)

HAMPTON

HAMPTON COURT PALACE

☎ 8781 9500; www.fhrp.org.uk; East Molesy; all-inclusive ticket adult/child aged 5-15/senior & student/family £10.80/7.20/8.50/32.30; ☻ 10.15am-6pm Mon, 9.30am-6pm Tue-Sun mid-Mar–late-Oct, 10.15am-4.30pm Mon, 9.30am-4.30pm Tue-Sun late-Oct–Feb; rail Hampton Court

In 1514 Cardinal Thomas Wolsey, Lord Chancellor of England, decided to build himself a palace in keeping with his lofty sense of self-importance. Unfortunately, even Wolsey couldn't persuade the pope to grant Henry VIII a divorce from Catherine of Aragon and relations between king and chancellor soured rapidly. Given that background, you only need to take one look at Hampton Court Palace to realise why Wolsey felt obliged to present it to Henry, a monarch not too fond of anyone trying to muscle in on his mastery of all he surveyed, some 15 years later. The hapless Wolsey was charged with high treason but died before his trial in 1530.

As soon as he acquired the palace, Henry set to work expanding it, adding the **Great Hall**, the **Chapel Royal** and the sprawling **kitchens**. By 1540 this was one of the grandest and most sophisticated palaces in Europe. In the late 17th century, King William and Queen Mary employed Sir Christopher Wren to build extensions. The result is a beautiful blend of Tudor and 'restrained Baroque' architecture.

Today the palace is England's largest and grandest Tudor structure, knee-deep in history, with superb **gardens** and a famous 300-year-old **maze**. You should set aside plenty of time to do it justice, bearing in mind that if you come by boat from central London the trip will have eaten up half the day already.

At the ticket office by the main **Trophy Gate** you can purchase joint tickets to the palace and the Tower of London, or tickets for just the gardens or the maze, as well as the all-inclusive Hampton Court Palace ticket. Be sure to pick up a leaflet listing the daily programme, which will help you plan your visit; this is important as some of the free guided tours require advance booking.

As you walk up the path towards the palace you'll have a fine view of the lengthy red-brick façade with its distinctive Tudor chimneys and sturdy gateway. Passing through the main gate you arrive first in the Base Court and then the Clock Court, named after the fine 16th-century Astronomical Clock that shows the sun revolving round the earth. The Fountain Court is next. From the Clock Court you can follow signs to the six sets of rooms in the complex.

The stairs inside Anne Boleyn's Gateway lead up to **Henry VIII's State Apartments**, including the Great Hall, the largest single room in the palace, decorated with tapestries and a spectacular hammer-beam roof from which tiny painted faces peep down. A hallway hung with antlers leads to the Great Watching Chamber where guards controlled access to the king; this is the least altered of all the rooms dating from Henry's time. Leading off from the chamber is the smaller Pages' Chamber and the Haunted Gallery. Arrested for adultery and detained in the palace in 1542, Henry's fifth wife Catherine Howard managed to evade her guards and ran screaming down the corridor in search of the king. Her woeful ghost is said to do the same thing to this day.

Further along the corridor you'll come to the beautiful Chapel Royal, built in just nine months. A Royal Pew forming part of the state apartments looks down over the altar. The blue-and-gold vaulted ceiling was originally intended for Christ Church, Oxford, but was installed here instead, while the 18th-century reredos was carved by Grinling Gibbons.

Also dating from Henry's day are the Tudor kitchens, again accessible from Anne Boleyn's Gateway and originally able to rustle up meals for a royal household of some 1200 people. The kitchens have been fitted out to look as they might have done in Tudor days and palace 'servants' turn the spits and stuff the bustards. Don't miss the Great Wine Cellar, which handled the 300 barrels each of ale and wine consumed here annually in the mid-16th century.

Returning again to the Clock Court and passing under the colonnade to the right you reach the **King's Apartments**, built by Wren for William III towards the end of the 17th century. These apartments were badly damaged by fire in 1986 but have now been extensively restored.

A tour of the apartments takes you up the grand King's Staircase painted by Antonio Verrio in about 1700 and flattering the king by comparing him to Alexander the Great. You'll emerge into the King's Guard Chamber, which is decked out with guns, bayonets and swords and leads to the King's Presence Chamber. This room is dominated by a throne backed with scarlet hangings and by an equestrian portrait of William III by Godfrey Kneller.

Next on the tour is the King's Eating Room where William would sometimes have dined in public, beyond which you'll find the King's

Privy Chamber, where ambassadors were received; the chandelier and throne canopy have been carefully restored after suffering terrible damage in the 1986 fire. Beyond this is the King's Withdrawing Room, where more intimate gatherings took place, and the King's Great Bedchamber, a splendid room, its bed topped with ostrich plumes, where the king was ceremonially dressed each morning. William actually slept in the Little Bedchamber beyond.

The back stairway beyond the King's Closet leads to three more wood-panelled closets furnished with paintings and more carvings by Grinling Gibbons. You then walk through an orangery to the King's Private Drawing Room and Dining Room, which is decorated with Kneller's paintings of the Hampton Court Beauties.

William's wife, Mary II, had her own separate **Queen's Apartments**, which are accessible up the Queen's Staircase, decorated by William Kent. When Mary died in 1694 work on these rooms was incomplete; they were finished under George II's reign. The rooms are shown as they might have been when Queen Caroline used them for entertaining between 1716 and 1737.

In comparison with the King's State Apartments, those for the queen seem rather austere, although the Queen's Audience Chamber has a throne as imposing as that of the king. Pass through the Queen's Drawing Room and you come to the State Bedchamber, where the queen took part in levees (royal morning meetings) rather than sleeping. The Queen's Gallery is hung with a set of 18th-century tapestries depicting the adventures of Alexander the Great.

Also upstairs and ringing Wren's graceful Fountain Court are the **Georgian Rooms** used by George II and Queen Caroline on the court's last visit to the palace in 1737. The first rooms you come to were designed to accommodate George's second son, the Duke of Cumberland, whose bed is woefully tiny for its grand surroundings. The Wolsey Closet was restored and repanelled in 1888 to give an idea of what one of the palace's smaller rooms might have looked like in Tudor times. The Communications Gallery was built for William III and is decorated with Peter Lely's portraits of the Windsor Beauties, the most beautiful women at the court of Charles II. Beyond that is the Cartoon Gallery where the Raphael Cartoons (now in the Victoria & Albert Museum; p134) used to hang; nowadays you have to make do with late-17th-century copies.

Hampton Court Palace (opposite)

Beyond the Cartoon Gallery are the Queen's Private Rooms: her drawing room and bedchamber, where she and the king would sleep if they wanted to be alone. Particularly interesting are the Queen's Bathroom, with its tub set on a floor cloth to soak up any spillage, and the Oratory, with its 16th-century Persian carpet.

Once you're finished with the palace interior there are still the wonderful gardens to appreciate. Carriage rides round the gardens are available; they cost £9 and last 20 minutes. Look out for the **Real Tennis Court**, dating from the 1620s and designed for real tennis, a rather different version of the game from that played today. The restored 24-hectare Riverside Gardens are spectacular. Here you'll find the **Great Vine** planted in 1768 and still producing around 300kg of grapes per year; it's an old vine, no doubt about it, but not the world's oldest, as they say it is here. The **Lower Orangery** in the gardens houses Andrea Mantegna's nine *Triumphs of Caesar* paintings, bought by Charles I in 1629; the Banqueting House was designed for William III and painted by Antonio Verrio. Look out, too, for the iron screens designed by Jean Tijou.

No-one should leave Hampton Court without losing themselves in the famous 800m-long maze, which is made up of hornbeam and yew planted in 1690. In case you're wondering, the average visitor takes 20 minutes to reach the centre.

There are trains every half-hour from Waterloo to Hampton Court station. The palace can also be reached from Westminster Pier in central London on one of three river boats operated by **Westminster Passenger Services Association** (☎ 7930 4721; www.wpsa.co.uk) from April to September, with reduced sailings in October. For details p379.

ISLEWORTH

OSTERLEY PARK & HOUSE Map p414

☎ 8232 5050; www.nationaltrust.org.uk; Osterley Park, off Jersey Rd; house adult/child aged 5-15/family £4.30/2.15/10.50, park free; ☺ house 1-4.30pm Wed-Sun Apr-Oct, park 9am-dusk year-round; tube Osterley

Set in 120 hectares of landscaped park and farmland, Osterley House started life in 1575 as the country retreat of Thomas Gresham, the man responsible for the Royal Exchange, but was extensively remodelled in the mid-18th century by Robert Adam. There are wonderful paintings, plasterwork and furniture, but many people rate the downstairs kitchen and the Tudor Grand Stables as even more interesting.

To get there from Osterley tube, walk eastward along the Great West Rd and turn left into Thornbury Rd, bringing you to Jersey Rd and the park entrance. The house is 500m to the north.

PITSHANGER MANOR Map p414

☎ 8567 1227; www.ealing.gov.uk/pitshanger; Walpole Park, Mattock Lane W5; admission free; ☺ 10am-5pm Tue-Sat; tube/rail Ealing Broadway

This manor was bought by the architect John Soane in 1800 and rebuilt in the Regency style. Parts of the manor now house a collection of pottery, designed by the Martin Brothers of Southall in the late 19th century. Not everyone will care for their grotesque designs, although the owl jars with swivel heads are undoubtedly good fun. There is also an adjacent art gallery that houses temporary exhibits.

Walking Tours

Walking Tours

There is no better way to see London than by foot. Londoners pour into many parts of central London at the weekends to enjoy the historic buildings, parkland and river walks that the capital has to offer, and visitors should too. Being London, museums are nearly always free, so you can just pop your head in for a noncommittal glance if you don't feel like trawling through an entire collection. On foot, you'll be able to see the city up close and personal, and, most importantly, enjoy its many pubs with a well-earned drink at the end of each tour.

THE SOHO WALK

Where better to wander than the seedy, bohemian and chaotic streets of Soho, the village at the heart of modern London? The world-famous streets that collectively make up the oddly named neighbourhood nestle between the thoroughfares of Oxford St, Regent St, Shaftsbury Ave and Charing Cross Rd, and are several worlds rolled into one.

Starting at the transport and advertising hub of **Piccadilly Circus** (p92), walk up Sherwood St and look into the **Warwick 1** pub on the left; this unassuming place was a haunt of Soho's gangland leaders throughout the '50s and '60s. They would frequently meet in the upstairs room where you can now enjoy a good pub lunch.

Coach & Horses pub (p265)

Turn right onto Brewer St and follow it towards Great Windmill St, passing lap-dancing clubs and 'bookshops'. Juxtaposed against them are nevertheless some great shops: **Anything Left Handed 2** (No 57) and the **Vintage Magazine Store 3** (No 39–43) both sell a great range of potential presents, while **Arigato 4** Japanese supermarket (No 48–50) is a great place to pick up something special for a picnic.

Continue along Brewer St, then turn left up Lexington St and you'll arrive at the **John Snow 5** pub, named after the local doctor who isolated the water pump on Broadwick St as the source of the Soho cholera outbreak in 1854. There's a replica water pump on the site of the original, to commemorate the 5000 people who died before Snow made the vital connection. Turn right from Broadwick St into Berwick St, with its lively **market 6** (p333) and sense of real community (between the prostitutes and the drug addicts, some might cynically say). There is a great crepe stand on the corner of Berwick and Newburgh Sts for a lunchtime snack.

Keep walking down Berwick St, where aside from the market stalls there are some excellent record shops selling very good-value CDs and a huge selection of underground dance music on vinyl. As you approach the end of Berwick St, the concentration of sex shops and sleaze suddenly reaches its peak in the appropriately named

Walk Facts

Best time Weekend mornings, when Soho is at its most 'village'
Start Piccadilly Circus tube station
End Leicester Square tube station
Food en route Crepe from the stand on the corner of Berwick and Newburgh Sts
Drink en route Coach & Horses
Distance 1 mile (1.6km)
Time About an hour

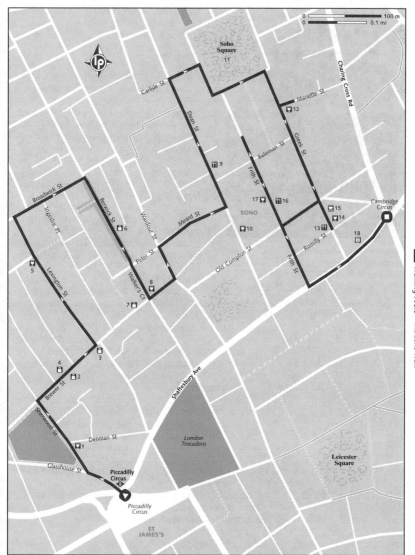

Walker's Ct that links the end of Berwick St to Brewer St. Walk through Walker's Ct to absorb yet another aspect of Soho life, then make a quick right turn back on to Brewer St and, if your crepe won't provide enough fuel for the walk, a snack from the superb Italian deli **Lina 7** (No 18) definitely will. Walk back past Walker's Ct to the fabled nightspot of **Madame Jo Jo's 8** (p296). This is one Soho institution that shows no sign of flagging – it's seamy, glamorous, fun and camp all at once, with cabaret and dancing every night.

At the end of Brewer St turn left up Wardour St, one of Soho's busiest arteries, and then turn right into Meard St, a gorgeous side street with original Georgian town houses perfectly preserved and still inhabited today. You'll come out onto Dean St, former home of Karl Marx, who moved to No 28 in 1851, above what is now the beautiful **Quo Vadis 9** (p224)

Ronnie Scott's jazz club (p308)

restaurant. Marx's name appears here in large letters on the wall. The interior has obviously improved since Marx's day, when a Prussian agent visited Marx, only to report back:

> Everything is broken, tattered and torn, finger-thick dust everywhere, and everything in the greatest disorder…it is dangerous to sit down. But nothing of this embarrasses Marx or his wife in the least…a spirited conversation makes up for the domestic defects and in the end you become reconciled because of the company…

Dean St plays host to two of Soho's fabled private members' clubs: literary Black's (No 67) and the media-luvvy **Groucho Club 10** (No 44), where you can see celebrities come and go any night of the week. Having turned left onto Dean St, follow the road up as far as Carlisle St – turn right here and you'll walk into **Soho Square 11**, the graceful and charming green lung of Soho. On a summer's day, office workers in their hundreds crowd every available square inch of the lawns to enjoy lunch, but the rest of the year it's usually far quieter and is a lovely place to sit and people-watch.

Having walked through the gardens and seen the curious mock Tudor 'house' at the centre, walk out of the square down Greek St. This happening strip of bars and restaurants was once home to Casanova, and you can take a diversion through the archway on your left onto Manette St, where Francis Bacon's regular haunt, the **Pillars of Hercules 12**, on the corner of Manette, still packs them in.

Crossing over Old Compton St, the epicentre of London's sprawling gay scene, Greek St continues – look out on the right for Oscar Wilde's frequent haunt, the pizza restaurant **Kettner's 13** (p224), a large and rather gaudily furnished eatery founded in 1868 by Napoleon III's chef. It's something of a disappointment to eat in today, as not only is it virtually devoid of atmosphere, but it is also now part of a ubiquitous pizza chain. More interesting is the **Coach and Horses 14** (p265) pub across the road – Peter O'Toole can often be spotted propping up the bar and the play *Jeffrey Barnard Is Unwell*, first performed starring O'Toole, is set here. Next door, **Maison Bertaux 15** (p225) is a favourite among the 'boho' set who love to drink tea all day long in this little cake house.

Turn left into chilled-out Old Compton St and try to guess which bars are gay. Even the straight bars in Soho are quite gay, so it's often a bit hard to tell. Turn right onto Frith St and you'll find post-clubbing institution **Bar Italia 16** (p225), immortalised by Jarvis Cocker in the eponymous Pulp song, and a place in which revellers have been enjoying cappuccinos for decades. Above Bar Italia, John Logie Baird changed the world as we know it by giving the first ever demonstration of television in 1926 in front of an audience of 50 scientists. Mozart lived next door (No 20), opposite the world-famous **Ronnie Scott's 17** nightclub (No 47; p308). Every jazz great has performed here at some time since it was founded in 1959 by the unfortunately named Ronald Schatt, who came up with a suitable tweak to his name to make it sound just right. The essayist William Hazlitt lived and died at No 6 and is buried in St Anne's Churchyard on Lower Wardour St, where a monument to him was restored in 2003.

To end the walk, stroll back down Frith St all the way to Shaftesbury Ave. Turn left up the avenue, past the wonderful **Curzon Cinema 18** (p293) to Cambridge Circus, where the walk ends and you emerge from the village of Soho back into the rush of London streets and heavy traffic. For those wanting to wander further on, stroll up Charing Cross Rd and drop into some of its many second-hand bookshops.

THE WORLD IN LONDON WALK

This walk is a long route through some of the less-visited areas of the capital, but a good stretch of it can be done by bus if you're unwilling to do the whole thing on foot. It takes in a few of London's welcoming but still very tight-knit ethnic minority communities in East London, from the Bengali community in Shoreditch, to the West African hub of Dalston, the Turkish diaspora in Stoke Newington, and the fascinating Orthodox Jewish quarter of Stamford Hill.

Starting at Aldgate East tube station, make your way left onto Osborn St from Whitechapel High St and follow the road up as it becomes Brick Lane. In 1550 this was just a country road leading to brickyards, and by the 18th century had been paved and lined with houses and cottages inhabited by the Spitalfields weavers. Today, this vibrant street is taken up almost entirely by curry houses, all of which offer cheap and varied variations on cuisine from the Indian subcontinent. During festivals the street is beautifully lit and festooned with decorations. There are plenty of interesting shops on both sides of the street selling a huge range of fabrics and clothing, as well as knick-knacks and other Bengali exotica. All the street names are in Bengali as well as English (along with Chinatown and Southall, this is one of the few bilingual areas of London).

Halfway up you'll pass the trendy **Vibe Bar 1** (p269) and the **Truman Brewery 2** (p118). The Truman was the biggest brewery in London by the mid-18th century and the Director's House standing to the left dates from 1740. The old **Vat House 3** (p118), which dates from the turn of the 19th century and has a hexagonal bell tower, is across the road. Next to it stands the **Engineer's House** (p118) of 1830 and a row of former stables. The brewery shut down in 1989 and the Truman today is now an arts centre that showcases the work of up-and-coming young artists from all media. Unsurprisingly, the Vibe Bar is a haunt for the same artists, as well as wannabes and local trendies.

There's an excellent **flea market 4** (p334) on Sundays at Brick Lane around Shoreditch tube station, where some good bargains can be had, particularly for furniture.

At the far end of Brick Lane, some of the original Jewish families who settled the neighbourhood continue to dwell, and there are a couple of excellent bagel outlets; proof of their proficiency is provided by the endless queues of people coming from all over the surrounding areas to buy up fresh supplies. Try **Brick Lane Beigel Bake 5** (p239), which operates 24 hours a day and is usually busy with Shoreditch clubbers throughout the night.

Walk Facts

Best time Any time
Start Aldgate East tube station
End Dalston Kingsland train station
Food en route Fried king prawns and sweet chilli sauce at Columbia Road Flower Market
End-of-walk drink Birdcage pub
Distance 3 miles (4.8km)
Time 3 hours

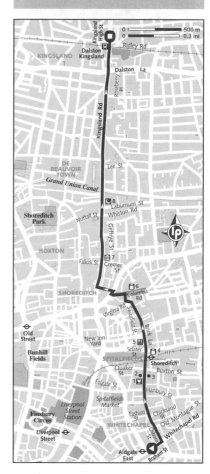

From Brick Lane, if it's a Sunday, cross Bethnal Green Rd and go up Swanfield St until you get to Columbia Rd, scene of London's most colourful **market 6** (p334). Here, every Sunday from dawn, market stalls selling freshly cut flowers, plants and orchids feed flora-starved Londoners who come in their

Columbia Rd flower market (above)

droves. Arrive early to see the market in all its glory, and, if you aren't too hung over from Saturday night, make a beeline for the food stalls behind the main flower sellers. Here you can enjoy fried king prawns and sweet chilli sauce as a perfectly exotic London breakfast.

Make your way east down Columbia Rd until you reach Hackney Rd; cross over and follow your way to Kingsland Rd. This now achingly cool strip boasts a big range of bars, clubs and cafés, and the planned new Hoxton tube station and endless series of warehouse conversions make it pretty certain that property prices here will continue to soar.

The **Geffrye Museum 7** (p117), on the right as you walk up the road, is an imposing inlet of Victorian almshouses, which now hosts a fascinating museum devoted to English furniture through the ages. It's a museum about London as much as about furniture, and it can be seen in half an hour.

After the Geffrye Museum you can either walk the stretch of road up to Dalston or take the bus (all buses on the side of the road opposite the museum stop in Dalston). The walk to Dalston takes about 15 minutes and includes the impressive **Sulemaniye Mosque 8** at 212–216 Kingsland Rd and the Grand Union Canal that flows under the road as you head north.

Dalston, hardly an impressive sight at first, starts with a slew of fried-chicken takeaways. However, as you approach Dalston Junction you suddenly begin to wonder what country you are in. The chaos, brilliant colour and animation of the African community here are all-encompassing. The traffic is always chaos, Ridley Rd Market (p334) is always chaos, Dalston is always chaos – it's unlike any other part of London. Kingsland Rd sweeps up to Stoke Newington, where the African community is replaced gradually by the enormous Turkish diaspora that has established itself across northeast London from Haringey to Islington.

We recommend you stop here, but should you have still have some life in your legs, carry on to atmospheric, rambling Abney Park Cemetery (p187), whose residents don't have any life left at all. Reward yourself with a well-deserved pint at the Birdcage in Stamford Hill.

THE SQUARE MILE WALK

No part of London is so thoroughly riddled with history as the 'Square Mile' – the ancient city of London that is now the financial district of the British capital. The wild juxtaposition of steel and glass skyscrapers and medieval churches is so commonplace that few of the workers who flood the area from nine to five Monday to Friday barely give it a second glance, and yet to approach the city with fresh eyes, and preferably over the weekend when it is almost eerily quiet, is to see a remarkable survey of London past and present.

Starting from St Paul's tube station, you'll find one of the city's most recognisable landmarks, Sir Christopher Wren's **St Paul's Cathedral 1** (p106). Walking the nearby streets, you can imagine the crowds and excitement that accompanied the wedding of Prince Charles and Lady Diana here in 1981. From the Cathedral entrance, follow St Paul's Chyd onto Cannon St and on arrival at Mansion House tube station, take Queen Victoria St until you reach the **Temple of Mithras 2** (p110) on your right. These remains of an ancient Roman temple, dating from AD 240 and devoted to the Persian god Mithras, look almost comical, situated on this busy street in front of a Japanese banking corporation's anonymous-looking headquarters. Yet this is the very essence of the city in all its glorious incongruity.

Continuing up Queen Victoria St you reach the heart (if not the soul) of the Square Mile (p110) – the imposing buildings of the **Bank of England 3**, **Royal Exchange** and **Mansion House**. Stop here and admire the last, the official residence of the Lord Mayor of London, which distinguishes itself as the only private residence in the country to have its own law courts and prison cells. It is also the scene of the Chancellor of the Exchequer's annual address to the great and the good of the City. The Bank of England has a fascinating history and the **museum** (p110) it houses (enter from Bartholomew's Lane) is free and of great interest, including a display of British money through the ages.

Leaving Bank, as this traffic-packed confluence of streets has been dubbed due to the tube station it masks below ground, walk down genteel King William St until you reach Monument tube station. Cross over to the other side of the road and walk down until you reach the **Monument 4** (p112). Wren

Walk Facts

Best time Any time on the weekend
Start St Paul's tube station
End Whitechapel tube station
Food en route Snacks at the Spitalfields Market stalls
End-of-walk drink Blind Beggar
Distance 3 miles (4.8km)
Time 2 hours

and Robert Hooke erected this commemorative Doric column between 1671 and 1677 to mark the 1666 Great Fire. Imagine how it dominated the skyline of the city in the late 17th century, standing at a then-enormous 66m. It is now dwarfed by surrounding buildings and is a virtually forgotten footnote to London history. Views over the river and the city's high-rises are well worth the £2 entry charge, although the trip to the top is not for the even faintly vertiginous.

Walking north from the Monument up Gracechurch St, a small detour down Leadenhall St will allow you to wander the fascinating **Leadenhall Market 5** (p111), built in the 14th century and now covered by a beautifully painted arcade. Many unique shops – including fine-soap merchants and perfumeries – survive, although, in a nod to the inevitable, chain stores have been moving in gradually over the past decade. Further along you can ogle at the striking **Lloyds of London 6** (p111) building on Lime St, designed by Richard Rogers.

Turn back along Leadenhall St and turn right into Bishopsgate, the old Roman road that leads all the way to York. Here you'll pass the city's transport hub of Liverpool St Station. Turn right into Folgate St, lined with fine Georgian houses. It was in this area that Protestant Huguenots settled in the late 17th century, bringing with them their skills as silk weavers. Street names such as Fleur-de-Lis St and Nantes Passage recall their presence.

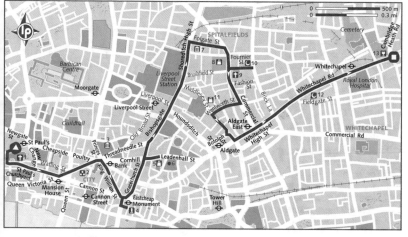

Walking Tours – The Square Mile Walk

211

At 18 Folgate St is **Dennis Severs' House 7** (p117), named after the late American eccentric who restored it to its 18th-century splendour. If you don't mind having your wits frightened out of you, join the 'Silent Night' candlelit tour (p117), held on Monday evenings.

Turn right (south) along Commercial St and you'll see hip **Spitalfields Market 8** (p117) on the right, part of which has been snatched from the hands of redevelopers. On Sundays, one of London's more interesting markets takes place in the arena.

On Commercial St, virtually opposite the market, you can't miss the arresting façade of **Christ Church, Spitalfields 9** (p117). A magnificent English-Baroque structure, it was designed by Nicholas Hawksmoor and completed in 1729 for the Huguenot weavers who lived in the area. Ongoing restoration work is coming to an end and it's worth timing your visit for the brief opening hours.

Leadenhall market shop window (p334)

Turn down Fournier St, to the left of Christ Church, and check out the beautifully restored Georgian houses with their wooden shutters. Most were built between 1718 and 1728 for wealthy London merchants, and were later taken over by the silk weavers and their families.

At the Brick Lane end of Fournier St is one of the most interesting buildings in Spitalfields, the New French Church, built for the Huguenots in 1743. In 1899 the church became the Great Synagogue for Jewish refugees from Russia and central Europe. In 1975 it changed faiths again, becoming the **Great Mosque 10** (p118) of the Bengali community.

Back on Commercial St, you can either turn right and have a pint at the shamelessly traditional Golden Hart pub – with its marvellous fish and chips and kind landlady who adopts newcomers to Spitalfields – or wander left down the ramshackle rows of clothing bulk-buy outlets and fabric shops to Wentworth St. This will take you to Middlesex St, where the enjoyable **Petticoat Lane Market 11** (p334) operates on Fridays and Sundays. Unlike the swish organic food stalls of Spitalfields Market, Petticoat Lane is a true East End tradition where you'll find cheap clothing, beauty products and leather goods.

The back of the market leads you into Aldgate, the site of the old eastern gate to London. Walk down Aldgate to Whitechapel High St – you have now entered Jack the Ripper territory. The 19th-century serial killer's identity remains a mystery, adding to the interest in him and his crimes. What is certain is that in 1888 he butchered five prostitutes in the wretched backstreets of the Victorian East End: Mary Anne Nichols died in Bucks Row (now Durward St) north of Whitechapel; Annie Chapman in Hanbury St near the Ten Bells pub opposite Christ Church, Spitalfields; Elizabeth Stride in Berner St (now Henriques St) south of Commercial Rd; Catherine Eddowes in Mitre Square near Aldgate; and Mary Kelly in Miller's Court (now a car park). For more on the gory crimes, see the Ripping Yarns boxed text, and for details on organised tours of the murder sites, p168.

Travel along Whitechapel High St, which becomes Whitechapel Rd, and turn right onto Fieldgate St, where you'll find some good Pakistani restaurants and the Fieldgate Great Synagogue, now part of the modern **Whitechapel Mosque 12**. Alternatively, continue east on Whitechapel Rd to the junction with Cambridge Heath Rd and you'll see the **Blind Beggar 13** (p167) pub at No 337, notorious for being the place where Ronnie Kray shot George Cornell in 1966 in a gang war over control of the East End's organised crime. Whitechapel tube is a short distance west of the pub.

THE SOUTH BANK WALK

The South Bank of the Thames has developed gradually into a fascinating place to visit. The late 1990s saw a huge increase in the area's popularity, from the opening of the fantastic Tate Modern and Shakespeare's Globe to the London Eye. All these factors have made the South Bank one of the most popular weekend spots in which Londoners can wander and chill out, and a walk down the Thames, dipping in and out of museums and cafés, should not be missed.

Starting from the hyper-modern **Westminster tube station 1**, cross Westminster Bridge, which gives you spectacular views of the House of Commons and Big Ben. **County Hall 2** (p157) – once the power base of the so-called

Walk Facts

Best time Any time
Start Westminster tube station
End Tower Hill tube station
Food en route Borough Market for a gourmet picnic
End-of-walk drink Tower Thistle Hotel bar
Distance 2 miles (3.2km)
Time 2 hours

'loony left' Greater London Council (GLC) under the leadership of 'Red' Ken Livingstone – is the imposing 1922 building at the end of the bridge, now containing a hotel, the superb **London Aquarium** (p158) and a small Salvador Dalí museum, **Dalí Universe** (p158). The GLC was finally dissolved by Margaret Thatcher after it dared disagree with her one too many times. However, while Lady Thatcher is rarely heard from these days, Ken Livingstone has gone on to take the ultimate prize, becoming mayor of London, and is now basing his operations in the equally imposing Greater London Authority Building next to Tower Bridge. The stretch of the embankment from Westminster Bridge to the **British Airways London Eye 3** (p157) is packed with tourists and tat-stalls – one of the few noticeably tacky and touristy areas

in the city (avoided by many other London sights through strict planning permission requirements). Although the London Eye offers unbeatable views of the capital from on high, queues can be long, so it's better to book in advance.

The Thames curves gracefully towards Waterloo here, and you'll walk past the new **Hungerford footbridge**, which is particularly stunning at night when floodlit. Follow the Thames' path, and you'll see the South Bank complex on your right. The unfortunate concrete buildings belie the fact that some of London's best films, plays, art and concerts can be seen within their walls. The complex houses the National Film Theatre (NFT; p294), which has an excellent programme of new and repertory films; the National Theatre, which is always putting on new and challenging productions; and the Royal Festival Hall, one of the world's best-known concert venues.

On weekends the brilliant Riverside **secondhand book market 4** (p334) under Waterloo Bridge offers excellent bargains. The NFT café has outdoor seating that can be a lovely spot for a drink if the weather is good.

Continuing along the Thames, you'll pass the recently redeveloped **Oxo Tower 5** (p159). This handsome building hosts plenty of shops and art galleries, as well as the eponymous restaurant on the 5th floor (p240). Past

Riverside book market (p334)

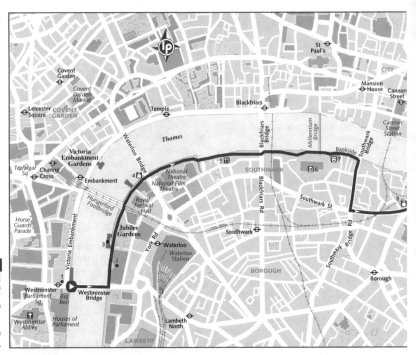

Blackfriars Bridge you enter Bankside, until recently a rather forgotten and quiet neighbourhood that has suddenly become the last word in stylish London living – to which the sheer number of yuppie flats attests. The centrepiece of the now-lively quarter is Sir Giles Gilbert Scott's magnificent Bankside Power station, which, like its Battersea counterpart, had lain empty for years before it was remodelled for the millennium as the **Tate Modern 6** (p160).

Take advantage of the free admission and wander through this incredible space – even if just to look into the enormous turbine hall where temporary exhibits of unfeasible proportions are often displayed. The permanent displays are interestingly curated by theme rather than in the more obvious chronological style, and the restaurant and members' room on the top floors have breathtaking views across the river to the city.

In front of Tate Modern, the **Millennium Bridge** (p160), a fabulous Norman Foster creation, spans the Thames to the prestigious City of London Boys School. Famously, the bridge had to be closed almost as soon as it opened when it began to sway under the strain of huge crowds; it took a year and a half to re-open. It's a great place to cross the river and affords magnificent views of St Paul's Cathedral on the other side. However, stay on the

Borough Market (p334)

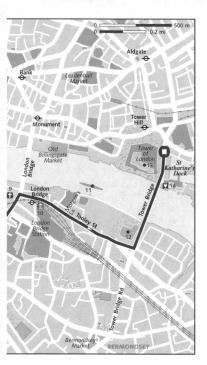

south bank and continue east to **Shakespeare's Globe Theatre 7** (p161), a replica of the London theatre that William Shakespeare co-owned. The idea may sound tacky to some, but everyone is in agreement – this replica, which burned down during a performance of *Henry V* in 1613, is definitely worth a visit. You can wander through the fascinating exhibition that charts the history of the theatre, take a guided tour, and even better, watch a matinee performance.

From here walk down Bankside to Southwark Bridge. Take Southwark Bridge Rd south to Southwark St and turn left into the smart neighbourhood of Borough. This wonderful area has a village feel, and a sense of community that is a rare find in London. Its centrepiece is the fantastic **Borough Market 8** (p334), where food has been sold since the 13th century. On Fridays and Saturdays, the market is abuzz with shoppers checking out a fantastic range of gourmet stalls, where you can buy everything from cured Spanish meats to organic country quiches to fresh sea bass. This is a great place to pick up a picnic lunch, which you can enjoy in the lovely grounds of the **Southwark Cathedral 9** (p162) – walk up Borough High St towards the Thames and you'll see the cathedral to your left. This captivating place is wonderful to walk around and has an

incredible amount of history. Most notably it was used as a pigsty after the Reformation, and previous to that was the scene of Protestant martyrdom under Mary Tudor.

From London Bridge, take Tooley St towards Bermondsey. There is plenty of interest around here, including the **London Dungeon 10** (p164) and **HMS Belfast 11** (p164) at the end of Morgan's Lane. Tooley St brings you into Tower Bridge Rd, giving you wonderful views of the bridge as you approach. The **Greater London Authority Building 12**, next to Tower Bridge, will compete for your attention, but while it's an interesting building in a faintly ridiculous way, it's no contest to London's best-known river crossing.

Wander across the bridge and enjoy the views of the Tower of London. You can even go into the 'roof' of **Tower Bridge** (p116) – the views are arguably the main reason for doing this, rather than the fairly uninteresting history of the bridge's unique mechanics. Once back north of the river, the truly hardy could tackle the **Tower of London 13** (p112), while most will prefer to have a drink at the **Tower Thistle Hotel 14**, or one of the other smart bars in nearby St Katharine's Dock.

THE HIGHGATE & HAMPSTEAD WALK

One of the loveliest areas of London, the hilly, leafy villages of Highgate and Hampstead (p184) have long enchanted visitors, as well as being home to the city's moneyed intellectuals. This walking tour begins in Highgate, with a visit to the world-famous cemetery, and takes you across glorious Hampstead Heath to old Hampstead village.

Starting from Archway tube station, walk northwest up **Highgate Hill**. This was the spot where, according to legend, Dick Whittington heard Bow Bells (the church bells of St Mary-le-Bow, in the East End) ringing out 'turn again, Whittington, Lord Mayor of London', and dutifully he did, going on to fulfil his destiny as Lord Mayor four times. While obviously untrue – being able to hear Bow Bells on Highgate Hill would have been some achievement, not to mention rendering the posh local residents cockneys – it's a nice story and there is the **Whittington Stone 1** (p78) to mark the 'event'.

Hampstead Heath (p185)

Continuing up Highgate Hill, turn left into Dartmouth Park immediately after you pass the distinctive **St Joseph's Church 2** on your left. The entrance to the lovely **Waterlow Park** is then a little way down the road on the right. Waterlow Park is a beautiful, uncrowded spot to wander, with lovely ponds and hills. It was donated to London at the end of the 19th century by Sir Sydney Waterlow and takes you out onto bucolic Swain's Lane. It's hard to believe you are still in London here, and that was obviously the intention behind the building of **Holly Village**, a private residential enclave erected in 1865. It's off Swain's Lane to your left after Highgate Cemetery.

Walk left down Swain's Lane and you will come to Highgate's most famous spot, its **cemetery 3** (p184). Of the two halves, the western section can be visited only on a guided tour (such as are its complexities), however, you are free to stroll at leisure in the eastern section. Most famous of all the greats buried here is Karl Marx, and the cemetery was something of a pilgrimage spot for communists during the 20th century. Nowadays, diplomats from the few surviving communist governments in the world are the only people who seem to bring flowers.

If you have time to join the tour of the western cemetery, it's definitely the highlight of the two, being far more atmospheric and magical with its catacombs and maze-like pathways adorned with elaborate family crypts.

Follow the pretty curve of Swain's Lane down to the right, and it will lead you straight to **Hampstead Heath** (p185) and onto **Parliament Hill**, with its glorious views over the centre of London. Hampstead Heath offers almost endless leisure activities – you can swim at numerous ponds and at

Walk Facts

Best time Any day during the summer months
Start Archway tube station
End Hampstead tube station
Food en route A posh café or restaurant on Hampstead High Street
End-of-walk drink The Hollybush pub
Distance 3 miles (4.8km)
Time 3 hours

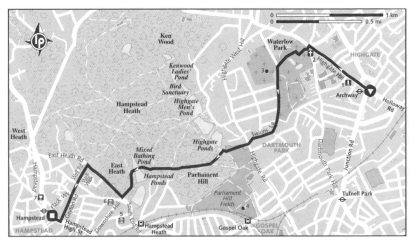

the wonderful **Parliament Hill Lido 4** (p305), play football, ride bikes, rollerblade or just drink in the scenery.

But as you're already doing plenty of exercise on this walk, you might want to just head to **Keat's House 5** (p185). Make your way across Parliament Hill and down towards Hampstead Ponds, then leave the heath at Southend Rd and walk down to Keats Grove to see the house – this is where the poet lived for two years until 1820. From Keats House, take South End Rd back towards the heath and wander up East Heath Rd.

Lovers of modernism may be interested in the unique building at **No 2 Willow Rd 6** (p186), which is on the left as you walk up, just off Downshire Hill. The international modernist building style was pioneered by Ernö Goldfinger and this fascinating example is now maintained by the National Trust.

Carrying on up East Heath Rd, wander the incredibly village-like side streets of Well Rd and Well Walk, where beautiful little ivy-clad cottages vie with one another to be the most attractive. Walking down Well Walk will take you through Gayton Rd to **Hampstead High St** . This is the centre of

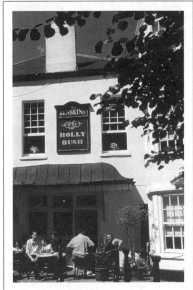

Hollybush tavern (p275)

village Hampstead and a great place to stop for a spot of lunch and a well-earned drink. You'll do well to try one of Hampstead's best-loved taverns, the **Hollybush 7** (p275) on Holly Mount.

THE FLEET STREET & STRAND WALK

This walk takes you from Fleet St to the Strand, the roads that have linked London's two opposing worlds for centuries: the business-minded City of London and political Westminster, with the sniping press wedged between the two.

From Ludgate Circus, walk westwards along Fleet St, one-time home to the nation's national newspapers. Most editorial offices have now moved east to the Docklands in search of more space and cheaper rent, but there are still plentiful reminders of the press hub that once was. The office of Reuters – the only remaining media organisation left nowadays – is at No 85. On the northern side of the street at No 135 is **Peterborough Court 1** (p60), the former *Daily Telegraph* building, built in 1928 and variously described as 'jazz modern' and 'neo-Greek'. Next door, at No 129, is **Salisbury Court 2**, the Art Deco erstwhile home of the *Daily Express*, one of the most stylish and atmospheric early 20th century structures in London. The bars and pubs on Fleet Street still pack in hacks day and night.

Farther along on the northern side is a narrow alleyway called Wine Office Court (where the excise office stood until 1665), which leads to Dr Johnson's local, **Ye Olde Cheshire Cheese 3** (p267). This pub is wonderfully atmospheric, and it is worth a pint at any time of day – the spirits of its many famous regulars seem to hang over the tiny little rooms with cosy fireplaces that make up the pub. The numerous pilgrims who have drunk where Dr Johnson once drank include Charles Dickens and Mark Twain among their number.

Walk Facts

Best time any time
Start Blackfriars tube
End Temple tube
Food en route A sandwich at the Somerset House café, with tables overlooking the Thames
End-of-walk drink Ye Olde Cheshire Cheese
Distance 1 mile (1.6km)
Time About an hour

Walk back to Fleet St and continue westward along the same side. At No 154 you pass **Bouverie House 4**, once home to the *Sun* newspaper, the publication that gave the world the Page Three girl and pioneered the crass headline. Turn right at narrow Johnson's Court, which leads to Gough Square and **Dr Johnson's House 5** (p82); the wooden chair on which he used to sit while drinking at **Ye Olde Cock Tavern 6** is preserved on the 1st-floor landing. The tavern, the oldest in Fleet St, is a short distance to the west on the other side of the street at No 22 and was a favourite of the poet TS Eliot. The colourful cockerel on its pub sign is said to have been designed by Grinling Gibbons, whose work adorns many London churches, including St Paul's Cathedral. Pepys, Dr Johnson, Goldsmith and Charles Dickens all drank here – when they weren't knocking them back at Ye Olde Cheshire Cheese.

Opposite the Cock stands **St Dunstan-in-the-West 7** which was built by John Shaw in 1832 and boasts a spectacular octagonal lantern tower. Look out for Elizabeth I on the façade, the only such outdoor statue of the Virgin Queen, which stood on Ludgate until it was demolished in 1760. You can't miss Gog and Magog in the recess above the clock outside; on the hour they swing round and club the bells beside them.

Further west, at No 17, is **Prince Henry's Room 8**, one of the few buildings to survive both the Great Fire of London and the Blitz, although its exterior was rebuilt after the war. Here James I's son Henry ran his duchy of Cornwall, before succumbing to typhoid at the age of 18, meaning he never ascended the throne. Beyond that an archway leads to **Temple Church 9** (p100) in the Inner Temple.

In the centre of Fleet St, a statue of a griffin bestriding an elaborately carved plinth marks the site of the original **Temple Bar 10**, where the City of Westminster becomes the City of London. The plinth is decorated with statues of Queen Victoria and her husband, Prince Albert, together with symbols of Art and Science, and War and Peace.

The **Wig & Pen Club 11** (p98) at No 229–230 on the Strand dates from 1625 and is the only Strand building to have survived the Great Fire of 1666; it's now a restaurant. Have a look at the symbolic wigs and pens in the external plasterwork.

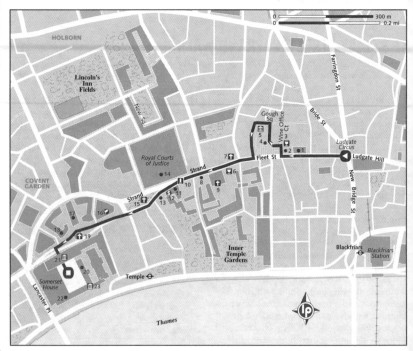

As you proceed westward, look up to appreciate the fine architecture. A few doors west of the Wig & Pen, at No 222–225, an Art Deco branch of **Lloyd's Bank 12** has carved fish twined around its circular windows and elaborate tiles adorning the recess now housing its cash machines. Just beyond on the same side at No 216 is **Twinings 13** (p98), a tea shop opened by Thomas Twining in 1706 and believed to be the oldest company in London still trading on the same site and owned by the same family. On the northern side of the Strand is the extraordinary neo-Gothic confection of the **Royal Courts of Justice 14** (p99), containing over 1000 rooms and three miles of hallways. You'll often see the street outside packed with a media scrum and gawping bystanders when high-profile criminal and libel cases come to be decided. In 2003 Catherine Zeta-Jones and Michael Douglas controversially won damages from *Hello!* magazine here, and this has also been a place for many an unhappy end in more serious criminal trials.

The church in the centre of the road is **St Clement Danes 15** (☎ 7242 8282; ⏰ 8.30am-4.30pm Mon-Fri, 9am-3.30pm Sat, 9am-12.30pm Sun; p100). The original church was designed by Sir Christopher Wren in 1682, with the steeple added by James Gibbs in 1719; only the walls and steeple survived the bombings of 1941. In 1958 the church was rebuilt for the Royal Air Force; 800-plus slate badges of different squadrons and units of the RAF are set into the nave pavement. At 9am, noon, 3pm and 6pm the church bells chime out the old nursery rhyme 'Oranges and Lemons' (p100). The statue in front of the church is that of the controversial Sir Arthur 'Bomber' Harris, Marshall of the Royal Air Force, who led the bombing raids over Germany during WWII – including Dresden, where 10,000 civilians were incinerated.

Continue west along the Strand, with **Australia House 16**, designed by Marshall Mackenzie between 1912 and 1918, and strikingly modernist **Bush House 17**, built in 1920, on your right. The latter houses the BBC World Service, which broadcasts daily to an audience of over 150 million in 43 different languages. The World Service, described by UN Secretary General Kofi Annan as 'Britain's greatest gift to the world', began broadcasting overseas as early as 1932, when it was known as the Empire Service. Since then it has grown so

Somerset House (p220)

vastly that new premises are currently being built to house it next to Broadcasting House in Oxford Circus. The equally imposing **India House 18** next door dates from 1930 and is decorated inside with fascinating murals by four Bengali artists. There is a bust of Nehru, India's first prime minister, in the small passageway connecting the Strand to Aldwych.

In the centre of the road is **St Mary-le-Strand 19**, designed by James Gibbs between 1715 and 1724, and the church of the Women's Royal Naval Service. St. Mary's was supposed to have no steeple, but instead a column with a statue of Queen Anne on top. However, this idea was dropped when Queen Anne died in 1714 and the imposing steeple was built. Imagine the maypole that entertained the common folk on the green where the church now stands until Puritans burned it in 1644. It was replaced after the Restoration only to be bought by none other than Sir Isaac Newton as a telescope support!

Facing off Bush House on the other side of the road is the monstrous face of King's College's Strand campus, which belies the fact that this is one of the oldest London colleges, founded by King George IV in 1829. Despite its rather unsightly exterior, walking into its courtyard is worth it to see the Georgian façade, a place often used by film companies making costume drama, who enjoy its unspoilt regency feel.

Next door is even more graceful: **Somerset House 20** (p98), designed by Sir William Chambers in 1774 and completed in 1835. Walk into the impressive courtyard that now houses playful fountains in the summer and an ice rink in the winter. You can also walk out the far door onto the walkway overlooking the Thames, and have a bite to eat on the terrace café. Somerset House now houses three impressive museums: the **Courtauld Gallery 21** (p99), **Hermitage Rooms 22** (p99) and **Gilbert Collection of Decorative Arts 23** (p99). Further down the Strand on your left you'll see the Savoy Hotel. As well as housing the world famous Savoy Grill (where Churchill lunched so frequently at table 4 that on his death they left it empty for a year out of respect), Savoy Street – the small conduit leading from the Strand to the hotel – is famous for being the only street in Britain where driving is on the right, due to the room needed to manoeuvre a car from the Strand into the hotel forecourt and back out again.

The walk ends as the Strand fills up with high street shops and pours into Trafalgar Square. From here you can wander south to Whitehall, west to Buckingham Palace or north to Soho for a spot of retail therapy.

Eating

Eating

Dining out has become unfathomably fashionable in London over the last decade (p16) and there has never been a better time to explore the local foodscape. In this chapter, we steer you towards the best restaurants and cafés that are distinguished by their location, unique features, original settings, value for money and, of course, outstanding grub. Our list ranges from breakfast cafés that are convenient for nursing a hangover to scintillating world-beaters worthy of the most special occasion.

'Gastropubs' were all the rage in the capital a few years ago and you'll find many of the establishments listed in the Drinking chapter are also worthy food destinations (although most of them are not).

Goddards Pie House, Greenwich (p246)

Tipping

Tipping has become a bit of a grey area here in recent years. Most restaurants now automatically tack on a 'recommended' 12.5% service charge and, cheekily, *still* leave space for a tip on the credit card slip. Whether or not the servers are benefiting from this service charge is questionable – they're probably not – and it's up to you whether you want to leave something extra or not. If the service wasn't up to scratch, just refuse to pay the service charge. The system sucks.

Hours & Meal Times

Londoners follow fairly loose fuelling schedules although, in contrast to people in continental Europe, they like to eat their evening meal early, generally between 7pm and 9.30pm. Most places serve lunch between noon and 2.30pm and dinner from 7pm and 10pm although many mid-range restaurants stay open throughout the day. Hours can change from place to place – for example many restaurants in Soho close Sunday, and those in the City for the whole weekend – and we've noted with each venue where places stray from the standard. However, if you're going out of your way, it's always safest to call first and check.

Booking Tables

Making reservations has become just about compulsory for all central restaurants from Thursday to Saturday and for the hippest ones at any time. A good Internet booking service is www.toptable.co.uk, which is reliable and often offers substantial discounts. Many of the highest-end places – the ones that cost the most and where you'd most like to linger – run the exceedingly annoying system of multiple sittings, where you have the option of an early or late slot, for example 7pm to 9pm or 9pm to 11pm. It's probably best to go for the later window and not be rushed.

Smoking

Most restaurants – at least mid-range and upwards – provide no-smoking areas but you won't always have that luxury, and smokers at the next table won't hesitate in sparking up even if you're half way through your main. More and more venues are turning smoke-free but if you're a heavy nonsmoker, make sure to say so when you book.

How Much?

Perhaps the most compelling reason for scouring this chapter and choosing your restaurant carefully is that dining out here is outlandishly expensive compared with the US, Australia and most of Europe. And if you don't earn sterling, chances are that you'll rarely get what you consider value for money. Go to a top restaurant, have a martini at the bar, order three courses à la carte and wash it down with a decent European red, and two of you will be lucky to get change out of £250. Then again, you could have an excellent meal for half that if you avoided the restaurants *du jour*, but neither of you are likely to cherish the memories of a meal that costs less than £50 here. The West End and south central are the most expensive places to eat.

Self-Catering

Along with Londoners' new-found passion for dining out comes a greater appreciation for food in general, and if you're keen to self-cater you'll find lots of great little farmers markets, continental delis and ethnic and organic stores dotted all over town.

Vegetarian Dining

Vegetarianism has long been integral to London dining – not least because of the customary health scares over British meat – and the vast majority of places listed here offer choice and flavour for meat-free diners. For dedicated vegetarian joints, try Food for Thought (p226), the Gate (p255), Mildred's (p224), Oshobasho Café (p251), the Place Below (p235), Rasa (p252), Raw Deal (p250), Red Veg (p229) and Woodlands (p248).

THE WEST END

Many of London's most eclectic, fashionable and often expensive restaurants are dotted around the thrilling West End. There's a huge concentration of places to eat along the main tourist drags, although the best places are often on the back streets and the most prominent ones are generally the worst. New restaurants open here weekly, but if they're good you'll rarely be able to walk in off the street without a prior booking. Chinatown, as you might guess, is a great spot for inexpensive Chinese and Japanese food. There are a few well-known vegetarian places in the likeable Neal's Yard, although price and quality have been heading in opposite directions in recent years so we've dropped them from our list.

SOHO

BACK TO BASICS Map pp426-7   *Fish*
☎ 7436 2181; 2a Foley St W1; mains £12.95-14.95;
🕑 closed Sat & Sun; tube Oxford Circus

There are other options on the menu but fish is the focus at this superb corner restaurant, which you'll find cosy or cramped, loud or just lively depending on your mood. A dozen varieties of exceedingly fresh fish, and a dozen ways to cook 'em, are chalked up on a blackboard daily but you won't always get our favourite of monkfish with spicy, garlicky prawn couscous.

CRITERION Map p428   *French*
☎ 7930 0488; 224 Piccadilly W1; mains £12-20;
🕑 closed Sun; tube Piccadilly Circus

This beautiful Marco Pierre White restaurant is all chandeliers, mirrors, marble and sparkling mosaics – one breathless wag has compared it to the inside of a Fabergé egg – but its most spectacular feature is the modern French food, which ranges from the delicate mussel and saffron soup to a hefty and heavenly steak tartare. Unfortunately, it's one of those places where dinner is in shifts; arrive for the second sitting so you won't be so rushed. Vegetarians shouldn't arrive at all.

GARLIC & SHOTS Map p428   *Novelty*
☎ 7734 9505; 14 Frith St W1; mains £9-13; 🕑 dinner until 1am Thu-Sat; tube Tottenham Court Road

Your tolerance for garlic – and your plans for later in the evening – will determine how much you enjoy this novelty place, popular with a largely black-clad and partly red-coiffed crowd. Its dedication to the odorous bulb knows no bounds as all the dishes are infused with it, even the cheesecake for chrissakes. Its other focus is getting hammered on flavoured vodka shots (try the bloodshot). There's outdoor seating and a very loud vampire bar downstairs.

GAY HUSSAR Map p428   *Hungarian*
☎ 7437 0973; 2 Greek St W1; mains £12-18; tube Tottenham Court Road

Elegant without being stuffy, the Gay Hussar brings you back to the Soho of the 1950s via Budapest, where dinner is served in a wood-panelled dining room with brocade and sepia prints on the walls, and a conspiratorial ambience. The menu is rich, authentic and meaty, and the portions are colossal. The 'Gypsy quick dish' of pork medallions, onions and green peppers is a stand-out.

KETTNERS Map p428   *Pizza*
☎ 7734 6112; 29 Romilly St W1; dishes £7-11; tube Leicester Square

Although part of Pizza Express, Kettners charges a couple of quid more for their pizzas than the mother ship but the quality and vibe is more than twice as good. The glamorous decor of this decadent old hotel, established in 1867 and long a Soho institution, and the everyday fare of pizzas and burgers make for a charming contrast, one that you can mull over while trying to choose from 50 different champagnes and listening to the tinkling of a piano in the background.

LINDSAY HOUSE Map p428   *Irish*
☎ 7439 0450; 21 Romilly St W1; set lunch/dinner £23/48; tube Leicester Square

Richard Corrigan is the Irish chef and character behind this superb restaurant, where you'll be won over to 'new Irish cuisine' – no sniggering, it's something to behold. Dishes are simple and hearty but exquisitely executed (like poached *ballotine* of sea bass with pickled cabbage and oysters). The restaurant still has the atmosphere of the 18th-century residence it occupies; you have to ring the bell to get in, and the decor comprises all natural materials and tones. Service is warm and sincere. Typical of Irish hospitality.

MEZZO Map p428   *Modern European*
☎ 7314 4000; 100 Wardour St W1; mains £14-18; tube Piccadilly Circus

Another of Terence Conran's ventures that attracts London's media crowd and the wannabes that cling to them, Mezzo is so big that you might not find your way back from the loo. The main restaurant in the basement is fun and noisy, and the food and service are outstanding for the price (as long as you don't let the occasional bitchy waitress put you off). Mezzonine is a more casual, cheaper eatery on the ground floor.

Top Five – West End

- J Sheekey (p227)
- Lindsay House (left)
- Mildred's (below)
- Sketch (p225)
- Zipangu (p227)

MILDRED'S Map p428   *Vegetarian*
☎ 7494 1634; 45 Lexington St W1; mains £5-7; tube Tottenham Court Road

This is central London's best veggie restaurant and is a treat for carnivores and herbivores alike. Mildred moved into bigger premises recently but lunchtimes are still heaving. Don't be shy about sharing tables or you'll miss out on excellent, inexpensive and hugely portioned wholesome veggie fare from salads and stirfries to beanburgers and a memorable ale pie. Drinks include juices, coffees, beers and organic wines, and the staff are friendly and unruffled.

PIZZA EXPRESS Map p428   *Pizza*
☎ 7439 8722; 10 Dean St W1; pizzas £5-8; tube Tottenham Court Road

It's getting a bit of stick about resting on its laurels but this chain is still much loved by Londoners and has about 50 branches dotted around town, all serving reliable, undistinguished pizzas in a family-friendly environment. This branch, however, is as well known for its nightly jazz in the basement as it is for doughy discs.

QUO VADIS Map p428   *Italian*
☎ 7437 9585; 26-29 Dean St W1; mains £14-32; tube Tottenham Court Road

This used to be a cosy arrangement between super chef Marco Pierre White and Britartist Damien Hirst. After a very public spat in 1999, Marco got rid of Damien's art from the walls and replaced it with his own parodies. It has settled back into a very snazzy groove these days, exuding elegance and intimacy in its light and airy interior. Marco is only executive chef these days, so he can't take all the credit for the excellent food (try the mushroom risotto or skate with capers). Service is warm and extremely well organised – an all-round winner.

SAIGON Map p428   *Vietnamese*
☎ 7437 7109; 45 Frith St W1; meals £11; tube Tottenham Court Road

This place is required dining for anyone on a gastronomic tour of Asia, via Chinatown.

Top Five Soho Cafés

Soho presents the nearest thing London has to a sophisticated café culture to match that of its Continental neighbours. The area has been synonymous with sipping, smoking and schmoozing since the Victorians established the first coffee houses here. Its café heyday came with the mod hangouts of the '60s, but whatever your inclination or mood, there are still plenty of places from which to choose. These five will get you started.

BAR ITALIA Map p428
☎ 7437 4520; 22 Frith St W1; sandwiches £3.50-5; 🕐 24hr; tube Leicester Square

Pop into this Soho favourite at any time of day or night – or in any state – and you'll see slumming celebrities lapping up reviving juices and hunky paninis amid cool 1950s decor. It's always packed and buzzing but you can normally get a seat, after 1am.

MAISON BERTAUX Map p428
☎ 7437 6007; 28 Greek St W1; cakes about £3; tube Tottenham Court Road

Bertaux has exquisite confections, unhurried service, a French bohemian vibe and 130 years of history on this spot.

MONMOUTH COFFEE COMPANY Map p430
☎ 7836 5272; 27 Monmouth St WC2; tube Tottenham Court Road/Leicester Square

Essentially a shop selling beans from just about every coffee-growing country in the world, characterful Monmouth also has a few wooden alcoves at the back where you can squeeze in, sit and savour the blends from Nicaragua and Guatemala to Kenya and Ethiopia (although you'd probably catapult through the window after all that). This place is the antithesis of the café chains in every way.

PATISSERIE VALERIE Map p428
☎ 7437 3466; 44 Old Compton St W1; sandwiches £3.50-5.95; tube Tottenham Court Road/Leicester Square

This sweet Soho institution was established in 1926 and has delicious, delicate pastries, stylish sandwiches, filled croissants and strictly no phones le mobile. There are four more branches around town and you'll be lucky to get a seat at any of them.

STAR CAFÉ Map p428
☎ 7437 8778; 22 Great Chapel St W1; mains £5-8; tube Tottenham Court Road

So Soho, this wonderfully atmospheric café has vintage advertising and continental decor that makes it feel like not much has changed since it opened in the 1930s. It's best known for brekky, particularly the curiously named Tim Mellor Special of smoked salmon and scrambled eggs. Cold roast lamb and new potatoes makes a terrific lunch as well, and the service is bright and friendly whatever the time of day.

While London isn't particularly well endowed with good Vietnamese eateries – and Saigon might not cut the *mu tac* (mustard) in another town – it manages to satisfy body and soul with authentic tastes and furnishings.

SKETCH Map p428   *Modern European*
☎ 0870 777 4488; 9 Conduit St W1; Lecture Room mains £50-75; Gallery mains from £10; tube Oxford Circus

The name suggests something rough and unfinished but this place is anything but. *The* trendiest place in London – at the time of writing, at least – and host to all the hottest parties, Sketch is a design enthusiast's wildest dream.

Shimmering white rooms, designer Tulip chairs, toilets in the form of individual white eggs and walls ablaze with video imagery – and that's just the downstairs video art gallery, which becomes a buzzy and inexpensive restaurant at night, and a funky club after midnight. Daintily portioned dishes here hint at what you could be enjoying upstairs in the Lecture Room, the most expensive eatery in London, where a starter could set you back £65. Menus come in his and hers varieties (with and without prices) but the restaurant's most outstanding feature – apart from crystal-encrusted loos – are the sensational tasters from chef Pierre Gagnaire, who won three Michelin stars for his restaurant in Paris.

On the High Teas

Going out for 'afternoon tea' is something dear to the heart of many English folk, for whom a trip to the centre of London wouldn't be complete without a visit to one of its atmospheric tea rooms. A traditional tea comes with a selection of delicate sandwiches (cucumber or smoked salmon), freshly baked scones with cream and jam and a selection of assorted sweet nibbles all washed down with lashing of tea. It will cost you about £25 per person and the best places to indulge are the Ritz (p344), Brown's Hotel (p343), Claridges (p343) and the venerable department store Fortnum & Mason.

SPIGA Map p428 — *Italian*
☎ 7734 3444; 84-86 Wardour St W1; pizzas & pastas £6-9, mains £12.50-14; tube Tottenham Court Road

The small, upmarket chain is the place to come when you want modern Italian food in smart casual surroundings and don't want to pay the world for it. Feisty pizzas, perky pastas, excellent vegetarian antipasto and refined cheese platters make this a rare and well-priced West End treat.

SUGAR CLUB Map p428 — *Fusion*
☎ 7437 7776; 22 Warwick St W1; mains £13.80-25; tube Oxford Circus

This popular place concentrates on Pacific Rim dishes – grilled scallops with sweet chilli sauce, roast duck on wok-fried black beans give you an idea – that cleverly mix and match traditions from East and West. The ground floor is slightly cluttered and possibly too lively for couples, who'll prefer the more discreet basement.

COVENT GARDEN & LEICESTER SQUARE

1997 Map p428 — *Chinese*
☎ 7734 2868; 19 Wardour St W1; mains £6.50-9; ⏰ open until 4am; tube Leicester Square

Named after the year Hong Kong was reclaimed by China, 1997 does a perky Peking Duck and comforting soup noodles beneath pictures of distinguished communists and, er, Princess Diana. You know you're onto a winner when the place is heaving with Chinese students.

ATLANTIC BAR & GRILL
Map p428 — *Modern British*
☎ 7734 4888; 20 Glasshouse St W1; mains £12-20; tube Piccadilly Circus

This buzzy and atmospheric place boasts high ceilings, a large Art Deco dining area, two bars and a menu of splendid pasta, meat and fish dishes, as well as more wines and cocktails than you could shake your credit card at.

CALABASH Map p430 — *African*
☎ 7836 1973; Africa Centre, 38 King St WC2; mains £5-8; tube Covent Garden

This easy and relaxed eatery in the Africa Centre pulls in flavours from all over the continent, and has a descriptive menu to guide the uninitiated on a gastronomic tour from *egusi* (Nigerian meat stew) to *yassa* (Senegalese chicken).

CHUEN CHENG KU Map p428 — *Chinese*
☎ 7437 1398; 17 Wardour St W1; dim sum £2, mains £6-12; tube Leicester Square

This Chinatown champ is ideal for the uninitiated as all the dishes – dumplings, noodles, paper-wrapped prawns – are trundled, sometimes raced, around on trolleys so you can just point out what you want (and then cross your fingers). The dim sum starters are mostly moist and perky while the main courses burst with flavour. There are lots of vegetarian options, even if 'crabmeat and tofu' doesn't quite fit the bill.

FOOD FOR THOUGHT
Map p430 — *Vegetarian*
☎ 7836 0239; 31 Neal St WC2; mains £3-6.50; tube Covent Garden

This valued vegetarian joint is big on sociability and flavour and small on price and space. Food ranges from soups and salads to stir fries and traditional Indian *thalis* (mixed plates). It's earthy, unpretentious, and deservedly packed.

IVY Map p430 — *Modern British*
☎ 7836 4751; 1 West St WC2; mains £10-25; tube Leicester Square

With its liveried doorman and celebrity clientele, just managing to snag a table at the Ivy is a showbizzy event in itself. Once you're in, well you're in. Whether you're Brad Pitt or Arm Pit, the service is courteous and unpretentious, and the fare consists of glorious versions of British staples such as shepherd's pie (doubtless the best in town so probably the best in the world), steak tartare and kedgeree.

Eating – The West End

J SHEEKEY Map p430 *Fish*
☎ 7240 2565; 28-32 St Martin's Crt WC2; mains £10-25; tube Leicester Square

A jewel of the local scene, this incredibly smart restaurant has four elegant, discreet and spacious wood-panelled rooms in which to savour the riches of the sea, cooked simply and exquisitely. Waiters are tall and handsome while the menu is short and select; haddock with potatoes, fried egg and crispy bacon never disappoints.

ORSO Map p430 *Italian*
☎ 7240 5269; 27 Wellington St WC2; mains £13-16; tube Covent Garden

This refined, polished and middle-aged Italian eatery is especially popular with journalists by day (perhaps drawn by the free Bloody Mary with the set lunch) and tourists on their way to the theatre in the evening. The fare is reliable if nothing special although the waiters *are* especially handsome.

OSIA Map p428 *Asian/Australian*
☎ 7976 1313; 11 Haymarket SW1; mains £12-20; tube Piccadilly Circus

Among the steakhouses and chain bars of Haymarket, Osia is a beacon of sophisticated cool. So-called because it's supposedly a fusion of Australian and Asian influences (the food is mostly Australian, the prices Japanese), Osia has a gorgeous dining room in which to enjoy some of the most exquisite food in London, and a sexy little bar at the back for cocktails and seduction. Standouts include pan-fried halibut with leeks, pumpkin and parsnips and an elaborate pavlova (Australia's contribution to the world table, although it could be from New Zealand). The staff are bright, breezy and chatty.

LA PERLA Map p430 *Mexican*
☎ 7240 7400; 28 Maiden Lane WC2; mains £8.95-12.50; tube Covent Garden

You mightn't think the tiny kitchen visible from this 'bar' could be up to much – and the other punters normally seem more interested in drinking than eating – but like us you might be so pleased with the huge portion of chicken stir-fry fajitas that you come back for the tacos and stay for the tequila.

ROCK & SOLE PLAICE Map p430 *Fish*
☎ 7836 3785; 47 Endell St WC2; mains £6-13; tube Covent Garden

Established in 1871 and possibly London's oldest fish and chip shop, this Covent Garden landmark does a steady stream of business at its takeaway and restaurant. Along with the old favourite – and increasingly rare – cod you can get dover sole, scotch salmon or tuna steak between crispy batter along with good, thick and crispy chips.

RULES Map p430 *Traditional British*
☎ 7836 5314; 35 Maiden Lane WC2; mains £18-24; tube Covent Garden

Established in 1798, this very posh and very British establishment is London's oldest restaurant and specialises in classic game cookery, serving up some 18,000 birds a year. Despite the history, it's not a museum piece and its sustained vitality attracts locals as well as the tourist masses.

TOKYO DINER Map p430 *Japanese*
☎ 7287 8777; 2 Newport Pl WC2; set meals £5.90-8.50; tube Leicester Square

Everyday Japanese food at everyday prices is what Tokyo Diner's all about, and you can't ask for fairer than that. The waiters are all Japanese, so discreet and graceful in their service, and knowledgeable about the food. The miso is ordinary but the Japanese-style curry is tops. All-round this is a terrific place to pop in for a quick bowl of noodles or plate of sushi. However, at the rate they've been scribbling things out of the menu, there might be nothing left by the time you get there.

WONG KEI Map p428 *Chinese*
☎ 7437 3071; 41-43 Wardour St W1; mains £4.50-7.50, set menus from £6; tube Leicester Square

'What you want? Coming 'ere all de time, wha' u wan?' This place is legendary for the rudeness of its waiters, although they're really not that bad (or good, depending on what you're after). It's really just a pantomime these days. The Cantonese food is cheap and a little stodgy but as good a value as you'll find on a (plastic) plate and the communal table is good for making friends.

ZIPANGU Map p430 *Japanese*
☎ 7437 5042; 8 Little Newport St WC2; set dinner £10-14; tube Leicester Square

It's not much to look at but Zipangu has three storeys of outstandingly tasty, constantly fresh and exceedingly good food and graceful service. While it won't win any awards for style, apart from the bunker this place is the epitome of cheap and cheerful.

HOLBORN & THE STRAND

ADMIRALTY Map p430 *French*
☎ 7845 4646; Somerset House, Strand WC2; set lunch £25; tube Embankment

The flagship restaurant of the restored Somerset House has a traditional interior and modern French food. There's a lovely terrace outside overlooking the Thames, and the degustation menus – including a vegetarian one – are sublime.

SIMPSON'S-IN-THE-STRAND
Map p430 *Traditional British*
☎ 7836 9112; 100 Strand WC2; mains £15; tube Covent Garden

If you have a craving for traditional English roasts and joints off the trolley (we're still talking about meat) head to this rather stuffy old stalwart, which has been dishing up fleshy fare in a fine panelled dining room since 1848.

BLOOMSBURY & FITZROVIA

ABENO Map p430 *Japanese*
☎ 7405 3211; 47 Museum St WC1; mains £5-25; tube Tottenham Court Road

This understated little restaurant specialises in *okonomiyaki*, a kind of Japanese savoury pancake that is combined with the ingredients of your choice (there are over 20 varieties with anything from sliced meats and vegetables to egg, noodles and cheese) and cooked in front of you on the hotplate that makes up most of your table. It can get a little warm and the staff can go a bit overboard with the sauces, but the food is tasty, making this an interesting and novel gastronomic diversion.

BAM-BOU Map p428 *Vietnamese*
☎ 7323 9130; 1 Percy St W1; mains £10-14; tube Goodge Street

This listed Georgian house attracts the media darlings from all over Fitzrovia with its winning colonial French-Vietnamese cuisine. It can feel a little cliquish and some of the staff are less

---

Top Five – Designer Eats

- Baltic (p241)
- E&O (p252)
- Hakkasan (right)
- Nobu (p238)
- Sketch (p225)

---

than welcoming but the mostly modern Vietnamese fare (sesame prawns, pan-fried duck) is a winner.

HAKKASAN Map p428 *Chinese*
☎ 7907 1888; 8 Hanway Pl W1; mains £6-30; tube Tottenham Court Road

This place – hidden down a lane like all the most fashionable haunts should be – combines celebrity status, stunning design, persuasive cocktails and surprisingly sophisticated Chinese food. It was the first Chinese restaurant to get a Michelin star. The low, nightclub-style lighting makes it a good spot for dating, or interrogating, while the long, glinty bar is a great place to suck on a Belvedere Beauty. Ahem, that's a martini made with Belvedere vodka and lychee that was created here for one Kate Moss. It's a pity the place takes itself so seriously, though; you're not allowed take photographs among yourselves in case you frighten the glitterati. There's more informal dining in the Ling Ling lounge.

HAN KANG Map p428 *Korean*
☎ 7637 1985; 16 Hanway St W1; mains average £12; tube Tottenham Court Road

You wouldn't expect to find a culinary gem on dodgy Hanway St, which wears its seediness on its sleeve, but Han Kang is the very thing. It's not much to look out – and nonsmokers might not be able to cope with the uninterrupted cloud left by Korean students – but the food here is a revelation, from *kimchi* (hot pickled, spicy cabbage) to *bulgogi* (literally 'fire meat', marinated slices of beef).

NORTH SEA FISH RESTAURANT
Map pp420-1 *Fish*
☎ 7387 5892; 7-8 Leigh St WC1; mains £8-17; tube Russell Square

This restaurant cooks fresh fish and potatoes, a simple ambition that it realises with aplomb. Look forward to jumbo-sized plaice or halibut steaks, deep-fried or grilled, and a huge serving of chips. The setting is characterless but the charisma of the staff more than makes up for it.

PIED A TERRE Map pp426-7 *French*
☎ 7636 1178; 34 Charlotte St W1; 3-course set lunch/dinner £24/47; tube Goodge Street/Tottenham Court Road

After losing one of its two Michelin stars a few years ago – probably for being too fancy-pants – a new head chef came in and revamped the menu, stripped it back to simpler, more cohesive and ultimately tastier dishes, and the Pied deservedly retrieved its star. Chilled celeriac soup with a dob of pesto is a summer hit, although this being French you can expect mostly meaty mains from snails to veal. The outstanding wine list suggests food and drink combos.

RASA SAMUDRA Map p428   Indian
☎ 7637 0222; 5 Charlotte St W1; mains £8-13; tube Goodge Street

Behind Rasa Samudra's loud interior, this under-appreciated restaurant showcases the tantalising seafood cuisine of Kerala from the southern tip of India, supported by a host of more familiar vegetarian staples. The fish soups are outstanding, the breads superb and the various curries heavily and heavenly spiced. The staff are cheeky and charming.

CHEAP EATS

CAFÉ IN THE CRYPT Map p430   Café
☎ 7839 4342; St Martin-in-the-Fields, Duncannon St WC2; mains £3.95-6.50; tube Charing Cross/Embankment

This is an atmospheric crypt in which to rest weary bones and enjoy excellent food from soups to casseroles (with plenty for vegetarians). Lunchtime is mental.

FRANX SNACK BAR Map p430   Café
☎ 7836 7989; 192 Shaftesbury Ave WC2; meals £3; tube Tottenham Court Road

This is as authentic a London 'caff' as you'll find in these parts; expect eggs and bacon and other artery-clogging one-plate specials.

IKKYU Map p430   Japanese
☎ 7439 3554; 7-9 Newport Pl WC2; sushi £1.50-2.50, noodle dishes £5-8; tube Leicester Square

This Chinese-owned restaurant with Japanese cooks has à la carte sushi, sashimi and noodle

dishes, but the great draws for budget travellers are the four different set lunches and the all-you-can-eat Japanese buffet from 5pm.

KULU KULU Map p428   Japanese
☎ 7734 7316; 76 Brewer St W1; sushi £1.20-3; tube Piccadilly Circus

Bare and bustling, this is the best inexpensive conveyor-belt sushi place in the city. There are no menus and you just grab colour-coded plates of whatever takes your fancy before it rushes past on the carousel. Portions are petite so it can quickly cease to be a cheap eat if you lose the run of yourself.

POLLO Map p428   Italian
☎ 7734 5917; 20 Old Compton St W1; mains £4-8; tube Leicester Square

This popular cheapie draws a regular and relaxed crowd with reasonable pastas, risottos and pizzas. Despite the name, there isn't a shred of chicken to be seen.

RED VEG Map p428   Vegetarian Fast Food
☎ 7437 3109; 95 Dean St W1; mains £3-5; tube Tottenham Court Road

NoName nuggets and organic pop are typical of this unique vegetarian place, which has corny communist decor and a solid line in vegetarian fast food from oriental noodles to falafel.

SOBA Map p428   Japanese
☎ 7734 6400; 38 Poland St W1; noodle & rice dishes around £6; tube Oxford Circus

It's been described as Japanese junk food – the service is blindingly fast – but this is a great place for a fruit juice or Asahi beer with a quick bowl of noodles (try the *yaki-soba* with meat and veg).

EAST CENTRAL

Five years ago, culinary boundaries between the City, with its expense-account diners, and the hip Hoxton scene were clearly drawn. Now, the lines between 'establishment' and 'stylish' have started to blur. While Shoreditch's most singular outlet is the glittery, over-the-top Les Trois Garçons, Clerkenwell has been developing a cluster of noteworthy restaurants: from the delicate Club Gascon to meaty St John's, via the exotic spices of Moro and the smokey flavours of Souvlaki & Bar. By comparison, Islington, once the capital's foodie hubs, is falling a little behind.

Top Five – East Central

- Bonds (p230)
- Café Spice Namaste (p230)
- Club Gascon (p232)
- Les Trois Garçons (p231)
- Real Greek (p231)

THE CITY

An influx of stylish venues notwithstanding, restaurants in the City are still very much geared to the population of financial execs and office workers when it comes to opening hours. That means very little weekend opening, although exceptions do exist.

1 LOMBARD STREET Map pp432-3   French
☎ 7929 611; 1 Lombard St EC3; ☺ breakfast, lunch & dinner Mon-Fri 7.30am-3pm & 6-10pm Mon-Fri; mains £28-30; tube Bank

A totally impressive temple of power dining, 1 Lombard St used to be a bank. Now it's an airy, Michelin-starred restaurant (thanks to chef Herbert Berger) and serves a great combination of seafood, meat and poultry. The menu includes fillets of lamb, beef, venison and roast turbot fish on the bone, as well as such delicacies as caramelised lobster with Thai risotto, plus lobster and coconut velouté. The restaurant is good for impressing clients; the bar mixes a weekday crowds of suits with the occasional celebrity party. There's set lunches for £32 to £38, and a set dinner for £34.

BONDS Map pp432-3   Central European
☎ 7657 8088; 5 Threadneedle St EC2; ☺ lunch & dinner Mon-Fri; mains £18-22; tube Bank

There are two good reasons for coming to this very smart and corporate hotel restaurant: one is to glimpse the awe-inspiring circular lobby of the Threadneedles Hotel; the other, more important, reason is the food. The chef likes to mix the traditional with the unusual, summed up in dishes like braised pigs' cheeks with chorizo and garlic and parsley mash, or smoked haddock tortellini with black pudding and buttered leeks. There's a set lunch for £24.

CAFÉ SPICE NAMASTE Map pp432-3 Indian
☎ 7488 9242, 16 Prescot St E1; ☺ lunch & dinner, closed lunch Sat & Sun; mains £9.50-15; tube Tower Hill

This restaurant is too good, really, for its predominantly City-worker customers to have to themselves. Admittedly, it's a bit off the beaten track, but it is only a 10-minute walk from Tower Hill. Parsee chef Cyrus Todiwala has taken an old magistrates' court, and spiced it up in bright-patterned Oriental colours. The Parsee/Goan menu is famous for its superlative *Dhansaak* (traditionally lamb, but now also vegetable, stew with rice, lentils and vegetables). However, there are plenty of other pleasant surprises, such as the *papeta na pattice* – mashed potato cakes, filled with green peas, grated coconut, chopped nuts and spices.

GRAND CAFÉ & BAR
Map pp432-3   Modern European
☎ 7618 2480; Royal Exchange, Threadneedle St EC2; ☺ breakfast, lunch & dinner Mon-Fri; dishes £5.50-£14.50; tube Bank

This newish Conran venue is really just a very swish pavement café, but its excellent location in the middle of the beautiful Royal Exchange building makes it a great place for an informal business meeting. The food ranges from sandwiches (crab, honey-roasted ham, lobster toasted ciabatta etc) to dishes such as leek and fontina tart and langoustines with mayonnaise.

PRISM Map pp432-3   Modern European
☎ 7256 3888; 147 Leadenhall St EC3; ☺ lunch & dinner, closed lunch Sat & Sun; mains £6-13; tube Bank

Part of the Harvey Nichols empire, this is a more welcoming place than many in the City, even though it's still generally crammed full of expense-account diners. The room is large and airy, with modern art on the walls; the menu is strong on seafood.

SWEETING'S Map pp432-3   Seafood
☎ 7248 3062; 39 Queen Victoria St EC4; ☺ lunch Mon-Fri; mains £10-£22; tube Bank, rail Cannon Street

Old-fashioned Sweeting's is a long-standing City institution, more than 50 years old. It still carries a sense of history with its small sit-down restaurant area, mosaic floor and narrow counters, behind which stand waiters in white aprons. Dishes include wild smoked salmon, oysters (in season from September to April) and even eels.

HOXTON, SHOREDITCH & SPITALFIELDS

ARKANSAS CAFÉ
Map pp432-3   North American
☎ 7377 6999; Unit 12, Spitalfields Market, 107b Commercial St E1; ☺ lunch, closed Sat; mains £4-12.50; tube Liverpool Street/Aldgate East

Good ole, down-home country cookin' is served up in this unprepossessing unit on edges of Spitalfields market (reached via the inside of the market). Whether you're tucking into ribs, corn-fed chicken or steak, you can rest assured they'll be of truly excellent quality, with lots of potatoes, coleslaw and stuff on the side. It's the kind of place to give vegetarians a real fright, but meat-loving City workers flock here in droves.

EYRE BROTHERS Map pp420-1 *Spanish/African*
☎ 7613 5346; 70 Leonard St EC2; ✆ lunch & dinner, closed lunch Sat & Sun; mains £16-25; tube Old Street
Geographically located in Shoreditch, but stylistically with one foot in the City, this dark panelled, low-ceilinged den excels with an interesting range of Spanish/Portuguese/Mozambiquean food. Slightly older diners tuck into a largely vegetarian-unfriendly menu, including home-cured salt cod, clams with jamón Serrano, grilled Mozambique prawns with piri-piri sauce or lamb marinated with anchovy, garlic and rosemary. There are set menus for £5.50 (starters) and £13.50 (mains). The eponymous Eyre brothers were behind London's first gastropub, the Eagle. They still know what they're doing.

FIFTEEN Map pp420-1 *British/Italian*
☎ 7251 1515, 9.30am-5.30pm Mon-Fri; 15 Westland Pl N1; ✆ lunch & dinner, closed lunch Sat & Sun; mains £11-26; tube Old Street
It seems a little uncharitable to diss Jamie Oliver's not-for-profit venture to train and employ 15 young underprivileged people as chefs, so we're assuming some of the mixed reviews just after it opened were down to first-night nerves. In any case, people like to visit this bright, cartoonish venue just to say they've been to the cheeky chappy Naked Chef's place. You can walk into the deli bar (8am to 11pm Monday to Friday, 8am to 5pm Sunday), but you need to book about three months ahead for the restaurant (using possibly the most irritating booking system in town).

GREAT EASTERN DINING ROOM
Map pp420-1 *Modern Asian*
☎ 7613 4545, 54-56 Great Eastern St EC2; ✆ lunch & dinner, closed lunch Sat & Sun; mains £9-12; tube Old Street
With dark wood laminate paired with dandelion chandeliers in the dining area, and with red chairs in the bar, this place looks very 'new establishment'. It still appears to have a hefty percentage of expense account customers

– even if they work for funky new media companies and dress down – but the cuisine has shifted from Italian to modern Asian.

LES TROIS GARÇONS Map pp420-1 *French*
☎ 7613 1924; 1 Club Row E1; ✆ dinner Mon-Sat; mains £17-22; tube Liverpool Street
The animal trophies – antelopes, a tiger and even a giraffe – wearing diamante tiaras and necklaces all join forces with the long, square hanging chandeliers, the crowned alligator carrying a sceptre and a centrepiece of hanging handbags to make this converted pub as camp as Christmas. The food – largely French but with a modern twist – is very good. Although the service can sometimes be so attentive as to be almost overbearing, it's still the place for a memorable evening.

REAL GREEK Map pp420-1 *Greek*
☎ 7739 8212; 15 Hoxton Market N1; ✆ lunch & dinner, closed Sun; mains £15-17; tube Old Street
The newfangled menu certainly doesn't seem to be what most of us understand as authentic Greek food (usually Greek Cypriot), but when it comes to sheer deliciousness, this is the real deal. Mains might include dishes such as *giouvarlakia* (meat dumplings) or pot-roasted pork with pickled flat cabbage, served with Greek pasta and Cretan goat's cheese. The real delight is the range of smaller *fagaki* and mixed *mezedes* dishes (around £8) from octopus casserole to rocket, leek, caper and filo pie. You can try out the cuisine for about £2 to £6 per tapas-style dish in the more casual Mezedopolio café attached.

CLERKENWELL
CLERKENWELL DINING ROOM
Map pp426-7 *Modern International*
☎ 7253 9000; 69-73 St John St EC1; ✆ lunch & dinner, closed lunch Sat & Sun; mains £13-15; tube Farringdon
Up there with Club Gascon and St John in producing some of Clerkenwell's best food, the Dining Room is a little less formal and expensive than those two. Chef Andrew Thompson once worked at the famous L'Escargot where his cooking won him a Michelin star. His menu here, although regularly changing, sticks fairly closely to classic combinations with dishes like salmon with sorrel sauce and lamb with rosemary jus. There's a set menu lunch and early-evening deal of two/three courses for £12.50/£15.50.

CLUB GASCON Map pp426-7   *French*
☎ 7796 0600; 57 West Smithfield EC1; ✌ lunch & dinner, closed lunch Sat & Sun; tapas £5-25; tube Farringdon/Barbican

Indisputably Clerkenwell's leading restaurant since it was awarded a Michelin star in 2002, Club Gascon takes a different approach to fine dining, with a selection of tapas-style portions (that would, naturally, leave an ordinary tapas restaurant for dust). There's duck, squid, cassoulet and an entire menu section devoted to foie gras. A set meal costs £35, but if you go off piste you're looking at more like £50 and up per head.

CICADA Map pp420-1   *Modern Asian*
☎ 7608 1550; 132-136 St John St EC1; ✌ lunch & dinner, closed lunch Sat & Sun; mains £8-11; tube Farringdon

A hip-looking open-plan bar/restaurant, with plenty of outside seating, Cicada serves a pan-Asian menu, from Japanese tempuras to Thai salads. It can be pretty hectic in this restaurant, sister to Notting Hill's E&O and Hoxton's Great Eastern Dining Room, so book early to grab one of the brown leather booths.

EAGLE Map pp420-1   *Mediterranean*
☎ 7837 1353; 159 Farringdon Rd EC1; ✌ lunch & dinner, closed dinner Sun; mains £4.50-14; tube Farringdon

London's first gastropub is still going strong. Even though the original owners and many chefs have left, the customers still come, at lunch or after work, for its Mediterranean-influenced food. As it's no long part of the 'scene' per se, the atmosphere is nicely relaxed.

GAUDÍ Map pp426-7   *Spanish*
☎ 7608 3220; 63 Clerkenwell Rd EC1; ✌ lunch & dinner, closed lunch Sat & Sun; mains £12-22; tube Farringdon

This restaurant in the Turnmills club building takes its cue from Catalan architect Gaudi's designs to provide a backdrop for what has been dubbed New Spanish cuisine. Fish plays a big role here, beside venison, lamb, pork and duck. There's a good Spanish wine list. A two-course set lunch menu costs £15.

LE CAFÉ DU MARCHÉ Map pp426-7   *French*
☎ 7608 1609; 22 Charterhouse Sq, Charterhouse Mews EC1; ✌ lunch & dinner, closed lunch Sat & Sun; 3-course set menu £26; tube Farringdon

This quaint, authentic French bistro might become less of a state secret with the new Malmaison hotel (p343) across Charterhouse Sq. Then again, tradition is a watchword in this exposed brick warehouse, from the hearty steaks, garlic and rosemary-flavours to the piano playing and jazz upstairs, so hopefully it won't change. Meals are set-menu only.

MORO Map pp420-1   *North African/Spanish*
☎ 7833 8336; 34-36 Exmouth Market N1; mains £11-15.50; tube Farringdon

The exulted Moro's reputation precedes it, especially since it released a book of its North African, Spanish and Portuguese fusion cuisine. And the weight of expectation is probably why opinions are so mixed. Some diners love it, while others complain about odd seasonings and small portions. The only answer is to try it yourself. The constantly changing menu might include dishes such as crab *brik*, a crispy deep-fried packet served with piquant harissa sauce, wood-roasted red mullet with sharp Seville orange and char-grilled lamb with artichokes.

QUALITY CHOP HOUSE
Map pp420-1   *British*
☎ 7837 5093; 92-94 Farringdon Rd EC1; ✌ lunch & dinner, closed lunch Sat; mains £6.75-24; tube Farringdon

Hmmm. The self-description as 'a progressive working-class caterer' is a bit pretentious, but the food is good and we see what they mean. This former workmen's caff, with a white-and-black tiled floor and wooden benches, now serves old-fashioned British staples to a middle-class media crowd. Starters include eels, while Toulouse sausages and mash, lots of red meat and the widely recommended salmon fish cakes are among the mains.

ST JOHN Map pp426-7   *British*
☎ 7251 0848; 26 St John St EC1; ✌ lunch & dinner, closed lunch Sat & Sun; mains £15-18; tube Farringdon

Vegetarians would do well to skip this review, and that's because Fergus Henderson reaches parts of an animal that other chefs do not reach. Indeed, this much-acclaimed restaurant really is for adventurous carnivores wanting to sample Ye Olde English cuisine. The signature dish is bone marrow salad, and the changing daily menu includes things like calf's liver, ox tongue and pig's spleen. There are more familiar choices like duck, fish and even lentils (one of a few token veggie dishes, but much too late!). However, St John, with its minimalist white dining room and patient staff, is overwhelmingly a Rabelaisian experience.

SMITHS OF SMITHFIELD

Map pp426-7   *Modern British*

☎ 7236 6666; 67-77 Charterhouse St EC1;
🕐 breakfast, lunch & dinner Mon-Fri, dinner Sat;
mains £3.50-29; tube Farringdon

After the hubbub of the cavernous bar and
café on the ground floor, where you can grab
breakfast and lunch (all-day breakfast £3.50 to
£6.50), there's two quieter places to dine: the
brasserie on the 2nd floor (mains all £10.50)
and the rooftop dining room (mains £19 to
£29) which has great views of St Paul's. The
linking factor is a focus on top-quality British
meat and organic produce.

SOUVLAKI AND BAR Map pp420-1   *Greek*

☎ 7253 7234; 142 St John St EC1; 🕐 10am-11pm
Mon-Sat; tapas £2.80-5.50, grills £6-12, souvlaki £3.75-
9.25; tube Farringdon

The Greek tapas are as tasty as at mother ship
Real Greek (p236) and better value than the
grills. Souvlakis are pork or lamb, depending
on season. However, this pleasant, smart
casual place is better for a light lunch/snack
and a drink (*metaxa*, ouzo and vodka cocktails
or surprisingly good Greek wine), rather than
a full-on meal.

ISLINGTON

ALMEIDA Map pp420-1   *French*

☎ 7354 4777; 30 Almeida St N1; mains £11-20; tube
Angel

The Terence Conran empire marches on. This
particular outlet is one of the restaurateur's
better examples, and has been a big hit with
locals. Trolleys of pâtés and terrines for starters and tarts for dessert parade around the
decent-sized dining room; the classic French
mains are reliably good – although you might
need the staff's help in translating the largely
French-language menu.

DUKE OF CAMBRIDGE

Map pp420-1   *Gastropub*

☎ 7359 9450; 30 St Peter's St N1; 🕐 lunch &
dinner, closed lunch Mon; mains £6.50-15; tube Angel

It has a typical London gastropub feel, with
bare wooden boards, tables and sofas, but
there's something different about the Duke of
Cambridge. Everything here, even the lager,
is organic, making it the first of its kind in
the UK. The Italian/French/Spanish-influenced
menu can be a little inconsistent in quality,
but generally it's worth coming here for more
than just the novelty.

FREDERICK'S

Map pp420-1   *Modern International*

☎ 7359 2888; Camden Passage; 🕐 lunch & dinner,
closed lunch Sat & Sun; mains £9.50-19; tube Angel

Probably Islington's premier upmarket eatery
and popular with the expense-account brigade, Frederick's is more establishment than
cutting edge. The main dining room is under
a glass-vaulted roof and overlooks a garden,
much like a conservatory. Within the eclectic
menu, the pepper-roasted duck is widely recommended, although you'll also find lots of
fish, beef and lamb. There's a set lunch/early
evening dinner menu at £12.50/£15.50 for
two/three courses.

GIRAFFE Map pp420-1   *International*

☎ 7359 5999; 29-31 Essex Rd N1; 🕐 breakfast, lunch
& dinner; mains £8-13; tube Angel

It's a chain. It's always jam-packed with middle-
class young families. We love it anyway – for
the food. The great potato wedges aren't
greasy, the rice paper rolls are brilliantly fresh
and the curries spicy. Really, you'd be unlucky
to go wrong with anything on the menu in this
cheerful brasserie. Prices quoted are for dinner;
lunches and brunches are slightly cheaper.

HOUSE Map pp420-1   *Gastropub*

☎ 7704 7410; 63-69 Canonbury Road N1; 🕐 lunch &
dinner, closed Sun, lunch Mon; mains £9.50-17; tube
Highbury & Islington, rail Essex Rd

House combines a funky bar with an informal
dining room. The menu is strong on seafood
dishes like risotto of calamari with mascarpone
and salt cod *mariniere*, as well as an excellent
range of starter salads, such as the version with
peppered beef fillet, stilton and red onion.

LOLA'S Map pp420-1   *Modern International*

☎ 7359 1932; The Mall, Camden Passage, 359 Upper St
N1; 🕐 lunch Mon-Sat, dinner; mains £15-20; tube Angel

The usual complaint recently about upmarket
Lola's is that you wait so long for your food.
On our visit to its elegant airy dining room,
the service couldn't have been more helpful
and attentive. However, unusually, we weren't

Top Five – For the Kids

- Banners (p251)
- Giraffe (above)
- New Culture Revolution (p250)
- Pizza Organic (p239)
- Tootsies (p257)

Worth a Trip...South

Although the street is still awash with the aromas of turmeric, cumin and garam masala, it's no longer considered as cool as it once was to head to Brick Lane for a curry, and in truth the standard of cooking has deteriorated over the years. But never mind, for Tooting is the new Brick Lane.

If you have time for the journey to surburban SW17, head to Tooting Broadway or Tooting Bec tube stations; you'll be rewarded by a similar promenade through neighbouring curry houses. Even better, as opposed to Brick Lane where the restaurants are mainly Bengali, in Tooting there's an array of sub-continental cuisine, from north to south, from Bangladeshi to Sri Lankan. You want more? This great cuisine is generally pretty cheap. Some of the best places to try:

Jaffna House (☎ 8672 7786; 90 Tooting High St SW17) The Sri Lankan and South Indian food here is mild and great for veggies.

Kastoori (☎ 8767 7027; 188 Upper Tooting Rd SW17) Excellent Gujerati cuisine, by way of Africa.

Lahore Karahi (☎ 8767 2477; 1 Tooting High St SW17) Cheap-as-poppadums Pakistani café.

Masaledar (☎ 8767 7676; 121 Upper Tooting Rd SW17) Tandoori house with East African specialities.

Radha Krishna Bhavan (☎ 8767 3462; 86 Tooting High St SW17) Serving superlative Keralan cuisine.

so sure about the food. It seemed a trifle over-fussy, although the restaurant's reputation made an excellent comeback with dessert. Still Lola's remains a leading venue for business lunches; there's a set meal at lunch and early evening for £15/18 for two/three courses.

METROGUSTO Map pp420-1   *Italian*
☎ 7226 9400; 11-13 Theberton St N1; ☾ dinner Mon-Sat, lunch Fri-Sun; mains £13-16; tube Angel
This Islington branch is just as great as the Battersea original (p259). The chef's superb attention to detail with the progressive, modern Italian cuisine attracts a good mix of happy diners.

PASHA Map pp420-1   *Turkish*
☎ 7226 1454; 301 Upper St N1; mains £6.95-14; tube Highbury & Islington/Angel
The Ottoman wall paintings, the fountain and decadent, cushion-filled alcoves convey that this is an upmarket kind of Turkish restaurant and it doesn't disappoint. The meze, while smallish, is great. Mains run the gamut of seafood tagine, lamb couscous and auber-gine pilaf.

THE SOCIAL Map pp420-1   *Gastropub*
☎ 7354 5809; Arlington Sq N1; ☾ dinner Mon-Sun, lunch Sat & Sun; mains £9-13; tube Angel, rail Essex Rd
This grown-up venue for late 20- and 30-somethings – plus the odd B- or C-list celeb – serves excellent gastropub fare. If you come on a Friday, Saturday (usually) or Sunday (always) evening, you can enjoy your crisp roast belly of pork, chargrilled rib eye steak, roast salmon in polenta crumb or risotto cake with butternut squash while a DJ spins funky laid-back tunes in the corner. The name over the door says Hanbury Arms, which can't be changed as it's listed.

CHEAP EATS

AFGHAN KITCHEN Map pp420-1   *Afghani*
☎ 7359 8019; 35 Islington Green N1; ☾ lunch & dinner Tues-Sat; mains £ 5.50-6; tube Angel
This tiny gem serves up such Afghan delights as *dogh*, a yoghurt and mint concoction, and lamb cooked with spinach.

BRICK LANE BEIGEL BAKE
Map pp420-1   *Bakery*
☎ 7729 0616; 159 Brick Lane E2; ☾ 24 hrs; bagels 12p- £1.70; tube Old St
Renowned round-the-clock bakery turning out some of London's springiest, chewiest bagels, and attracting daytime and after-club crowds. It's a slice of real London, but not ko-sher (in the Jewish sense).

GALLIPOLI Map pp420-1   *Turkish*
☎ 7359 0630; 102 Upper St N1; mains £4-10; tube Angel/Highbury & Islington
A crammed, popular, cheek-by-jowl restaurant with funky Turkish decorations and not bad food, from the meze to the spicy vegetarian moussaka. There's an overspill restaurant, Gallipoli Again, at 120 Upper St.

LE MERCURY Map pp420-1   *French*
☎ 7354 4088; 140a Upper St N1; mains £5.95; tube Angel/Highbury & Islington
Given the low prices here and the more-than-reasonable food, it's all the more surprising that this budget French eatery favours silver-ware and white linen over the usual rustic decor. There are occasional specials, as well as set meals (£5.45/6 for two/three courses).

LITTLE BAY

Map pp420-1   *Modern International*
☎ 7278 1234; 171 Farringdon Rd EC1; ⏰ 8.30am-
midnight; mains before/after 7pm £5.45/£7.95; tube
Farringdon
Slightly kitsch Little Bay has gargoyles, pieces of
netting on the walls and chandeliers made from
stripped electrical wire and marbles. And you
could pay a lot more for meals this satisfying.

PLACE BELOW Map pp432-3   *Vegetarian*
☎ 7329 0789; St Mary-le-Bow Church, Cheapside EC2;
⏰ lunch Mon-Fri; tube Bank
In a church crypt, this pleasant veggie restaurant is of the old school. Think spinach and
mushroom quiche, celeriac and blue cheese
gratin and (steady on, getting a bit modern
here) sun-dried tomatoes and rice salad.

PREEM Map pp420-1   *Indian*
☎ 7247 0397; 120 Brick Lane E1; ⏰ noon-2am; mains
£6.50-8.50; tube Liverpool Street/Aldgate East
The cuisine is generally less oily than most, and
tastier, making this one of the best curry houses
on Brick Lane. Filling set meals are £10.

RAVI SHANKAR Map pp420-1   *Indian*
☎ 7833 5849; 422 St John St EC1; mains £4-7.50;
tube Angel
Serving delicious, but mildly spiced, Indian
vegetarian food. Try the *bhel poori* or *dahi*

vada starters or thalis for a full meal. There's
another branch near Euston station (☎ 7388
6458, 133–5 Drummond St).

SÔNG QUÊ Map pp420-1   *Vietnamese*
☎ 7613 3222; 134 Kingsland Rd E2; mains £3.50-8.50
tube Old Street, then bus 55 or 243
The critics are right, this is London's best
Vietnamese restaurant. However, the much-
lauded competition is in fact terribly poor
– Chinese really – so connoisseurs beware
that this accolade doesn't say as much as
it could.

TINSELTOWN Map pp426-7   *American*
☎ 7689 2424; 44-46 St John's St EC1; ⏰ 24 hr; mains
£5-10; tube Farringdon
Tinseltown is a 24/7 American-style basement
diner, serving average pastas, burgers and
grills. It's very popular with after-club crowds
who want milkshakes more than gourmet
food.

WAGAMAMA Map pp432-3   *Japanese*
☎ 7256 9992; 22 Old Broad St EC2; ⏰ lunch & dinner
Mon-Fri; mains £6-9.50; tube Bank/Liverpool St
The relatively new City branch of this classic
noodle bar chain is reckoned by some to be
the best. Next to NatWest's Tower 42, it has
floor-to-ceiling glass walls.

SOUTH CENTRAL

Naturally, quality gravitates to where the money is and you'll find some of London's finest establishments in the swanky hotels and ritzy mews of these areas, particularly Mayfair
and Chelsea. The king of them all, Gordon Ramsay, has three Michelin stars in its crown
and resides in Chelsea. Many of London's most dazzling new restaurants have sprung up
around Mayfair, while chic and cosmopolitan South Kensington has always been reliable
for pan-European options. Cheap eats are few and far between but a walk along Chelsea's
King Rd should see you right.

MAYFAIR & ST JAMES'S

BENARES Map pp426-7   *Indian*
☎ 7629 8886; 12 Berkeley Sq W1; mains £8-14; tube
Green Park
This splendid restaurant, in a prime Mayfair location, is the first independent project of Atul
Kochar, who a few years ago became only
the second Indian chef in the world to earn a
Michelin star (at Tamarind; p236). The interior
is made up of dark wood, taupe upholstery
and cream walls, while the small but choice
menu brings together the four corners of India
with contemporary dash. Kochar has an expert
touch when it comes to spicing although he

needs some help sorting out his service, which
is a little scatty.

GORDON RAMSAY AT CLARIDGES
Map pp426-7   *Modern British*
☎ 7499 0099; 53 Brook St W1; set menu £50;
⏰ breakfast, lunch & dinner; tube Bond Street
The coming together of London's most-
celebrated chef and its grandest hotel was
probably a match made in heaven and sent
down as His way to apologise for the historic
awfulness of British food. All is forgiven. A meal
in this gorgeous Art Deco dining room is a
special occasion indeed; the Ramsay flavours
will have you reeling, from the veloute of baby

turnips with a fricassee of cèpes, artichokes and rocket all the way to the cheese trolley, whether you choose the one with French, British or Irish number plates.

LOCANDA LOCATELLI Map pp422-3 *Italian*
☎ 7935 9088; 8 Seymour St W1; pastas £10, mains £18-27; tube Marble Arch
The waiters at this Michelin-starred joint need a firecracker up their collective backside but at least when they do arrive they deliver *molto bellissimo* Italian food like Mama would have made had she been an award-winning cook. Tagliatelle with sardines and sultanas is much better than it sounds. The low-lit interior is elegant and creamy with large fish-eye mirrors. The man behind this operation is the gregarious Italian, Giorgio Locatelli, who has been responsible for establishing many of the city's best Italian restaurants.

MENU AT THE CONNAUGHT
Map pp426-7   *British*
☎ 7592 1222; The Connaught Hotel, 16 Carlos Pl W1; set lunch/dinner £25/45; tube Bond Street
This bastion of fine dining got a brilliant new team recently although, thankfully, not a modernist makeover. Gordon Ramsay protégé Angela Hartnett and designer Nina Campbell have imbued the restaurant and menus with a subtle 21st-century elegance that appeals to young and old. The menu melds Italian chic with old-fashioned *haute* luxury in dishes like sweet prawns and soft scallops on an earthy artichoke purée. The dress code has loosened a little although jackets are still 'preferred'.

MOMO Map p428   *North African*
☎ 7434 4040; 25 Heddon St W1; mains £10-20; tube Piccadilly Circus
The souk comes to the West End at this wonderfully atmospheric and maximalist North African restaurant, which is stuffed with cushions and lamps and manned by all-dancing, tambourine-playing waiters. It's a funny old place that manages to be all things to all diners, from romantic couples to raucous office party ravers. Service is very friendly and the dishes are as exciting as you dare to be, so eschew the traditional and ordinary *tagine* and tuck into the splendid Moroccan speciality of nutmeg and pigeon pie. They also make a mean *mojito*.

QUAGLINO'S Map p428   *Modern European*
☎ 7930 6767; 16 Bury St SW1; mains £11-16.50; tube Green Park/Piccadilly Circus
This glamorous Conran fixture is in a former ballroom and was once a pioneer of London's

foodie scene. Newer, hipper establishments have largely eclipsed this leading light but it's still a wonderful choice for all things crustacean.

SARTORIA Map p428   *Italian*
☎ 7534 7000; 20 Savile Row W1; mains £14-16.50, set lunch Sat £23; tube Piccadilly Circus
Calm and cosy, elegant and sophisticated, discreet and spacious, this Conran restaurant in the home of English tailoring perfectly weaves simple and delicious Italian food with English hospitality. The menu changes daily but always includes familiar Italian staples and is never too convoluted.

TAMARIND Map p428   *Indian*
☎ 7629 3561; 20 Queen St W1; mains £10-30; tube Green Park
This is one of those places where you're passed along a chain of assorted staff before you actually get to park your bum (beneath huge inverted tea-lights), not quite Bobby de Niro in *GoodFellas* but you get the picture. The slightly older crowd is froufrou in keeping with the beautiful restaurant and neighbourhood, while the food – a cavalcade of Indian classics – is out of this world.

WESTMINSTER & WHITEHALL
CINNAMON CLUB Map pp426-7   *Indian*
☎ 7222 2555; Old Westminster Library, 30 Great Smith St W1; mains £10-18; tube St James's Park
Domed skylights, high ceilings, parquet flooring and a book-lined mezzanine evoke an atmosphere reminiscent of when this place was the Westminster Library. Hushed, eager-to-please waiters hover like anxious footmen, although they really have no need to be concerned because the Indian food here is consistently of the highest quality and fit for a rajah.

VICTORIA & PIMLICO
KEN LO'S MEMORIES OF CHINA
Map pp440-1   *Chinese*
☎ 7773 7734; 67-69 Ebury St SW1; mains £5-29; tube Victoria
This is where fine Chinese food arrived in London, with the late Ken Lo many moons ago, and if food is more important than buzz this is still the best Chinese restaurant in the city. The interior is elegant, oriental minimalism and the noise levels are agreeably low because this place isn't filled with highly

strung first dates like London's more fashionable restaurants. There are several set menus – including a veggie one and an unforgettable 'Gastronomic Tour of China' – and all the well-proportioned dishes feature a splendidly light touch and wonderful contrasts of flavours and textures.

OLIVO Map pp440-1 *Italian*
☎ 7730 2505; 21 Eccleston St SW1; mains £9-15; tube Victoria/Sloane Square

This colourful restaurant specialises in the food and wine of Sardinia and Sicily, and has a dedicated clientele of sophisticates who, quite frankly, would rather keep it to themselves. Not surprising really because it's a little gem. As a general rule, drink Sicilian and eat Sardinian, particularly the famous spaghetti bottarga (which is a delicacy with mullet roe served simply with oil, garlic, parsley and flakes of red pepper).

CHELSEA & BELGRAVIA
GORDON RAMSAY
Map pp436-7 *Modern European*
☎ 7352 4441; 68-69 Royal Hospital Rd SW3; set lunch/dinner/degustation £35/65/80; tube Sloane Square

One of Britain's finest restaurants, and the only one in the capital with three Michelin stars, this is hallowed turf and obviously the creation of man of the moment, Mr Ramsay himself. This is as close to perfect as we may ever experience, a blissful treat right through from the taster to the truffles. The only quibble is that you don't get time to savour it. Bookings are made in specific eat-it-and-beat-it slots and, if you've seen the chef on television, you won't argue for fear he might come rushing out of the kitchen with a meat cleaver.

LA POULE AU POT Map pp440-1 *French*
☎ 7730 7763; 231 Ebury St SW1; mains £14-19; tube Sloane Square

Some Londoners claim the 'Chicken in the Pot' is the best country-style French restaurant in town and we've yet to prove them wrong

(although we could name five places that offer better value). What you're paying for here is the romantic, candlelit ambience – which makes it virtually impossible to read the menu – although it might all backfire if your accent isn't as sexy as zee waiter's.

KNIGHTSBRIDGE, SOUTH KENSINGTON & HYDE PARK
BIBENDUM Map pp436-7 *Modern European*
☎ 7581 5817; 81 Fulham Rd SW3; mains £16-27; tube South Kensington

This restaurant occupies the striking Art Nouveau Michelin House (1911), one of the finest settings in London. Upstairs dining is in a spacious and light room with stained glass windows, where you can savour fabulous and creative food, and tolerate very ordinary service. Downstairs in the Bibendum Oyster Bar, you can really feel at the heart of the architectural finery while lapping up terrific native and rock oysters.

BOXWOOD CAFÉ
Map pp422-3 *Modern European*
☎ 7235 1010; Berkeley Hotel, Wilton Pl SW1; mains £13-16; tube Knightsbridge

A couple of strides ahead of the posse as usual, Gordon Ramsay recently extended his empire to this New York–style café, which is his mostly successful attempt to kick back with the young folk and make fine dining in London 'a little bit more relaxed'. It's the kind of place you can come for a single course or a glass of

Bibendum, South Kensington (above)

wine and while the layout is a little flat – even dreary down in the depths of the main restaurant – the food is generally first rate. Simple starters like fried oysters, fennel and lemon are generally tastier than the fussier mains.

COLLECTION Map pp436-7 *Modern European*
☎ 7225 1212; 264 Brompton Rd SW3; mains £11-25; tube South Kensington

Flaming torches greet you at the door to this converted warehouse and former gallery (that doesn't quite seem to work architecturally), where the main dining room sits on a balcony overlooking a vivacious bar filled with the kind of people you'd think would say 'work hard, play hard'. The fusion food is unremarkably good – take roast organic salmon with steamed asparagus as an example – and the cocktails are chirpy even if the bar staff are not.

DAPHNE'S Map pp436-7 *Italian*
☎ 7589 4257; 112 Draycott Ave SW3; mains £10-22; tube South Kensington

Long popular with frocked-up Sloane Rangers, this attractive restaurant is buzzy without being brash, and intimate without being too discreet. The pan-Italian menu never disappoints although you're probably paying as much for the good looks of your fellow diners and the opportunity to gawk at celebrities as you are for the grub.

DAQUISE Map pp436-7 *Polish*
☎ 7589 6117; 20 Thurloe St SW7; mains £5.50-12.50; tube South Kensington

A wonderful little find, this attractively dowdy Polish diner is as authentic and charming as you're likely to find in the centre of London these days. Staff are welcoming and friendly, and the menu consists of lots of vegetarian as well as meat options. Two standouts are the borsch (beetroot and bean soup) and, for dessert, the delicious *Pancake à la Daquise* (with vanilla ice cream, orange caramel sauce and almond flakes) that's big enough for two.

FIFTH FLOOR CAFÉ
Map pp422-3 *Modern European*
☎ 7823 1839; Harvey Nichols, 109-125 Knightsbridge SW1; mains £19.50-24; tube Knightsbridge

On the same floor as the food hall, sushi bar and glitzy designer restaurant, this café used to be one of the most fashionable places to be seen and one of the most fashionable scenes to be talking about. These days it's less trendy and more practical, and there are few places

Top Five – Celebrity Spotting
- Bar Italia (p225)
- Gordon Ramsay (p237)
- Nobu (below)
- River Café (p255)
- Sketch (p225)

better to drop after a shop. You can enjoy light and innovative Mediterranean meals beneath a stunning metal and glass ceiling canopy or out on the terrace if the weather is fine.

HARD ROCK CAFÉ Map pp426-7 *American*
☎ 7629 0382; 150 Old Park Lane W1; dishes £8-15; tube Hyde Park Corner

The original Hard Rock Café has been here since 1971 and is largely a Londoner-free zone because tourists are the only ones with the time to queue. Tried, tested and huge burgers are the staple, impressive rock memorabilia the decor and loud tackiness the overall vibe.

NAHM Map pp426-7 *Thai*
☎ 7333 1234; Halkin Hotel, Halkin St SW1; mains £25-30; tube Hyde Park Corner

Aussie chef David Thompson is one of the world's pre-eminent authorities on Thai food and responsible for the scandalously good tucker at this hotel restaurant, the only Thai eatery outside the kingdom to have a Michelin star. Eating here is like taking a pulse-pounding gastronomic tour of Thailand, and the menu comprises Thai classics like jungle curry of monkfish as well as more exotic fare like crab and pomelo with roasted coconut and caramel dressing. The staff are enthusiastic and friendly, which more than makes up for the slightly sterile setting.

NOBU Map pp426-7 *Japanese*
☎ 7447 4747; Metropolitan Hotel, 19 Old Park Lane W1; mains £5-28; tube Hyde Park Corner

Not so much a Japanese restaurant as a London designer's *idea* of a Japanese restaurant, this is nonetheless a strong contender for the best Asian food in town. It's comfortably minimalist in decor, anonymously efficient in service, and out of this fricken world when it comes to exquisitely prepared and presented sushi and sashimi. The black cod is worth sneaking past customs. Amorous couples thinking about sharing the chocolate *bento* box (a cake shell packed with gooey chocolate) might want to order a cab first, and have it waiting.

RACINE Map pp436-7 *French*
☎ 7584 4477; 239 Brompton Rd SW3; mains £11-15; tube Knightsbridge

The key to the success of this splendid 2003 creation is that it limits its ambitions and then achieves them with panache. Regional French cooking is the vehicle and all-round, dedicated service to the customer the destination. Expect the likes of cream of Jerusalem artichoke soup, Morecambe Bay shrimps and smoked duck. Being French, dishes might feel heavy to some, but the sauces, the very foundation of 'la cuisine', are spot on.

TOM AIKENS Map pp436-7 *Modern European*
☎ 7584 2003; 43 Elystan St SW3; set lunch £25, à la carte £75; tube South Kensington

A notorious firebrand in the kitchen, the Tom of the title made his name by picking up two Michelin stars at Pied a Terre by the time he was only 26. He disappeared for a few years but returned with an enormous splash in mid-2003 with this handsome and understated restaurant. The food is fab, and the pork belly and truffle starter is just about the best darn starter we've ever had. Mains hop along the lines of rabbit confit, and frogs' legs are equally good. The *Evening Standard*'s Fay Maschler, London's most important reviewer, bestowed upon it the extremely rare honour of three stars.

ZAFFERANO Map pp440-1 *Italian*
☎ 7235 5800; 15-16 Lowndes St SW1; 3-course set lunch/dinner £25/42; tube Knightsbridge

This glamorous place, sparkling with diamonds and wall-to-wall with perma-tans, serves excellent seasonal and inspired Italian dishes that succeed every time. That said, the service is sometimes snooty and they might try to fob you off with an inferior table.

ZUMA Map pp422-3 *Japanese*
☎ 7584 1010; 5 Raphael St SW7; typical meal without drinks £35; tube Knightsbridge

The 'opulently minimalist' decor at this jolly Japanese place features glass, steel, teak and swathes of granite, and it's a favourite setting for celebrities out for a quick bite and a slow cocktail. The exceptionally long menu is outstanding from top to tail; all the dishes are bursting with flavour, especially anything that's just come from under the robata grill (chicken wings, pork skewers, tiger prawns etc). You can dine at the counter with the plebs or at the chef's table, but the most delicious display of eye candy can be found around the rectangular bar. Unfortunately, the bar is understaffed and the staff aren't overfriendly.

CHEAP EATS

Cheap is relative and in Old Money London, the following qualify.

CHELSEA KITCHEN Map pp436-7 *European*
☎ 7589 1330; 98 King's Rd SW3; mains £3-6; tube Sloane Square

This Spartan place – part of the Stockpot empire which has branches all around town – has some of the cheapest food in London and is *almost* like eating out at a restaurant. Sturdy staples include the likes of French onion soup, spaghetti bolognese, lasagne and steak.

HENRY J BEAN'S Map pp436-7 *American*
☎ 7352 9255; 195 King's Rd SW3; mains £6-8; tube Sloane Square/South Kensington

Essentially this is just a loud and lively pub with American paraphernalia serving American-style fare (burgers, steaks etc) a paper-cut above the pub norm. The main draw, however, is the enormous beer garden and the cute young things it attracts in summer. But all said, it's still just a pub and it's most definitely not worth waiting for a table.

JAKOB'S Map pp436-7 *Armenian*
☎ 7581 9292; 20 Gloucester Rd SW7; main courses £5-8; tube Gloucester Road

If you want to spend your money on shopping rather than restaurant frills like decor and menus, this charismatic Armenian restaurant is a revelation. It serves delicious and wholesome salads, falafel and kebabs that are a treat for your palate and relief for your purse.

JENNY LO'S TEA HOUSE
Map pp440-1 *Chinese*
☎ 7259 0399; 14 Eccleston St SW1; mains £5-7.50; tube Victoria

This simple place in Westminster – established by the daughter of the late Chinese food supremo Ken Lo – is very good value for the neighbourhood. It serves soups and rice dishes but noodles are the speciality.

PIZZA ORGANIC Map pp436-7 *Pizza*
☎ 7589 9613; 20 Old Brompton Rd SW7; pizzas £5-8; tube South Kensington

At this family-friendly place on a busy corner of South Kensington, a squadron of black-clad waiters are primed to spring into action. The actual pizzas occupy a delicious middle ground between Roman-style pizzas, with thin crusts, and Neapolitan, with thick and moist crusts.

SHEPHERD CAFÉ BAR Map pp426-7   *Italian*
☎ 7495 5509; 7 Shepherd Market W1; tube Green Park
The Shepherd Café Bar is a friendly Italian joint that has outdoor tables and is long on pasta, short on ceremony. Meals are around £4.

ALONG THE SOUTH BANK

Dining in this part of London can be as much about the view as it is the food. The panorama – of St Paul's and the City – that's laid out before you at the Oxo Tower Restaurant is one of London's most memorable, although the People's Palace on the South Bank is equally famous for its, admittedly lower-level, outlook. Since the advent of the Tate Modern art gallery (which has its own cafés, p160), designer venues like Baltic have sprung up in the streets away from the river. If that all sounds too chi-chi for your tastes, head towards the area around Borough Market, where you'll still find down-to-earth workers' cafés and the occasional pie-and-mash shop.

SOUTH BANK CENTRE & WATERLOO

BAR + KITCHEN
Map pp426-7   *Modern International*
☎ 7928 5086; 131 Waterloo Rd SE1; ☽ lunch & dinner, closed lunch Sat & Sun; mains lunch £7-10, dinner £10-13; tube Southwark/Waterloo
As lived-in and unpretentious as its name, this small boozer and quiet restaurant has a menu encompassing a global range of food from chargrilled tuna Niçoise and vegetable skewers with melted mozzarella to lamb wimbourne sausages and steak & kidney pie. Its wooden tables are complemented by modern art on the walls.

CUBANA Map pp426-7   *Spanish/Caribbean*
☎ 7928 8778; 48 Lower Marsh SE1; tapas £3.45-4.45, mains £6.95-10.95; tube Waterloo
The Cuban-influenced tapas – with additions such as plantain, black beans and mango salsa – are more average-tasting than they sound. However, vegetarians are well catered for and the colourful decor and rum cocktails make this a fun place to be. There's live salsa Friday and Saturday evenings, with free lessons from 5pm to 6pm Sunday. Set lunches are £5.95/7.95 for two/three courses.

LIVEBAIT Map pp426-7   *Seafood*
☎ 7928 7211; 43 The Cut SE1; mains £8-17; tube Southwark/Waterloo
A one-time award-winning, now fairly wellworn, stand-by for fish, shellfish and more, Livebait is no longer as universally appealing as its neighbours, Tas and Mesón Don Felipe. Cod and chips for £14 is a bit cheeky, but Livebait does have its loyal fans. The tiled green-and-white interior is reminiscent of more downmarket

pie-and-mash shops. Set menus are £13/16 for two/three courses.

MESÓN DON FELIPE Map pp426-7   *Spanish*
☎ 7928 3237; 53 The Cut SE1; tapas £3.95-4.95; ☽ lunch & dinner, closed Sun; tube Southwark/Waterloo
It's a shock to learn that this tapas bar is owned by an Englishman; it tastes (and, thanks to the Spanish staff, feels) so authentically Iberian. Because the bar occupies much of the room's central space, there's often a bit of a scrum in here. You're likely to find yourself perching on a stool, oblivious to people pushing by as you enjoy some of the best *patatas bravas* in town.

OXO TOWER RESTAURANT & BRASSERIE
Map pp426-7   *Modern International*
☎ 7803 3888; 8th fl, Barge House St SE1; mains £16-27; ☽ lunch & dinner, closed lunch Sun; tube Waterloo
The Oxo Tower is about event dining, with the emphasis a teensy bit more on the event than the food. Magnificent views over the Thames, focused on St Paul's Cathedral, guarantee a night to remember in this modern dining room, but the menu of French, with a spice of oriental, cuisine is unfortunately less uni-

---

Top Five – Along the South Bank

- Baltic (opposite)
- Delfina (p242)
- Le Pont de la Tour (p243)
- Oxo Tower (above)
- People's Palace (opposite)

formly reliable, despite a revamp. Experience and word-of-mouth suggest that selecting a fish or seafood dish, of which there are many, is perhaps the safest route. There's a reasonably extensive choice of global wines, and a three-course lunch menu for £29.

PEOPLE'S PALACE
Map pp426-7   *Modern International*
☎ 7928 9999; Level 3, Royal Festival Hall, South Bank SE1; mains £14-18; tube Waterloo

Forget the proletarian-sounding moniker, the People's Palace is really pretty classy. The bright, white 1950s-style dining room (with red and blue lounge chairs and early Conran dining chairs) is cavernous, with a high ceiling and picture windows overlooking the Thames. The food is Modern British with Mediterranean influences, ranging from lamb rump to sea bream with crab mash and Tuscan bean casserole.

RIVER WALK RESTAURANT
Map pp426-7   *Modern International*
☎ 7928 2884; 2nd fl, Barge House St SE1; mains £6.50-13; ☽ lunch & dinner, closed lunch Sat & Sun; tube Waterloo

The River Walk Restaurant has comfy, wine-coloured sofa-style seating and a pan-Asian menu with lots of vegetarian choices. Otherwise, the crispy duck breast, crunchy tofu and Earl Grey essence is very appealing, as is the citrus clam curry. However, the view from this level isn't a patch on that from Oxo Tower Restaurant on the 8th floor above. There's a set menu for lunch (£13/20 for two/three courses).

RSJ
Map pp426-7   *French*
☎ 7928 4554; 13A Coin St SE1; mains £11-17; ☽ lunch & dinner, closed lunch Sat & Sun; tube Waterloo, rail Waterloo East

With pale green carpet and cheap replica Arne Jacobsen chairs mixed with a couple of old-looking exposed beams, RSJ ain't easy on the eye. Fortunately, it's kinder to the palate, with basically French cuisine, including dishes like breast of duck *magret* or supreme of chicken in morel vinaigrette. And that odd name? It's an industrial term meaning 'rolled steel joist' – presumably something to do with the metal running along the exposed beams. Set menus are £16/17 for two/three courses.

TAS
Map pp426-7   *Turkish*
☎ 7928 1444, 7928 2111; 33 The Cut SE1; mains £6.55-£15; tube Southwark/Waterloo

The owners describe Tas as Anatolian, and at the very least it's Turkish with a difference,

with excellent hummus, tabouli, wonderfully flavoured olives and grilled meats with herby casseroles, couscous and fish dishes. It's a great place for vegetarians, while the straightforward modern surrounds mean everyone can just relax and really enjoy their meal.

BANKSIDE

BALTIC
Map pp426-7   *East European*
☎ 7928 1111; 74 Blackfriars Rd SE1; mains £9.50-14; ☽ lunch & dinner, closed lunch Sun; tube Southwark

Baltic starts off as achingly hip and sci-fi surreal, but as you follow the vodka-lined stainless steel bar around to the restaurant area, things start to look a little more ordinary. Only a little, though, as the high-ceilinged roof has exposed, inverted V-shaped aabeams, there's a chandelier of rough-hewn chips of amber and the food is Eastern European. Starters include blinis, herrings, *pierogi* and caviar, as well as Polish black pudding, smoked eel, seared ox tongue and crayfish in vodka. Mains (Georgian lamb shashlik, pork and sauerkraut) are a little less left of centre.

FISH!
Map pp432-3   *Seafood*
☎ 7407 3803; Cathedral St SE1; mains £8.95-17; tube London Bridge

Situated in an all-glass Victorian pavilion overlooking Borough Market and Southwark Cathedral, fish! serves fish that is fresher-than-fresh and seafood that is prepared simply, uncluding steamed or grilled swordfish, cod, skate, squid (or whatever is ticked off on the placemat) served with one of five sauces.

Baltic restaurant (above)

BOROUGH & BERMONDSEY

Options here range from workers' caffs and pie-and-mash shops to more exotic (and expensive) choices. Culinary highlights include Terence Conran's gastronomic palaces at Shad Thames.

BERMONDSEY KITCHEN

Map pp432-3   *International*
☎ 7407 5719; 194 Bermondsey St SE1; mains £9-12; ✆ lunch & dinner, closed dinner Sun; tube London Bridge

A short walk from the Fashion and Textile Museum, Bermondsey Kitchen is a trendy but relaxed eatery, with an open grill, rough-hewn tables and chairs, comfy sofas and groovy 1960s-style lampshades over the bar. Ruth Quinlan, formerly of London's original gastropub the Eagle, serves up a short but changing menu, which might include lemon sole, roast Gloucester Old Spot pork or lamb kofte. Eggy brunch comes with Bloody Marys, although it's a shame that only white bread is served.

BLUE PRINT CAFÉ Map pp432-3 *International*
☎ 7378 7031; Design Museum, Butler's Wharf SE1; mains £13-19; ✆ lunch & dinner, closed dinner Sun; tube Tower Hill

Throughout the following listings, you'll see that Sir Terence Conran has had a large say in Butler's Wharf and its restaurants. In keeping with its Design Museum location, this is one of his mid-range outlets, in a minimalist style and serving a changing range of modern international food, which might include grilled ox tongue or skate with horseradish and chives. The emphasis is on fresh produce, but the restaurant's best feature is still the view over the Thames and Tower Bridge. With binoculars at each table, diners can peer through them out the window, as in some Spanish surrealist film.

Blue Print Café (above)

BUTLER'S WHARF CHOP HOUSE

Map pp432-3   *Modern British*
☎ 7403 3403; Butler's Wharf Bldg, 36E Shad Thames SE1; mains £13.50-17; ✆ lunch & dinner, brunch Sat & Sun, closed dinner Sun; tube Tower Hill

Conran's upmarket reworking of the British working café, the Chop House sits on an indisputably touristy strip; however, if you do manage to grab an outdoor table on the riverside in summer, you won't give a hoot about that. The hearty food, mixing things like pork chops with garlic mash, hot smoked eel with horseradish and bacon, and turning out a signature steak, kidney and oyster pudding, acts as an excellent ambassador for Modern British cuisine. The bar offers a pared-down menu and there are cheap set menus.

CANTINA DEL PONTE Map pp432-3 *Italian*
☎ 7403 5403; Butler's Wharf Bldg, 36C Shad Thames SE1; mains £5.50-15; ✆ lunch & dinner, brunch Sat & Sun, closed lunch Sun; tube Tower Hill

The general consensus is that the most affordable Conran establishment at Butler's Wharf is the most disappointing. Sometimes a lack of detail in the accompaniments just spoils a salad or pasta dish, at other times a meat or fish dish just doesn't turn out right. The pizzas (from £5.50) generally pass muster, though. Set meals come at £11/13.50 for two/three courses.

DELFINA Map pp432-3 *International*
☎ 7357 0244; 50 Bermondsey St SE1; mains £9.95-14; ✆ lunch Mon-Fri; tube London Bridge

Not the only artists' co-operative canteen in the world, but certainly one of the most chic, with large photos and paintings on its white walls, polished floorboards, green tables and modern international cuisine. The menu changes fortnightly and might include slow-roasted shank of lamb, monkfish with horseradish polenta or rosemary roasted pumpkin with butter beans Coffee and cakes are served 10am to noon and 3pm to 5pm.

FINA ESTAMPA Map pp432-3 *Peruvian*
☎ 7403 1342; 150 Tooley St SE1; mains £12-16; ✆ lunch & dinner, closed lunch Sat & Sun; tube London Bridge

No longer the only place to get Peruvian cuisine in London, this uncluttered restaurant remains a sentimental favourite, nonetheless. It churns out good portions of *cebiche* (white fish marinated in lemon juice), *seco* (lamb or chicken in coriander sauce) and *carapulcra* (dried Peruvian potatoes served with pork, chicken and yucca). Pisco sour cocktails (£3.50) are also served.

GARRISON Map pp432-3   *Gastropub*
☎ 7089 9355; 99 Bermondsey St SE1; mains £6-13; ⏰ lunch & dinner, brunch Sat & Sun; tube London Bridge

Another phoenix rising on the ashes of an old favourite, the Garrison is a new gastropub on the site of the Honest Cabbage, with the ambience of a French country kitchen, but serving honest, basic Modern British food. It's across from the Fashion and Textile Museum, so it's inevitably going to be busy at lunchtimes.

LAUGHING GRAVY
Map pp426-7   *Modern International*
☎ 7721 7055; 154 Blackfriars Rd; mains £9-14; ⏰ closed lunch Sat & Sun; tube Southwark

This casual pub is named after silent comedians Laurel and Hardy's dog, apparently, the expression itself being a Prohibition-era term for whisky. Some critics contend it's not just the name that's too clever by half, but the surprisingly ambitious menu, too. True, output like escalope of jerked wild boar with tropical fruit and coriander compote is fussy, but many dishes nevertheless come off very well. The paintings, plants, piano and large sauce-bottle display give the place a relaxed lived-in feel.

LE PONT DE LA TOUR Map pp432-3   *French*
☎ 7403 8403; Butler's Wharf Bldg, 36d Shad Thames SE1; mains £18-27; ⏰ lunch & dinner, closed lunch Sat; tube Tower Hill

Where Bill and Tony (Clinton and Blair) once dined, Le Pont de la Tour continues to turn out exquisite food within sight of Tower Bridge. There's an excellent selection of seafood and luscious meat dishes like chateaubriand, all whisked to your table in the hands of friendly and efficient staff. Formal without being intimidating, the restaurant also boasts a strong selection of fine wines. There's a three-course set lunch for £29.50 and a pared-down bar menu.

TAS Map pp432-3   *Turkish*
☎ restaurant 7403 7090, café 7403 8557; 72 Borough High St; restaurant mains £6.55-£15, café snacks £1.75-4.50; ⏰ breakfast, lunch & dinner; tube London Bridge

You'll find pretty much the same Anatolian/ Turkish deal here as at the branch on The Cut (p241). However, in addition, there's also a cheaper café attached , where you can get toasted Turkish sandwiches (with cheese or cheese and *suchuk* sausage), mezes, wraps, salads and extremely syrupy baklava and other sweets.

CHEAP EATS
BOROUGH MARKET CAFÉ
Map pp432-3   *English*
☎ 7407 5048; Borough Market; mains £2-5; ⏰ lunch Thu-Sat; tube London Bridge

The successor to the Borough Café (a Jamie Oliver hang-out) will still sell the same mix of breakfasts (bacon, eggs, tomatoes, bubble and squeak) and other filling meals – this time to market customers.

EL VERGEL Map pp432-3   *Latin American*
☎ 7357 0057; 8 Lant St SE1; mains £4.50-6.50; ⏰ 8.30am-3pm Mon-Fri; tube Borough

This small café is most notable for its breakfasts of fried Chilean bread and bacon, but also does specialities like *empanadas*, tacos and Peruvian flat bread sandwiches, all to the tune of a funky beat.

KONDITOR & COOK
Map pp426-7   *International*
☎ 7620 2700; 66 The Cut SE1; mains £6.25-7.95; ⏰ for meals 8.30am-7.30pm Mon-Fri, 10.30am-7.30pm Sat; tube Southwark/Waterloo

Some of the most delightfully sinful chocolate cake (£2.85) this side of Vienna, as well as whiskey orange bombe, almond fruit tart and other sorts of *küchen*. Accompanied by the likes of sausage and mash, caesar salad and potato cakes in the company of performers, local businesspeople or theatre-goers.

MANZE'S Map pp416-7   *English*
☎ 7407 2985; 87 Tower Bridge Rd SE1; mains around £3; ⏰ lunch, closed Sun; tube Borough/Bermondsey

Not the oldest, but one of the prettiest remaining pie shops in London has been going strong for over a century and is handy for Bermondsey Market. In its pleasantly tiled interior you'll find jellied eels, pie and mash and liquor.

Eating – Along the South Bank

THE EAST END

While Brick Lane is now a landscape of restaurant 'greeters' trying to entice you inside, and lads out on the piss trying to outdo each other in competitions as to who can eat the hottest vindaloo, real curry fans have moved on to Whitechapel. The East End's famous multiculturalism means its ethnic cuisine doesn't stop there, either. You'll find pretty well anything – from Turkish and Latin American, even Russian and Georgian.

BETHNAL GREEN & HACKNEY

ARMADILLO Map pp416-7 *Latin American*
☎ 7249 3633; 41 Broadway Market E8; mains £10-15; ⏰ dinner; rail London Fields, bus 106, 253, 26, 48, 55
Armadillo is the jewel in the crown of Broadway Market's increasingly funky scene, a simple neighbourhood restaurant that people travel across London to visit. There's a constantly changing mix of excellent Argentinean, Brazilian and Peruvian food, a friendly vibe and sparse decoration with Latino-kitsch touches (beaded curtains with pictures of Jesus and Frida Kahlo, lizard-shaped toilet-roll holders). Typical dishes might include Argentinean chorizo with croquettes and peppers *picante*, Peruvian duck *seco* and fried cassava or pancakes with *dulce de leche* (a sweeter, thicker condensed milk).

CROWN ORGANIC Map pp416-7 *Gastropub*
☎ 8981 9998; 223 Grove Rd E3; mains £7.50-15; tube Mile End, bus 8 or 277
The cooking is a little more variable at this offshoot of Islington's Duke of Cambridge (p233), but with its elegant upstairs dining room and its pleasant balcony, it's a bit of a boon in this area.

LITTLE GEORGIA Map pp416-7 *Georgian*
☎ 7249 9070; 2 Broadway Market E8; mains £12-15; ⏰ dinner Tue-Sat; rail London Fields, bus 106, 253, 26, 48, 55
That's Georgia, part of the former USSR, not Georgia, Atlanta. After a period as simply a café Little Georgia should have reverted to being a full-blown restaurant by the time you read this, but ring to check. The plan is to serve things like blinis, borscht, chicken *satsivi* in walnut sauce, spicy lamb with aubergine and other Greek/Turkish-style specialities, as well as to return to a more traditional Georgian decor. On our visit at least the service was already perfectly Soviet-style – ie frustratingly slow and disorganised.

CHEAP EATS

LAHORE KEBAB HOUSE
Map pp432-3 *Indian*
☎ 7488 2551; 2 Umberston St E1; mains £5-6; tube Whitechapel/Aldgate East
This smoky glass-walled restaurant is not an aesthetic experience and ever since City workers discovered this local the standard of cooking seems to have slipped a little bit. Still, it's okay for a fast and functional fill-up of curry or lamb kebabs.

LAHORE ONE Map pp432-3 *Indian*
☎ 7791 0112; 218 Commercial Rd E1; mains £2.95-4.95; tube Whitechapel
You'll be lucky to bag a table at this tiny outlet, but it does takeaway anyhow. The proprietors boast that the food is made to order with no artificial or packet sauces, in charcoal-fired ovens, and they're certainly doing something right. Spicy lamb kebabs (60p each) are a popular starter, while mains are mostly meat and veggie biryanis or *karahai* (their spelling) wok dishes.

LMNT Map pp416-7 *International*
☎ 724 9 6727; 316 Queensbridge Rd E8; mains before/after 7pm £5.45 /7.95; rail London Fields
The ornate Egyptian interior with seating in elevated alcoves in the corners, over the bar or inside a huge gilt jar, comes as a shock as you enter from the nondescript street. The food is also good and plentiful at this less-wealthy person's Les Trois Garçons (p231).

MANGAL Map pp420-1 *Turkish*
☎ 7275 8981; 10 Arcola St E8; mains £6.50-8.50; rail Dalston Kingsland
Mangal serves some of the best Turkish meze, grilled lamb chops, pigeon and salads in north London. Gilbert & George, *enfants terribles* of the British art scene, are in here every day, we're informed.

Top Five – East End

- Armadillo (above)
- LMNT (right)
- Mangal (right)
- New Tayyab (opposite)
- Whitechapel Art Gallery Café (opposite)

Eating – The East End

NEW TAYYAB Map pp432-3 *Indian*
☎ 7247 9543; 83 Fieldgate St E1; mains £3-10;
☾ dinner; tube Whitechapel

From the enticing aroma on entering, it's clear this buzzing Punjabi restaurant is not like its nearby Brick Lane equivalents; it's in another league. Seekh kebabs, masala fish and other starters served on sizzling hot-plates are delicious, as are accompaniments like naan, raita and mango lassi. But meat mains are definitely the strong point here.

The vegetarian *karahi* wok dish, while tasty, is atypically oily. BYO alcohol.

WHITECHAPEL ART GALLERY CAFÉ
Map pp432-3 *Mediterranean*
☎ 7522 7888; 80-82 Whitechapel High St E1; mains £5.10-6; ☾ lunch Tue-Sun; tube Aldgate East

Upstairs from the gallery, this is a nice respite from art observation, where you can partake of dishes like parma ham and mushroom tart and spinach, chicken and veggie *tarte tatin*.

DOWN RIVER

It would be easy to think of Docklands as an area strictly serving meals to financial workers who've been in for the nine-to-five, but as more people move back into the neighbourhood it turns out to have some magnificent culinary surprises. In Greenwich on the other hand, many restaurants are geared towards the passing tourist trade. Walking 10 minutes or so, however, will unearth a few gems.

DOCKLANDS

LIGHTSHIP TEN Map pp432-3 *Danish*
☎ 7481 3123; 5a St Katherine's Way, St Katherine's Docks E1; ☾ lunch Tue-Fri, dinner Tue-Sat; mains £12-15; tube Tower Hill

A memorable restaurant aboard the world's oldest lightship, serving, wait for it, nouveau Danish cuisine. You can lunch on dishes such as crab and salmon *frikadeller* or Copenhagen meatballs in the lacquer-red dining room of the middle deck, or retire to the even more atmospheric lower deck for dinner. Starters include gravalax on poppyseed *knaekbrot* (crispbread), and we'll certainly be back for more elderflower and fresh berry jelly with subtly liquorice ice cream.

Royal China restaurant (above)

ROYAL CHINA Map p435 *Chinese*
☎ 7719 0888; 30 Westferry Circus E14; dim sum £1.90-3.80, 4-course set meal £25; tube Canary Wharf, DLR Westferry

Part of the city's number one dim sum chain, the Westferry branch is reckoned by some punters to be a cut above the rest. Certainly, the view of the Thames is impressive, and it's quieter on weekends here than at the famous Queensway branch, so you won't need to queue. At weekday lunchtimes, when Canary Wharf is busy it's good to book, however. Classic dim sum is accompanied by more inventive varieties, such as steamed prawn and sweet-corn dumplings.

UBON Map p435 *Japanese*
☎ 7719 7800; 34 Westferry Circus E14; ☾ lunch Mon-Fri, dinner Mon-Sat; mains £5-30; tube Canary Wharf, DLR Westferry

Not as starry as its big sister Nobu (p238), Ubon compensates with breathtaking views over the Thames. The prices are just as high, however, and the food just as excellent. The Nobu classic of cod with miso is, naturally, on the menu.

WAPPING FOOD
Map pp432-3 *Mediterranean*
☎ 7680 2080; Wapping Wall E1; ☾ lunch & dinner, brunch Sat & Sun, closed dinner Sun; mains £11-18, brunch £4-8; tube Wapping

It's not just another converted industrial premise; this trendy Mediterranean restaurant has a winning difference. Wapping Food has left the hydraulic equipment *in situ*, so the smartly dressed patrons dine atmospherically in between turbines and giant wheels. The staff are very pleasant, the wine list all-Australian and the ingredients fresh. Wonderful.

GREENWICH

INSIDE Map p435   *Modern European*

☎ 8265 5060; 19 Greenwich South St SE10; mains £12-17; ☾ brunch Sat & Sun, lunch Wed-Sun, dinner Mon-Sat; DLR Cutty Sark

At Inside, clean, crisp design meets clean, crisp cuisine. So while it's busy at brunch on market days, its white and aubergine walls, modern art and linen table cloths also make it good for a relatively formal meal. The menu is ever-changing, but typically includes dishes like fresh-tasting pea soup or truffle and mixed mushroom risotto, and desserts such as dark chocolate tart with white chocolate ice cream. Set menus (£15/18 for two/three courses) are available at most weekday lunches and for early dinners.

TRAFALGAR TAVERN

Map p435   *British/Mediterranean*

☎ 8858 2437; Park Row SE10; mains £8.30-13; DLR Cutty Sark

To be honest, many of the restaurants right near Cutty Sark Gardens are a bit pikey, so you're better off walking the extra distance to Inside (above) or the recently revamped restaurant here. While you tuck into the celebrated whitebait (for which Parliament used to come to a halt when it first came into season) or one of the extensive range of fish dishes, you enjoy an excellent view of the river. The British staple of bangers and mash with red onion and gravy is also on the menu.

CHEAP EATS

GODDARDS PIE HOUSE

Map p435   *Traditional English*

☎ 8293 9313; 45 Greenwich Church St SE10; pies 95p-£2.70; ☾ 10am-6pm Mon-Thu, 10am-8pm Fri & Sat; DLR Cutty Sark

Carnivores and vegetarians alike can wallow in traditional English cuisine at Goddards, the city's oldest pie shop, established in 1890. Of course, soy 'Banks' pie and veggie-friendly packet gravy are relative newcomers to the chalkboard menu, otherwise littered with steak & kidney pie, shepherd's pie, green peas and jellied eels. It's no gourmet experience, but Goddards is tops for comfort food.

PETER DE WIT'S Map p435   *British*

☎ 8305 0048; 21 Greenwich Church St; snacks £2.50-5; ☾ 10am-6pm Mon-Thu, 10am-8pm Fri & Sat; DLR Cutty Sark

This small, Spartan, unpretentious café attracts student and boho customers with its hearty soups, sandwiches and cream teas (£5). There are jazz performances on weekends and a tiny seating area out back where patrons can sun themselves in the warmer months.

Part of the Food Chain

Until recently, 'chain' was a dirty word in the context of eating out – and still is if you think along the lines of McDonald's and Starbucks – but a new breed has infiltrated London in recent years. Trying to woo the capital's cash-rich and time-poor with clear style statements in food and atmosphere, these places are irresistibly convenient to the text-messaging generation looking for a post-work rendezvous. None of the production-line meals are particularly exciting but if you need a hole filled in a hurry, these will do the job.

At the elegant and *awfully English* Brown's (mains average £13) you'll get good value, British soul food such as bangers and mash, and steak & kidney pie amid bright, colonial surroundings. Popular with business lunchers, Chez Gerard (mains £9-16) is a smart brasserie chain serving French staples and steaks. Giraffe (mains £7-10) manages to be at once funky and family-friendly and serves a global gamut from curries to burgers. Jamies (mains £8-12) has a clutch of classy wine bars serving inventive global mains. Pizza Express (pizzas £5-8) has a knack for snapping up architecturally interesting buildings and filling them with polished metal furniture and plain pizzas. Stockpot (mains £4-6) is a London institution and one of the few places where you can get three courses (pasta or meat-and-two-veg) for under a tenner. Noodle-factory Wagamama (mains £5.50-9) attracts the longest queues and is the place to knock back a bowl of Japanese noodles while sitting at communal tables listening to anything but your own thoughts (which you won't be able to hear). Yo! Sushi (sushi £2-4) represents high-tech conveyor belt dining but is more impressive for its merchandising than for its occasionally limp sushi.

NORTH CENTRAL

Marylebone and Camden are by far the most important gustatory tracts in these neighbourhoods, although there are a few other options sprinkled about elsewhere. In general terms, Marylebone is on the way up and Camden is on the way down but the denizens of each are still spoiled for choice.

MARYLEBONE & REGENT'S PARK

GOLDEN HIND Map pp426-7   *Fish & Chipper*
☎ 7486 3644; 73 Marylebone Lane W1; mains £5-10; tube Bond Street

This 90-year-old chippie has a classic interior, chunky wooden tables and contractors sitting alongside pin-striped business types. From the vintage fryer comes quite possibly the best cod and chips in London. Attentive service and fresh fish cooked well – could you ask for anything more? Well, maybe those signed celebrity pix could come down off the walls – they kinda put you off your scran. BTW, it's BYO.

LA FROMAGERIE CAFÉ Map pp426-7   *Café*
☎ 7935 0341; 2-4 Moxon St W1; mains £6.50-9.50; tube Baker Street/Bond Street

Walking into this wonderful new café/shop is like entering celebrated food writer and owner Patricia Michelson's own kitchen, with bowls of delectable salads, antipasto, peppers and beans scattered about the long communal table with huge slabs of bread just inviting you to tuck in, and all the while the heavenly waft from the cheese room beckons. Sensational food, smiley service, sensible prices.

ORRERY Map pp426-7   *Modern European*
☎ 7616 8000; 55 Marylebone High St W1; mains £15-30; tube Baker Street/Regent's Park

Worth every point of its Michelin star, this Conran gem has perhaps the best service of any of London's fine dining establishments – friendly, efficient, never in the way and always there when you need them. The French-leaning food is also outstanding, with dishes like seared sea scallops with pork belly and caviar-covered cauliflower a thorough treat. But Orrery's star attraction is its selection of some 40 cheeses that you'll remember long after your gig here is over.

OZER Map pp426-7   *Turkish*
☎ 7323 0505; 5 Langham Pl W1; 🕐 lunch & dinner Mon-Sat ; mains £7.50-13; tube Oxford Circus

The 'Ottoman cuisine' here is lighter and more refined than the Turkish norm, as local workers

Top Five – North Central

- La Fromagerie Café (left)
- Ozer (left)
- Orrery (left)
- Providores (below)
- Raw Deal (p250)

and shoppers fully appreciate. This restaurant's Ankara sibling is supposed to be one of the best in Turkey. Portions are 'elegant' (okay, that means small) but mains like roasted shoulder of lamb with kumquat marmalade are powerful. It's a classy joint but if you don't agree, complain to Ozer, whose mobile number is on the table!

PROVIDORES Map pp426-7   *Spanish Fusion*
☎ 7935 6175; 109 Marylebone High St W1; tapas £2-10, mains £10-15; tube Baker Street/Bond Street

A couple of Kiwis are the kitchen alchemists behind this sassy, sociable and sexy place, which gives fusion back its good name. The restaurant is split over two levels, with tempting tapas grazers on the ground floor and full meals along the same innovative lines – Spanish and just about everything else – in the elegant and understated dining room above.

QUIET REVOLUTION Map pp426-7   *Café*
☎ 7487 5683; 28 Marylebone High St W1 (behind Avenda); 🕐 closes 6pm; mains £5-9; tube Baker Street/Bond Street

Just walking into this wholly organic place is enough to lift flagging spirits and put the spring back in your step. It's a terrific place to unwind and fill up during the day on vigorous juice combos, creative but simple brekkies like herb omelettes and zingy salads and mouth-watering quiches for lunch. Bills come with a free promotional beauty product from Aveda.

SPIGHETTA Map pp426-7   *Italian*
☎ 7486 7340; 43 Blandford St W1; mains average £10; tube Baker Street

Not a misspelt spaghetti house – *spighetta* actually means wheat – but a large basement

Farmers Markets

For fruit, vegetable, dairy and other foodstuffs that taste the way they did when you were a kid (ie with flavour), head to one of the growing number of weekend farmers markets that have been springing up around London. Here producers sell their own wares, the atmosphere is sociable and the plumpest, crispiest produce guaranteed. You can check out all the markets online at www.lfm.org.uk; these are some of the best and most central:

- **Blackheath** (station car park; 10am-2pm Sun; rail Blackheath)
- **Islington** (Map p444; Essex Rd, opposite Islington Green; 10am-2pm Sun; tube Angel) The original market, which sells organic produce.
- **Marylebone** (Map p666; Cramer St car park; 10am-2pm Sun; tube Baker Street/Bond Street)
- **Notting Hill** (Map p555; Kensington Pl, car park behind Waterstone's; 9am-1pm Sat; tube Notting Hill Gate)
- **Palmer's Green** (station car park; 10am-2pm Sun; rail Palmer's Green)
- **Peckham** (Peckham Sq, Peckham High St; 9.30am-1.30pm Sun; rail Peckham Rye)
- **Pimlico Road** (Map p011; Orange Sq, cnr Pimlico Rd & Ebury St; 9am-1pm Sat; tube Sloane Square)
- **Swiss Cottage** (Map p 333; next to Camden Library; 10am-4pm Wed; tube Finchley Road)
- **Wimbledon** (Havana Rd; 9am-1pm Sat; tube Wimbledon Park)

buzzing with activity and serving all sorts of Italian standards including excellent pizza, pasta and puddings. The table linen is crisp, the service friendly and the atmosphere one of workerlike refinement. There's a clutch of good restaurants on this strip.

VILLANDRY Map pp426-7 *Modern European*
☎ 7631 3131; 170 Great Portland St W1; mains £10-20; tube Great Portland Street
You pass through a shop to reach this restaurant and leaving empty-handed can be quite a challenge. On your way out, it's all too tempting to buy up large from the admirably stocked shelves in an attempt to recreate the invariably lovely meal you've just had in the simple and stylish dining room. Well worth sampling is the rustic white bean stew flavoured with shavings of black truffle, and you should finish with the celebrated cheese platter.

WOODLANDS Map pp426-7 *Veg/Indian*
☎ 7486 3862; 77 Marylebone Lane W1; mains £5-13; tube Bond Street
In India the 'Voodies' chain is pretty decent but here, it's wow. Superb *thalis* (all-you-can-eat mixed plates) and *dosas* are highlights but there are no real duds on the South Indian menu. Their rallying call is 'let vegetation feed the nation' and they put up a persuasive argument.

PADDINGTON & BAYSWATER

COUSCOUS CAFÉ Map pp422-3 *Moroccan*
☎ 7727 6597; 7 Porchester Gardens W2; mains £8-15; tube Bayswater
If Moroccan is your cup of mint tea then get yourself down to this vividly decorated place, which does a faultless line in familiar favourites

from all over North Africa but really excels with tangy tagines, sweet pastries and slightly exaggerated service.

MANDARIN KITCHEN Map pp422-3 *Chinese*
☎ 7727 9468; 14-16 Queensway W2; mains £5.95-25; tube Bayswater/Queensway
This perennially popular Cantonese restaurant specialises in seafood and keeping customers waiting ages for their table. With that gripe out of the way – oh, and the decor's not up to much – we can focus on the fare, which is most likely the best Chinese seafood in the big smoke. The lobster noodle with ginger and spring onion is, well, you'll just have to wait and sea.

SATAY HOUSE Map pp422-3 *Malaysian*
☎ 7723 6763; 13 Sale Pl W2; mains £4.50-9.50; tube Edgware Road/Paddington
The only time we ventured into Paddington was to catch the Heathrow Express until we discovered Satay House. Pretty and unpretentious, it serves the most authentic and delicious Malaysian food this side of Kuala Lumpur (well, in north London) with the Malay chicken curry a personal favourite.

KING'S CROSS & EUSTON
DIWANA BHEL POORI HOUSE
Map pp418-9 *Indian*
☎ 7387 5556; 121 Drummond St; mains £3-6.50; tube King's Cross
The first of its kind – and still the best on this busy street, according to many – Diwana specialises in Bombay-style *bhel poori* (a sweet and sour, soft and crunchy 'party mix' snack) and *dosas* (filled pancakes). There's an all-you-can-eat lunch-time buffet for £6.

EL PARADOR Map pp418-9   *Spanish*
☎ 7387 2789; 245 Eversholt St NW1; tapas £4-5.50;
tube Mornington Crescent

This laid-back Spanish place has a huge selection of tapas – including mucho vegetarian titbits – from all over Spain. There's a walled garden for when the sun's out and you're feeling moderately Mediterranean (the reasonably priced *rioja* might help). The only thing we don't like about this place is the odd booking protocol: fewer than three can forget it.

CAMDEN

BAR GANSA Map pp418-9   *Spanish*
☎ 7267 8909; 2 Inverness St NW1; tapas £2.50-4,
mains £12; tube Camden Town

This place bears more than a passing resemblance to a traditional Spanish tapas joint; it's smoky, loud, cramped and the staff often seem to speak a different language. Whether you feel like picking or porking out, the menu ranges from tasty titbits to manly mains. This is a focal point of the Camden scene, has a late licence and is howlingly popular. It's good but we could cope with a little less attitude.

CAFÉ CORFU Map pp418-9   *Greek*
☎ 7269 8088; 7-9 Pratt St NW1; mains £8-12; tube
Camden Town

Corfu is among the best of a host of Greek restaurants around here. Decor is sleek and simple, the delicious food feels light but fills, and there's more than retsina to slake your thirst. A belly dancer helps with digestion on the weekend but be warned, on her second spin the buxom beauty takes partners.

CAFÉ DELANCEY Map pp418-9   *French*
☎ 7387 1985; 3 Delancey St NW1; mains £7-15; tube
Camden Town

The granddaddy of French-style brasseries in London, Delancey offers the chance to get a decent cup of coffee with a snack or a full meal in relaxed European-style surroundings complete with newspapers. The cramped toilets, bickering staff and Charles Aznavour crooning in the background seem suitably Parisian.

Top Five – Outdoor Tables

- Butlers Wharf Chop House (p242)
- Engineer (right)
- Jason's (p252)
- Lauderdale House (p251)
- Terrace café at Somerset House (p98)

Trojka restaurant, Camden (p250)

COTTONS RHUM SHOP, BAR &
RESTAURANT Map pp418-9   *Caribbean*
☎ 7482 1096; 55 Chalk Farm Rd NW1; mains £10-15;
tube Chalk Farm

Easily more enticing than it sounds, Cottons is one of the most authentic Caribbean eateries in town, and offers island specials like jerk chicken and curried goat, head-banging rum-based cocktails and a friendly atmosphere in cheerful surroundings.

ENGINEER Map pp418-9   *Gastropub*
☎ 7722 0950; 65 Gloucester Ave NW1; mains £10-15;
tube Chalk Farm

One of London's original and best gastropubs, the Engineer serves up consistently good international cuisine – from tempura prawns to racks of lamb – and is hugely popular with impeccably hip north Londoners. The pub itself is quite decadent with red velvet curtains and gold candelabras hanging from the high ceilings upstairs, although the splendid walled garden is the highlight.

LEMONGRASS Map pp418-9   *Thai*
☎ 7284 1116; 243 Royal College St; mains £5-8; tube
Camden Town

When you want to eat out without *putting* yourself out, try this cute and calming little place where you can tuck into a solid and inexpensive line of fresh and tasty authentic Thai classics (with Cambodian twists). There's a vegetarian menu, no smoking and chirpy staff.

MANGO ROOM Map pp418-9 *Caribbean*
☎ 7482 5065; 10 Kentish Town Rd NW1; mains £9-12; tube Camden Town

Among the litter and lowlife of this part of Camden, Mango Room is a relaxed Caribbean experience popular with everyone from preclubbers to the occasional brigade of silver-haired ladies out for a special occasion. It's kind of de-caf Caribbean, although there's no holding back with the food, especially things fishy or with mango – grilled goat's cheese with mango and pesto, and grilled barracuda with courgettes and coconut sauce were highlights. The early ska/Jamaican jazz soundtrack is wicked.

TROJKA Map pp418-9 *Eastern European*
☎ 7483 3765; 101 Regent's Park Rd NW1; mains £6-9; tube Chalk Farm

This Primrose Village place serves good-value Eastern European/Russian dishes such as herrings with dill sauce and Russian salad, Polish *bigosz* (a cabbage 'stew' with mixed meats) and salt beef in an attractive, sky-lit restaurant frequented by local bohos. Avoid the house wine by bringing your own.

CHEAP EATS

ADDIS Map pp420-1 *African*
☎ 7278 0679; 42 Caledonian Rd N1; mains £4.50-8.50; tube King's Cross

It always feels like summer in Addis with its golden sunset hues, cheery staff and very laid-back vibe. It's normally full of Ethiopian and Sudanese punters, which is a good sign, and serves up a lip-smacking parade of exotic fare like *ful masakh* (a salad with feta and spicy falafel), the best sign of all.

ALI BABA Map pp418-9 *Egyptian*
☎ 7723 7474; 32 Ivor Pl NW1; mains £3; tube Baker Street

Looking more like a laundry than somewhere to eat, this tiny Egyptian double take is buried

in between terraced houses in residential Marylebone – a most unlikely place to find such good (for the price) hummus, falafel and kebabs. You can takeaway or sit in a tiny room and watch Arab TV.

ASAKUSA Map pp418-9 *Japanese*
☎ 7388 8533; 265 Eversholt St NW1; mains £5-10; tube Mornington Crescent

This scruffy but clean place has cheap sushi for £1 to £2 per piece, along with more elaborate reasonably priced set menus.

CASTLE'S Map pp418-9 *Traditional British*
☎ 7485 2196; 229 Royal College St NW1; dishes £2-4; tube Camden Town

One of a dying breed, Castle's is a traditional pie-and-mash caff with Formica tables, plastic chairs, and a complete absence of airs or graces. Pies with liquor and mash, jellied eels, and the whole gamut of ye olde London food right here.

NEW CULTURAL REVOLUTION
Map pp436-7 *Asian*
☎ 7352 9281; 305 King's Rd SW3; mains £6; tube Sloane Square

This is a popular dumpling and noodle bar, which has changing veggie specials as well as brisk and helpful service.

RAW DEAL Map pp422-3 *Vegetarian*
☎ 7262 4841; 65 York St W1; main & 2 salads £6.50; tube Baker Street

Kooky and compelling, Raw Deal occupies a glass corner of a Marylebone backstreet and feels like the café on a Victorian railway platform where trains never come (it must have been a looooong day). Anyway, it's run by friendly South American smoothies who dish up robust and hearty salads along with premade hot dishes that never disappoint.

TERRA BRASIL Map pp418-9 *Brazilian*
☎ 7388 6554; 36-38 Chalton St NW1; set buffet £5; tube Euston

Don't think less of Terra because of the bracket it's in; this is the best eatery in the whole of Euston (although we concede that that's a bit like saying the best slalom skier in the desert). It's a particularly warm and homely place, where the *caipirinha* cocktails are mighty and the plates laden with tasty Brazilian fare like *feijoada* (an assorted platter of thinly sliced meats with black beans, rice and citrus slices).

Top Five – Veggie

- Food for Thought (p226)
- Gate (p255)
- Mildred's (p224)
- Rasa (p252)
- Raw Deal (p250)

THE NORTHERN HEIGHTS

None of these restaurants are destinations in themselves but a visit to any one of them will certainly improve your outing. A couple are in parks while most of the others are on the 'high streets' of each of the different neighbourhoods; Stoke Newington Church St, Crouch End Broadway and Muswell Hill Broadway are particularly good strips.

HAMPSTEAD & HIGHGATE

JIN KICHI Map p415   *Japanese*
☎ 7794 6158; 73 Heath St NW3; mains £5.50-13; tube Hampstead

A disproportionate number of London's Japanese live in Hampstead, and a disproportionate number of them eat at this slightly shabby and cramped little place, regarded as one of the best Japanese restaurants in north London. It's a particularly good bet for grilled meats and other nonstandard Japanese flavours, none of which you'll be able to enjoy unless you book.

LAUDERDALE HOUSE Map p415   *Café*
☎ 8348 8716; Waterlow Park, Highgate Hill N6; mains £6; tube Archway

The best place to eat in Highgate during the day – and only a short walk from the cemetery – Lauderdale House is a lovely 16th-century residence that doubles as a community arts centre. The outdoor tables in the big garden that leads out into the park are much coveted on sunny weekend afternoons by families and hungover funsters. Standard dishes include reasonable fish cakes, chips, salads and lasagnes although the creative specials like stuffed avocado are often your best bet. The coffee is very good.

OSHOBASHO CAFÉ
Map p415   *Café/Vegetarian*
☎ 8444 1505; Highgate Wood, Muswell Hill Rd N10; no food Mon; mains £5; tube Highgate

Smack bang in the middle of Highgate Wood, this lovely café (which feels like it's just outside London) is set in a pavilion, has a huge outdoor terrace surrounded by trees and is perfect for a sunny afternoon. Pastries, desserts and coffee are the mainstays but there are also decent hot dishes like pasta bake, tortilla and vegetable curry.

Top Five – Traditional Fish & Chips

- Costa's Fish Restaurant (p253)
- Geales (p253)
- Golden Hind (p247)
- Rock & Sole Plaice (p227)
- Toff's (right)

Top Five – Northern Heights

- Blue Legume (p252)
- Café on the Hill (below)
- Jin Kichi (left)
- Rasa (p252)
- Toff's (below)

MUSWELL HILL

CAFÉ ON THE HILL   *Modern European*
☎ 8444 4957; 46 Fortis Green Rd N10; mains £8-14; tube Highgate, then bus 134

Largely organic and very veggie it may be but this ain't no hippy, hippy shake; it's just all you could hope for in a local café – seasonal menus, all-day brekkies, good coffee, light lunches, afternoon tea, substantial evening meals, newspapers and a welcoming atmosphere.

TOFF'S   *Fish & Chipper*
☎ 8883 8656; 38 Muswell Hill Broadway N10; closes 7pm; mains £9-17; tube Highgate, then bus 134

This former British chipper of the year has a rather smelly takeaway counter at the front and a more salubrious dining room out back. The staff are very friendly and Toff's is renowned for providing large quantities of fresh fish, beautifully battered and flawlessly fried.

STOKE NEWINGTON & FINSBURY PARK

BANNERS   *Modern European*
☎ 8348 2930; 21 Park Rd N8; mains £8-11; tube Finsbury Park, then bus W7

They say some people move to Crouch End to be closer to this café although we suspect that 'they' might be the owners. It's always buzzing – too much so when the babies and infants start acting up – and it's got an inexplicable magnetic power. The food can be hit and miss (veggie sausages and mash hit, cooked brekkies generally miss), the smoothies are invigorating, and the staff are friendly to locals and polite to strangers.

Eating – The Northern Heights

251

BLUE LEGUME
Vegetarian

☎ 7923 1303; 101 Stoke Newington Church St N16; mains £5-8; rail Stoke Newington, bus 73

Buzzing with familiarity, this lively and laid-back local has mosaic tables and slightly kooky decor (such as a big plaster sun hanging from the ceiling) although there's nothing odd about the big, late breakfasts or the selection of satisfying smoothies. Throughout the day there are light veggie snacks such as ciabatta and crostini, hot specials like courgette burgers and trays of delicate, delicious pastries.

RASA Map p414
Indian/Vegetarian

☎ 7249 0344; 55 Stoke Newington Church St N16; mains £4-6; rail Stoke Newington, bus 73

This superb South Indian vegetarian restaurant can't be missed (not with that shocking pink facade anyway). Friendly service, a calm atmosphere, jovial prices and outstanding food from the Indian state of Kerala are its distinctive features. Don't bother with the menu and just bring on the three-course feast. Rasa Travancore, across the road, is more of the same but with fish and meat.

NORTHWEST LONDON

Notting Hill is the epicentre of this zone and offers a superb range of eateries whatever the size of your belly or purse, from venerated chippers to fashionable fusion.

ST JOHN'S WOOD & MAIDA VALE

GREEN OLIVE Map pp422-3
Italian

☎ 7289 2469; 5 Warwick Pl W9; 3-course set lunch/dinner £15/45; tube Warwick Avenue

The Maida Vale cognoscenti hold this neighbourhood Italian place in high esteem. Dishes, although creative and very tasty, are rather daintily portioned so you don't want to arrive with a mean appetite. The plain brickwork and bubbly staff give it an upmarket rustic kinda vibe.

Sausage & Mash Café (opposite)

JASON'S Map pp422-3
Fish

☎ 7286 6752; Jason's Wharf, opposite 60 Blomfield Rd W9; mains £12-20; tube Warwick Avenue

One to remember when the sun's out, canal-side Jason's has cosy outside tables, as well as its main dining room in a high wooden-ceilinged boathouse that is basic but feels almost alfresco in itself. Happily the exotic fare is more reliable than the weather; you can expect superb fish and seafood dishes with French, Mauritian and Creole influences and overtones.

NOTTING HILL & WESTBOURNE GROVE

ASSAGI Map pp422-3
Italian

☎ 7792 5501; 39 Chepstow Pl W2; mains £16-20; tube Notting Hill Gate

Although you'll still see the occasional showbiz straggler here, above a charming Chepstow pub, Assagi's days as a happening celebrity hangout are long gone. It's now settled into the more relaxed groove of an elegant and tasteful neighbourhood joint with reliable if unrivetting Italian cooking that focuses on the best ingredients cooked simply (dishes such roast lamb and sea bass).

E&O Map pp422-3
Asian Fusion

☎ 7229 5454; 14 Blenheim Cres W11; mains £6-20; tube Notting Hill Gate/Ladbroke Grove

This Notting Hill hot spot is about the best – certainly the trendiest – of a notable neighbourhood. The Eastern & Oriental presents fusion fare, which usually starts with an Asian base, and then pirouettes into something resembling Pacific Rim, eg red pumpkin, aubergine and lychee curry. The decor is stark and minimalist but you'd better appreciate it at lunch because the evenings are mental. You can dim sum at the bar.

GEALES Map pp422-3   *Fish & Chipper*
☎ 7727 7528; 2 Farmer St W8; fish & chips £10; tube **Notting Hill Gate**
Gregarious Geales was established in 1939 and has become a popular faux seaside fixture with locals and tourists alike. It prices everything according to weight and season, and while it's more expensive than your everyday chipper, it's a lot better and worth every penny.

MANDOLA Map pp418-9   *African*
☎ 7229 4734; 139-141 Westbourne Grove W2; mains £5-7; tube Bayswater
This bright and breezy Sudanese joint offers staples such as *tamia* (a kind of falafel), *fifilia* (a vegetable curry) and meat dishes such as the unusual *shorba fule* (a meat and peanut soup). The owners are so relaxed they sometimes can't be bothered opening.

MARKET THAI
Map pp422-3   *Thai*
☎ 7460 8320; The Market Bar, 240 Portobello Rd; mains £5-8; tube Ladbroke Grove
Drippy white candles, carved arches and wrought-iron chairs set out the interior in this delightful restaurant, which occupies the first floor of the Market Bar but feels way, way, way beyond the market crowds. Hospitable staff and fresh, delicately spiced Thai cuisine make this place a little money very well spent.

TAWANA Map pp422-3   *Thai*
☎ 7229 3785; 3 Westbourne Grove W2; mains £6-18; tube Bayswater/Royal Oak
Try the delicious chicken satay and succulent king prawn dishes at this diminutive Thai place, decorated with potted plants and rattan chairs. The exceedingly friendly waiters

---

> ## Top Five – Northwest London
> - E & O (opposite)
> - Geales (above)
> - Mandalay (right)
> - Market Thai (above)
> - Sausage & Mash Café (right)

---

will help you make some sense of the huge menu – including a large veggie section – should you need help. Or you could just take our advice.

CHEAP EATS

CHURRERÍA ESPAÑOLA Map pp422-3   *Café*
☎ 7727 3444; 177 Queensway W2; mains £3-6; tube **Bayswater**
This unlikely café serves a variety of cheap dishes from English breakfasts to a range of Spanish staples including paella and several veggie specials. There are a few outdoor tables.

COSTA'S FISH RESTAURANT
Map pp422-3   *Fish & Chipper*
☎ 7229 3794; 12-14 Hillgate St W8; mains £4-7; tube **Notting Hill Gate**
This fondly regarded local puts a Cypriot spin on the traditional chippy and has a huge array of fresher-than-fresh fish dishes at market prices, which many prefer to the more upmarket Geales nearby.

MANDALAY
Map pp422-3   *Burmese*
☎ 7258 3696; 444 Edgware Rd W2; mains £4-7; tube **Edgware Road**
Unbelievably good-value, Mandalay looks like a cross between a down-at-heel solicitor's office and a fortune teller's parlour and is London's only Burmese restaurant. Try the spicy *mokhingar* soup with noodles redolent of shrimp paste and fish sauce.

MANZARA Map pp422-3   *Turkish*
☎ 7727 3062; 24 Pembridge Rd W11; mains £5-8; tube Notting Hill Gate
There is cheap, fresh and well-prepared Turkish food, with great *pides*, kebabs, pseudo pizzas and lots of vegetarian options at this simple place.

SAUSAGE & MASH CAFÉ
Map pp422-3   *Traditional British*
☎ 8968 8898; 268 Portobello Rd W10; mains £5-7; tube Ladbroke Grove
Under the elevated Westway, this S&M club takes the British favourite of bangers and mash to new levels. There is not just a choice of different sausages, as you'd expect, but also variations of creamy mounds of mash and even gravy.

WEST LONDON

The sheer variety on offer in multicultural west London makes it rich pickings for some truly excellent restaurants. Shepherd's Bush in particular is constantly abuzz with new openings and revamps of old favourites, while Earl's Court offers a good range of cheaper options and some great people-watching. Hammersmith makes up for its lack of sights with some unique eateries, including the superb Gate vegetarian restaurant.

EARL'S COURT & WEST BROMPTON

TROUBADOUR Map pp436-7   *Home Cooking*
☎ 7370 1434; 265 Old Brompton Rd SW5; mains £6-7;
☽ breakfast, lunch & dinner; tube Earl's Court

Bob Dylan and John Lennon have performed here, and Troubadour remains a wonderfully relaxed bohemian hangout decades later – great for coffee or a reasonably priced, home-cooked meal. There's still live music most nights and a large pleasant garden for summer. Come for the atmosphere and the friendly service and to make new friends with other boho inhabitants of West London. The Troubadour deli next door offers a sumptuous array of fresh foodstuffs for sale.

LOU PESCADOU Map pp436-7   *Fish*
☎ 7370 1057; 241 Old Brompton Rd SW5; mains £14-15; ☽ dinner; tube Earl's Court

Simplicity and elegance meet at this wonderful seafood restaurant, which stands out among the many neighbouring eateries on Old Brompton Rd. Should you have trouble understanding the all-French menu, the staff are surprisingly democratic about assisting you, and the results usually very rewarding. A particularly great place in summer, when the menu is simple and light, Lou Pescadou is always a treat.

BALANS WEST Map pp436-7   *Brasserie*
☎ 7224 8838; 293 Old Brompton Rd SW5; mains £8-9; ☽ 8am-1am; tube Earl's Court

More relaxed than its Old Compton St cousin, this gay-friendly bar-grill is pleasant, although pricey for the fare it serves. Eye candy waiters may be little else than that, but it's a nice spot from which to watch the world go by. The menu ranges from simple sandwiches to the more standard brasserie fare of well-realised salads and grills.

MR WING Map pp436-7   *Chinese*
☎ 7370 4450; 242-244 Old Brompton Rd SW5; mains £7-10; tube Earl's Court

The oddly-named Mr Wing is a very smart Asian fusion place offering Chinese cuisine with elements of Thai and Mongolian cooking. It has a plush, dark interior, helpful staff and a basement where live jazz is played to recommend it. This is one of London's more interesting Chinese restaurants, yet Mr Wing is surprisingly well priced.

SHEPHERD'S BUSH & HAMMERSMITH

BRACKENBURY   *Modern European*
☎ 8748 0107; 129-131 Brackenbury Rd W6; mains £9-15; ☽ lunch & dinner, closed dinner Sun; tube Goldhawk Road/Hammersmith

The Brackenbury is very much a neighbourhood restaurant with a friendly vibe and relaxed atmosphere. Its modern European menu is enticing, with some imaginative starters and a good selection of wines from reasonable prices, ensuring the Brackenbury stands out from the many gastropubs in the immediate vicinity.

BUSH BAR   *Modern European*
☎ 8746 2111; 45a Goldhawk Rd W12; mains £10-15; ☽ lunch & dinner, closed dinner Sun; tube Goldhawk Road

You have to search for this trendy media hangout, down an alleyway off Goldhawk Rd and housed in a converted warehouse. It's light and breezy and the decent restaurant attracts a BBC crowd after work with its great cocktails as much as its food. The menu is inventive and particularly strong on fresh fish and salads.

COTTO   *Modern European*
☎ 7602 9333; 44 Blythe Rd W14; mains £13-17; ☽ lunch Mon-Fri, dinner Mon-Sat; tube Goldhawk Road/Kensington Olympia

This hyper-sleek west London eatery is generally recognised to be the finest in Shepherd's Bush, and that's quite something when there are so many great places to eat locally. Simplicity and understatement are the main themes here, running from the stark decor to the Modern European food. This is the antithesis of the mid-'90s London fusion restaurant, and well worth a visit.

DOVE
British

☎ 8748 5405; 19 Upper Mall W6; ☺ lunch & dinner, closed dinner Sun; tube Hammersmith/Ravenscourt Park

The perfect place to stop off for a hearty pub lunch on a walk down the river, this 17th-century pub is also famed for having the smallest bar in England. Legend has it that *Land of Hope and Glory* was written between these walls, although most visitors will be more impressed that this was Graham Greene's local. The dark wood interiors are charming, but if the sun is shining, fight for a place on the terrace and enjoy traditional English food overlooking the Thames.

ESARN KHEAW
Thai

☎ 8743 8930; 314 Uxbridge Rd W12; ☺ lunch Mon-Fri, dinner; mains £5-8.50; tube Shepherd's Bush

Welcoming you back into the '70s is the green and kitsch interior of this superb Thai restaurant, which has won awards consistently throughout the last seven years. The fish-cake starters are sublime and the staff extremely friendly. The biographical detail on the menu that traces the owner's journey from Thailand to owning his own restaurant via Trusthouse Forte is a gem.

GATE
Vegetarian

☎ 8748 6932; 51 Queen Caroline Rd W6; ☺ lunch & dinner Mon-Fri, dinner Sat; mains £8-11; tube Hammersmith

Widely considered among the best vegetarian restaurants in town, the Gate has an unlikely location rented from the next-door church. The staff are exceptionally friendly and welcoming, and the relaxed atmosphere, despite being full most nights of the week, contributes to the uniqueness of this place. Surprisingly enough, it's the cheesecake that gets recurring rave reviews, as does the stuffed aubergine, the simple but inspired starters and fine wine list. A good place to convert meat-eaters. Bookings advisable.

RIVER CAFÉ
Map pp416-17 *Italian*

☎ 7386 4200; Thames Wharf, Rainville Rd W6; ☺ lunch & dinner, closed dinner Sun; mains £22-31; tube Hammersmith

The restaurant that spawned the world-famous cookbooks, the River Café is a serious treat off Fulham Palace Rd, overlooking Barnes across the river. The simple, precise cooking showcases seasonal ingredients sourced with fanatical expertise, although the arrogance of the staff has in the past been cause for complaint. Booking is essential, as it's still a hot favourite of the Fulham set, not to mention the New Labour elite, as the wine list and prices will confirm.

CHEAP EATS

A. COOKE'S
Traditional English

☎ 8743 7630; 48 Goldhawk Rd W12; ☺ lunch; mains £3-5; tube Shepherd's Bush/Goldhawk Road

For a slice of the real London, drop into A. Cooke's – a no-frills English establishment where the queue for pies and jellied eels snakes around the corner every lunch time. Delicious and cheap fare, although it can only be taken away as there are no eat-in facilities.

BENJY'S
Map pp436-7 *Traditional English*

☎ 7373 0245; 314 Earl's Court Rd SW5; ☺ breakfast, lunch & dinner; min charge £3.30, mains £3-5; tube Earl's Court

Benjy's is a great place for a filling breakfast, the local greasy spoon of note, and one of the few places in London to have adopted the North American tradition of multiple refills for tea and coffee without charge. Nothing amazing, just good cheap food for hungry travellers.

BLAH BLAH BLAH
Modern European

☎ 8746 1337; 78 Goldhawk Rd W12; ☺ lunch & dinner, closed lunch Sun; mains £8-£10; tube Goldhawk Road

This vegetarian institution has been packing them in for years with imaginative, well-realised food and a great, informal atmosphere. You can bring your own bottle, which makes an already medium-priced night out very good value indeed. Crayons are supplied for doodling on your table while wait for your order.

KRUNGTAP
Map pp436-7 *Thai*

☎ 7259 2314; 227 Old Brompton Rd SW10; mains £4-6; tube Earl's Court

Krungtap is the Thai name for Bangkok, and this eponymous restaurant is a busy, friendly café-style undertaking serving very good value Thai food. There is also karaoke from 7pm to midnight Friday to Sunday, so be warned.

Top Five – West London

- Cotto (opposite)
- Esarn Kheaw (left)
- Gate (left)
- Lou Pescadou (opposite)
- River Café (left)

Eating – West London

SOUTHWEST LONDON

Although not universally known for its cuisine, this area of London can lay claim to a number of decent gastronomic outposts, some of which are well worth crossing town for. If you're in Fulham, wander down the Fulham Rd, up New King's Rd and along Wandsworth Bridge Rd for a good choice. In Putney, head down the High St or the roads heading off it.

FULHAM & PARSON'S GREEN

ATLAS Map pp436-7   *Mediterranean*
☎ 7385 9129; 16 Seagrove Rd SW6; mains £8-12; tube Fulham Broadway

This Victorian gastropub is a small, perfectly formed gem with a cosy, relaxed feel contributed to by a clientele of well-behaved locals in their late-20s and 30s, out for a quiet meal with friends. The food is delicious, although you might find the menu descriptions slightly over the top, and there's a lovely little courtyard.

BLUE ELEPHANT Map pp436-7   *Thai*
☎ 7385 6595; 4-6 Fulham Broadway SW6; mains £10-17; ☽ lunch Mon-Thu & Sun, dinner Mon-Thu, Sat & Sun; tube Fulham Broadway

The sumptuous surroundings, attentive staff and excellent food make dining at the Blue Elephant a memorable experience. The atmosphere is romantic with candlelit tables, fountains and lush foliage. It's wise to book for dinner.

GHILLIES Map pp436-7   *Fish*
☎ 7371 0434; 271 New King's Rd SW6; mains £8-12; ☽ breakfast, lunch & dinner, closed dinner Sun; tube Parson's Green

Ghillies is a great place to while away the hours on a grey London day. This is a laid-back and friendly little place with lots of regulars and the affable staff will make you feel welcome. Tuck into a plate of scampi and chips while watching the football on a Saturday afternoon or treat yourself to oysters and champagne on a Friday evening.

IL PAGLIACCIO Map pp436-7   *Italian*
☎ 7371 5253; 184 Wandsworth Bridge Rd SW6; mains £6-12; tube Fulham Broadway

If you come to Il Pagliaccio you must be prepared to get into the spirit – quite literally on tequila nights. This is a favourite for birthday parties and hen's nights and can get very rowdy – great fun if you're out to get drunk and friendly with locals. Oh, and the food's pretty decent too.

JOE'S BRASSERIE Map pp436-7   *Brasserie*
☎ 7731 7835; 130 Wandsworth Bridge Rd SW6; mains £10-14; tube Fulham Broadway

The menu at Joe's includes all the usual brasserie favourites (fish cakes, duck salad, steak sandwiches) but they all taste good so you can forgive Joe's for not being more imaginative with the menu. The continental atmosphere and pleasant staff make for a genial meal out.

MIRAGGIO CLUB Map pp436-7   *Italian*
☎ 7384 3142; 510 Fulham Rd SW6; mains £8-12; ☽ dinner, lunch Sat & Sun; tube Fulham Broadway

With partners in Rome and Fregene this delightful little restaurant is genuinely Italian. The food is cooked with fresh ingredients and is excellent value. The rustic decor only adds to the charm of this firm favourite.

MISSION Map pp436-7   *Modern European*
☎ 7736 3322; 116 Wandsworth Bridge Rd SW6; mains £7-9; ☽ dinner Mon-Sat; tube Fulham Broadway/Parson's Green

Put on your trendiest togs for dining at stylish Mission because this is the in place for food and a few drinkies in Fulham. Although very cool, this place is not intimidating and you shouldn't pass up the opportunity to sample the desserts – out of this world!

NAPULÉ Map pp436-7   *Italian*
☎ 7381 1122; 585 Fulham Rd SW6; mains £5-10; ☽ dinner, lunch Sat & Sun; tube Fulham Broadway

This busy little restaurant is full of Italians, which in itself is a good recommendation, and the antipasto and wood-fired pizzas certainly deserve their praise. Booking is advisable in the evenings.

Eating – Southwest London

NAYAAB Map pp436-7 — *Indian*
☎ 7731 6993; 309 New King's Rd SW6; mains £6-12;
tube Putney Bridge

Don't come to Nayaab for a cheap curry after a
heavy night on the booze – this accomplished
Punjabi restaurant is too good for that.

SALISBURY TAVERN
Map pp436-7 — *Modern British*
☎ 7381 4005; 21 Sherbrooke Rd SW6; tube Fulham
Broadway

At this pub-cum-restaurant the food is far from
the soggy microwaved lasagne school of pub
grub. The dishes are of excellent quality and
the staff are highly professional. There's also a
great atmosphere as you are still very much
part of the busy pub. You'll definitely need to
book your table in advance.

CHEAP EATS

209 CAFÉ Map pp436-7 — *Thai*
☎ 7385 3625; 209 Munster Rd SW6; ☽ dinner; mains
£4-7; tube Fulham Broadway/Parson's Green

This tiny little Thai restaurant is perfect for
good food on a small budget, but it's not a
secret so head down early if you don't want
to wait for a table.

CASBAH CAFÉ Map pp436-7 *Traditional English*
☎ 7385 2865; 101 Farm Lane SW6; ☽ breakfast &
lunch; mains £3; tube Fulham Broadway

Don't blink or you'll miss it – tucked out of the
way in a little backstreet and hidden behind
wire mesh, the Casbah Café doesn't shout
about its presence. However, for cheap sandwiches or a filling plate of fried egg, sausage
and chips it can't be beat.

TOOTSIES GRILL Map pp436-7 — *American*
☎ 7736 4023; 177 New King's Rd SW6; ☽ brunch,
lunch & dinner; mains £6-10; tube Parson's Green

When you think Saturday night's over indul-
gence may just get the better of you head
down to Tootsies for Sunday brunch and feed
that hangover; a fry-up with all the trimmings
should do the trick.

PUTNEY & BARNES

DEL BUONGUSTAIO Map pp416-7 — *Italian*
☎ 8780 9361; 283-285 Putney Bridge Rd SW15;
mains £5.90-16.90; 3-course lunch £12.75; tube Putney
Bridge

There's some argument among locals as to
whether standards at this perennially popular

Italian restaurant have slipped over recent
years, but there are enough Putneyites still
singing its praises to warrant its entry here.
Its trick is to serve up a constantly changing
menu (one week it'll be duck breast with
strawberry balsamic vinaigrette, the next
ravioli of wild guinea fowl) in simple, faux-
rustic surrounds. Most weekends it's full of
Italian families that don't ever seem to leave
– testament to the genial atmosphere, at least,
if not the food.

ENOTECA TURI — *Italian*
☎ 8785 4449; 28 Putney High St SW15; ☽ lunch
Mon-Fri, dinner Mon-Sat; mains £10; tube Putney
Bridge

And, relax...you've arrived at a little oasis of
calm on the High St. The atmosphere is serene, the service is charming and the interior
is all understated elegance (linen tablecloths,
don't you know). Enoteca Turi devotes equal
devotion to the grape as to the food, which
means that each dish, be it a shellfish tagli-
olini or calf's liver, comes recommended with
a particular glass of wine (or you can pick
from the 300-strong wine menu if you think
you know best).

LA MANCHA — *Spanish*
☎ 8780 1022; 32 Putney High St SW15; tapas £3.50-
6.95, mains £8.25-12.95, 2-course set lunch £7.50; tube
Putney Bridge

La Mancha is the place to visit for some good
wholesome fun and at weekends it's packed
with young Putneyites having exactly that. It
serves up a vast variety of tapas from all over
Spain, from old favourites such as *patatas
bravas* to dishes you're less likely to see on the
Costa del Sol (poached octopus with olive oil
and paprika for one).

MA GOA Map pp416-7 — *Indian*
☎ 8780 1767; 242-244 Upper Richmond Rd 15;
☽ dinner, closed Mon; mains £6.50-9.50; tube Putney
Bridge

What's different about Ma Goa? There's a
clue in the name – the speciality here is the
Portuguese-influenced cuisine of Goa, served
up in terracotta bowls by cheery staff. Sausages may not be the first dish that springs
to mind when you think of the subcontinent,
but the cinnamon-infused pork snags are
worth the booking alone. With plenty more
intriguing options you'll understand why
this restaurant is repeatedly voted Putney's
favourite Indian.

PUTNEY BRIDGE
French

☎ 8780 1811; 2 Lower Richmond Rd SW15; mains £7.50-24.50, 2-course lunch £15.50, degustation menu £49, Sunday lunch menu £22.50; tube Putney Bridge

Glassy, ship-shaped Putney Bridge brought a RIBA architectural award and a Michelin star to this stretch of the river when it first opened here. It's still premier stuff, serving up a stunning menu, expansive views of the river from every table in the house, service as polished as all that glass and an effortlessly stylish interior. If you have trouble deciding what to pick from the short but ever-changing menu, take note that the game is always particularly gorgeous.

CHEAP EATS

MOOMBA WORLD CAFÉ
Global

☎ 8785 9151; 5 Lacy Rd SW15; mains £6.25-8.95; 🕑 brunch, lunch & dinner

Taking its name from the Aboriginal word meaning 'to get together and have a good time', Moomba is a convivial place to spend a few weekend hours. Locals loll about on pavement chairs or at scatty wooden tables inside, occasionally breaking from conversations to pick up crayons and puzzles (provided by Moomba) for their offspring. Brunch here is our favourite – try eggs Florentine or the mushroom risotto cakes.

SOUTH LONDON

This part of south London's best retort to all those sniffy jokes by north Londoners is its wonderful restaurant scene. You'd actually travel here just to visit some of the restaurants in Clapham and Wandsworth, while Brixton lays out a reasonably-priced multicultural spread.

BRIXTON

BRIXTONIAN HAVANA CLUB
Map p439　　　　　　　　　　　*Caribbean*

☎ 7924 9262; 11 Beehive Pl SW9; mains £14; tube Brixton

There are them folk that come to this club late for its *caipirinhas*, rum punches and dancing, and them that head upstairs earlier for the food. If you're a connoisseur of Caribbean nosh, it's certainly worth joining the latter group and trying dishes like roast pepper and ginger soup and baked ham with sweet sorrel sauce. Each month, the kitchen highlights the cuisine of a different island in the Caribbean.

BUG BAR Mapp439　　*Modern International*

☎ 7738 3366; St Matthew's Church SW2; mains £7.50-10.50; 🕑 dinner, lunch Sun; tube Brixton

Seated on a red leather chair in the crypt of St Matthew's Church – with arches, candles and gilt mirrors all creating an ecclesiastical theme – you can feel quite virtuous tucking into Bug's organic, vegetarian or free-range meat cuisine. The signature dish is Cantonese mock duck, but the changing menu also includes things like nut Wellington, swordfish or chicken satay. Sunday roasts, nut or meat, have become a permanent fixture on the local scene.

FUJIYAMA Map p439　　　　　　*Japanese*

☎ 7737 2369; 5-7 Vining St SW9; mains £5-10; 🕑 dinner, lunch Sat & Sun; tube Brixton

The lazy and sceptical person's route to a feeling of total well-being, Fujiyama is the sort of

Top Five – South London

- Brixtonian Havana Club (left)
- Chez Bruce (opposite)
- Gourmet Burger Kitchen (p260)
- Thyme (opposite)
- Tsunami (p260)

restaurant where you can walk in decidedly rundown and leave uplifted by a lip-smacking meal. Part of that's down to the usual cleansing rush that Japanese food brings. However, there's also something ritualistically relaxing about the dark-red interior, communal benches and lacquer bento boxes. Apart from a large choice of bento boxes, noodles, tempuras, *gyoza* dumplings, miso soup and fantastic juices are also on the placemat-style menu.

BATTERSEA & WANDSWORTH

This part of south London, with its lovely park and expensive mansion blocks, tends to have more upmarket restaurants than areas to the east and west.

BUCHAN'S Map pp436-7　　*Modern Scottish*

☎ 7228 0888; 62-64 Battersea Bridge Rd SW11; mains £11-17; tube Sloane Square, then bus 19, 49, 239, 319 or 345

This fairly formal wine bar and restaurant specialises in traditional Scottish food such as haggis (£4.95/8.95 as starter/main course) and the accompanying neeps and tatties and smoked salmon. With the range of Caledonian dishes being fairly limited, it ventures into the Modern British arena too.

CHEZ BRUCE Map p414 *French*
☎ 8672 0114; 2 Bellevue Rd SW17; fixed-price 3-course weekday lunch/weekend lunch/dinner £21.50/25/30; ☺ lunch, dinner Sat & Sun; rail Wandsworth Common

The Bruce in question is chef Bruce Poole and people still, rightly, trek across London to visit his Michelin-starred abode. The cuisine is principally French, with mains such as chateaubriand and pot-roast rabbit leg, interspersed with more international starters such as risotto or tuna – although the menu changes regularly. The restaurant's rustic facade, beside Wandsworth Common, belies a modern interior, where diners are professionally attended to. The fixed-price only set-up means there's no need to scrimp on desserts, but selecting a fine French wine on top of your food can double the bill.

LE GOTHIQUE Map p414 *French*
☎ 8870 6567; Royal Victoria Patriotic Bldg, Fitzhugh Grove, Trinity Rd SW18; ☺ lunch Mon-Fri, dinner Mon-Sat; rail Wandsworth Common/Clapham Junction

This restaurant serves pretty reasonable food, but you come here for the romance and atmosphere of the gothic-style Royal Victoria Patriotic Building. There's a courtyard where you can dine outside on a summer's evening, too.

METROGUSTO Map pp440-1 *Italian*
☎ 7720 0204; 153 Battersea Park Rd SW11; mains £13-16; ☺ lunch & dinner, closed Sun; rail Battersea Park

This excellent Italian continues to command a loyal following, even after several years. The food is not as cutting-edge or experimental as it used to be. However, you can rely on tasty pizzas, as well as mains including *carne del giorno* and *pesce di mercato* (meat and fish of the day) and dishes like duck breast with wild garlic, tarragon and vegetable mash or tagliatelle with southern meat ragu.

RANSOME'S DOCK
Map pp436-7 *Modern European*
☎ 7223 1611; 35-7 Parkgate Rd SW11; mains £10-20; ☺ lunch & dinner, closed Sun; tube Sloane Square, then bus 19, 49, 239, 319 or 345

Diners flock here not because it's on a narrow inlet of the Thames but for the superbly prepared Modern British food: smoked Norfolk eel with buckwheat pancakes and crème fraîche, noisettes of English lamb, and calf's liver with Italian bacon and field mushrooms.

CLAPHAM

The area around Clapham in particular has its own little happening restaurant scene.

BOMBAY BICYCLE CLUB Map p414 *Indian*
☎ 8673 6217; 95 Nightingale Lane SW12; mains £6.50-12; ☺ dinner, closed Sun; tube Clapham South

A million miles from the flock wallpaper and mock sitar music of the typical cheap Indian nosh house, this long-standing local favourite has tall vases of flowers and palm trees that allow it to call itself 100% nonauthentic Indian. Whatever, the spicy chicken *murgh mangalore* and milder *pasanda khybari*, lamb in a sweet creamy sauce, taste pretty good.

THE DRAWING ROOM
Map p414 *Modern International*
☎ 7350 2564; 103 Lavender Hill SW11; mains £10-14; ☺ lunch Sat & Sun, dinner Tue-Sun; rail Clapham Junction

This quirky little restaurant is one whose looks entice you in. It's not a bad choice if you're passing, either, because its curio-shop appearance – full of tapestries, clocks, candelabras and other bric-a-brac (it was formerly an antique store) – is matched by decent everyday food. This runs the gamut from goat's cheese in filo to chicken and spinach gnocchi, but you can also simply have a coffee in the adjacent, aptly named Sofa Bar.

ECO Map pp416-7 *Italian*
☎ 7978 1108; 162 Clapham High St SW4; mains £5.50-10.50; tube Clapham Common

Eco made a name for itself with some of the best pizza south of the river, but there are always mutterings about its attitude and its trendy, but self-conscious, design – all blonde wood and sculpted iron. Strangely, the more complicated pizzas, including spicy chicken and fiorentina, seem to be better than the simpler margheritas and marinaras. Antipasto, pasta, calzone and salads are also up for grabs.

THYME Map pp416-7 *French*
☎ 7627 2468; 14 Clapham Park Rd SW4; ☺ dinner; mains £6-10, set dinner £30, with wine £55; tube Clapham Common

As at Clerkenwell's Club Gascon, dishes are starter size only, and served tapas style. So, although the prices look low, this is a mid-range place if you're in any way hungry. It's worth the outlay, though, because the tastes at this multi-award-winning gem are innovative, subtle and divine. Listen to some smitten critics: 'Sweet Jesus but it's good.' (Jay Rayner in the *Observer*) 'I think I'm in love.' (Terry Durack in the *Independent on Sunday*). Book ahead.

TSUNAMI Map pp416-7   *Japanese*
☎ 7978 1610; 5-7 Voltaire Rd SW4; ⏰ dinner
Mon-Sat; mains £8-17, 5-course set dinner £35; tube Clapham North
The food at this accolade-laden restaurant exhibits the style and taste you'd expect from an ex-Nobu chef, with exquisite sushi, sashimi and tempura from Singi Nakamura. But it's the more unusual dishes, like *ebi* prawns wrapped in Greek pastry and butternut squash, green-tea ice cream and especially the mint-tea duck with pear and sweet honey miso that will really bowl you, whirlwind-like, off your feet. Stepping from a fairly drab, rail-side street into a minimalist interior of white walls and wooden benches, you wonder if this is how Alice in Wonderland felt going through the looking glass.

KENNINGTON, OVAL & STOCKWELL

CAFÉ PORTUGAL Map p415   *Portuguese*
☎ 7587 1962; 5a-6a Victoria House, South Lambeth Rd SW8; ⏰ breakfast, lunch & dinner; mains £6.50-13; tube Vauxhall/Stockwell
One of the classiest options in Little Portugal (ie the Stockwell neighbourhood), Café Portugal serves Lusitanian favourites such as *porco à Alentejana*, a tasty casserole of pork and clams, and *arroz de marisco* (seafood rice), with the occasional nod to big brother Spain.

CHEAP EATS

ASMARA Map p439   *Eritrean*
☎ 7737 4144; 386 Coldharbour Lane SW9; ⏰ dinner; mains £4-7.50; tube Brixton
Asmara is one of the more unusual offerings among Brixton's culinary melting pot, with its

focus on spicy meat and vegetable Eritrean dishes – which are eaten by using a piece of sourdough pancake, *injera*, to scoop up your meal. There is also a nod to the former colonial power, Italy, with a smattering of pasta, on top of basic desserts and wonderful coffee. Staff cut a dash moving through the stripped pine room in their traditional costumes.

BAMBOULA Map p439   *Caribbean*
☎ 7274 8600; 12 Acre Lane SW9; mains £6-8.50; tube Brixton
Bamboula is a highly rated Caribbean takeaway and restaurant that is cheap and usually very cheerful. Even some of the menu listings raise a little smile: Satisfaction (quarter of a jerk chicken, rice & peas, plantain and a soft drink); Hungry Man (the same with half a jerk chicken) and 'rundown' vegetables and chicken. Inside this green-walled grotto you'll also find oxtail and curried goat, while great ackee and saltfish, and bread pudding laced with rum do the trick, too. From 5pm to 8pm, Monday to Thursday Bamboula has a special £10 deal for any starter, main course and soft drink.

GOURMET BURGER KITCHEN
Map p414   *International*
☎ 7228 3309; 44 Northcote Rd SW11; burgers £5-7; rail Clapham Junction
It's tricky saying somewhere is the best of its kind in a huge city moving at London's breakneck speed, but if you find better burgers than here let us know. Big, plump sesame buns, imaginative fillings, vibrantly coloured salad...well, you know you ain't at McDonald's here.

PEPPER TREE Map pp416-7   *Thai*
☎ 7622 1758; 19 Clapham Common South Side SW4; mains £4-5; tube Clapham Common
This noodle-bar style canteen, with communal benches, is great for a functional fill-up. The adequate Thai food includes curries listed according to colour (red, yellow, green) and variety (beef, chicken, vegetable etc).

UP RIVER

In keeping with its very high standard of living, restaurants in this part of London tend to be aimed at the wealthy and are usually exquisitely presented, featuring superlative food and wine lists with price tags to match. Don't miss out on the full French experience at La Trompette or Glasshouse. Don Fernando's in Richmond serves up wonderfully fresh and tasty tapas.

CHISWICK

DUMELA
South African

☎ 8742 3149; 42 Devonshire Rd W4; mains £10-24; ☽ dinner Mon-Sat; tube Turnham Green

Bravely situated just down the road from the superb La Trompette in Chiswick is the less remarkable, but nevertheless still popular Dumela, which was formerly known as the Springbok Grill. This South African place allows you to try most animals barbecued while washing them down with a South African wine from its large list.

LA TROMPETTE
French

☎ 8747 1836; 5-7 Devonshire Rd W4; 3-course set lunch/dinner £19.50/£30; tube Turnham Green

This upscale French restaurant stands out as one of the few places to visit Chiswick for, on a side street off the disappointing Chiswick High Rd. Its sleek interior and terrace attract both locals and visitors again and again with its stunning menu of traditional French cuisine with imaginative trimmings, as well as the impressive wine list. It won *Time Out*'s best local restaurant award in 2002 and is a culinary landmark of West London. Bookings advisable.

RICHMOND

CANYON Map p439
American

☎ 8948 2944; The Tow Path, Richmond; mains £10-16; ☽ lunch & dinner, closed lunch Sun; tube/rail Richmond

Canyon's superb location on the Thames is just one reason to visit – the food is excellent without being showy and the staff are friendly. The theme is Arizona, with the garden crafted to look like the American West (as much as the Thames embankment can). Our only complaint is that the waiter refused to bring our wine before the food was served, which seemed rather odd, but not enough to deter us from recommending Canyon heartily – the American menu borrows enough from modern European cuisine to make it pleasingly inventive while familiar.

CHEZ LINDSAY Map p439
French

☎ 8948 7473; 11 Hill Rise, Richmond; 2/3-course set lunch/dinner £6/15; tube/rail Richmond

The location of this excellent Breton hideaway is the key to its success – just off the tow path where Londoners often come to walk and relax on a good day, although the food here is of a standard that will draw visitors in any weather. The seafood is a particular strength of the house, and the variety of crepes for dessert is sumptuous.

DON FERNANDO'S Map p439
Spanish

☎ 8948 6447; 27f The Quadrant, Richmond; tapas £3-6, mains £8-10; ☽ lunch & dinner, closed Mon & Tue lunch; tube/rail Richmond

Richmond station seems an unlikely place for one of the best tapas bars in London, but the Izquierdo family have been serving superb cuisine from their native Andalucia for 13 years now, and things are still looking very good. With a good house red and an exhaustive list of Spanish specialities, this makes a great place for a good lunch or a slow supper. The sardines and king prawns are marvellous and the staff very friendly.

KOZACHOK Map p439
Russian

☎ 8948 2366; 10 Red Lion St; mains £9-12; ☽ dinner Tue-Sat; tube/rail Richmond

Despite being a well-known Richmond establishment, visits to this Russian restaurant can be hit and miss, with quality varying from one day to the next. However, the interior is charmingly kitsch, the food authentic and the Slavic matriarch very welcoming. One of the few places in London to serve *tri medvedi* beer, as well as a great range of vodkas.

KEW

GLASSHOUSE
Modern European

☎ 8940 6777; 14 Station Pd W9; 3-course set lunch/dinner £17.50/30; ☽ lunch & dinner, closed Sun lunch; tube Kew Gardens

Thankfully, not many people seem to know about this unique restaurant next to Kew Gardens tube station. It may look rather pompous and expensive from the outside, but the reality couldn't be more different. Like its sister establishment, Chiswick's La Trompette, the Glasshouse gives you a set menu, with a choice of nine dishes for each course. The simple, elegant cuisine combines traditional English mainstays with modern European innovation and the bright, airy interior and perfect acoustics all seem like footnotes to a great meal.

NEWENS MAIDS OF HONOUR
Traditional English

☎ 8940 2752; 288 Kew Rd W9; set tea £5; ☽ 9.30am-6pm Tue-Sun; tube Kew Gardens

The name of this quirky Kew tearoom comes from its famed dessert, supposedly created by

Anne Boleyn, Henry VIII's ill-fated second wife. It is made of puff pastry, lemon, almonds and curd cheese, and anyone visiting should try it. The incongruous establishment looks far more like it belongs in a Cotswolds Village, but is in fact just a short distance from the main entrance to Kew Gardens at Victoria Gate.

TWICKENHAM

BRULA   *Modern European*
☎ 8892 0602; 43 Crown Rd, Middlesex; mains £10-15; lunch & dinner, closed dinner Sun; rail St Margaret's

This attractive and upmarket restaurant near Marble Hill House seems to get it just right. The service and elegant decor complement the fantastically fresh and clever menu of modern French cooking and the stained-glass windows give the place a unique feel that keeps the locals coming in droves.

McCLEMENTS   *Modern European*
☎ 8744 9610; 2 Whitton Rd, Middlesex; set 3-course lunch/dinner £19/29; lunch & dinner, closed dinner Sun; rail Twickenham/Whitton

This elaborate restaurant is one for an occasion, serving a heady mix of traditionally prepared European dishes, from elegant fresh crab to

Top Five – Up River

- Brula (left)
- Canyon (p261)
- Don Fernando's (p261)
- Glasshouse (p261)
- La Trompette (p261)

suckling pig. The two menus, *traditionnel* and gourmand, allow you the choice between four and eight courses – and four is quite enough for anyone. Enjoy the Art Nouveau exterior, good service and the equally laudable food.

CHEAP EATS

TURNHAM GREEN THAI   *Thai*
☎ 8994 3839; 57 Turnham Green Tce W4; mains £5; dinner Tue-Sat; tube Turnham Green

This bring-your-own-bottle place functions as an ordinary greasy-spoon-type joint, serving Thai food in the evenings and belying its rather shabby decor to surprise with excellent and good value cooking. The friendly staff make you feel right at home, and with only 20 places, it's easy to believe you are. No cards – cash only.

Drinking

Drinking

The pub is the heart of London's social existence; it's the great leveller where status and rank are made redundant, where generation gaps are bridged, inhibitions lowered and tongues loosened. Virtually every Londoner has a 'local' and some go by the quality of the nearest pubs when deciding on whereabouts in this massive city to pitch themselves. Sampling a range of boozers is, for our money, one of the highlights of any visit to this great city. From ancient and atmospheric taverns to slick DJ bars, London has much to offer the discerning tippler, no matter how hard the themed and chain bars try to take over.

Cubana, Waterloo (p240)

Britain – along with Ireland – is the very cradle of pub culture and you'll find some of the world's greatest drinking dens here, carrying on their business the way they have for centuries. Their histories are often writ all over their walls and etched in the occasionally bloated and bloodshot faces of the regulars who prop up their bars.

Just like just about every other facet of London life, the drinking culture has been undergoing something of a transformation in recent decades and these days there's a huge choice of sensational venues, whether you're swilling beers, sipping cocktails or quaffing wine. DJ bars, in particular, have been springing up all over the shop, and many are now destinations in their own right (as opposed to pre-club warm-ups).

But while *every* change in the restaurant scene has been an improvement, the dictates of fashion have not been universally kind to the drinking culture. Some atmospheric and traditional old boozers have sadly been converted into alcoholic theme parks, cocktail lounges, bland gastropubs and whatever else has been the flavour of recent days. Then there are the myriad chain pubs that have taken over high streets all over the city. These are, quite clearly, the deeds of the devil. Learn to walk past establishments that look vaguely like pubs and feature the words 'slug', 'lettuce', 'all', 'bar', 'one', 'firkin', 'parrot', 'O'Neills', 'Hog's' and 'Head' in their names, and your holiday will be immeasurably improved.

We reckon it's the traditional pubs that make drinking in London so special, although throughout these pages we've tried to provide an even spread of the timeless and the hip. We've provided info on many of *our* favourite drinking dens here although there's no substitute for individual research – your liver's the only limit.

Opening Hours

Of course you'll be familiar with England's arcane drinking laws, which mean that most pubs – those without special licences – close at 11pm Monday to Saturday and at 10.30pm Sunday. These restrictive supping times were introduced during WWI to get workers out of the pubs and back into the munitions factories, and it's ludicrous that they are still in force. Just before closing time in pubs throughout London (and the country) there's a mad rush as customers stockpile the drinks, only to be ushered out onto the street with an incessant 'time ladies and gentlemen please!' a few minutes later. It can also get a bit lively/aggro just after closing time in pubs where young crowds predominate and, Mr Blair, is it any bloody wonder? There's been talk – and very little else – about relaxing the licensing hours for the last few years but still this modern capital is expected to go night-nights at 11pm.

In this chapter, we've noted the pubs that have later licensing hours. In central areas it's always possible to kick on after closing time, but having to shift locations or work out a plan can often spoil the mood, so you might prefer to set yourselves up in a late drinking venue in the first place.

THE WEST END

In the words of one incredulous local, 'only tourists and nutters go out drinking in the West End on the weekend'. A bit harsh perhaps, but certainly if you're going out around Soho, Covent Garden or Leicester Square on a Friday or Saturday night you'd better be pumped and ready for lots of company. Also, have a plan B for getting home because getting a cab is a nightmare. Things are much more gratifying around the fringes in Bloomsbury, Fitzrovia and Holborn.

SOHO

AKA Map p430
☎ 7836 0110; 18 West Central St W1; ◔ until 3am Tue-Fri, 7am Sat, 4am Sun; tube Holborn
In one of the West End's deadest parts, you'll find one of its liveliest DJ bars, which, despite its six years, is still managing to cling to its cred by filling its cavernous interior with a chunky sound system and a young, good-looking clientele propelled by precision-made cocktails.

ALPHABET Map p428
☎ 7439 2190; 61-63 Beak St W1; tube Oxford Circus
Besides the bunch of advertising nobs who seem to be a permanent feature at the bar here, this is a groovy Soho solution with two rooms, leather sofas and a huge floor map of London that will help you plot your way home (although not on the weekend when you'll barely see it for fashionable shoes).

COACH & HORSES Map p428
☎ 7437 5920; 29 Greek St W1; tube Leicester Square
Famous as the place where *Spectator* columnist Jeffrey Bernard drank himself to death, this small, busy and thankfully unreconstructed boozer retains an old Soho bohemian atmosphere with a regular clientele of soaks, writers, hacks, tourists and those too pissed to lift their heads off the counter. Pretension will be prosecuted.

French House (see above)

FRENCH HOUSE Map p428
☎ 7437 2799; 49 Dean St W1; tube Leicester Square
This decadent and charming bar (it doesn't serve pints so doesn't deserve the moniker of pub) was the meeting place of the Free French Forces during WWII and De Gaulle is said to have drunk here often. More importantly, renowned drinkers such as Dylan Thomas, Brendan Behan and Peter O'Toole frequently ended up on its wood floors. There's red wine and a regular clientele of curiosities.

INTREPID FOX Map p428
☎ 7494 0827; 99 Wardour St W1; tube Leicester Square/Piccadilly Circus
So not Soho, this loud and arrestingly unaffected rock 'n' Goth pub will be recognisable from the demented gargoyle above the door, the fake spiders and bats along the walls and the motley human assembly of Goths, punks and metalheads with indoor complexions and impressive cleavages. The music is loud, the toilets grubby, beer inexpensive and bullshit is barred.

SHAMPERS Map p428
☎ 7437 1692; 4 Kingly St W1; tube Oxford Circus/Piccadilly Circus
It's standing room only in this traditional wine bar at the back of a more contemporary dining room, and it's packed most nights with punters jostling between dark green walls lined with bottles and sampling the terrific and educational changing wine menu.

TWO FLOORS Map p428
☎ 7439 1007; 3 Kingly St W1; tube Oxford Circus/Piccadilly Circus
Unrecognisable from the outside – as cool bars need to be – Two Floors attracts an unfailingly cool mix of bohemian and trendy types, and always seems to be playing the music that you've just got into. The bar staff are friendly and sassy, the decor loungey and scruffy, and drinks restricted to bottled beers and cocktails.

Drinking – The West End

ZEBRANO Map p428

☎ 7287 5267; 14-16 Ganton St W1; tube Oxford Circus

What's black and white and red all over? A newspaper. And the basement of this sexy bar, which has red-tinged zebra prints as a backdrop for some very handsome, sharply dressed men with smooth gazes. It's about drinking cocktails and being coquettish, although the ground-level café lets you look out onto the street if you'd rather play hard to get.

COVENT GARDEN & LEICESTER SQUARE

CORK & BOTTLE WINE BAR Map p430

☎ 7734 7807; 44-46 Cranbourn St WC2; tube Leicester Square

Londoners have taken to wine in a big way over recent years, although most of them don't know much about it, which is why Kiwi Chairman Don does so well with this downstairs stone-floor cellar where you can sip or swig from hundreds of his personal favourites and nibble on a buffet of cheeses and cured meats amid bustling conviviality.

FREEDOM BREWING CO Map p430

☎ 7240 0606; 41 Earlham St WC2; tube Covent Garden

Even though it was recently refitted and the beer is brewed elsewhere these days, the attractions of London's most popular microbrewery haven't changed; tasty beers (particularly the pale ales), a cosy semi-chic interior, considerate lighting and staff who, oddly for a London bar, seem intent on serving customers the best way they can.

FREUD Map p430

☎ 7240 9933; 198 Shaftesbury Ave WC2; tube Covent Garden

Make this the first stop on your crawl because there's no way you'll make it down the stairs (not much more than a ladder) after a few bevvies. It's a small basement bar/café/gallery with the sort of beige walls that could look just plain dirty but there are purposefully arty pictures to head off scrutiny. The decor and punters are suitably scruffy and arty, and the cocktails are fat and fancy while beer is only by the bottle.

LAMB & FLAG Map p430

☎ 7497 9504; 33 Rose St WC2; tube Covent Garden

This historic pub is everyone's Covent Garden 'find' so it's always ridiculously packed. It was

built in the 17th century, when it was called 'the Bucket of Blood', and was also the scene where the poet John Dryden was attacked for penning some less than complimentary words about Charles II's mistress.

PUNCH & JUDY Map p430

☎ 7379 0923; 40 The Market WC2; tube Covent Garden

Inside Covent Garden's central market hall itself, this two-level pub is another very busy option, but it has a balcony that lets you look down on St Paul's Church and the buskers.

SHERLOCK HOLMES Map p430

☎ 7930 2644; 10 Northumberland St WC2; tube Charing Cross

This is where Sir Arthur Conan Doyle is said to have written many of his most famous stories (and there's a glassed-off museum of Holmes memorabilia upstairs). It's a classic English pub until the coachloads of middle-aged tourists trundle through the door.

HOLBORN & THE STRAND

LAMB Map pp426-7

☎ 7405 0713; 94 Lamb's Conduit St WC1; tube Russell Square

There are two great pubs on this oddly monikered strip; the venerable and atmospheric Lamb has a central mahogany bar with etched-glass 'snob screens' and terrific tucker while the younger, groovy Perseverance has rather fetching – and ironic – ivory-and-ruby flocked wallpaper; very little chance of getting a seat and equally good food upstairs.

PRINCESS LOUISE Map p430

☎ 7405 8816; 208 High Holborn WC1; tube Holborn

Indulge us for a moment. W-O-W! We might have used the word gem before but we take all of the other instances back. This late-19th-century Victorian boozer is spectacularly decorated with a riot of fine tiles, etched mirrors, plasterwork and a stunning central horseshoe bar. There are invariably more bums than seats until the after-workers split.

BLOOMSBURY & FITZROVIA

BRADLEY'S SPANISH BAR Map p428

☎ 7636 0359; 42-44 Hanway St W1; tube Tottenham Court Road

Low ceilings, cramped quarters, vaguely Spanish decor, a vintage vinyl jukebox and a convivial atmosphere are the features of this charming hostelry, which is one of the most ordinary boozers in the West End and therefore among the best. Although it's tucked away behind Oxford St, enough punters know about it and they regularly spill out onto the street. Treat yourself to the Cruzcampo.

MUSEUM TAVERN Map p430
☎ 7242 8987; 49 Great Russell St WC1; tube Tottenham Court Road
This is where Karl Marx used to retire for a sup after a hard day in the British Museum Reading Room. It's an atmospheric traditional pub and if it was good enough for him...

QUEEN'S LARDER Map pp426-7
☎ 7837 5627; 1 Queen Sq WC1; tube Russell Square
In a lovely square southeast of Russell Square, this pub is so-called because Queen Charlotte, wife of 'Mad King' George III, rented part of the pub's cellar to store special foods for him while he was getting treatment nearby. There are benches outside for fair weather fans and a good dining room upstairs.

EAST CENTRAL

If super club Fabric (p297) has helped make Clerkenwell one of London's hottest nightspots, then – on weekends at least – we prefer slightly older-hat Hoxton, where there's less of a tendency for surrounding bars to charge an entry fee on the slightest pretext (ie one of the owner's mates spinning a few discs in the corner). Whichever way you look at it, this eastern district is still the capital's most happening nightlife hub. (Apart from the City, of course, where even the trendier bars pretty well work a Monday to Friday roster.)

THE CITY

JAMAICA WINE HOUSE Map pp432-3
☎ 7626 9496; 12 St Michael's Alley EC3; ☾ closed Sat & Sun; tube Bank
Not a wine bar at all but a historic Victorian pub, the 'Jam Pot' stands on the site of what was the first coffee house in London (1652), and consequently is more a place to enjoy beer rather than wine.

NYLON Map pp432-3
☎ 7600 7771; 1 Addle St EC2; ☾ closed Sun; tube Moorgate
This humungous bar brings a bit of Shoreditch interior design to the City, with its overwhelming orange retro decor, plus dark-wood panelling, fish tanks and a huge chandelier. Behind the Mayfair-style VIP entrance, the crowds are still fairly typical City crowds, though.

VERTIGO 42 Map pp432-3
☎ 7877 7842; 25 Old Broad St EC2; ☾ closed Sat & Sun; tube Bank
The stratospheric views from this 42nd-storey bar (the UK's highest) are matched by the stratospheric prices, and for security reasons you *must* book well in advance. Seats are arranged around the glass-walled circular space, where you quaff champagne while taking in an unforgettable view.

YE OLDE CHESHIRE CHEESE Map pp426-7
☎ 7353 6170; Wine Office Court, 145 Fleet St EC4; tube Blackfriars
The entrance to this historic pub is via a picturesque alley. Cross the threshold and you'll find yourself in a wood-panelled interior (the oldest bit dates from the mid-17th century) with sawdust on the floor and divided up into various bars and eating areas.

The Cocktail Revolution

Dispel thoughts of flaming Molotovs being hurled through the windows of ghastly chain pubs because we're talking about the fervour with which London has taken to martinis, Manhattans and *mojitos*. Long gone are the days when drinkers, particularly women, might pause at the bar before grudgingly ordering a limp G&T because there were no more appealing options. And in are the days when new bars promote their specialist cocktail staff, the media get into a excited tizz about new concoctions, punters are savvy enough to know their Smirnoff from a Belvedere (one of them is a luxurious and little-known vodka, the other is not) and nobody seems to mind paying £10 for a fancy-sounding drink served in a martini glass topped with a gooseberry. While many Londoners traditionally have a reputation for drinking whatever will quench a thirst rather than tastes good, the new breed of cosmopolitan city-slicker is a connoisseur indeed.

HOXTON, SHOREDITCH & SPITALFIELDS

BAR KICK Map pp420-1

☎ 7739 8700; 127 Shoreditch High St E1; tube Old Street

A much larger sister venue to Clerkenwell's Café Kick (p269), this place has a slightly edgier Shoreditch vibe. This time, too, there's some floor space left over after they installed four footie tables, leather sofas and simple tables and chairs. Meals are served.

BLUU Map pp420-1

☎ 7613 2793; 1 Hoxton Sq N1; tube Old Street

When you first walk in, Bluu might feel cold and unwelcoming; that's the effect of all that exposed concrete. Sink into one of the comfy seats and knock back a few cocktails, though, and you see why locals regard it fondly as a comfy old favourite.

BRICKLAYERS ARMS Map pp420-1

☎ 7739 5245; 63 Charlotte Rd EC2; tube Old Street

A determinedly down-to-earth stalwart of the Hoxton scene, the Bricklayers Arms attracts an unpretentious but cool-looking, generally mid-to-late 20s crowd. This essentially old-style pub is often seen as a solid place to start the evening, before heading off elsewhere

Vibe Bar (opposite)

CANTALOUPE Map pp420-1

☎ 7613 4411; 35-43 Charlotte Rd EC2; tube Old Street/Liverpool Street

One of the first of the new generation of Hoxton bars and *the* bar that focused the media's eyes on it in the late 1990s, the Cantaloupe was a bit hectic during the dotcom boom. Now you're no longer likely to rub shoulders with cast members from seminal 20-something drama *This Life* here, it's just a pleasant and not unfashionable gastropub.

CARGO Map pp420-1

☎ 7729 6818; 83 Rivington St EC2; tube Old Street/Liverpool Street

Housed beneath three railway arches, the excellent Cargo advertises itself as a combined MDF (music, drinks, food) experience. During the week, you can park yourself on its dishevelled sofa benches to enjoy a quiet drink – or else head to the courtyard with its hammock – but on weekends the club room takes precedence.

CHARLIE WRIGHT'S INTERNATIONAL BAR Map pp420-1

☎ 7490 8345; 45 Pitfield St N1; tube Old Street

The clientele is the main draw at Ghanaian powerlifter Charlie Wright's bar – a true local institution. They're a mixed cast of characters, but all up for a good time.

DRAGON BAR Map pp420-1

☎ 7490 7110; 5 Leonard St N1; tube Old Street

Dragon's super-cool, in that louche, moody (as opposed to overtly posey) Hoxton way. It's easy to miss it, as the name is only embossed on the entrance stairs, but once inside it's all exposed brick, Chinese lanterns, velvet curtains and, a suitably ironic touch here, one of those illuminated waterfall pictures you buy on Brick Lane. A place where you feel comfortable in the latest street style, but definitely not in a suit.

DREAMBAGSJAGUARSHOES Map pp420-1

☎ 7739 9550; 34-36 Kingsland Rd E2; tube Old Street

Despite the unusual moniker this is a typical example of Shoreditch shabby-chic; wooden floors, exposed brick/concrete walls, leather and canvas sofas rescued from somewhere like a skip, with lads wearing that mussed-up 'just got out of bed' hair look and sleeker-looking gals. Check out the graffiti wall downstairs.

FOUNDRY Map pp420-1

☎ 7739 6900; 84-86 Great Eastern St EC2; tube Old Street

The eccentric Foundry so genuinely doesn't give a hoot about being hip that it manages to be impossibly hip and welcoming to all simultaneously. The ramshackle furniture, makeshift bar and piano renditions of, oh, say, vintage David Bowie, are reminiscent of an illegal squat bar somewhere in Eastern Europe. Brilliant.

GRAND CENTRAL Map pp420-1

☎ 7613 4228; 91-93 Great Eastern St EC2; tube Old Street

The 'grand' in the name applies to the back bar wall towering some 6.5m above you and the streaks of white, red, green, yellow and brown light running along the front of the bar, rather than overall size, as this elegant place is rather small. It's central all right, though. Right on the corner of Great Eastern St, it attracts a slightly upmarket mix of suits and trendies.

HOME Map pp420-1

☎ 7684 8618; 100-106 Leonard St EC2; tube Old Street/Liverpool Street

Another early arrival on the scene, this downstairs bar and restaurant is not quite as shabby as it once was. In fact, the lounge chairs are now comfy and new, and if you can grab one (not always possible), they're a great place to sit back, enjoy a beer or cocktail and observe the Hoxton scene in full swing.

LOUNGELOVER Map pp420-1

☎ 7012 1234; 1 Whitby St E1; rail/tube Liverpool St

Evincing the same sparkly, 'junk shop re-arranged by a gay stylist' look of its sister establishment Les Trois Garçons, trendy Loungelover is totally over the top and addictive. It's like stepping into another world, where chandeliers, antiques, street lanterns and comfy lounge chairs material-ise just seconds away from the run-down streets outside. Coming here once is never enough, even though the drink prices are pretty high.

MEDICINE BAR Map pp420-1

☎ 7739 7110; 89 Great Eastern St EC2; tube Old Street

This larger offshoot of the Islington bar (p271) has been welcomed in Hoxton. Its upstairs room is pleasant enough and it attracts a cool

crowd, but it's the downstairs DJ bar that's the main draw. Those to have played here include Norman Cook (Fatboy Slim), Norman Jay, Jon Carter (Radio 1 DJ Sara Cox's main squeeze), Sancho Panza and Ashley Beedle. There's a cover charge of £6 after 9pm on Fridays and Saturdays.

SHOREDITCH ELECTRICITY SHOWROOMS Map pp420-1

☎ 7739 6934; 39a Hoxton Sq N1; tube Old Street

Now that the queues to get in of a weekend aren't so ridiculous, the Showrooms have backed off on some of their posey attitude. The ever-changing mural behind the bar, de-picting everything from elephants to the Alps, still provides a focal point.

SOSHO Map pp420-1

☎ 7920 0701; 2 Tabernacle St EC2; tube Old Street/Moorgate

The best of the Match bar chains, this glam former photographic studio in South Shoreditch (hence Sosho) serves brilliant cock-tails to a very hip crowd. Downstairs DJs spin the disks, with a tendency towards jazzy house. Saturday's cover charge is £3.

VIBE BAR Map pp432-3

☎ 7377 2899; The Truman Brewery, 91-95 Brick Lane E1; tube Old Street/ Aldgate East

An epicentre of the Hoxton scene, the Vibe is part bar, part club. On quieter nights, drinkers can still enjoy themselves in the spacious bar, which has scuffed leather sofas, arcade games and computer terminals, even. The courtyard is just perfect for a sunny afternoon.

CLERKENWELL

CAFÉ KICK Map pp420-1

☎ 7837 8077; 43 Exmouth Market EC1; tube Farringdon

It's fairly bare-boards Spartan really, but hardly anyone at this buzzing, tiny continental-style bar notices, because most attention is focused on the three 'baby foot' tables and the Nastro Perroni and other good bottled beers. When major football matches are on, you can watch them on TV.

CHARTERHOUSE 38 Map pp426-7

☎ 7608 0858; 38 Charterhouse St EC1; tube Farringdon

Charterhouse 38 is a tiny but convivial wedge-shaped bar and you usually find yourself bumping into someone to get to the bar.

Entrance is always free, but the music can get a little loud in here on weekends, when you'll find yourself shouting 'What?' repeatedly.

DUST Map pp426-7
☎ 7490 0537; 27 Clerkenwell Rd EC1; tube Farringdon
Because it's not quite as popular as it used to be, there's more often room to breathe here. The decor is a typically urban mix of brick walls and comfy sofas, with a few mosaic-top tables and pieces of art. There's a door tax (£4 to £5) on weekends, when DJs spin the disks.

FLUID Map pp426-7
☎ 7253 3444; 27 Charterhouse St EC1; tube Farringdon
Behind its vibrant neon sign, this Japanese-themed bar oozes laid-back, unpretentious cool. In the dim light, punters sit sipping raspberry-flavoured Tokyo martinis, losing the freestyle sushi off their chopsticks or necking Asahi beer, while others play the '70s video arcade games or investigate the mothballed beer-dispensing machine. Downstairs there's a DJ space with a Tokyo photomontage on the wall. On Saturdays, there's a cover charge (£5).

JERUSALEM TAVERN Map pp426-7
☎ 7490 4281; 55 Britton St EC1; tube Farringdon
It's hard to know what to rave about most at the small Jerusalem Tavern – the 18th-century decor where plaster walls are adorned with occasional tile mosaics, or the range of drinks, which includes organic bitters, cream stouts, wheat and, mmm, fruit beers.

SMITHS OF SMITHFIELD Map pp426-7
☎ 7236 6666; 67-77 Charterhouse St EC1; tube Farringdon
You know the saying 'any port in a storm'? Well, on weekends this is it. During the week, the enormous downstairs at Smiths is a fairly pleasant, suity bar. But on Saturday it's one of the few places locally without a cover charge, and it fills up with bored-looking 20-somethings then. Fine for a beer; steer clear of the cocktails.

THREE KINGS OF CLERKENWELL
Map pp420-1
☎ 7253 0483; 7 Clerkenwell Close EC1; tube Farringdon
A friendly pub near Clerkenwell Green, the Three Kings is festooned with pâpiér-mache models, including a giant rhino head above the fireplace.

YE OLDE MITRE Map pp426-7
☎ 7405 4751; 1 Ely Ct, off Hatton Garden EC1; tube Chancery Lane/Farringdon
A delightfully cosy historic pub, tucked away in a backstreet, Ye Olde Mitre was built for the servants of Ely Palace. There's still a memento of Queen Elizabeth, in the shape of the stump of a cherry tree around which she once danced. There's no music, so the snug rooms only echo to the sound of amiable chit-chat.

ISLINGTON

ALBION Map pp420-1
☎ 7607 7450; 10 Thornhill Rd N1; tube Angel/Highbury & Islington
Renowned for its wisteria-covered beer garden out back, which makes it seem like a true country pub, the Albion's best suited for a drink on a sunny weekend afternoon. It's a magnet then for young families and children.

BAR FUSION Map pp420-1
☎ 7688 2882; 45 Essex Rd N1; tube Angel
Islington is a good place for gay bars, but many of them are either lesbian or gay. Bar Fusion can really be called mixed, although there's a separate women's section out back. Decor-wise it's nothing special, but it's friendly and there's plenty of seating outside.

ELBOW ROOM Map pp420-1
☎ 7278 3244; 89-91 Chapel Market N1; tube Angel
Don't be fooled by the row upon row of pool tables, this place is packed on the weekends with punters just as interested in the cocktails, beer, bar food and DJs. It's relaxed, unposey and reckoned by many men to be a top place to meet members of the opposite sex. Entrance on Saturday costs about £5.

EMBASSY Map pp420-1
☎ 7359 7882; 119 Essex Rd N1; tube Angel, bus 38, 56 or 73
Behind those black walls and smokey windows, cool muso and meejah types quaff beer in the comfy sofas or enjoy the DJs in the street level bar and more recent basement bar. The buzz about the street-cred Embassy has grown, so it's now one of Islington's premier venues; there's a cover charge (£3) on weekends. Get there early.

Drinking – East Central

KING'S HEAD Map pp420-1
☎ 7288 2666; 115 Upper St N1; tube Angel
Even if you're not coming to a theatre production, this rather Spartan-looking pub, with just one open space, is a nice spot to knock back a beer.

MEDICINE BAR Map pp420-1
☎ 7704 9536; 181 Upper St N1; tube Highbury & Islington
Still one of the coolest bars along Upper St, the Medicine Bar attracts thirty-something clubbers and drinkers, as well as a younger crowd. One reason you'd come to this converted dark-red pub, with low sofas and dim lighting, is its music, ranging from jazzy funk to hip-hop; another attraction is minor celebrity spotting – you might catch sight of your fave DJ, model or TV star (if you can see through the crowds, that is).

SOCIAL Map pp420-1
☎ 7837 7816; 418 Arlington Sq N1; tube Angel
Heavenly Records' second pub venture is a lot more relaxed than its Noho cousin, with a fairly local feel. While it's also a gastropub (p234), the largish horseshoe bar is quite rightly a destination in its own right.

SOUTH CENTRAL

Although a few slick new bars have opened up around here in recent years, the traditional pubs are so beautiful and atmospheric that they can't be toppled from our best-of list.

MAYFAIR & ST JAMES'S

CHE Map pp426-7
☎ 7747 9380; 23 St James's St W1; tube Green Park
Named after the happy-go-lucky Cuban guerrilla this chummy cigar bar below a plush, trendy restaurant has an enviable collection of vintage rums, tequilas and whiskies and a floor-to-ceiling humidor with more than 70 different cigar types and a spectacular list of cocktails.

GUINEA Map pp426-7
☎ 7409 1728; 30 Bruton Pl W1; tube Green Park
Top-quality (Young's) beers, famous autographs on the toilet walls and the whiff of money define this quiet and out-of-the-way pub in London's most exclusive neighbourhood of Mayfair. There are very few places to sit and it sometimes feels little more than a waiting room for the rear restaurant (renowned for its pies).

KNIGHTSBRIDGE, SOUTH KENSINGTON & HYDE PARK

CHURCHILL ARMS Map pp422-3
☎ 7727 4242; 119 Kensington Church St W8; tube Notting Hill Gate
This lovely traditional tavern is stuffed with Winston memorabilia and assorted bric-a-brac. Although it feels like a museum pub, it's hugely popular with locals as well as tourists, perhaps drawn by the excellent Thai restaurant upstairs and the calming conservatory out back.

COOPERS ARMS Map pp436-7
☎ 7376 3120; 87 Flood St SW3; tube Sloane Square/ South Kensington
This classic Chelsea pub just off King's Rd, decorated with stuffed critters and vintage railway advertising, has a bright and sunny bar, a mixed clientele and bonhomie by the barrel.

CUBA Map pp422-3
☎ 7938 4137; 11-13 Kensington High St W8; tube High Street Kensington
If you're really into traditional English pubs but have somehow strayed onto these pages, you might enjoy a romp through this Latin theme bar which positively fizzes with a combination of lethal rum-based cocktails, sexy samba dancers and leery Latino lads. Dress to sweat.

GRENADIER Map pp426-7
☎ 7235 3074; 18 Wilton Row SW1; tube Knightsbridge
Down a quiet and rather exclusive mews, this pub is pretty as a picture from the outside and welcoming within (despite the sabres and bayonets on the walls).

NAG'S HEAD Map pp426-7
☎ 7235 1135; 53 Kinnerton St SW1; tube Hyde Park Corner
In a serene mews not far from bustling Knightsbridge, this gorgeously genteel early-19th-century drinking den has eccentric decor, a sunken bar and no mobile phones. A dreamy delight; don't bother if you're not pure of pub heart.

STAR TAVERN Map pp422-3

☎ 7235 3019; 6 Belgrave Mews West SW1; tube Knightsbridge/Sloane Square

This cheery place is best known for West End glamour and East End skulduggery; it's where Christine Keeler and John Profumo rendezvoused for the scandalous Profumo Affair and where the Great Train Robbers are said to have planned their audacious crime. These days, it's just a lovely boozer with reliable Fuller's beers.

WINDOWS Map pp426-7

☎ 7493 8000; Hilton Hotel, 28th fl, Park Lane W1; tube Hyde Park Corner

If you make one observation in London, it should probably be from this 28th floor bar of the Hilton Hotel. The views of the city are breathtaking, particularly at dusk, and there are drinks from beer to cocktails and cognac to slake your thirst.

WINDSOR CASTLE Map pp422-3

☎ 7243 9551; 114 Campden Hill Rd W11; tube Notting Hill Gate

This memorable pub has oak partitions separating the original bars, with doors so tiny that big drinkers may have trouble getting past the front bar (but, sure isn't that always the case?). It also has one of the loveliest walled gardens (with heaters in winter) of any pub in London.

WESTMINSTER & WHITEHALL

RED LION Map pp426-7

☎ 7930 5826; 48 Parliament St SW1; tube Westminster

This is a classic turn-of-the-century pub with polished mahogany and etched glassware where the TV shows parliamentary broadcasts, muted, just in case it kicks off in the house and the MPs have to rush back.

ALONG THE SOUTH BANK

Most of the drinking establishments in this area are good, down-to-earth boozers, which just happen to have been here for hundreds of years. While the sleek punters at Baltic are trying to choose between the reams of different vodkas – and finding it more difficult after each shot – those in the historic pubs are generally raising a real ale. Cheers!

BANKSIDE

ANCHOR BANKSIDE Map pp432-3

☎ 7407 1577; 34 Park St SE1; tube London Bridge

Come rain or shine, this 18th-century pub is the business. If the weather's poor you can shelter in its warren of historic rooms, including one where Samuel Johnson (1709–84) wrote part of his famous dictionary. When it's sunny, the riverside terrace is justifiably popular.

BOROUGH & BANKSIDE

BALTIC Map pp426-7

☎ 7928 1111; 74 Blackfriars Rd SE1; tube Southwark

There are many vodka bars in London these days, but this is definitely one of the chicest-looking with 28 or 29 different varieties (many with indecipherable Cyrillic labels) all lined up above the glowing, silver futuristic bar. The clientele can get a bit messily drunk though, and the service a little heavy-handed – should the waiters decide to treat you (as they did us) as if you're constantly about to do a runner.

FAMOUS ANGEL Map pp432-3

☎ 7237 3608; 101 Bermondsey Wall East SE16; tube Bermondsey

Another great historic pub, this 17th-century venue is known for being where Captain Cook prepared for his trip to Australia.

Famous Angel, Bermondsey (left)

MARKET PORTER Map pp432-3
☎ 7407 2495; 9 Stoney St SE1; ⏲ 6.30-8.30am Mon-Fri; tube London Bridge

This pub opens early on weekdays, from for the traders at Borough's wholesale market. It's good during normal opening hours, too, for its convivial atmosphere, plus real ales and bitters.

GEORGE INN Map pp432-3
☎ 7407 2056; Talbot Yard, 77 Borough High St SE1; tube Borough/ London Bridge

It doesn't even fully explain the 'wow' factor of the George to say it's London's last surviving galleried coaching inn and a National Trust pub; you have to see its low-ceilinged, dark-panelled rooms for yourself. Dating from 1676, it's mentioned in Charles Dickens' *Little Dorrit*.

ROYAL OAK Map pp432-3
☎ 7357 7173; 44 Tabard St SE1; tube Borough

Restored to its full Victorian grandeur of etched glass and mahogany benches, the Royal Oak is among London's nicest historic pubs and sells good cask beer.

THE EAST END

DOVE FREEHOUSE & KITCHEN
☎ 7275 7617; 24 Broadway Market; rail London Fields, bus 106, 253, 26, 48 or 55

On a Sunday winter's evening, it's lovely to come here for a comforting roast. Okay, this rambling series of rooms is good at any time for its wide range of Belgian beer, but there's something about its dim back room, with its ethnic boho chic, that makes this pub a great place to hunker down against the chill.

DOWN RIVER

If you're looking for pubs straight out of Dickens, this area can oblige – and throw in some wonderful views, to boot.

DOCKLANDS

GRAPES Map p435
☎ 7987 4396; 76 Narrow St E14; DLR Westferry

One of Limehouse's renowned historic pubs – just follow the street signs from the DLR – the Grapes is cosy and snug. Actually, it's absolutely tiny, especially the riverside terrace, which can only really comfortably fit four to six people. However, it reeks olde worlde charm.

MAYFLOWER Map pp432-3
☎ 7237 4088; 117 Rotherhithe St SE16; tube Rotherhithe

This 15th-century pub is named after the ship that took the Pilgrims to America in 1620, because the ship set sail from Rotherhithe, and the captain supposedly charted out its course here while supping schooners. There's now a long jetty, from which you can view the river.

PROSPECT OF WHITBY Map pp432-3
☎ 7481 1095; 57 Wapping Wall E1; tube Wapping

Although undeniably touristy, the 16th-century Whitby is still a lovely atmospheric old pub, with dim lighting, flagstone floor and pewter bar. You need to be pretty lucky to grab one of the tables by the windows over looking the Thames, but there's a river terrace. One of London's oldest surviving drinking houses, the pub also features an upstairs restaurant and open fires in winter.

WHITE SWAN Map pp416-17
☎ 7780 9870; 556 Commercial Rd E14; DLR Limehouse

If you're interested in barrow boys (some real, most *faux*) with buzz cuts, check out the East End's friendliest, cruisiest gay pub/club (especially the night BJ's, 10pm to 3am Saturday).

GREENWICH

NORTH POLE Map p435
☎ 8853 3020; 131 Greenwich High Rd SE10; DLR/rail Greenwich

This funky Greenwich bar attracts a fairly trendy crowd. It's over two levels. Upstairs is all animal-print sofas and a warm red glow. Downstairs, at the South Pole, there's an aircraft theme. There's a mix of R'n'B and garage on the DJs' decks.

TRAFALGAR TAVERN Map p435
☎ 8858 2437; Park Row SE10; DLR Cutty Sark, rail Maize Hill

Charles Dickens once drank at this historic pub and mentions it in *Our Mutual Friend*. Prime ministers Gladstone and Disraeli used to dine on the celebrated whitebait. Today, it still has an historic feel, with dark-wood panelling and curved windows overlooking the Millennium Dome. However, the nearby University of Greenwich has brought in a large student clientele during term time. In summer, tourists take over.

NORTH CENTRAL

Marylebone and Camden Town – on their way up and down respectively – are the two busiest neighbourhoods for drinking options here, although there are a few celebrated 'locals' scattered elsewhere.

MARYLEBONE & REGENT'S PARK

DUSK Map pp426-7
☎ 7486 5746; 79 Marylebone High St W1; tube Baker Street

Everyone looks more attractive at dusk, and we're not just talking about that moment when demanding day slides into sensual night. This newish (well, recently made over) bar feels designer on both sides of the counter and has polished floorboards, boutique beers and choice cocktails.

MASH Map p428
☎ 7637 5555; 19-21 Great Portland St W1; ✆ until 2am Mon-Sat; tube Oxford Circus

With a microbrewery and café, Mash is an all-day and all-week affair although the main, huge and high-ceilinged bar requires a crowd to take off and is probably best kept for the weekend. It's a futuristic bar set in an old car showroom, and the mechanics make mean *mojitos*.

O'CONNOR DAN Map pp426-7
☎ 7935 9311; 88 Marylebone Lane W1; tube Bond Street

A great Irish pub free of bullshit and blarney, O'Connor Dan is big, dark and handsome with table service, scuffed wooden surfaces and bar and restaurant food that is several cuts above the pub norm.

EUSTON

HEAD OF STEAM Map pp418-19
☎ 7383 3359; 1 Eversholt St NW1; tube Euston

You probably won't head to Euston especially for a tipple – unless you're a thirsty train-spotter with a penchant for railway memorabilia – but if you are in the neighbourhood or waiting for a train, this is a convivial, blokeish place for an express tour through an extensive range of real ales.

CAMDEN

BARTOK Map pp418-19
☎ 7916 0595; 78-79 Chalk Farm Rd, Camden Town NW1; ✆ until 1am Mon-Thu, 2am Fri-Sat, midnight Sun; tube Chalk Farm/Camden Town

We love the fact that in Camden, the cradle of Britpop, you can head to this bar and savour a pint with a little classical concerto for audible company. Named after the Hungarian composer and pianist, Bartok has low comfy sofas, intimate lighting and huge drapes as the setting for some brilliant DJ sets blending jazz, classical and world music.

BAR VINYL Map pp418-19
☎ 7681 7898; 6 Inverness St NW1; tube Camden Town

Although deeply chilled and effortlessly cool, this archetypal DJ bar has a very welcoming vibe and propping up on a bar stool or plopping into comfy retro chairs here is a genuine treat midweek, accompanied by unfailingly groovy sounds. It's equally good at the weekend, just without the chance of a seat.

CROWN & GOOSE Map pp418-19
☎ 7485 8008; 100 Arlington Rd NW1; tube Camden Town

One of our favourite London pubs, this square room has a central wooden bar between British racing green walls studded with gilt-framed mirrors and illuminated by big shuttered windows. More importantly, it combines a good-looking crowd, easy conviviality, top tucker and good, inexpensive beer.

PEMBROKE CASTLE Map pp418-19
☎ 7483 2927; 150 Gloucester Ave NW1; tube Chalk Farm

This light, airy and welcoming place has stained-glass windows and an all-embracing, down-to-earth vibe in which you can feel comfy whether you're sipping wine or skolling beer. There's a big-screen TV upstairs, a good spot for watching football, or a few pavement tables outside if the sun is out.

QUEEN'S Map pp418-19
☎ 7586 0408; 49 Regent's Park Rd NW1; tube Camden Town

While the ghost of actress, royal 'friend' and former next door neighbour Lilly Langtree is said to reside in the cellar of this spirited joint, the pub proper is haunted by contemporary beauties like Jude Law and the other fashionistas of Primrose Hill. The food and drinks won't disappoint and there's plenty to look at among the clientele but if you hanker after something more, head across the road to the hill and splendid views of London.

WORLD'S END Map pp418-19
☎ 7482 1932; 174 Camden High St NW1; tube Camden Town

'Meetcha at the World's End, the one beside Camden tube station,' are the famous last words uttered by tourists every day before they find themselves (and nobody else) in this huge, boisterous and manically popular pub that claims to sell a million pints of beer a day. Hell knows what the decor looks like but it sure feels lively.

Drinking Strips

With some 4000 drinking dens throughout the city, you won't have to search far for something to slake your thirst. However, if you want to try a few different great pubs in the same session, you should head towards the likes of Upper St and Essex Rd in Islington, Westbourne Grove and Portobello Rd in Notting Hill. All of these are blessed with boozers.

THE NORTHERN HEIGHTS

Head to the hills if you want to savour pubs that haven't changed in centuries, incoherent celebrities and regular north Londoners at play.

HIGHGATE & HAMPSTEAD

BOOGALOO Map p415
☎ 8340 2928; 312 Archway Rd N6; tube Highgate

Unquestionably the oddest location we'll send you, Archway Rd is most definitely not somewhere that gets a lot of passing tourist trade. This old local was converted in recent years from a very cool local frequented by some of London's best musicians and comedians to a more self-consciously cool place, albeit with great music. The jukebox is regularly reprogrammed by celebrity musicians.

FLASK Map p415
☎ 8348 7346; 77 Highgate West Hill N6; tube Highgate

About the best pub in Highgate Village, the refurbished Flask is very popular but has lots of nooks and crannies for intimate tête-à-têtes. Don't fret if you mistakenly end up in the equally good pub of the same name on the other side of the heath in Hampstead village. If you're in Highgate on an evening and longing for a late lock-in, you could bring things to a head, down the hill a little on the left.

HOLLYBUSH Map p415
☎ 7435 2892; 22 Holly Mount (above Heath St, reached via Holly Bush Steps) NW3; tube Hampstead

A beautiful pub that makes you envy the privileged residents of Hampstead, Hollybush has an antique Victorian interior, a lovely secluded hilltop location, open fires in winter and a knack for making you stay longer than you had intended at any time of the year.

SPANIARD'S INN Map p415
☎ 8731 6571; Spaniards Rd NW3; tube Hampstead, then bus 21

This marvellous tavern dates from 1585 and has more character than a West End musical. Dick Turpin, the dandy highwayman (or was

that Adam Ant?) was born here and used it as a hangout, while more-savoury sorts like Dickens, Shelley, Keats and Byron also availed of its charms. There's a big, blissful garden and the food ain't half bad (English for good).

WRESTLERS Map p415
☎ 8340 4397; 98 North Rd N6; tube Highgate

Another great, great local where the ambience, beer, food and decor just combine to make you happy to be alive, although when the very friendly Irish governor gets chatting you can begin to have second thoughts.

STOKE NEWINGTON & FINSBURY PARK

AULD SHILLELAGH
☎ 7249 5951; 105 Stoke Newington Church St N16; bus 73

Light relief for heavy drinkers, the Auld Shillelagh is one of the best Irish pubs in London. Typically, it's many things to many people; a theatre and a cosy room, centre stage and a sanctuary, a debating chamber and a place for silent contemplation. What's more, the staff are sharp, the Guinness is good, and the live entertainment frequent and varied.

HARRINGAY ARMS
☎ 8340 4243; 153 Crouch Hill N8; tube Finsbury Park, then bus W7

As far as you can get from tourist London, this convivial, charismatic and vaguely Irish boozer provides a great opportunity to sample genuine London life and the life of a genuine London local. It's small but perfectly formed, and filled most nights with sociable dogs and local wags. Say hi to Jim, Sheila and Liz (and guarantee this author a few free pints when he's back in town).

NORTHWEST LONDON

Notting Hill has the greatest concentration of great pubs in London – we can't be much more unequivocal than that.

ST JOHN'S WOOD & MAIDA VALE

WARRINGTON HOTEL Map pp422-3
☎ 7266 3134; 93 Warrington Cres W9; tube Warwick Avenue

This former hotel and brothel is now an ornate Art Nouveau pub with heaps of character and an atmosphere that's so laid-back it's virtually horizontal. The huge saloon bar, dominated by a marble-topped hemispherical counter with a carved mahogany base, is a fabulous place to sample a range of real ales. There is outdoor seating for fair weather fans and good Thai restaurant upstairs.

WARWICK CASTLE Map pp422-3
☎ 7432 1331; 6 Warwick Pl W9; tube Warwick Avenue

The attraction of this place is that it doesn't try too hard and it's a lovely, low-key local on a quiet street near the canal. It's one of a dying breed of London pubs actually owned by a landlord rather than a brewery or corporation.

NOTTING HILL & WESTBOURNE GROVE

COW Map pp422-3
☎ 7221 5400; 89 Westbourne Park Rd W2; tube Westbourne Park/Royal Oak

Owned by Tom Conran, the son of renowned restaurateur Sir Terence, this superb pub was transformed from a dilapidated old side-street boozer into a unique and thrilling gastropub with outstanding food and a jovial pub-is-a-pub atmosphere. Seafood is a highlight (predictably, the fresh oysters with Guinness are a speciality, a pint of prawns and mayonnaise is a delight) and the staff are much friendlier than you'd expect from such a perpetually hip hangout.

ELBOW ROOM Map pp422-3
☎ 7221 5211; 103 Westbourne Grove W2; tube Notting Hill Gate/Bayswater

A casual pool hall mixed with a cocktail bar and club sounds like a pretty ambitious plan, but these guys managed to pull it off here at the original Elbow Room, where the decor is post-industrial, the atmosphere unhassled and the tables gone early.

LONDSDALE Map pp422-3
☎ 7228 1517; 44-48 Londsdale Rd W11; tube Notting Hill Gate/Westbourne Park

The super-slick Londsdale looks like Buck Rogers' pad with glossy black progressing to lush red beneath a stunning oval skylight. Cocktails are customary, dahling, although there are also drinks for boys and great if rather exxie bars snacks. The punters are exceptionally well groomed and the staff, even the doorman, are friendly.

MARKET BAR Map pp422-3
☎ 7229 6472; 240a Portobello Rd W11; tube Ladbroke Grove

The unofficial base for Carnival and market-goers, this deconstructed boho bar chills out

Market Bar (above)

Drinking – Northwest London

during other days with a steady stream of locals and tourists supping stout and coffee respectively, and gets mobbed in the evenings when the music's cranked up (by DJs Friday and Saturday, and a jazz band late on Sunday afternoon). There's a more than decent Thai restaurant upstairs (p253).

WESTBOURNE Map pp422-3
☎ 7221 1332; 101 Westbourne Park Villas W2; tube Royal Oak/Westbourne Park

This is another great pub. The Westbourne is virtually opposite the Cow and the summer crowds spilling out from both boozers sometimes get within touching distance. The Westbourne has the larger outdoor area although inside it's more cramped and there is a little more attitude.

SOUTH LONDON

Brixton pub regulars turn up their noses at all the pretentious posing that goes on in many of London's neighbourhoods du jour, but nearby Clapham has a style bar or two.

BRIXTON

BRIXTONIAN HAVANA CLUB Map p439
☎ 7924 9262; 11 Beehive Pl SW9; tube Brixton

While it is a restaurant (p258), and sort of a club too (with DJs), most punters seem to come for the cocktails, which oil the wheels of a super-friendly atmosphere. Take your pick from *mojitos, caipirinhas,* rum punches or even just stick to beer.

BUG BAR Map p439
☎ 7738 3366; St Matthew's Church SW2; tube Brixton

This sumptuously Gothic bar in a church crypt is a good place to shelter with friends and a glass of wine – possibly even switching over to the restaurant at some point for a meal (p258).

DOGSTAR Map p439
☎ 7733 7515; 389 Coldharbour Lane SW9; tube Brixton

Downstairs, this long-running local institution has a cavernous bar, always mobbed with a young, casual and trendy South London crowd loudly milling around the tables around the floor. Upstairs, there's a house music club, open to 3am; after 9pm on Friday and Saturday a cover charge applies. And there are queues.

PLAN B Map p439
☎ 7733 0926; 418 Brixton Rd SW9; tube Brixton

It doesn't have to be plan B, it could be an evening's plan A, if you're looking for a friendly low-key DJ bar on a Thursday to Sunday night.

Even on Tuesday and Wednesday, the decent cocktails are enough to woo you to this large room, decorated in an urban minimalist style of all concrete, exposed brick and benches with frosted-glass side panels.

VAUXHALL TAVERN Map pp440-1
☎ 7582 0833; 372 Kennington Lane SE11; tube Vauxhall

This scruffy gay pub is open every night, even though it's best known for the madcap 'post-gay' cabaret and eclectic tunes of Duckie, Saturday's long-running night (admission £5).

WANDSWORTH

SHIP Map pp416-17
☎ 8870 9667; 41 Jew's Row SW18; rail Wandsworth Town

Though the Ship is right by the Thames, the views aren't spectacular (unless you're partial to retail parks and workaday bridges). Still, the outside area is large, the summertime BBQs a treat and the conservatory bar fun in any weather.

CLAPHAM

ARCH 635 Map pp416-17
☎ 7720 7343; 15-16 Lendel Tce SW4; tube Clapham North

On the less pretentious, more down-to-earth side of Clapham, this brick-and-stainless-steel bar under the railway arches is a great place to shoot a few balls, knock back a beer and listen to the trains rumble overhead.

BREAD & ROSES Map pp416-17

☎ 7498 1779; 68 Clapham Manor St SW4; tube Clapham Common/Clapham North

Run by the Worker's Beer Company, which caters to all the UK's major music festivals such as Glastonbury, this bright airy pub is a delight. It's pretty family friendly during the day, but also serves real ales and Belgian and Czech beer, which make it worth visiting at night. There's a regular pan-African night and lots of comedy, poetry, music and political events.

SAND Map pp416-17

☎ 7622 3022; 156 Clapham Park Rd SW4; tube Clapham North

Sand sure is sleek and good-lookin', with sand-textured walls, Islamic-style room dividers, leather pouffes, low-slung tables and lots of interesting features, like wall alcoves, candles, breeze blocks and a huge sand timer. The mood is quite cosy and relaxed on weekdays, mobbed on weekends, when there are DJs (entrance £5 after 9pm).

SO.UK Map pp416-17

☎ 7622 4004; 165 Clapham High St SW4; tube Clapham Common

Owned by two celebs (including Leslie Ash of *Men Behaving Badly* fame), So.uk is a stylish Moroccan-themed bar that's light and airy and serves unusual cocktails, like Harissa-tinis. It's extremely popular, with the chance to spot a few well-known faces. Otherwise, you couldn't put it any better than the *Independent* newspaper, which called this a pulling place for Clapham professionals.

WEST LONDON

Away from the 'trustafarian' hang outs of Notting Hill and Fulham, the bars and pubs of the more down-to-earth areas of west London are a refreshing departure. Shepherd's Bush is particularly lively, although Earl's Court attracts young travellers, particularly from Australia, as well as a small but visible gay crowd.

EARL'S COURT

COLEHERNE Map pp436-7

☎ 7244 5951; 261 Old Brompton Rd SW5; tube Earl's Court

This is the centre of the Earl's Court's gay scene – an open plan, welcoming place on Old Brompton Rd that makes a quiet place for a drink during the day with its small crowd of regulars, becoming very busy in the evenings. A world away from Soho gay bars, and the disco lights over the pool table are pure genius.

COURTFIELD Map pp436-7

☎ 7370 2626; 187 Earl's Court Rd SW5; tube Earl's Court

The Courtfield is a fun place to have a drink with a great atmosphere and friendly crowd, and in this light it stands out against many of the seedy and dull pubs of the neighbourhood. The service is good, and the clientele are a pleasant blend of locals and visitors.

PRINCE OF TECK Map pp436-7

☎ 7373 3107; 161 Earl's Court Rd SW5; tube Earl's Court

This Earl's Court mainstay is nearly always packed with travellers and is festooned with Australiana (well, stuffed kangaroos, anyway). It's large and comfortable and has big screens for sports events on both floors. This is the default pub for young Aussies and Kiwis in the neighbourhood.

SHEPHERD'S BUSH & HAMMERSMITH

ALBERTINE

☎ 8743 9593; 1 Wood Lane W12; mains £6-9; tube Shepherd's Bush

This pleasant wine bar just off Shepherd's Bush Green has a great wine list and is a laid-back place for a drink and meal amid the humming conversation of after-work drinkers. The room upstairs is quieter and often empty for those in a decent-sized group. The menu is largely French, but incorporates other European cuisines into quite a few dishes.

GINGLIK

☎ 8749 2310; www.ginglik.co.uk; 1 Shepherd's Bush Green W12; tube Shepherd's Bush

In a converted Victorian public convenience under Shepherd's Bush Green lurks the local smart set's drinking tavern in the form of Ginglik, a private member's bar populated by the arty and the gorgeous. You'll have to be taken by a well-connected friend, or else apply in advance for temporary membership through their website. Either way, this place makes for a fun and offbeat night out – the bar plays host to various underground DJs and has regular showings of cult films.

HAMPSHIRE
☎ 8748 3391; 227 King St W6; tube Ravenscourt Park
The Ravenscourt Park pub of choice, the Hampshire is an unpretentious but upmarket bar on the main road into Hammersmith. There is a nice beer garden, a well-staffed bar and a pub cat who mixes happily with all the drinkers. Not one to travel for, but a great place for a pint if you are staying in the area.

HAVELOCK TAVERN
☎ 7603 5374; 57 Masbro Rd W14 ; tube Kensington Olympia
Perhaps the best gastropub in the neighbourhood, the Havelock does a busy trade with both diners and drinkers all day long. Friendly staff and a relaxed atmosphere make it a great weekend spot.

WALKABOUT INN
☎ 8740 4339; 58 Shepherd's Bush Green W12; tube Shepherd's Bush
Part of the Australian Walkabout pub chain, this huge venue has a licence for over 1000 punters, and is now undoubtedly *the* place to go for ex-pats looking for a heavy night out. Its extended opening hours mean that it's hugely popular and will always guarantee you a party.

OLD SHIP
☎ 8748 2593; 25 Upper Mall W6; tube Hammersmith
This funky towpath pub is packed at weekends with families and couples getting some liquid refreshment during their walks down the Thames. Its position is its greatest selling point, looking south across the lazy bend of the river towards Putney. It's popular the rest of the week too, with its outdoor dining area, terrace and 1st-floor balcony letting you make the most of the sun.

RIVERSIDE STUDIOS
☎ 8237 1000; Crisp Rd W6; tube Hammersmith
Perfect for chilling out after one of the many cultural events at the Riverside, the large bar area is the hub of the whole studio complex. You don't need to have seen a play or film, however – the great Thames-view terrace and relaxed and friendly vibe make the Riverside one of Hammersmith's few cool places to be.

SOUTHWEST LONDON
Going out in Fulham is mainly about cheesy nights with lots of drinking, dancing on tables and generally behaving badly. Don't head to this part of town if you want a classy evening. Putney and Barnes offer an altogether more sedate experience – there are few more enjoyable ways to spend a sunny afternoon in London than whiling away the hours in a pub on the river.

FULHAM & PARSON'S GREEN
ECLIPSE Map pp436-7
☎ 7731 2142; 108-110 New King's Rd SW6; ⏰ noon-late; tube Parsons Green
This cool, but comfortable, cocktail bar looks pretty swanky but the Fulhamites always manage to drag the party down to their level. You won't find any uptight Sloanes giving you the cold shoulder in here, just sociable locals having a fun night out.

FIESTA HAVANA Map pp436-7
☎ 7381 5005; 490 Fulham Rd SW6; ⏰ Mon-Sat 5pm-2am, Sun 5pm-midnight; tube Fulham Broadway
The epitome of a cheesy night out, you'll have to be up for it to enjoy yourself at Havana. If you're looking to pull, success is almost guaranteed: Havana has a reputation as a meat market so be prepared to fight off unwanted attention if snogging a stranger wasn't what you had in mind. The music's great though (groovy Latin beats) and there are free dance classes at the beginning of the evening.

MITRE Map pp436-7
☎ 7386 8877; 81 Dawes Rd; tube Fulham Broadway
A decent pub with a large semi-circular bar and walled courtyard at the back, the Mitre gets very crowded in the evenings and at the weekends, mainly with toffs, but don't let that put you off – they're generally pretty friendly.

WHITE HORSE Map pp436-7
☎ 7736 2115; 1-3 Parson's Green; tube Parsons Green
Right on the green, the White Horse is an inviting pub with a diverse clientele. Come here for the good hearty fare, BBQs during summer,

the warm and friendly atmosphere and the extensive range of beers. Belgian Trappist beers feature heavily, along with a selection of draught ales and every year in November the White Horse is host to the Old Ales Festival when you can sample traditional ales.

PUTNEY & BARNES

BIER REX
☎ 8394 5901; 22 Putney High St SW15; tube Putney Bridge

Going for a shabby-chic vibe with torn-up leatherette booths, frayed tables and chairs and a pool table out the back, Bier Rex is a

The British beer experience

dark little hang-out popular with 20- and 30-somethings who are so over the on-the-piss and on-the-pull behaviour encouraged by other pubs on Putney High St.

COAT & BADGE
☎ 8788 4900; 8 Lacey Rd SW15; tube Putney Bridge

The Coat & Badge has gone for a tried and tested lounge-room approach (large sofas, second-hand books on shelves, sport on the telly, impartial decor) which seems to please local Aussies. It has a short but excellent menu (the Sunday roasts are particularly good) and a fantastic large terrace out the front – someone was spewing in it on our visit and, judging by the reaction of the slightly cooler-than-thou staff, this wasn't a unique event.

DUKE'S HEAD
☎ 8788 2552; 8 Lower Richmond Rd SW15; tube Putney Bridge

One of many Young's pubs in the area, the Duke's is set apart by its location – right slap-bang on the river. On sunny days, punters spill out onto the Embankment, creating a merry atmosphere on the river bank. Inside, the bar fronting the Thames is the nicest, with high ceilings, huge windows and a puzzling number of lamps (just you count them).

GREEN MAN
☎ 8788 8096; Putney Heath; tube Putney Bridge, train Putney, then bus 14 or 85

This tiny little pub on the heath is your real local's local, with old men perched on bar stools, chewing the fat with anyone who happens to be in vocal range. It's decidedly battered inside but has a certain rough charm nonetheless. The pub's walled garden is *vast* and gorgeous and hosts BBQs in the summer.

JOLLY GARDENERS
☎ 8780 8921; 61-63 Lacey Rd SW15; tube Putney Bridge, train Putney

The antithesis to formulaic decorating and a tribute to all things chilled, this is our favourite pub in Putney. And it's not even on the river. It's been lovingly and eclectically kitted out (you'd never guess that Victorian oak cabinets go quite so well with Art Deco lamps or that thick drapes look good next to bare bricks and wood-panelled walls). Jolly Gardeners plays host to amiable 30-somethings and boasts a cheeky little wine menu and innovative food.

Its large terrace fronting a quiet road compensates for the lack of riverside location.

PUTNEY BRIDGE
☎ 8780 1811; Embankment SW15; tube Putney Bridge, train Putney

The restaurant (p258) above the bar is the main attraction at Putney Bridge, but this place is still popular with sleek young locals after a taste of designer cool. Its striking, curved bar, offering an extensive cocktail menu and bar snacks (posh nuts, posh spring rolls, posh Samosas), runs parallel to the Thames and along much of the length of the room; most heads, though, are turned towards the river itself.

YE WHITE HART
☎ 8876 5177; The Terrace SW13; train Barnes

Of the three Young's pubs in Barnes, this is the nicest. It has a lovely terrace on the river, somewhat marred by the busy road outside and the view of the mother ship upstream, the source of the pint in your hand perhaps. If you have been to any of Young's pubs before, you will know exactly what the interior looks like: just think swirly carpets, fruit machines, old man at bar smoking B&Hs.

UP RIVER

Quieter and more traditional, the pubs up river are often real neighbourhood hubs, unlike the more anonymous pubs in central London where the transience of both staff and punters is a major theme. Often centuries-old, many of the best pubs overlook the river and make a great place to stop for a drink at any time of day.

CHISWICK

BOLLO PUB & DINING ROOM
☎ 8994 6037; 13 Bollo Lane W4; tube Chiswick Park

Out of the way even by Chiswick's high standards, this new gastropub has been a huge success, run by local restaurateurs who redeveloped it from a simple local. This is not the place to catch up with disaffected youth (they're probably all at boarding school anyway) but a great place for an older, wealthier crowd looking for a pub and dining room rolled into one.

PACKHORSE & TALBOT
☎ 8994 0360; 145 Chiswick High Rd W4; tube Turnham Green

The oddly named Packhorse is justly one of Chiswick's most popular pubs. It's in the top 20 best pubs in Britain, as voted by beer lovers' website www.beerintheevening.com. It's a big place in the centre of Chiswick, with a great beer garden and a very popular landlord. There are big screens for sports events too.

RICHMOND

DYSART Map p439
☎ 8940 8005; 135 Petersham Rd, Richmond; rail/tube Richmond

Formerly the Dysart Arms Hotel, the newly refitted Dysart is a great family pub facing Richmond Park's Petersham entrance. Apart from the mock-Gothic interior, which is a serious breach of good taste, the Dysart succeeds on all fronts: families are made to feel welcome, although children are not allowed to run riot, the food is good and the large terrace is packed on a warm afternoon.

OLD SHIP Map p439
☎ 8940 3461; 3 King St, Richmond; tube/rail Richmond

This charming old pub in the centre of Richmond attracts a down-to-earth crowd who seem largely oblivious to the toffs and suits of Richmond. There's a firm emphasis on sports with several large screens, but also the nice traditional elements of the old English pub. It's packed on match days, but you can usually get a seat the rest of the week.

ORANGE TREE Map p439
☎ 8940 0944; 45 Kew Rd, Richmond; tube/rail Richmond

The eponymous theatre next door is one of the best in London outside the West End, and the Orange Tree pub is a decent place to come for a drink at anytime, with its large open front and wooden fittings. On rugby match days though, it's completely packed and not too pleasant, due to its proximity to the station.

WHITE SWAN Map p439
☎ 89400959; Old Palace Lane, Richmond; tube/rail Richmond

Facing the site of Richmond Palace, this great little pub nestles between the Thames towpath and Richmond Green. Its historic façade gives way to a modern, airy interior, but it's friendly and comfortable, with good Thai food and a pleasant garden.

TWICKENHAM
BARMY ARMS
☎ 8892 0863; The Embankment, Twickenham; rail Twickenham

This a popular local pub that gets packed to capacity on international match days. It's just by Eel Pie Island and also has decent pub food and a charming beer garden to recommend it.

WHITE SWAN
☎ 8892 2166; Riverside, Twickenham; rail Twickenham

This pub is a London classic with a fantastic riverside location, great selection of beer and a loyal crowd of locals. It overlooks Eel Pie Island, a funky hippy hangout that still attracts the alternative crowd, despite its heyday being long-gone. If you are in Twickenham, the White Swan is a local treat, and if you're not too far, this is one pub worth a detour.

WIMBLEDON
BAR SIA
☎ 8540 8339; 105-109 The Broadway SW19; tube Wimbledon

This is one of the best-designed and funkiest bars in London, and its location above a Turkish bath that used to serve the actors of Wimbledon Theatre is completely unique. Bar Sia has two bars and a dance floor, features leather sofas and sleek green decor with white tiling and is quite unlike most places you'll drink in. Undoubtedly the best table is the one at the bottom of the empty plunge-pool! Makes Wimbledon seem cool.

FOX AND GRAPES
☎ 8946 5599; 9 Camp Rd SW19; tube Wimbledon

This traditional Wimbledon inn started serving pints in 1787 and is one of the most popular locals. The low-ceilinged bar is no smoking, while the bigger bar (converted from the stables) is beautiful with high beams and brimming with traditional atmosphere. The Pacific Rim bar menu is also worth a look.

1 Coffee and cake, Soho (p225)
2 Mayfair dining (p230)
3 Villandry, Regent's Park (p248) 4 Window display, Borough Market (p333) 5 Fish and chips (p251)

283

1 Oxo Tower Restaurant & Brasserie, Waterloo (p240)
2 Baltic restaurant, Bankside (p241) 3 Café in the Crypt, St Martin-in-the-Fields (p229)
4 Bar life, Soho (pp265-6)
5 Borough Market (p333)

1 *Le Pont de la Tour restaurant, Butler's Wharf (p243)* 2 *Bibendum Oyster Bar, South Kensington (p231)* 3 *Brixton Market, Brixton (p334)* 4 *Rock & Sole Plaice, Covent Garden (p227)*

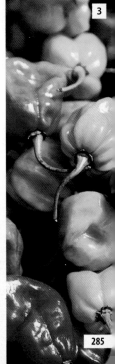

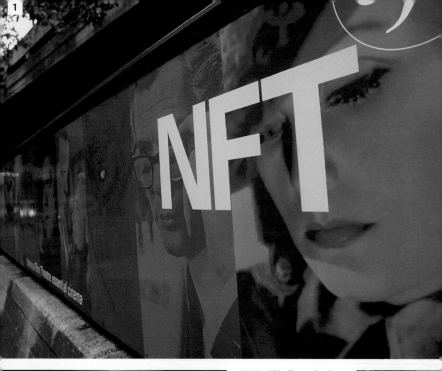

1 National Film Theatre, South Bank (p294) **2** Fiesta Havana, Fulham (p279) **3** Ronnie Scott's jazz club, Soho (p308) **4** Cubana restaurant, South Bank (p240)

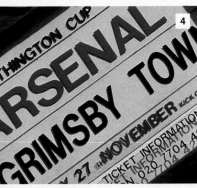

1 Duke of York's Theatre, Covent Garden (p315) 2 The Cross, Kings Cross (p298) 3 Underworld, Camden (p307) 4 Arsenal Stadium, Highbury (p310)

1 Hamleys store, Covent Garden (p322) **2** The Tea House, Covent Garden (p321) **3** Antiquarius antique dealers, Chelsea (p318) **4** Harvey Nichols store, Knightsbridge (p325)

1 Camden High St (p333)
2 Borough Market, Borough (p333)
3 Foyles Bookstore, Soho (p326)
4 Covent Garden Market (p333)

1 Brown's hotel, Mayfair (p343)
2 Great Eastern Hotel, Hoxton (p342) 3 St David's Hotel, Paddington (p352) 4 Claridges hotel (p343) 5 The Rookery hotel (p343)

Entertainment

Entertainment

Okay, this is the bit that many people come to London for, and with several lifetimes needed to exhaust all the city's going-out possibilities, you won't be disappointed. Despite pubs that shut at 11pm, and despite an Underground system that won't get you home much past midnight, you can still find yourself in the wee hours of a Sunday morning enjoying the vibe on Fabric's 'bodysonic' dance floor, watching a big name spin the disks at glam club Pacha, or bouncing around happily at 93 Feet East. It'll cost you, of course, but in return the capital can offer priceless memories, say, catching a hip star like DJ Yoda, or even a mainstream one like Fatboy Slim, at a 300-capacity venue.

Shaftesbury Avenue, Soho

There are plenty of cutting-edge bars round the super-chilled Hoxton and Shoreditch districts. Alternatively, if you simply want a cheesy good time, London lets you relive your hormonally charged teenage years at School Disco or transports you back to the 1970s at Car Wash. Hoxton, Brixton, Notting Hill and Soho also act as nightlife hubs.

For those looking for slightly less frenetic pursuits, the capital is steeped in culture. Not only is there a good chance of watching a major Hollywood star like Gwyneth Paltrow or Kevin Spacey strut their stuff on a stage in the West End, but there's also a wealth of home-grown talent. British actors who've gained international movie stardom, such as Dame Judi Dench, Sir Ian McKellen, Ralph Fiennes and Rhys Ifans, still tread the boards here. What's even more impressive is that they're backed by well-trained supporting casts and visionary directors who arguably make London theatre the best on the planet.

The Royal Shakespeare Company, the Royal Opera, the Royal Ballet and four major orchestras all cater to discerning highbrow tastes, while popular musicals like *Chicago, Bollywood Dreams, Phantom of the Opera* and *Mamma Mia* woo the crowds. However, London also excels at producing the adventurous, the experimental and the unexpected genius. In recent years, for example, it's been the crucible for the world-famous, all-male ballet *Swan Lake* and it's thrown up an entirely new genre by adapting the confessional TV show into *Jerry Springer – the Opera*.

The city harbours the unique experience of seeing Shakespeare staged in a bawdy Elizabethan manner, in an authentic reconstruction of the theatre where the bard worked. It also has plenty of fun with the English language's most revered playwright: the Reduced Shakespeare Company has managed to compress his works into a mere 90-minute performance, while others have turned his works into hip-hop comedies.

When it comes to cinema, American visitors might at first throw down the London film listings in disgust, thinking they've seen all the movies months before. But read on beyond the Hollywood blockbusters and you'll find an amazing diversity. French arthouse, Asian martial arts, African dramas, East European black comedies and Latin American love stories all get plenty of screen-time here.

Finally, there's London's live rock and pop music scene, which simply can't be beat. Creatively, the city is in a lull, with the best bands and records being produced elsewhere, but anyone who's anyone plays the English capital at some time. Among its hundreds of venues, there's bound to be a performance to grab your attention nearly every night. New York might boast that it's the city that never sleeps, but London brushes off its archaic licensing laws and somnolent public transport to party just as hard.

CINEMA

While UK film critics still complain that distributors release movies in Britain later than in other countries, the choice of movies to watch in London is frankly dazzling. That's because many of the old-style independent film houses have held out and continue to show world cinema in repertory, despite the inevitable march of American-style multiplexes.

Of course, if you want nothing more challenging than the latest Hollywood blockbusters, there are plenty of those in town. Check newspaper or magazine listings for the Warner Villages, Odeons or UGCs – and be prepared to pay up to £12 for a first-run film. Many major premieres are held in Leicester Square, the sort of place you might spot J.Lo posing in a revealing dress or Tom Cruise talking on fans' mobile phones.

If your tastes are a little more eclectic, try one of the cinemas below. They're not necessarily cheaper than the multiplex chains, but certainly offer greater choice.

Typically, in either arthouse or mainstream cinemas, there are price discounts on Mondays and for most weekday afternoon screenings.

If you are in town in October or November, do keep an eye out for the **Times' London Film Festival** (www.rlff.com), Europe's largest of its kind, with plenty of previews, debates and talks.

National Film Theatre, South Bank (p294)

Entertainment – Cinema

BARBICAN Map pp432-3
☎ info 7382 7000, bookings 7638 8891; Silk St EC2; tube Moorgate/Barbican

The cinemas here operate at a handicap – the Barbican Centre is out of the way and difficult to negotiate – yet they still manage to pull in the crowds with innovative and unusual programming, regular film festivals and talks by directors and stars.

CINÉ LUMIÈRE Map pp436-7
☎ 7838 2144; 17 Queensberry Pl SW7; tube South Kensington

If you simply must see a subtitled French film this week, this cinema at the French Institute can provide it.

CLAPHAM PICTURE HOUSE Map pp416-17
☎ info 7498 2242, bookings 7498 3323; 76 Venn St SW4; tube Clapham Common

One of the capital's best local cinemas, the Picture House has four screens and the kind of café/bar where locals arrive well before the film starts just so they can hang out for a bit. The programme runs the gamut from first-run blockbusters to Chinese arthouse cinema.

CURZON MAYFAIR Map pp426-7
☎ info 7495 0501, bookings 7495 0500; 38 Curzon St W1; tube Hyde Park Corner/Green Park

Posher and not quite so relaxed as its Soho sister (see following), the original Curzon nevertheless shows an interesting range of mostly new independent and foreign films.

CURZON SOHO Map p430
☎ info 7439 4805, bookings 7734 2255; 93-107 Shaftesbury Ave W1; tube Leicester Square/Piccadilly Circus

The Curzon beats other West End cinemas hands down, and that's not even because of its good taste and arthouse leanings in the programming department. Upstairs it has a great coffee counter, also serving herbal tea and cakes, while downstairs you'll find the coolest movie-house bar in the centre of town – all of which should be even better after its refurbishment.

ELECTRIC CINEMA Map pp422-3

☎ 7908 9696 or 7229 8688; 191 Portobello Rd W1; tube Ladbroke Grove/Notting Hill Gate

A night out at this Rolls Royce of cinemas is no ordinary evening at the pics. The Edwardian building, the UK's oldest purpose-built cinema, has been luxuriously fitted out with leather armchairs, footstools, tables for food and drink in the auditorium, and an upmarket brasserie. Of course, such pampering comes at a slightly higher cost; on full-price nights the seats are £12.50, or £30 for a two-seater sofa.

EVERYMAN HAMPSTEAD Map p415

☎ 08700 664 777; 5 Holly Bush Vale NW3; tube Hampstead

This cosy arthouse cinema has two screens. The newer, smaller auditorium downstairs can seat 90 people in comfy armchairs and will screen slightly older foreign or left-of-centre films, while the main feature is shown in the original hall upstairs.

GATE Map pp422-3

☎ 7727 4043; 87 Notting Hill Gate W1; tube Notting Hill Gate

The Gate's single screen has one of London's most charming Art Deco cinema interiors – although the bar area is a little squished. It's the programming it prides itself on, however, introducing new arthouse and independent films.

ICA Map pp426-7

☎ 7930 3647; Nash House, The Mall SW1; tube Charing Cross/Piccadilly Circus

The ICA has two screens: one of them extremely, erm, intimate (ie small), the other more capacious and with a bit more leg room. Both show rarer, arty flicks from the likes of Finland's Aki Kaurismäki, the USA's Harmony Korine and Czech surrealist animator Jan Svankmajer.

NATIONAL FILM THEATRE Map pp426-7

☎ 7928 3232; South Bank SE1; tube Waterloo/Embankment

The large auditorium at Britain's national repository of film is often used for directors and actors – occasionally including major Hollywood stars – to present and talk about their films, both new releases and golden oldies dusted off for retrospectives. There are two other, smaller screens, a good bookshop and a pleasant café/bar.

OTHER CINEMA Map p428

☎ info 7437 0757, bookings 7734 1506; 11 Rupert St W1; tube Piccadilly Circus/Leicester Square

Formerly the Metro, the Other Cinema has continued its predecessor's tradition of programming quirky independent cinema. It still hosts the Latin American Film Festival and shows movies by new directors, documentaries and short films.

PRINCE CHARLES Map p428

☎ info 0901 272 7007 (25p per min), bookings 7494 3654; Leicester Place WC2; tube Leicester Square

Central London's cheapest cinema (tickets generally cost from £2.50 to £3.50) is not for highbrow cinema buffs but for self-proclaimed movie geeks. You can gorge on several episodes of *Star Wars*, *Harry Potter* or *Lord of the Rings*, catch up on cult classics like *Amélie*, or revisit cool directors like Steven Soderbergh, Paul Thomas Anderson and the Coen brothers. Famously, the cinema also transformed *The Sound of Music* into a phenomenal – and very camp – sing-a-long hit. The audience, gay and straight, still dress up as nuns or schoolgirls in plaits, mimicking Maria and booing Baron von Trapp (7.30pm Friday, admission £13.50).

RENOIR Map pp420-1

☎ 7837 8402; Brunswick Centre, Brunswick Sq WC1; tube Russell Square

A basement-level oasis of mainly French chic in the drab, concrete Brunswick Centre, the Renoir has a good range of arthouse videos on sale in the lower foyer, and serves warming

Ritzy cinema, Brixton (opposite)

coffee and cake. As well as a healthy dose of French film, you'll also be able to catch all sorts of international cinema, from Iranian morality tales to Taiwanese love stories.

RIO Map pp416-17
☎ 7241 9410; 107 Kingsland High St E8; rail Dalston Kingsland
Dalston's Rio was thoroughly modernised in the late '90s, but you can still see traces of the lovely Art Deco theatre it was in its single-screen auditorium. It shows a range of new releases, arthouse pics and classic cinema, and is where you'll find the Spanish, Kurdish and Turkish film festivals (in April, Autumn and December respectively).

RITZY Map p439
☎ 7733 2229; Brixton Oval, Coldharbour Lane SW2; tube Brixton
A renovation in the mid-'90s saw a move towards the multiplex model, with four new screens added to this 1911 building, but Brixton's local cinema still has plenty of style. The large original auditorium, with its proscenium arch, survived the conversion (making for five screens in all) and there is a funky bar and café.

RIVERSIDE STUDIOS Map p414
☎ 8237 1111; Crisp Rd W6; tube Hammersmith
Once a film and TV studio itself, where classics like *Dr Who* and *Hancock's Half-Hour* were shot,

the cinema at the Riverside now shows classic arthouse flicks and those you might have missed a few months back. Unusual events, such as a programme of international ads, are also sometimes held here.

SCREEN ON BAKER ST Map pp422-3
☎ info 7486 0036, bookings 7935 2772; 96 Baker St NW1; tube Baker Street
Cosy *and* anonymous, this smallish central cinema gives you the chance to catch up with recent independent releases or films you might have missed a month or so back.

SCREEN ON THE GREEN Map pp420-1
☎ 7226 3520; 83 Upper St N1; tube Angel
At a bustling junction of Islington's busy nightlife, this film house has a single auditorium with one large screen, attracting a trendy, upmarket crowd with a taste for edgy independent cinema (and good ice cream).

SCREEN ON THE HILL Map p415
☎ 7435 3366; 203 Haverstock Hill NW3; tube Belsize Park
The Screen on the Hill caters for the chattering classes of Hampstead and Belsize Park – this comfy, licensed cinema intersperses its generally highbrow programme with the occasional mainstream blockbuster. Think *The Talented Mr Ripley* or *The Pianist*. Jane Austen is huge, too, with *Sense and Sensibility* one of the biggest-ever hits.

CLUBBING

With pubs shut at 11pm, London's clubs become one of the city's biggest draws, playing to the wee hours. You pay for the privilege of staying out until 4am, 5am or 6am, however. Admission prices vary from £3 to £10 Sunday to Thursday, but on Friday and Saturday rise to between £14 and £20.

Dress codes vary widely. The reviews below should give you some idea, but ring ahead if you're unsure. Trainers/sneakers are fine for somewhere like Fabric or 93 Feet East, less so for Pacha. Many of the specific club nights mentioned have already moved venue several times, so it's always a good idea to check up-to-date listings in *Time Out* or the *Evening Standard*.

THE WEST END

As one of the hubs of London's thriving lesbian and gay scene, Soho has a higher-than-average proportion of leading gay clubs.

ASTORIA Map p428
☎ 7434 9592, 7434 6963; 157 Charing Cross Rd WC2; ☺ 10.30pm-4am Mon & Thu, 11pm-4am Fri, 10.30pm-5am Sat; tube Tottenham Court Road
This dark, sweaty and atmospheric venue hosts London's largest gay club, G-A-Y (good as you).

Saturday is the big night, with commercial beats and various Kylie/Dannii parties. There's a Pink Pounder cheap night on Monday, Thursday night is Music Factory and Friday night is Camp Attack.

BAR RUMBA Map p428
☎ 7287 2715; 36 Shaftesbury Ave W1; ☺ 10.30pm-3am Mon & Wed; 8.30pm-3am Tue, Thu, Fri; 9pm-5am Sat; 8pm-1.30am Sun; tube Piccadilly Circus
A small club in the heart of Soho with a loyal following, Bar Rumba is best known

for Monday's THIS! (That's How It Is), where celeb DJ Gilles Peterson and colleagues Ben Wilcox and Raw Deal push the envelope with an eclectic mix of drum 'n' bass, jazz, hip hop and global beats.

END Map p430
☎ 7419 9199; 18 West Central St WC1; ✆ 10pm-3am Mon & Wed, 10pm-4am Thu, 10pm-5am Fri, 9.30pm-6am Sat; tube Holborn

The End is a glam club – with minimalist industrial decor – situated in a West End back street. Fridays and Saturdays are devoted to guest DJs, including big names like Darren Emerson or LTJ Bukem. Wednesday's Swerve with Fabio is mega-popular, and the rest of the week includes Sunday's hard-house Riot and Monday's disco/glam/punk/'80s electronica Trash.

GHETTO Map p428
☎ 7287 3726; 5-6 Falconberg Ct W1; ✆ 10pm-3pm Mon-Thu, from 10.30pm Wed, 10.30pm-4.30am Fri & Sat; tube Tottenham Court Rd

In a sweaty basement, this leading gay club has nevertheless garnered compliments from *Face* magazine, with its 1950s American milk bar–style white seats and red walls. The most talked about night is Nag, Nag, Nag, where both Boy George and Yoko Ono have appeared, followed by Friday's in-yer-face Cock. There's also Thursday's indie-music Missshapes and Saturday's trashy Wig Out.

HEAVEN Map p430
☎ 7930 2020; Under the Arches, Villiers St WC2; ✆ 10.30pm-3am Mon & Wed, 10pm-3am Fri, 10pm-5am Sat; tube Embankment/Charing Cross

This long-standing and perennially popular gay club has always had some mixed nights, evidenced by the fact that the very mixed School Disco (uniform absolutely essential) has moved here for Friday nights. Saturday is still the flagship night for gay clubbers who like very commercial house music.

ICA Map pp426-7
☎ 7930 3647; The Mall SW1; ✆ box office noon-9.30pm; tube Embankment/Charing Cross

This trendy art gallery cum cinema also hosts bands and the occasional club night. One special event worth looking out for is DJ Cliffy's Brazilian night Batmacumba, appearing every one or two months.

MADAME JO JO'S Map p428
☎ 7734 3040; 8 Brewer St W1; ✆ 10.30pm-3am Wed-Fri, from 9.30pm Thu, cabaret 7pm-10pm & club 10pm-3am Sat; tube Leicester Square/Piccadilly Circus

The renowned transvestite cabaret and all its sleazy, fun kitsch gives way to a deep house/nu-jazz club night on Saturdays. But Keb Darge's deep-funk night on Fridays is equally legendary, attracting a cool crew of breakers, jazz dancers and people just out to have a good time.

PACHA Map pp440-1
☎ 7834 4440; Terminus Pl SW1; ✆ 10pm-6am Fri & Sat; tube/rail Victoria

The London outpost of the seminal 'Ibeefa' club is one of London's most sumptuous venues, eschewing the 'industrial' look that dominates London clubland for the oak-wood panelling, upholstered booths and stunning stained-glass ceiling of a 1920s gentleman's club. Sleek, glammed up customers chuck on lots of bling for Friday's regular Urbandeluxe, with its mix of pole-dancers (yes, really) and soul, funky disco, boogie and hip hop. Changing Saturday nights include the monthly Kinky Malinki.

EAST CENTRAL

333 Map pp420-1
☎ 7739 5949; 333 Old St EC1; ✆ 10pm-5am Fri, 10pm-4am Sat, 10pm-4am Sun; tube Old Street

A real Hoxton old-timer, 333 might have three different shambling levels of breakbeats, techno and funk, however its attitude is determinedly down to earth. Just off Hoxton Square, it's one of the area's less pretentious clubs. On the top floor is the Mother bar (✆ 8pm-2am) which is often a destination in itself.

93 FEET EAST Map pp432-3
☎ 7247 3293; 150 Brick Lane E2; ✆ bar 11am-11pm, 11am-2am Fri & Sat, club Thu-Sat 8pm-2am; tube Liverpool Street/Aldgate East

Probably the most popular club in Hoxton, 93 Feet East runs some top music nights, particularly Way Out East and Groove Armada's mega-successful monthly residency Lovebox. The venue itself is appealing too: there's a courtyard, three good-sized rooms packed with a typically cool East London crowd, and an outdoor terrace. However, all those doormen milling around menacingly are a little bit of overkill.

Top Five Club Nights

- **Fabric Live** (Fabric; 😊 Fri; www.fabriclondon.com) Proving itself to be the only one of several so-called 'super-clubs' to live up to its name, Fabric Live continues to impress with cutting-edge line ups and a cool party crowd. You won't hear music like this anywhere else – look no further for the cool London clubbing experience.
- **Nag Nag Nag** (Ghetto; 😊 Wed) The cream of London's club world comes to this superb weekly event, where electro meets punk and models meet pop stars. Come early and expect to queue if you have the audacity not to be on the guest list. Kate Moss and Björk are regulars, so the wannabe factor is understandably high.
- **Progression Sessions** (The End; 😊 every 2nd Fri; www.glo.uk.com) London's best drum'n'bass/alternative beats night. It's run by the Good Looking Organisation and features big-name DJs at one of London's most enduringly hip venues.
- **Club Type** (Cross; 😊 every 2nd Sat; www.clubtype.com) Balearic fest helmed by superstar Seb Fontaine, who cut his teeth here before hitting the big time. The Cross is one of London's best venues, with a great chill-out area outside and three dance floors. Expect a friendly, up-for-it crowd.
- **School Disco** (😊 Fri at Heaven, Sat at Hammersmith Palais; www.schooldisco.com) Cheese-o-rama night for a drunken, debauched after-work office crowd with a serious school-uniform fetish. Entrance is only for those in approved English school wear. This the place to relive all those prefect fantasies in full Technicolor.

AQUARIUM Map pp420-1
☎ 7251 6136, 0870 246 1966; 256-260 Old St EC1; 😊 10pm-3am Sat, 10pm-4am Sun; tube Old Street
The Saturday night hitch-up between '70s disco evening Carwash and this converted gym seems like an excellent match: clubbers dressed in sexy, retro gear – compulsory, but disco wigs not allowed – now mingle around the huge pool or in the trendy bar. The following evening is host to Absolutely Sunday, with a focus on old-school house, garage and R&B.

BRIDGE & TUNNEL Map pp420-1
☎ 7729 6533; 4 Calvert Ave E2; 😊 7pm-midnight, 7pm-2am Fri & Sat; tube Liverpool Street/Old Street
The guys who own Nuphonic records own this, as they did Hoxton's original Blue Note. It's an industrial-looking venue peopled by a trendy Shoreditch crowd. The music's always good, but Sunday is particularly notable for Goldie's Metalheadz and their drum 'n' bass evening.

CARGO Map pp420-1
☎ 7739 3440; 83 Rivington St EC2; 😊 noon-1am Mon-Thu, noon-3am Fri, 6pm-3am Sat, noon-midnight Sun; tube Old Street
One of the area's best clubs, Cargo has three different spaces under brick railway arches. The music policy is pretty innovative, with a rolling programme of Latin house, nu-jazz, funk, groove and soul, DJs, global (particularly Latin) bands, up-and-coming bands, demos and rare grooves.

FABRIC Map pp426-7
☎ 7336 8898 or 7490 0444; 77A Charterhouse St EC1; 😊 9.30pm-5am Fri & Sun, 10pm-7am Sat; tube Farringdon
This good-looking superclub is still one of the best in town as the lengthy queues attest (worst from about 9 to 11pm). A smoky warren of three floors, three bars, many walkways and unisex toilets, it has a kidney-shaking 'sonic boom' dance floor where you can feel the music, literally. The crowd is hip but fairly casual, the music mainly electro, techno and breakbeats. Top Friday-night resident DJs James Lavelle and Ali B are regularly joined by big names ranging from the Chemical Brothers to Andrew Weatherall and beyond.

HERBAL Map pp420-1
☎ 7613 4462; 10-14 Kingsland Rd E2; 😊 9pm-2am Wed, Thu & Sun; 9pm-3am Fri; 10pm-3am Sat; tube Old Street
You'll recognise Herbal by all the plastic grass stapled to its front wall. Inside is a two-level bar/small club. The laid-back, grown-up loft upstairs has a small dance floor, seating and a window overlooking Shoreditch. Downstairs is more minimalist and can get very sweaty. There's a mix of drum 'n' bass, house, funk house and hip hop, interspersed with live shows.

PLASTIC PEOPLE Map pp420-1
☎ 7739 6471; 147-149 Curtain Rd EC2; 😊 10pm-2am Thu, 10pm-3am Fri & Sat; tube Old Street
Afrobeat, jazz dance, future dance, broken beats and garage are all on the playlist in

this small downstairs club with Balance on Saturday nights. On Fridays, it's an even more eclectic mix of punk, funk, acid disco, sleazy electro and leftfield for the night And Did We Mention Our Disco?.

TURNMILLS Map pp426-7
☎ 7250 3409; 63 Clerkenwell Rd EC1; ☼ 6pm-midnight Tue, 10.30pm-7.30pm Fri, 9pm-5am Sat; tube Farringdon
This long-running house institution still manages to pull in big-name DJs, including the likes of Judge Jules, Sister Bliss and Roger Sanchez, with its kickin' beats.

ALONG THE SOUTH BANK
MINISTRY OF SOUND Map pp432-3
☎ 7378 6528; 103 Gaunt St SE1; ☼ 10.30pm-6am Fri, midnight-9am Sat; tube Elephant & Castle
No longer a mere club, but an enormous global brand, the Ministry of Sound naturally doesn't have the edge it once did. However, it has been trying to grab back some of that revolutionary feel since a major refurbishment in late 2003, which included a total overhaul of its main room, new bars, luxurious loos and a green, glass box apparently floating in mid-air. Join the queue.

NORTH CENTRAL
CAMDEN PALACE Map pp418-19
☎ 7387 0428; 1A Camden High St NW1; ☼ 10pm-2.30am Tue 10pm-6am Fri & Sat; tube Mornington Crescent
With a huge dance floor overlooked by four to five levels of balcony, the Palace is a rite-of-initiation sort of club, so the crowd can be fairly young (generally early 20s or less; over 26s will feel ancient). The leading night is Friday's Peach, when clubbers move to the sounds of trance and uplifting, roof-raising house. Saturday varies, while Tuesday is devoted to indie rock.

CROSS Map pp420-1
☎ 7837 0828; Goods Way Depot, York Way N1; ☼ 10.30pm-5am Fri & Sat, 10.30am-4pm Sun; tube King's Cross/St Pancras
This is one of London's leading venues, hidden under the arches off York Way, and with an outdoor terrace. Friday has mixed/gay Fiction, with soulful funk and garage. Sunday is run by Vertigo, which is a Continental-style

Top Five Gay Club Nights

- **The Cock** (Ghetto; ☼ Fri) Innovative, democratically weird and highly enjoyable pop/electro extravaganza, featuring new DJs every week playing for a crowd of punks, trannies, muscle boys and fashionistas. The Ghetto is the coolest gay venue in town at the moment.
- **DTPM** (Fabric; ☼ Sun) The name apparently stands for Drugs Taken Per Minute, and that has some resonance when you see the crowd who roll up here on Sunday night – none of them appear to have slept since Thursday. However, the atmosphere of hedonism is incredible, with superb music in a superb venue.
- **Popcorn** (Heaven; ☼ Mon) Cheapest and least pretentious gay club in London, aimed at students and slackers. You can get drunk for £10 and enjoy the full run of Heaven, with indie, house and R'n'B rooms.
- **Fiction** (Cross; ☼ Fri) Some of the best music on the gay scene for a cool, carefree crowd of serious clubbers. Come early, as the queues can be huge. Enjoy the excellent range of music, spread over three small dance floors, in this beautifully converted space in the King's Cross wasteland.
- **Popstarz** (Scala; ☼ Fri) The granddaddy of alternative gay clubbing is no longer hip, but it's still fun, with three dance floors playing indie/rock, '80s and '90s pop, and R&B. Entry is free before 11pm – one of the weekend's best deals.

clubbing operation, who bring over lots of Italian guest DJs.

EGG Map pp420-1
☎ 7428 7574; 5-13 Vale Royal, off York Way N1; 10pm-4am Fri, 10pm-5am Sat; ☼ tube King's Cross
One of London's newer, hotter venues, omnisexual Egg has been likened to a club in New York's meat-packing district because of its bare walls and exposed concrete. There are three floors, two roof terraces and an outside courtyard. Friday is gay/mixed, with Zerox (electro-punk, funk with classic electronic). On weekends after 11pm, a free shuttle bus runs from King's Cross to the venue every 30 minutes.

SCALA Map pp420-1
☎ 7833 2022; 275 Pentonville Rd N1; ☼ 10pm-5am Fri & Sat; tube King's Cross
On Friday, this multi-level former cinema hosts Popstarz, a laidback, gay/mixed potpourri of

indie, alternative and kitsch. On Saturday, it's UK garage night Cookies and Cream. Occasionally, there are promotional nights during the week.

WEST LONDON

CHERRY JAM Map pp422-3
☎ 7727 9950; 58 Porchester Rd W2; ⊙ 6pm-late Mon-Sat, 4pm-11pm Sun; tube Royal Oak

Whether you want to call it a DJ bar or a club, there are three things certain about Cherry Jam: it's small, usually crowded and super fine. Part-owner Ben Watt (Notting Hill Arts Club – see below – and formerly of pop duo Everything but the Girl) is one of the DJs on Saturdays. Other club nights are from Wednesday to Sunday, and include Thursday's famous Yo-Yo. Bands play Tuesdays, while on Mondays there are readings and other arty events.

NEIGHBOURHOOD Map pp422-3
☎ 7524 7979; 2 Acklam Rd W10; ⊙ 6pm-late Thu-Sun; tube Ladbroke Grove

On the site of the long-running Subterania, Cherry Jam and Notting Hill Arts Club supremo Ben Watt has decided to open yet another undoubtedly excellent venue.

NOTTING HILL ARTS CLUB Map pp422-3
☎ 7460 4459; 21 Notting Hill Gate W11; ⊙ 6pm-1am Tue-Sat, 6pm-2am Fri & Sat, 4pm-11pm Sun; tube Notting Hill Gate

This laid-back, funky basement club attracts an eclectic crowd. Anyone from dreadlocked students to the occasional celebrity can be found between its white walls. Sunday's legendary Lazy Dog has been replaced with house night Underdog, with the result that the media have now focused on Wednesday's Death Disco – a rock 'n' roll, indie and punk evening from Creation Records founder Alan McGee, which has attracted celebs like Courtney Love.

PO NA NA HAMMERSMITH Map p414
☎ 8600 2300; 242 Shepherd's Bush Rd W6; ⊙ 10pm-3am Sat; tube Hammersmith

If you didn't get enough kissing behind the bicycle sheds and other school disco action at Heaven on a Friday night (p296), there's more tonight at Po Na Na. A uniform is compulsory or you'll be expelled.

SOUTH LONDON

CRASH Map pp416-17
☎ 7820 1500; 66 Goding St SE11; ⊙ 10.30pm-6am Sat; tube Vauxhall

If Vauxhall in general is one of London's newest gay hangouts, then Crash, in particular, is its Muscle Mary heaven. There's two dance floors churning out hard beats, four bars and even a few go-go dancers.

DOGSTAR Map p439
☎ 7733 7515; 389 Coldharbour Lane SW9; 9pm-3am Fri & Sat; tube Brixton

You'll have to push your way through the huge downstairs bar of this converted pub to get to the house-music club upstairs, but that's what a hell of a lot of Southside clubbers do.

THE FRIDGE Map p439
☎ 7326 5100; 1 Town Hall Pde SW2; ⊙ 9pm-2.30am Mon-Thu & Sun, 10pm-6am Fri & Sat; tube Brixton

This is one of London's longest-running venues and it is still extremely popular. The Fridge is an excellent bar and club venue that is not too big and not too small. It runs a wide variety of club nights and live music ranging from African Gospel and Cuban salsa to reggae and punk. On weekends, though, the music's generally a mix of trance and hard house.

MASS Map p439
☎ 7737 1016; St Matthew's Church SW2; ⊙ 10pm-6am Fri & Sat; tube Brixton

Mass is an appropriately named venue, situated in St Matthew's Church, with its vaulted ceilings, pews and frescoes. Friday night is Fetish Night, while Saturday rolls around for Dekefex, an award-winning mix of drum 'n' bass and hip hop.

SUBSTATION SOUTH Map p439
☎ 7737 2095; 9 Brighton Tce SW9; ⊙ 10pm-late; tube Brixton

This gay place's no-nonsense approach to cruising is not for the faint of heart during the week, especially with Monday's underwear-only Y Front, Wednesday's Boot Camp and Friday's Dirty Dishes. The attention turns a little more to music and dancing with Queer Nation's house night on Saturday and indie evening Marvellous on Sunday.

Entertainment – Clubbing

COMEDY

Comedy in London is bigger than in just about any other city we've ever visited, and there are more than 20 major clubs hosting regular gigs and big names from the circuit, along with countless other venues – including pubs that try and get in on the act at least one night a week. Some of the world's most famous comedians hail from, or made their names in, London. To whet your appetite a quick roll call from recent decades might include Peter Sellers, Peter Cook, Spike Milligan, Dudley Moore, Tommy Cooper, Dawn French, Lenny Henry, Ben Elton, Alexei Sayle, Harry Enfield, Victoria Wood, Julian Clary, Rowan Atkinson, Reeves & Mortimer, Eddie Izzard and Ali G.

Comedy Café, Hoxton (see opposite)

Up until the early '80s comedy was largely restricted to fat stand ups in working men's clubs, who usually told sexist and racist jokes (sometimes combining the two for rousing encores), as well as comedy revues made up of college-educated, middle-class larrikins (the likes of Monty Python and the Young Ones).

So-called 'alternative comedy' – a term that sounds positively quaint these days – swept to prominence in the early 1980s when a wave of politically savvy and brilliantly innovative comedians arrived to challenge the ethos, strictures and downright dreariness of Thatcher's Britain. The circuit mushroomed, the media labelled comedy the new rock 'n' roll (what *hasn't* been at some stage?) and this new generation of comics went on to shape a golden age in British TV comedy.

While the heyday of English comedy has probably passed, the comedy continues unrelenting, and London now has a motley crew of chuckle merchants from all around the world. While some are comedy stalwarts going through the same patter they have for years, London continues to be at the sharp end and it's cutting edge is often the world's best. You'll find no better place if you're into having your funny bone tickled, your perceptions challenged and possibly your conscience pricked. Look out for London-based American comedian Rich Hall who, for our money, is the greatest stand-up of his time. Ross Noble is a uniquely gifted, sonic-waffling Geordie whose stream of consciousness shtick should come with a health warning, while musician, poet and Luton-towner, John Hegley, is the uncrowned king of rhythm on the London circuit. Other names that will guarantee memorable moments are Mark Thomas, Richard Herring, Bill Bailey, Daniel Kitson and Simon Munnery.

You'll often have to visit the bigger theatres and venues to see the highest profile performers, although they sometimes mingle with the new and establishing talent in the clubs. If you're in town for June and July you might see big names in small clubs as they fine tune their shows for the Edinburgh's comedy festival in August, when the laughs are somewhat stifled in London. If you fancy yourself as a contender for the world's hardest gig, there are always try-out nights in the smaller clubs and pub venues. *Time Out* has the complete listings.

AMUSED MOOSE

☎ 8341 1341; Barcode below, 3 Archer St; ☿ Sun-Mon, Wed-Thur; admission £6-11; tube Piccadilly Circus
One of the city's best small clubs, Amused Moose is popular with audiences and co-medians alike, perhaps helped along by the fact that heckling is 'unacceptable' and all of the acts are 'first date–friendly' in that they're unlikely to humiliate the front row.

BANANA CABARET

☎ 8673 8904; Bedford Arms, 77 Bedford Hill SW12;
☿ Fri & Sat; admission £10-13; tube Balham
Touted as the finest pub comedy club in south London, this drum-shaped venue has been going for decades and always has fairly reliable, established acts – although you're not likely to discover the next big thing. A post-gig DJ cranks it up until 2am.

BOUND & GAGGED
☎ 8450 4100; The Fox, 413 Green Lanes N13; ☿ Fri & Sat; admission £10; rail Palmers Green

This 200-seater has long been one of the best rooms in London comedy and will doubtlessly be improved by a 2003 refurbishment. Expect to see some of the best of the moment.

CANAL CAFÉ Map pp422-3
☎ 7289 6054; Bridge House, 13 Westbourne Terrace Rd W2; ☿ Thu-Sun; admission £5-10; tube Warwick Avenue

Although it's pretty, er, unkempt, this 25-year-old fringe venue continues in the satirical spirit of some of Britain's best – you'll see some huge talent on this tiny Little Venice stage.

CHUCKLE CLUB Map pp426-7
☎ 7476 1672; Three Tuns Bar, London School of Economics (LSE), Houghton St; ☿ Sat; admission around £10; tube Holborn

The comedian's favourite, this club has a great atmosphere thanks to comedy stalwart, resident host and all-round lovely bloke, Eugene Cheese, who begins every night with the Chuckle Club warm-up song.

COMEDY CAFÉ
☎ 7739 5706; 66-68 Rivington St EC2; ☿ Wed-Sat; admission Wed free, Sat up to £14; tube Old Street

We really don't like the whole meal-and-show vibe and think this purpose-built comedy club in Hoxton is a little too try-hard and wacky for our tastes, but it has some good comedians and the Wednesday night try-out spots are excruciatingly entertaining.

COMEDY STORE Map p428
☎ 7344 4444; Haymarket House, 1A Oxendon St SW1; ☿ Tue-Sun; admission £13/8; tube Piccadilly Circus

This was one of the first (and still one of the best) comedy clubs in London. It was established down the road in Soho in 1979, the year Margaret Thatcher came to power, which we're sure was no coincidence. Although it's a bit like conveyor-belt comedy, it gets some of the biggest names, plus the Comedy Store Players, the most famous improv outfit in town, on Wednesday and Sunday.

DOWNSTAIRS AT THE KING'S HEAD
Map pp420-1
☎ 8340 1028; 2 Crouch End Hill N8; ☿ Sat-Sun; admission £7; tube Finsbury Park, then bus W7

Another club that has thrived thanks to the efforts of its dedicated manager, Downstairs

is a busy, smokey and intimate room with a giving atmosphere and top acts.

HEADLINERS
☎ 8566 4067; The George IV, 185 Chiswick High Rd W4; ☿ Fri & Sat; admission £10; tube Turnham Green

The first purpose-built venue in West London, Headliners is comfortable and has a traditional shape in that the compere introduces the act and scarpers, try-outs open the night, and the best is saved until last.

JONGLEURS Map pp418-19
☎ 0870 78 70707; Dingwalls, 11 East Yard, Camden Lock NW1; ☿ Fri-Sat; admission from £15; tube Camden Town

The McDonald's of the comedy world, this international chain combines eating, drinking and laughing and is so popular you'll probably have to book for Friday and Saturday night (there are other venues in Battersea and Bow). The bill normally features one terrific, big-name comic and a couple of guys on unicycles (or thereabouts).

LEE HURST'S BACKYARD
COMEDY CLUB Map pp416-17
☎ 7739 3122; 231-237 Cambridge Heath Rd E2; ☿ Fri & Sat; admission £10-13; tube Bethnal Green

Established and maintained by the likeable comic and dedicated promoter of the venue's name, this place benefits by being one of those that the comics most like to play.

RED ROSE CLUB
☎ 7281 3051; 129 Seven Sisters Road N7; ☿ Sat; admission £7/5; tube Finsbury Park

This club is gloriously traditional, meaning there is no food, no DJ, and no airs or graces. Red Rose is housed at the back of a Labour club in an slightly seedy neighbourhood and is reliable for 24-carat comedy.

UP THE CREEK Map p435
☎ 8858 4581; 302 Creek Rd SE10; ☿ Fri & Sat; admission £10-14; rail Greenwich

Without meaning to encourage them, sometimes the hecklers are funnier than the acts at this great club, run and occasionally still compered by the legendary Malcolm Hardee, the patron sinner of British comedy, who stole Freddie Mercury's 40th birthday cake and donated it to his local old folks home.

DANCE

London is home to five major dance companies and a host of small, experimental ones. The Royal Ballet, the best classical-ballet company in the land, is based at the Royal Opera House in Covent Garden; the London Coliseum is another venue for ballet at Christmas and in summer.

The annual contemporary dance event in London is Dance Umbrella (p12). For more information about dance in the capital visit the London Dance Network's website at www.londondance.com.

Other occasional dance venues include the Riverside Studios and the ICA (p124) and the home of the English National Opera, the London Coliseum. For more information about dance in London, p53.

BARBICAN Map pp432-3

☎ 7638 8891; www.barbican.org.uk; Silk St EC2; admission £6.50-30, (students & over-60s on day of performance £6.50-9); tube Moorgate/Barbican

Increasingly, the Barbican is staging dance performances, particularly through its multi-disciplinary BITE festival (Barbican International Theatre Events), which runs the year through.

LABAN Map p435

☎ 8691 8600; www.laban.org; Creekside SE8; admission £1-15; tube Deptford/DLR Greenwich

This is an independent dance training school, but it also presents student performances, graduation shows, and regular pieces by its resident troupe Transitions, as well as other assorted dance, music and physical performances. Its £22-million home was designed by Tate Modern's architects Herzog & de Meuron.

PEACOCK THEATRE Map p430

☎ 7863 8222; www.sadlers-wells.com; Portugal St WC2; admission £10-37; tube Holborn

This small venue in the West End is part of the Sadler's Wells complex (opposite). It hosts things like parodies of modern dance or performances from the less established companies.

THE PLACE Map pp418-19

☎ 7387 0031; www.theplace.org.uk; 17 Duke's Rd WC1; admission £5-15; tube Euston

The birthplace of modern British dance (a Martha Graham–style school was established here in 1969), the Place concentrates on challenging, contemporary and experimental choreography, with a regular dash of Asian influences and dance theatre. Behind the late-Victorian facade, you'll find a recently refurbished 300-seat theatre, an arty, creative café atmosphere and six training studios.

ROYAL BALLET Map p430

☎ 7304 4000; www.royalballet.co.uk; Royal Opera House, Bow St WC2; admission £4-80; tube Covent Garden

Although it has modernised its programme around the edges, classical ballet is still, as one newspaper critic has put it, 'the mother lode of the Royal Ballet's identity'. So this is where to head if you want to see traditional performances like *Giselle* or *Romeo & Juliet*, performed by stars such as Darcey Bussell (once she recovers from an injured ankle), Sylvie Guillem, Irek Mukhamedov or Tamara Rojo. Standing tickets are £4 to £5. There are same-day tickets, one per customer, from 10am for £8 to £40, and half-price standby tickets.

SADLER'S WELLS Map pp420-1

☎ 7863 8000; www.sadlers-wells.com; Rosebery Ave EC1; admission £10-40; tube Angel

Sadler's Wells has a long and distinguished history. It dates from 1683, but more recently it's been credited with making modern dance mainstream by staging Matthew Bourne's revolutionary all-male *Swan Lake*. (More is expected by stars such as Bourne's New Adventures troupe.) Reopened in 1998 after a major make-over, this glittering modern venue attracts renowned international dancers. The Rambert Dance Company are regulars and worth seeing. The smaller Lilian Baylis Theatre stages more left-of-centre studio productions.

SOUTH BANK CENTRE Map pp426-7

☎ 7960 4242; www.rfh.org.uk; Belvedere Rd SE1; admission £6-60; tube Waterloo

Every August, the spotlight is put on dance for the Summer on the South Bank community dance festival. The Royal Festival Hall, Queen Elizabeth Hall and Purcell Room are also regular venues for the Dance Umbrella city-wide festival.

SPOKEN WORD

As one of the epicentres of the English language, Londoners treat their literati like glitterati and London is an extremely good place to see writers read their own work. It's not just home-grown UK talent like Monica Ali, Louis de Bernieres, Patrick Neate, Zadie Smith, Tony Parsons, Will Self or even occasionally JK Rowling you might find here, but international writers like Bill Bryson, Douglas Coupland or Aleksander Hemon on promotional tours. (Hemon's first book reading in London, for *The Question of Bruno,* was part-organised by Renee Zellwegger as she practised undercover for her role in the film *Bridget Jones's Diary.*)

As they tend to rely on the author's availability, many of these readings are organised on an ad hoc basis, so if you're interested it's best to keep an eye on the listings in *Time Out* or the *Evening Standard Metro Life* supplement on Thursdays. Chain bookstores, particularly Waterstone's and Books Etc, often have readings, and some major authors now appear at the South Bank Centre (p157). Meanwhile, some clubs like Cargo (last Sunday of the month, p297), Cherry Jam (Mondays once a month, p299) and Vibe Bar (p269) have spoken-word performances, open-mic sessions, poetry slams and similar events.

Otherwise, the following venues most regularly appear in spoken word listings pages.

ENTERPRISE Map pp418-19

☎ 7485 2659; 2 Haverstock Hill NW3; tube Chalk Farm

A weekly writers' session is held every Wednesday at this pub. From small beginnings in 1996, the Express Excess evening every Wednesday has since managed to attract top names in British writing. John Cooper Clarke, John Hegley, Will Self and Murray Lachlan Young have all appeared in the cosy room at the top of this typically grungy Camden pub.

ICA Map pp426-7

☎ 7930 3647; Nash House, The Mall SW1; tube Charing Cross/Piccadilly Circus

Writers in all media, from books to film and beyond, give readings from their books here.

A roster of well-known writers, from the hip to the seriously academic, often appear here to read from and discuss their work. The best events are those in the wonderful, high-ceilinged Nash Room upstairs.

POETRY CAFÉ Map p430

☎ 7420 9888; 22 Betterton St WC2; tube Covent Garden

With performances by established poets and a regular poetry and jazz evening every Saturday, it's little wonder this is a favourite destination for lovers of the spoken word. You can also polish your own prose at writing workshops or show what you've learnt on Tuesday's Poetry Unplugged open mike evening.

HEALTH & FITNESS

In a city famed for its drinking and nightlife, it's reasonable to expect Londoners to eschew such puritan pastimes as going to the gym in favour of shameless hedonism. In fact, many people indulge in both, and you will never be far from some sports facility or swimming pool. In fact, gym attendance in London has never been higher, with up-market chains being the order of the day, often staying open until late at night for the convenience of office workers. Like most other things in London, keeping fit in the capital can be expensive and riddled with snobbery – the gym you're a member of says a lot about you.

Gyms are either council-run at the bottom end of the market, or private enterprises at the top, with the latter often coming in large chains. Gyms with swimming pools can send membership rates soaring in the increasingly space-conscious city, although not in all cases.

In all cases, opening hours vary hugely even within certain leisure centres, where some facilities open or close before others. As a rule, most gyms are open until at least 9pm at night. However, it's best to call ahead.

GYM CHAINS

FITNESS FIRST

☎ 01202 845000; www.fitnessfirst.co.uk

Despite the fact that they shamelessly state 'there are no strangers at Fitness First, just friends you haven't met yet' on their website, this pan-London chain has a reputation as a good middle-range gym chain. Handily, you can use any Fitness First club, no matter where you joined up. With branches all over London, this chain is the most popular with short-term visitors to London.

HOLMES PLACE

☎ 7795 4100; www.holmesplace.co.uk

This yuppie behemoth spans the classier areas of London, and offers top-notch facilities for people with more money than time. Locations include several in the city, Docklands, Notting Hill, Putney and throughout suburban London. Tariffs vary from club to club, and it costs £80 per month just for the honour of using another branch of the pan-London network.

LA FITNESS

☎ 7366 8080, www.lafitness.co.uk

With over 20 gyms in all areas of London, from Victoria to the City, LA Fitness is another big player on the scene. Its gyms are modern and well equipped and their membership packages flexible.

INDIVIDUAL GYMS

CENTRAL YMCA Map p428

☎ 7343 1700; 112 Great Russell St WC1; per day/week £15/42.50; tube Tottenham Court Rd

The gym at London's YMCA remains a very popular place and is always busy. Membership also gives you the chance to use the pool. The YMCA compares favourably with many of the more expensive and elitist London gyms, and of course it's very friendly. It is not, however, a youth hostel!

EQVVS PERSONAL TRAINING Map pp436-7

☎ 7838 1138; 43A Cheval Place SW7; tube Knightsbridge

This personal training centre offers top-of-the-range facilities and orientates itself squarely toward models, actors and other unworldly beings that are able to pay for the personal services of Marco Bellagamba. The centre offers more alternative therapies as well, from yoga to reflexology. Prices are high and vary upon the services required.

QUEEN MOTHER SPORTS CENTRE

Map pp440-1

☎ 7630 5522; 223 Vauxhall Bridge Rd SW1; per day £7.10; tube Victoria

This place is another reliable, central London gym, featuring three pools and comprehensive sporting facilities.

SEYMOUR LEISURE CENTRE Map pp422-3

☎ 7723 8019; Seymour Pl W1; per day £7.15; tube Marble Arch

The Seymour is an unimpressive but perfectly functional place that is well equipped and friendly. Its main advantage is its central London location and its reasonable prices, which mean it's always quite busy.

THIRD SPACE Map p428

☎ 7439 6333; 13 Sherwood St W1; per month £250; tube Piccadilly Circus

The Groucho Club of gyms, this pretentiously named Piccadilly Circus establishment is the last word in gym chic, make no mistake. The sumptuous facilities provide everything necessary for your busy Soho media exec to relax in or work up a sweat on. All at a hefty price, naturally, and the minimum time period for membership is one month.

SWIMMING POOLS

There are a huge number of swimming pools in London and listed below are some of the best. The Art Deco lidos built in the first 30 years of the 20th century are of particular interest. Obviously, these open-air pools are best in the summer, although most are open all year round for the hardy. Often, you have to be a member of the local swimming club in order to use the pool. The prices listed below are adult/concession.

BROCKWELL PARK LIDO Map pp416-17

☎ 7274 3088; Dulwich Rd SE24; ☉ 6.45am-7pm mid-Jun–Aug, otherwise weather dependent; before/after 10am £3/4; rail Herne Hill

A beautifully designed 1930s lido, Brockwell is hugely popular in the summer months and was recently fully restored with funding from Evian, who now sponsor the pool.

IRONMONGER BATHS Map pp420-1

☎ 7253 4011; Ironmonger Row EC1; £2.90/1.30; tube Old Street

This council-run gym and pool complex is popular but not too crowded, and has a great pool and friendly atmosphere.

OASIS Map p430
☎ 7831 1804; 32 Endell St WC2; £3/1.10; tube Tottenham Court Road/Covent Garden

This bizarre pool has the advantage of being right in the heart of London. It's often very crowded, although the experience of swimming outdoors on the roof should not be missed. There's an indoor pool for fresher London days.

PARLIAMENT HILL LIDO Map p415
☎ 7485 3873; Hampstead Heath, Gordon House Rd NW5; admission 7-9am free, 10-6pm £3.60/1.80; rail Gospel Oak

This classic lido on Hampstead Heath is a wonderful place to come for a bracing morning swim free of charge during the summer months. It attracts a friendly but dedicated bunch of local devotees and also boasts a children's paddling pool and sunbathing area.

SERPENTINE LIDO Map pp422-3
☎ 7298 2100; Hyde Park W2; tube Hyde Park Corner/Knightsbridge

Perhaps the ultimate London pool, the fabulous Serpentine Lido is usually open in July and August each summer. Prices and times are always subject to change, so best to call ahead.

TOOTING BEC LIDO
☎ 8871 7198; Tooting Bec Rd SW17; ☺ May-Sep; adult/conc/under 5 £3.65/£2.50/free; tube Tooting Bec

The first-ever public lido in London, Tooting Bec was built in 1906 and remains one of the largest in Europe at 90 by 36 metres. It was refurbished in 2002 and now includes Jacuzzis and saunas.

SPAS

ELEMIS DAY SPA Map pp426-7
☎ 8909 5060; 2-3 Lancashire Ct; tube Bond Street

This incredible Mayfair spa recently won European day spa of the year, and it's not hard to see why. The place is almost ridiculously elaborate and features themed suites – Balinese, Moroccan, the purple room and the emerald room, for example. Upmarket and offering a huge range of services, this is one hell of a place to treat yourself. Make sure you book ahead.

K SPA
☎ 7674 1000; Richmond Way W12; day membership basic/luxury £25/£35; tube Shepherd's Bush

The K Spa is an important part of the K West Hotel, and has a good range of facilities – a Jacuzzi, eucalyptus steam room, sauna and two gyms. Alternatively you can also choose from a range of exotic treatments such as the Espa hot stone treatment, as well as a full range of massages and body and facial treatments. One of the best complexes in West London.

PORCHESTER BATHS Map pp422-3
☎ 7792 2919; Porchester Centre, Queensway W2; day membership £18.95; tube Bayswater

The Porchester Centre contains a spa, pool and gym and is one of the cheaper places to go and spend the day pampering yourself. The place has seen better days, as is visible from the swimming pool's ceiling, but it's often next to empty, which makes swimming a joy.

MUSIC
POPULAR

Britpop is *so* over that former *Select* magazine editor John Harris has even written a book about it *(The Last Party)*. However, it would be a mistake to think that without Blur, Oasis and Pulp, London's music scene has died. The recent crop of US new wave and punk bands go down well here and like to visit. Other major groups continue to consider London an essential place to tour. As well, there's always a core of up-and-coming local bands, and some superstars of the 1980s and 1990s (from Dave Gahan to Steve Strange) have even reappeared. Together, these artists and bands keep London's wide range of rock and pop venues – from the aircraft-hangar sized Earl's Court or Wembley Arena to the tiny Borderline or Barfly – humming and full. For a more in-depth round-up of London music, p43.

If you can, it's best to buy direct from the venue to save yourself commission charges. However, events in London sell out astonishingly quickly and agencies tend to have tickets after the venue has sold out. Ticketmaster (☎ 7344 4444; www.ticketmaster.co.uk), Stargreen (☎ 7734 8932; www.stargreen.co.uk) and Ticketweb (☎ 7771 2000; www.ticketweb.co.uk) all have 24-hour telephone and online booking. Be wary of ticket touts outside the venue on the night, even if you're really desperate to get in. The price will be exorbitant and sometimes the ticket turns out to be forged.

ASTORIA Map p428

☎ 7434 0044; www.meanfiddler.com; 157 Charing Cross Rd WC2; tube Tottenham Court Road

An extremely popular, although not particularly salubrious venue, the Astoria hosts an array of performers from the likes of Kylie to Thin Lizzy. At the time of writing, it was struggling to keep its licence, so check weekly listings. The adjacent Mean Fiddler, at No 165, is actually a better venue, but doesn't get used as much.

BRIXTON ACADEMY Map p439

☎ 7771 2000; www.brixton-academy.co.uk; 211 Stockwell Rd SW9; tube Brixton

It's hard to have a bad night at the Brixton Academy, even if you leave with your soles sticky with beer, as this cavernous former theatre (holding 4000) alway thrums with bonhomie. There's a properly sloping floor for good views, as well as plenty of bars. You can catch international acts of the ilk of Madonna (once), but more likely bands are Beck, Queens of the Stone Age or the Dandy Warhols.

EARL'S COURT EXHIBITION CENTRE

Map pp436-7

☎ 7385 1200 or 0870 903 9033; Warwick Rd SW5; tube Earl's Court

The kind of large, soulless venue that gave stadium rock its bad name, Earl's Court has nevertheless scored a coup in recent years by playing host to the annual Brit music awards – where Justin Timberlake was famously photographed pawing Kylie Minogue's bum.

FORUM Map p415

☎ 7344 0044; www.meanfiddler.com; 9-17 Highgate Rd NW5; tube Kentish Town

Once the famous Town and Country Club, this medium-sized hall, with stalls and a mezzanine, remains one of the better places in town to see the newly famous, and keeps the ticket touts swarming around Kentish Town tube.

GARAGE Map pp420-1

☎ 7607 1818; www.meanfiddler.com; 20-22 Highbury Corner N5; tube Highbury & Islington

Ever since the likes of the Strokes and the Vines announced the return of guitar-based rock, this indie-kid venue has been enjoying a minor renaissance – although in truth it never went away. The smaller, upstairs room is slightly less heaving and sweaty than the main floor.

HACKNEY OCEAN Map pp416-17

☎ 8533 0111; www.ocean.org.uk; 270 Mare St E8; tube Bethnal Green/rail Hackney Central

This renovated former library has superb facilities in its three halls, although the setting is not particularly atmospheric – it feels a bit like a bingo hall or leisure centre. Still, it's a good place to catch everything from world music to two-step, UK garage and R&B (with a little '80s nostalgia thrown in occasionally).

LONDON ARENA Map p435

☎ 7538 1212; www.londonarena.co.uk; Limeharbour, Isle of Dogs E14; DLR Crossharbour & London Arena

The fact that, in a land of football, it has to boast about being the home of the London Knights ice hockey team says all about the Arena you need to know. Large, new, unatmospheric and not very conveniently located.

UNION CHAPEL Map pp420-1

☎ 0870 120 1349; www.unionchapel.org.uk; Compton Tce N1; tube Highbury & Islington

A place that doubles as a church and a venue for gigs and parties, the Union Chapel is worth visiting for its atmosphere alone. The acoustics aren't brilliant, but the octagonal-shaped room with its pews and carved banisters is breathtaking. It's for quieter, folksier performers; in recent years, Cerys Matthews (ex-Catatonia) and Rufus Wainwright have appeared.

Borderline (opposite)

SHEPHERD'S BUSH EMPIRE Map pp416-17

☎ 7771 2000; www.shepherds-bush-empire.co.uk; Shepherd's Bush Green W12; tube Shepherd's Bush

The mid-sized Empire is certainly one of the cleanest and most civilised music venues in town. It's the sort of place you'll find a slightly older, chilled but still hip crowd watching the likes of Interpol, The Handsome Family, Nitin Sawhney, or comeback artists like Evan Dando and Dave Gahan. One gripe: the floor doesn't slope, so if you're under 6ft tall, it's a little difficult to see from up the back in the stalls.

WEMBLEY ARENA Map pp416-17

☎ 8902 0902; Empire Way, Wembley; tube Wembley Park

A huge, unappealing barn that's a bit of a schlep to reach – you'd really only bother going to this 10,000-plus capacity venue if your favourite band was on.

Smaller places that have a more club-like atmosphere and are worth checking out for up-and-coming bands.

BARFLY @ THE MONARCH Map pp418-19

☎ 7691 4244, 7691 4245; www.barflyclub.com; Monarch, 49 Chalk Farm Rd NW1; tube Chalk Farm/ Camden Town

Barfly, Charles Bukowski, lounge lizards – you get the picture. This typically grungy, although not unpleasant, Camden venue is full of small-time artists looking for their big break. Alternative music radio station Xfm and music weekly *NME* host regular nights.

BORDERLINE Map p428

☎ 7734 2095; www.borderline.co.uk; Orange Yard, off Manette St W1; tube Tottenham Court Road

Through the Tex-Mex entrance and down into the basement, you'll find a packed, 275-capacity venue that really punches above its weight. Read the writing on the walls (literally, there's a gig list): Crowded House, REM, Blur, Counting Crows, PJ Harvey, Lenny Kravitz, Debbie Harry, plus many anonymous indie outfits, have all played here. The crowd's equally diverse, but full of music journos and talent-spotting record-company A & Rs.

BULL & GATE Map p415

☎ 7485 5358; 389 Kentish Town Rd NW5; tube Kentish Town

An old-skool, smokey music venue, despite recent renovations, the legendary Bull & Gate still

pulls in the punters with lots of guitar bands hoping to be the next big thing.

CARGO Map pp420-1

☎ 7739 3440; 83 Rivington St EC2; tube Old Street

Multi-talented Cargo spices up its club nights (p268) with performances from up-and-coming bands or visiting cult bands from overseas.

DINGWALLS Map pp418-19

☎ 7267 1577; 11 East Yard, Camden Lock Pl NW1; tube Camden Town

More a comedy venue (p301) and better suited to that really, Dingwalls does however host indie acts on the less busy days from Sunday to Thursday.

DUBLIN CASTLE Map pp418-19

☎ 7485 1773; 94 Parkway NW1; tube Camden Town

This famous pub is where a lot of successful bands cut their indie teeth. Madness launched their careers here and the likes of Blur and Ash have passed through.

HALF MOON

☎ 8780 9383; www.halfmoon.co.uk; 93 Lower Richmond Rd SW15; tube Putney Bridge

It's an unlikely location for a legendary London venue, but the Half Moon has seen the likes of the Stones, U2 and Elvis Costello on its stage. It's more likely to book tribute bands these days, but check the website for listings (the Hamsters and My Vitriol played recently).

SPITZ Map pp432-3

☎ 7392 9032; 109 Commercial St E1; tube Aldgate East/Liverpool Street

In the row of buildings lining Spitalfields market, Spitz is a restaurant and café/music venue. It's pretty relaxed in both demeanour and music policy, with the latter including anything from beats-driven jazz fusion to experimental Icelandic singing and everything in between.

UNDERWORLD Map pp418-19

☎ 7482 1932; 174 Camden High St NW1; tube Camden Town

An underground warren beneath the World's End pub (p275), only mid-sized but with plenty of nooks and crannies, Underworld has indie and rock bands performing and fills in the blanks with similarly tuned club nights.

Entertainment – Music

JAZZ

London has always had a thriving jazz scene, and – with its recent resurgence thanks to acid jazz, hip hop, funk and swing – is stronger than ever.

100 CLUB Map p428
☎ 7636 0933; 100 Oxford St W1; tube Oxford Circus
This legendary London venue concentrates on jazz, but once showcased the Stones and was at the centre of the punk revolution. There are still free lunch-time jazz sessions from noon to 3pm Friday.

JAZZ CAFÉ Map pp418-19
☎ 7916 6060; 5 Parkway NW1; tube Camden Town
The jazz club that's really made the most of jazz's crossover to the mainstream, this trendy industrial-style restaurant mixes its jazz with afro, funk, hip, R&B and soul styles.

PIZZA EXPRESS JAZZ CLUB Map p428
☎ 7439 8722; 10 Dean St W1; tube Tottenham Court Road
It's a bit of a strange arrangement, having a small basement venue beneath the main chain restaurant, but it seems to work well. Patrons listen attentively to modern jazz.

RONNIE SCOTT'S Map p428
☎ 7439 0747; 47 Frith St W1; tube Leicester Square
One of the world's most famous jazz clubs, Ronnie Scott's survived the death of its namesake

owner in 1996. His business partner Pete King now does the introducing and tells the bad jokes that give the place a bit of atmosphere.

VORTEX Map p414
☎ 7254 6516; 139-141 Stoke Newington Church St N16; bus 73,76, 106, 243
This is a relaxed and pleasant local venue, where you'll find British jazz musicians playing nightly.

FOLK & WORLD MUSIC

AFRICA CENTRE Map p430
☎ 7836 1973; 38 King St WC2; tube Covent Garden
The centre offers African music concerts most Friday nights and there are one-offs on other nights.

CECIL SHARP HOUSE Map pp418-19
☎ 7485 2206; 2 Regent's Park Rd NW1; tube Camden Town
The headquarters of the English Folk Dance and Song Society, this is *the* venue for English folk music (an acquired taste, it must be said), especially at 8pm on Tuesday when the folk club meets.

CLASSICAL MUSIC

London is a major classical-music capital, with four world-class symphony orchestras, two opera companies, various smaller ensembles, brilliant venues, reasonable prices and high standards of performance.

There's so much on that you may have trouble deciding what to pick. On any night of the year, the choice will range from traditional crowd-pleasers to new music and 'difficult' composers. Opera is naturally more costly. However, despite recent hiccups at the English National Opera, the overall standard is high.

BARBICAN Map pp432-3
☎ 7638 8891; www.barbican.org.uk; Silk St EC2; admission £6.50-30, students & over-60s on day of performance £6.50-9; tube Moorgate/Barbican
The Barbican Centre has plenty to offer the classical music buff: it's the home of the wonderful London Symphony Orchestra, but scores of leading international musician also perform here every year. The lesser-known BBC Symphony Orchestra, City of London Symphonia and English Chamber Orchestra are also regulars. The halls' acoustic qualities

Wigmore Hall (opposite)

Church Venues

Many churches host evening concerts or lunch-time recitals year round or during the summer months. Sometimes they are free (with a suggested donation requested); at other times there is a charge. A few of the city's redundant churches now serve as concert halls.

St James's Piccadilly (Map p428; ☎ 7734 4511; 197 Piccadilly W1; £7.50-17; tube Piccadilly Circus) Concerts at 1.10pm on Mon, Wed and Fri; donation requested. Evening concerts at 7.30pm (days vary).

St John's, Smith Square (Map pp440-1; ☎ 7222 1061; Smith Square SW1; £6; tube Westminster) Concerts at 1pm on Mon.

St Martin-in-the-Fields (Map p430; ☎ 7839 8362; Trafalgar Sq WC2; lunchtime/evening donations requested/ £6-20; tube Charing Cross) Concerts at 1.05pm on Mon, Tue and Fri. Evening concerts by candlelight Thu to Sat at 7.30pm.

St Paul's Cathedral (Map p432-3; ☎ 7236 4128; New Change EC4; organ recitals £6; tube St Paul's) Organ recitals at 5pm on Sun. Evensong 5pm Mon to Sat, 3.15pm Sun, special events permitting.

Southwark Cathedral (Map pp432-3; ☎ 7367 6700; Montague Close SE1; tube London Bridge) Organ recitals at 1.10pm on Mon, other concerts at 1.10pm on Tue. Evensong weekdays at 5.30pm (excluding Mon and Wed), 4pm Sat and 3pm Sun.

Westminster Abbey (Map pp426-7; ☎ 7222 5152; www.westminster-abbey.org; Dean's Yard SW1; tickets are usually £5-18; tube Westminster) Free organ recitals every Sun 5.45pm. Evensong weekdays at 5pm (excluding Wed), at 3pm Sat & Sun. Ring or check website for details of spring/summer organ festival sometime between May and August.

were greatly improved by renovations a few years back.

KENWOOD HOUSE Map p415

☎ 7413 1443; www.ticketmaster.co.uk, Hampstead Lane NW3; admission £16.50-24.50; tube Archway/ Golders Green, then bus 210

A highlight of any sunny summer is to attend an outdoor concert in the grounds of Hampstead's Kenwood House, for Proms on the Heath. People sit on the grass or on deck chairs, eat strawberries, drink chilled white wine and listen to classical music and opera (staying for the fireworks) on selected weekend evenings in July and August.

ROYAL ALBERT HALL Map pp422-3

☎ 7589 8212; www.royalalberthall.com; Kensington Gore SW7; admission £5-150, Proms admission £4-75; tube South Kensington

This splendid Victorian concert hall hosts many classical-music, rock and other performances, but is most famous as the venue for the (BBC) Proms – one of the world's biggest classical-music festivals, still with a touch of flag-waving 'Rule Britannia' patriotism on the last night. Booking is possible, but from mid-July to mid-September, Proms punters also queue for £4 standing (or 'promenading') tickets that go on sale one hour before curtain up. Otherwise, the box office and pre-paid ticket collection counter are both through door No 12 on the

south side of the Hall leading up from Prince Consort Road.

SOUTH BANK CENTRE Map pp426-7

☎ 7960 4242; www.rfh.org.uk; Belvedere Rd SE1; admission £6-60; tube Waterloo

The ears have it. The **Royal Festival Hall** is one of London's premier concert venues simply because the acoustics are superb. Home to the Philharmonia orchestra and the London Philharmonic, it's also where leading symphony orchestras visiting London come (alongside the Barbican). The smaller **Queen Elizabeth Hall** and **Purcell Room** host chamber groups or solo performances. Sometimes, during certain festivals, even bands like the Fun Lovin' Criminals or Asian Dub Foundation might appear at the South Bank. Standby tickets (from £6 to £10) are available for some performances.

WIGMORE HALL Map pp426-7

☎ 7935 2141; www.wigmore-hall.org.uk; 36 Wigmore St W1; admission £6-35; tube Bond Street

This Art Nouveau hall has possibly even better acoustics than the Royal Festival Hall, and its traditional atmosphere and exquisite Art Deco detailing make it one of the best concert venues in London. There's a great variety of concerts and recitals. The recitals at 11.30am on Sunday (£10) are particularly good. There are lunchtime concerts at 1pm on Monday (adults/seniors £8/6).

OPERA

ROYAL OPERA Map p430

☎ 7304 4000; www.royaloperahouse.org; Royal Opera House, Bow St WC2; admission £6-150, midweek matinees £6.50-50; tube Covent Garden

The once starchy Royal Opera House has been attracting a younger, wealthy audience since its £210 million redevelopment at the turn of the century, with more adventurous programming, including operas like *Woyczek*. The renovated Floral Hall is now open to the public during the day, with free lunch-time concerts at 1pm on Monday, exhibitions and daily tours.

ENGLISH NATIONAL OPERA Map p430

☎ 7632 8300; www.eno.org; Coliseum, St Martin's Lane WC1; admission £3-65; tube Leicester Square/ Charing Cross

Generally renowned for making opera modern and relevant, the ENO has recently suffered a quadruple whammy of bad reviews, personnel woes, financial difficulties and media flak. It's back at the now refurbished Coliseum from February 2004 (after a Barbican sojourn) and is hopefully finding its way artistically again. Same-day tickets (£3) are the cheapest deal, but prices could rise.

OPERA HOLLAND PARK Map pp422-3

☎ 0845 230 9769; www.operahollandpark.com; Holland Park, off Kensington High St W8; admission £25-40; tube Kensington High Street

An 800-plus seat canopy is erected temporarily every summer for a nine-week season in the middle of Holland Park, and it's an excellent place to see opera. The atmosphere's relaxed, you're in a beautiful setting and you can enjoy a picnic beforehand. The programme mixes crowd-pleasers like *Tosca* or *Fidelio* with rare works like *L'Arlesiana* and attracts older and younger guests.

SPORTS

As capital of a sports-mad nation, you can expect London to be brimming over with sporting spectacles throughout the year. As always the entertainment weekly *Time Out* is the best source of information on fixtures, times, venues and ticket prices.

Clubs in the Capital

Football is at the very heart of English culture, and attending a game is one of the highlights of any visit to London. Whether you're after the glamour of a premiership tie or the old-fashioned atmosphere of the lower divisions, there's ample opportunity to adopt a team and join the cheering throngs. At the time of writing, Arsenal, Charlton, Chelsea, Fulham and Tottenham Hotspur were all in the Premiership with seven others aspiring to the same heights. For more on football in London, p20.

Arsenal (☎ 7413 3366; www.arsenal.com, Avenell Rd N5; admission £25-45; tube Arsenal)

Charlton Athletic (☎ 8333 4010; www.cafc.co.uk; The Valley, Floyd Rd SE7; admission £15-40; rail Charlton)

Chelsea (☎ 7385 5545, tickets 7386 7799; www.chelseafc.co.uk; Stamford Bridge Stadium, Fulham Rd SW6; admission £11-40; tube Fulham Broadway)

Crystal Palace (☎ 8771 8841; www.cpfc.co.uk; Selhurst Park, Whitehorse Lane SE25; admission £20-26; rail Selhurst)

Fulham (☎ 7893 8383, tickets 7384 4710; www.fulhamfc.co.uk; Craven Cottage, Stevenage Rd SW6; admission £25-40; tube Putney Bridge)

Leyton Orient (☎ 8926 1111; www.leytonorient.com; Matchroom Stadium, Brisbane Rd E10; admission £12-16; tube Leyton)

Millwall (☎ 7231 9999; www.millwallfc.co.uk; The Den, Zampa Rd SE16; admission £16-25; rail South Bermondsey)

Queens Park Rangers (QPR; ☎ 8740 2575; www.qpr.co.uk; Loftus Rd W12; admission £14-20; tube White City)

Tottenham Hotspur (☎ 8365 5000, tickets 08700 112222; www.spurs.co.uk; White Hart Lane N17; admission £12-55; rail White Hart Lane)

Watford (☎ 01923 496010; www.watfordfc.com; Vicarage Rd, Watford; admission £10-25; rail Watford Junction)

West Ham United (☎ 8365 5000, tickets 8548 2700; www.westhamunited.co.uk; Boleyn Ground, Green St E13; admission £22-39; tube Upton Park)

Wimbledon (☎ 8771 8841; www.wimbledon-fc.co.uk; Selhurst Park, Whitehorse Lane SE25; admission £18-27; rail Selhurst) There has been talk in recent years of the Dons moving from their temporary South London home to the satellite town of Milton Keynes so if you want to be one of the 'hundreds' that go to watch this team, you should telephone ahead.

FOOTBALL

Wembley Stadium, in northwest London, has been the premier national stadium since it was built in 1923, and is where England traditionally plays its international matches and where the FA Cup Final is contested in mid-May. Its greatest moment came when the victorious England captain, Bobby Moore, held the World Cup trophy aloft in 1966. But sadly and controversially, the great stadium and its two landmark towers were demolished in 2001; a new 80,000-capacity, state-of-the-art complex is being erected in its place, due for completion some time in 2005. It will become the premier venue for football, rugby league and athletics competitions, but until it's ready, important internationals are being played at various venues around the country, with the FA Cup Final held at Cardiff's Millennium Stadium.

There are a dozen league teams in London and usually around five or six play in the Premier League, meaning that on any weekend of the season – from August to mid-May – top-quality football is just a tube or train ride away (if you can manage to get hold of a ticket). If you really want to see a match, you might consider dropping a division and going to see one of the first division teams, for which you can normally just rock up on the day.

CRICKET

If you're hot and bothered from seeing the sights, you could do a lot worse than packing up a picnic and spending a day enjoying the thwack of leather on willow and savouring the atmosphere of this most English of sports. Although the game was invented here, the England team has struggled on the international stage in recent years, although of late there have been promising signs and the game of gentlemen continues to flourish.

The **English Cricket Board** (☎ 08705 338833; www.ecb.co.uk) has full details on schedules and tickets, which cost between £20 and £50 and can be difficult to get. Tests are regularly played at the venerable Lord's and Oval grounds (the latter is known for its distinctive gasholders). Tickets (£5-10) are a lot easier to come by for county games; county teams compete in four-day, one-day and twenty-over matches between April and September.

LORD'S Map pp418-19
☎ tours office 7616 8585, switchboard 7616 8500; www.lords.org; St John's Wood Rd NW8; tube St John's Wood
Home to county team Middlesex.

OVAL Map pp440-1
☎ 7582 7764; www.surreycricket.com; Kennington Oval SE11; tube Oval
County side Surrey plays at the Oval.

RUGBY UNION & RUGBY LEAGUE

Between January and March England competes against Scotland, Wales, Ireland, France and Italy in the Six Nations Championship, and there are always three games at Twickenham Stadium.

TWICKENHAM RUGBY STADIUM
☎ 8892 2000; www.rfu.com; Rugby Rd, Twickenham; tube Hounslow East then bus 281, or rail Twickenham
The shrine of English rugby union. For tours of the stadium and its museum.

LONDON BRONCOS Map p414
☎ 8853 8001; www.londonbroncos.co.uk; The Valley, Floyd Rd SE7; rail Charlton
This is only place in southern England to see rugby league.

Union fans should head to southwest London, where mighty teams like the Harlequins and Wasps play from August to May. London Irish and Saracens are also in the Premiership. Most matches are played on Saturday and Sunday afternoons.

HARLEQUINS
☎ 8410 6000; www.quins.co.uk; Stoop Memorial Ground, Langhorn Dr, Twickenham; admission £12-25; rail Twickenham

LONDON IRISH
☎ 01932 783034; www.london-irish.com; Bennet Rd, Reading; admission £7-16; rail Reading

WASPS
☎ 8740 2545; www.wasps.co.uk; Twyford Avenue Sports Ground, Twyford Ave, Acton W3; admission £7-18; tube Ealing Common

SARACENS
☎ 01923 496200; www.saracens.com; Vicarage Rd, Watford; admission £12-35; rail Watford High Street

TENNIS

Tennis and Wimbledon, in southeast London, are almost synonymous.

WIMBLEDON

☎ 8944 1066, 8946 2244; www.wimbledon.org; Church Rd SW19; tube Southfields/Wimbledon Park

The All England Lawn Tennis Championships have been taking place here in late June/early July since 1877. Most tickets for the Centre and Number One courts are distributed by ballot, applications for which must be made the preceding year. Try your luck by sending a stamped addressed envelope to **All England Lawn Tennis Club** (☎ 8944 1066, info 88946 2244; www.wimbledon.org; PO Box 98, Church Rd, Wimbledon SW19 5AE). Limited tickets go on sale on the day of play although queues are painfully long. The nearer to the finals, the higher the prices; a Centre Court ticket that costs £25 a week before the final will cost twice that on the day. Prices for outside courts are under £10, reduced after 5pm. You might be better off going to the men's warm-up tournament at **Queen's Club** (☎ 7385 3421; www.queensclub.co.uk; Palliser Rd, Hammersmith W14; admission per day £12; tube Barons Court), which takes place a couple of weeks before Wimbledon.

ATHLETICS

England, and London in particular, has a rich history in athletics and continues to produce world champions. There are major international meets each summer at the grand old venue of Crystal Palace in southeast London, which has been the site of many magical moments in recent years and where every international athlete worth his or her salt has competed.

CRYSTAL PALACE NATIONAL SPORTS CENTRE Map p414

☎ 8778 0131; www.crystalpalace.co.uk; Ledrington Rd SE19; rail Crystal Palace

Athletics and swimming meetings attracting major international and domestic stars take place here regularly throughout the summer.

BASKETBALL

'B ball' is becoming more popular in the capital and there are two local teams, **London Leopards** (☎ 01277 230231; Brentwood Leisure Centre, Doddinghurst Rd, Essex; rail Brentwood) and **Kinder London Towers** (☎ 8776 7755; www.london-towers.co.uk; Crystal Palace National Sports Centre, Ledrington Rd SE19; rail Crystal Palace) in the British Basketball League. Tickets are about £8.

HORSE RACING

There are plenty of racecourses within striking distance of London for those who want to have a flutter. The flat racing runs from April to September, while you can see the gee-gees scaling fences from October to April.

ASCOT

☎ 01344 622211; Berkshire; admission from £6; rail Ascot

Best known for the regal fashion circus of Royal Ascot in June.

EPSOM

☎ 01372 470047; Epsom, Surrey; admission from £5; rail Epsom Downs

Epsom has much more racing credibility than Ascot. The famous racetrack's star-turn is Derby Day in June, although it has meetings throughout the year.

KEMPTON PARK

☎ 01932 782292; Staines Rd East, Sunbury-on-Thames, Middlesex; admission from £6; rail Kempton Park

Kempton has meetings all year but is particularly good for its evening events in summer.

ROYAL WINDSOR RACECOURSE

Greyhound Racing

If you're looking for a cheap and cheesy night out, consider going to the dogs. Greyhound racing, in which six to eight skinny mutts chase a mechanical rabbit around an oval track, costs as little as £1.50 to £5 for a 12-race meeting and is Britain's second most popular sport after football. A flutter or two will guarantee excitement, and you'll rub shoulders with a London subculture both welcoming and slightly shady.

Catford Stadium (☎ 8690 8000; Adenmore Rd SE6; rail Catford Bridge)

Walthamstow Stadium (☎ 8531 4255; Chingford Rd E4; rail Highams Park)

Wimbledon Stadium (☎ 8946 8000; Plough Lane SW17; tube Wimbledon Park)

☎ 01753 865234; Maidenhead Rd, Windsor, Berkshire; admission from £6; rail Windsor

Beside the castle, an idyllic spot for a day at the races.

SANDOWN PARK

☎ 01372 463072; Portsmouth Rd, Esher, Surrey; admission from £12; rail Esher

This is generally considered to be the finest racecourse in the southeast.

THEATRE

In recent years, London has definitely snatched from New York's Broadway the accolade of being the world's greatest centre for theatre (p40). Hollywood stars such as Nicole Kidman, Madonna, Gywneth Paltrow, Woody Harrelson and Matthew Perry have certainly voted with their manicured and well-shod feet, willingly accepting a measly pay cheque for all the street cred that performing in a play here brings.

In recent years the risk-taking and innovation normally seen in fringe theatre has infused and enthused the West End, often leaving audiences on the edge of their seats. At the same, if you just want good-time entertainment, musicals like *Les Miserables*, *Phantom of the Opera*, *Chicago* and *Mamma Mia!* carry on.

For a comprehensive look at what's being staged, pick up the free *Official London Theatre Guide* or visit www.officiallondontheatre.co.uk.

Booking Agencies

Shows sell out fast in London, so book as far in advance as you can. You can go directly through a theatre's box office or, for a booking fee, through agencies **Ticketmaster** (☎ 7344 4444, www.ticketmaster.co.uk) or **First Call** (☎ 7420 0000, www.firstcalltickets.co.uk). Most box offices open around 10am to 8pm Monday to Saturday, but almost never on Sunday. If the production is sold out, you may be able to buy a returned ticket on the day of the performance, although for something really popular you might need to start queuing before the returns actually go on sale.

On the day of performance only you can buy discounted tickets, sometimes up to 50% off, for West End productions from the **Tkts Booth** (Map p430; ☿ 10am-7pm Mon-Sat, noon-3pm Sun; tube Leicester Square) in the clock tower on the south side of Leicester Square. It's run by the non-profit **Society of London Theatre** (SOLT; ☎ 7836 0971) and wholly legitimate, although it levies a £2.50 service charge per ticket and has a limit of four tickets per customer. Payment is by cash or credit/debit card (Visa, Mastercard, American Express, Switch).

Be wary of commercial ticket agencies nearby, particularly those along Cranbourn St, which advertise half-price tickets without mentioning the large commission added to the price. Student stand-by tickets are sometimes available on production of identity cards one hour before the performance starts. Phone the Student Theatre Line on ☎ 7379 8900 for more details.

ROYAL NATIONAL THEATRE Map pp426-7

☎ 7452 3000; www.nationaltheatre.org.uk; South Bank SE1; admission Olivier & Lyttelton £10-34, Cottesloe £10-25; tube Waterloo

Britain's flagship theatre showcases a mix of classic and contemporary plays performed by excellent casts. It has three auditoria: **Olivier**, **Lyttelton** and the smaller **Cottesloe** studio. New artistic director Nicholas Hytner is not only using exciting stagings and plays to attract new audiences, but has also slashed ticket prices. For six months during his first annual season, three-quarters of the seats in the Olivier were being sold for £10. Whether such Easyjet-style bargains will be repeated is still being decided, but same-day tickets are sold for £10 in any case. Stand-by tickets (usually £17) are sometimes available two hours before the performance. Students or the unemployed must wait until just 45 minutes before the curtain goes up to purchase stand-by tickets at a concession price of around £9. Registered disabled visitors are eligible for discounts.

Behind the scenes tours (£5) of the theatre are available at 10.15am, 12.15pm (or 12.30pm) and 5.15pm (or 5.30pm) Monday to Saturday. You're supposed to ring ☎ 7452 3400 or 7452 3333 for details, but we could never get through, so try the main number above or book in person.

BARBICAN Map pp432-3

☎ 7638 8891; www.barbican.org.uk; Silk St EC2; admission to theatre/Pit £5-30/£15; tube Moorgate/Barbican

The Barbican's been valiantly working to fill its two auditoria – the Barbican Theatre and the smaller Pit – since the formerly resident Royal

Entertainment – Theatre

Shakespeare Company left. It's not done too badly either, especially with its BITE (Barbican International Theatre Events) programme. Besides music and dance shows, overseas drama companies and local fringe theatre troupes also perform. Stand-by tickets are available on the day of the performance to students, seniors and the unemployed for about £12.

ROYAL COURT Map pp436-7
☎ 7565 5000; www.royalcourttheatre.com; Jerwood Theatre, Sloane Sq SW1; admission Tue-Sun/Mon 10p-£26/£7.50; tube Sloane Square

Forever associated with John Osborne's *Look Back In Anger* and similar revolutionary postwar pieces, the Royal Court continues to concentrate exclusively on fresh, surprising new writing.

The company's own theatre, the Jerwood, was refurbished during the latter half of the 1990s and now has two comfy modern auditoria, upstairs and downstairs. All tickets on Monday are £7.50; there's a general price for students, under 21s, seniors, and the unemployed of £9.50; and 10p standing tickets for eight people are sold just before the performance in the downstairs theatre. Stand-by tickets are sold an hour before the performance, but at full price.

SHAKESPEARE'S GLOBE Map pp432-3
☎ 7401 9919; www.shakespeares-globe.org; admission seated/standing £13-29/£5; 21 New Globe Walk SE1; tube London Bridge

The Globe is the home of authentic Shakespearean theatre, not only in the sense that it's a near-perfect replica of the building Shakespeare himself worked in from 1598 to 1611, but because it also largely follows Elizabethan staging practices. The building is a wooden 'O', with no proper roof over the central stage area. Although there are covered wooden bench seats in tiers around the stage, many people elect to emulate the 17th-century 'groundlings' who stood in front of the stage, shouting and cajoling as they wished.

The building is quite open to the elements and you may have to wrap up. No umbrellas are allowed, but cheap macs are on sale. The theatre season runs from May to September, including works by Shakespeare, his contemporaries such as Christopher Marlowe, and at least one new work every year.

A warning: two pillars holding up the stage canopy (the 'Heavens') obscure much of the view in section D; you'd almost do better to

stand. In winter, plays are staged in the new indoor **Inigo Jones Theatre**, a replica Jacobean playhouse at the Globe.

OFF WEST END & FRINGE

London's most challenging and ultimately headline-creating theatre is often found in its many off–West End and fringe-theatre productions. Offering a selection of the amazing, the life-enhancing and the downright ridiculous, some of the better venues include:

ALMEIDA THEATRE Map pp420-1
☎ 020 7359 4404; www.almeida.co.uk; Almeida St N1; tube Angel

It's got refurbished seats and a new artistic director in Michael Attenborough, but the tiny Almeida hasn't lost its edge. Previous productions have included Natasha Richardson doing Ibsen, the world premiere of a play by Neil LaBute (director of films *In the Company of Men* and *Nurse Betty*), and several versions of Franz Wedekind's tale of the irresistible temptress *Lulu*.

BATTERSEA ARTS CENTRE Map pp416-17
BAC; ☎ 7223 2223; www.bac.org.uk; Lavender Hill SW11; tube Clapham Common, rail Clapham Junction, bus 77, 77A or 345

This is a friendly, down-to-earth community theatre where staff chat to you and the actors mingle in the bar with the audience postshow. Its innovative work has won it plaudits, too. Past hits have included the Gecko company's *Taylor's Dummies*, a winning piece of physical theatre, and *Jerry Springer – the Opera*, which transferred to the National.

BUSH THEATRE Map pp416-17
☎ 7610 4224; www.bushtheatre.co.uk; Shepherd's Bush Green W12; tube Shepherd's Bush

For what is essentially a pub theatre, the Bush is exceptionally good. Its success is down to strong writing from the likes of Tina Brown, Jonathan Harvey, Conor McPherson and Stephen Poliakoff. It also attracts top actors. The seating has been renovated, so you no longer have to clamber over other people to reach yours. A move in 2005 is possible, so ring ahead.

DONMAR WAREHOUSE Map p430
☎ 7369 1732; www.donmar-warehouse.com; 41 Earlham St WC2; tube Covent Garden

When Sam Mendes was artistic director and Nicole Kidman was administering 'theatrical viagra' nightly by peeling off her clothes in *The Blue*

West End Theatres

Every summer the West End theatres stage a new crop of plays and musicals, but some performances really do run and run. Addresses and box-office phone numbers of individual theatres are given below. We've noted where shows have taken up long-term residence at a particular theatre. Where no show is noted, consult *Time Out* to see what's on.

Adelphi (Map p430; ☎ 7344 0055; Strand WC2; tube Charing Cross) Where to see *Chicago*, and all that jazz.

Albery (Map p430; ☎ 7369 1740; 85 St Martin's Lane WC2; tube Leicester Square)

Aldwych (Map p430; ☎ 0870 400 0805; 49 Aldwych WC2; tube Holborn) *Fame – The Musical*. Is it going to live forever?

Apollo (Map p428; ☎ 7494 5070; 39 Shaftesbury Ave W1; tube Piccadilly Circus) Bollywood fans come here to indulge their *Bombay Dreams*.

Cambridge (Map p430; ☎ 7494 5080; Earlham St WC2; tube Covent Garden)

Comedy (Map p428; ☎ 7369 1731; Panton St SW1; tube Piccadilly Circus)

Criterion (Map p428; ☎ 7413 1437; Piccadilly Circus W1; tube Piccadilly Circus) The Reduced Shakespeare Company trots out the Bard's complete works in a hilarious 90 minutes.

Dominion (Map p428; ☎ 0870 607 7400; 268-269 Tottenham Court Rd W1; tube Tottenham Court Road) Queen's greatest hits are melded together by Ben Elton in *We Will Rock You*.

Duke of York's Theatre (Map p430; ☎ 7836 4615; St Martin's Lane WC2; tube Leicester Square)

Fortune (Map p430; ☎ 7836 2238; Russell St WC2; tube Covent Garden) *The Woman in Black* continues to send a chill down the spine.

Garrick (Map p430; ☎ 7494 5085; 2 Charing Cross Rd WC2; tube Charing Cross)

Gielgud (Map p428; ☎ 7494 5065; 33 Shaftesbury Ave W1; tube Piccadilly Circus)

Her Majesty's (Map p428; ☎ 7494 5400; Haymarket SW1; tube Piccadilly Circus) *The Phantom of the Opera's* regular haunt is Her Majesty's.

London Palladium (Map p428; ☎ 7494 5020; 8 Argyll St W1; tube Oxford Circus) *Chitty Chitty Bang Bang* – the kids will love you.

Lyceum (Map p430; ☎ 7420 8100; 21 Wellington St WC2; tube Covent Garden)

Lyric (Map p428; ☎ 7494 5045; Shaftesbury Ave W1; tube Piccadilly Circus)

New Ambassadors (Map p430; ☎ 7369 1761; West St WC2; tube Leicester Square) *Stones in his Pocket*, about a Hollywood film being shot in Ireland, keeps them chuckling.

New London (Map p430; ☎ 7405 0072; Drury Lane WC2; tube Holborn)

Palace (Map p430; ☎ 7434 0909; Shaftesbury Ave W1; tube Leicester Square) *Les Miserables* are still singing about a revolution.

Phoenix (Map p430; ☎ 7369 1733; 110 Charing Cross Rd WC2; tube Tottenham Court Road) Willy Russell's *Blood Brothers* is set in Liverpool.

Piccadilly (Map p428; ☎ 7478 8800; Denman St W1; tube Piccadilly Circus)

Prince Edward (Map p428; ☎ 7447 5400; 30 Old Compton St W1; tube Leicester Square) *Mamma Mia!* indeed: the enduring appeal of Abba strikes again in this long-running musical.

Prince of Wales (Map p428; ☎ 7839 5987; 31 Coventry St W1; tube Piccadilly Circus)

Queen's (Map p428; ☎ 7494 5040; Shaftesbury Ave W1; tube Piccadilly Circus)

St Martin's (Map p430; ☎ 7836 1443; West St WC2; tube Leicester Square) Agatha Christie's *The Mousetrap* doesn't look like snapping shut, even after more than 50 years.

Shaftesbury (Map p430; ☎ 7379 5399; 210 Shaftesbury Ave WC2; tube Tottenham Court Road/ Holborn)

Savoy (Map p430; ☎ 7836 8888; Savoy Court, Strand WC2; tube Charing Cross)

Strand (Map p430; ☎ 7836 4144; Aldwych WC2; tube Covent Garden)

Theatre Royal Drury Lane (Map p430; ☎ 7494 5060; Catherine St WC2; tube Covent Garden) With a little bit of luck, you'll still be able to catch *My Fair Lady*.

Theatre Royal Haymarket (Map p428; ☎ 0870 901 3356; Haymarket SW1; tube Piccadilly Circus)

Whitehall (Map p430; ☎ 7321 5400; 14 Whitehall SW1; tube Charing Cross)

Wyndham's (Map p430; ☎ 7369 1736; Charing Cross Rd WC2; tube Leicester Square)

Room, the Donmar really was the hottest ticket in town. Now it's under the direction of Michael Grandage from Sheffield Theatres, who seems to be adding a European flavour. The theatre's reputation is way out of proportion to it tiny size, so book ahead. Actor Rhys Ifans has compared performing here to 'doing it in a lift'.

HACKNEY EMPIRE Map pp416-17
☎ 8985 2424; 291 Mare St E8; rail Hackney Central
Only rarely a venue for serious theatre, the newly renovated Empire stages lots of variety and comedy shows, benefits and world music.

HAMPSTEAD THEATRE Map pp418-19
☎ 7722 9301; www.hampsteadtheatre.com; 98 Avenue Rd NW3; tube Swiss Cottage
Known for producing the works of new and emerging writers, including some new plays by Harold Pinter in the 1960s, the Hampstead Theatre also features the occasional well-known face, such as actor Ewan McGregor. Its now has a funky new modern building, with two auditoria – one seating 80, the other 325.

KING'S HEAD Map pp420-1
☎ 7226 1916; 115 Upper St N1; tube Highbury & Islington
Its informal, down-to-earth atmosphere means this theatre pub is not ideally suited to serious drama, but it's great for cabaret and the like.

LYRIC HAMMERSMITH Map p414
☎ 08700 500 511; www.lyric.co.uk; King St W6; tube Hammersmith
A modern glass entrance leads to a plush, red historic auditorium, seating 550 and a smaller 180-seat studio. Expect innovative versions of historic European plays, such as *Pericles*, and mixed-media performances with film projection, dance and music. The studio is aimed at audiences under 20.

OLD VIC Map pp426-7
☎ 7928 7616; Waterloo Rd SE1; tube Waterloo
The Old Vic might be in a state of disrepair, but help is on the way. New artistic director Kevin Spacey kicked off the fundraising as early as 2003, and has given the box office a boost by promising to perform here twice a year.

OPEN AIR THEATRE Map pp418-19
☎ 7486 2431; www.openairtheatre.org; Inner Circle, Regent's Park NW1; admission £10-26; tube Baker Street
From June to early September, it's fun to take in a Shakespearean play or musical at this outdoor theatre.

SOUTHWARK PLAYHOUSE Map pp432-3
☎ 7620 3494; 62 Southwark Bridge Rd SE1; tube Southwark
The Southwark Playhouse, a relatively new 70-seat theatre, has been getting rave reviews for its challenging work under young artistic director Thea Sharrock. One of the biggest hits to date has been *Through the Leaves* starring Simon Callow, which later transferred to the West End.

TRICYCLE THEATRE Map pp416-17
☎ 7328 1000; www.tricycle.co.uk; 269 Kilburn High Rd NW6; tube Kilburn
A venue that knows its local audience well, the Tricycle stages top-class productions with an Irish or black theme, and mostly with a strong political angle. There's a nice cinema and bar on site, too.

YOUNG VIC Map pp426-7
☎ 7928 6363; 66 The Cut SE1; tube Waterloo
Associate director Rufus Norris has been called one of the boldest and the best in new British Theatre, and has instigated such typically creative Young Vic hits as a reworking of *Sleeping Beauty* and a translated Spanish play *Peribanez*. The audience sits close to the actors, giving this wonderful theatre an intimate feel.

Shopping

Shopping

'My brother (sister/mother/daughter/boyfriend etc) went to London and all I got was this lousy T-shirt.' It's an infamous souvenir, but who wants to limit their shopping to *that* in one of the world's great retail meccas? There's hours of endless fun in having a proper rummage through this city's consumer delights, whether you're looking for Harrods' English breakfast tea or the latest in Vivienne Westwood clothes.

It's not *quite* correct that if you can't find something in London, it probably doesn't exist (but near enough, damn it). There are

Camden Canal Market (p333)

antiques and clothes along Portobello Rd Market, a dozen libraries' worth of books along Charing Cross Rd, design stores, furniture stores and world-renowned department stores like Fortnum & Mason and Harvey Nichols. Let's not forget Camden Market, rated among the top five sights to see. So, in short, if retail is therapy, then London is a great big sympathetic couch (designer, of course).

True, London rarely offers the value found in New York, and shopaholic Londoners themselves frequently cross the Atlantic on cheap jeans-buying sprees. However, even if pricey, this city has plenty of retail strengths. Take its fashion – apart from jeans – as an example. It's not only represented by the reinvented classic brands like Burberry and the reinvigorated tailoring of Savile Row, nor by the whole host of hot young British designers, from Antoni Berardi and Alexander McQueen to Stella McCartney and Julien Macdonald. Rather, London's real flag-carrier is its cutting-edge streetwear. You'll see this around you, on almost every street, but such fashion's spiritual homes these days appears to be Hoxton, including the boutiques around Brick Lane and Spitalfields.

Even along touristy **Oxford St** (Map p428), you'll find plenty of clothes – they'll be from chain stores, but in such number as you rarely see. Bond St is lined with expensive global brands, while High St Kensington mixes posh and trendy styles. Covent Garden isn't all twee souvenir outlets, either; there are plenty of great stores in Floral St, Monmouth Gardens, Shorts Gardens, Neal St and Neal's Yard.

Fashion aside, other streets have their own specialities. Jewellery lovers will find nirvana in Clerkenwell, record collectors will discover second-hand heaven in Hanway St and Notting Hill. Tottenham Court Rd is synonymous with computer shops and furniture stores. Chelsea (particularly the Antiquarius Antiques Centre), Islington and Kensington are the top places to head for antiques.

Of course, some of London's bigger stores are tourist attractions in their own right. Harrods is usually top of the list, but most people also know 'Harvey Nicks' (Harvey Nichols). Older customers tend to love Fortnum & Mason, while younger shoppers are usually bowled over by Selfridges. Customers so young they need to bring their parents reckon the toy emporium Hamleys to be the best show in town.

For more details, try the annual *Time Out Shopping Guide* (£8.99), with details of hundreds of the capital's shops.

Opening Hours

The good news is that you can go shopping every day of the week. The slightly bad news is that this is not universally true throughout the city.

Generally, shops open from 9am or 10am to about 6pm or 6.30pm Monday to Saturday, at least. Shops in the West End (Oxford St, Soho and Covent Garden) open late (normally to 8pm) on Thursday; those in Chelsea, Knightsbridge and Kensington open late on Wednesday.

In the West End and Chelsea, Knightsbridge and Kensington, many shops are now also open on Sunday, typically from noon to 6pm but sometimes 10am to 4pm. Sunday trading is also common in Greenwich and Hampstead and along Edgeware and Tottenham Court Rds.

Conversely, some shops in the square mile, or the City of London, only open Monday to Friday. Additionally, smaller designer stores tend to keep hours to suit their owners, opening later of a morning and often closing on a Monday or Tuesday to stay open on weekends. It's a good idea to ring ahead with these places, too, as they often have last-minute changes.

If there's a major market on a certain day – say, Columbia Road Flower Market on a Sunday morning – it's a good bet that neighbouring stores will fling open their doors.

Duty free

In certain circumstances, visitors from non-EU countries are entitled to claim back the 17.5% value added tax (VAT) they have paid on purchased goods. The rebate only applies to items purchased in stores displaying a 'tax free' sign (there are plenty of these along Bond St) – to claim it, visitors must be staying in the UK for less than six months.

The procedure to follow is relatively simple: don't forget to pick up the relevant form in the shop at the time of sale and then hand it in at the airport when you leave.

Best Areas to Shop

London's famous Oxford St can be slightly disappointing, testing your patience as you elbow your way through the crowds. Similarly, litter-strewn and packed Camden is somewhat less fabulous than its reputation might admit. Carnaby St was the heart of the Swinging '60s, but Austin Powers movies notwithstanding, that's all a long way in the past. Instead, the best places to head with your wallet or credit card are:

Charing Cross Rd It's been immortalised in TV and film, and while London's most famous book of streets now features more chains (Books Etc, Borders, Waterstones) they complement existing independent stores to provide both quantity and quality. For special interest browsing, try Murder One (crime novels), Sports Pages (every sport possible) and Zwemmer's (art, architecture, photography).

Covent Garden Away from the touristy old market hall, you'll find a whole host of cool fashion, including Ted Baker, Camper and Paul Smith (in and around Floral St), Koh Samui and Poste Mistress (Monmouth Gardens), hip menswear shop Duffer of St George (Shorts Gardens), Diesel, and Australian surfwear label Mambo (Neal St and Earlham St). Luxury cosmetics store Space NK is also in Earlham St, while the four-floor Dr Marten emporium is located back towards the market on King St.

High St Kensington The less crowded, more salubrious alternative to Oxford St, this has all the high-street chains from BHS, Boots, French Connection, H&M and Jigsaw to Kookai, Marks & Spencer, Warehouse and Zara. Trendy stores, including Diesel (no 38a) and Urban Outfitters (no 36), can also be found here, while towards Church St there's even the chance of snapping up some antiques.

Hoxton, Shoreditch and Spitalfields Home on Sunday to the happening Spitalfields market, this area is increasingly important as a London shopping 'hood. Up-and-coming designers tout clothes, cutting-edge jewellery and household objects, plus there are oodles of classic furniture pieces for sale. It's a place for adventurous shoppers, who don't mind searching out small boutiques for something unique, cool and slightly ahead of the game.

King's Rd A far cry from its 1960s mod heyday, King's Road is still strong on household goods, with the Designer's Guild (No 269), Habitat (No 206) and Heal's (No 234). Children are well catered for, too; Daisy & Tom (No 181) and Trotters (No 34) provide distractions such as a carousel (D&T) and express train (Trotters), while offering designer children's clothes, toys and haircuts.

Knightsbridge Harrods is a national institution, and even sceptics should see its food halls and Egyptian Hall of gifts at least once. Harvey Nichols is within easy reach, and there are many nearby stores for cashed-up fashionistas. Hand-bag store Mulberry (Brompton Rd) and the Queen's lingerie supplier Rigby and Peller (Hans Rd) are home-grown concerns, while Italian design gets an airing at Emporio Armani (Brompton Rd).

THE WEST END

This is the heart of London shopping, where you'll find the greatest concentration of stores across every type and budget. If there's a label worth having, you'll find it between the West End and South Central. Shopping options are well scattered, although some streets are renowned for their specialities. Dedicated followers of fashion will already know that the area around Covent Garden has all the best in urban and streetwear (Newburgh, Floral and Carnaby Sts are particularly worth checking out), while Oxford St is *the* quintessential High St, and the area around Sloane Square is where to look for high-end couture. The twee shops and stalls inside the old market building at Covent Garden itself tend to be pricey and tourist-oriented, but the streets running off it remain a happy hunting-ground whether you're in the market for undies, books, music, homewares or cheese.

DEPARTMENT STORES

SELFRIDGES Map pp426-7
☎ 7629 1234; 400 Oxford St W1; tube Bond Street
This is the funkiest and most vital of London's one-stop shops, where fashion runs the gamut from street to formal, the food hall is unparalleled and the cosmetics hall is the largest in Europe. Some say it's what Harrods was before it became a self-parody.

FASHION & DESIGNER

ANYA HINDMARCH Map pp422-3
☎ 7838 9177; www.anyahindmarch.com; 15 Pont St; tube Sloane Square
Colourful, stylish and humorous bags are the Hindmarch trademark and have become icons of the fashionistas. She also does more formal accessories and has recently started designing shoes along the same themes.

BLACKOUT II Map p430
☎ 7240 5006; 51 Endell St WC2; tube Covent Garden
Two floors crammed with designer retro gear from the '50s to the '80s for men and women.

DUFFER OF ST GEORGE Map p430
☎ 7836 3722; 29 Shorts Gardens, Covent Garden WC2; tube Covent Garden
The *meisters* of London menswear, Duffer has two stores within a few doors of each other here, purveying 'shield' formal wear like shirts and classic Italian handmade suits, as well as more urban sweats, bags and accessories.

EMMA HOPE'S SHOES Map pp422-3
☎ 7259 9566; www.emmahope.co.uk; 53 Sloane Sq SW1; tube Sloane Square
Multi-award-winning designer Emma Hope is renowned for lovingly detailed and gorgeous girlie shoes made with luxurious materials such as suede and silk. Now, you can also wear her beautiful designs over your shoulder.

FRENCH CONNECTION UK Map pp426-7
☎ 7629 7766; 396 Oxford St W1; tube Oxford Circus
The high prince (and price) of London high street, FCUK is an in-your-face chain with an aggressive PR department leading the way in street-chic style, including everything from T-shirts to slinky party dresses.

HIGH JINKS Map p430
☎ 7240 5580; Thomas Neal Centre, Earlham St WC2; tube Covent Garden
A temple for street wear, this emporium is crammed with labels from established skate and street labels as well as struggling young designers, who are more than a little keen to sell their imaginative and low-slung rags.

MANOLO BLAHNIK Map pp436-7
☎ 7352 3863; 49-51 Old Church St SW3; tube Sloane Square
Fans of footwear should scuttle to this marvellous place that looks more like a gallery than a mere shop. On display are the kind of shoes that Madonna reckons are 'better than sex' and the girls on *Sex & the City* drool over.

PAUL SMITH Map p430
☎ 7379 7133; 40-4 Floral St WC2; tube Covent Garden
Great for a browse even if you don't intend to spree, Paul Smith represents the best of British classic with innovative twists. Glorious garments and attractive accessories for men, women and children.

PHILIP TREACY Map p440-1
☎ 7824 8787; www.philiptreacy.co.uk; 69 Elizabeth St SW1; tube Sloane Square
Hats off to this wonderful Irish milliner who dresses the heads of some of the world's most exclusive customers and provides an affordable ready-to-wear range for mere mortals, including his famous 'bisexual' cap.

POSTE
Map pp426-7

☎ 7499 8002; 10 South Molton St; tube Bond Street

On one of London's most fashionable streets, this very cool shop is aimed at boys who like good shoes, and stocks everything from vintage street labels to razor-sharp Italian imports. Staff are very friendly and ridiculously good-looking.

TOP SHOP
Map p428

☎ 7636 7700; www.topshop.co.uk; 36-38 Great Castle St W1; tube Oxford Circus

The inimitable 'Toppers' is a high street icon and an outstanding British chain store for youth-market fashion. It's always right on the nail with its cheap and cheerful approach to designer dressing on a shoestring. It nurtures young design talent and always has some worthy, throwaway pieces whatever your taste, style or spending power. Topman gets equally, frenetically busy on Saturdays.

ZARA
Map p428

☎ 7534 9500; 118 Regent St W1; tube Piccadilly Circus/Oxford Street

The Spanish name synonymous with high-quality clothes for men and women has a carefully commercialised fashion edge, and won't cost you an arm and a leg.

FOOD & DRINK

ALGERIAN COFFEE STORES
Map p428

☎ 7437 2480; 52 Old Compton St W1; tube Leicester Square

This is *the* place to go to buy all sorts of tea and coffee, including Maragogype (aka the Elephant Bean), the biggest coffee bean in the world.

ANGELUCCI COFFEE MERCHANTS
Map p428

☎ 7437 5889; 23b Frith St W1; tube Tottenham Court Rd

This friendly and atmospheric shop is one of the oldest Italian family-run businesses in Soho and has been plying its trade since the 1920s. Its own blend, Mokital, is excellent.

GERRY'S
Map p428

☎ 7734 4215; 74 Old Compton Rd W1; tube Leicester Square

This place stocks a frankly frightening array of alcohol gathered from far-flung parts. Come here if you just can't manage without a bottle of Peruvian *pisco*, Polish *zubrowka*, Stoli Razberi or 70% absinthe.

Clothing Sizes
Measurements approximate only, try before you buy

Women's Clothing

Aust/UK	8	10	12	14	16	18
Europe	36	38	40	42	44	46
Japan	5	7	9	11	13	15
USA	6	8	10	12	14	16

Women's Shoes

Aust/USA	5	6	7	8	9	10
Europe	35	36	37	38	39	40
France only	35	36	38	39	40	42
Japan	22	23	24	25	26	27
UK	3½	4½	5½	6½	7½	8½

Men's Clothing

Aust	92	96	100	104	108	112
Europe	46	48	50	52	54	56
Japan	S		M	M		L
UK/USA	35	36	37	38	39	40

Men's Shirts (Collar Sizes)

Aust/Japan	38	39	40	41	42	43
Europe	38	39	40	41	42	43
UK/USA	15	15½	16	16½	17	17½

Men's Shoes

Aust/ UK	7	8	9	10	11	12
Europe	41	42	43	44½	46	47
Japan	26	27	27½	28	29	30
USA	7½	8½	9½	10½	11½	12½

MILROY'S OF SOHO
Map p428

☎ 7437 9311; 3 Greek St W1; tube Tottenham Court Road

This shop stocks over 500 whiskies, including 350 malts and 30 Irish whiskeys.

NEAL'S YARD DAIRY
Map p430

☎ 7240 5700; 17 Shorts Gardens WC2; tube Covent Garden

One of the best cheesemongers in London, this is the place to get local specialist farmhouse cheeses from throughout the British Isles, as well as condiments, pickles, jams and chutneys.

PAXTON & WHITFIELD
Map p428

☎ 7930 0259; 93 Jermyn St SW1; tube Piccadilly Circus

London's oldest cheesemonger has built up a hugely loyal following since opening the doors and letting the smell of its strong-smelling cheese waft out the door in 1797.

THE TEA HOUSE
Map p430

☎ 7240 7539; 15a Neal St WC2; tube Covent Garden

A quaint and attractive shop with a huge range of teas, tisanes and impractically cute pots to brew them in.

HOUSEHOLD

HABITAT Map pp426-7
☎ 7631 3880; 196 Tottenham Court Rd W1; tube Goodge Street
The chain that brought design into British homes has furniture as well as great home accessories. There are Habitat branches throughout London.

HEAL'S Map pp426-7
☎ 7636 1666; 196 Tottenham Court Rd W1; tube Goodge Street
This long-established furniture and homewares store is like Habitat's more *responsible* older brother, with more practical and conservatively classy designs, along with a great kitchenware section.

KITSCHEN SYNC Map p430
☎ 7497 5129; 7 Earlham St WC2; tube Covent Garden
Specialising in 'everything that is flashy and trashy for the home', this place is so tacky that it almost comes out the other side and becomes fun. You can buy groovy retro kitchenware such as shocking-pink kettles, heart-shaped chairs and Union Jack toilet seats.

ROYAL DOULTON Map p428
☎ 7734 3184; 154 Regent St W1; tube Piccadilly Circus
Try here for classic English bone-china and cut glassware.

JEWELLERY

JESS JAMES Map p428
☎ 7437 0199; www.jessjames.com; tube Oxford Circus
This great jewellery emporium showcases the elegant and diverse works of dozens of local designers as well as Jess herself.

MAPPIN & WEBB Map p428
☎ 7734 3801; www.mappin-and-webb.co.uk; 170 Regent St W1; tube Oxford Circus/Piccadilly Circus
This traditional jewellers has been in business since 1774 and today produces both contemporary and classic pieces including the fairly recent introduction of designer watches. There's also a watch repair service.

SPECIALIST STORES

AGENT PROVOCATEUR Map p428 *Lingerie*
☎ 7439 0229; 6 Broadwick St W1; tube Oxford Circus
For women's knickers to die for, die over and die in, pull up to this wonderful shop, which stocks sexy and saucy corsets, bras and nighties for all shapes and sizes and exudes confident and positive sexuality. The window displays are stunning.

ANN SUMMERS Map p428 *Lingerie*
☎ 7434 2475; 79 Wardour St W1; tube Piccadilly Circus
Roll up here for your lacy lingerie, leopard-skin handcuffs, breast enhancers, G-strings, leather whips and nurse uniforms. Much of the lingerie is geared towards play rather than towards practicality, although it *is* rather fetching.

JAMES SMITH & SONS
Map p430 *Accessories*
☎ 7836 4731; 53 New Oxford St WC1; tube Tottenham Court Road
Nobody makes and stocks umbrellas, canes and walking sticks as elegant as those behind this beautiful shop exterior.

LONDON SILVER VAULTS
Map pp426-7 *Silverware*
☎ 7242 3844; Chancery House, 53-63 Chancery Lane WC2, enter from Southampton Bldgs; ⊗ closes 1pm Sat; tube Chancery Lane
The 40 subterranean shops collectively known as the London Silver Vaults form the largest single concentration of silver in the world, where you'll find everything from jewellery and picture frames to candelabra and tea services.

TOYS

BENJAMIN POLLOCK'S TOY SHOP Map p430
☎ 7379 7866; 1st floor, 44 The Market, Covent Garden WC2; tube Covent Garden
For traditional toys – from Victorian theatres to handmade puppets – you won't find any better store (see also Pollock's Toy Museum on p103).

HAMLEYS
☎ 7494 2000; 188-96 Regent St W1; tube Oxford Circus
This is an Aladdin's cave of toys and games, with friendly, helpful and patient staff, and some sort of activity always going on.

KITE STORE Map p430
☎ 7836 1666; 48 Neal St WC2; tube Covent Garden
When you want to get the wind in your sails, select from hundreds of different kites here, from the traditional to the unrecognisable.

EAST CENTRAL

The City remains something of a retail desert, dotted mainly with chain stores, but the neighbouring districts of Hoxton and Clerkenwell more than make up for that.

Hoxton, in particular, is where to head for the latest in London's much vaunted street fashion. Spitalfields Market (p117) every Sunday is a meeting place for creative types churning out the new and unique and those interested in buying their wares. Each June and November, there's also a major showcase of the latest products, clothes, jewellery and art at the Atlantis Gallery of the Truman Brewery. This usually features something inspiring and unforgettable and is a good place to talent-spot future design stars. See www.eastlondondesignshow.co.uk.

Not too far away, Clerkenwell is another repository of hip clothes and homewares. However, it is most known for its jewellery. For classic settings and unmounted stones, visit **Hatton Garden** (Map pp426-7; tube Chancery Lane). The area's funky modern jewellers tend to be, literally, on the other side of the railway tracks. The **Clerkenwell Green Association** (cnr Clerkenwell Green & Clerkenwell Rd; www.cga.org.uk) provides an excellent starting point.

THE CITY

MOLTON BROWN Map p432-3

☎ 7621 0021; www.moltonbrown.co.uk; 27 Royal Exchange, Threadneedle St EC2; ⏰ 9am-7pm Mon-Fri; tube Bank

Much loved by (and much nicked from the bathrooms of) stylish boutique hotels, this British brand of natural beauty and skincare products offers plenty of pampering for men and women. There are other stores in Chelsea, Mayfair, Notting Hill and Covent Garden, but in the shopping desert of the City, this is in the best oasis – the Royal Exchange.

HOXTON, SHOREDITCH & SPITALFIELDS
Clothes

HOXTON BOUTIQUE Map pp420-1

☎ 7684 2083; www.hoxtonboutique.co.uk; 2 Hoxton St; ⏰ 10am-6pm Mon-Fri, 11am-5pm Sat, noon-5pm Sun; tube Old Street

This place has a kind of take-no-prisoners, dedicated attitude to stocking the absolute latest in women's streetwear – even if that's, say, an '80s revival. Two gnome statues welcome you to a minimalist room stocking the likes of Future Classics, Tatty Devine and Sophie Malig, and you could be looking at £90 to £100 for a pair of combat trousers.

JUNKY STYLING Map p432-3

☎ 7247 1883; www.junkystyling.co.uk; 12 Dray Walk, Old Truman Brewery, 91 Brick Lane E1; ⏰ 11am-5.30pm Mon-Fri, 10.30am-6pm Sat & Sun; tube Liverpool Street/Aldgate East

Junky has a different interpretation of 'recycled' clothes to most. It buys new designer gear at warehouse closing-down sales and gives them a total makeover, turning a man's suit jacket, for example, into a woman's halterneck top. You bring your own clothes in for the same treatment.

LADEN SHOWROOMS Map p432-3

☎ 7247 2431; www.laden.co.uk; 103 Brick Lane E1; ⏰ noon-6pm Mon-Fri, 10.30am-6pm Sat & Sun; tube Liverpool Street/Aldgate East

Go here for the latest in ironic flat-cap wearing, pointy-toed, satin-ruched combat-trousered Hoxton fashion. Laden stocks reasonably priced women's wear and menswear by young designers. Many of them also sell at Spitalfields Market, but here things are on sale all week.

TIMOTHY EVEREST Map p432-3

☎ 7377 5770; 32 Elder St E1; ⏰ by appointment only 9am-5.30pm Mon-Fri, 9am-3.30pm Sat; tube Liverpool Street

One of the most successful London tailors outside Savile Row, Everest counts David Beckham, Jarvis Cocker and Tom Cruise among his clients. A bespoke suit will cost at least £1,500, but it's possible to buy off the peg shirts for as little as £100, too. The showroom really looks more like a private house and, to prevent overcrowding, it's safest to book an appointment.

Household
EAT MY HANDBAG BITCH Map p432-3

☎ 7375 3100; www.eatmyhandbagbitch.co.uk; 6 Dray Walk, Old Truman Brewery, 91 Brick Lane E1; ⏰ 11am-6pm daily, but closed alternate Sundays; tube/rail Liverpool Street

Attention-grabbing name, but, strangely, not a handbag in sight. However, you won't care once you see the assortment of retro furniture and other 20th-century design classics on offer, as well as some particularly stylish replica '70s vases. They're fairly pricey, though. Ring to make sure the shop is open if you're going on a Sunday.

LASSCO ST MICHAEL'S Map pp420-1
☎ 7749 9944; www.lassco.co.uk; St Michael's Church, Mark St EC2, enter from Leonard St; 🕑 9.30am-5.30pm Mon-Fri, 10am-5pm Sat; tube Old Street
Lassco stands for London Architectural Salvage and Supply Co and it lays out a recycler's dream. Unique items from slate tiles and oak floorboards to enormous marble fireplaces and garden follies are up for sale, having been salvaged from historic buildings under demolition.

MATHMOS Map pp420-1
☎ 7549 2700; www.mathmos.co.uk; 22-24 Old St EC1; 🕑 9.30am-6pm Mon-Fri; tube Old Street/Barbican
Purveyors of the original Lava Lamp since the 1960s, Mathmos has experienced something of a revival in recent years. This huge, white showroom offers a range of sizes and designs, from original to rocket-shaped lava lamps, to glowing outdoor 'aduki' shapes. The cursed things are all so mesmerising, however, making it difficult to choose.

CLERKENWELL
Clothes
ANTONI & ALISON Map pp420-1
☎ 7833 2002; www.antoniandalison.co.uk; 34 Roseberry Ave EC1; 🕑 10.30am-6.30pm Mon-Fri, noon-4pm Sat; tube Farringdon
The main attraction here is the dozens of quirky T-shirt transfers. Pick a T-shirt (men's or women's) to go with them and they put the two together for you downstairs. Bank on paying £40-50. Cartoon purses are a good sideline.

Household
INFLATE Map pp420-1
☎ 7713 9096; www.inflate.co.uk; 28 Exmouth Market St EC1; 🕑 9.30am-6pm Mon-Fri; tube Farringdon
This unique shop sells a range of funky inflatables, from blow-up boiled-egg holders and postcards to lampshades and fruit bowls. There are also squidgy plastic objects, including knapsacks, piggy banks, salt-and-pepper shakers and wine-bottle corks. Genius, and a true one-off.

Jewellery
EC ONE Map pp420-1
☎ 7713 6185; www.econe.co.uk; 41 Exmouth Market St EC1; 🕑 10am-6pm Mon-Fri, 10.30am-6pm Sat; tube Farringdon
Goldsmith Joe Skeates makes eye-catching use of stones, particularly in his necklaces and rings, but it's the bracelets that have won the most attention, ever since movie star Cameron Diaz bought a bulk lot. Commissions are also accepted.

LESLEY CRAZE GALLERY Map pp420-1
☎ 7608 0393; www.lesleycrazegallery.co.uk; 33-35a Clerkenwell Green EC1; 🕑 10am-5.30pm Mon-Sat; tube Farringdon
This is considered one of European's leading centres for arty, contemporary jewellery and it's certainly one of the best in Clerkenwell. Much of the collection focuses on exquisitely understated, and sometimes pricey, metal designs. However, there's a smaller selection of mixed-media bangles, broaches, rings and the like (to the right of the main door) where prices start from about £15.

ISLINGTON
Clothes
COMFORT AND JOY Map pp420-1
☎ 7359 3898; 109 Essex Rd N1; 🕑 10am-6pm Mon-Sat; tube Angel
In this enticing, well-laid out small store, as you try on one of the extremely well tailored retro A-line print skirts, or perhaps one of the lovely floral tops, you can hear more of them being sewn with love and care. There's also a menswear section with similarly retro-styled clothes.

Household
ARIA Map pp420-1
☎ 7704 1999; 295-6 Upper St N1; 🕑 10am-7pm Mon-Fri, 10am-6.30pm Sat, noon-5pm Sun; tube Angel
Lots of lovely mugs, plates, toasters, Alessi kitchen equipment and so on. In the sister store across the road (No 133), you can even buy yourself crockery stamped with the faces of players from the local football team, Arsenal.

GET STUFFED Map pp420-1
☎ 7226 1364; 105 Essex Rd N1; 🕑 1pm-5pm Mon-Fri, 1.30pm-3.30pm Sat; tube Angel
This taxidermy shop is certainly something to see, whether you would consider buying here or not. It makes the point that all the animals

stuffed died of natural causes. Ring ahead, as opening hours sometimes change.

PAST CARING Map pp420-1
76 Essex Rd, N1; ⏱ noon-6pm Mon-Sat; tube Angel
Stuffed full of second-hand retro bric-a-brac, from ashtrays to curtain material, this shop has been a fave of Jarvis Cocker. Prices are good, and so is the stock. There's no phone, 'for obvious reasons' the assistant told us snottily, but we're still not quite sure why.

Toys
CHEEKY MONKEYS Map pp420-1
☎ 7288 1948; 38 Cross St N1; ⏱ 9.30am-5.30pm Mon-Fri, 10am-5pm Sat, 11am-5pm Sun; tube Angel
There are a few stores for children, including clothes stores, in and around Cross St. This sells a good range of toys, from stuffed Cats in the Hat to T-shirts and lots of outdoor garden stuff for children, like picnic tables and watering cans.

SOUTH CENTRAL

The chains and department stores of Regent St preserve traditional tastes and standards. Kensington High St has a nice mix of chains and boutiques; South Molton St is the strip for urban chic from local and international designers; Chelsea's famously chic King's Rd still has stylish shops; while Bond St is the fat end of the high-fashion wedge with designer outlets and classic jewellers. Of course, you know your tailor-made suit will fit more sharply if it comes from Savile Row, the home of English bespoke tailoring. Meanwhile, Knightsbridge draws the hordes with *orfully* English department stores and chichi boutiques. You'll find venerable and atmospheric stores dotted around that have spent centuries catering to the whims and vanities of the refined folk who live here.

DEPARTMENT STORES
FORTNUM & MASON Map p428
☎ 7734 8040; www.fortnumandmason.co.uk; 181 Piccadilly W1; tube Piccadilly Circus
Bywords for quality and service from a bygone area, Fortnum & Mason is steeped in almost 300 years of tradition, and is especially noted for its old-world, ground-floor food hall where Britain's elite come for their cornflakes and bananas. Exquisite picnic and gift hampers are available from the basement. It is also renowned for its outstanding range of teas and establishment fashion. This is where Scott stocked up before heading off to the Antarctic.

HARRODS Map pp422-3
☎ 7730 1234; www.harrods.com; 87 Brompton Rd SW1; tube Knightsbridge
This unique store is like a theme park for fans of the British establishment. It is always crowded with slow tourists and there are more rules than at an army boot camp, but even the toilets will make you swoon, the food hall will make you drool, and if they don't stock what you want you probably don't really want it.

HARVEY NICHOLS Map pp422-3
☎ 7235 5000; www.harveynichols.com; 109-25 Knightsbridge SW1; tube Knightsbridge
This is London's temple of high fashion, where you'll find all the names that matter in local and international high couture. There's a great

food hall and café on the 5th floor, a softly lit lingerie department, an extravagant perfume department and exquisite jewellery worth a short prison sentence.

LIBERTY Map p428
☎ 7734 1234; www.liberty-of-london.com; 210-20 Regent St W1; tube Oxford Circus
An irresistible blend of contemporary styles in an old-fashioned mock-Tudor atmosphere, Liberty has a huge and recently refurbished cosmetics department, along with a new lingerie section on the 1st floor – you can't leave London without some 'Liberty Florals' (printed fabrics).

PETER JONES
☎ 7730 3434; Sloane Square SW1; tube Sloane Square
Peter Jones and John Lewis on Oxford St are the slightly more upmarket, very English versions of Ikea, where you come to meet household needs rather than find cutting-edge design.

FASHION & DESIGNER
AMANDA WAKELY Map pp436-7
☎ 7590 9105; www.amandawakeley.com; 80 Fulham Rd SW3; tube South Kensington
Simple ideas expressed strongly is the defining characteristic at this store, showcasing the creations of one of Britain's best designers. She's also highly regarded for her international Sposa collection of ready-to-wear bridal clobber.

Books

Anyone who read the book or saw the film *84 Charing Cross Road* will know which street to head for when looking for books. Although its character is threatened by greedy landlords who are forcing out many specialist booksellers, Charing Cross Rd – and the little laneways leading off it – is still the best place to head for reading material old or new. Sadly typical of the times, 84 Charing Cross Rd, the best address imaginable for a bookstore is instead a soulless chain pub. Following are some more excellent addresses.

Al-Hoda (Map p430; ☎ 7240 8381; 76-78 Charing Cross Rd WC2; tube Leicester Square) The largest Muslim and Arab bookshop in central London.

Blackwell's (Map p430; ☎ 7292 5100; www.bookshop.blackwell.co.uk; 100 Charing Cross Rd WC2; tube Tottenham Court Road) This shop is primarily for academic titles but also stocks general books.

Books for Cooks (Map pp422-3; ☎ 7221 1992; www.booksforcooks.com; 4 Blenheim Cres W11; tube Ladbroke Grove) An enormous collection of cookery books. There's also a café with a test kitchen where you can sample recipes.

Borders (Map p430; ☎ 7379 8877; www.bordersstores.com; 120 Charing Cross Rd WC2; tube Tottenham Court Road) This branch of the American chain has a good selection of general titles as well as academic ones. The bigger Oxford St store has four floors of books, magazines, newspapers from around the world and CDs, tapes and DVDs.

Daunt Books (Map pp426-7; ☎ 7224 2295; 83-84 Marylebone High St W1; tube Baker Street) A beautiful old sky-lit shop with a wide selection.

Forbidden Planet (Map p428; ☎ 78364179; www.forbiddenplanet.com; 71-75 New Oxford St WC1) A trove of comics, videos and magazines.

Foyle's (Map p430; ☎ 7437 5660; www.foyles.co.uk; 113-119 Charing Cross Rd WC2; tube Tottenham Court Road) One of the biggest – and certainly the most confusing – bookshops in London, but it often stocks titles you may not find elsewhere and has recently set up a version of the Silver Moon Women's bookshop on the same premises.

French Bookshop (Map pp436-7; ☎ 7584 2840; www.frenchbookshop.com; 28 Bute St SW7; tube South Kensington) Head here for books *en français* and about France.

Garden Books (Map pp422-3; ☎ 7792 0777; 11 Blenheim Cres W11; tube Ladbroke Grove) Great place for green-thumbing your way through books on gardening.

Gay's the Word (Map pp420-1; ☎ 7278 7654; www.gaysthoword.co.uk; 66 Marchmont St WC1; tube Russell Square) This shop stocks guides and literature for, by and about gay men and women.

Gosh! (Map p430; ☎ 7636 1011; 39 Great Russell St WC1; tube Tottenham Court Road) Try this place for comics, cartoons and playing cards. The basement contains the London Cartoon Gallery where you'll find books on cartoon art.

Grant & Cutler (Map p428; ☎ 7734 2012; www.grantandcutler.com; 55-57 Great Marlborough St W1; tube Oxford Circus) This is the best foreign-language bookshop in London.

Helter Skelter (Map p430; ☎ 7836 1151; www.skelter.demon.co.uk; 4 Denmark St WC2; tube Tottenham Court Road) Just off Charing Cross Rd, this excellent shop has very helpful staff and specialises in books about popular music.

Housmans (Map pp420-1; ☎ 7837 4473; 5 Caledonian Rd N1; tube King's Cross) Great radical store, which stocks books you won't find anywhere else. Also good stationery section.

Magma (Map pp426-7; ☎ 7242 9503; 117-119 Clerkenwell Rd EC1; ⏱ 10am-7pm Mon-Fri; tube Farringdon) Full of design books and magazines, including tomes on typography from Büro Destruct, portraits by London cartoonist Julian Opie (who designed the *Best of Blur* album cover) and loads on Japanese design and cartoons. There are also T-shirts, Jimmy Corrigan toys and things like *Mr Lunch* address books. Also in Covent Garden (☎ 7240 8498; 8 Earlham St)

Motor Books (Map p430; ☎ 7836 5376; www.motorbooks.co.uk; 33 St Martin's Court WC2; tube Leicester Square) A dream come true for revheads, trainspotters and anyone with an interest in things to do with transport and mechanics.

Murder One (Map p430; ☎ 7734 3485; 71-73 Charing Cross Rd WC2; tube Leicester Square) Head for Murder One if crime fiction, science fiction and romance light your candle.

Shipley (Map p430; ☎ 7836 4872; www.artbook.co.uk; 72 Charing Cross Rd; tube Leicester Square) Atmospheric and friendly shop specialising in current and out-of-print books on fine arts, architecture and design.

Sportspages (Map p430; ☎ 7240 9604; www.sportspages.co.uk; 94-96 Charing Cross Rd; tube Leicester Square) Fanzines, signed biographies, videos and all sorts of books relating to a range of sports.

Spread Eagle Bookshop (Map p435; ☎ 8305 1666; 8 Nevada St SE10; ⏱ 10.30am-5.30pm daily; DLR Cutty Sark) In this browser's paradise of vintage books and plays, you can unearth ancient 'Boy's Own' annuals, or classic copies of *Picture Post* and *Life*. In the basement, there's a collection of antique curios.

Stanford's (Map p430; ☎ 7836 1321; www.stanfords.co.uk; 12-14 Long Acre WC2; tube Covent Garden) One of the largest selections of maps, guides and travel literature in the world.

Travel Bookshop (Map pp422-3; ☎ 7229 5260; www.travelbookshop.co.uk; 13 Blenheim Cres W11; tube Ladbroke Grove) London's best 'boutique' travel bookshop has all the new travel guides as well as out-of-print and antiquarian gems.

Waterstone's (Map p428; ☎ 7851 2400; www.waterstones.co.uk; 203-206 Piccadilly W1; tube Piccadilly Circus) The chain's megastore is the biggest bookshop in Europe and has knowledgeable staff, organised shelves and serene surrounds.

Zwemmer Design & Architecture (Map p430; ☎ 7240 1559; www.zwemmer.com; 72 Charing Cross Rd WC2; tube Leicester Square) Zwemmer branches each have their own speciality. At number 80 on the same street is the media outlet, which has stacks of excellent books on everything from art and fashion to film and photography.

AQUASCUTUM Map p428
☎ 7675 8200; 100 Regent St W1; tube Piccadilly Circus
When the heavens open up and the cold sets in, dash along to Aquascrutum for stylish overgear, especially retro-inspired pea jackets and storm coats.

BETTY JACKSON Map pp436-7
☎ 7589 7884; 311 Brompton Rd SW3; tube South Kensington
This British designer has been at the head of the pack for over two decades and has attracted a fervent following among women about town with her fashionable and unfussy lines, particularly in linen, suede and knits.

BURBERRY Map pp426-7
☎ 7839 5222; 21-23 New Bond St SW1; tube Bond Street/Oxford Circus
Slick but casual, Burberry almost became a victim of its own success with its famous signature plaids suffering overload around the world. They've pulled their heads in a little and the pattern is being used much more sparingly these days. A very 'London' item of clothing is the Burberry tartan macintosh.

NICOLE FARHI Map pp426-7
☎ 7499 8368; 158 New Bond St W1; tube Bond Street
This London-based, French-born Algerian designer is renowned for clean, classical and sensual styling. Among her most famous lines are chunky knits much favoured by Nicole Kidman and men's tweeds favoured by Ewan McGregor. There's also a restaurant here, should you require a mid-shop pit stop.

PRINGLE Map pp426-7
☎ 0800 360 200; 112 New Bond St W1; tube Bond Street
Difficult as it is to believe, the sort of jumpers that even golfers had long ago deemed passé have suddenly been made hip again and Pringle, benefiting no doubt from the success of rival Burberry, has become one of the most recent indispensable style labels thanks to risqué marketing, careful sponsorship and a fresh new look (although we're still to be convinced that the pink range is going to be 'the next big thing').

STELLA McCARTNEY
☎ 7518 3100; 30 Bruton St W1; tube Green Park
Celebrity designer Stella McCartney (yes, daughter of the Beatle) opened her debut London store in mid-2003 and is beginning to make a splash with her collections – including lingerie and vegetarian footwear – as well as her celebrity dom and famous friends. This shop has the novelty of an in-house tailor for men and women, and is a stunning browse in itself, with Art Deco chandeliers and a glasshouse garden.

VIVIENNE WESTWOOD Map pp426-7
☎ 7629 3757; 6 Davies St W1; tube Bond Street
The woman who dressed the punk generation is still designing clothes as bold, innovative and provocative as ever. Upon receiving an OBE from the Queen at Buckingham Palace, cheeky Viv did a twirl in front of the cameras to reveal that she wasn't wearing any knickers.

JEWELLERY
GARRARD Map pp426-7
☎ 7758 8520; www.garrard.com; 24 Albemarle St W1; tube Bond Street
Working hard at updating its traditional image, this classic jewellers has extended its range to include much more funky and contemporary pieces – jewel-encrusted clothing and gift items are sold upstairs.

TIFFANY & CO Map p428

☎ 7409 2790; 25 Old Bond St W1; tube Green Park

The quintessential English charmer, Tiffany specialises in simple, elegant and exquisite jewellery that only *looks* a million dollars. It's great for picking up luxurious bits and pieces that make great gifts.

WRIGHT & TEAGUE Map pp426-7

☎ 7629 2777; www.wrightandteague.com; 1A Grafton St, Mayfair; tube Green Park

This couple met while studying at St Martins School of Art more than 20 years ago and have been working, living and designing together ever since. Their highly emotive, original and elegant pieces are mainly in silver and gold.

SPECIALIST STORES

DAISY & TOM

Map pp436-7   *Children's Department Store*

☎ 7352 5000; 181-183 Sloane St SW3; tube Sloane Square

This superb children's department store has a marionette show, carousel rides, rocking horses, play areas, traditional and modern toys, and a big book room where kids can loll about while flicking through the latest Harry Potter. Upstairs there are fashion labels fit for (your) little princes and princesses.

DAVIDOFF OF LONDON Map pp426-7 *Cigars*

☎ 7930 3079; 35 St James's St SW1; tube Green Park

This posh shop is the best for pipes, pipe equipment and a wide range of cigars, including its own brand from the Dominican Republic.

DR HARRIS Map pp426-7 *Perfumer/Herbalist*

☎ 7930 3915; 29 St James's St SW1; tube Green Park

Operating as chemists and perfumers since 1790, this shop stocks such esoteric goods as moustache wax, tiny beard-combs and DR Harris Crystal Eye Drops to combat the visual effects of late nights, early starts and jetlag. Best of all, it has its own hangover cure: a bitter herbal concoction called DR Harris Pick-Me-Up. If it works for us, it will work for you.

JANE ASHER PARTY CAKES

Map pp436-7   *Cakes*

☎ 7584 6177; 22-24 Cale St SW3; tube South Kensington/ Sloane Street

Jane Asher, actress and cookery-book writer, best known for her liaison with erstwhile Beatle Paul McCartney in the 1960s, has the cake-decorating market cornered in London. There are thousands of designs to choose from

---

London's Auction Houses

Fancy a spot of upmarket shopping without the hassle of fixed price tags or actually buying? Visit one of the following auction houses to watch paintings, historic relics, manuscripts and more change hands for thousands of pounds or more. Be careful not to fidget though, otherwise you might find yourself buying something for which you require an emergency bank loan!

- **Bonhams** (Map pp422-3; ☎ 7393 3900; www.bonhams.com; Montpelier St SW7; tube Knightsbridge)
- **Christie's** (Map pp426-7; ☎ 7839 9060; www.christies.com; 8 King St SW1; tube Green Park/Piccadilly Circus)
- **Criterion** (Map pp420-1; ☎ 7359 5707; www.criterion-auctioneers.co.uk; 53 Essex Rd N1; tube Angel)
- **Phillips** (Map pp426-7; ☎ 7629 6602; www.phillipsauctions.com; 101 New Bond St W1; tube Bond Street)
- **Sotheby's** (Map pp426-7; ☎ 7293 5000; www.sothebys.com; 34-35 New Bond St W1; tube Bond Street)

or, if you can provide 10 days' notice, you can give them your own design. The rest of the shop is taken up with Sugarcraft, an emporium of baking utensils and cookbooks.

RIGBY & PELLER Map pp436-7 *Underwear*

☎ 7589 9293; 2 Hans Rd SW3; tube Knightsbridge

This old-fashioned place's main claim to fame is that it makes the Queen's bras. You can get both off-the-peg and made-to-measure bras, corsets and swimwear fit for regal buns, while there is also a fitting and alteration service.

ROCOCO Map pp436-7 *Chocolates*

☎ 7352 5857; 321 King's Rd SW3; tube Sloane Square

Choc fans will feel like they've gone to cocoa heaven when they see – never mind taste – the wares in this glorious shrine to sweet things. There are also vegan and organic varieties.

TAYLOR OF OLD BOND ST

Map p428   *Men's Grooming*

☎ 7930 5321; www.tayloroldbondst.co.uk; 74 Jermyn St SW1; tube Green Park

This shop has been plying its trade since the mid-19th century and has contributed as much as any other to the expression 'well-groomed gentlemen'. It stocks every sort of razor, shaving brush and flavour of shaving soap imaginable.

ALONG THE SOUTH BANK

As the Tate Modern art gallery, the London Eye and the Saatchi art gallery have all renewed attention on this area, new shopkeepers have thrown open their doors to welcome in the crowds. Their premises tend to be clustered in two areas, however: along Lower Marsh and at the Oxo Tower, the latter being the true jewel in the South Bank's shopping crown.

SOUTH BANK & WATERLOO
Clothes
WHAT THE BUTLER WORE Map pp426-7
☎ 7261 1353; 131 Lower Marsh SE1; 🕑 11am-6pm Mon-Sat; tube Waterloo
One of several retro shops along Lower Marsh, this is full of '60s and '70s retro clothes, including handbags, shoes and some outrageously outsized sunglasses.

Food
KONDITOR & COOK Map pp426-7
☎ 7261 0456; 22 Cornwall Rd SE1; 🕑 7.30am-6.30pm Mon-Fri; 8am-2.30pm Sat; tube Waterloo
One of the best specialist bakeries in London, this is where to find excellent German/Austrian-style cakes.

Konditor & Cook (left)

BANKSIDE
There are two floors of small British design shops in the Oxo Tower building, turning out clothes, jewellery, furniture and other products. The following are three favourite examples.

Household
BLACK + BLUM Map pp426-7
☎ 7633 0022; www.black-blum.com; Unit 2:07 (2nd floor), Oxo Tower Wharf, Bargehouse St SE1; 🕑 9am-5pm Mon-Fri, Sat & Sun 11am-4pm; tube Southwark/London Bridge
This Anglo-Swiss partnership turns out entertaining and affordable products, from 'James the Doorman', a human-shaped doorstop, to 'Mr and Mrs Hang-up', anthropomorphic coat hangers that can indicate your mood. The firm's strength, however, is lights. 'Reading light' is a bulb with wire arms and legs, 'reading' its newspaper-shaped shade. 'Bag of light' is a floor light that can be carried like a handbag. Very cute.

BODO SPERLEIN Map pp426-7
☎ 7633 9413; www.bodosperlein.com; Unit 1:05 (1st floor), Oxo Tower Wharf, Bargehouse St SE1; 🕑 10am-6pm Mon-Fri, 1pm-5pm Sat & Sun; tube Southwark/London Bridge
Bodo's fine, white-bone china, in modern designs and with subtle patterns, has earned him international praise, from the *New York Times* to German *Vogue*.

JOSEPH JOSEPH Map pp426-7
☎ 7261 1800; Unit 1:21 (1st floor), Oxo Tower Wharf, Bargehouse St SE1; 🕑 9am-6pm Mon-Sat; tube Southwark/London Bridge
Home to the wonderful Snack, Tokyo Snack and Optic Snack range of glass plates decorated with cartoons or Japanese graphics – you might recognise them when you see them.

THE EAST END
Clothes
BURBERRY FACTORY SHOP Map pp416-17
☎ 8985 3344 or 8328 4320; 29-53 Chatham Place E9; 🕑 11am-6pm Mon-Fri, 10am-5pm Sat, 11am-5pm Sun; tube Bethnal Green, then bus 106 or 256 to Hackney Town Hall
You'll find it's pot luck at this large warehouse-style outlet, depending on what stock has been sent here recently. Sometimes there'll be seconds and samples of this year's fashions from the reborn-as-trendy Brit brand, sometimes you'll find stuff from last season. Only classic gear, like rainwear, is a given. Prices can be up to 50% to 70% off those in the West End, with the best deals on accessories.

Music

Per head, Britons buy more music than any other nation on earth and a disproportionate concentration of this spending is in London, in part propelled by these great shops.

Blackmarket (Map p428; ☎ 7437 0478; www.blackmarket.co.uk; 25 D'Arblay St W1; tube Oxford Circus) Small, cramped and brilliant for dance music, with listening decks and the best international stock.

Daddy Kool (Map p428; ☎ 7437 3535; www.daddykoolrecords.com; 12 Berwick St W1; tube Oxford Circus) Best shop in central London for all sorts of black music, particularly reggae, original ska and classic dub.

Haggle Vinyl (Map pp420-1; ☎ 7354 4666; www.haggle.freeserve.co.uk; 114 Essex Rd N1; ☽ 9am-7pm Mon-Sat, 10am-5.30am Sun; tube Angel) An excellent collection or rare and not-so rare vinyl records, from as little as £2 for the stuff that has spilled over into the boxes on the floor. From 1950s crooners to early hip-hop.

Harold Moores (Map p428; ☎ 7437 1576; www.hmrecords.co.uk; 2 Great Marlborough St W1; tube Oxford Circus) London's finest classical music store stocks an extensive range of vinyl, CD and video.

Honest Jon's (Map pp422-3; ☎ 8969 9822; 276-278 Portobello Rd W10; tube Ladbroke Grove) Two adjoining shops with jazz, soul and reggae.

HMV (Map p428; ☎ 7631 3423; www.hmv.co.uk; 150 Oxford St W1; tube Oxford Circus) Three floors for all tastes.

Music & Video Exchange (Map pp422-3; ☎ 7243 8573; 38 Notting Hill Gate W11; tube Notting Hill Gate) Second-hand store par excellence.

Mole Jazz (Map pp420-1; ☎ 7278 8623; 311 Gray's Inn Rd WC1; tube King's Cross) Great shop for traditional jazz and second-hand CDs.

DOWN RIVER

As a place more of work than leisure, Docklands has few shops apart from chains. Greenwich, on the other hand, is the capital of retro and second-hand goods. That's true whether you're talking household knick-knacks and furniture, or Austin Powers–style clothes. Yeah, baby.

DOCKLANDS
Clothes
FROCKBROKERS Map p435
☎ 7538 0370; Port East Bldg, West India Quay E14; ☽ 11am-7pm Mon-Fri, to 8pm Thurs, 11am-5.30pm Sat, noon-6.30pm Sun; DLR West India Quay

This eminently browsable, girly boutique has end-of-season outfits from the likes of Adolfo Dominguez, BRZ and Shelley Fox at great discounts. You will also find a collection of beaded and appliquéd handbags, flip-flops, strappy sandals and a rack of formal party frocks.

GREENWICH
Clothes
EMPORIUM Map p435
☎ 8305 1670; 332 Creek Rd SE10; ☽ 10.30am-6pm Wed-Sun; DLR Cutty Sark

A very pleasant vintage shop (unisex), with glass cabinets of paste jewellery and old perfume bottles (under the Shell advertising lamp), straw caps or trying on the jackets and blazers.

THE OBSERVATORY Map p435
☎ 8305 1998; 20 Greenwich Church St; ☽ 10.30am-6pm Mon-Sun; DLR Cutty Sark

There's a small collection of new, but retro-style, clothing at the front of this long, narrow store. Further back and upstairs, it moves into real vintage territory, stocking both men's and women's clothes.

Gifts
COMPENDIA Map p435
☎ 8293 6616; www.compendia.co.uk; Shop 10, Greenwich Market; ☽ noon-5.30pm Mon-Fri, 10.30am-5.30pm Mon-Fri; DLR Cutty Sark

It's brilliantly piled high with board and other games from around the world, so discovering this place means you'll never be bored. There's backgammon, chess, Scrabble, solitaire and Car-rom (the sit-down Indian version of pool).

Household
DECOMANIA Map p435
☎ 8858 8189; 9 College Approach SE10; ☽ 10.30am-5pm Wed-Sun; DLR Cutty Sark

An impeccable cavern of lovingly restored furniture and *objets d'art*, this is every Art Deco fan's

On the Beat (Map p428; ☎ 7637 8934; 22 Hanway St W1; tube Tottenham Court Road) Mostly '60s and '70s retro, and helpful staff.

Ray's Jazz Shop (Map p430; ☎ 7440 3205; www.foyles.co.uk; first floor, Foyles, 113-119 Charing Cross Rd WC2; tube Tottenham Court Road) Quiet and serene with friendly and helpful staff, this is one of the best jazz shops in London.

Reckless Records (Map p428; ☎ 7437 4271; www.reckless.co.uk; 26 & 30 Berwick St W1; tube Oxford Circus) Huge range from indie to dance and soul to metal at these two great stores.

Tower Records (Map p428; ☎ 7439 2500; www.towerrecords.co.uk; 1 Piccadilly Circus W1; ⏰ until midnight Tues-Fri; tube Piccadilly Circus) Though this massive store stocks a lot of everything, the jazz and folk music sections are particularly extensive.

Rough Trade (Map pp422-3; ☎ 7229 8541; 130 Talbot Rd W11; tube Ladbroke Grove/Notting Hill Gate) This famous store was at the forefront of the punk explosion in the 1970s and still the place to come for underground specials, vintage rarities and pretty much anything of an indie or alternative bent.

Sister Ray (Map p428; ☎ 7287 8385; www.sisterray.co.uk; 94 Berwick St; tube Oxford Circus) Great stop for experimental and innovative stuff across the genres.

Smallfish Records (Map pp420-1; ☎ 7739 2252, 372 Old St E1; www.smallfish.co.uk; ⏰ 11am-8pm Tues-Sat, noon-5pm Sun, 3-8pm Mon; tube Old Street) Electronica, funk, hip hop and house records and some CDs sold by guys who really know their stuff. There's an excellent record-cleaning service – £1 to clean out static and hiss, plus the place stocks the renowned free fanzine *Shoreditch Twat*.

Virgin Megastore (Map p428; ☎ 7631 1234; www.virgin.com; 14-30 Oxford St W1; ⏰ until 10pm Mon-Sat; tube Tottenham Court Road) The largest of the megastores, with four floors and massive Top 40 displays.

dream. It's expensive, so maybe skip the chairs, lamps and sideboards, and lash out instead on a patterned vintage perfume holder or aeroplane paperweight. Ring ahead, as times can vary.

FLYING DUCK ENTERPRISES Map p435

☎ 8858 1964; 320-322 Creek Rd SE10; ⏰ 11am-6pm Tue-Fri, 10.30am-6pm Sat & Sun; DLR Cutty Sark
A little grotto of kitsch, with two small rooms mainly lit by retro lamps and jam-packed with everything from snow domes, 'super swirly' drinks coasters and bakelite telephones, to Tretchikoff paintings of exotic women, 1960s and '70s cocktail sets and 1950s Homemaker crockery with black-and-white graphics. There's some newer stuff, including Elvis washbags and genuinely vintage comic annuals.

NAUTICALIA Map p435

☎ 8858 1066; www.nauticalia.com; 25 Nelson Rd SE10; ⏰ 10am-6pm Mon-Fri; DLR Cutty Sark
Nauticalia boasts that it is 'the first shop in the world' because of its almost zero longitude. This maritime outlet features a good range of stripey Bretong shirts and sailing caps, as well as ship clocks, bells, barometers and all other manner of equipment. The most amazing thing you can buy here, though, is beautiful original china rescued from the wreck of the *Tek Sing* – it costs about £50 to £180 apiece. The *Tek Sing* sunk after leaving China in 1822 and was famously discovered in 1999 – it's considered the oriental version of the *Titanic*.

WEST LONDON

With the lion's share of the cool and the chic being located in Notting Hill and Knightsbridge, the remainder of west London is a fairly drab place to shop. Some quirkier highlights include the various multi-ethnic shops of the Goldhawk Rd in Shepherd's Bush – from Moroccan couscous to Polish vodkas there's plenty of offbeat interest to be found here, as well as the fantastic **Shepherd's Bush Market** (⏰ 9.30am-5pm Mon-Sat, Thu 9.30am-1pm) that runs underneath the Hammersmith and City Line, between Goldhawk Road and Shepherd's Bush tube stations. It's a focal point for the many different ethnic groups in the area, and you can purchase everything from West African food to Asian delicacies.

Earl's Court has limited shopping – mainly corner shops and chain stores – but it does boast the superb **Troubadour Delicatessen** (☎ 7341 6341; 267 Old Brompton Rd SW5; tube Earl's Court), next to the famous local eatery of the same name. You'll find a superb selection of mainly Italian delicacies here, perfect for a gourmet picnic.

Hammersmith is dominated by high-street chains and offers little out of the ordinary, although King St is a decent place to shop for clothes and shoes.

SOUTHWEST LONDON

Your average Londoner isn't going to be racing this way on pay day, anxious to relieve themselves of their hard-earned cash, but there are some nice little shops in the area.

FULHAM & PARSON'S GREEN

The shopping in Fulham and Parson's Green is uninspiring apart from the designer furniture and fabric shops that are dotted along the Fulham Rd, Wandsworth Bridge Rd and the western end of the King's Rd. One of the best of these is **Mufti** (☎ 7610 9123; 789 Fulham Rd SW6; ☺ 10am-6.30pm Mon-Sat; tube Parson's Green), where they sell exclusive hand-made furniture and household accessories from natural raw materials. You can also commission custom pieces for your home. For antiques head to the northern end of Munster Rd, where there's a cluster of little shops with everything from battered leather sofas to old vinyl records.

For your basics, head to **North End Road Market** (☺ Mon-Sat 9am-5pm) for fruit and veg, cheap clothing and household goods. There's also a sparkling new shopping centre next to Fulham Broadway tube – most of it taken up with a nine-screen cinema – but the ground floor has a Sainsbury's supermarket, Boots chemist, Books Etc. and Virgin Megastore.

PUTNEY & BARNES

Skip Putney (it's full of grim chains) and head to Church Rd and the High St in Barnes. Of the many shops lining these adjoining roads, our picks are: **Blue Door** (74 Church Rd), with gorgeous Swedish textiles and home furnishings; **Question Air** (86 Church Rd), offering laidback designer fashion; **The White Room** (55 Barnes High St); and **Tom Foolery** (100 Church Rd), selling contemporary jewellery. Anyone wishing to indulge their snappers could try children's toy shops **The Farmyard** (63 Barnes High St); **Bradford** (53 Barnes High St); **Bug Circus** (153 Church Rd); and the paint-your-own-pottery workshop, **Brush & Bisque It** (77 Church Rd).

SOUTH LONDON

UP RIVER

Richmond is a big shopping draw for the already well-heeled residents of the area, but one unlikely to excite visitors. The High St consists largely of chain clothing stores, which can be found in larger incarnations in central London, although there are some interesting places if you look down side streets and do some wandering. Of the pleasingly eccentric second-hand bookshops, look out for **WA Houben Booksellers** (☎ 8940 1055; 2 Church Court; tube/rail Richmond), where you can find an interesting selection of old and new books.

Swankier Richmond Hill is a great place to check out antiques, as well as expensive independent clothes designers. However, this is more likely than not to be window-shopping, as you aren't going to find bargains here.

Chiswick High Rd is also a disappointment from the shopper's perspective. Despite having all the necessary ingredients for a lively and unusual range of shops, the majority are outlets from national chains or are rather twee home furnishing establishments. However, one very enjoyable shopping experience is the **Chiswick Farmer's and Fine Foods Market** (Masonian Bowls Hall, Duke's Meadow W4; ☺ 10am-2pm Sun; rail Chiswick, tube Turnham Green) Here, you'll deal directly with the producers, many of whom use organic farming methods and offer the kind of sophisticated products you'd rightly expect to see on sale in Chiswick – from luxury cheeses to fresh honey and olives.

Space allows us to give you only a small taste of South London's retail delights, although many locals swear you needn't head north to bag yourself some bargains. The biggest draw in this area, of course, is Brixton market (p334).

Clothes

JOY Map p439

☎ 7787 9616; 432 Coldharbour Lane SW11; ☺ 10am-7.30pm Mon-Sat, 1pm-7pm Sun; tube Brixton

Elle magazine has called this store 'Biba for the 21st century', but it sure doesn't limit itself to clothes. On top of quirky new outfits, from stylish red macs to men's and women's T-shirts, you'll find lots of accessories, books and household objects.

Food

THE HIVE Map p414

☎ 7924 6233; 93 Northcote Rd SW11; ⏰ 10am-5pm Mon-Fri, to 6pm Sat; tube Clapham South

This shop boasts an enormous selection of honey, with more than 40 different varieties, plus a cutaway section through a hive, so you can see the bees buzzing about. It also carries royal jelly, beeswax candles and other apiarian products.

Gifts

OLIVER BONAS Map pp416-17

☎ 7720 8272; www.oliverbonas.com; 23 The Pavement SW4; ⏰ 10am-6.30pm Mon-Fri, to 6pm Sat, noon-6pm Sun; tube Clapham Common

Oliver Bonas runs the gamut from brown suede cushions and chrome tables to jewellery, Swiss army knives and greetings cards. It's part of a chain, and also has a branch in the City near St Paul's (☎ 7329 3939; Ludgate Broadway).

Markets

London's markets are treasure troves full of knick-knacks, clothes, foodstuffs and all sorts of mystical ephemera and earthly accoutrements; they're also a delightful slice of city life. Even if you don't snaffle the antique you wanted at Portobello Rd or can't pick up the latest slashed fashion at Camden Market by getting 'dawhn wiv the geezers' at Bermondsey or Borough markets, or imbibing the floral perfumes along Columbia Rd, you'll take away an experience you'll never forget.

Camden

This **market** (Map pp418-19; www.camdenlock.net/markets; tube Camden Town) is one of London's top tourist attractions. It's busiest at weekends, especially Sundays, when the crowds elbow each other all the way north from Camden Town tube station to Chalk Farm Rd. It's composed of several separate markets, which all tend to merge.

Camden Market (Cnr Camden High & Buck Sts NW1; ⏰ 9am-5.30pm Thu-Sun) This covered market houses stalls for fashion, clothing, jewellery and tourist tat.

Camden Canal Market (Cnr Chalk Farm & Castlehaven Rds NW1; ⏰ 10am-6pm Sat & Sun) Farther north and just over the canal bridge, Camden Canal Market has bric-a-brac from around the world. If you're pushed for time, this is the bit to skip.

Camden Lock Market (Camden Lock Pl NW1; ⏰ 10am-6pm Sat & Sun, indoor stalls 10am-6pm daily) Right next to the canal lock with diverse food, ceramics, furniture, oriental rugs, musical instruments, designer clothes...

The Stables (Chalk Farm Rd, opposite Hartland Rd NW1; ⏰ 8am-6pm Sat & Sun) Just beyond the Railway Arches, the Stables is the best part of the market, with antiques, Asian artefacts, rugs and carpets, pine furniture, and '50s and '60s clothing.

Covent Garden

While the shops in the **Covent Garden Piazza** (Map p430; tube Covent Garden/Leicester Square/Charing Cross) are open daily, several markets also take place here.

Apple Market (Map p430; Covent Garden Piazza, North Hall WC2; ⏰ 9am-5pm daily) This touristy market sells handicrafts and curios.

Jubilee Market (Map p430; Jubilee Hall, cnr Covent Garden & Southampton St WC2; ⏰ 9am-3pm Mon, 9am-5pm Tue-Sun) Monday is for antiques and collectables, Tuesday to Friday for general tat, and Saturday and Sunday for quality crafts.

Other Markets

Bermondsey (Map p432-3; Bermondsey Square; ⏰ 5am-1pm Fri; tube Borough/Bermondsey) This curios market has mythic status because it's reputedly legal to sell stolen goods before dawn – which maybe (or maybe not) explains why most of the action is over by 8am. Knick-knacks like bowling balls, hatpins, costume jewellery and porcelain sit alongside a better selection of silverware. Adjacent warehouses shelter more delicate furnishings and objects.

Berwick St (Berwick St W1; ⏰ 8am-6pm Mon-Sat; tube Piccadilly Circus/Oxford Street) South of Oxford St and running parallel to Wardour St, this fruit-and-vegetable market has managed to hang on to its prime location since 1830, and is a great place to put together a picnic or shop for a prepared meal and to hear cockney accents straight out of Central Casting.

Borough Market (Map p432-3; Cnr Borough High & Stoney Sts SE1; ⏰ 9am-6pm Fri, 9am-4pm Sat; tube London Bridge) 'London's Larder' has been here in some form since the 13th century, and it has enjoyed a dazzling renaissance in recent years, featuring prominently in the successful creations of Jamie Oliver. It's a superb – and moody – food market, where you'll find everything from organic falafel to a boar's head.

Brick Lane (Map p432-3; Brick Lane E2; ☺ 8am-1pm Sun; tube Aldgate East) In the last few years, this market has really become two. Things are more expensive along the main drag, but under the arches and in the side streets you'll still find a few bargains. Goods on sale range from clothes, fruit and vegetables to household goods, paintings, bric-a-brac.

Brixton (Map p439; Reliance Arcade, Market Row, Electric Lane & Electric Ave SW9; ☺ 8am-6pm Mon-Sat, 8am-3pm Wed; tube Brixton) This market is a heady, cosmopolitan mix of everything from the Body Shop and reggae to slick Muslim preachers, South American butcher shops, exotic fruits and the overpowering smell of incense. On Electric Ave and in the covered Granville Arcade you can buy eels, unusual foods such as tilapia fish and Ghanaian eggs (really a type of vegetable), unusual spices, homeopathic root cures and sugar cane.

Camden Passage (Map pp420-1; Camden Passage N1; ☺ 7am-2pm Wed, 8am-4pm Sat; tube Angel) Not to be confused with Camden Market (p183), this is a series of four arcades selling antique and curios, located in Islington, at the junction of Upper St and Essex Rd. Stallholders know their stuff so real bargains are rare. Wednesday is the busiest day, but it's worth coming along on Sunday for the Islington Farmers Market between 10am and 2pm.

Columbia Rd Flower Market (Map pp420-1; Columbia Rd E2; ☺ 7am-1pm Sun; tube Bethnal Green/rail Cambridge Heath/bus 26, 48 or 55) London's most fragrant market shouldn't be missed. Between Gosset St and the Royal Oak pub, merchants lay out their blooms, from everyday geraniums to rare pelargoniums .

Greenwich (Map p435; College Approach SE10; ☺ 9am-5pm Thur, 9.30am-5.30pm Sat & Sun; DLR Cutty Sark) Greenwich market is ideally suited for a relaxed few hours' rummaging through its second-hand household objects, glass, rugs prints and wooden toys. In between, you can snack on speciality foods in the food court. Thursday is the day for antiques, while the general market is open on weekends. You will also find general stalls open Wednesday and Friday. Stores around the market open daily, but weekends are the best time to come.

Leadenhall Market (Map p432-3; Whittington Ave, off Gracechurch St EC1; ☺ 7am-4pm Mon-Fri; tube Bank) As well as being an attraction in its own right, thanks to Horace Jones' 1881-designed Victorian hall, this market has clothes stores and curio shops, as well as bars and restaurants, a fishmonger, a butcher and a cheesemonger. As it principally serves a City clientele, prices tend to be high.

Leather Lane (Map pp426-7; Leather Lane EC1; ☺ 10.30am-2pm Mon-Fri; tube Chancery Lane/Farringdon) This market south of Clerkenwell Rd, running parallel to Hatton Garden, attracts local office workers with its suspiciously cheap videos, tapes and CDs, household goods and clothing sold by archetypal cockney stallholders.

Petticoat Lane (Map p432-3; Middlesex & Wentworth Sts E1; ☺ 8am-2pm Sun, Wentworth St only 9am-2pm Mon-Fri; tube Aldgate/Aldgate East/Liverpool Street) It's a shame the famous lane itself has been renamed Middlesex St. The market, however, soldiers on, selling cheap consumer items and clothes to East Enders and tourists alike.

Portobello Rd (Map pp422-3; Portobello Rd W10; ☺ 8am-6pm Mon-Wed, 9am-1pm Thur, 7am-7pm Fri & Sat, 9am-4pm Sun; tube Notting Hill Gate/ Ladbroke Grove) After Camden, this is London's most famous street market. Antiques, jewellery, paintings and ethnic stuff are concentrated at the Notting Hill Gate end of Portobello Rd. Stalls move downmarket as you move north. Beneath the Westway a vast tent covers more stalls selling cheap clothes, shoes and CDs, while the Portobello Green arcade is home to some cutting-edge clothing and jewellery designers. Though shops and stalls open daily, the busiest days are Friday, Saturday and Sunday. There's an antiques market on Saturday, and a flea market on Portobello Green on Sunday morning. Fruit and veg are sold all week at the Ladbroke Grove end, with an organic market on Thursday.

Ridley Rd Market (Map pp416-17; Ridley Rd E8; ☺ 8.30am-6pm Mon-Sat; rail Dalston) As colourful and diverse as the Afro-Caribbean community it serves, this market has all the usual bric-a-brac and household usefuls, but is valuable for the wealth of exotic fruit and vegetables, as well as pickles and pickles and specialist meat products like pig's tails.

Riverside Walk (Map pp426-7; Outside the National Film Theatre, Riverside Walk SE1; ☺ 10am-5pm Sat & Sun; tube Waterloo/Embankment) Great for cheap second-hand books long out of print, this book market is held come rain or shine outside the South Bank under the arches of Waterloo Bridge. In summer, it really adds to the impression that the South Bank is becoming a little like Paris' Left Bank. Occasionally, individual dealers set up their stalls during the week.

Smithfield (Map pp426-7; West Smithfield EC1; ☺ 4am-noon Mon-Fri; tube Farringdon) Although this is London's last surviving meat market (cattle were slaughtered in front of customers here in the 14th century), it was recently refurbished in a £70 million project to become the most modern in Europe. You'll see hardly a speck of blood these days.

Spitalfields (Map pp420-1; Commercial St, between Brushfield & Lamb Sts, E1; ☺ 9.30am-5.30pm Sun; tube Liverpool Street) Maybe not as famous as Camden or Portobello, Spitalfields is these days London's premier market for those in the know. It's where young clothes designers tout their wares and where you'll find everything from candles to retro furniture, wheatgrass to funky T-shirts, coconuts to saucy underwear. There's an organic market on Friday.

Sleeping

Sleeping

No matter how fat your wallet, where you stay is going to be a huge chunk out of your travel budget. It's unlikely that you'll ever get what you consider good value for money because accommodation in just about every bracket is more expensive in London than in virtually any other European city. Once you've packed and stored that piece of information, however, you can look forward to staying in some great places that will enrich your visit immeasurably. But make sure you plan and book ahead. Even when tourism has been slow in recent years, demand frequently outstrips supply at the better places, particularly at the lower end of the market. You'd be stark raving bonkers to arrive in summer (between June and August) without having reserved accommodation in advance. You'll be expected to pay at least 10% as a deposit and, once you

The Rookery, Clerkenwell (p343)

arrive, many establishments prefer that you pay up front (and don't do a runner). If you're travelling solo, bear in mind that single rooms are scarce and most places are reluctant to let a double room – even during quiet periods – without adding a hefty surcharge or even charging the full rate.

WHICH LONDON?

Where you choose to shelter will have a huge bearing on the image of London you'll take home, so geography should be as important a consideration as level of comfort, style or expense when choosing your accommodation. Base yourself anywhere in the West End and you'll soon get into the throbbing rhythm of London at play. If theatre's your temptation, base yourself around Covent Garden and compete for space with dedicated shoppers. If you want to immerse yourself in gritty multiculturalism, pitch your tent around Brixton or the East End, whereas you'll find the more-polished version around Notting Hill or South Kensington. Hoxton, Clerkenwell and Shoreditch are where it's at right now, and there are a few good places to stay here at London's cutting edge. If royal London's your reason for visiting, get close to the Windsors around St James's. For traditional London and the whiff of aristocracy, make Knightsbridge or Mayfair your domain. New money and a sense for fashion go together in Chelsea, while the comfortably well off live quietly around Maida Vale and Primrose Hill. If you want to feel how most Londoners live, you might hang your hat out in Camden or the Northern Heights – if you don't care how Londoners live, you might pause with the travelling circus in Earl's Court and parts of Victoria. For our money, the best value and overall picture of London today can be had around Marylebone.

TYPES OF ACCOMMODATION

If you're looking for luxury, London has a superb range of deluxe hotels (£300+) and you'll be spoiled for choice of old classics that combine the best in traditional atmosphere and modern comforts. There's also good choice at the next level down (£150 to £300), which offers superior comforts without the prestige. Also in this bracket you'll find many of the boutique and style hotels that have sprung up over the last decade, now providing

London with as many *Wallpaper** Magazine cover stories as most of Europe put together. But from here there's a long and sudden slide in quality and choice. Of course there are terrific places to rest your head without haemorrhaging your hard-earned – there's just not nearly enough. And if you were budgeting to spend less than £100 a night on your room, you'll get a TV and telephone but, let's just say, your lodgings probably won't provide the most cherished memories of your trip. The best B&Bs come in at around this price and, while many are characterful and cosy, most occupy former residential homes so rooms are invariably small. The cheap options (listed under 'Cheap Sleeps' in this chapter) are limited to hostels and student residences, and these provide only the most basic of facilities and are largely for backpackers and anyone seriously skimping.

Each year the **London Tourist Board & Convention Bureau** (☎ 7932 2000; www.londontouristboard.com) publishes *Where to Stay & What to Do in London* (£4.99), which lists approved hotels, B&Bs, guesthouses and apartments. You can also check out www.frontdesk.co.uk, www.hotelsoflondon.co.uk and www.londonlodging.co.uk.

Serviced Apartments

If you are visiting for a few weeks or several months, staying in a serviced apartment is the best way to get a sense of living in the city, although short-term rentals can cost anywhere from £700 a week and up. There are several specialist agencies including **Aston's Apartments** (☎ 7590 6000; www.astons-apartments.com; 31 Rosary Gardens SW7; tube Gloucester Road), which has a range of accommodation from standard to designer on its books and **Vancouver Studios** (☎ 7243 1270; www.vienna-group.co.uk; 30 Princes Square W2; tube Bayswater), which has 45 quality serviced studios in a block that has also has the convenience of a hotel.

Long-Term Rentals

Monthly rents vary dramatically according to the neighbourhood but, on average, you'll find leasing expensive. At the very bottom end of the market, bedsits (£300 to £500) are single furnished rooms, usually with a shared bathroom and kitchen, and they are always pretty grim. A step up is a self-contained studio (£500+), which normally has a separate bathroom and kitchen. You won't get a two-bedroom flat for less than £900. Shared houses and flats generally offer the best value, anywhere from £300 and upwards. Most landlords demand a security deposit (normally one month's rent) plus a month's rent in advance.

To get abreast of current prices, consult the classifieds such as *Loot*, *TNT*, *Time Out* and the *Evening Standard*'s Wednesday supplement *Homes & Property*. Capital Flat Share is a free service run by **Capital Radio** (☎ 7484 8000), which collects lists of people willing to share their flats (deadline: 6pm Monday) and publishes the list in *The Guide*, an entertainment-listings magazine that comes with Saturday's *Guardian*. If you prefer to use an agency, the **Jenny Jones Agency** (☎ 7493 4801; 40 South Molton St W1; tube Bond Street), charges the landlord rather than the tenants.

BOOKING OFFICES & OTHER RESOURCES

The **London Tourist Board** (☎ 7932 2020; www.visitlondon.com; ☾ 9am-5.30pm Mon-Fri, 10am-2pm Sat) runs an efficient booking service for which it charges £5. The **British Hotel Reservation Centre** (24 hrs ☎ 0800 282888; www.bhrconline.com; ☾ 6am-11.30pm) is on the main concourse of Victoria train station. There's a kiosk on the mezzanine level of the Britain Visitor Centre as well as at Euston, King's Cross and Victoria stations, Gatwick Airport and South Kensington Tube.

If you want to stay in a B&B or private home, reservations can be made for a minimum of three nights and a 5% booking fee through the reliable **London Homestead Services** (☎ 8949 4455; www.lhslondon.com) or **London Bed & Breakfast Agency** (☎ 7586 2768; www.londonbb.com).

You can book a hostel through the **YHA central reservations system** (☎ 0870 8818; lonres@yha.org.uk), although you still pay the individual hostel directly; the staff will know what beds are available where and when.

Sleeping

THE WEST END

The Soho/Covent Garden area is the epicentre of London life and you'll pay more for the privileged location. There are some good bargains to be had around the fringes, in places like Gower and North Gower Sts in Fitzrovia, while Bloomsbury is a haven of B&Bs and guesthouses.

BLOOMSBURY & FITZROVIA

ACADEMY HOTEL Map pp426-7 *Hotel*
☎ 7631 4115; www.etontownhouse.com; 21 Gower St WC1; d from £150; tube Goodge Street
Orrrfully English, the renovated Academy has 49 large and individually decorated rooms set in five Georgian town houses, and a pleasant back garden in which to recline after a hard day's yakka at the British Museum.

ALHAMBRA HOTEL Map pp420-1 *Hotel*
☎ 7837 9575; www.alhambrahotel.com; 17-19 Argyle St WC1; basic d £45, with bathroom £60; tube King's Cross St Pancras
About the best budget option around here, the Alhambra has 52 simple and spotless rooms, friendly French- and English-speaking staff and is close to two mainline stations for getaways.

ARRAN HOUSE HOTEL Map pp426-7 *Hotel*
☎ 7636 2186; arran@dircon.co.uk; 77-9 Gower St WC1; dorms £13.50- 21, d with bathroom £85; tube Goodge Street
This welcoming place is in the heart of literary Bloomsbury and provides excellent value for the location. Lodgings range from the most basic dormitory-style accommodation to bright and cosy well-furnished doubles with bathrooms, although the atmosphere never feels like anything but a small and welcoming hotel. The rose garden is a pleasant bonus in the summer.

BLOOMS TOWNHOUSE HOTEL
Map pp426-7 *Hotel*
☎ 7323 1717; www.bloomshotel.com; 7 Montague Street WC1; d £145, ste from £180
This elegant and airy 18th-century townhouse has the feel of a country home, which belies its position in the heart of London (in what used to be the grounds of the British Museum, in fact). Think floral prints, classical music, a delightful garden and staff who 'really, sorry about this, but if you wouldn't mind, awfully sorry, it's just…'

CHARLOTTE STREET HOTEL
Map p428 *Hotel*
☎ 7806 2000; www.firmdale.com; 15 Charlotte St W1; standard d £220, ste from £340; tube Tottenham Court Road
Another doozy from the folks at Firmdale, this is where Laura Ashley goes postmodern and comes up smelling of roses. It's a favourite with visiting media types (ie those in the know). The bar buzzes by night while Oscar restaurant is a delightful spot any time of day, but particularly for afternoon tea.

CRESCENT HOTEL Map pp418-19 *Hotel*
☎ 7387 1515; www.crescenthoteloflondon.com; 49-50 Cartwright Gardens WC1; s from £46, d with bathroom £89; tube Russell Square
In the middle of academic London, this friendly, family-owned hotel was built in 1810 and overlooks a private square flanked by student residences. While the rooms range from pokey singles without facilities to relatively spacious doubles with bathrooms, all are as comfortable as can be and the staff are very hospitable.

HARLINGFORD HOTEL Map pp418-19 *Hotel*
☎ 7387 1551; www.harlingfordhotel.com; 61 Cartwright Gardens WC1; d from £75, f £110; tube Russell Square
Comprising three 19th-century town houses and a bewitching chain of halls and stairways, the Harlingford is a jolly good hotel on a pleasant Georgian crescent lined with more basic lodgings. The further up the stairs you go (there's no lift) the rooms generally get bigger and brighter, but bathrooms are all small.

HOTEL CAVENDISH Map pp426-7 *Hotel*
☎ 7636 9079; www.hotelcavendish.com; 75 Gower St WC1; basic d £48, with bathrooms £66; tube Goodge Street
Spick, span and run by an amiable family, this hotel has lovely, simple purple and burgundy-

hued rooms, along with a pleasant walled garden and a reasonable English cooked breakfast (included with the price). If the Cavendish is full, you'll be referred to its sister hotel, the Jesmond, nearby, with similar rates and standards.

JENKINS HOTEL Map pp418-19 *Hotel*
☎ 7387 2067; www.jenkinshotel.demon.co.uk; 45 Cartwright Gardens WC1; s from £52, d £85; tube Russell Square

Close to the British Museum, this smoke-free hotel has pretty rooms with washbasin, TV, phone and fridge. The rooms are small but the welcome is huge. All prices include breakfast, which you are welcome to work off on the tennis courts across the road.

MORGAN HOTEL Map p430 *Hotel*
☎ 7636 3735; 24 & 40 Bloomsbury St WC1; d from £90, ste £125; tube Tottenham Court Road

In a row of 18th-century Georgian houses alongside the British Museum, this is one of the best mid-priced hotels in London where the warmth and hospitality more than make up for the slightly cramped guest quarters. The rooms have been recently refurbished and the standard ones are a little chintzy, while the suites are more tasteful and well worth the few extra bob.

RIDGEMOUNT HOTEL Map pp422-3 *Hotel*
☎ 7636 1141; www.ridgemounthotel.co.uk; 65-67 Gower St WC1; basic d £50, with bathroom £65; tube Goodge Street

This old-fashioned hotel offers a warmth and consideration that you don't come across very often in the city these days. Half of its 30 utilitarian rooms have bathrooms. Rates include a decent breakfast, and there's a laundry.

ST MARGARET'S HOTEL Map pp426-7 *Hotel*
☎ 7636 4277; www.stmargaretshotel.co.uk; 26 Bedford Pl WC1; basic d £63, with bathroom £95; tube Russell Square/Holborn

Young and not so young are catered for at this huge 60-room family-run hotel, which occupies a classic Georgian town house. Rooms are bright and comfortable, there are relaxing lounges and a lovely rear garden.

SANDERSON Map p428 *Hotel*
☎ 7300 1400; www.ianschragerhotels.com; 50 Berners St W1; standard d from £205, loft ste £500; tube Oxford Circus

Concealed behind the none-too-inviting aluminium and glass facade of a 1960s corporate HQ, prolific duo Ian Schrager and Philippe Starck – of St Martin's Lane – are responsible for this 'urban spa', which comes with a lush bamboo-filled garden, artworks and installations, 18th-century theatre curtains, sheets with a 450-thread count and a jumble of personality furniture. It's a little quirky, almost surreal, and completely gorgeous. Parisian superchef Alain Ducasse continues the theme in Spoon restaurant.

Cheap Sleeps

AROSFA Map pp426-7 *Hotel*
☎ 7636 2115; 83 Gower St WC1; basic d £50, with bathroom £75; tube Euston Square/Goodge Street

Diminutive Arosfa (Welsh for 'a place to stay') is a breath of fresh air on this very busy strip because it's one of the few where smoking is banned. The 16 rooms cover the basics and light sleepers might prefer one at the back.

ASHLEE HOUSE Map pp420-1 *Hostel*
☎ 7833 9400; www.ashleehouse.co.uk; 261-5 Gray's Inn Rd WC1; dm from £13, s £34; tube King's Cross St Pancras; 🖳

This welcoming place is a clean and well-maintained backpackers' hostel with 180 beds on three floors close to King's Cross station. Dorms (most with bunks) can be cramped, but there is double-glazing on the windows, a laundry, decent-sized kitchen, free left-luggage room and Internet access.

GENERATOR Map pp420-1 *Hotel*
☎ 7388 7655; www.the-generator.co.uk; Compton Place, 37 Tavistock Place WC1; dm £12.50-17, s £37; tube Russell Square; 🖳

One of the liveliest budget options in central London, the Generator has industrial decor and looks like an updated set from Terry Gilliam's film *Brazil*. Along with 207 rooms (830 beds), it has flirtatious staff and a bar that stays open until 2am – but they don't necessarily go together. There's also pool tables, Internet access, safe-deposit boxes and a large eating area, but no kitchen. All prices include breakfast.

SOHO

HAZLITT'S Map p428 *Hotel*
☎ 7434 1771; www.hazlittshotel.com; 6 Frith St W1; standard d £205, Baron Willoughby's ste £300; tube Tottenham Court Road

One of London's most characterful cribs, this stunningly stylish hotel in the middle of Soho consists of three 18th-century terraced houses, including one where the great essayist

William Hazlitt lived. Twenty-three rooms are named after former residents and guests to the house, and boast a wealth of seductive details, including mahogany four-poster beds, Victorian claw-foot tubs, sumptuous fabrics, winsomely wonky floors and impeccable taste throughout. Bear in mind that this is a listed building so there's no lift. Some of the rooms aren't large but look at the quality!

WEST STREET Map p430 *Hotel*
☎ 7010 8600; www.weststreet.co.uk; 13-15 West St WC2; r £350-630; tube Leicester Square

In the heart of theatreland, this new uber-chic members' hotel has three exquisite and highly individualised suites above a glass restaurant and bar. The White Room is exactly how it sounds, as is the Stone Room with its own terrace large enough for cocktails (or a barbie depending on your inclination), while the Loft occupies the entire fourth floor. Each room is filled with designer everything and the staff are hell-bent on catering to your every whim.

Cheap Sleeps

OXFORD ST YHA Map p428 *Hostel*
☎ 7734 1618; oxfordst@yha.org.uk; 3rd fl, 14 Noel St W1; dm £18/22; tube Oxford Circus/Tottenham Court Road

The most central of London's hostels is basic, clean, welcoming and loud. There is a large kitchen but no meals are served apart from a packed breakfast. The majority of the 75 beds are twins.

COVENT GARDEN, LEICESTER SQUARE & HOLBORN

COVENT GARDEN HOTEL Map p430 *Hotel*
☎ 7806 1000; www.firmdale.com; 10 Monmouth St WC2; standard d £245, loft ste £795; tube Covent Garden/Tottenham Court Road

Combining gorgeous graphics, Asian fabrics and English warmth, this hospital-turned-charming-boutique-hotel is unquestionably one of the finest places to stay in London. It is another gem from talented hoteliers and gifted interior designers Tim and Kit Kemp of the Firmdale chain of small hotels, who have single-handedly made London an altogether more beautiful place to stay in recent years. There are also two splendid and charming restaurants, and the Firmdale trademarks of style, comfort and service are all here in spades.

FIELDING HOTEL Map p430 *Hotel*
☎ 7836 8305; www.the-fielding-hotel.co.uk; 4 Broad Court, Bow St WC2; standard d £110; tube Covent Garden

You can almost feel the pulse of the West End at this hotel, located in a pedestrianised court in the heart of Covent Garden. It was named after the novelist Henry Fielding (1707–54) who lived on the street. Space is at a premium and the decor is shop bought, but there's no better place to be located if you want to take in a lot of London in just a few days.

KINGSWAY HALL Map p430 *Hotel*
☎ 7309 0909; www.kingswayhall.co.uk; Great Queen St WC2; standard d weekdays/weekends £240/165; tube Holborn

Tipping its cap fairly determinedly at the professional traveller, Kingsway nonetheless manages to provide smart, comfortable and very central lodgings for anyone with less business and more play on their mind. The atmosphere is more relaxed on the weekend, when rates are considerably cheaper, and the fitness centre's not full of barrel-chested types on schedules.

ONE ALDWYCH Map p430 *Hotel*
☎ 7300 1000; www.onealdwych.co.uk; 1 Aldwych WC2; standard d £315, 2-bedroom deluxe ste £1045; tube Covent Garden/Charing Cross

Luxurious and trendy, One Aldwych has spacious, stylish rooms replete with raw silk curtains, natural tones and modern art, along with bath tubs big enough for two. The highly regarded Axis Restaurant & Bar hosts jazz mid-week and is a place to be seen, while the superb health club and pool is superb for preparing to be seen.

REGENT PALACE HOTEL Map p428 *Hotel*
☎ 0870 400 8703; fax 7734 6435; Piccadilly Circus, Cnr Glasshouse St W1; s with shared facilities from £50, d with bathroom from £80; tube Piccadilly

The location is this massive hotel's strongest *and* weakest point: being so central is great for the sights but rather too frenetic for most people's idea of a holiday. Dealing with almost 1000 rooms, the hotel lobby is just as busy and the whole place feels rather impersonal and even institutional. But if you're only looking for shelter, it's certainly central and cheap.

ST MARTIN'S LANE Map p430 *Hotel*
☎ 7300 5500, toll free ☎ 0800 634 5500; www.ian schragerhotels.com; 45 St Martin's Lane; standard d £195, garden r £270; ste from £300; tube Covent Garden/Leicester Square

This joint effort between international hotelier Ian Schrager and French designer

Philippe Starck is so cool you'd hardly notice it was there. Rooms have floor-to-ceiling windows with sweeping West End views, the public rooms are bustling meeting points, and everything (and everyone) is beautiful. Unquestionably the best place for lift encounters with supermodels.

SAVOY Map p430 *Hotel*
☎ 7836 4343; www.savoy-group.co.uk; Strand WC2; s/d/ste from £149/159/319; tube Charing Cross

Still one of the swankiest addresses in London, the Savoy stands on the site of the old Savoy Palace, which was burned down during the Peasants' Revolt of 1381. Some have been so taken with its palatial grandeur that they've taken up permanent residence. Many rooms have spectacular views of the Thames; Monet was so impressed that he painted it from his room. The forecourt is the only street in Britain where motorists drive on the right.

WALDORF MERIDIEN Map p430 *Hotel*
☎ 0870 400 8484; www.lemeridien-hotels.com; Aldwych WC2; r £140-330; tube Temple/Covent Garden/Charing Cross

Now part of the Meridien chain, the Waldorf is another grand old dame glorying in her Edwardian splendour, which is typified by the wonderful Palm Court, a splendid lounge famous for its weekend tea dances, which are an almost century-old tradition of high tea and nostalgic music. Just think of the ballroom scenes in the film *Titanic*, which were actually shot here. There are lots of polished marble floors and chandeliers in the public rooms although the guest rooms can be relatively poky and comparably drab.

EAST CENTRAL

Traditionally the preserve of business travellers flying in for assignments in the City, this area has seen the addition of both boutique hotels and budget chains in recent years – particularly in the hip, trendy districts of Hoxton and Clerkenwell. Days on the weekend can seem quiet, particularly in the heart of the City, but do provide a respite from the hustle and bustle of the West End.

THE CITY

CITADINES APART'HOTEL
BARBICAN Map pp432-3 *Hotel/Apartments*
☎ 7566 8000, central reservations ☎ 0800 376 3898; www.citadines.com; 7-21 Goswell Rd EC1; studios/apartments £110/165; tube Barbican

This apart'hotel (part of a global chain) is set up for longer stays, as nightly rates reduce once you've stayed more than a week (studios £100, apartments £145). In these reasonably comfortable, if not massively new, rooms you can at least do your own cooking. In the studios, however, the only bed is the sofa bed in the living room.

GRANGE CITY HOTEL Map pp432-3 *Hotel*
☎ 7233 7888; www.grangehotels.co.uk; 10 Coopers Row EC3; r from £260; tube Tower Hill

If you're just staying a weekend, Grange City is a terrific find. It's a classy, new, five-star hotel with some character. Many of the rooms have close-up views of Tower Bridge and the Tower of London, for as little £90 for a room per night (if you stay three nights, Friday to Sunday)! The rooms are decorated in rich red and warm gold tones. During the week, rates rise to those quoted above. The chain has other hotels – most four-star, however – with comparable weekend deals. Ring the central reservations number listed here.

THISTLE TOWER Map pp432-3 *Hotel*
☎ 7481 2575, central reservations ☎ 0800 181 716; www.thistlehotels.com; St Katharine's Way E1; s from £250, d £270; tube Tower Hill

The South Bank Centre of hotels, this ugly concrete monolith has some 800 rooms, so it's rarely fully booked. Another plus is that many of those rooms have great views of the river and Tower Bridge. Once again, although this is not quite as nice as the Grange City, it's the weekend rates that are the clincher. A single/double can cost as little as £65/90 Thursday to Sunday.

THREADNEEDLES Map pp432-3 *Hotel*
☎ 7657 8080; www.thetoncollection.com; 5 Threadneedle St EC2; r from £270; tube Bank

This centrepiece of this discreetly located boutique hotel is its grand circular lobby, which is furnished in a vaguely Art Deco style and covered with a 19th-century hand-painted glass dome. However, the rooms in this converted bank are just as elegant. Richly coloured blankets over duvets and monogrammed pillows are complemented by light, sandy-coloured bathrooms, flat-screen TVs and arty photography. Weekday rates don't include breakfast; weekend rates, starting at £140, do.

Cheap Sleeps

CITY OF LONDON YHA Map pp426-7 Hostel
☎ 7236 4965; city@yha.org.uk; 36 Carter Lane EC4; 3-15 bed dm £15-26; s £24-30, 2-6 bed f £55-£140; tube St Paul's

Clean, quiet and yet very close to St Paul's Cathedral, the only odd thing about this otherwise impeccable 193-bed hostel is that some bunk beds are at right angles over each other, so, with your feet covered, you sometimes feel like you're sleeping in a half-open drawer.

BARBICAN YMCA Map pp432-3 Hostel
☎ 7628 0697; www.barbicanymca.com; 2 Fann St EC2; s/tw £27/50; tube Barbican

In the heart of the concrete jungle, this large YMCA has okay rooms, although the shared bathroom floors look a little cracked and discoloured. Bring a pair of flip flops for your feet.

LONDON CITY YMCA Map pp420-1 Hostel
☎ 7628 8832; www.londoncityY.org; 8 Errol St EC1; s with shared bathroom £33, tw with bathroom £60; tube Barbican

Much nicer than its Barbican counterpart, this YMCA has better bathrooms and newer bedrooms with TVs and a phone for incoming calls. It's very handy for the Shoreditch and Hoxton areas, but you should book about one month ahead.

HOXTON, SHOREDITCH & SPITALFIELDS

GREAT EASTERN HOTEL Map pp432-3 Hotel
☎ 7618 5010; www.great-eastern-hotel.co.uk; Liverpool St EC1; s/d from £225/265; tube/rail Liverpool Street

Just the right mix of hip and classic, and without any unnecessary attitude, the Great Eastern is one of the most stylish hotels in town. Even if you're not too sure about the neon sign declaring 'You make my heart go boom boom' over the dark-wood reception desk, go with it – after one night in the super-comfy beds you'll be won over. Rooms on this Conran hotel's lower floors have a more masculine feel with dark wood and reddy earth tones, while

Great Eastern Hotel, Hoxton (below)

those on floors five and six have a subtly maritime theme, with blonde wood, sunnier tones and porthole windows. Weekend rates (for doubles only, excluding breakfast but with tax) begin at £140.

EXPRESS BY HOLIDAY INN
Map pp420-1 Hotel
☎ 7300 4300; www.holidayinn.co.uk; 275 Old St EC1; s & d £110, tr £140; tube Old Street

The only hotel in the heart of trendy Hoxton and Shoreditch, this budget chain hotel is one level up from a Travel Inn and feels less impersonal. The rooms are decorated in blue and yellow with blonde wood. The breakfast room and lounge look similar, adding colourful lounge chairs and glass bricks. (Indeed, it's the sort of place Steve Coogan's comic creation Alan Partridge set up home in when thrown out of his apartment in his last TV series.) There are some 10 Holiday Inn Express hotels in London, including one in Southwark behind Tate Modern (☎ 7401 2525).

TRAVELODGE Map pp432-3 Hotel
☎ 0870 191 1689, central reservations ☎ 08700 850 950; www.travelodge.co.uk; 1 Harrow Place E1; r from £80; tube Liverpool Street

Another budget hotel within easy reach of the bars and clubs of Hoxditch, the Travelodge sits in a quiet street off Petticoat Lane, just a few minutes from Liverpool Street station. The emphasis here is strictly on functionality, as the reception is tiny and there is no lounge. The rooms themselves are fairly smartly decorated, however, and there is a breakfast room/café, where you can buy yourself a continental or cooked morning meal. There are another five or so Travelodges in London, contactable through the central reservations number above.

CLERKENWELL

MALMAISON CLERKENWELL
Map pp426-7 *Hotel*
☎ 7012 3700; Charterhouse Sq EC1; r from £165; tube Farringdon

Although it's less than a minute from the hustle and bustle of Charterhouse Street (near Smithfields meat market), this new boutique hotel could be in another world; it sits on a quiet and leafy square, among historic buildings. Inside, the rooms are individually designed in a hip, contemporary style. Weekend rates should start at £100. However, at the time of writing the hotel hadn't officially opened, so ring just to be sure.

THE ROOKERY Map pp426-7 *Hotel*
☎ 7336 0931; www.rookeryhotel.com; Peter's Lane, Cowcross St EC1; s/d from £215/245; tube Farringdon

Tucked away in a little Clerkenwell corner, this higgledy-piggledy warren of 33 period rooms just oozes charm and character. Each room is individually decorated and, as the hotel is built in a row of once-derelict, 18th-century Georgian houses, each has a wildly different layout and shape. The *piece de resistance* is the two-floor Rook's Nest suite, where the ceiling/floor slides back and forth. The Victorian bathrooms and small garden are also sweet. Weekend rates start at £145 for a double room, Friday through to Sunday.

SOUTH CENTRAL

This is where London's most splendid deluxe digs are located, hotels so grand that many of them are tourist attractions in their own right. If you're not from old money yourself, you'll get more punch for your pound in the areas of Victoria and Pimlico.

MAYFAIR & ST JAMES

41 Map pp440-1 *Hotel*
☎ 7300 0041; www.redcarnationhotels.com; 41 Buckingham Palace Rd SW1; standard d £160, split-level ste from £300

If you're not likely to get a call-up for Buckingham Palace itself, you can console yourself by getting the royal treatment at this nearby club-style hotel, which offers 20 classically designed black-and-white rooms, the services of two full-time butlers working around the clock, 24-hour hot and cold buffets as well as all the business facilities high-fliers should require.

BROWN'S Map p428 *Hotel*
☎ 7493 6020; www.brownshotel.com; 30 Albemarle St W1; d/ste from £160/315; tube Green Park

This five-star stunner was created from a dozen houses in 1837, by a former manservant to Lord Byron who was familiar with the comforts required by well-groomed gentlemen. It was the first lodgings in London to have a lift and is now the capital's longest-operating deluxe hotel. Furnishing and atmosphere evoke the past although comforts are very much of the now.

CHESTERFIELD Map pp426-7 *Hotel*
☎ 7491 2622; www.redcarnationhotels.com; 35 Charles St W1; standard d/ste from £100/165; tube Green Park

Just a block from Berkeley Square, the Chesterfield comprises five floors of refinement and lustre hidden behind a fairly plain Georgian townhouse. It has moulding ceilings, marble floors and period-style furnishing as you'd expect from one of the grand dames of London digs. Bonuses are the lush and lovely Conservatory restaurant, themed suites (like the musical one featuring instruments and tasteful paraphernalia), doggy meals for spoilt poochies and outstanding value for money.

CLARIDGES Map pp426-7 *Hotel*
☎ 7629 8860; www.the-savoy-group.com; Brook St W1; d from £179, ste from £319; tube Bond Street

Thankfully leftover from a bygone era, Claridges is one of the greatest of London's five-star hotels. Many of the Art Deco features of the public areas and suites were designed in the late 1920s and some of the 1930s furniture once graced the staterooms of the lost *SS Normandie*. Celebrated chef Gordon Ramsay recently took over the kitchen (p235) while the bar is *the* place to sip martinis whether you're a paying guest or not.

CONNAUGHT Map pp426-7 *Hotel*
☎ 7499 7070; www.the-savoy-group.com; Carlos Place W1; d/ste from £179/319; tube Green Park

The Connaught steadfastly refuses to cut its clothes to suit this year's fashion and concentrates on its tried-and-tested formula of yesteryear style, coddling comforts and legendary hospitality. Think crystal chandeliers, antiques, gilt-frames, mahogany panelling, Wedgwood and guests who never stray far from the lap of comfort.

The Ritz, St James (right)

DORCHESTER Map pp426-7 *Hotel*
☎ 7629 8888; www.dorchesterhotel.com; Park Lane W1; d from £330, ste £500; tube Hyde Park Corner
There's no better place to play the recalcitrant rich kid than this most lavish of London foyers at the 'Dorch'. Monumental floral arrangements and faux-marble columns dominate the public areas, while most of the guest rooms feature huge four-poster beds piled high with pillows, along with all the gadgets, products and niceties required for a prestigious pampering.

METROPOLITAN Map pp426-7 *Hotel*
☎ 7447 1000; www.metropolitan.co.uk; 19 Old Park Lane W1; d from £275, ste £585; tube Hyde Park Corner
In the same stable as The Halkin, the 155-room Metropolitan is another minimalist hotel – 'stripped of nonessentials' (as they say) and decorated in shades of cream and muesli – that attracts a super-trendy, well-heeled crowd (more rock star than royal, really). The hotel's Japanese restaurant Nobu is outstanding (p238). The Met Bar's day as the nocturnal in-scene for the glitterati has passed although it's still nigh on impossible to get in without pull or profile.

NUMBER 5 MADDOX STREET
Map p428 *Hotel*
☎ 7647 0200; 5 Maddox St W1; ste £230-575; tube Victoria
Perhaps because its direction is so focussed, this hotel achieves its aim to provide a contemporary, urban sanctuary with considerable élan – they make you feel more like you're 'super styling' in your own rented pad than staying in a hotel. On show are Eastern themes, natural tones and an exquisite eye for detail along with all the technical facilities the contemporary traveller could require, including free a broadband Internet connection in every room.

PARK LANE SHERATON HOTEL
Map pp426-7 *Hotel*
☎ 7499 6321; Piccadilly W1; d from £140, ste £430; tube Green Park
Although taken over and upgraded by the Sheraton Corporation in the late '90s, this grand dame of London hotels retains its essential Englishness, with refurbished rooms that boast upgraded comforts while retaining an old-fashioned mood. The hotel was used for parts of that most English of television dramas, *Brideshead Revisited*.

THE RITZ Map pp426-7 *Hotel*
☎ 7493 8181; www.theritzlondon.com; 150 Piccadilly W1; d/ste from £320/600; tube Green Park
Considering the world renown of this most ritzy of establishments, you might expect it to rest on its laurels, don some slippers and discreetly fade out. Not so. While it's still the royal family's home away from home, such is the Ritz's unyielding cred that even the new generation of cultural elite can't get enough of it. The rooms are predictably opulent while the restaurant is decked out like a rococo boudoir. 'Puttttting on my top hat, puttttting on my white tie…'

TRAFALGAR HILTON Map p430 *Hotel*
☎ 7870 2900; www.thetrafalgar.hilton.com; 2 Spring Gdns SW1; standard d/ste from £179/390; tube Charing Cross/Embankment
Since making a splash when it opened as the Hilton's first 'style' hotel in 2001, the tastefully minimalist Trafalgar continues to appeal to a young, hip and fashionable crew behind its traditional 19th-century facade. Large windows offer some of the greatest views over the square and the London cityscape, while the cool and spacious Rockwell bar specialises in more than 80 different brands of bourbon (in case views aren't your thing).

Sleeping – South Central

KNIGHTSBRIDGE, KENSINGTON & SOUTH KENSINGTON

BASIL ST HOTEL Map pp422-3 *Hotel*
☎ 7581 3311; www.thebasil.com; Basil St SW3; s/d from £145/205; tube Knightsbridge

This family-owned hotel has been taking care of guests for almost a century. It's a lovely, antique-stuffed hideaway in the heart of Knightsbridge, perfectly placed for carrying heavy bags back from Harrods, Harvey Nicks or Sloane St. It's decidedly low-tech – baths instead of showers, no lifts etc – but it's a delightful vision of little England in big London.

BLAKES Map pp436-7 *Hotel*
☎ 7370 6701; www.blakeshotels.com; 33 Roland Gdns SW7; d/ste from £140/235; tube Gloucester Road

Five Victorian houses were knocked into one to create London's original boutique, opened by designer Anoushka Hempel in the 1970s. Rooms are elegantly decked out and individually wrapped with four-poster beds, rich fabrics and antiques. They are gorgeous, if sometimes a little impractical (beds facing away from the TV for example). It's renowned as the stars' hideout from the paparazzi, but it would be much better if staff took more care of their no-name clientele with half as much enthusiasm.

FIVE SUMNER PLACE Map pp436-7 *Hotel*
☎ 7584 7586; www.sumnerplace.com; 5 Sumner Pl SW7; d £130; tube South Kensington

On a quiet leafy road not far from South Kensington tube, this hotel is restful, refined and elegant. It has 13 well-equipped rooms (any room with a drinks cabinet is 'well-equipped'), and there's an attractive conservatory and a tiny courtyard garden. Only two rooms have baths and the others have little showers you'll have to squeeze into. Also, request a double bed or you might get two conjoined singles.

THE GORE Map pp422-3 *Hotel*
☎ 7584 6601; www.gorehotel.co.uk; 189 Queen's Gate SW7; d from £190, Tudor r £295; tube Gloucester Road

Charismatically kooky, slightly threadbare and irresistibly romantic, this 54-room hotel is a veritable palace of polished mahogany, Turkish carpets, bronze statues, antique-style bathrooms, aspidistras, thousands of portraits and prints and a great bar. The dark-panelled Tudor Room is gorgeous, with stained glass and a four-poster bed. The attached Bistrot 190 is a wonderful place for brunch.

THE HALKIN Map pp426-7 *Hotel*
☎ 7333 1000; www.halkin.co.uk; 5 Halkin St SW1; d/ste from £305/475; tube Hyde Park Corner

The 41-room Halkin is for business travellers of a minimalist bent: lots of burlwood, marble and round glass things. Bedrooms are wood-panelled and stylishly uncluttered; staff strut about in Armani uniforms.

HOTEL 167 Map pp436-7 *Hotel*
☎ 7373 0672; www.hotel167.com; 167 Old Brompton Rd SW5; d from £90; tube Gloucester Road

The new paint job on the outside of this hotel only makes the interior look a little more frayed around the edges. That said, though, this is a quiet and pleasant hotel with mostly friendly service and unusually clutter-free rooms. There's no lift but the highest – and the best – room is on the 3rd floor.

KNIGHTSBRIDGE HOTEL Map pp436-7 *Hotel*
☎ 7584 6300; 10 Beaufort Gdns SW3; www.firmdale.com; d/ste from £175/335; tube Knightsbridge

Another masterpiece from the Kitts, this hotel occupies a 200-year-old house just around the corner from Harrods and has elegant and beautiful interiors done in a sumptuous, subtle and modern English style. Some of the rooms, although beautifully furnished, are too small for the price so you might want to double check when booking. There's a self-service 'honesty bar' in a pleasant study and the staff is young, good-looking, friendly and capable.

LANESBOROUGH *Hotel*
☎ 7259 5599; www.lanesborough.com; Hyde Park Corner; d from £310; tube Hyde Park Corner

This is where visiting divas doze and Regency opulence meets state-of-the-art technology. The Royal Suite, the most expensive digs in town, comes with a chauffeured Bentley and costs £6,213, although you could probably get a couple of quid off if you haggle. The service, as you might expect, is impeccable.

NUMBER SIXTEEN Map pp436-7 *Hotel*
☎ 7589 5232; www.numbersixteenhotel.co.uk; 16 Sumner Place SW7; d from £165; tube South Kensington

Even by Firmdale's lofty standards, this recently refurbished hotel is outstanding. With cool grey, muted colours, tasteful clarity and choice art throughout, it's a stunning place to repose and that's even before you see the idyllic back garden set around a fish pond with a few cosy snugs; or have breakfast in the conservatory; or read the newspaper in front of the fire in the drawing room.

SWISS HOUSE HOTEL Map pp436-7 *Hotel*
☎ 7373 2769; www.swiss-hh.demon.co.uk; 171 Old Brompton Rd SW5; d from £89; tube Gloucester Road
The hushed Swiss House is an outstanding place for the price, set in a Victorian terrace house festooned with flowers. Staff are gracious and welcoming, and the amply sized rooms are cosily shabby chic. Rooms at the rear look out over a pleasant garden and don't get any noise from the street.

Cheap Sleeps
HOLLAND HOUSE YHA HOSTEL
Map pp422-3 *Hostel*
☎ 0870 770 5866; hollandhouse@yha.org.uk; Holland Walk W8; dm £22; tube High Street Kensington
This hostel has 201 beds and is built into the Jacobean wing of Holland House, overlooking Holland Park. It's large, very busy and rather institutional, but the position is unbeatable. There's a café and kitchen, and breakfast is included.

CHELSEA & BELGRAVIA
ANNANDALE HOUSE HOTEL
Map pp436-7 *Hotel*
☎ 7730 5051; Sloane Gdns SW1; tube Sloane Square
This discreet, traditional hotel is just south of Sloane Square and an excellent choice for the noise-sensitive. All rooms have a TV and phone.

TOPHAMS BELGRAVIA Map pp440-1 *Hotel*
☎ 7730 8147; www.tophams.co.uk; 28 Ebury St SW1; d/4 posters from £130/150; tube Victoria
Cosy and calm, Tophams has been run by the same family since it opened for business in 1937 and although it was significantly renovated in the '90s the furnishings evoke a sense of yesteryear. It's made up of five small, inter-connected houses giving it a delightfully higgledy-piggledy feel.

VICTORIA & PIMLICO
CHESHAM HOUSE HOTEL *B&B*
☎ 7730 8513; 64-66 Edbury St SW1; basic d £55, with bathroom £70; tube Victoria
Situated on a lovely street in elegant Belgravia, this terrific B&B has a pair of striking,

old-fashioned carriage lamps flanking its door, through which you'll find well-maintained quarters with bathroom and washing facilities on every floor and some good value bathrooms.

HAMILTON HOUSE HOTEL Map pp440-1 *Hotel*
☎ 7821 7113; www.hamiltonhousehotel.com; 60 Warwick Way SW1; basic d £65, with bathroom £90; tube Victoria
This friendly place is close to the transport options of Victoria and is good value for the facilities. Many of the 40 rooms are a little small but they're bright and cheerful, and there's a decent restaurant on site.

LUNA & SIMONE HOTEL Map pp440-1 *Hotel*
☎ 7834 5897; www.lunasimonehotel.com; 47-9 Belgrave Rd SW1; d with bathroom £80; tube Victoria
Central, spotlessly clean and comfortable, Luna & Simone is about the best on this busy street. A full English breakfast is included, and there are free storage facilities if you want to leave bags while travelling. If all of London's budget hotels were like this, we'd probably stay longer.

MORGAN HOUSE Map pp440-1 *Hotel*
☎ 7730 2384; www.morganhouse.co.uk; 120 Ebury St SW1; basic d £66, d with bathroom £86, f £122; tube Victoria
There are many places to stay on this street. The same people who run Woodville House own this one – rooms are brighter and cosier here, but the management has its moody days.

VICARAGE HOTEL Map pp422-3 *B&B*
☎ 7229 4030; www.londonvicaragehotel.com; 10 Vicarage Gate W8; basic d £78, with bathroom £102; tube High Street Kensington
One of London's most highly regarded B&Bs, Vicarage is very good although it's beginning to lose a little of its lustre. On the positive side, you'll find old-fashioned and affordable English charm, a sociable guest lounge, hearty breakfasts (kippers if you like) and a top location, while the only real minuses are the faint, musty whiff and the complete lack of private loos.

WINDERMERE HOTEL Map pp440-1 *Hotel*
☎ 7834 5163; www.windermere-hotel.co.uk; 142-4 Warwick Way SW1; d from £84; tube Victoria
The award-winning Windermere has 22 small, singularly designed and spotless rooms in a sparkling, white mid-Victorian town house that offers character and warmth in an area not exactly renowned for such. There's a reliable and reasonably priced restaurant on site. The Victorian house occupies what used to

be Abbot's Lane, a thoroughfare connecting Westminster Abbey and the Abbot's residence, along which the abbot and kings would have trod in medieval times.

Cheap Sleeps
VICTORIA HOTEL   *Hotel*
☎ 7834 3077; www.astorhostels.com; 71 Belgrave Rd SW1; dm £16; tube Pimlico

This recently and funkily refurbished hostel has 60 beds so it's busy without being too impersonal. It's staffed by pausing travellers, has Internet and 24-hour reception, and is within easy walking distance of the Tate Britain and Westminster Abbey.

WELLINGTON HALL
Map pp440-1   *Student Residence*
☎ 7834 4740; 71 Vincent Sq SW1; basic s/tw £28/42; tube Victoria

Just a few minutes' walk from Westminster and Victoria's transport stations, this sterile but clean student residence has 125 beds in single and twin rooms, and is very handy when all you require is shelter.

ALONG THE SOUTH BANK
A decade ago, the South Bank was all but bereft of accommodation. Now hotels keep popping up to meet the demands of those who wish to stay near Tate Modern, the London Eye or Waterloo International train station.

SOUTH BANK CENTRE & WATERLOO
COUNTY HALL TRAVEL INN
CAPITAL Map pp426-7   *Hotel*
☎ 0870 238 3300; www.travelinn.co.uk; Belvedere Rd SE1; r up to 2 adults & 2 children £85; tube Waterloo

At the back of County Hall, this Travel Inn is well-located near the London Eye and Saatchi Gallery but lacks river views. It has about as much style as a fast-food restaurant, with lots of purple paint, vinyl flooring, laminated menus and large vending machines, but you'll still need to book well ahead to get a room. Numbers 10 to 20 on each floor are the quietest, apparently. If you can't get in here, there are about a dozen Travel Inns throughout the capital, including one at Tower Bridge (☎ 0870 238 3303). Check the website for details.

LONDON MARRIOTT HOTEL
COUNTY HALL Map pp426-7   *Hotel*
☎ 7928 5200, 0870 400 7200; www.marriott.co.uk/lonch; Westminster Bridge Rd SE1; s/d from £210, with river views £230; tube Westminster

This elegant, luxury hotel is famed for its fabulous, close-up views of the Thames and the Houses of Parliament. This was formerly the headquarters of the Greater London Council and the florally, traditional rooms still have a halls-of-power feel. That's to say you'll feel uncomfortable dressing *too* casually here. The sweeping, circular driveway seems miles away from the bustle of Westminster Bridge outside.

WELLINGTON AT WATERLOO HOTEL
Map pp426-7   *Hotel*
☎ 7928 6083, wellington@regents-inn.plc.uk; 81-3 Waterloo Rd SE1; s/d/f £70/80/90; tube Waterloo

The traditional façade of the hotel is appealing and rooms look refreshingly comfortable and modern, if a trifle small. However, this hotel is on a busy road and near to a railway line, so it's not great for guests who are very sensitive to noise. The bars downstairs have been recently refurbished, but retain their impressive mural of the Battle of Waterloo.

Cheap Sleeps
STAMFORD STREET APARTMENTS
Map pp426-7   *Student Residence*
☎ 7848 2960; www.kcl.ac.uk/kcvb; 127 Stamford St SE1; s with bathroom £34; tube Waterloo

This is a modern and central 543-bed student residence. Rooms are available from the end of June to mid-September. Student, group and long-stay rates are available.

BANKSIDE
NOVOTEL CITY SOUTH Map pp432-3 *Hotel*
☎ 7089 0400; www.novotel.com; 51-61 Southwark Bridge Rd SW1; s/d £140/160; tube Southwark/London Bridge

The first of Novotel's new trendier properties, with slightly small, modern and stylish rooms; think two-tone duvets, brightly coloured cushions, tinted green glass in the bathroom and blonde wood. All mod cons, from ironing board to hairdryer to minibar are provided. There's a swish bar and restaurant. Rates above don't include breakfast, weekend rates of £100 do.

MAD HATTER Map pp426-7 *Hotel*

☎ 7401 9222; www.madhatterhotel.com; 3-7 Stamford St SE1; tube Southwark; r £100

Its rooms are actually quite generic, but the Mad Hatter feels slightly homier than most chain hotels, thanks to its traditionally styled reception area and the adjacent pub. There's a decent level of comfort, and although the hotel is at a fairly major road junction, inside it doesn't seem too noisy. It's possible to accommodate three people in some rooms for an extra £12 a night. Weekend rates for singles/doubles are £80.

SOUTHWARK ROSE HOTEL

Map pp432-3 *Hotel*

☎ 7015 1480; www.southwarkrosehotel.co.uk; 43-47 Southwark Bridge Rd SW1; tube Southwark/London Bridge; r £105

Claiming to be London's first budget boutique hotel, the Southwark Rose looks pretty good. The downstairs lobby is all white walls, rose lounge chairs, grey-fleck rugs, silver and rose domed light shades and sexy Japanese photography. Rooms are stylishly decorated with big fluffy duvets and large, textured headboards. The pay-off is that they are fairly small. Rates don't include breakfast (£4.50/8 for continental/English). Rooms start at £95 on weekends.

Cheap Sleeps

BANKSIDE HOUSE *Student Residence*

☎ 7633 9877; www.lse.ac.uk/collections/vacations; 24 Sumner St SE1; tube Blackfriars; s shared bathroom £31, with bathroom £45, tr/q £60/80

This 800-bed hall is the largest in the LSE stable . Rooms available early July to mid-September.

THE EAST END

Decent accommodation is thin on the ground in the East End, but there is one option if you simply must be near the curry houses of Brick Lane and the market at Spitalfields.

CITY HOTEL Map pp432-3 *Hotel*

☎ 7247 3313; www.cityhotellondon.co.uk; 12 Osborn St E1; tube Aldgate East; s/d from £140/150, f £190

The public spaces in this hotel, unfortunately, have a little more character than the rooms. Often, you'll open the door after checking in, to find the beds laid out in regimental lines. Other times, however, the layout is fine, and at least you can be sure the place is clean and comfortable. The street is a little busy, so ask for a room at the back.

BOROUGH & BERMONDSEY

Cheap Sleeps

DOVER CASTLE HOSTEL Map pp432-3 *Hostel*

☎ 7403 7773; www.dovercastlehostel.co.uk; 6a Great Dover St SE1; tube Borough; 3-12 bed dm £10-15

This 55-bed hostel in a four-storey Victorian terrace house has a Caribbean-theme bar below. It has a TV lounge, kitchen facilities, luggage storage and Internet access.

ST CHRISTOPHER'S INN

Map pp432-3 *Hostel*

☎ 7407 1856; www.st-christophers.co.uk; 163 Borough High St SE1; tube Borough/London Bridge; 4-12 bed dm £15-19, tw £45

This 164-bed place is the flagship of an excellent hostel chain with basic, but cheap and clean, accommodation, and friendly service. There's a roof garden with sauna, solarium, hot tub and excellent views of the Thames. Nearby branches (same contact details) include **St Christopher's Inn** (121 Borough High St SE1), with 48 beds, a pub below the hostel, small veranda and chill-out room, and the **Orient Espresso** (59-61 Borough High St SE1), with 36 beds, a laundry and café. Prices are slightly cheaper in winter and there are sometimes ridiculously cheap Internet deals, so check the website.

159 GREAT DOVER ST

Map pp432-3 *Student Residence*

☎ 7403 1932; www.kcl.ac.uk/kcvb; 159 Great Dover St SE1; tube Borough; s/tw £29/49

This modern student residence has 280 rooms from the end of June to mid-September. Ring for student, group and long-stay rates.

BUTLER'S WHARF RESIDENCE

Map pp432-3 *Student Residence*

☎ 7407 7164; butlers.wharf@lse.ac.uk; 11 Gainsford St SE1; tube Tower Hill/London Bridge; s/tw £23/40

The rooms in this 281-bed student hall don't have private bathrooms, so you will find yourself sharing. The rooms are available from the first week of July to the third week in September.

DOWN RIVER

London's answer to La Defense in Paris, Docklands is almost a world unto itself, and without your own car, you'll find it difficult to get back to late at night. Greenwich is also a little difficult to reach after hours, but has a decent cluster of reasonably priced, archetypically English hotels and B&Bs.

DOCKLANDS

FOUR SEASONS CANARY
WHARF Map p435 *Hotel*

☎ 7510 1999; www.fourseasons.com; Westferry Circus, Canary Wharf E14; s/d from £280; tube Canary Wharf

It no doubt hosts many financial wizards jetting into Canary Wharf and has an excellent river frontage, but it's hard not to feel that this striking hotel is wasted a little in Docklands. Still, it's excellent if you need/want to stay in the area. The exterior, by Philippe Starck, looks like an oversized doll's house, with its row upon row of square windows, large panels of wood on either side of the door, slightly A-line shape and green architectural quiff. Inside, it's still modern, but slightly more discreet. The service, as ever at Four Seasons, is superb.

GREENWICH

GREENWICH PARKHOUSE HOTEL
Map p435 *Hotel*

☎ 8305 1478; www.greenwich-parkhouse-hotel.co.uk; 1 & 2 Nevada St SE10; s/d £33/40, d with bathroom from £45, tr with hall bathroom £55; tube DLR Cutty Sark

This is a tiny, family-run B&B. It's not flash by any means – its old fashioned rooms have TVs and tea-making facilities, but no in-room phones. However, the place has price and location going for it – it's next to Greenwich Park. Book well ahead as there are only eight rooms, and reservations for three nights or more are preferred. Credit cards are not accepted.

HAMILTON HOUSE HOTEL Map p435 *Hotel*

☎ 8694 9899; www.hamiltonhousehotel.co.uk; 14 West Grove SE10; s/d from £100/120; tube DLR Cutty Sark

About five minutes beyond the Royal Observatory and Greenwich Park, this is a remarkable hilltop Georgian house that has been restored to its original elegance. Once home to two London Lord Mayors, it now has nine hotel rooms, some of which look over to Canary Wharf, others towards Blackheath. There's a lovely garden and four rooms with four-poster beds (£150 per night). All of this makes it very popular with wedding parties, so book ahead.

MITRE Map p435 *B&B*

☎ 8355 6760; fax 8355 6761; 291 Greenwich High Rd SE10; s/d/f £60/80/100; tube DLR Cutty Sark

Another family-run B&B, a little larger and more comfortable than the Greenwich Parkhouse hotel, but also more prone to noise. The rooms are also rather old-fashioned looking: think immediate post-war style, but with bathrooms and mod cons like direct-dial phone, TV and kettle. However, that's all part of the charm; actually, the rooms have been refurbished and are definitely clean. There's a traditional English bar below (there's a lift) and the building's on a main road, so it's hard to imagine things quietening down until well past midnight.

Cheap Sleeps

ROTHERHITHE YHA Map pp432-3 *Hostel*

☎ 7232 2114; www.yha.org.uk; 20 Salter Rd SE16; 4-10 bed dm £15-24, tw/q £55/145; tube Rotherhithe

The facilities at this large, flagship YHA are very good, but the location is a bit remote. There's a bar, restaurant, kitchen facilities and a laundry, plus four bedrooms adapted for disabled visitors. All rooms have private bathrooms.

ST CHRISTOPHER'S INN Map p435 *Hostel*

☎ 7407 1856; www.st-christophers.co.uk; 189 Greenwich High Rd SE10; 4-12 bed dm £15-19, tw £45; tube DLR Cutty Sark

The Greenwich branch of this well-respected chain of hostels.

NORTH CENTRAL & THE NORTHERN HEIGHTS

Marylebone is a great place to stay – it's very central and convenient for shopping and for West End nightlife, although at the same time it has a local atmosphere as well as local prices. If you'd rather visit urban London by day and return to 'little England' at night, there are a few good options around Hampstead and Highgate, while Camden makes a good base if you're into live music or the weekend market.

66 CAMDEN SQUARE Map pp418-19 *B&B*
☎ 7485 4622; 66 Camden Sq NW1; B&B £90; tube Camden Town

This glass-and-teak B&B combines space, light and comfort in a quiet north London square, not far from Camden Town and Regent's Park. The owners are fans of things Japanese and the whole house is attractively minimalist.

30 KING HENRY'S ROAD *B&B*
☎ 7483 2871; 30 King Henry's Rd; B&B £100; tube Chalk Farm

This large mid-Victorian family home has snug and spacious rooms, and a great position between loud and lively Camden and dreamy, romantic Primrose Hill. A healthy and delicious continental-style breakfast (with fruit salads and yoghurt) is served in a cosy kitchen, looking onto a well-tended garden (and a well-groomed greyhound).

BRYANSTON COURT HOTEL
Map pp422-3 *Hotel*
☎ 7262 3141; www.bryanstonhotel.com; 56-60 Great Cumberland Pl W1; standard d £120; tube Marble Arch

Open fireplaces, leather armchairs, creaky floors and oil paintings give this place a hushed and traditional English atmosphere. There are 60 pleasantly furnished rooms, although the ones at the back are quieter and brighter.

CAMDEN LOCK HOTEL Map pp418-19 *Hotel*
☎ 7267 3912; www.camdenlockhotel.co.uk; 89 Chalk Farm Rd; d from £70; tube Chalk Farm

It's not much to look at, but if you want to be in or at least near the thick of Camden commotion, this blue-collar business hotel will do the job. The decor is reminiscent of suburbia but the rooms are relatively spacious and the staff are very friendly.

DURRANTS HOTEL Map pp426-7 *Hotel*
☎ 7935 8131; www.durrantshotel.co.uk; George St W1; standard d £145, ste £285; tube Bond Street

The same family has owned this quintessentially English gem since 1921 and the long-serving and uniformed staff – night porters worked here for 40 years – gives it a unique atmosphere. The hotel is luxurious, sprawling, traditional and soothing, and the rooms are charmingly old-fashioned. It's located directly behind the wonderful Wallace Collection and only a shopping bag's swing from Oxford Street.

DORSET SQUARE HOTEL Map pp426-7 *Hotel*
☎ 7723 7874; www.dorsetsquare.co.uk; 9-40 Dorset Sq NW1; d £160, 4-poster r £240; tube Baker Street

Two combined Regency town houses contain this enchanting hotel overlooking leafy Dorset Square, where the very first cricket ground was laid in 1814 (which explains the cricket memorabilia on the walls). Guest quarters are predictably small but almost dreamily decorated with a blend of antiques, sumptuous fabrics, crown-canopied beds, and mahogany/marble bathrooms.

EDWARD LEAR HOTEL Map pp422-3 *Hotel*
☎ 7402 5401; www.edlear.com; 28-30 Seymour St W1; basic d £70, d with bathroom £89; tube Marble Arch

Once home to the famous Victorian painter and limerick writer Edward Lear, this hotel's best qualities are its location, a short walk from Hyde Park Corner, and full English breakfasts, featuring meat from HRH's traditional butcher. Rooms and furnishings are a little threadbare and there are four floors and no lifts.

LA GAFFE Map p415 *Hotel*
☎ 7435 8965; www.lagaffe.co.uk; 107-11 Heath St NW3; d £90, honeymoon room £125; tube Hampstead

Near Hampstead Heath, La Gaffe has eccentric and comfortable lodgings in an early 18th-century cottage above a popular Italian restaurant of the same name. The hotel's rooms are granny-chic, and there's a lovely honeymoon room with a Jacuzzi and four-poster bed.

HAMPSTEAD VILLAGE GUEST HOUSE *Guesthouse*
☎ 7439 8679; www.hampsteadguesthouse.com; 2 Kemplay Rd NW3; basic d £72, d with bathroom £82; tube Hampstead

Only 20 minutes by tube from the centre of London, this is a lovely pad with a quirky character, rustic and antique decor and furnishing, comfy beds and a delightful back garden in which you can enjoy a cooked breakfast (if you pay the extra £7). There's also a studio flat, which can accommodate up to five people.

HOUSE HOTEL Map p415 *Hotel*
☎ 7431 3873; 2 Rosslyn Hill NW3; d from £110; tube Belsize Park; **P**

This free-standing hotel at the foot of Rosslyn Hill has 23 (mostly) spacious and elegantly furnished rooms with marble bathrooms, and offers the rare opportunity to park your car around these parts.

SANDRINGHAM HOTEL
Hotel

☎ 7435 1569; 3 Holford Rd NW3; d from £100; tube Hampstead

Another Hampstead bargain, this hotel occupies an period home and has some characteristic English, frilly clutter in its rooms.

WIGMORE COURT HOTEL
Map pp442-3
Hotel

☎ 7935 0928; www.wigmore-court-hotel.co.uk; 23 Gloucester Pl W1; d from £80; tube Marble Arch

One-time residence of former PM William Pitt, this place manages to be sombre and over-the-top, a gloomy Victorian structure awash with pink decor! It is well organised and guests have access to a kitchen and self-service laundry. On the down side, there's no lift for the four floors and the reception is understaffed.

NORTHWEST LONDON

Notting Hill is particularly well endowed when it comes to stylish and eccentric lodgings, although the closest budget travellers will get is likely to be the less-fashionable Paddington or Bayswater.

BALMORAL HOUSE HOTEL
Map pp422 *Hotel*

☎ 7723 7445; www.balmoralhousehotel.co.uk; 156 & 157 Sussex Gardens W2; basic d £48, with bathroom £68; tube Paddington

This immaculate hotel is made up of two properties opposite one another on a street lined with small hotels and lots of traffic. Double-glazing might protect light sleepers, although you may be kept awake by the garish decor.

COLONNADE TOWN HOUSE
Map pp422-3
Hotel

☎ 7286 1052; www.etontownhouse.com; 2 Warrington Crescent W9; d from £118, 4-poster £143; tube Warwick Avenue

A charmer in lovely Little Venice, the Colonnade is the handsome Victorian structure where Sigmund Freud sheltered after he fled Vienna. Apart from two in the basement, rooms are light, spacious and relaxing, and there are nice touches like the provision of slippers and gowns.

GATE HOTEL
Map pp422-3
Hotel

☎ 7221 0707; www.gatehotel.com; 6 Portobello Rd W11; d from £65; tube Notting Hill Gate

Many of the rooms are barely bigger than the beds, the continental breakfasts aren't worth a bleary eye, the staff are frequently gruff and you can't check in before 2pm – but this is still

Cheap Sleeps

ST CHRISTOPHER'S INN CAMDEN
Map pp418-19
Hostel

☎ 7388 1012; www.st-christophers.co.uk; 48-50 Camden High St NW1; dm from £14

This 54-bed branch of the popular hostel chain is five minutes from Camden High St, atop the very busy Belushi's bar, which has a 2am license. The staff is very friendly, there's no curfew and the lodgings are nice and clean although some of the private rooms are very small.

ST PANCRAS INTERNATIONAL YHA
Map pp418-19
Hostel

☎ 0870 770 6044; stpancras@yha.org.uk; 79-81 Euston Rd NW1; dm £24, private tw from £50; tube King's Cross St Pancras/Euston

The area itself isn't great, but this 152-bed hostel itself is modern, with kitchen, restaurant, lockers, cycle shed and lounge, and it's in the hub of London's transport links.

a worthy option for inexpensive lodgings on fashionable Portobello Rd, and the lovely floral window boxes are pleasant to return to.

HEMPEL
Map pp422-3
Hotel

☎ 7298 9000; www.the-hempel.co.uk; 31-35 Craven Hill Gdns W2; d from £210, studio £360; tube Lancaster Gate/Queensway

One of London's most stunning sanctuaries, designer Anouska Hempel's hotel combines Renaissance proportions with Zen-like synchronicity in the public spaces, guest quarters and bathrooms. The monochrome tones, white-on-white spaces and crisp fabrics won't be to everyone's tastes, but high-flying business folk certainly seem to dig it. The super-slick I-Thai restaurant continues the minimalist theme, although it's a bit too self-conscious to be fun.

INVERNESS COURT HOTEL
Map pp422-3
Hotel

☎ 7229 1444; www.cghotels.com; Inverness Tce W2; d from £190; tube Queensway

This structure was commissioned by Edward VII for his 'confidante' Lillie Langtry, and came with a private theatre that's now a cocktail bar. Panelled walls, stained glass and huge open fires give it a Gothic feel, but most rooms – some overlooking Hyde Park – are modern and pretty ordinary.

MANOR COURT HOTEL Map pp422-3 *Hotel*
☎ 7792 3361, ☎ 7727 5407; fax 7229 2875; 7 Clanricarde Gdns W2; basic d £50, with bathroom £65; tube Notting Hill Gate

Probably due for a nip and tuck, this hotel (and neighbourhood) nonetheless still provides decent accommodation at decent prices, and it's not far from the lights and life of Notting Hill. Some rooms are better than others so have a look around if you can. You can get a fiver off this rate in the off-season.

MILLER'S RESIDENCE Map pp422-3 *Hotel*
☎ 7243 1024; www.millersuk.com; 111a Westbourne Grove, enter from Hereford Rd W2; r from £150; tube Bayswater/Notting Hill Gate

More a five-star B&B than a hotel, this '18th-century rooming house' is chock-a-block with curiosities and antique furnishings, and quite literally brimming with personality. Every available surface is plastered with *objets d'art* and the Victorian-style drawing room has to be seen to be believed (preferably by candle-light). Rooms come in all shapes, sizes and shades of antique opulent, but they all offer terrific value and ample opportunity for a romantic sojourn.

OXFORD HOTEL Map pp422-3 *Hotel*
☎ 7402 6860; www.oxfordhotellondon.co.uk; 13-14 Craven Tce W2; d £66, f £83; tube Lancaster Gate

Although tastelessly furnished with horrible floral bed spreads and curtains, this hotel offers excellent value – particularly for families – as far as rates/facilities go, and there's a welcoming atmosphere helped along by the friendly family who runs it, as well as sociable pets and a convivial guests' lounge.

PAVILION HOTEL Map pp422-3 *Hotel*
☎ 7262 0905; www.msi.com.mt/pavilion; 34-6 Sussex Gdns W2; d from £100; tube Paddington

'Fashion, Glam & Rock 'n' Roll' is the motto of this place, so if you'd like to cap off your holiday by throwing a TV set out the window, this could be for you. There are 30 individually themed rooms ('Honky Tonky Afro' has a Moorish theme, Casablanca has a 1970s theme). It's fun and good value, although cheesily B-list.

PEMBRIDGE COURT Map pp422-3 *Hotel*
☎ 7229 9977; 34 Pembridge Gdns W2; d from £185; tube Notting Hill Gate

Behind an elegant neoclassical facade in Notting Hill is this sweet and soothing contender for London's best small hotel. A bright and breezy welcome sets the tone although you'll probably best remember the pet cat, floral drapery, Victorian knick-knacks and sumptuous furnishings. The best rooms are up the top and the small singles are *very* small.

PORTOBELLO HOTEL Map pp422-3 *Hotel*
☎ 7727 2777; www.portobello-hotel.co.uk; 22 Stanley Gdns W11; d from £160; tube Notting Hill Gate

This famous place has been a firm favourite with rock and rollers and movie stars down the years. Rooms and furnishing are eccentric in a funky, haphazard, devil-may-care fashion and there's a 24-hour bar to fuel guests on their merry way. The most coveted room is number 16, featuring a round bed which has seen action from the likes of Johnny Depp and Kate Moss who stayed here a few years back. Rumour has it that a romantic Johnny filled the Victorian claw bath with champagne for Kate, only for a shocked maid to pull the plug and drain the 'dirty bathwater'.

ST DAVID'S HOTEL Map pp422-3 *Hotel*
☎ 7723 4963; www.stdavidshotels.com; 16-20 Norfolk Sq W2; basic d £59, with bathroom £69; tube Paddington

Not that there's necessarily anything *wrong* with this neighbourhood (read: it's scruffy) beside the train station, but if St David's had smarter surrounds, you'd probably pay around 20% more for the facilities (TVs, phone, breakfast). The hotel is cobbled together from four terraced houses, the decor of the tight-fitting rooms is comfortably dowdy and the welcome is genuine.

WESTBOURNE HOTEL Map pp422-3 *Hotel*
☎ 7243 6008; 65 Westbourne Grove W11; d from £180; tube Notting Hill Gate

Trendsetters and followers among you will probably be flicking through this guide while waiting for room service at this cool and stylish urban inn in perpetually hip Notting Hill. Spontaneously modern and cosy, the Westbourne combines loungey decor with stark modern artworks and retro furniture to great effect.

Cheap Sleeps
LEINSTER INN Map pp422-3 *Hostel*
☎ 7229 9641; www.astorhostels.com; 7-12 Leinster Square W2; dm from £17; tube Bayswater

In a big, old house northwest of Bayswater tube station and close to Portobello Rd Market, this 372-bed hostel is the largest in the Astor stable and has a café, laundry, Internet lounge and bar with a 4am licence and monthly theme parties.

WEST LONDON

Earl's Court has been a haven for travellers from Australia since the 1940s, earning itself the nickname 'Kangaroo Valley' by the 1960s. In postwar Britain many from down under faced discrimination from a very narrow-minded British public, and therefore sought to build their own community in West London. While the discrimination no longer exists today, Earl's Court remains the obvious place for young Australians, New Zealanders and South Africans to stay when visiting London, with plenty of chances to meet others in the same situation. While Earl's Court offers a wealth of accommodation options, from the most basic to comfortable three-star hotels, it's wise to get feedback from other travellers, as places can change overnight. There are a large number of complete dives that are not recommended, and are listed in the appropriate section. It's usually evident from the entrance halls and general atmosphere how clean and safe a place will be, and in Earl's Court in particular, trust your instincts. Elsewhere in the area there is little accommodation available, although Shepherd's Bush is quickly becoming another favourite with backpackers due to its great transport links and buzzing local scene.

EARL'S COURT

The main streets for hotels and hostels are off the Earl's Court Road – particularly Penywern Road for budget travellers and beautiful Barkston Gardens for middle-range options.

BARMY BADGER BACKPACKERS
Map pp436-7 *Hostel*

☎ 7370 5213; barmybadger@hotmail.com; 17 Longridge Rd SW5; 2-/4-/8-bed dm £17/16/15; tube Earl's Court
The Badger is a fun, family-run hostel offering great deals for the budget traveller, including a bed in a twin room for £95 per week. Book in advance, as it fills up during the summer. An affordable laundry service is also available.

BEAVER HOTEL Map pp436-7 *Hotel*

☎ 7373 4553; fax 7373 4555; 57-9 Philbeach Gdns, SW5; s/d/tr £60/85/99; tube Earl's Court
This hotel is nestled on the far end of Philbeach Gardens, towards Cromwell Road. It was remarkably quiet and smelt quite strange when we visited, but the receptionist was very helpful and the rooms are simple but clean. For its standards, the Beaver offers good rates for triple rooms.

BOKA HOTEL Map pp436-7 *Hotel*

☎ 7370 1388; www.bokahotel.activehotels.com; 33-5 Eardley Crs SW5; s/d £36/48; tube Earl's Court
This unshowy little place is in a quieter area of Earl's Court, but is very reasonably priced. Guests have access to a kitchen and TV place and the general atmosphere is relaxed. There are good cheap deals on triples and dorms, as well as competitive weekly rates.

BURNS HOTEL Map pp436-7 *Hotel*

☎ 7373 3151; www.vienna-group.co.uk; 18-26 Barkston Gdns SW5; s/d £115/160; tube Earl's Court
This converted mansion was once home to the actress Ellen Terry, and now houses the equally grand Burns Hotel, with its well-appointed rooms in the traditional English style and a pleasant garden and restaurant for guests.

EARL'S COURT YHA Map pp436-7 *Hostel*

☎ 7373 7083; earlscourt@yha.org.uk; 38 Bolton Gdns SW5; dm adult/under 18 £19/16.75; s £52, 4-bed r £76; tube Earl's Court; 💻
The Earl's Court Youth Hostel has a great atmosphere and friendly staff, and has been the starting point for many Australians' trips to Britain. The kitchen has just been redone and the whole place is cheerful but basic: most accommodation is in dorms, and small but clean four-bedroom rooms with bunks. There is a nice garden out the back for the summer and Internet access from the lounges. Book ahead.

HENLEY HOUSE HOTEL Map pp436-7 *Hotel*

☎ 7370 4111; www.henleyhousehotel.com; 30 Barkston Gardens SW5; s/d £69/89; tube Earl's Court
Overlooking a lovely garden square on this row of plush middle-range hotels, Henley House is a slice of England rather than London – indeed, whether the full-on chintz furnishings will inspire a love or hate reaction will influence your decision to stay here. The place is clean and well appointed and the staff very helpful.

HOTEL EARL'S COURT Map pp436-7 *Hotel*

☎ 7373 7079; www.hotelearlscourt.com; 28 Warwick Rd, SW5; s £28-45, d £45-60; tube Earl's Court
Despite looking vaguely insalubrious, the Earl's Court gets positive feedback from visitors who value its good location and say it is better than most of the other accommodation on this street. Breakfast is included.

LONDON TOWN HOTEL Map pp436-7 *Hotel*
☎ 7370 4356; www.londontownhotel.com; 15 Penywern Rd, SW5; s/d/tr/q £49/69/118/138; tube Earls Court
The rooms here are small but clean, and the management offers a 10% discount for anyone staying more than three nights. This place is a good bet for budget travellers in a group, as they have a large number of triples and quads available.

MERLYN COURT HOTEL Map pp436-7 *Hotel*
☎ 7370 4986; london@merlyncourt.demon.co.uk; 2 Barkston Gdns, SW5; s/d £45/75; tube Earl's Court
Perhaps the best value of the numerous smart hotels on Barkston Gardens, the Merlyn Court is not as plush and traditionally English as its neighbours, but it is a good bet for a decent and well-appointed room without having to pay through the nose.

MOWBRAY COURT HOTEL Map pp436-7 *Hotel*
☎ 7373 8285; mowbraycrthot@hotmail.com; 28/32 Penywern Road; s/d incl breakfast £52/67; tube Earl's Court
Its brochure looks more like one produced by a down-at-heel Warsaw youth hostel in the 1980s, but unfortunately the room rates do not reflect this. The Mowbray Court is decidedly sleazy, but it does offer out-of-season walk-in discounts for those who just turn up on their door, so it may be worth a shot for budget travellers.

PARAGON HOTEL Map pp436-7 *Hotel*
☎ 7385 1255; www.paragonhotel.co.uk; 47 Lillie Rd, SW6; s/d £150/175 ; tube West Brompton; P
This top-end hotel is very well appointed, but a typically soulless business hotel. The main lobby looks like a disused set from *Dynasty* and some of the clientele not unlike extras. Its location is not central, down the road in the nether regions of West Brompton, but it is quiet. However, it's popular with tour groups and reductions can be had if you are a good negotiator.

PHILBEACH HOTEL Map pp436-7 *Hotel*
☎ 7373 1244; www.philbeachhotel.freeserve.co.uk; 30/31 Philbeach Gardens, SW5; s/d with bathroom incl breakfast £65/90; tube Earl's Court
The Philbeach Hotel stands out from the crowd as a characterful and pleasant place to stay on a quiet residential street away from the Warwick Road. This is one of London's few gay hotels, and its interiors are suitably stylish and unique. The garden restaurant, Wilde About Oscar, and

Jimmy's bar, on the lower ground floor, are both popular with the local gay crowd.

WINDSOR HOUSE Map pp436-7 *Hotel*
☎ 7373 9087; www.windsor-house-hotel.com; 12 Penywern Rd, SW5; d £25.80; tube Earl's Court
The Windsor House is rather shabby, although it hardly stands out as any worse than the other hotels on the street, and service is friendly, if basic. However, they offer good reductions for advance bookings and have a kitchen that guests can use for self-catering.

YORK HOUSE HOTEL Map pp436-7 *Hotel*
☎ 7373 7519; yorkhh@aol.com; 28 Philbeach Gardens, SW5; s/d £34/54, with bathroom £47/73; tube Earl's Court
On a pretty and unassuming Earl's Court crescent, this small place has seen better days, but it's good value, particularly if you are happy to share your facilities. The staff are friendly and welcoming and the location quiet.

SHEPHERD'S BUSH
ST CHRISTOPHER'S *Hostel*
☎ 7407 1856; www.st-christophers.co.uk/bush/htm; 13-15 Shepherd's Bush Green; 2-/3-/4-/8-bed dm £23/29/18.50/15; tube Shepherd's Bush
One of a number of UK hostels run by St Christopher's, their Shepherd's Bush operation is right in the middle of the action and offers some of the best value about. The accommodation is rather cramped, but special offers can mean beds at under £10 per night. No curfew, a sprawling Australian sports pub next door and the tube at your doorstep – this is the place to stay if you are a young party animal seeking a base for your debauchery.

HILTON LONDON KENSINGTON *Hotel*
☎ 7603 3355; www.kensington-hilton.com; 177-199 Holland Park Ave; s/d £105/£155; tube Shepherd's Bush; P
The Hilton Group should get a prize for marketing skills – the Hilton London Kensington is on the Shepherd's Bush roundabout, although it just about qualifies for its title with its swanky address at the very end of one of London's poshest thoroughfares. This is a particularly smart hotel, even by Hilton standards, with liveried staff, over 600 rooms, three restaurants and the usual plush and beautifully appointed accommodation. Breakfast is not included.

K WEST
Hotel

☎ 7674 1000; www.k-west.co.uk; Richmond Way, W14; s/d £109/121; tube Shepherd's Bush; [P]

The former Kensington Hotel, K West is a sleek and stylish place that is just off Shepherd's Bush Green. The minimalist decor and fleet of staff on duty at reception can be a little disconcerting at times, but they are friendly and polite. The hotel's room rates are surprisingly reasonable, given the clientele it is obviously aiming for, and many people come to stay here to take advatnage of the spa alone. Prices are for accommodation only, although all guests can use the extensive spas, saunas and Jacuzzis and enjoy the weird and wonderful natural treatments. This is the place to come if you like being covered in mud and then discussing it at length over a £10 cocktail.

HAMMERSMITH
EXPRESS BY HOLIDAY INN LONDON
Hotel

☎ 8746 5100; www.hiexpress.co.uk 124 King Street, W6; r £99.95; tube Hammersmith;

Holiday Inns may not be the most exciting hotels, but they are reliable and often offer good discounts; check the website for London availability. The Hammersmith Holiday Inn looks just like any other, and while its location is not ideal – a 600m walk to Hammersmith tube – it is functional and reliable for this part of town, on the main shopping area of King Street.

SOUTHWEST LONDON

There are quite a number of B&Bs dotted throughout Fulham and Parson's Green, the best of which are listed below. Residential Putney and Barnes offer less in the way of tourist accommodation and it's a bit of a trek into town if you're only here for a short time, but there are a couple of options if a bed near(ish) the river appeals.

FULHAM & PARSON'S GREEN
CHELSEA VILLAGE HOTEL
Hotel

☎ 7565 1400; Fulham Road SW6; www.chelsea village.com; s/d incl breakfast from £65/79; tube Fulham Broadway

Built into one end of the Stamford Bridge stadium with some rooms overlooking the pitch, this is a smart, essentially business, hotel. If football, and Chelsea in particular, is your thing then this is your hotel. Rooms can cost up to £180 for a double, but you can also get some fabulously cheap deals out of season.

FULHAM GUESTHOUSE
B&B

☎ 7731 1662; 55 Wandsworth Bridge Rd; www.ful hamguesthouse.com; s/d £42/65 incl breakfast; tube Fulham Broadway/Parson's Green

The Fulham Guesthouse is run by a friendly and welcoming couple in a tastefully renovated Victorian town house. Although none of the rooms has their own bathroom they are all clean and functional.

LUXURY IN LONDON
B&B

☎ 7736 7284; 3 Bradbourne St; www.luxuryin london.co.uk; s/d with bathroom incl breakfast £55/80; tube Parson's Green

Luxury in London is a beautifully decorated and very comfortable B&B. With only three guest rooms there's an intimate feel to the place, and in the summer breakfast is served in the pretty garden.

PUTNEY & BARNES
LODGE HOTEL PUTNEY
Hotel

☎ 8874 1598; 52-54 Upper Richmond Rd SW15; www.thelodgehotellondon.com; s £89-99, d £108-128, tr/q £138/144, breakfast £6

This predictably styled hotel from the Best Western stable has 65 functional but comfortable rooms with bathroom, as well as an on-site bar and restaurant. Note that the 'executive' rooms are far from that, although they have been recently spruced up and are slightly more individual than the standard variety rooms.

SELECT HOMES IN LONDON
B&B

8412 9402; 1a Terrace Gardens SW13; www.users .waitrose.com/~selecthomes/home.htm; s £32-57, d £59-94, self-catering apartment from £500

This booking agent offers a selection of family-run B&Bs throughout southwest London, including ten in Barnes and four in Putney. You will find that the standard of accommodation can vary, although it tends to veer away from chintz and towards something altogether more tasteful.

UP RIVER

Suburban West London is not an obvious place to base yourself for a trip to London – it's quite a slog to the centre, noticeably more expensive than other parts of suburbia and definitely not known for offering budget accommodation. Anyone wanting to stay in a quieter, more-refined part of London will be right at home here – and there are a number of very comfortable and pleasant places to stay, all in near reach of greenery and the river.

CHISWICK
CHISWICK HOTEL   *Hotel*
☎ 8994 1712; www.chiswick-hotel.co.uk; 73 High Rd, W4; s/d £82/110; tube Turnham Green; **P**

It would be hard not to prejudge this hotel due to its particularly ghastly pink paint job, but this is a well-located, comfortable hotel, a short walk from the Thames and the busy bars and restaurants of Chiswick High Rd. A good range of services includes babysitting and 24-hour room service, and the bedrooms are individually designed, and, thankfully, not all pink. The staff is remarkably helpful and welcoming.

RICHMOND
RICHMOND PARK HOTEL   *Hotel*
☎ 8948 4666; fax 8940 7376; 3 Petersham Road, Richmond, Surrey; s/d £79/89; tube/rail Richmond

This 22-bedroom hotel at the bottom of Richmond Hill is a pleasant mid-range place for anyone wanting to be in the centre of Richmond. All rooms have private facilities and are comfortably furnished with TVs and telephones. While continental breakfast is included, the owners will do a full calorific English slap-up for a small supplement. This hotel has rate reductions at the weekends.

RICHMOND GATE HOTEL   *Hotel*
☎ 8940 0061; www.corushotels.co.uk/richmondgate; Richmond Hill, Surrey; s/d £160/170; tube/rail Richmond

The superb position of this large hotel complex is its selling point, overlooking the Thames and just seconds from the wide-open spaces of Richmond Park. The hotel is an amalgamation of Georgian mansions that have been gradually taken over – and both the facilities and decoration are excellent. Rooms are large, light and comfortable, while the facilities include a pool and health club. It's a great place for a pampering getaway within London.

Excursions

Excursions

Leaving London's staggering ethnic, religious, architectural and social variety, the real England suddenly emerges from the chaos: picturesque medieval towns, market squares, thatched-roofed cottages and the green and pleasant land that makes the English countryside so unique. Leaving London is your choice, but anyone wanting to see England – as opposed to its wildly unrepresentative capital – can do so with ease. In an easy day trip from London, the possibilities are almost endless of seeing vibrant and historic towns, the wonderful English countryside and incredible stately homes. Trains and buses, despite the constant gripes you'll hear in London about public transport, are still a good and reliable way to travel outside the capital, and much is within easy reach of the city centre by train.

HISTORIC TOWNS & CITIES
Where to begin in England? You could start by immersing yourself in **Cambridge** (below) and **Oxford** (p361). Both are just over an hour away from London, and parts of the cities remain unchanged after eight centuries of learning and tradition. Or there's Georgian **Bath**, perhaps the most attractive town in the whole of England (p363) – an unfeasibly beautiful West Country city nestled among some wonderful scenery, and an ancient settlement that predates the arrival of the Romans in Britain two millennia ago. Commanding **Canterbury Cathedral** (p364) may also take your fancy, while few places have the literary history of **Stratford-upon-Avon** (p366), home of William Shakespeare.

THE SEASIDE
The weather may be unreliable, but that makes English seaside towns try all the harder. From piers to shopping to clubbing, **Brighton** (p367) has it all, and if you are there during the summer you can even swim at its lovely rocky beach. Less obviously, the former fishing village of **Whitstable** (p369) offers some more laidback charms – there's not much to do here, and that's entirely the point. Then there's always **Rye** (p370), a perfect example of the quintessential English town.

CASTLES, PALACES & STATELY HOMES
As if to prove the saying that an Englishman's home is his castle, successive kings, queens, princes, dukes and barons have outdone each other building some of the finest country houses in the world over many hundreds of years. **Windsor** (p371), official residence of the Queen, is the oldest inhabited castle in the world, while **Stowe** (p372) and **Blenheim** (p373) both have amazing landscaped gardens and fine Georgian architecture. **Leeds Castle** (p373) in Kent, on the other hand, is happy with the simple sobriquet 'the loveliest castle in the world', and with one look at its moat and fairytale turrets you'll have to agree.

CAMBRIDGE
☎ 01223

The university at Cambridge was founded in the 13th century, several decades later than Oxford. There is a fierce rivalry between the two cities and their universities, and an ongoing debate over which is the best and most beautiful. One thing is for sure: Cambridge is far wealthier, with assets of more than £1.2 billion against Oxford's £800 million, according to a 2001 *Times of London* survey.

If you have time, you should visit both cities. But if you only have time for one, choose Cambridge. Oxford draws far more tourists and sometimes seems like a provincial city that happens to have a university. Cambridge, an architectural treasure-trove, always feels just like an English university town (and indeed it is!).

The centre of Cambridge lies in a wide bend of the River Cam. The best-known section of riverbank is the mile-long Backs, which combines lush scenery with superb views of half a dozen colleges (the other 25 colleges are scattered throughout the city).

Starting at Magdalene Great Bridge to the north, walk southeast along Bridge St until you reach the **Round Church**, built in 1130 to commemorate its namesake in Jerusalem. Turn right down St John's St to **St John's College**. On the other side of the gatehouse (1510) are three beautiful courtyards, the second and third dating from the 17th century. From the third court, the picturesque **Bridge of Sighs**, named after the one in Venice, spans the Cam. Stand in the centre and watch the punts float by.

Transport

Distance from London 54 miles (87km)

Direction North

Travel time 2hr by bus, 55min by train

Car The M11 connects the London Orbital Motorway (M25) to Cambridge. Take Exit 13 onto A1303 (Madingley Rd) and follow it towards the city centre.

Bus National Express runs hourly shuttle buses (£8 day return).

Train There are trains every 30min from King's Cross and Liverpool Street stations (£14.50 day return).

Just south of St John's, **Trinity College** is one of the largest and most-attractive colleges, not to mention the wealthiest. It was established in 1546 by Henry VIII, whose statue peers out from the top niche of the great gateway (he's holding a chair leg instead of the royal sceptre, the result of a student prank). The **Great Court**, the largest in Cambridge or Oxford, incorporates some fine 15th-century buildings. Beyond the Great Court are the cloisters of Nevile's Court and the dignified **Wren Library**, built by Sir Christopher in the 1680s.

Next comes Gonville and Caius (pronounced keys) College and **King's College** and its chapel, one of the most sublime buildings in Europe. The **chapel** was begun in 1446 by Henry VI and completed around 1516. Henry VI's successors, notably Henry VIII, added the intricate fan vaulting and elaborate wood-and-stone carvings of the interior. The chapel comes alive when the choir sings and there are services during term time and in July.

Continue south on what is now King's Pde (which becomes Trumpington St) and the **Fitzwilliam Museum**, which houses ancient-Egyptian sarcophagi and Greek and Roman art in the lower galleries and a wide range of paintings upstairs.

Taking a punt along the Backs is great fun, but it can also be a wet and hectic experience, especially on a busy weekend. The secret to propelling these flat-bottomed boats is to push gently on the pole to get the punt moving and then to use it as a rudder to keep on course. The cheapest boats are those at **Trinity Punt Hire**. Trinity also does chauffeured tours of the river. Another punting company, **Scudamore's**, has punts for hire and chauffeured rides.

SIGHTS & INFORMATION

TIC (Tourist Information Centre; ☎ 322640; www.cam bridge.gov.uk; Wheeler St; ☼ 10am-6pm Mon-Fri, 10am-5pm Sat, 11am-4pm Sun Apr-Sep, 10am-5.30pm Mon-Sat Oct-Mar) Just south of Market Square, TIC staff can arrange accommodation in town for £3, and two-hour walking tours (adult/child £6/4 or £7/4 including King's College), leaving at 1.30pm year-round, with more during summer.

Geoff's Bike Hire (☎ 365629; 65 Devonshire Rd; ☼ 9am-6pm Apr-Sep, 9am-5.30pm Mon-Sat Oct-Mar; bikes £8/15 per day/week, deposit £25)

Round Church (Church of the Holy Sepulchre; ☎ 518218; cnr Round Church & Bridge Sts; ☼ 10am-5pm summer, 1-4pm winter)

St John's College (☎ 338676; St John St; ☼ 10am-5pm)

Trinity College (☎ 332500; www.trin.cam.ac.uk; Trinity Lane; adult/senior, student & child aged 12-17 £2/1; ☼ 10am-5pm)

Wren Library (☼ noon-2pm Mon-Fri, 10.30am-12.30pm Sun)

King's College & Chapel (☎ 331100; King's Pde; adult/senior & child aged 12-17 £3.50/2.50; ☼ 9.30am-4pm) Evensong is at 5.30pm Mon-Sat (men's voices only on Wed), and 3.30pm Sun. There's also a choral service at 9.30am Sun.

Fitzwilliam Museum (☎ 332923; www.fitzmuseum.cam .ac.uk; Trumpington St; admission free; ☼ 10am-5pm Tue-Sat, 2.15-5pm Sun) Guided tours of the museum at 2.45pm on Sun cost £3.

Trinity Punt Hire (☎ 338483; Garret Hostel Lane; £6 per hr plus £25 deposit) Chauffeured tours of the river cost £6 to £8 per person.

Scudamore's (☎ 359750; Grant Pl; £12 per hr plus £60 deposit) Chauffeured rides cost £10/person. From Apr-Oct you can keep punts overnight for £60 (plus £60 deposit).

EATING

In addition to the places listed below, a number of cheap Indian and Chinese eateries can be found where Lensfield Rd meets Regent St in the direction of the train station.

Browns (☎ 461655; 23 Trumpington St; pasta dishes & salads £6.85-8.95, mains £7.35-13.95, set lunch £5.95 noon-4pm Mon-Fri) This lovely restaurant, once the outpatient department of a hospital built in 1914, is full of plants and light and boasts excellent pies.

The Eagle (☎ 505020; Bene't St; lunch £6) Just down from the TIC, this place is where you should head for a pub lunch. American airmen left their signatures on the ceiling of the back bar during WWII.

Loch Fyne Oyster Bar (☎ 362433; The Little Rose, Trumpington St; mains £6.95-34.95) This cosy place serves all types of seafood, but oysters (£5.95 to £7.45 per half dozen) are its speciality.

Nadia's (☎ 568336; 11 St John's St or ☎ 568335; 16 Silver St; filled bagels & baps £1.85-2.35) A small, local chain of excellent-value takeaway bakeries, offering sandwiches and cakes.

Rainbow (☎ 321551; 9A King's Pde; soups £2.75, salads £4.25, mains £6.75) Across the road from King's College and down a narrow passageway is Rainbow, a good gluten-free and vegetarian restaurant that serves dishes such as Thai green vegetarian curry and mushroom-and-nut crumble.

OXFORD

☎ 01865

Oxford grew from the ancient site on the river Cherwell, where farmers led their cows across the river, and gradually developed from a Saxon village to become England's first university town. The students of the first colleges in the early 12th century would probably have trouble recognising the place today, with its busy shopping streets, heavy traffic and hoards of tourists in the summer months. However, Oxford still retains a huge amount of charm, despite the onslaught of

Christ Church Cathedral, Oxford

time. The poet Matthew Arnold described Oxford as 'that sweet city with her dreaming spires' and they continue to dream today. The city's superb architecture and the unique atmosphere of the colleges, courtyards and gardens remain major attractions.

Oxford's 36 colleges and five 'halls' are scattered around the city, but the most important – and beautiful – ones are in the centre. **Carfax Tower**, part of the now-demolished Church of St Martin that dated from medieval times, makes a useful central landmark. There's a great view from the top (99 steps).

Walk south from the tower along St Aldate's, past the **Museum of Oxford**, which offers an easy introduction to the city's long history, and **Christ Church**, the grandest of the colleges, founded in 1525. The main entrance to Christ Church is below Tom Tower, the top of which was designed by Sir Christopher Wren in 1682. However, the visitors' entrance is further down St Aldate's via the wrought-iron gates of the Memorial Gardens and Broad Walk, which faces Christ Church Meadow. The college chapel, **Christ Church Cathedral**, is the smallest cathedral in the country and a wonderful example of late-Norman architecture.

From Broad Walk continue eastwards then turn left (north) up Merton Grove to Merton St. On your right is **Merton College**, founded in 1264. In the college's 14th-century **Mob Quad** is the oldest medieval library still in use in the UK. **Corpus Christi College** is on the left of Merton St.

Head north up Magpie Lane to High St. Just opposite, at the corner of High and Catte Sts, is the **University Church of St Mary the Virgin**. Its 14th-century tower offers views of the city's spires. From St Mary's, walk east along the High St, with its fascinating mix of architectural styles, to **Magdalen College** (pronounced *maud*-len) on the River Cherwell. Magdalen is one of the richest colleges and has huge grounds, including a deer park. It also has stunning cloisters, whose strange gargoyles and other carved figures inspired CS Lewis' stone statues in *The Chronicles of Narnia*.

If you retrace your steps and walk north up Catte St, you'll come to the circular, Palladian-style **Radcliffe Camera** (1749), which is a reading room for the **Bodleian Library**, just to the north across the courtyard (enter via the Great Gate on Catte St).

Continue north along Catte St, passing the **Bridge of Sighs** (a 1914 copy of the famous one in Venice) that spans New College Lane. When you reach Broad St you have one of two options. Walking north along Parks Rd for about 500m will bring you to the **Oxford University Museum of Natural History**, famous for its dinosaur and dodo skeletons, and the renovated **Pitt Rivers Museum**, crammed to overflowing with everything from a sailing boat to a collection of South American shrunken heads.

However, if you go west along Broad St you'll pass Sir Christopher Wren's first major work (1667), on your left, the **Sheldonian Theatre**. This is where important ceremonies, including graduations, take place. On the right is **Trinity College**, founded in 1555, and next to it, at the corner with Magdalen St, is **Balliol College**. The wooden doors between the inner and outer quadrangles still bear scorch marks from when Protestant martyrs were burned at the stake in the mid-16th century. Opposite the college is a hokey, 40-minute romp through Oxfordiana, the multimedia **Oxford Story**.

A short distance north up Magdalen St to St Giles is the **Ashmolean Museum**. Opened to the public in 1683, the Ashmolean is Britain's oldest museum and houses extensive displays of European art and Middle Eastern antiquities.

There's no better way to soak up Oxford's atmosphere than to take to the river in a punt. **Magdalen Bridge Boathouse** hires out punts, but if you're not up to punting yourself, try a chauffeured boat for up to five people, with a bottle of wine thrown in for free.

SIGHTS & INFORMATION

TIC (☎ 726871, www.visitoxford.org; 15-16 Broad St; ☽ 9.30am-5pm Mon-Sat, 10am-1pm & 3.30-5.30pm Sun Apr-Sep) Staff can book accommodation for a £2.50 fee (plus 10% deposit); two-hour guided walking tours of the colleges (adult/child £6.50/3) leave TIC at 11am and 2pm.

Carfax Tower (☎ 792653; Queen & Cornmarket Sts; adult/child aged 6-16 £1.20/60p; ☽ 10am-5.30pm Apr-Oct, 10am-3.30pm Nov-Mar)

Museum of Oxford (☎ 815559; St Aldate's; adult/senior & student/child/family £2/1.50/50p/£5; ☽ 10am-4pm Tue-Fri, 10am-5pm Sat, noon-4pm Sun)

Christ Church (☎ 276150; adult/child £4/3; ☽ 9am-5pm Mon-Sat, 1-5.30pm Sun)

Merton College (☎ 276310; admission free ☽ 2-4pm Mon-Fri, 10am-4pm Sat & Sun)

University Church of St Mary the Virgin (☎ 279112; www.university-church.ox.ac.uk; tower admission adult/child £1.60/80p; ☽ 9am-7pm Jul-Aug, 9am-5pm Sep-Jun)

Magdalen College (☎ 276000; adult/child £2/1 Apr-Sep, admission free Oct-Mar; ☽ noon-6pm mid-Jun–Sep, 2pm-sunset rest of year)

Balliol College (☎ 01865 277777; web.balliol.ox.ac.uk; Balliol College, Oxford)

Bodleian Library & Divinity School (☎ 277000; ☽ 9am-5pm Mon-Fri, 9am-12.30pm Sat)

Bodleian Exhibition Room (☽ 9.30am-4.45pm Mon-Fri, 9.30am-12.30pm Sat; guided tours (☎ 277224; £3.50)

10.30am, 11.30am (Mar-Oct) & 2pm & 3pm Mon-Fri, 10.30am & 11.30am Sat) Guided tours should be booked at least an hour in advance at busy times.

Oxford University Museum of Natural History (☎ 272950; www.oum.ox.ac.uk/; Parks Rd; admission free; ☽ noon-5pm)

Pitt Rivers Museum (☎ 270927; www.prm.ox.ac.uk/; Parks Rd; admission free; ☽ 1-4.30pm Mon-Sat, 2-4.30pm Sun)

Sheldonian Theatre (☎ 798600; www.sheldon.ox.ac.uk/; adult/child £1.50/1; ☽ 10am-12.30pm & 2-4.30pm Mon-Sat)

Trinity College (☎ 01865 279900; www.trinity.ox.ac.uk; Broad St, Oxford)

Oxford Story (☎ 728822; www.oxford story.co.uk; 6 Broad St; adult/child/senior & student/family £6.75/5.25/5.75/22; ☽ 9.30am-5pm Jul & Aug, 10am-4.30pm Mon-Sat, 11am-4.30pm Sun Sep-Jun)

Ashmolean Museum (☎ 278000; www.ashmol.ox.ac.uk; Beaumont St; admission free; ☽ 10am-5pm Tue-Sat, noon-5pm Sun)

Magdalen Bridge Boathouse (☎ 202643; Magdalen Bridge; punting £10/hr, deposit £30; chauffeured boat, max 5 people £20; ☽ 10am-sunset Mar-Oct)

EATING

In addition to the following places, there are lots of eateries – from Indian to Jamaican to Lebanese – along Cowley Rd, which leads off the High St southeast of Magdalen College.

Café Bohème (☎ 245858; 73 High St; mains £6.50-15) This French-ish café with real, live French staff serves decent breakfasts as well as upmarket sandwiches (£4.50 to £6) and salads (£4 to £8.50).

Café Coco (☎ 200232; 23 Cowley Rd; pizzas £5.35-7.50, salads £6.95-8.65) Come here for a buzzy, nontouristy atmosphere.

Chutneys (☎ 724241; New Inn Hall St; mains £4.10-6.45, lunchtime buffet £7.50) This mostly vegetarian south Indian brasserie attracts customers as much by its brightly coloured exterior as its affordable and tasty fare.

Grand Café (☎ 204463; 84 High St; sandwiches £5.90-7.50, lunches £4.95-8.75, teas £6.50-12.50) This museum-piece of a cafe, on the site of England's first coffee house (1650), is a wonderful place to break during a tour of Oxford.

Quod Bar & Grill (☎ 202505; 92-4 High St; pizzas £6.95-7.95, pasta dishes £4.95-8.50, mains £7.35-12.95) This is an incredibly popular place with locals for its stylish Italian cuisine and comfortable surroundings.

BATH

☎ 01225

Bath is perhaps the most sumptuous and graceful town in England, and has been a tourist attraction for the moneyed classes for centuries. Indeed, the incredibly wide pavements were apparently designed to enable two ladies in their huge dresses to pass one another easily. While Bath was rejuvenated in the 18th century as a society spa resort, under the direction of Beau Nash, its curative waters were favoured earlier by the Romans,

Roman Baths and Museum

and the place where the town itself now stands was originally settled by the Celts. A trip to Bath from London will mean staying overnight here. There is a huge amount to see and do, but there are some obvious must-sees. However, part of the city's charm is its consistent beauty, so slowing down and strolling aimlessly here is a real pleasure.

Bath's most popular attraction is the **Roman Baths and Museum**, which can be very crowded so try to get there early. Head along the Baths' raised walkway to the **Great Bath**, complete with Roman paving and surrounded by 19th-century arcading. A series of excavated chambers beneath street level leads off in several directions and allows you to inspect the remains of other smaller baths and heating systems. One of the most picturesque corners of the complex is the 12th-century **King's Bath**, built around the original sacred spring – through a window there are views of the pool, and 1.5 million litres of hot water pour into the pool every day. You can see the ruins of the **Sulis Temple of Minerva** under the **Pump Room**, and recent excavations of the **East Baths** give an insight into its 4th-century form.

Bath Abbey held the coronation of the first-ever king of a united England, King Edgar in AD 973. The current edifice was constructed much later, though, between 1499 and 1616, making it the last great medieval church raised in England. The abbey boasts 640 wall monuments, second only to Westminster Abbey, and hosts the graves of Reverend Thomas Malthus and Bath godfather Beau Nash.

No visit to Bath would be complete without a visit to the stunning **Royal Crescent** built between 1767 and 1771. This hilltop, crescent-shaped row of houses overlooks the city, and the Palladian town house at **No 1 Royal Crescent** has had its interior restored to make it exactly as it would have been in the late 18th century. The servants' quarters are of as much interest as the unbridled luxury that characterises the upstairs accommodation.

Excursions – Bath

SIGHTS & INFORMATION

Roman Baths Museum (☎ 477784; www.roman baths.co.uk; Stall St; adult/child £8/4.60; ⌚ 9am-5pm Mar-Jun, Sep & Oct, 9am-9pm Jul & Aug, 9.30am-4.30pm Nov-Feb)

Bath Abbey (☎ 422262; next to the Roman Baths entrance; requested donation £2; ⌚ 9am-6pm Mon-Sat Easter-Oct, 9am-4.30pm Nov-Easter, afternoons only on Sun)

No 1 Royal Crescent (☎ 428126; adult/child £4/3.50; ⌚ 10.30am-5pm Tue-Sun Mar-Oct, 10.30am-4pm Tue-Sun Nov)

EATING

It's quite easy to gather together a picnic lunch from the **Guildhall Market** on High St next to the Guildhall, where crepes and other takeaway food are readily available. For dinner or a more substantial lunch, try one of the following:

Bathtub Bistro (☎ 460593; 2 Grove St; mains £7.50-12; closed lunch Mon) A Tardis-like eatery by Pulteney Weir, dishing up good world food, vegetarian gems and specials such as wild boar steak.

Demuth's (☎ 446059; 2 North Pde Passage; mains £5.50-6.50) Serves vegetarian and vegan curries, wraps and outstanding tapas.

Le Beaujolais (☎ 423417; 5 Chapel Row; mains £12-16; ⌚ closed Sun) This place is very popular with Bath residents who enjoy their regional French cuisine.

The Olive Tree (☎ 447928; Russell St; 2-/3-course lunch £13.50/15.50, 3-course dinner £26) Beneath the Queensbury Hotel, this chic and slick modern British restaurant is one of the finest in Bath.

Transport

Distance from London 106 miles (170km)
Direction Southwest
Travel time 3½hr by bus, 1½hr by train
Bus National Express buses run from London Victoria (return £21, 10 daily).
Train There are frequent trains from London Paddington (return £40).

SLEEPING

Bath's distance from London and wealth of attractions make it a good place to spend the night. There are plenty of B&Bs as well as more upscale accommodation. It's best to book ahead at weekends, as Bath is a popular getaway spot.

Henry Guest House (☎ 424052; 6 Henry St; rms per person £22) This place is located right in the heart of Bath. Don't be put off by the exterior – it's much more promising inside, and the staff is friendly. All eight bedrooms share bathrooms.

Koryu (☎ 337642; 7 Pulteney Gdns; s/d incl breakfast £28/48) Owned by an Anglo-Japanese couple, this is an excellent place – bright, friendly and modern. Most rooms have bathrooms.

Old Boathouse (☎ 466407; Forester Rd; d with bathroom £55-65, 4-person cottage £100) A delightful converted Edwardian boating station, this place is in an idyllic location beside the Avon, just north of Sydney Gardens. Some rooms have river-view balconies.

Royal Crescent Hotel (☎ 823333; fax 339401; 16 Royal Cres; d £230) Bath's top hotel is at the city's most exclusive address, and features a pool and spa as well as period furnishing.

CANTERBURY

☎ 01227

Canterbury, in Kent, makes a relatively easy day-trip from the capital. Its greatest treasure is its magnificent **cathedral**. While Canterbury's bustling city centre is atmospheric and lively, most of your day should definitely be spent at the cathedral. Like most great cathedrals, it evolved over the centuries and reflects several architectural styles.

The current-day church is the successor to the original that St Augustine built after he began converting the English to Christianity in AD 597. Following the martyrdom of archbishop Thomas Becket in 1170, the cathedral became the focus of one of Europe's most important medieval pilgrimages, which was immortalised by Geoffrey Chaucer in *The Canterbury Tales*.

The traditional approach to the cathedral is along narrow Mercery Lane to Christ Church Gate. Once inside the gate, turn right and walk east to get an overall picture.

The main entrance is through the **southwest porch**, built in 1415 to commemorate the English victory at Agincourt. From the centre of the nave there are impressive views eastwards down the length of the church, with its ascending levels, and westwards to the **window** with glass dating from the 12th century.

Beneath **Bell Harry tower** (with its beautiful fan vaulting) is even more impressive stained glass. A 15th-century screen, featuring six kings, separates the nave from the choir.

Thomas Becket is believed to have been murdered in the northwest transept; a modern **altar and sculpture** mark the spot. The adjoining **Lady Chapel** has beautiful perpendicular fan vaulting. Descend a flight of steps into the Romanesque crypt, the main survivor of the Norman cathedral.

Transport

Distance from London 56 miles (90km)

Direction Southeast

Travel time 1hr 50min by bus, 1¾hr by train

Bus National Express buses has 16 daily shuttle buses (£9 day return)

Train Canterbury East train station is accessible from London Victoria, and Canterbury West is for trains to/from Charing Cross and Waterloo (£12.50/16 day return to Canterbury East/Canterbury West).

The **Chapel of Our Lady** at the western end of the crypt has some of the finest Romanesque carving surviving in England. St Thomas was entombed in the Early English (Gothic) eastern end until 1220. This is where Henry II allowed himself to be whipped in penance for having provoked Becket's murder with the infamous words 'Who will rid me of this turbulent priest?', and is said to be the site of many miracles. The **Chapel of St Gabriel** features 12th-century paintings, while the **Black Prince's Chantry** is a beautiful perpendicular chapel, donated by the prince in 1363.

In the southwest transept the **Chapel of St Michael** includes a wealth of tombs, including that of archbishop Stephen Langton, who helped persuade King John to seal the Magna Carta in 1215. The superb 12th-century choir stalls rise in stages to the High Altar and Trinity Chapel. The screen around the choir stalls was erected in 1305 and evensong, the choral service of worship in the Church of England, has been sung here every day for more than 800 years. **St Augustine's Chair**, dating from the 13th century, is used to enthrone archbishops.

The stained glass in **Trinity Chapel** is mostly 13th century, celebrating the life of St Thomas Becket. On either side are the tombs of Henry IV, buried with wife Joan of Navarre, and of the Black Prince, with its famous effigy that includes the prince's shield, gauntlets and sword.

Opposite **St Anselm's Chapel** is the **tomb of Archbishop Sudbury** who, as Chancellor of the Exchequer, was held responsible for a hated poll tax in the 14th century. He was beheaded by a mob during the Peasants' Revolt of 1381; his body lies here but his head is in a church in Suffolk.

Walk around the eastern end of the cathedral and turn right into Green Ct, which is surrounded on the eastern (right) side by the Deanery and on the northern side (straight ahead) by the early 14th-century **brewhouse and bakehouse**. In the northwestern corner (far left) is the much celebrated **Norman Staircase** (1151).

If you get through the cathedral in less than a day, and are keen to immerse yourself in even more history, check out **The Canterbury Tales**, an automated historical recreation of Chaucer's famous stories.

Or you could visit Canterbury's only remaining city gate, **West Gate**, which dates from the 14th century and survived because it was used as a prison. It now houses a small **museum** with collections of arms and armour.

For a last dose of history before returning to the buzz and bright lights of London, take yourself over to **Canterbury Heritage Museum**. Located in a converted 14th-century building, it gives good, but rather dry, coverage of the city's history. The building, once the Poor Priests' Hospital, is worth visiting in its own right.

Excursions – Canterbury

SIGHTS & INFORMATION

TIC (☎ 766567, ☎ 767744; www.canterbury.co.uk; 34 St Margaret's St; ☼ 9.30am-5.30pm Mon-Sat, 10am-4pm Sun Apr-Oct, 9.30am-5pm Mon-Sat, 10am-4pm Sun Nov & Dec, 9.30am-5pm Mon-Sat Jan-Mar). Guided tours of 1½hr (adult/senior, student & child/family £3.50/3/8.50) leave TIC at 2pm Apr-Sep, plus 11.30am Jul & Aug.

Canterbury Cathedral (☎ 762862; www.canterbury -cathedral.org; Sun St; adult/child aged 5-16 £3/2;

☼ 9am-6.30pm Mon-Sat, 12.30-2.30pm & 4.30-5.30pm Sun Easter-Sep, 9am-5pm Mon-Sat, 12.30-2.30pm & 4.30-5.30pm Sun Oct-Easter) Since the cathedral's treasures are tucked away in corners and all have their associated stories, a one-hour guided tour costing adult/senior & student/child/family £3.50/2.50/1.50/6.50 is recommended. It leaves at 10.30am, noon & 2.30pm Monday to Saturday Easter to September, and 10.30am, noon & 2pm October to Easter. If the crowd looks daunting, you can take a 30-minute audioguide tour costing adult/child

£2.95/1.95. Choral evensong is 5.30pm Monday to Friday and 3.15pm Saturday and Sunday.

Canterbury Tales (☎ 454888, ☎ 479227; St Margaret's St; adult/senior, student & child/family £6.50/5/20; ⌚ 9.30am-5.30pm Apr-Oct, 10am-4.30pm Nov-Mar)

West Gate Museum (☎ 452747; St Peter's St; adult/child £1/65p; ⌚ 11am-12.30pm & 1.30-3.30pm Mon-Sat)

Canterbury Heritage Museum (☎ 452747; Stour St; adult/child £1.90/1.20; ⌚ 10.30am-5pm Mon-Sat, 1.30-5pm Sun Jun-Oct, 10.30am-5pm Mon-Sat Nov-May)

EATING

Flap Jacques (☎ 781000; 71 Castle St; crepes £2.75-6.50) This is a small French bistro serving Breton-style savoury and sweet pancakes.

Il Vaticano (☎ 765333; 33-5 St Margaret's St; pasta dishes £4.50-8.50) This place has a wide range of pastas and a lovely courtyard.

Thomas Becket (☎ 464384; Best Lane; lunch £4-6) If you love traditional pub food, this is the place to come. Make sure you try its Sunday roast.

STRATFORD-UPON-AVON
☎ 01789

Anyone with limited time and a love for William Shakespeare will not mind the effort involved in visiting his charming hometown. Staying overnight is the best option, allowing time to take in a relaxed show at the Royal Shakespeare Company in the evening.

Stratford is a quiet Norman market town on the river Avon, and its fortunes would have been quite different were it not for William Shakespeare's birth in 1564. While some may find the industry that has grown up around Britain's greatest writer akin to a personality cult, there is plenty of scope for an interesting trip. It's best to avoid the area around Sheep St, a textbook tourist trap full of souvenir shops and over-priced eateries.

Start your tour with **Shakespeare's Birthplace** in the town centre, where the atmosphere of a well-to-do 16th-century family home has been well preserved (not to mention 'refreshed' in a recent revamp). There is also an adjacent **Shakespeare Exhibition** included in the entry price, giving all the possible background on the Shakespeare enigma.

The other Shakespeare houses (those used by the bard and his family) include the remains of **New Place** on the corner of Chapel St and Chapel Lane, and **Nash Place** next door, home to Shakespeare's granddaughter Elizabeth. New Place was Shakespeare's final home but unfortunately it was demolished in 1759 and is now a pretty garden. The Elizabethan townhouse of Shakespeare's daughter Susanna, **Hall's Croft**, is next to Holy Trinity Church and includes a fascinating display devoted to the medical practices in use during Shakespeare's lifetime. Finally, **Anne Hathaway's Cottage** is a must-see – the home of Shakespeare's wife before the couple was married is situated 1.5km outside the town centre. The cottage is in a gorgeous location and has a traditional thatched roof, as well as an orchard and the **Shakespeare Tree Garden** where all the trees mentioned in the bard's plays stand proud. **Holy Trinity Church** is the resting place of Shakespeare and his wife, and also features a bust of the playwright, crafted seven years after his death. The church also holds his baptism and burial records.

Stratford is home to the Royal Shakespeare Company (RSC) and the three theatres it maintains: **The Royal Shakespeare Theatre**, **The Swan** and **The Other Place**. These can be the highlight of any trip, as there can be no better proof of Shakespeare's endurance than seeing one of the RSC's usually very high-quality performances of his work. You'll need to book well ahead unless you are very lucky, but the chance to take in one of the company's productions should not be missed.

SIGHTS & INFORMATION

TIC (☎ 293127; www.shakespeare-country.co.uk; ⌚ 9.30am-5.30pm Mon-Sat, 10.30am-4.30pm Sun Apr-Oct, 9.30am-5pm Mon-Sat, 10am-3pm Sun Nov-Mar) Close to the river on Bridgefoot.

Shakespeare's Birthplace & Exhibition (☎ 01789 204016; Henley St)

Royal Shakespeare Company (☎ 403404; www.rsc.org.uk)

EATING

Although you'll do well to avoid Sheep St at all costs, you'll still have plenty of choice – that's because the sheer volume of visitors ensures there are no shortages of eateries.

Edward Moon'sn (☎ 267259; 9 Chapel St) A stylish place with a tasty menu from around the globe, including superb desserts.

Transport

Distance from London 93 miles (150km)

Direction Northwest

Travel time 3½hr by bus, 2hr by train

Car Take the M40 North, turning off at Junction 15, onto A46 South towards Stratford-upon-Avon.

Bus National Express buses depart Victoria Central Station three times daily (£16.50 day return).

Train There are a few direct train services from London Paddington (one way £23.30). It's also possible to get a train from Marylebone station – you will have to change at Banbury or Leamington Spa.

Havilands (☎ 415477; 5 Meer St; cream tea £3.95; ⏱ 9am-5pm Mon-Sat) This is a small, cosy spot for lunch or just for indulging in coffee and home-made cake.

Lemon Tree (☎ 292997; 2 Union St; panini & baguettes £3.50; ⏱ closed Sun) Happy, breezy lunch spot.

SLEEPING

There is a huge variety of accommodation on offer in Stratford, often in attractive Victorian houses. Popular streets for B&Bs include Evesham Pl, Grove Rd, Broad Walk and Alcester Rd. In summer, when accommodation is hard to come by, the TIC charges £3 to find you a room, and requires a 10% deposit. You should book a few weeks ahead for summer visits.

Arrandale (☎ 267112; 208 Evesham Rd, r per person £16-18) This B&B is one of the cheapest options, and just a 10-minute walk from the town centre.

Carlton Guest House (☎ 293548; 22 Evesham Pl; s with shared facilities £18-22, d with bathroom £40-48) This guesthouse has airy rooms and even singles are spacious.

The Shakespeare (☎ 0870 400 8182; shakespeare@macdonald-hotels.co.uk; Chapel St; r £57-115) Comprised of beautiful historic buildings, The Shakespeare is four-star. Some bedrooms even boast four-poster beds.

BRIGHTON

☎ 01273

Brighton, with its heady mix of seediness and a certain amount of sophistication, is London's favourite seaside resort.

The town's character dates from the mid-1780s when the dissolute, music-loving Prince Regent (later King George IV) began indulging in lavish parties by the sea. Brighton still has some of the hottest clubs and venues outside London as well as a vibrant student population, excellent shopping, a thriving arts scene, a gay scene and countless restaurants, pubs and cafés.

Indian palace on the outside and over-the-top chinoiserie on the inside – the **Royal Pavilion** is an extraordinary folly. The first pavilion, built in 1787, was a classical villa. It wasn't until the early 19th century, when things Asian became all the rage, that the current confection began to take shape. The final Mogul-inspired design was produced by John Nash, architect of Regent's Park and its surrounding crescents, and was built between 1815 and 1822. George is said to have cried when he first saw the Music Room, with its nine lotus-shaped chandeliers and Chinese murals in vermilion and gold. It was badly damaged by arson in 1975 and by a great storm in 1987, but has since been lovingly restored.

The entire edifice is not to be missed, but have a good look at the **Long Gallery**, **Banqueting Room** (with its domed and painted ceiling), superb **Great Kitchen** and restored **Music Room** on the ground floor and the **South Galleries** and **Queen Victoria's Apartments** (including her water closet) on the 1st floor. Keep an eye out for Rex Whistler's humorous painting *HRH The Prince Regent Awakening the Spirit of Brighton* (1944), in which the overweight (and all-but-naked) prince is rousing a nubile 'Brighton' with a lascivious look in his eye. It's in the Adelaide Corner on the 1st floor just before the entrance to the Queen Adelaide Tearoom.

Transport

Distance from London 51 miles (82km)

Direction South

Travel time 1hr 50min by bus, 50min by fast train

Car Visitors driving from London and the north should follow the M23/A23 road towards Brighton, which runs straight into the town centre.

Bus National Express runs a shuttle service at least hourly from London (£8 day return).

Train There are about 40 fast trains a day from London Victoria station (£13 day return) and slightly slower Thameslink trains from Blackfriars, London Bridge and King's Cross.

Originally designed as an indoor tennis court, the **Brighton Museum & Art Gallery** (☎ 290900; Church St; admission free; ⏱ 10am-5pm Mon, Tue & Thu-Sat, 2-5pm Sun), which has been undergoing a £10 million redevelopment, houses a quirky collection of Art Deco and Art Nouveau furniture, archaeological finds, surrealist paintings and costumes.

Palace Pier, known locally as Brighton Pier, has amusement rides such as the Helter Skelter, takeaway food and penny arcades. It is the very essence of Brighton. This is the best spot to buy sticks of the famous boiled sweet called Brighton Rock.

West Pier, built in 1866 and closed since 1975 due to safety fears, finally began to collapse into the sea in December 2002. While this was a dramatic end to a historic structure, a £30 million renovation budget had already been approved, and the West Pier trust is confident that it can fully restore the pier to its former glory by 2006.

SIGHTS & INFORMATION

Guide Friday (☎ 294466) This company runs bus tours every 20 minutes from 10am to 5pm or 5.30pm mid-June to August & every half-hour till 3.30pm or 4.30pm September to mid-June. Tours cost adult/senior & student/child aged 5-14/family £6.50/5.50/2.50/15.50.

TIC (☎ 0906 711 2255; www.visitbrighton.com; 10 Bartholomew Sq; ⏱ 9am-5.30pm Mon-Fri, 10am-5pm Sat, 10am-4pm Sun Mar-Oct, 9am-5pm Mon-Fri, 10am-5pm Sat Nov-Feb) The TIC sells the useful *Brighton Town Centre Map & Visitor's Guide* (£1).

Royal Pavilion (☎ 290900; Pavilion Pde; adult/senior & student/child aged 5-15/family £5.20/3.75 /3.20/13.60; ⏱ 10am-6pm Jun-Sep, 10am-5pm Oct-May) Tours of the Royal Pavilion (£1.25) leave at 11.30am & 2.30pm, with additional departures at 1pm & 1.30pm Saturday and Sunday in summer. Free summer band concerts take place in the restored Pavilion Gardens at 3pm on Sunday from late June to early September.

Palace Pier (www.brightonpier.co.uk; Madeira Dr; admission free; ⏱ daily)

EATING

Brighton is jam-packed with decent eateries. Wander around the Lanes, a maze of alleyways crammed with shops and restaurants just north of the TIC, or head down to Preston St, which runs back from the seafront near the disused and crumbling West Pier and has a lot of restaurants.

Fishbowl (☎ 777505; 74 East St; mains £4.95-7.95) This small and groovy place serves everything from satay to paella.

Gingerman (☎ 326688; 21a Norfolk Square; 1-/2-/3-course set lunch £9.95/12.95/14.95, 2-/3-course set dinner £21/23.50) This small but stylish restaurant serves seasonal and contemporary food. It's one of the top places in Brighton so book ahead.

The King & I (☎ 773390; 2 Ship St; mains £5.65-7.95) This place by the waterfront serves decent Thai food and has a lunchtime special for £4.95.

The Little Shop (☎ 325594; 48a Market St; sandwiches £1.75-3.95) Award-winning sandwiches and filled baguettes.

Regency Tavern (☎ 325652; 32 Russell Sq; lunch £4.95) This outwardly modest place from the outside hides what looks like a room from the Royal Pavilion: striped wallpaper, cameo portraits and brass palm trees.

Terre à Terre (☎ 729051; 71 East St; mains £11.50) A gourmet vegetarian restaurant is not an oxymoron; we discovered some of the most inventive meatless dishes ever at this very popular eatery.

SLEEPING

You should book ahead for weekends in summer and during the Brighton Festival in May.

Genevieve Hotel (☎ 681653; genevievehotel@aol.com; 18 Madeira Pl; r per person £25-45) This place has clean, comfortable rooms. The rate includes a continental breakfast.

Royal Pavilion, Brighton (left)

Oriental Hotel (☎ 205050; fax 821096; info@orientalh otel.co.uk; 9 Oriental Pl; d Mon-Fri/Sat & Sun £55/90) A real breath of fresh air among B&Bs. Decorated with bright colours, home-made furniture and cool decor.

Old Ship Hotel (☎ 329001; fax 820718; oldship@para mount-hotels.co.uk; Kings Rd; s/d from £70/80) The ultimate doyen of Brighton's hotels, refurbished in ultra-cool style.

De Vere Grand Hotel (☎ 224300; fax 224321; reser vations@grandbrighton.co.uk; King's Rd; r from £100) Headlines were made in 1983 when the IRA tried to kill Margaret Thatcher and her cabinet here at the De Vere Grand Hotel by exploding a huge bomb. The hotel has been restored to its former splendour and remains the top spot in town.

WHITSTABLE
☎ 01227

This overgrown fishing village overlooking Whitstable Bay is nicknamed the 'Pearl of Kent'; it's famous for its seafood (particularly oysters) and relatively unspoilt charm. Weatherboarded cottages line the lanes off High St, which have odd names like Squeeze Gut Alley, recalling Whitstable's main pastime. To the east of town are the cliff-top lawns of Tankerton Slopes, lined with multicoloured beach huts and perfect views of The Street, which is actually a narrow shingle ridge stretching half a mile out to sea (but only visible at low tide).

Whitstable isn't really a museum or church place. People come to soak up the atmosphere, swim (in good weather) and just hang around. It's a nice to stay the night, particularly if the Big Smoke wears you out, so we've included a few accommodation options below. If you need to see something, the **Whitstable Museum & Gallery** has pretty good exhibits on Whitstable's fishing industry, with a special emphasis on oysters.

In recent years, Whitstable has developed a vibrant artistic scene, and there are plenty of **art galleries** that you can wander into for a look. Most of the best ones line Harbour St, on the seafront.

Since 2001 the **Whitstable Oyster Festival** has been held in the third week in July. It's an arts and music extravaganza where you can wash down oysters with pints of Guinness or glasses of champagne. The programme of events is varied and interesting, featuring everything from jazz bands and classical quartets to how-to demonstrations of various crafts. The whole town lends a hand and it's the highlight of the summer. For info on upcoming events, contact the TIC.

Transport

Distance from London 44 miles (73km)
Direction East
Travel time 1-2hr
Car Follow the M2; at Margate/Ramsgate sign, follow the Thanet Way
Bus Five daily departures (outward 10.30am-8.30pm, return 8.05am-5.55pm); duration 2hr; £10.50 day return
Train Departures every 30 mins (outward 5.41-12.04am, return 12.56-22.27pm); duration 1¼-2hr; £15.60 day return

SIGHTS & INFORMATION

TIC (☎ 275482; 7 Oxford St; ☺ 10am-5pm Mon-Sat Jul & Aug; 10am-4pm Mon-Sat Sep-Jun) Has free accommodation booking service.

Whitstable Museum & Gallery (☎ 276998; 8 Oxford St; admission free; ☺ 10am-4pm Mon-Sat year-round & 1-4pm Sun Jul & Aug)

EATING

Hope you like seafood...

Pearson's Crab & Oyster House (☎ 272005; The Horse-bridge; seafood platter £15.95) The most atmospheric of Whitstable's restaurants.

Royal Native Oyster Stores (☎ 276856; The Horsebridge; mains £8, seafood platter £13) Has a terrific seafood platter.

Wheelers Oyster Bar (☎ 273311; www.whitstable -shellfish.co.uk/wheelers_oyster_bar.htm; 8 High St; mains £7-13; ☺ 10.30am-9pm Mon, Tue, Thu & Fri; 10am-10pm Sat, 11am-9pm Sun) Make sure you try the oysters!

SLEEPING

Hotel Continental (☎ 280280; fax 280257; 29 Beach Walk; d from £55, fisherman's cottages from £260) An Art Deco building on the seafront with elegantly appointed double rooms; it also rents out delightful fisherman's cottages on the beach.

Wavecrest B&B (☎ 770155; wavecrestbandb@aol.com; 2 Seaway Cottages; s/d from £45/55) A marvellously bohemian place right on the beach.

The Windmill (☎ 265963; Miller's Crt; s/d from £30/50) A large windmill, complete with working sails. Rooms at the top of the mill have panoramic views over town.

RYE

☎ 01797

Rye is almost impossibly beautiful. This desperately picturesque medieval town looks like it has been preserved in historical formaldehyde. Not even the most talented Hollywood set designers could have come up with a better representation of Ye Olde Englishe Village: the half-timbered Tudor buildings, winding cobbled streets, abundant flowerpots and strong literary associations should be enough to temper even the most hard-bitten cynic's weariness of the made-for-tourism look.

Such beauty *has* made it a tourist magnet, but most people wander about the town in almost muted appreciation, lest their gasps of surprise disturb the air of genuine tranquillity and perfection. If you do visit (and you absolutely should) avoid summer weekends. The town is easily covered on foot and you can start your tour of the town at the TIC's **Rye Town Model Sound & Light Show**, which gives a half-hour theatrical introduction to the town's history.

Around the corner from the TIC, in Strand Quay, are a number of **antique shops** selling all kinds of wonderful junk. From here walk up cobbled **Mermaid St**, one of the most famous streets in England, with timber-framed houses dating from the 15th century.

Turn right at the T-junction for the Georgian **Lamb House**, mostly dating from 1722. It was the home of American writer Henry James from 1898 to 1916 (he wrote *The Wings of the Dove* here). Continue around the dogleg until you come out at Church Square. This gorgeous square is

Transport

Distance from London 54 miles (90km)

Direction Southeast

Travel time 1-2hr

Car Follow the M2, M20 then A20

Train Departures from Charing Cross every 40min (outward 7am-9pm, return 9.43am-9.43pm) duration 2hr; £18.80 day return

surrounded by a variety of attractive houses, including the **Friars of the Sack** on the southern side at No 40. Now a private residence, it was once part of a 13th-century Augustinian friary. The **Church of St Mary the Virgin** incorporates a mixture of ecclesiastical styles. The turret clock is the oldest in England (1561) and still works with its original pendulum mechanism. There are great views from the **church tower.**

The town celebrates its medieval heritage with a two-day **festival** each August, and in September there is the two-week **Festival of Music and the Arts**.

EATING

There's a surprisingly diverse range of eateries for a small English town.

Flushing Inn (☎ 223292; 4 Market St; mains £8.80-13.50) The Inn has local wines and a '1066 Maritime Menu', comprised mostly of seafood.

The Lemongrass (☎ 222327; 1 Tower St; curries £7) The only Thai restaurant in town, and a pretty good one at that.

Mermaid Street Coffee House (☎ 224858; cnr Mermaid & West Sts) The place to try a smorgasbord of coffee and snacks, with cake and coffee for £3.

The Old Borough Arms (☎ /fax 222128; info@oldborough arms.co.uk; The Strand) This 300-year-old former smuggler's inn is a truly lovely guesthouse with an excellent café. It serves great sandwiches for £2.50 and cream teas for £2.95.

Tudor Room Bar & Bistro (☎ 223065; Mermaid St) Part of the Mermaid Inn, this tiny, low-ceilinged, half-timbered pub has an outdoor terrace. Try the baked local fish pie with smoked cheese for £7.95.

SIGHTS & INFORMATION

TIC (☎ 226696; fax 223460; www.rye-tourism.co.uk/ heritage; Strand Quay; ☽ 10am-5pm Mon-Sat Apr-Oct, 10am-4pm Mon-Sat Nov-Mar) Rye Town Walk gives a detailed history of the town's buildings and costs £1. There's also an audio tour costing £2.50/1.50 per adult/child. For guided walks around town phone ☎ 01424-882343 or ☎ 01424-882466.

Rye Town Model Sound & Light Show (TIC building, Strand Quay; adult/child £2.50/1)

Lamb House (☎ 224982; www.nationaltrust.org.uk; West St; adult/child £2.60/1.30; ☽ 2-6pm Tue-Sat Apr-Oct)

Rye Hire (☎ 223033; Cyprus Pl) You can rent bikes from £9 per day, with a £25 deposit. A cycling map of East Sussex is available from the TIC.

Church of St Mary the Virgin (tower views adult/child £2/1; ☽ 9am-4pm winter, 9am-6pm rest of the year)

WINDSOR

☎ 01753

Windsor Castle is one of the nation's finest tourist attractions. Easily accessible by rail and road, it crawls with tourists in all seasons. If possible, avoid visiting on weekends and during the peak months of July and August. Across the River Thames from Windsor is Eton and its celebrated college.

Windsor Castle overlooks the Thames, with the town of Windsor fanning out to the west. Eton is essentially a small village linked to Windsor by a pedestrian bridge over the Thames.

Transport

Distance from London 23 miles (37km)

Direction West

Travel time 1hr by bus, 55min by train

Bus Green Line buses leave Victoria Coach Station between five and 10 times a day from 7.45am (from 9am Sat, from 9.40am Sun) to about 2pm (adult/child aged 5-15 £7.50/4 day return).

Train Trains run from Waterloo to Riverside station every 30 mins, hourly on Sun (£6 day return).

Standing on chalk bluffs overlooking the Thames, and home to British royalty for over 900 years, **Windsor Castle** is one of the greatest surviving medieval castles in the world. It started out as a wooden motte-and-bailey castle (one built on a mound, surrounded by a wall) in 1070, was rebuilt in stone in 1165 and was successively extended and rebuilt right through to the 19th century.

The **State Apartments** combine formal rooms with museum-style exhibits. In 1992, a fire badly damaged St George's Hall and the adjacent Grand Reception Room. £37 million restoration was completed in 1998.

After the **Waterloo Chamber**, created to commemorate the Battle of Waterloo and still used for formal meals, and the **Garter Throne Room**, the **King's Rooms** begin with the **King's Drawing Room**, also known as the Rubens Room, after the three paintings hanging there. The **King's State Bedchamber** has paintings by Gainsborough and Canaletto, but Charles II actually slept in the **King's Dressing Room** next door. Some of Windsor's finest paintings hang here, including works by Holbein, Rembrandt, Rubens and Dürer. **The King's Closet** was used by Charles II as a study and contains works by Canaletto, Reynolds and Hogarth.

From the King's Rooms you come to the **Queen's Rooms**. The **Queen's Ballroom** has a remarkable collection of paintings by Van Dyck. Only three of the 13 Verrio ceiling paintings from Charles II's time survive, and one of them is in the **Queen's Audience Chamber**. Gobelins tapestries and another Verrio ceiling can be found in the **Queen's Presence Chamber**.

Queen Mary's Doll's House was the work of architect Sir Edwin Lutyens and was built on a 1:12 scale in 1923. It's complete in every detail, right down to running water in the bathrooms.

One of Britain's finest examples of early English architecture, **St George's Chapel** was begun by Edward IV in 1475 but not completed until 1528. The nave is a superb example of the perpendicular style, with gorgeous fan vaulting arching out from the pillars. The chapel contains **royal tombs**, including those of George V and Queen Mary, George VI and Edward IV. The **Garter Stalls** are the chapel's equivalent of choir stalls. Dating from the late 15th century, the banner, helm and crest above each stall indicate the current occupant. Plates carry names of earlier knights who have occupied the stalls since the 14th century.

Cross the River Thames by the pedestrian Windsor Bridge to reach another enduring symbol of Britain's class system: **Eton College**. This famous public (ie private) school has educated no fewer than 18 prime ministers, and modern-day princes William and Harry. Several buildings date from the mid-15th century. One-hour tours are £4/3 (adult/child) at 2.15pm and 3.15pm. If you are here in term time you can spot the pupils by their anachronistic black uniforms and white shirts, and they are well used to being stared at: hoards of girls searching out the young princes used to plague the town, although both William and Harry have now left the school.

On High St beside Castle Hill, Windsor's **Guildhall** was built between 1686 and 1689, its construction completed under Sir Christopher Wren's supervision. The central columns in the open area don't actually support the 1st floor; the council of the day insisted upon them despite Wren's conviction that they were unnecessary. Wren left a few centimetres of clear space (still visible) to prove his point.

Some of the oldest parts of Windsor lie along cobbled streets behind the Guildhall, including **Queen Charlotte St**, the shortest road in Britain. The leaning **Market Cross House** is next to the Guildhall. Nell Gwyn, Charles II's favourite mistress, lived at 4 Church St (now a restaurant).

The 1920-hectare **Windsor Great Park**, where in 1999 Elizabeth II's husband, Prince Philip, had an avenue of ancient trees beheaded because they got in the way of his horse and buggy, extends from behind the castle almost as far as Ascot.

SIGHTS & INFORMATION

TIC (☎ 743900; www.windsor.gov.uk; 24 High St; ☺ 10am-5pm Mon-Sat, 10am-4.30pm Sun Apr-Jun & Sep-Oct, 9.30am-6pm Jul & Aug, 10am-4pm Nov-Mar)

Guide Friday (☎ 01789-294466; adult/senior & student/child aged 5-14/family £6.50/5.50/2.50/15.50) Open-top double-decker bus tours of Windsor

French Brothers (☎ 851900; www.boat-trips.co.uk; Clewer Ct Rd; adult/child/family £4.40/2.20/12.10; ☺ every half hr 11am-5pm Easter-Oct) This company runs 35-minute boat trips from Windsor to Boveney lock.

Windsor Castle (☎ 869898, 831118; www.the-royal -collection.org.uk; adult/senior/child aged 5-16/family £11/9/5.50/27.50 or £5.50/4.50/2.70/13.70 when State Apartments are closed; public areas ☺ 9.45am-5.15pm Mar-Oct, 9.45am-4.15pm Nov-Feb, changing of the guard 11am Mon-Sat May & Jun (weather permitting), alt days from Mon-Sat Jul-Apr)

Eton College (☎ 671177; www.etoncollege.com; Baldwins Shore; adult/child £3/2; ☺ 2-4.30pm term-time, 10.30am-4.30pm Easter & summer holidays) **Windsor Great Park** (☎ 860222; admission free; ☺ 8am-sunset)

EATING

Peascod St and its extension, St Leonard's Rd, are good hunting grounds for restaurants.

Crooked House (☎ 857534; 51 High St; sandwiches £5-7) From the tiny, precarious-looking Market Cross House, this café turns out excellent sandwiches and baguettes.

Crosses Corner (☎ 862867; 73 Peascod St; lunch £5.25-6) This pub pulls in the lunch crowds.

Francesco's (☎ 863773; 53 Peascod St; pizzas & pasta dishes £5-15, 3-course lunch £6.95) A very popular place.

Ha! Ha! Bar & Canteen (☎ 770111; Windsor Royal Station; snacks £4-4.50, meals £6.50-10) This branch of a London chain in the old Royal railway station is Windsor's current place to be seen.

The Viceroy (☎ 858 005; 49-51 St Leonard's Rd; mains £5.50-11.95, Sunday buffet adult/child £8.50/4.99) This place serves great Indian food but the service can be cavalier at times.

STOWE HOUSE & LANDSCAPED GARDENS

Stowe is in a remote position in north Buckinghamshire, which ensures it is never overrun by tourists. It was once the country seat of the Temple family who rose with incredible speed from being local landowners to becoming the Dukes of Buckingham and Chandos by the 18th century. They went bankrupt in 1848 and were forced to sell the contents of the house in a 40-day auction, although in the preceding two centuries they managed to create a staggering work of landscaping and perhaps the most important 18th-century gardens in the country.

Don't come here expecting to see flowers – Stowe is where Lancelot 'Capability' Brown cut his teeth developing English landscape gardening in the 18th century, in which naturalism triumphed over French formalism. Earlier, James Gibbs and St John Vanbrugh crafted temples and follies through the grounds, as well as a staggering main house, which has housed the Stowe School since 1923. It is still possible to visit the larger state rooms, and although none of the original furniture remains, the art collection, ceilings and views make this

Transport

Distance from London 75 miles (121km)

Direction Northwest

Travel time 1hr by train, then 30min by bus & 10min by taxi from Buckingham

Car Take the M40 out of London, until junction 10, then take the A43 towards Northampton. Turn off onto the A422 signposted for Buckingham and Stowe Landscape Gardens, from there follow signposts to the grounds. On arrival, drive up the main drive, and continue straight on until you get to the National Trust car park.

Train Take a train from Euston to Milton Keynes (£13.40), from where there are hourly buses from the bus station across the road to Buckingham. From Buckingham bus station, a taxi to Stowe will cost about £6.

worthwhile. Particularly notable is **Marble Hall** with its incredible glass dome and sculptures of everyday Roman life. The **Music Room** and **Library** are fine examples of Georgian design, and the view from the **South Front Portico** over the **Octagan lake** and to the **Corinthian Arch** is breathtaking. The National Trust now runs the grounds (but not the house) and has spent much of the past decade rectifying the neglect the temples have suffered.

SIGHTS & INFORMATION

Stowe (☎ house 01280 822850, gardens 01280 818282; www.nationaltrust.org.uk; near Buckingham, Buckinghamshire; house adult/child/family £3/1.50/12.50, gardens adult/child £5/2.50; ☼ 10am-5.30pm Wed-Sun Mar-Oct, 10am-4pm Wed-Sun Nov & Dec) Call for opening hours.

EATING

There is a small National Trust café behind the Temple of Concorde and Victory that serves sandwiches and other light meals for between £4 and £5 per person, open 10am until the grounds close every day.

BLENHEIM PALACE

The fabulous Oxfordshire home of the Dukes of Marlborough, **Blenheim Palace** is another creation of Vanbrugh and Brown, the only nonroyal residence in the country to be called a palace. You'd be forgiven for thinking this was the home of royalty, as the impressive, sumptuous interiors are perfectly preserved by the current Duke who still resides at Blenheim today.

Blenheim is famous as Winston Churchill's birthplace; his bedroom is included on the interesting guided tour of the house. The tapestries made for the first duke in the aftermath of his incredible military feats at Blenheim against the French are perhaps the highlight, and a walk in the landscaped gardens (including the fantastic hedge maze, the UK's biggest) is the perfect counterbalance to the in-your-face luxury. Be warned, Blenheim is a huge tourist draw, mainly because of its proximity to Oxford, and this can detract from the experience in summer.

Blenheim Palace

SIGHTS & INFORMATION

Blenheim Palace (☎ 01993 811325; www.blenheimpalace.com; near Woodstock, Oxfordshire; palace, park & gardens adult/child/senior & student £11.50/6.50/9.50, park only £10/car, pedestrian adult/child £3.50/2.50; ☼ palace & gardens 10.30am-4.45pm mid-Mar–Oct, park 9am-4.45pm year-round)

EATING

There is an on-site café where you can buy sandwiches and snacks for £3 to £4.

Transport

Distance from London 60 miles (97km)

Direction Northwest

Travel time 1hr by train to Oxford, then 30min by bus

Train Take the train to Oxford (p363), from where there are regular buses to Blenheim leaving from Gloucester Green bus station.

LEEDS CASTLE

This magnificent Kentish castle has been dubbed 'the loveliest castle in the world'. Like something from a fairytale, it stands on two small islands in a Kentish lake surrounded by rolling wooded hills. The building dates from the 9th century, but Henry VIII transformed it from a fortress into a palace. Its curious name (Leeds is several hundred miles north of Maidstone) derives from a nearby village. The castle was colloquially known as 'Ladies Castle', being home to many queens over the centuries, from Philippa of Hainult

(Edward III's wife) to Catherine de Valois, Catherine of Aragon and even Elizabeth I, who was imprisoned here before she took the throne.

Walking around the castle will explode some of the more outlandish myths of castle life: instead of dank, rat-infested chambers, the huge rooms, roaring fires and walls hung with tapestries give out an air of comfort well in keeping with its queenly past. However, the grounds are the most striking feature of the castle, from the glorious moat to the gardens and hedge maze.

SIGHTS & INFORMATION

Leeds Castle (☎ 01622-765400, ☎ 0870 600 8880; www.leeds-castle.com; Maidstone, Kent; castle, park & gardens admission adult/child aged 4-15 /senior & student/ family £11/7.50/9.50/32; ☺ 10am-7pm, last admission 5pm, Mar-Oct, 10am-5pm, last admission 3pm, Nov-Feb)

Transport

Distance from London 43 miles (70km)

Direction Southeast

Travel time 1¼hr by bus, 1hr by train

Car 7 miles east of Maidstone. Take the M20 from London, coming off at Junction 8 and following signs for Leeds Castle.

Bus National Express has a daily direct service from Victoria Coach Station leaving at 9am (adult/senior & student/child aged 5-15 £10/8/5 or adult/child £14/11 including castle admission). Green Line has a similar inclusive deal with buses departing 9.35am Mon-Fri (adult/child £14/8).

Train The nearest train station is Bearsted. Take the combined rail-travel, coach-transfer and admission ticket from Victoria or Charing Cross train stations with Connex Rail (adult/child £20.50/10.30).

Directory

Directory

TRANSPORT

AIRLINES

London is served by nearly every international airline, and the vast majority have offices in the city. The main airline numbers are listed below.

Aer Lingus ☎ 0845 084 4444; www.aerlingus.com
Aeroflot ☎ 7355 2233; www.aeroflot.com
Air Canada ☎ 0870 524 7226; www.aircanada.com
Air France ☎ 0845 084 5111; www.airfrance.com
Air New Zealand ☎ 8741 2299; www.airnz.com
Alitalia ☎ 0870 544 8259; www.alitalia.com
American Airlines ☎ 0845 778 9789; www.aa.com
British Airways ☎ 0845 773 3377; www.british-airways.com
British European ☎ 0870 567 6676; www.flybe.com
British Midland ☎ 0870 607 0555; www.flybmi.com
Cathay Pacific Airways ☎ 7747 8888;
   www.cathaypacific.com
Continental Airlines ☎ 0800 776 464; www.continental.com
Delta Air Lines ☎ 0800 414 767; www.delta.com
EasyJet ☎ 0870 600 0000; www.easyjet.com
El Al Israel Airlines ☎ 7957 4100; www.elal.com
Iberia ☎ 0845 601 2854; www.iberia.com
Icelandexpress ☎ 0870 850 0737;
   www.icelandexpress.com
KLM UK ☎ 0870 507 4074; www.klm.com
Lufthansa Airlines ☎ 0845 773 7747; www.lufthansa.com
Olympic Airways ☎ 0870 606 0460; www.olympicair
   ways.com
Qantas Airways ☎ 0845 774 7767; www.qantas.com
Ryanair ☎ 0870 156 9569; www.ryanair.com
Scandinavian Airlines (SAS) ☎ 0845 607 2772; www.sas.se
Singapore Airlines ☎ 0870 608 8886;
   www.singaporeair.com
SN Brussels Airlines ☎ 0870 735 2345; www.flysn.com
South African Airways ☎ 7312 5000; www.flysaa.com
TAP Air Portugal ☎ 0845 601 0932; www.tap.pt
Thai Airways International ☎ 0870 606 0911;
   www.thaiair.com
Turkish Airlines ☎ 7766 9300; www.turkishairlines.com
United Airlines ☎ 0845 844 4777; www.ual.com
Virgin Atlantic ☎ 01293 747747; www.virgin-atlantic.com

AIRPORTS

London is served by five major airports: Heathrow (the largest), Gatwick, Stansted, Luton and London City.

HEATHROW AIRPORT

LHR; ☎ 0870 000 0123; www.baa.co.uk/heathrow
Fifteen miles (24km) west of central London, Heathrow is the world's busiest commercial airport. It currently has four terminals, with a fifth one due. Two Piccadilly line tube stations serve the airport: one for Terminals 1, 2 and 3, the other for Terminal 4. Each terminal has competitive currency-exchange facilities, information counters and accommodation desks.

There are some 15 international hotels at or near Heathrow, should you be arriving or leaving at a peculiarly early or late hour. To reach them from Heathrow you must take the Heathrow **Hotel Hoppa bus** (☎ 0870 574 7777; one way £2.50; ⊗ 6am-11pm), running every 10 to 15 minutes for the first three terminals and every 30 minutes for Terminal 4.

There are also left-luggage facilities:

Terminal 1 ☎ 8745 5301; ⊗ 5am-11pm
Terminal 2 ☎ 8745 4599; ⊗ 5.30am-10.30pm
Terminal 3 ☎ 8759 3344; ⊗ 24 hrs
Terminal 4 ☎ 8745 7460; ⊗ 5am-11pm

The charge is £3.50 per item for the first 12 hours and £4 per item for up to 24 hours. All branches can forward baggage.

Here are options for getting to/from Heathrow airport:

Heathrow Express (☎ 0845 600 1515; www.heathrowe xpress.co.uk; one way/return £12/23, cheaper if booked in advance; trains depart every 15 min; journey time 15 min) An ultramodern train that whisks passengers from Heathrow Central station (serving Terminals 1 to 3) and Terminal 4 station to Paddington station. The Heathrow Central train runs between 5.12/5.08am and 11.32/11.37pm Mon-Sat/Sun, while the Terminal 4 train runs between 5.07/5.03am and 11.32/11.37pm Mon-Sat/Sun. The first train leaves Paddington at 5.10am, the last at 11.40pm. Many airlines, including British Airways (BA) and United Airlines, have check-in facilities at Paddington.

Underground (☎ 7222 1234; www.thetube.com; one way £3.70; return trains every 2-8 min; journey time from central London 1 hr) This remains the cheapest way of getting to Heathrow, though the journey takes a lot longer and is less comfortable than the Express. It runs between 5.30am and 11.45pm. You can buy tickets from machines in the baggage reclaim areas of the Heathrow terminals, so you don't have to queue in the station.

Airbus A2 (☎ 0807 574 7777; www.nationalexpress .com; one way/return £5/£10; tickets valid 3 months; buses depart every 30 min to 1pm then once an hour; journey time 1hr 15 min) The Airbus links King's Cross station with Heathrow about 30 times a day. The first bus leaves Terminal 4 at 5.30am via Terminals 3, 2 & 1, with the last departure at 9.45pm. The first bus leaves King's Cross at 4am, the last at 8pm.

Black cabs A metered trip to/from central London (Oxford St) will cost about £35.

GATWICK AIRPORT
LGW; ☎ 0870 000 2468; www.baa.co.uk/gatwick
Gatwick is located some 30 miles (48km) south of central London, and is smaller and better organised than Heathrow. The North and South terminals are linked by an efficient monorail service, with the journey time about two minutes. Gatwick also has left-luggage facilities:

North Terminal ☎ 01293-502013; ⏱ 6am-10pm
South Terminal ☎ 01293-502014; ⏱ 24hr

The charge is £3.50 per item for the first six hours and £4 per item for up to 24 hours.

Here are options for getting to/from Gatwick airport:

Gatwick Express (☎ 0870 530 1530; www.gatwickexp ress.co.uk; one way/return £10.50/20; trains depart every 15 min 5am-midnight, otherwise hourly; journey time 30 min) Trains link the station near the South Terminal with Victoria station. BA and American Airlines passengers can check in at Victoria station.

Connex South Central train service (☎ 0845 748 4950; www.connex.co.uk; one way/return £8.20/4.10; trains depart every 15 to 30 min, once an hour from 1am to 4am; journey time 45 min) This service runs from Victoria station to both terminals and takes a little longer than the Express.

Thameslink service (☎ 0845 748 4950; www.thames link.co.uk; one way/return £9.80/4.95) This service runs from King's Cross, Farringdon and London Bridge train stations.

Airbus No 5 (☎ 0807 574 7777; www.nationalexpress .com; one way/return £8.50/10; tickets valid 3 months; journey time 90 min) Runs from Gatwick to Victoria Coach Station 16 times a day between 4.15am and 9.15pm (between 6am and 11pm from Victoria to Gatwick).

Black cabs A metered trip to/from central London will cost around £70.

STANSTED AIRPORT
STN; ☎ 0870 000 0303; www.baa.co.uk/stansted
About 35 miles (56km) northeast of central London, this is London's third busiest international gateway. Here are options for getting to/from Stansted airport:

Stansted Express (☎ 0845 748 4950; www.standsted express.com; one way/return £13/21; trains depart every 15-30 min; journey time 45 min) Links the airport and Liverpool Street station. From the airport, the first train goes at 6am, the last just before midnight. Trains depart Liverpool Street station from 5am (4.45am Sat) to 11pm. If you need to connect with the tube, change at Tottenham Hale for the Victoria line or stay on to Liverpool Street station for the Central line.

Airbus A6 (☎ 0807 574 7777; www.nationalexpress .com; one way/return £7/10; tickets valid 3 months; journey time 1½ hrs) Links to Victoria Coach Station about 40 times a day round the clock. From the airport buses leave every half-hour between 3.30am and 11.30pm and then once an hour. They depart the coach station half-hourly between 4.05am and 11.35pm and then hourly.

Black cabs A metered trip to/from central London will cost £70 to £80.

LONDON CITY AIRPORT Map p414
LCY; ☎ 7646 0000; www.londoncityairport .com
Six miles (10km) east of central London, London City Airport is in the Docklands by the Thames. It has flights to 20 continental European cities as well eight destinations in the British Isles (Aberdeen, Belfast, Dublin, Dundee, Edinburgh, Glasgow, Isle of Man and Jersey). Here are options for getting to/from London City airport:

Blue airport Shuttlebus (☎ 7646 0088; www.londoncit yairport.com/shuttlebus; one way/return to/from Liverpool Street station £6/12; buses depart every 10/15 min Mon-Fri/Sat & Sun; journey time 25 min) Connects the airport with Liverpool Street station via Canary Wharf between 6.50am (11am Sun) and 10pm (1.15pm Sat). The first bus leaves Liverpool Street at 6.15am (10.30am on Sun); the last departs 9pm weekdays (12.45pm Sat).

Green airport Shuttlebus (☎ 7646 0088; www.londonc ityairport.com/shuttlebus; adult/child one way £2/1; buses depart every 10 min; journey time 5 min) Links the airport and Canning Town station, which is on the Jubilee tube, DLR and Silverlink lines, from 6am (10.05am on Sun) until 10.20pm (1.15pm on Sat).

Black cabs A metered trip to/from central London will cost about £20.

LUTON AIRPORT

LTN; ☎ 01582-405100; www.london-luton.co.uk
A smallish airport some 35 miles (56km) north of London, Luton caters mainly for cheap charter flights, though the discount airline easyJet operates scheduled services from here.

Here are options for getting to/from Luton airport:

Thameslink (☎ 0845 748 4950; www.thameslink.co.uk; adult/child one way £9.50/4.75; trains depart every 5-15 min 7am-10pm; journey time 30-40 min) Runs trains from King's Cross and other central London stations to Luton Airport Parkway station, from where an airport shuttle bus will take you to the airport in eight minutes.

Green Line bus No 757 (☎ 0870 608 7261; www.greenline.co.uk; one way/return £8/13; journey time 55 min) Buses to Luton run from Buckingham Palace Rd south of Victoria station, leaving every half-hour from 7.05am (7.35am Sat & Sun) to 10pm, then hourly to 6.30am. They depart Luton every half-hour 8am to 8pm, then hourly to 7.30am.

Black cabs A metered trip to/from central London will cost £70 to £80.

Websites

As well as airline websites (p376), there are a number of efficient online resources for buying good-value plane tickets. Some of the best include www.ebookers.com, www.opodo.com and www.cheapflights.co.uk.

BICYCLE

Cycling around London is one way of cutting transport costs but it can be grim, with heavy traffic and fumes detracting from the pleasure of getting a little exercise. The **London Cycling Campaign** (LCC; ☎ 7928 7220) is working towards improving conditions, campaigning to establish the London Cycle Network, which is up and running in parts of the South Bank and in Bankside. The LCC produces the map called *Central London Cycle Routes*. It's advisable to wear a helmet, and many Londoners also wear facemasks to filter out pollution.

Hire

The following places hire out mountain or hybrid bikes in mint condition. Each demands deposits of £100 to £200 (credit cards are accepted), however short or long the rental period.

BIKEPARK Maps p430 & pp436-7

Covent Garden: ☎ 7430 0083; www.bikepark.co.uk; 11 Macklin St WC2; tube Holborn. Chelsea: ☎ 7731 7012; 63 New Kings Rd SW6; tube Fulham Broadway
The minimum charge at both Bikeparks is £12 for the first day, £6 for the second day and £4 for subsequent days. You can also hire bikes for a week or more; the first week costs £38 and subsequent ones £28.

LONDON BICYCLE TOUR COMPANY Map pp426-7

☎ 7928 6838; www.londonbicycle.com; 1a Gabriel's Wharf, 56 Upper Ground SE1; tube Blackfriars
Rentals cost £2.50 per hour or £12 for the first day, £6 for subsequent days, £36 for the first week and £30 per week after that. It also offers daily three-hour bike tours of London (2pm Sat & Sun) for £12 including the bike or £9 if you have your own. The routings are on its website.

Bicycles on Public Transport

Bicycles can be taken only on the District, Circle, Hammersmith & City and Metropolitan tube lines outside the rush hour – outside being 10am to 4pm and after 7pm Monday to Friday. Folding bikes can be taken on any line, however. Bicycles can also travel on the above-ground sections of some other tube lines and the Silverlink line. But on the DLR, bicycles are banned.

Restrictions on taking a bike on suburban and mainline trains vary from company to company so you need to check before setting out. For details call ☎ 0845 748 4950.

Pedicabs

These three-wheeled cycle rickshaws that seat two or three people arrived on the scene in Soho in 1998 and have gained popularity since then. Starting at around £2 per person for a short trip within Soho to £15 for a ride to King's Cross, they're less 'a mode of transport' than a nice gimmick for tourists and other pleasure-trippers. The best-known company is nonprofit **Bugbugs** (☎ 8675 6577; www.bugbugs.co.uk; 7pm–2am Mon-Fri, 7pm–5am Sat & Sun). Daytime trips can be booked in advance.

BOAT

With the drive to make use of London's often overlooked 'liquid artery', companies running shuttle boats on the river have been sprouting up in recent years. There's good news for Travelcard holders (p384): you get one-third off all fares listed below. Private boat operators crowd the piers and will often tout for customers – you'll find them around Embankment, Westminster and even down as far as Richmond.

For something more romantic, there is no shortage of dinner cruises, offering dancing, music and fine food against a backdrop of the city at night. Try www.thames-dinner-cruises.co.uk (prices start at £16.50 per person).

Eastward along the Thames

BATEAUX LONDON – CATAMARAN CRUISERS LTD

☎ 7987 1185 or 7925 2215; www.bateauxlondon.com; River Pass adult/child £10.50-11.50/5.50-6.50; 🕐 every 30 min 10am-6pm

Offers a similar service to City Cruises, linking Embankment, Tower and Greenwich Piers for £5.70 to £9 (adult) and £3.50 to £5.50 (child) return depending on the stage and season. The River Pass allows one day's unlimited use of the service. Schedules vary according to season, with six or seven daily departures in winter.

CIRCULAR CRUISE

☎ 7936 2033; www.crownriver.com; adult/child aged 5-15/student & senior/family £6/3/5/15.80; 🕐 every 30-40 min 11am-7pm Apr-Sep, 11am, 12.20pm, 1.40pm & 3pm Oct-May

Offers a service from Westminster Pier as far as St Katharine's Pier in Wapping. Vessels call at London Bridge City Pier and, on weekends in the summer season, at Festival Pier on the South Bank. Fares are cheaper between just two stages (eg Westminster Pier to/from London Bridge City Pier costs £4.30/2.20/3.20/11).

CITY CRUISES

☎ 7740 0400; www.citycruises.com; River Red Rover Day Ticket adult/child aged 5-16/family £7.50/3.75/19.50; 🕐 every 20-40 mins 10/10.30am-5/6pm

A year-round ferry service from Westminster Pier to Tower Pier, or Tower Pier to Greenwich Pier for £5/2.50 (adult/child) one way or £6/3 return, and Westminster Pier to Greenwich for £6/3 (adult/child) one way or £7.50/3.75 return.

A River Red Rover Day Ticket allows you to hop off and on. Schedules vary widely depending on the route and the season, with later departures in summer (June to August) and fewer sailings in winter (November to March).

TATE-TO-TATE

See p160.

THAMES CLIPPERS

☎ 7977 6892; www.thamesclippers.com; adult/child single £2 /1, return £3/1.50; 🕐 6.30am-7pm, every 20 minutes early morning, every hour after 9am

Serving more as commuter boats than tourist boats, these are cheap and fast, giving you access to lots of the river sights. They run from Savoy Pier at Embankment to Masthouse Terrace in Docklands, passing Tower Bridge, the Tate Modern, Shakespeare's Globe and Canary Wharf.

WESTMINSTER TO GREENWICH THAMES PASSENGER BOAT SERVICE

WGTPBS; ☎ 7930 4097; www.westminsterpier.co.uk; one way adult/child/senior/family £6.50/3.25/5.25/17.50, return £8/4/6.50/21.50; 🕐 every 30 min 10am-4/5pm peak season

These cruise boats leave Westminster Pier for Greenwich, passing the Globe Theatre, stopping at the Tower of London and continuing under Tower Bridge and past the docks. The last boats return from Greenwich at about 5pm (6pm in summer).

Westward along the Thames

WESTMINSTER PASSENGER SERVICE ASSOCIATION

☎ 7930 4721; www.wpsa.co.uk; Royal Botanic Gardens one way adult/child/senior £7/3/6, return £11/5/9, journey time 1½ hrs; Hampton Court one way adult/child/senior £10/4/8, return £14/7/11, journey time 3½ hrs

These boats go upriver from Westminster Pier, an enjoyable excursion although it takes much longer and is not (perhaps) as interesting as the trip east. The main destinations are the Royal Botanic Gardens at Kew and Hampton Court Palace. It's possible to get off the boats at Richmond in July and August. No boats run in this direction from the end of October until the end of March. Boats to the Royal Botanic Gardens at Kew sail from Westminster Pier via Putney up to five times a day from 10.15am to 2pm from late March to September with limited services in October. Boats to Hampton Court leave Westminster Pier at 10.30am, 11.15am and noon April to September/October. See p90 for information on canal trips.

BUS

If you're not in much of a hurry, travelling round London by double-decker bus can be more enjoyable than using the tube. Even though they were privatised in 1994, London's 5500-odd buses are under the Transport for London umbrella. About 3.5 million people travel on them every day.

Information

There are about three dozen separate (and free) bus guides available to areas as far-flung as Harrow, Romford and Hounslow. Most visitors, however, will find the *Central London* bus guide, essentially a map and available from most transport travel information centres, sufficient. If you can't get to a centre, ring ☎ 7371 0247 to have one sent or write to London Buses (CDL), Freepost Lon7503, London SE16 4BR. For general information on London buses call ☎ 7222 1234 (24 hrs). For more information on how services are running, phone Travelcheck on ☎ 7222 1200.

The wheelchair-accessible **Stationlink buses** (☎ 7941 4600), which have a ramp operated by the driver, follow a similar route to that of the tube's Circle Line (p383), joining up the mainline stations – from Paddington, Euston, St Pancras and King's Cross to Liverpool Street, London Bridge, Waterloo and Victoria. People with mobility problems and those with heavy luggage may find this easier to use than the tube, although it operates only once an hour. From Paddington there are services clockwise on the SL1 from 8.15am to 7.15pm and anticlockwise (the SL2) from 8.40am to 6.40pm.

Night Buses

Trafalgar Square is the focus of two-thirds of the more than 60 night buses (prefixed with the letter 'N') that come on duty when the tube shuts down and the daytime buses return to the barn; if you're not familiar with the routes, head to Trafalgar Square or check any of the bus-stop information boards. Night buses run from about midnight to 7am, but services can be infrequent and stop only on request, meaning you must signal clearly to the driver to stop.

Networks & Useful Routes

One of the best ways to explore London is to buy a Travelcard and jump on a bus, especially the double-decker Routemaster buses, which have a conductor, and an access platform at the rear to make jumping on and off easy.

Some of the most useful bus routes include the following:

No 24 This bus is especially good for travelling north to south (or vice versa). Beginning at South End Green in Hampstead Heath, it travels through Camden and along Gower St to Tottenham Court Rd. From there it goes down Charing Cross Rd, past Leicester Square to Trafalgar Square, then along Whitehall, past the Palace of Westminster, Westminster Abbey and Westminster Cathedral. It reaches Victoria station and then carries on to Pimlico, which is handy for the Tate Britain.

No 19 This is another north–south route worth trying. It departs from Finsbury Park tube station, travels down Upper St in Islington, through Clerkenwell, Holborn and Bloomsbury, then goes along New Oxford St and down Charing Cross Rd and Shaftesbury Ave to Piccadilly. It then travels along the northern edge of Green Park to Hyde Park Corner, before carrying on down Sloane St and along King's Rd. If you get off at the southern end of Battersea Bridge, you'll be well placed for Battersea Park.

No 8 From east to west, or the reverse, try this Routemaster bus. It comes from Bow in east London, then goes along Bethnal Green Rd and passes the markets at Spitalfields and Petticoat Lane, Liverpool Street station, the City, the Guildhall and the Old Bailey. It then crosses Holborn and enters Oxford St, travelling past Oxford Circus and turning down New Bond St to Piccadilly, Hyde Park Corner and Victoria.

Nos 9 & 10 These are also good bus routes, leaving Hammersmith and going through Kensington and Knightsbridge, passing the Albert Memorial, Royal Albert Hall and Harrods before reaching Hyde Park Corner. The **No 9** then goes along Piccadilly to Piccadilly Circus and Trafalgar Square before carrying on down the Strand to Aldwych (good for Covent Garden), where it terminates. The **No 10** heads northwards from Hyde Park Corner to Marble Arch and heads down Oxford St and then up Tottenham Court Rd to Euston, King's Cross and eventually Archway tube station.

Fares

Though the bus network is divided into four zones, this only affects holders of passes valid for a week or longer. Single-journey bus tickets cost £1 within central London (Zone 1) or for entering from anywhere in London, and 70p from any point to any point elsewhere in London; night bus fares are now the same as day fares. Children aged five to 15 pay a uniform 40p. Travelcards (p384) are valid on buses. Stationlink buses cost adult/child 70/40p though Travelcards, including those for Zone 1, are also valid. Travelcards are now valid on all night buses. Daily bus passes are valid for the whole network. By and large, if you live outside Zone 2, you'll want to use the tube or rail network to get into central London anyway, as buses are slow over long distances.

Since 2003, new plans to increase the speed of buses have meant that drivers no longer sell tickets. You must buy before you board, using the machines next to all bus stops. Frustratingly, these do not give change, so you'll need exact money, although they do sell daily bus passes. However, on routes with a conductor (ie any route where you board at the back of the bus), you can still purchase on board.

TRAVEL PASSES & DISCOUNT FARES

A **Saver** ticket (£3.90) is a book of six bus tickets valid on all buses, including those in central London and night buses. They are transferable but valid for one journey only.

If you plan to use only buses during your stay in London, you can buy a **one-day bus pass** valid throughout London for £2/1 (adult/child). Unlike the one-day Travelcards, these are valid before 9.30am. All-zone weekly/monthly passes are also available for £9.50/36.50 (adult) and £4/15.40 (child).

CAR & MOTORCYCLE

We do not advise driving in London: traffic jams are common, parking space is at a premium and the new **congestion charge** (right) adds to the expense of driving, including the already-high price of petrol. Traffic wardens and wheel clampers operate with extreme efficiency and if your vehicle is clamped you won't see much change from £100 to have it unclamped. Ring the 24-hour Clamping & Vehicle Section hotline

(☎ 7747 4747) if you do get clamped. If the car has been removed it's going to cost you at least £125 to get it back.

Driving
ROAD RULES

If you do plan to drive in London you should obtain the *Highway Code*, which is available at AA and RAC outlets as well as some bookshops and tourist information centres (TICs). A foreign driving licence is valid in Britain for up to 12 months from the time of your last entry into the country. If you bring a car from Europe make sure you're adequately insured. Note that all drivers and passengers must wear seatbelts and motorcyclists must wear a helmet.

THE CONGESTION CHARGE

In February 2003 London became the world's first major city to introduce a congestion charge to reduce the flow of traffic into its centre from Monday to Friday. While the number of cars entering the 'congestion zone' has fallen as a result, driving in London can still be very slow work.

As a rough guide, the charge zone is south of the Euston Rd, west of Commercial St, north of Kennington Lane and east of Park Lane. As you enter the zone, you will see a large letter 'C' in a red circle. If you enter the zone between 7am and 6.30pm Monday to Friday (excluding public holidays), you must pay the £5 charge before 10pm the same day (or pay £10 between 10pm and midnight the same day) to avoid receiving an £80 fine. Those living within the congestion zone receive a 90% discount on the charge, although you must be a registered resident to qualify. You can pay online, at newsagents, petrol stations or any shop displaying the 'C' sign, by telephone ☎ 0845 900 1234 and even by text message once you've registered online. For full details log on to www.cclondon .com.

Rental

Although driving in London is expensive and often slow, there is no shortage of rental agencies in the city centre and throughout Greater London. Competition is fierce, with easycar.com having significantly undersold many of the other more traditional companies over the past few years, forcing down prices. Compare prices, models and agency locations at one of the following websites: www.easycar.com; www.hertz.com; www.avis.com.

TAXI
Black Cabs

The black London taxicab (www.londonblackcabs.co.uk) is as much a feature of the cityscape as the red bus, although these days it comes in a variety of colours, bespattered with advertising. A new, streamlined black version has also been introduced.

Taxis come into their own at night, although prices are higher. Cabs are available for hire when the yellow sign above the windscreen is lit; just stick your arm out to signal one. Fares are metered, with a minimum charge of £1.40, and increments of 20p for each 219m (after the first 438m). There are additional charges for extra passengers, front-seat baggage and late-night trips. You can tip taxi drivers up to 10% but most people round up to the nearest pound.

Do not expect to hail a taxi in popular nightlife areas of London such as Soho late at night (and especially after pub closing time at 11pm). If you do find yourself in any of those areas, signal all taxis – even those with their lights off – and try to look sober. Many drivers are very choosy about their fares at this time of night. To order a cab by phone try Radio Taxis on ☎ 7272 0272; they charge what it costs to get to you, up to £3.80, as well as your actual fare.

Zingo Taxi (☎ 08700 700 700) is an innovative new scheme that uses GPS to connect your mobile phone to that of the nearest free black-cab driver – after which you can explain to the cabbie exactly where you are. This service costs £1.40, added to the price of the cab itself. It's perhaps a good idea late at night, when it's notoriously difficult to find a free cab.

Minicabs

Minicabs, some of which are now licensed, are cheaper, freelance competitors of black cabs. However, they are sometimes driven by untrained individuals who don't know their way around and who are often uninsured. Minicabs cannot legally be hailed on the street – they must be hired by phone or directly from one of the minicab offices

(every high street has at least one – look out for a flashing orange light). You may be approached by minicab drivers seeking fares; it's probably best to avoid this as there have been a number allegations of rape made against unlicensed cab drivers.

The cabs don't have meters, so it's essential to fix a price before you start (it's therefore not usual to tip minicab drivers). Make sure you bargain hard, as most drivers start at about 25% higher than the fare they're prepared to accept.

Ask a local for the name of a reputable minicab company, or phone a large 24-hour operator (☎ 7387 8888, 7272 2222, 7272 3322, 8888 4444). Women travelling alone at night can choose Ladycabs (☎ 7254 3501), which has women drivers. Freedom Cars (☎ 7734 1313) caters for the gay and lesbian market, although gay couples are extremely unlikely to experience open homophobia from drivers of black cabs.

TRAIN
Suburban Trains

Several rail companies operate passenger trains in London, including the Silverlink (or North London) line (☎ 0845 601 4867; www.silverlink-trains.com) and the crowded Thameslink (☎ 0845 748 4950; www.thameslink.co.uk), or 'sardine line'. Silverlink links Richmond in the southwest with North Woolwich in the southeast via Kew, West Hampstead, Camden Road, Highbury & Islington and Stratford stations. Thameslink goes from Elephant & Castle and London Bridge in the south through the City to King's Cross and as far north as Luton. Most lines connect with the Underground system, and Travelcards can be used on them.

If you're staying long-term in southeast London, where suburban trains are usually much more useful than the tube, it's worth buying a one-year Network Railcard. This card offers one-third off most rail fares in southeast England and on one-day Travelcards for all six zones. Travel is permitted only after 10am Monday to Friday and at any time on Saturday and Sunday. The card costs £20 and is available at most stations.

Most of the large mainline London stations have left-luggage facilities available, although due to the perceived threat from terrorists, baggage lockers have been phased out to oblivion. Excess Baggage (☎ 0800 783 1085;

www.excessbaggage.co.uk) has services costing £4 per bag per 24 hours or part thereof. These services operate from Paddington, Euston, Waterloo, King's Cross, Liverpool Street, and Charing Cross stations.

Docklands Light Railway

The independent, driverless **Docklands Light Railway** (DLR; ☎ 7363 9700; www.tfl.gov.uk/dlr) links the City at Bank and Tower Gateway at Tower Hill with Beckton and Stratford to the east and northeast and the Docklands (as far as Island Gardens at the southern end of the Isle of Dogs), Greenwich and Lewisham to the south. The DLR runs from 5.30am to 12.30am Monday to Friday, from 6am to 12.30am Saturday and from 7.30am to 11.30pm Sunday. Fares are the same as those on the tube though there is a host of daily, weekly, monthly and annual passes valid uniquely on the DLR.

For news of how services are running, call Travelcheck on ☎ 7222 1200.

TRAM

A small London tram network, Tramlink, was introduced to South London in 2000 and runs from Wimbledon through Croydon to Beckenham, where it has proven a popular mode of transport. New plans see the network being extended throughout the notoriously badly served South London area, all the way to Crystal Palace. There are also plans afoot for a cross-river scheme, linking South London to Euston and Camden. See the Transport for London website for the latest news: www.londontransport.co.uk/trams.

UNDERGROUND

The London Underground, or 'the tube' as it is universally known to Londoners, is normally the quickest and easiest way of getting round London. However, it is often slow and unreliable, and breakdowns are common. Sometimes entire sections of the tube are closed, and there's the constant threat of strikes by operators and other staff opposed to the government's proposed privatisation. Worst of all, it's expensive: compare the cheapest one-way fare in central London of £1.60 with those charged on the Paris metro and New York subway, and Londoners clearly pay over the odds.

Information

Underground travel information centres sell tickets and provide free maps. There are centres at all Heathrow terminals and at Euston, King's Cross St Pancras, Liverpool Street, Oxford Circus, Piccadilly Circus, St James's Park and Victoria tube and mainline train stations. There is also an information office at Hammersmith bus station. For general information on the tube, buses, the DLR or trains within London ring ☎ 7222 1234 or visit the Underground website at web www.thetube.com or the Transport for London website at www.transportforlondon .gov.uk. For news of how services are running, call Travelcheck on ☎ 7222 1200.

Network

Greater London is served by 12 tube lines, along with the independent (though linked) and privately owned DLR and an interconnected rail network. The first tube train operates at around 5.30am Monday to Saturday and around 7am Sunday; the last train leaves between 11.30pm and 12.30am depending on the day, the station and the line.

Remember that any train heading from left to right on the map is designated as eastbound, and any train heading from top to bottom is southbound – no matter how many squiggles and turns it makes. If your two stations are not on the same line, you need to note the nearest station where the two lines intersect, and it is here that you must change trains.

Tube lines vary in their reliability, and the Circle Line, which links most of the mainline stations and is therefore much used by tourists, has one of the worst track records. However, when it works, this line is very fast. Other lines low in the league tables are the Northern line (though improving) and the Hammersmith & City (often referred to as the 'Hammersmith & Shitty') line. The Piccadilly line to/from Heathrow is usually pretty good and the Victoria line, linking the station with Oxford Circus and King's Cross, is particularly fast.

Fares

The Underground divides London into six concentric zones. The basic (ie cheapest) fare for adults/children aged five to 15 years for Zone 1 is £1.60/60p; for Zones 1 and 2 £2/80p; for three zones £2.30/1; for four zones

£2.80/1.20; for five zones £3.40/1.40; and for all six zones £3.70/1.50. If you're travelling several times in one day or through a couple of zones, you should consider a Travelpass or some other discounted fare (below).

If you're caught on the Underground without a valid ticket (and that includes crossing into a zone that your ticket doesn't cover) you're liable for an on-the-spot fine of £10.

TRAVEL PASSES & DISCOUNT FARES

A Travelcard valid all day offers the cheapest way of getting about London and can be used after 9.30am on Monday to Friday and all day Saturday, Sunday and public holidays on all forms of transport in London: the tube, suburban trains, the DLR and buses (including night buses). Most visitors will find that a Travelcard covering Zones 1 and 2 (£4.10) will be sufficient. The card for Zones 1, 2, 3 and 4 costs £4.50 and the one for Zones 2, 3, 4, 5 and 6 costs £3.60. A card allowing travel in all six zones costs £5.10, just £1.40 more than a single-journey all-zone ticket – and you get to use it all day. A one-day Travelcard for children aged five to 15 costs £2 regardless of how many zones it covers but those aged 14 and 15 need a Child Photocard to travel on this fare. You can buy Travelcards from stations several days ahead.

There are also peak-time (not valid on suburban trains), weekend, family, weekly, monthly and annual Travelcards. Visit www.thetube.com for fares and conditions.

If you will be making a lot of journeys within Zone 1 only, you can buy a carnet of 10 tickets for £11.50/5 (adult/child) – a useful saving – although do remember that if you cross over into Zone 2 (eg from King's Cross St Pancras to Camden Town for the weekend market) you'll be travelling on an invalid ticket and therefore liable for a penalty fare.

TUBE FARES
One way, as of January 2004:

Zone 1 £2 (carnet £1.50)
Zone 2 (to Z1) £2.20
Zone 3 (to Z1) £2.50
Zone 4 (to Z1) £3.00
Zone 5 (to Z1) £3.50
Zone 6 (to Z1) £3.80

At the time of writing, children's ticket prices had not been finalised. Check www.tfl.gov.uk for further details.

PRACTICALITIES
ACCOMMODATION

The accommodation options in this guide are listed alphabetically by area for mid- and top-range hotels, followed by a separate cheap sleeps section. When budgeting for your trip remember that hotel rates often rise in the summer, while there are often some bargains to be had during the winter months.

Paying for accommodation in London will mostly likely make up a very significant chunk of your budget, however much money you have to spend. The average hotel rate is £70 to £100-plus per night, while hostels average about £30 to £40. The choice is enormous, but the lower end is consistently oversubscribed, so if your budget is limited it's a good idea to book well ahead.

Good resources for finding and booking hotels include www.hotelsoflondon.co.uk, www.londonlodging.co.uk and www.frontdesk.co.uk.

BABY-SITTING

All the top-range hotels offer in-house baby-sitting services. Prices vary enormously from hotel to hotel, so enquire with the concierges. You might also like to try www.babysitter.co.uk – membership costs £49 + VAT and sitters cost as little as £5.20 per hour. Two other sites you could also try are www.topnotchnannies.com and www.nicksbabysittingservice.co.uk (West London only).

BUSINESS

London is a world business hub, and doing business here (not including the media and new-technology industries) is as formal as you would expect from the English. Looking smart at all times is still seen as a key indicator of professionalism, along with punctuality and politeness. Business cards are commonplace.

Business Hours

While the City of London continues to work a very traditional Monday to Friday 9am to 5pm routine (the Square Mile is deserted at weekends), business hours elsewhere in the city are extremely flexible. Larger shops and chain stores are usually open until 7pm

Monday to Friday, as well as until at least 5pm Saturday and Sunday. Thursday is late-night shopping night in the West End.

Banks in central London are now usually open until 5pm, although counter transactions after 3.30pm are usually not processed until the next working day. Post offices vary in their opening times, but most are open from 9am to 5.30pm Monday to Saturday.

Pubs and bars usually open from midday until 11pm, shortly after which punters will have to leave unless the premises has a late licence.

Restaurants are usually open for lunch from noon until 2.30pm, and dinner from 7pm until 10pm. Those hours are for 'food served' rather than 'restaurant open'.

CHILDREN

London offers a wealth of sights and museums that are great for children. The London Dungeon, Madame Tussaud's, the Science Museum, the Tower of London, the London Aquarium and the London Eye just scratch the surface of the variety on offer. Take a look at p189. London is a city with many green spaces, often including safe areas for children to play, and swings and slides – although this all depends on the notoriously unpredictable English weather.

There is nearly always a special child's entry rate to paying attractions, although ages of eligibility may vary. Children also travel more cheaply on public transport.

The only places where children are traditionally not accepted are pubs, although many now have a family area, a garden or a restaurant where kids are welcome.

Nappies and all other baby essentials can be bought just about anywhere, from corner shops to supermarkets, so there's no need to import a huge amount.

CLIMATE

The old adage that 'London doesn't have a climate, it has weather' refers to the fickleness of the atmospheric conditions in this part of the world. Plan a picnic in a park in the morning and it will be raining by noon; go to a film to escape a wet and dreary afternoon, and you'll emerge to bright sunshine in a blue, cloudless sky. You just never know.

But London does have a climate – in fact, among the mildest in England – known as 'temperate maritime', with mild and damp

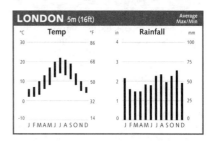

winters and moderate summers. It's wise to expect cloudy weather and rain even in the height of summer.

In July and August temperatures average around 18°C but can occasionally soar to 30°C or more. You'll wish they hadn't as the tube turns into the Black Hole of Calcutta and the heat concentrates the traffic fumes in the streets. A good many public buildings and venues are not air-conditioned. During most summers, however, you'll be lucky if the mercury tops the mid-20s.

Even so, the summer of 2003 was one of the hottest ever on record for Britain and much of Europe. London sizzled at a record-breaking 37.9C in August, breaking once and for all the stereotype of the mild English summer and making many locals feel bad for ever complaining about the usual July and August cool.

In spring and autumn temperatures drop to between 11° and 15°C. In winter they hover just below 6°C; it very rarely freezes in London these days and snow is a very infrequent visitor. It may seem mild, but the dampness can often make it feel twice or three times as cold.

For the Greater London weather forecast, ring Weathercall on ☎ 0906 654 3268, at a cost of 60p per minute.

COURSES

London is a centre of learning, and boasts countless colleges, universities and other educational institutions. The jewel in its crown is the huge University of London, whose world-renowned colleges include King's, University and Imperial Colleges as well as the London School of Economics.

Many people come to London to study English as a foreign language, and during any walk down Oxford St you are likely to be handed a flyer for one such establishment. The best source of information is the **British Council** (☎ 7930 8466;

www.british council.org; 10 Spring Gardens, SW1; tube Charing Cross), which publishes a free list of accredited colleges whose facilities and teaching reach the required standards. The Council can also advise foreign students on educational opportunities in the UK.

A huge number of London courses, from needlework to Nietzche, photography to politics, are listed in the biannual publication Floodlight (£3.75; www.floodlight.co.uk), available from most bookshops.

CUSTOMS

Like other nations belonging to the EU, the UK has a two-tier customs system: one for goods bought duty-free and one for goods bought in another EU country where taxes and duties have already been paid.

Duty-free

Duty-free sales to those travelling from one EU country to another were abolished in July 1999. For goods purchased at airports or on ferries outside the EU, you are allowed to import 200 cigarettes, 50 cigars or 250g of tobacco; 2L of still wine plus 1L of spirits over 22% or another 2L of wine (sparkling or otherwise); 50g of perfume, 250cc of toilet water; and other duty-free goods to the value of £145.

Tax & Duty Paid

Although you can no longer bring in duty-free goods from another EU country, you can bring in duty-paid goods that cost less than you'd pay for the same items in your destination country. The items are supposed to be for individual consumption but a thriving business has developed, with many Londoners making day trips to France to load up their cars with cheap grog and smokes. They often sell these back in the UK, and the savings can more than pay for the trip.

If you purchase from a normal retail outlet on the continent, customs uses the following maximum quantities as a guide to distinguish personal imports from those on a commercial scale: 800 cigarettes, 200 cigars, 1kg of tobacco, 10L of spirits, 20L of fortified wine, 90L of wine (of which not more than 60L is sparkling) and 110L of beer.

DISABLED TRAVELLERS

For many disabled travellers London is an odd mix of user-friendliness and downright disinterest. These days new hotels and modern tourist attractions are usually accessible by wheelchair, but many B&Bs and guesthouses are in older buildings that are hard (if not impossible) to adapt. This means that travellers who have mobility problems may end up having to pay more for accommodation than those who don't.

It's a similar story with public transport. Some of the newer trains and buses have steps that lower for easier access (such as the Stationlink buses that follow a similar route to that of the Circle Line – p383), but it's always wise to check before setting out. Transport for London's Unit for Disabled Passengers (☎ 7918 3312; lt.udp@ltbuses.co.uk) can give you detailed advice and it publishes *Access to the Underground*, which indicates which tube stations have ramps and lifts (all DLR stations do). To receive a copy ahead of your visit write to the Transport for London Unit for Disabled Passengers, 172 Buckingham Palace Rd, London SW1 9TN.

The Royal Association for Disability and Rehabilitation (RADAR; ☎ 7250 3222; www.radar .org.uk; Unit 12, City Forum, 250 City Rd, London EC1V 8AF) is an umbrella organisation for voluntary groups for the disabled and is a useful source of information about facilities. Many disabled toilets can be opened only with a special key, and this can be obtained from tourist offices or by sending a £3 cheque or postal order to RADAR, together with a brief statement of your disability.

Many ticket offices and banks are fitted with hearing loops to help the hearing-impaired; look for the ear symbol.

The Royal National Institute for the Blind (RNIB; 7388 1266; www.rnib.org.uk; 105 Judd Street, London WC1) can also be contacted via its confidential helpline ☎ 0845 766 9999 (9am-5pm Mon-Fri) and is the best point of initial contact for sight-impaired visitors to London. The Royal Nation Institue for the Deaf (RNID; ☎ freephone 0808 808 0123, freephone/textphone 0808 808 9000; www.rnid.org.uk; 19-23 Featherstone Street, London EC1) is a similar organisation for the deaf and hard of hearing, and publishes a large amount of helpful literature which it mails out for free.

DISCOUNT CARDS

Students studying full time in London are eligible for discounted travel on all London public transport. However, it takes some time to receive your discount card, as it needs to be sent by post for processing – ask for a form to fill out at any tube station. For details on travel cards offering discounts on public transport, p384.

Possibly of most interest to visitors who want to take in lots of sights and attractions is London Pass (www.londonpass.com). Passes start at £12 per day, although they can be altered to include use of the Underground and buses. They offer free entry and queue-jumping to all major attractions – check the website for details of how to select the card you want and how much it will cost.

ELECTRICITY

The standard voltage throughout the UK is 230/240V AC, 50Hz. Plugs have three square pins and can look rather curious to non-Brits. Adaptors for European, Australasian and American electrical items are available at any electrical store.

EMBASSIES

It's important to realise what your own embassy – the embassy of the country of which you are a citizen – can and cannot do to help you if you get into trouble.

Generally, it won't be much help if the trouble you're in is remotely your own fault. Remember that while in London you are bound by British law. Your embassy will not be sympathetic if you end up in prison after committing a crime locally, even if such actions are legal in your own country.

In genuine emergencies you might get some assistance, but only if other channels have been exhausted. For example, if you need to get home urgently, a free ticket home is highly unlikely – the embassy would expect you to have insurance. If you have all your money and documents stolen, it might assist with getting a new passport but a loan for onward travel is almost always out of the question.

The following is a list of selected foreign embassies and high commissions in London. For a more complete list check under 'Embassies & Consulates' in the central London *Yellow Pages* (www.yell.co.uk).

Australia (Map pp426-7; High Commission ☎ 7379 4334; fax 7240 5333, www.australia.org.uk; Australia House, Strand WC2; tube Holborn)

Belgium (Map pp440-1; Embassy ☎ 7470 3700; fax 7259 6213; 103 Eaton Sq SW1; tube Victoria)

Canada (Map p430; High Commission ☎ 7258 6600; fax 7258 6506; www.canada.org.uk; Macdonald House, 1 Grosvenor Sq W1; tube Bond Street)

France (Map pp436-7; Consulate-General ☎ 7838 2055; fax 7838 2046; 6a Cromwell Pl SW7; tube South Kensington)

Germany (Map pp422-3; Embassy ☎ 7824 1300; fax 7824 1435; 23 Belgrave Sq SW1; tube Hyde Park Corner)

Ireland (Map pp426-7; Embassy ☎ 7235 2171; fax 7245 6961; 17 Grosvenor Pl SW1; tube Hyde Park Corner; ☎ 7255 7700; Montpelier House, 106 Brompton Rd SW3; tube South Kensington)

Netherlands (Map pp426-7; Embassy ☎ 7590 3200; fax 7590 3334; 38 Hyde Park Gate SW7; tube High Street Kensington)

New Zealand (Map pp428; High Commission ☎ 7930 8422; fax 7839 4580; www.newzealandhc.org.uk; New Zealand House, 80 Haymarket SW1; tube Piccadilly Circus)

South Africa (Map pp430; High Commission ☎ 7451 7299; fax 7451 7284; www.southafricahouse.com; South Africa House; Trafalgar Sq WC2; tube Trafalgar Square)

Spain (Map pp426-7; Embassy ☎ 7235 5555; 39 Chesham Pl SW1; tube Hyde Park Corner)

USA (Map pp426-7; Embassy ☎ 7499 9000; fax 7495 5012; www.usembassy.org.uk; 5 Upper Grosvenor St W1; tube Bond Street)

EMERGENCIES

Dial ☎ 999 to call the police, fire brigade or ambulance in an emergency. For hospitals with 24-hour accident and emergency departments see p390.

GAY & LESBIAN TRAVELLERS

London is a mecca for gay travellers, who come here for the nightlife and relaxed atmosphere of its cafés and bars. It is rare to encounter any problems with couples sharing rooms or holding hands on the street. However, outside central London, discretion is often the best policy. In the event of an incident, the Metropolitan Police take homophobic crime very seriously indeed, ranking it as a 'hate crime' alongside racial harassment.

The tabloids *Boyz* and *QX*, as well as the more serious *Pink Paper*, are all available free in most gay bars and cafés. They include weekly listings for clubs, bars and other events, and often contain flyers for discounted entry to various venues. Magazines including *Gay Times*, *Diva* and *Attitude* are all available in newsagents throughout London, although some less enlightened proprietors still place them on the top shelf next to the pornography.

Check out the following websites:

www.whatsonwhen.com
www.queenscene.com
www.gaybritain.co.uk
www.rainbownetwork.com
www.gaypride.co.uk
www.londongay.co.uk

For information on gay-friendly taxis, see p382.

HOLIDAYS

Britons don't get a lot of holidays compared with other developed countries, although things are definitely a lot better than they were before the Bank Holidays Act was passed in 1871. Until then employers only allowed their workers to take off Christmas Day and Good Friday.

Public Holidays

Most attractions and businesses close for a couple of days over Christmas, and those that normally shut on Sunday will probably do so on Bank Holiday Mondays.

New Year's Day 1 January
Good Friday/Easter Monday late March/April
May Day Holiday first Monday in May
Spring Bank Holiday last Monday in May
Summer Bank Holiday last Monday in August
Christmas Day/Boxing Day 25 & 26 December

For details of the many festivals London hosts throughout the year, see p10.

School Holidays

These change from year to year and often from school to school. Moreover, public (ie private) school holidays tend to differ from those of state schools. As a general rule, however:

Summer holiday late July–early September
Autumn half term last week of October
Christmas holidays 20 December–6 January
Spring half term one week in mid-February
Easter holidays two weeks either side of Easter Sunday
Summer half term one week end of May/early June

INTERNET ACCESS

Logging onto the Internet shouldn't be a problem – if you have your own laptop you can go online with ease from your hotel room, and if you don't you can drop into any Internet café throughout the capital. The most important thing as a traveller with your own laptop is to buy an adaptor that slots onto the standard telephone cord to fit to the wider, thinner UK phone line. These are available in any hardware or electrical store for about £4. Some of the better-known and centrally located Internet cafés are listed below, but these are a fraction of those available.

BUZZ BAR Map pp422-3
☎ 7460 4906; www.portobellogold.com/internet; 95 Portobello Rd W11; tube Notting Hill Gate; £1/half-hour; 🕑 10am-midnight
Upstairs from the Portobello Gold Hotel, the Buzz Bar has six terminals available and has been pronounced 'the most relaxed internet café in London' by the *Evening Standard*.

CYBERG@TE Map pp420-1
☎ 7387 3810; www.c-gate.com; 3 Leigh St WC1; tube Russell Square; adult/student £1 for 20/30 min; 🕑 9am-11pm Mon-Sat, noon-8pm Sun
Cyberg@te's has another branch at STA Travel (☎ 7383 2282; 117 Euston Rd NW1; 🕑 10am-5pm Mon-Fri, 11am-5pm Sat).

CYBERIA
☎ 7209 0984; www.cyberiacafe.net; 39 Whitfield St W1; tube Goodge Street; 50p for 15 min; 🕑 9am-8pm Mon-Fri, 11am-7pm Sat
Cyberia has 14 terminals and was London's first Internet café.

EASYEVERYTHING Map pp440-1
☎ 7938 1841; www.easyeverything.com; 12-14 Wilton Rd SW1; tube Victoria; £1 for 20 min-1hr depending on time of day; 🕑 24hr
This chain of cybercafés is a division of the no-frills airline easyJet. Other branches include: **Tottenham Court Road** (Map p428; 9-16 Tottenham Court Rd W1; tube Tottenham Court Rd); **Kensington** (Map pp422-3; 160-166 Kensington High St W8; tube Kensington High St); **Oxford Circus** (Map p428; 358 Oxford St W1; tube Oxford Circus); **Trafalgar Square** (Map p430; 7 Strand WC2; tube Charing Cross); **Baker Street** (Map pp422-3; 122 Baker St, inside McDonald's; tube Baker Street); **Piccadilly Circus** (Map p428; 46 Regent St, inside Burger King; tube Piccadilly Circus) and

King's Road (Map pp436-7; Unit G1, King's Walk, 120 King's Rd; tube Sloane Square)

INTERNET EXCHANGE Map p428

☎ 7437 3704; www.internet-exchange.co.uk; London Trocadero, 1st floor, Piccadilly Circus W1; tube Piccadilly Circus; £3/4.20/hour 10am-noon/noon-midnight or £1.50/hr members, £1.50/half-hour nonmembers; 🕑 10am-midnight

This chain has branches as ubiquitous as those of easyEverything. Branches include **Covent Garden** (Map p430; ☎ 7836 8636; 37 The Market WC2; tube Covent Garden) and **Bayswater** (Map pp422-3; ☎ 7792 5790; 47-49 Queensway W2; tube Bayswater).

INTERNET LOUNGE Map pp436-7

☎ 7370 5742; 24a Earl's Court Gardens SW5; tube Earl's Court; £1 for 50 min; 🕑 9am-midnight

USIT CAMPUS Map pp440-1

☎ 0870 240 1010; www.usitnow.ie/services/uk.htm; 52 Grosvenor Gardens SW1; tube Victoria; £1/hr; 🕑 9am-6pm Mon-Fri, 10am-5pm Sat, 11am-3pm Sun

VIBE BAR Map pp432-3

☎ 7247 3479, 7377 2899; www.vibe bar.co.uk; The Brewery, 91-95 Brick Lane E1; tube Shoreditch/Aldgate East; usage free; 🕑 11am-midnight Mon-Sat, noon-midnight Sun

Seven terminals are available at no charge to customers.

VIRGIN MEGASTORE Map p428

☎ 7631 1234; 14-30 Oxford St W1; tube Tottenham Court Road; £1/50 min 9.30am-noon, £1/25 min noon-10pm; 🕑 9.30am-10pm Mon-Sat, noon-6pm Sun

This huge record store has access on 20 terminals.

LEGAL MATTERS

Should you face any legal difficulties while in London visit any one of the **Citizens Advice Bureaux** (www.nacab.org.uk) listed under 'Counselling & Advice' in the *Yellow Pages* or you can contact the **Community Legal Services Directory** (☎ 0845 608 1122; www.justask.org.uk).

Driving Offences

The laws against drink-driving have become tougher and are treated more seriously than they used to be. Currently you're allowed to have a blood-alcohol level of 35mg/100mL but there's talk of reducing the limit. The safest approach is not to drink anything at all if you're planning to drive.

Drugs

Illegal drugs of every type are widely available in London, especially in clubs. Nonetheless, all the usual drug dangers apply and there have been several high-profile deaths associated with ecstasy, the purity of which is often dubious. Cannabis has recently been reclassified as a Class C drug, which means possessing small quantities will not result in the user being arrested. However, there are still stiff penalties for dealing and handling large amounts of the drug. No other drugs have been reassessed, and be warned that other drugs are treated much more seriously.

Fines

In general you rarely have to cough up on the spot for an offence. The exceptions are trains, the tube and buses, where people who can't produce a valid ticket for the journey when asked to by an inspector can be fined there and then – £5 on buses and £10 on trains and the tube. No excuses are accepted.

At the time of writing, the British government was in the process of giving police new powers to impose on-the-spot fines for antisocial behaviour. These run from £40 for being drunk and disorderly, buying alcohol for under-18s or throwing fireworks in the street, to £80 for making false 999 calls or wasting police time.

MAPS

The *London A-Z* series produces a range of excellent maps and handheld street atlases. All areas of London mapped on this system can be accessed at www.streetmap.co.uk, one of London's most invaluable websites.

Lonely Planet also publishes a *London City Map*.

Stanford's Bookshop (Map p430; ☎ 7836 1321; 12-14 Long Acre; tube Covent Garden) has the widest selection of London maps on sale.

Other good bookshops with a wide selection of maps include **Foyles** (☎ 7437 5660; 113-119 Charing Cross Road WC2), **Waterstones** (☎ 7851 2400; 203-206 Piccadilly W1) and **Daunt's Bookshop** (☎ 7224 2295; 83 Marylebone High St W1).

MEDICAL SERVICES

Reciprocal arrangements with the UK allow residents of Australia, nationals of New Zealand, and residents and nationals of several other countries to receive free emergency medical treatment and subsidised dental care through the **National Health Service** (NHS; ☎ 0845 4647; www.nhsdirect.nhs.uk). They can use hospital emergency departments, GPs and dentists (check the *Yellow Pages*). Visitors of 12 months or longer, with the proper documentation, will receive care under the NHS by registering with a specific practice near their residence.

EU nationals can obtain free emergency treatment on presentation of an E111 form that has been validated in their home country.

Travel insurance, however, is advisable as it offers greater flexibility over where and how you're treated and covers expenses for an ambulance and repatriation that won't be picked up by the NHS.

HOSPITALS

The following hospitals have 24-hour accident and emergency departments:

Charing Cross Hospital (Map pp416-17; ☎ 8846 1234; Fulham Palace Rd W6; tube Hammersmith)

Chelsea & Westminster Hospital (Map p436-7; ☎ 8746 8000; 369 Fulham Rd SW10; tube South Kensington, then bus No 14 or 211)

Guy's Hospital (Map pp432-3; ☎ 7955 5000; St Thomas St SE1; tube London Bridge)

Homerton Hospital (Map pp416-17; ☎ 8919 5555; Homerton Row E9; rail Homerton)

Royal Free Hospital (Map p415; ☎ 7794 0500; Pond St NW3; tube Belsize Park)

Royal London Hospital (Map pp432-3; ☎ 7377 7000; Whitechapel Rd E1; tube Whitechapel)

University College Hospital (Map pp418-19; ☎ 7387 9300; Grafton Way WC1; tube Euston Square)

DENTAL SERVICES

To find an emergency dentist phone the **Dental Emergency Care Service** (☎ 7955 2186) between 8.45am and 3.30pm Monday to Friday, or call into **Eastman Dental Hospital** (☎ 7915 1000; 256 Gray's Inn Rd WC1; tube King's Cross).

METRIC SYSTEM

People in London use both the metric and imperial systems interchangeably. Some older people will not readily comprehend metric measurements and, similarly, some younger people will not readily understand imperial. To convert kilometres to miles, multiply by 0.062; to convert metres to feet, multiply by 3.28. To convert kilos to pounds, multiply by 2.2.

MONEY

Despite being a member of the EU, the UK has not signed up to the euro and has retained the pound sterling as its unit of currency. One pound sterling is made up of 100 pence (pronounced 'pee', colloquially). Notes come in denominations of £5, £10, £20 and £50, while coins are 1p, 2p, 5p, 10p, 20p, 50p, £1 and £2. Unless otherwise noted, all prices in this book are in pounds sterling. See p28 for an idea of the cost of living in London.

The pound is a stable and generally strong currency. In summer 2003 it stood at US$1.57, A$2.46, €1.44, C$2.21 and NZ$2.75. You can check out the latest rates on websites such as www.xe.com and www.oanda.com.

ATMs are a way of life in London, as the huge queues by them on Saturday nights in the West End attest. There is no area in London unserved by them, and they accept cards from any bank in the world that is tied into the Visa, MasterCard, Cirrus or Maestro systems, as well as some other more obscure ones. After a national campaign, most banks now allow their card holders to withdraw money from other banks' ATMs without charge, and vice versa. However, those without UK high-street bank cards should be warned that there is nearly always a transaction surcharge for cash withdrawals. You should contact your bank to find out how much this is before using ATMs too freely.

You can change money in most high-street banks and some travel agent chains, as well as at the numerous bureaux de change throughout the city. Compare rates and watch for the commission that is not always mentioned. The trick is to ask how many pounds you'll receive in all before committing – you'll lose nothing by shopping around.

Credit and debit cards are accepted almost universally in London, from restaurants and bars to shops and even some taxis. American Express and Diner's Club are less widely used than Visa and MasterCard, while most Londoners simply live off their Switch debit cards that can also be used to get 'cash back' from supermarkets, which saves making a trip to an ATM if you are low on cash.

NEWSPAPERS & MAGAZINES

Newspapers

For a good selection of foreign-language newspapers, try the newsstands in the Victoria Place shopping centre at Victoria train station, along Charing Cross Rd, in Old Compton St and along Queensway. See p387 for details of gay and lesbian publications.

DAILY PAPERS

Daily Express Middle-level tabloid.

Daily Mail Middle-level tabloid.

Daily Record Tabloid.

Daily Star Tabloid.

Daily Telegraph Broadsheet that far outsells its rivals. Excellent writing and world coverage.

Evening Standard Heavy focus on London news, with international and national events when they merit coverage.

Financial Times Business-oriented with a great travel section in its weekend edition.

Guardian Mildly left-wing and read by the liberal middle class – its review of the world media, *Editor*, which comes out as a supplement every Saturday, is required reading for anyone who wants to know what's happening outside Old Blighty. The Guide entertainment supplement (also with Saturday's *Guardian*) is worthwhile.

The Independent Politically correct (some say too much) and drier than an old bone in the Sahara.

International Herald Tribune Paris based and arguably the best brief source of international news available.

London Review of Books

Metro A marketing success story, *Metro* is a free paper produced by the publishers of the Daily Mail and given out free every morning at tube and train stations. You are most likely to find a used copy on the seat of a tube train later on in the day, as most copies have disappeared from the stands by 10am. Newswires of national and international news, but nothing heavy – lots of celebrity stories with TV listings and sport inside.

Mirror Fierce competitor to the *Sun*.

Sun Labour-supporting and gossip-loving tabloid.

The Times Conservative and influential, with good travel and sports sections.

SUNDAY PAPERS

News of the World Sister to the *Sun*, this is the ultimate scandal mag, with an enormous readership. Anathema to most literate liberal thinkers, its campaigns to unmask paedophiles, and its 'scoops' by investigative journalists – including the 'kidnap attempt' on Victoria Beckham and tricking the Countess of Wessex into promising royal connections – are legendary.

Observer Sunday-only paper similar in tone and style to the *Guardian*, which owns it.

Sunday Times Full of scandal and fashion. Probably destroys at least one rainforest per issue, but most of it can be arguably tossed in the recycling bin upon purchase.

Magazines

Good places to stock up are the kiosks in the mainline stations, where *Time* and *Newsweek* are also available.

Cosmopolitan

Dazed and Confused Jefferson Hack's bible of cool, where Rankin made his name as the ultimate 90s celebrity-portrait photographer. Good for fashion and the latest London buzz.

Elle

FHM 'For Him Magazine' is the ultimate lad's mag. Busty blonds on the cover and some vaguely sensible articles, as well as gadgets, cars and toilet humour.

Glamour

Heat The celebrity magazine that has out-manoeuvred its rivals and become a staple of doctors' waiting rooms and dental offices throughout the country.

i-D Once an über-cool London fashion/music gospel, *i-D* has gradually faded from the forefront of the scene, but still puts up a good fight.

I-Style

Loaded *FHM*'s major rival and a tongue-in-cheek look at everything blokey. A launch pad for seminaked female no-talents whose cover picture usually guarantees them a job in daytime television or a Top 40 single.

Loot This paper appears five times a week and is made up of classified ads placed free by sellers. You can find everything from kitchen sinks to cars, as well as an extensive selection of flat and house-share ads.

Marie Claire

Maxim

New Statesman Founded by Fabians Sidney and Beatrice Webb, this left-wing intellectual rag seems to go from strength to strength despite Labour's recent period in power. This is a favourite with middle-class liberal intellectuals and features some of the best writing on current events in Britain and abroad.

Private Eye (see p26) Satirical, rather public-school biweekly that gives a refreshing new perspective on the news. Many of its nicknames have become daily vernacular to Londoners – from the *Grauniad* (referring to the notoriously badly copy-edited *Guardian* newspaper) to Piers Moron (the *Eye*'s name for archnemesis *Daily Mirror* editor Piers Morgon). May be largely incomprehensible to a non-British readership, but is worth a shot for the front page alone.

Spectator Established in 1828, this traditionally upper-class right-wing magazine veers between tongue-in-cheek and very serious writing. It is edited by Tory MP and fop Boris Johnson, and attracts many big-name writers with controversial slants on politics. Worth its cover price for Mary Killen's hilarious etiquette problem page alone, providing the readership with answers to burning questions such as 'what puddings are currently fashionable?'

Time Out The London events magazine published every Wednesday – a complete listing of what's on and where.

TNT Magazine; Southern Cross; SA Times The weekly freebies with Australasian and South African news and sports results. Invaluable for any budget traveller, with entertainment listings, travel sections and useful classifieds covering jobs, cheap tickets, shipping services and accommodation. They can be picked up outside tube stations, mainly in Earl's Court, Notting Hill and Bayswater. *TNT Magazine* (www.tnt-live.com) is the glossiest and most comprehensive; ring ☎ 7373 3377 for the nearest distribution point.

Vogue

Wallpaper Created by the unlikely sounding Tyler Brûlé, *Wallpaper* was a huge '90s success story, creating a niche for a brand new kind of aspirant lifestyle magazine. Aimed at those with tonnes of cash, cheekbones and a love of chrome.

PHARMACIES

There's always one neighbourhood chemist that's open 24 hours, or you can check the *Yellow Pages* for one near you. Since all medication is readily available, either over the counter or on prescription, there's no need to stock up.

Most people will be instantly struck by the almost total monopoly enjoyed by Boots the Chemist. The Superdrug chain is the only potential rival, and individual dispensing pharmacies often lose out to the increasingly corporate face of UK medicine dispensing. That said, Boots are by far the best supplied and largest pharmacies in London, selling everything from hair dryers to camera film.

POST

Once the pride of Britain, the privatisation of the post office has resulted in the downgrading of a once superb delivery service. It's still generally very reliable, but it is no longer possible to take for granted the speed and accuracy that once was its hallmark.

For general postal enquiries ring ☎ 0845 722 3344 or visit www.royalmail.co.uk.

RATES

Domestic 1st-class mail is quicker but more expensive (28/42p per letter up to 60/100g) than 2nd class (20/34p).

Postcards and letters up to 20g cost a uniform 36p to send anywhere in Europe; to almost everywhere else, including the Americas and Australasia, it's 47/68p up to 10/20g. Packets and parcels up to 100/200g cost 89p/£1.34 to Europe and £1.17/2-2.13 to everywhere else. They must be taken to the post office for weighing.

Airmail letters to the USA or Canada generally take three to five days; to Australia or New Zealand, allow five days to a week.

POSTE RESTANTE

Unless you (or the person writing to you) specify otherwise, poste restante mail sent to London ends up at the Trafalgar Square post office (tube Charing Cross), 24–28 William IV St, WC2. It opens 8am to 8pm Monday to Saturday and 9am to 8pm on Saturday. Mail will be held for four weeks; ID is required. Amex offices will also hold clients' mail for free.

POSTCODES

The London postal code system is a remnant of the First World War and confuses Londoners themselves. The whole city is divided up into districts notated by a letter (or letters) and a number. For example, W1, the Mayfair and Soho postcode, stands for 'West London, district 1'. EC1, on the other hand, stands for East Central London, district 1. The numbers are assigned alphabetically throughout the districts and make little logical sense. However, postcodes are a good way of differentiating London streets that have identical names. For example, Harrow Road exists in E6, E11, NW10, W2, W10 and W9!

RADIO

For a taste of London on the airwaves, tune into the following stations:

BBC London Live (94.9kHz FM) Talk station with a London bias.

Capital FM (95.8kHz FM) The commercial equivalent of the BBC's Radio 1 and the most popular pop station in the city.

Capital Gold (1548kHz AM) Plays oldies from the '60s, '70s and '80s.

Choice FM (96.9kHz FM) Soul station.

Classic FM (100.9kHz FM) Yes, it's classical music.

Jazz FM (102.2kHz FM) For middle-of-the-road jazz and blues aficionados.

Kiss 100 (100kHz FM) Dance station.

LONDON POSTCODES

0 — 5 km
0 — 3 mi

To read a postcode from this map, determine lettered prefix **E** and add numbered suffix 3

Bow's postcode is E3, for example

— Prefix boundary
Suffix boundary

LBC (1152kHz AM) A talkback channel.

Magic FM (105.4kHz FM) Plays mainstream oldies.

News Direct (97.3kHz FM) An all-news station with full reports every 20 minutes.

Talk Sport (1089kHz AM) Self-descriptive!

Virgin (105.8kHz FM) Pop station.

Xfm (104.9kHz FM) An alternative, and generally very good, radio station that plays indie music.

TAXES & REFUNDS

Value-added tax (VAT) is a 17.5% sales tax levied on most goods and services except food, books and children's clothing. Restaurants must, by law, include VAT in their menu prices.

It's sometimes possible for visitors to claim a refund of VAT paid on goods, resulting in considerable saving. You're eligible if you have spent fewer than 365 days out of the two years prior to making the purchase living in the UK, and if you're leaving the EU within three months of making the purchase.

Not all shops participate in the VAT refund scheme, called the Retail Export Scheme or Tax-Free Shopping, and different shops will have different minimum purchase conditions (normally around £75 in any one shop). On request, participating shops will give you a special form (VAT 407). This must be presented with the goods and receipts to customs when you depart (VAT-free goods can't be posted or shipped home). After customs has certified the form, it should be returned to the shop for a refund (minus an administration or handling fee), which takes about eight to 10 weeks to come through.

TELEPHONE

British Telecom's (BT's) famous red phone boxes survive in conservation areas only (notably Westminster), while some private phone companies have painted theirs black and installed them around Piccadilly and Charing Cross. More common these days are the glass cubicles with phones that accept coins, phonecards and/or credit cards.

BT offers £3, £5, £10 and £20 phonecards that are widely available from retailers including most post offices and newsagents. A digital display on the telephone indicates how much credit is left on the card.

The following are some important telephone numbers and codes:

International dialling code	☎ 00
Local and national directory enquiries	☎ 118 500
International directory enquiries	☎ 153
Local and national operator	☎ 100
International operator	☎ 155
Reverse-charge/collect calls	☎ 155
Time	☎ 123
Weathercall (Greater London)	☎ 0906 654 3268

Be advised that some of the numbers above are charged calls. Some special phone codes worth knowing include:

Toll-free	☎ 0500/0800
Local call rate applies	☎ 0845
National call rate applies	☎ 0870
Premium rate applies (from 60p per minute)	☎ 09

Calling London

London's area code is 020 followed by an eight-digit number beginning with 7 or 8. You only need to dial the 020 when you are calling London from elsewhere in the UK.

To call London from abroad, dial your country's international access code, then 44 (the UK's country code), then 20 (dropping the initial 0) followed by the eight-digit phone number.

Local & National Call Rates

Local calls are charged by time alone; regional and national calls are charged by both time and distance. Daytime rates apply from 8am to 6pm Monday to Friday; the cheap rate applies from 6pm to 8am Monday to Friday; and the cheap weekend rate applies from midnight Friday to midnight Sunday. The last two rates offer substantial savings.

Calls to local and national directory enquiries cost 11p per minute from public phones (minimum deposit of 20p) and 40p from private phones.

International Calls & Rates

International direct dialling (IDD) calls to almost anywhere can be made from nearly all public telephones. To call someone outside the UK dial 00, then the country code, then the area code (you usually drop the initial zero if there is one) and then the number. For example, to ring Melbourne, where the area code is 03 and the code for Australia is 61, you would dial 00-61-3-1234 5678. To reach Boston, where area code is 617 and the code for the USA is 1, dial 00-1-617-123 4567.

Direct dialling is cheaper than making a reverse-charge (collect) call through the international operator (☎ 155). International directory enquiries (☎ 153) cost a whopping £1.50 per minute from private phones.

Some private firms such as Callshop offer cheaper international calls than BT. Try the Earl's Court branch of **Callshop** (Map pp436-7; ☎ 7390 4549; 181a Earl's Court Rd SW5; tube Earl's Court; ☽ 9am-11pm); in such shops you phone from a metered booth and then pay the bill. Some cybercafés and Internet access shops, such as Internet Lounge in Earl's Court, also offer cheap rates for international calls.

It's also possible to undercut BT international call rates by buying a special card (usually denominated £5, £10 or £20) with a PIN that you use from any phone, even a home phone, by dialling a special access number. There are dozens of cards available – with bizarre names such as Alpha, Omega, Banana Call, First National and Swiftlink – available from newsagents and grocers. To decide which is best you really have to compare the rate each offers for the particular country you want – posters with the rates of the various companies are often displayed in shop doors or windows.

Directory – Practicalities

Mobile Phones

The UK uses the GSM 900 network, which covers the rest of Europe, Australia and New Zealand, but is not compatible with the North American GSM 1900 or the totally different system in Japan (though many North Americans have GSM 1900/900 phones that do work here). If you have a GSM phone, check with your service provider about using it in the UK, and beware of calls being routed internationally (very expensive for a local call). You can also rent one from various companies, including **Mobell** (☎ 0800 243 524; www.mobell.com) and **Cellhire** (☎ 0870 561 0610; www.cellhire.com) from around £20 per week, depending on the hire period. In this case, however, you can't use your existing number.

TELEVISION

BBC1 Fame Academy, Walking with Dinosaurs, Eastenders

BBC2 Weakest Link, University Challenge, Newsnight

ITV Pop Idol, Who Wants to be a Millionaire, Tonight with Trevor Mcdonald, Stars in Their Eyes, Blind Date, Coronation Street, The Bill

C4 Countdown, Big Brother, Eurotrash, Hollyoaks, Channel 4 News, 15-to-1, Friends

C5 Mainly reruns of '80s B-movies

TIME

Wherever you are in the world, the time on your watch is measured in relation to the time at Greenwich in London – Greenwich Mean Time (GMT). British Summer Time, the UK's form of daylight-saving time, muddies the water so that even London is ahead of GMT from late March to late October. To give you an idea, San Francisco is usually eight hours and New York five hours behind GMT, while Sydney is 10 hours ahead of GMT. Phone the international operator on ☎ 155 to find out the exact difference.

TIPPING

Many restaurants now add a 'discretionary' service charge to your bill, but in places that don't you are expected to leave a 10% to 15% tip unless the service was unsatisfactory. Waiting staff are often paid derisory wages on the assumption that the money will be supplemented by tips. It's legal for restaurants to include a service charge in the bill but this should be clearly advertised. You needn't add a further tip (for more information on tipping in restaurants, p222). You never tip to have your pint pulled in a pub but staff at bars now often return change in a little metal dish, expecting some of the coins to glue themselves to the bottom.

If you take a boat trip on the Thames you'll find some guides and/or drivers importuning for a tip in return for their commentary. Whether you pay is up to you. See p382 for information on tipping taxi drivers.

TOILETS

Although many toilets in central London are still pretty grim, those at main train stations, bus terminals and attractions are generally good and usually have facilities for disabled people and those with young children. At train and bus stations you usually have to pay 20p to use the facilities, which is pretty irksome when you consider how much rail fares are. You also have to pay to use the self-cleaning concrete pods in places such as Leicester Square (and, yes, they do open automatically after a set amount of time, so no hanky-panky – or at least make it snappy).

In theory it's an offence to urinate in the streets, but arrests are rare. However, with the streets of Soho so frequently stinking of urine, Westminster council has pioneered an excellent scheme whereby public urinals are set up on the streets at weekends for those who can't make it to the next bar without relieving themselves. These can be found on Soho Square, Wardour Street and on the Strand, among other locations.

For information on toilets for the disabled, p386.

TOURIST INFORMATION

London is a major travel centre, so along with information on London, tourist offices can help with England, Scotland, Wales, Ireland and most countries worldwide.

Local Tourist Offices

TOURIST INFORMATION CENTRES

The tourist information centres (TICs) run by London Tourist Board (LTB) deal with direct queries and walk-in customers only; telephone enquiries are not possible. You can, however, phone LTB general enquiries (☎ 7932 2000) or make use of their London Line (☎ 0906 866 3344; premium-rate calls 60p/minute), which can fill you in on everything from tourist attractions and events (such as the Changing of the Guard) to river trips and tours, accommodation, eating, theatre, shopping, children's London and gay and lesbian venues. The LTB's comprehensive website is at www.londontouristboard.com.

As well as providing information, London's main TIC, in the forecourt of Victoria train station (Map pp440-1; tube Victoria; ☿ 8am-8pm Mon-Sat & 8am-6pm Sun Apr-Oct, 8am-6pm Mon-Sat & 9am-4pm Sun Nov-Mar), handles accommodation and travel bookings and can arrange national coach and theatre tickets. It can get positively mobbed in the peak season and in the past some staff have been less than welcoming.

There are much more helpful TICs in the arrivals hall at Waterloo International Terminal (Map pp426-7; tube Waterloo; ☿ 8.30am-10.30pm) and at Liverpool Street station (Map pp432-3; tube Liverpool Street; ☿ 8am-6pm). There's a TIC at the Heathrow Terminals 1, 2 & 3 Underground station (☿ 8am-6pm). Gatwick, Stansted, Luton and London City airports, Paddington train station and Victoria Coach Station all have information desks.

The City of London also has an **information centre** (Map pp432-3; ☎ 7332 1456; www.city oflondon.gov.uk; St Paul's Churchyard EC4, opposite St Paul's Cathedral; tube St Paul's; ☿ 9.30am-5pm Apr-Sep, 9.30am-5pm Mon-Fri & 9.30am-12.30pm Sat Oct-Mar).

A few London boroughs and neighbourhoods have their own TICs. These include:

Clerkenwell
☎ 7251 6311; fax 7689 3661; 53 Clerkenwell Close EC1R 0EA

Greenwich Map p435
☎ 0870 608200; fax 8853 4607; Pepys House, Old Royal Naval College, King William Walk SW10 9NN

Richmond
☎ 8940 9125; fax 8940 6899; Old Town Hall, Whittaker Ave, Richmond, Surrey TW9 1TP

Tower Hamlets Map p342-3
☎ 7364 4971; fax 7375 2539; 18 Lamb St E1 6EA

BRITAIN VISITOR CENTRE
This comprehensive **information and booking centre** (Map p428; 1 Regent St SW1; tube Piccadilly Circus; ☿ 9.30am-6.30pm Mon, 9am-6.30pm Tue-Fri & 10am-4pm Sat & Sun, 10am-5pm Sat Jun-Sep) includes the tourist boards of Wales, Scotland, Northern Ireland, the Irish Republic and Jersey as well as a branch of Stanford's map and guidebook shop on the ground floor. As with the TICs, it deals with walk-in enquiries only.

On the mezzanine level you'll find a **First Option** outlet, where you can arrange accommodation and tours as well as train, air and car travel, **Globaltickets** theatre ticket agency, a bureau de change, international telephones and a few computer terminals for accessing tourist information on the Web.

If you're not in the area and need information about Britain or Ireland ring British Tourist Authority (BTA) general enquiries on ☎ 8846 9000 or consult the BTA website at www.visitbritain.com.

VISAS
At present, citizens of Australia, Canada, New Zealand, South Africa and the USA are given, at their point of arrival, 'leave to enter' the UK for up to six months but are prohibited from working unless they secure a work permit. If you're a citizen of the EU, you don't need a visa to enter the country and may live and work here freely for as long as you like.

Visa regulations are always subject to change, so it's essential to check with your local British embassy, high commission or consulate before leaving home.

Immigration authorities in the UK are tough – dress neatly and be able to prove that you have sufficient funds to support yourself. A credit card and/or an onward ticket will help.

Visa Extensions
Tourist visas can only be extended in clear emergencies (eg an accident, death of a relative). Otherwise you'll have to leave the UK (perhaps going to Ireland or France) and apply for a fresh one, although this tactic will arouse suspicion after the second or third visa. To extend (or attempt to extend) your stay in the UK, ring the **Visa & Passport Information Line** (☎ 0870 606 7766 or 8649 7878; the Home Office's Immigration & Nationality Directorate, Lunar House, 40 Wellesley Rd, Croydon CR9 2BY; rail East

Croydon; 🕑 10am-noon & 2-4pm Mon-Fri) *before your current visa expires*. The process takes a few days in France/Ireland. Trying to extend within the UK takes a lot longer (no time scale).

Student Visas

Nationals of EU countries can enter the country to study without formalities. Otherwise you need to be enrolled in a full-time course of at least 15 hours per week of weekday, daytime study at a single educational institution to be allowed to remain as a student. For more details, consult the British embassy, high commission or consulate in your own country.

WOMEN TRAVELLERS

In general, London is a fairly laid-back place, and you're unlikely to have too many problems provided you take the usual city precautions. Apart from the occasional wolf whistle and unwelcome body contact on the tube, women will find male Londoners reasonably enlightened. There's nothing to stop women going into pubs alone, though this is not necessarily a comfortable experience even in central London. For details of the women-only taxi service, p382.

Safety Precautions

Solo women travellers should have few problems, although common sense caution should be observed, especially at night. It's particularly unwise to get into an Underground carriage with no-one else in it or with just one or two men, and there are a few tube stations, especially on the far reaches of the Northern Line, where you won't feel comfortable late at night. The same goes for some of the mainline stations in the south (such as Lambeth) and southeast (such as Bromley), which may be unstaffed and look pretty grim. In such cases you should hang the expense and take a taxi.

Information & Organisations

The Well Women Centre

Map pp426-7; ☎ 0845 300 8090; Marie Stopes House, 108 Whitfield St W1; tube Warren Street; 🕑 9am-5pm Thu-Mon, 9am-8pm Tue & Wed) Offers advice on contraception and pregnancy.

The Rape & Sexual Abuse Helpline

☎ 8239 1122; 🕑 noon-2.30pm, 7-9.30pm Mon-Fri & 2.30-5pm Sat & Sun

WORK

Even if you're unskilled you'll almost certainly find work in London, but you will have to be prepared to work long hours at menial jobs for relatively low pay. The trouble is, though, that without skills it's difficult to find a job that pays well enough to save money. You should be able to break even but will probably be better off saving in your home country. Remember also that you will be competing with recent arrivals from Eastern Europe, particularly Poles and nationals of the former Yugoslav republics.

Traditionally, unskilled visitors have worked in pubs and restaurants and as nannies. Both jobs often provide live-in accommodation, but the hours are long, the work exhausting and the pay not so good. A minimum wage (£4.10 per hour; £3.20 for those aged 18 to 21) was introduced in April 1999, but if you're working under the table no-one's obliged to pay you even that. Before you accept a job, make sure you're clear about the terms and conditions, especially how many (and which) hours you will be expected to work.

Accountants, health professionals, journalists, computer programmers, lawyers, teachers, bankers and clerical workers with computer experience stand a better chance of finding well-paid work. Even so, you'll probably need to have saved some money to tide you over while you search. Don't forget copies of your qualifications, references (which will probably be checked) and a CV (résumé).

Teachers should contact the individual London borough councils, which have separate education departments, although some schools recruit directly.

To work as a trained nurse or midwife you have to register (£56) with the United Kingdom Nursing & Midwifery Council, a long process that can take up to three months. Write to the Overseas Registration Department, UKNMC, 23 Portland Place, London W1N 4JT, or phone ☎ 7333 9333. If you aren't registered then you can still work as an auxiliary nurse.

The free *TNT Magazine* is a good starting point for jobs and agencies aimed at travellers. For au pair and nanny work buy the quaintly titled *The Lady*. Also check the *Evening Standard*, the national newspapers and government-operated Jobcentres, which are scattered throughout London and listed under 'Employment Services' in the phone directory. Whatever your skills, it's worth registering with a few temporary agencies.

If you play a musical instrument or have other artistic talents, you could try working the streets. As every Peruvian pipe-player (and his fifth cousin once removed) knows, busking is fairly common in London. It is now legal to perform in certain train and Underground stations provided the busker secures a licence (£20 per year) from Transport for London, which requires an audition. Buskers are assigned a marked pitch, where they can perform at specified times. The borough councils are also moving to license buskers at top tourist attractions and popular areas like Covent Garden and Leicester Square. You will still be able to play elsewhere, but those areas will be off-limits to anyone without a permit.

Tax

As an official employee, you'll find income tax and National Insurance are automatically deducted from your weekly pay packet. However, the deductions will be calculated on the assumption that you're working for the entire financial year (which runs from 6 April to 5 April). If you don't work as long as that, you may be eligible for a refund. Contact the **Board of Inland Revenue** (☎ 667 4001; Bush House, SW Wing, Strand WC2) or use one of the agencies that advertise in *TNT Magazine* (but check their fee or percentage charge first).

Work Permits

EU nationals don't need a work permit to work in London but everyone else does. If the main purpose of your visit is to work, you have to be sponsored by a British company.

However, if you're a citizen of a Commonwealth country and aged between 17 and 27, you may apply for a Working Holiday Entry Certificate, which allows you to spend up to two years in the UK and take work that is 'incidental' to a holiday. You're not allowed to engage in business, pursue a career or provide services as a professional sportsperson or entertainer.

You must apply to your country's British consulate or high commission before departure – Working Holiday Entry Certificates are not granted on arrival in Britain. It is not possible to switch from being a visitor to a working holidaymaker, nor can you claim back any time spent out of the UK during the two-year period. When you apply, you must satisfy the authorities that you have the means to pay for a return or onward journey and that you will be able to maintain yourself without recourse to public funds.

If you're a Commonwealth citizen and have a parent born in the UK, you may be eligible for a Certificate of Entitlement to the Right of Abode, which means you can live and work in Britain free of immigration control.

If you're a Commonwealth citizen with a grandparent born in the UK, or if the grandparent was born before 31 March 1922 in what is now the Republic of Ireland, you may qualify for a UK Ancestry Employment Certificate, which means you can work in the UK full time for up to four years.

Students from the USA who are at least 18 years old and studying full time at a college or university can get a Blue Card permit allowing them to work in the UK for six months. It costs US$250 and is available through the **British Universities North America Club** (BUNAC; ☎ 203 264 0901; wib@bunacusa.com; PO Box 430; Southbury CT 06488). Once in the UK, BUNAC can help Blue Card holders find jobs, accommodation and so on. BUNAC also runs programmes for Australians, Canadians and New Zealanders but you must apply before leaving home. For more details visit www.bunac.org.

If you have any queries once you're in the UK, contact the Home Office's Immigration & Nationality Directorate (p396).

Behind the Scenes

THE LONELY PLANET STORY

The story begins with a classic travel adventure: Tony and Maureen Wheeler's 1972 journey across Europe and Asia to Australia. There was no useful information about the overland trail then, so Tony and Maureen published the first Lonely Planet guidebook to meet a growing need.

From a kitchen table, Lonely Planet has grown to become the largest independent travel publisher in the world, with offices in Melbourne (Australia), Oakland (USA), London (UK) and Paris (France).

Today Lonely Planet guidebooks cover the globe. There is an ever-growing list of books and information in a variety of media. Some things haven't changed. The main aim is still to make it possible for adventurous travellers to get out there – to explore and better understand the world.

At Lonely Planet we believe travellers can make a positive contribution to the countries they visit – if they respect their host communities and spend their money wisely.

THIS BOOK

This edition was written by Martin Hughes, Sarah Johnstone & Tom Masters. The previous edition (third) of *London* was written by Steve Fallon. The first and second editions were written by Pat Yale. The guide was commissioned in Lonely Planet's London office, and produced by:

Commissioning Editor Amanda Canning
Coordinating Editor Simon Sellars
Coordinating Cartographer Jolyon Philcox
Coordinating Layout Designer Nicholas Stebbing
Editors & Proofreaders Imogen Bannister, Yvonne Byron, Melanie Dankel, Barbara Delissen, Joanne Newell, Stephanie Pearson, Diana Saad, Linda Suttie
Cartographers Joelene Kowalski, Wayne Murphy, Sarah Sloane, Simon Tillema
Layout Designers Pablo Gastar, Patrick Marris, Jacqui Saunders, Dianne Zammit
Cover Designer Maria Vallianos
Series Designer Nic Lehman
Series Design Concept Nic Lehman & Andrew Weatherill
Layout Manager Adriana Mammarella
Managing Cartographer Mark Griffiths
Managing Editor Martin Heng
Mapping Development Paul Piaia
Project Manager Andrew Weatherill
Regional Publishing Manager Katrina Browning
Series Publishing Manager Gabrielle Green
Series Development Team Jenny Blake, Anna Bolger, Fiona Christie, Kate Cody, Erin Corrigan, Janine Eberle, Simone Egger, James Ellis, Nadine Fogale, Roz Hopkins, Dave McClymont, Leonie Mugavin, Rachel Peart, Ed Pickard, Michele Posner, Howard Ralley, Dani Valent, Andrew Weatherill
Thanks to Ryan Evans, Kate McDonald, Darren O'Connell, Kalya Ryan

Cover Front: Great Court, British Museum – Neil Setchfield (top); Oxo Building – Doug McKinlay (bottom). Back: Canary Wharf Underground Station – Neil Setchfield.

Internal photographs by Lonely Planet Images and Neil Setchfield except for the following: p276 Juliet Coombe; p294 Elliot Daniel; p361 Christina Dameyer; p95 Lee Foster; p373 Veronica Garbutt; p65 Manfred Gottschalk; p161, p190, p363 Charlotte Hindle; p292 Richard I'Anson; p182 Doug McKinlay; p103 Martin Moos; p203 Guy Moberly; p153 (#6) Christine Osborne; p201, p368 David Tomlinson; p216 Lawrence Worcester. All images are the copyright of the photographers unless otherwise indicated. Many of the images in this guide are available for licensing from Lonely Planet Images: www.lonelyplanetimages.com.

ACKNOWLEDGMENTS

London Underground map: London Transport Museum © 2003.

THANKS
MARTIN

To Kirsti, Jeremy, Jane, Sean, Ardal, Melanie, Amanda, Emma, Marco, Gianfranco Zola and coauthors Sarah and Tom. Also, big thanks to Amanda, Fiona and Tom in the London office for their time, effort and expertise.

TOM

To everyone I know who make London the best place on earth, and especially Gray Jordan, Ruby Baker, Stephen Billington, Zeeba Sadiq, Mike Christie and Gabriel Gatehouse for help, advice and company while researching this book. Extra special thanks to Max Schaefer for comments and proofreading.

SARAH

Among others, thanks particularly to Max, Inkeri, Lou, Lisa, Peta, Martin – and Max the dog for taking me walkies past Alastair Campbell's (and scores of reporters) when my brain wouldn't function any more. On a more serious note, my sincere gratitude goes to RIBA President George Ferguson for taking time out of a busy schedule to talk to me.

OUR READERS

Many thanks to the travellers who used the last edition and wrote to us with helpful hints, useful advice and interesting anecdotes. Your names follow: Miho Aishima, Renata Alexander, Jane Allardice, Montse Basté-Kraan, Andre Berthy, Alison Blackbourne, Sarah Bonuomo, Francesco Borrelli, Clint Botha, Priscilla Bratcher, Bruce Breaden, A Bregman, Marcel Brulisauer, Vincent Brunst, John Vincent Burling, Gordon Callahan, Michelle Cassumbhoy, Andrea Cawley, Mona Chan, Mette Christiansen, Laurie Clamens, Sergio Conforti, Malcolm Craig, Donna Curry, Dave Dahms, Melissa Daniels, Sandra Dowd, Sharron Drinnan, Marietjie du Preez, Dianne Edlington,

S Edwards, Doug Eldred, Devin Farley, Kate Flood, Sandra Focken, Sandra Forde, Emma Foulger, Jimmy Franks, James Frey, Richard Game, D Gore-Harvey, Hugh Griffin, Karen Ha, Tricia Hammond, Paul Hanna, Stanley Hasegawa, Kerry Hawkins, Don Hershey, Keith Hughes, Andy Humphris, Jennifer Jameson, Nicklas Johansson, John Johnson, Robert Jones, Jason Kang, Warren Lear, Naryse Lechevalier, Norman Lee, Felicia Lim, Myra Loomer, Lawrence Manion, Jean Martino, Jon Milde, Linda Mills, John Moore, Frances Morrier, Suzie Muntz, Johanna Nilsson, Christina O'Callaghan, Virag Parkanyi, Vince Paul Jamie Pearson, Mary and Robert Perkins, Thomas G Power, Jerry Purcell, Kristin Redfern, Kathleen Reyes, Carlos Rivas, NW Rowan, Maeve Ryan, A Schneeberger, W Schuurman, Anna Shah, Jenny Sheffield, Duncan Shields, Pauline Simpson, Ben Smith, Christian Soelberg, Jamshid Soorghali, Tim Spanton, Cynthia Spencer, Anna-Maria Sviatko, Melissa Taylor, Patricia Teslak, Mohammad Tokhi, Wim Vandenbussche, Joan Vandewerdt, Niklas Varisto, Dag Eivind Vestbakkle, Neil Wallis, Ken Weingart, Andrew Wenrick, Mike Widener, Frank Weissbach, Ian Welbourn, Andrew Young, Ji Young

SEND US YOUR FEEDBACK

We love to hear from travellers – your comments keep us on our toes and help make our books better. Our well-travelled team reads every word on what you loved or loathed about this book. Although we cannot reply individually to postal submissions, we always guarantee that your feedback goes straight to the appropriate authors, in time for the next edition. Each person who sends us information is thanked in the next edition – and the most useful submissions are rewarded with a free book.

To send us your updates – and find out about LP events, newsletters and travel news – visit our award-winning website: www.lonelyplanet.com.

Note: We may edit, reproduce and incorporate your comments in Lonely Planet products such as guidebooks, websites and digital products, so let us know if you don't want your comments reproduced or your name acknowledged. For a copy of our privacy policy, see www.lonelyplanet.com/privacy.

Index

See also separate indexes for Eating (p408), Drinking (p409), Entertainment (p410), Shopping (p411) and Sleeping (p411).

000 photographs
000 map pages

Index

ENTERTAINMENT

Index

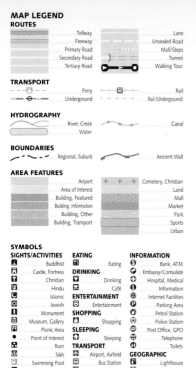

MAP LEGEND
ROUTES

Tollway
Freeway
Primary Road
Secondary Road
Tertiary Road

Lane
Unsealed Road
Mall/Steps
Tunnel
Walking Tour

TRANSPORT

Ferry
Underground

Rail
Rail (Underground)

HYDROGRAPHY

River, Creek
Water

Canal

BOUNDARIES

Regional, Suburb

Ancient Wall

AREA FEATURES

Airport
Area of Interest
Building, Featured
Building, Information
Building, Other
Building, Transport

Cemetery, Christian
Land
Mall
Market
Park
Sports
Urban

SYMBOLS
SIGHTS/ACTIVITIES

Buddhist
Castle, Fortress
Christian
Hindu
Islamic
Jewish
Monument
Museum, Gallery
Picnic Area
Point of Interest
Ruin
Sikh
Swimming Pool
Zoo, Bird Sanctuary

EATING

Eating

DRINKING

Drinking
Café

ENTERTAINMENT

Entertainment

SHOPPING

Shopping

SLEEPING

Sleeping

TRANSPORT

Airport, Airfield
Bus Station
Cycling, Bicycle Path
General Transport
Taxi Rank

INFORMATION

Bank, ATM
Embassy/Consulate
Hospital, Medical
Information
Internet Facilities
Parking Area
Petrol Station
Police Station
Post Office, GPO
Telephone
Toilets

GEOGRAPHIC

Lighthouse
National Park

Map Section

HAMPSTEAD & HIGHGATE

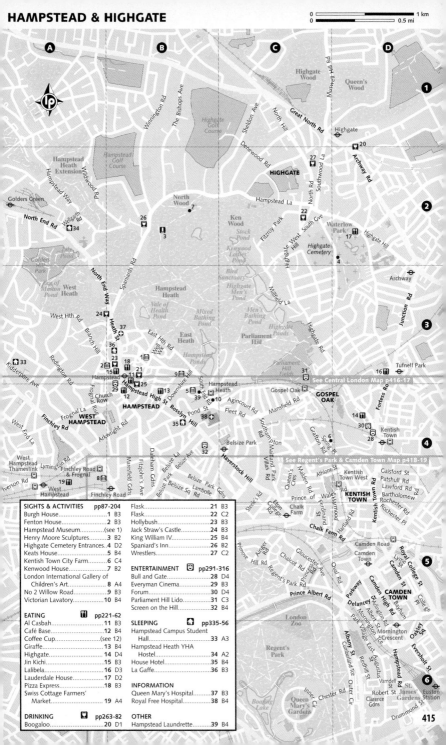

SIGHTS & ACTIVITIES	pp87–204
Burgh House	1 B3
Fenton House	2 B3
Hampstead Museum	(see 1)
Henry Moore Sculptures	3 B2
Highgate Cemetery Entrances	4 D2
Keats House	5 B4
Kentish Town City Farm	6 C4
Kenwood House	7 B2
London International Gallery of Children's Art	8 A4
No 2 Willow Road	9 B4
Victorian Lavatory	10 B4

EATING	pp221–62
Al Casbah	11 B3
Café Base	12 B4
Coffee Cup	(see 12)
Giraffe	13 B4
Highgate	14 D4
Jin Kichi	15 B3
Lalibela	16 D3
Lauderdale House	17 D2
Pizza Express	18 B3
Swiss Cottage Farmers' Market	19 A4

DRINKING	pp263–82
Boogaloo	20 D1

Flask	21 B3
Flask	22 C2
Hollybush	23 B3
Jack Straw's Castle	24 B3
King William IV	25 B4
Spaniard's Inn	26 B2
Wrestlers	27 C2

ENTERTAINMENT	pp291–316
Bull and Gate	28 D4
Everyman Cinema	29 B3
Forum	30 D4
Parliament Hill Lido	31 C3
Screen on the Hill	32 B4

SLEEPING	pp335–56
Hampstead Campus Student Hall	33 A3
Hampstead Heath YHA Hostel	34 A2
House Hotel	35 B4
La Gaffe	36 B3

INFORMATION	
Queen Mary's Hospital	37 B3
Royal Free Hospital	38 B4

OTHER	
Hampstead Laundrette	39 B4

See Central London Map p416–17

See Regent's Park & Camden Town Map p418–19

A B C D

1

Walm La
Shoot Up Hill
Willesden La
Kilburn
Brondesbury
48
Brondesbury
Park
Finchley Rd
WEST
HAMPSTEAD
West Hampstead
Thameslink
West
Hampstead
Finchley
Road &
Frognal
HAMPSTEAD
Hampstead
Heath
Gospel
Oak
GOSPEL
OAK
KENTISH
TOWN
Kentish
Town
Brecknock

See Regent's Park & Camden
Town Map pp418-19
Belsize Park
Belsize Park
Finchley
Road
Haverstock Hill
Kentish Town West
BELSIZE
PARK
Chalk
Farm
Camden
Road
Camden
Town

2

Harvist Rd
Kilburn High Rd
Kilburn
High Road
Kilburn
Kensal
Green
8
Queens
Park
Kilburn
Park
Maida Vale
Brondesbury
Park
KILBURN
Maida
Vale
MAIDA
VALE
St John's Wood Rd
Abbey Rd
ST
JOHN'S
WOOD
Wellington Rd
Avenue Rd
Prince Albert Rd
Primrose
Hill
London
Zoo
Regent's
Park
Boating Lake
Queen
Mary's
Gardens
Park Rd
CAMDEN
TOWN
Parkway
Mornington
Crescent
Albany St
Camden Rd
Kentish Town
Camden Town
Hampstead Rd
Everholt Rd
Warren
Street
Euston
Euston

See Hyde Park &
West London Map pp422-3
Warwick
Avenue
Marylebone
Baker
Street
Marylebone
Regent's
See The West End Map pp426-
Goodge
Street
Tottenham
Court Rd

3

Scrubbs La
Wood La
West
Cross
Route
Shepherd's
Bush
Goldhawk
Road
40
9
Ladbroke
Grove
Westbourne
Park
Royal Oak
Westbourne
Park Rd
Westway
Bishop's Bridge Rd
Praed St
Paddington
Sussex Gdns
Lancaster
Gate
Edgware Road
Marylebone
Edgware Rd
PADDINGTON
Gloucester Pl
Baker St
Oxford St
Oxford St
Bond
Street
Marble
Arch
Oxford
Circus
FITZROVIA
Tottenham
Court Road
Oxford St
SOHO
Piccadilly
Circus
Piccadilly
Circus
MAYFAIR
See Piccadilly & Soho
Map pp428
LADBROKE
GROVE
NOTTING
HILL
Ladbroke
Square
Gardens
BAYSWATER
Bayswater
Queensway
Notting
Hill Gate
Holland
Park
Holland
Park
Queensway
Bayswater Rd
Kensington
Gardens
Kensington
Palace
Green
The Long
Water
Hyde
Park
Park La
The Serpentine
Green
Park
Piccadilly
ST
JAMES
Pall Mall

Kensington
Church St
Kensington
Palace
Green
Rotten Row
Hyde Park
Corner
Grosvenor Pl
Buckingham
Palace
St James's
Park
St Jame
Park

KENSINGTON
Holland
Park
High Street
Kensington
Kensington Rd
KNIGHTSBRIDGE
Knightsbridge
Harrods
Brompton Rd

4

HAMMERSMITH
Hammersmith
15
Hammersmith
10
46
Holland Rd
Kensington High St
Kensington
(Olympia)
Warwick
Gdns
Cromwell Rd
Gloucester
Road
South
Kensington
SOUTH
KENSINGTON
Earl's
Court
Warwick Rd
Earls Ct Rd
Old Brompton Rd
Fulham Rd
Sloane
Square
Sloane St
BELGRAVIA
Eaton
Sq
Buckingham Palace Rd
Victoria
Belgrave
Rd
Vauxhall
Bridge
St James's
Park
Victoria
St James's
Park

Talgarth Rd
West
Kensington
Barons
Court
EARL'S
COURT
53
To Heathrow
Airport

5

BARNES
Wetland
Centre
FULHAM
24
Dawes Rd
Fulham Palace Rd
Lillie Rd
West Brompton
WEST
BROMPTON
Finborough Rd
Fulham
Broadway
WALHAM
GREEN
Parsons
Green
West Brompton
Gunter Grove
Fulham
Broadway
King's Rd
CHELSEA
Cheyne Wk
Battersea
Bridge
Albert
Bridge
Chelsea Embankment
Battersea Bridge Rd
Albert Bridge Rd
Chelsea
Bridge
PIMLICO
Pimlico
Pimlico Rd
PIMLICO
Grosvenor Rd
Battersea
Park
Battersea
Park Rd
Queenstown
Rd
BATTERSEA
NINE
ELMS
Nine El

6

Welland
Centre
3
Putney
Bridge
4
21
17
Putney High St
Thames
35
Wandsworth Bridge Rd
Parsons
Green
Battersea
Park
Queenstown
Rd
Wandsworth
Road
Latchmere Rd
Clapham
Junction
31
38
Lavender Hill
18
Cedars Rd
Long Rd
Clapham Common
Clapham
Common
CLAPHAM
28
51
41
19
25
23
Clapham
High
Stre
Clapha
Common

See Earl's Court & South Kensington Map pp436-7

Wandsworth
Common

SIGHTS & ACTIVITIES	pp87–204
Bethnal Green Museum of Childhood..1	G2
Freightliners Farm.....................2	E1
Fulham Football Club..................3	A5
Fulham Palace........................4	A6
Hackney City Farm....................5	G2
Hackney Museum......................6	G1
Jongleurs Bow Wharf..................7	H2
Kensal Green Cemetery................8	A2
Lamont Gallery.......................9	A3
London Ark Building..................10	A4
Ragged School Museum................11	H3
Stepping Stones Farm.................12	H3
Sutton House........................13	G1

EATING	pp221–62
Armadillo............................14	G2
Café................................15	A6
Crown Organic Pub...................16	H2
Del Buongustaio.....................17	B6
Drawing Room........................18	D6
Eco.................................19	D6
Little Georgia......................(see 14)	
LMNT................................20	G1
Ma Goa.............................21	A6
Mangal.............................22	F1
Pepper Tree........................23	D6
River Café.........................24	A5
Thyme..............................25	D6
Tsunami............................26	D6

DRINKING	pp263–82
Arch 635...........................27	E6
Bread and Roses....................28	D6

District............................29	G1
Dove Freehouse & Kitchen............(see 14)	
Eclipse (false position)............30	G1
Jongleurs Battersea.................31	C6
Lee Hurst's Backyard Comedy Club....32	G2
Royal Inn on the Park...............33	H2
Sand...............................34	E6
Ship...............................35	B6
So.uk..............................36	D6
White Swan.........................37	H3

ENTERTAINMENT	pp291–316
Battersea Arts Centre...............38	C6
Brockwell Park Lido.................39	E6
Bush Theatre.......................40	A4
Clapham Picture House...............41	D6
Hackney Empire.....................42	G1
Hackney Ocean......................43	G1
Mile End Climbing Wall..............44	H2
Pleasance Theatre..................45	E1
Po Na Na..........................46	A4
Rio Cinema.........................47	F1
Shepherd's Bush Empire..............(see 40)	
Tricyle Theatre....................48	B1
Unicorn Theatre for Children........49	E1

SHOPPING	pp317–34
Burberry Factory Shop...............50	G1
Oliver Bonas.......................51	D6
Ridley Rd Market...................52	G1

INFORMATION	
Charing Cross Hospital..............53	A5
Homerton Hospital...................54	G1

417

REGENT'S PARK & CAMDEN TOWN

SIGHTS & ACTIVITIES   pp87-204
Abbey Rd Zebra Crossing........1 B4
British Library..............................2 H5
Camden Market........................3 F3
Camley St Natural Park............4 H4
Entrance to London Zoo...........5 D4
Freud Museum..........................6 B1
Isokon Apartments....................7 D1
Jewish Museum.........................8 F3
London Central Islamic
  Centre & Mosque...................9 C5
London International Gallery
  of Children's Art...................10 A1
Percival David Foundation
  of Chinese Art........................11 H6
Petrie Museum of Egyptian
  Archaeology...........................12 G6
St Pancras New Church..........13 H5

EATING   pp221-62
Ali Baba...................................14 D6
Asakusa....................................15 G4
Bar Gansa................................16 F3
Café Corfu...............................17 F3
Café Delancey.........................18 F3
Castle's....................................19 G2
Cottons Rhum Shop,
  Bar & Restaurant..................20 E2
Diwana Bhel Poori House.......21 G5
El Parador................................22 G4
Engineer..................................23 E3
Lemongrass.............................24 G2
Mango Room...........................25 F3
Ravi Shankar...........................26 G5
Ruby in the Dust......................27 F3

SauCe..28 F2
Silks & Spice.............................29 F2
Taste of Siam............................30 F3
Terra Brasil................................31 H5
Thanh Binh...............................32 F2
Trojka..33 D2
Wagamama...............................34 F3

DRINKING   pp263-82
Bar Vinyl..................................35 F3
Bartok......................................36 E2
Belushi's Bar.............................37 F3
Black Cap.................................38 F3
Crown & Goose........................39 F3
Head of Steam.........................40 H5
Oh! Bar....................................41 F3
Pembroke Castle......................42 D2
Queen's...................................43 D3
Sir Richard Steele....................44 A5
Spread Eagle............................45 F3
Warrington Hotel....................46 A5
World's End..............................47 F3

ENTERTAINMENT   pp291-316
Barfly@the
  Monarch...............................48 E2
Camden Palace........................49 G4
Cecil Sharp House...................50 E3
Enterprise.................................51 E2
Hampstead Theatre.................52 B2
Jazz Café..................................53 F3
Lord's......................................54 B5
Open Air Theatre.....................55 E5
Place..56 H5
Underworld.......................(see 47)

SHOPPING   pp317-34
Sainsbury's Supermarket..........57 F3
Tower Records..........................58 F3

SLEEPING   pp335-56
66 Camden Square....................59 G1
Camden Lock Hotel..................60 E2
Crescent Hotel..........................61 H5
Euro Hotel..........................(see 61)
Euston Travel Inn Capital..........62 H5
Harlingford Hotel.....................63 H5
Hotels......................................64 G5
International Students House.....65 F6
Jenkins Hotel............................66 H5
John Adams Hall Student
  Residence.............................67 H5
Passfield Hall Student
  Residence.............................68 H6
St Christopher's Inn
  Camden...........................(see 37)
St Pancras International YHA....69 H5
University College Student
  Residences Office..................70 G6

TRANSPORT   pp376-84
Jenny Wren Cruises...................71 F2
London Waterbus Company......72 F2
Waterside Cafe....................(see 71)

INFORMATION
University College Hospital.......73 G6

OTHER
Forco Laundrette.......................74 F3
STA Travel.................................75 H5

KING'S CROSS & THE NORTH EAST

A **B** **C** **D**

1

Camden Park Rd
Marquis Rd
York Way
Market Rd
Caledonian Park
Brewery Rd
Blundell St
Agar Gve

Caledonian Road

Mackenzie Rd
Lough Rd
Sheringham St
Wentbourne St
Roman Way
BARNSBURY
Pentonville Prison
Bride St
Ellington St
Arundel Sq
Arundel Pl
Offord Rd
Furlong Rd
Highbury Corner
69
Highbury & Islington
Highbury Station Rd
Laycock St
Compton Ave
4
Canonbury Villas
78

2

68
Belitha Villas
Caledonian Road & Barnsbury
Huntingdon St
Barnsbury Park
Thornhill Rd
Bewdley Rd
Brooksby St
Barnsbury Sq
Lofting Rd
Barnsbury St
Ripplevale Gve
41
Liverpool Rd
Islington Park St
College Cross
58
108
ISLINGTON
81
6
Milner Sq
80
Florence St
Sebbon St
Halton Rd
25
Upper St

3

Pembroke St
Carnoustie Dr
Thornhill Sq
Hemingford Rd
Bingfield St
Havelock St
Bemerton St
Twyford St
Copenhagen St
67
Camley Garden St Natural Park
Camley St
Richmond Ave
Barnard Park
Cloudesley Rd
Barnsbury Rd
Cloudesley St
Cloudesley Pl
Gibson Sq
Theberton St
13
27
12
Almeida St
63
34
83
Cross St
72
22
31
42
86
23
77
Islington Green
26
St Peter's St

4

9
KING'S CROSS
Caledonian Rd
Carnegie St
Muriel St
Wynford Rd
PENTONVILLE
Chapel Market
82
52
White Lion St
Baron St
2
Dewey Rd
Ritchie St
Batchelor St
Tolpuddle St
Charlton Pl
30
21
Camden Passage
Duncan St
Gerrard Rd
Noel Rd
Devonia Rd
Colebrooke Row
Vincent Tce
Ella St
Angel
36
City Rd
Goswell Rd
Wakley St

York Way
Wharfdale Rd
48
Balfe St
Cheney Rd
King's Cross Station
90
11
Northdown St
Killick St
Cubitt St
Collier St
Cumming St
Donegal St
Cynthia St
Rodney St
Parton St
Pancras Rd
St Pancras Station
Midland Rd
Pentonville Rd
Penton Rise
Weston Rise
Mydelton St
Upper St
Islington High
Duncan Tce

5

British Library
Ossulston St
Euston Rd
King's Cross St Pancras
King's Cross Thameslink
76
97
100
St Chad's St
Argyle St
St Agnes Sq
101
Swinton St
Acton St
Frederick St
Leeke St
Britannia St
Wicklow St
Vernon Rise
Percy Circus
Gt. Percy St
Lloyd Sq
Lloyd Baker St
Amwell St
River St
FINSBURY
75
Rosebery Ave
Hardwick St
Myddelton Sq
Gloucester Way
Rawstone St
Spencer St
Percival St
Moreland
Hall St

6

Flaxman Tce
Bidborough St
Judd St
Hastings St
Thanet St
Sandwich St
Cartwright
Burton St
105
33
107
102
106
Tavistock
Marchmont St
Herbrand
Coram St
74
Brunswick Sq
Regent Sq
Cromer St
Harrison St
Sidmouth St
Ampton St
Cubitt St
ST PANCRAS
Woburn Pl
Bedford Way
BLOOMSBURY
Russell
Russell Square
St. George's Gardens
Heathcote St
Mecklenburgh Sq
St Pancras Coram's Fields
St. Andrew's Gardens
Gray's Inn Rd
Wren St
Calthorpe St
Margery St
King's Cross Rd
Phoenix Pl
Mount Pleasant
Rosebery Ave
Warner St
Eyre St Hill
Black Hill
Herbal Hill
Farringdon Rd
Easton
Exmouth Market
45
87
92
35
CLERKENWELL
29
18
79
Bowling Green La
Pear Tree La
Corporation Row
Compton St
Sekforde St
Aylesbury St
61
94
Clerkenwell Rd
Gt. Sutton St
93
39
15
1
Farringdon Rd
Clerkenwell Rd
St. John's La
Britton St
Turnmill St
Farringdon St
Skinner St
Spa Fields
Northampton St
Goswell Rd
Agdon St
Dallington St
Wharton St
Frederick St
Mydelton St

Guilford St
Gt. Ormond St
Lamb's Conduit
Millman St
Doughty St
3
Roger St
John's Mws
John St
Northington St
Theobald's Rd
Dombey St
Borwell St
Queen Sq
Portpool La
Leather Lane Market
Hatton Gdn
St Cross
Gt Ormond St

420

Harrow Rd

A **B** **C** **D**

1

Warrington Cres

Warw Aven

Wornington Rd

Elkstone Rd

St Ervan's Rd

Harrow Rd

Goldney Rd Maylands Rd Sutherland Ave Shirland Rd

Woodfield Rd

Clifton Villas

31 28
131
59

Senior St
Bourne Tce

Delamere Tce
Westbourne Tce

Grand Union Canal Westway

Ladbroke Gve Colborne Rd Bevington Rd Portobello Rd

66

2

Westbourne Park Alfred Rd

Royal Oak

127
61 Westbourne Park Villas

69
Porchester Rd

75

73

Tavistock Cres Great Western Rd

89
48

All Saints Rd Tavistock Rd St Luke's Rd Aldridge Rd Villas

Shrewsbury Rd Chepstow Rd

Kildare Tce Hereford Rd Alexander St Newton Rd

22 138
Bishop's Bridge Rd

Ladbroke Grove 19 65 21 18

63 Lancaster Rd Westbourne Park Rd Powis Gdns Talbot Rd

Westbourne Gve
49 24 34 52
107
35
Kensington Gdns Sq

Inverness Tce Queensway

3

25 82 92
44 96 86
95 71

Colville Tce Ledbury Rd Artesian Rd

Lonsdale Rd **NOTTING HILL**

118 62
30 116
93 54
17

Leinster Sq Prince's Sq Ichester Gdns

Moscow Rd St Petersburgh Pl

Porchester Gdns

64 85

Elgin Cres Arundel Gdns 91

Chepstow Villas Pembridge Villas

Pembridge Cres

58 39

Dawson Pl

32 113
124
Inverness Tce

Queensborough Tce

Leinster Tce

Porchester Tce

122 84

Ladbroke Gdns Stanley Gdns Stanley Cres 123

Pembridge Pl

114
138

BAYSWATER

Bayswater

Blenheim Cres Clarendon Rd

Kensington Park Gdns

Ladbroke Square Gardens

108 121
41 Pembridge Rd
Pembridge Gdns

Clanricarde Gdns Ossington St

Queensway

4

Lansdowne Rd Lansdowne Cres St John's Gdns Portland Rd Lansdowne Wk

Portobello Rd Kensington Park Rd

129 117

136 40
111
90 74
130

Kensington Palace Gdns Kensington Palace Mws

Ladbroke Tce Ladbroke Gve Hillgate St Aubrey Rd Campden Hill Rd

26 72
23 27
42
33

Notting Hill Gate

43

The Broad Wk

The Round Pond

53

Holland Park

Holland Park Ave Holland Park Mws Holland Park

68
Campden St
60

KENSINGTON

Campden Hill Rd Bedford Gdns Sheffield Tce Campden Hill

98
Vicarage Gate

Kensington Church St Brunswick Gdns Palace Gdns Tce

Kensington Palace

Kensington Palace Green

Palace Ave Palace Green

5

Addison Rd Abbotsbury Rd Aubrey Wk Aubrey Rd

Holland Park Duchess of Bedford's Walk Campden Hill Rd Hornton St Holland St

112

Opera Holland Park

16 70

Melbury Rd Holland Park High St Oakwood Ct Phillimore Gdns Argyll Rd Phillimore Wk

High Street Kensington

6

See Earl's Court & South Kensington Map pp436-7

Kensington (Olympia)

Holland Rd

Kensington (Olympia)

Olympia

Kensington High St

Wright's La

Fault St

Marloes Rd

Earls Ct Rd Allen St Kensington High St Scarsdale Villas

94 142 @ 135
141 140
134 50 6

5
St Alban's Gve
56
Stanford Rd Launceston Pl Victoria Rd Victoria Gve

Cornwall Gdns

422

HYDE PARK & WEST LONDON (pp422-3)

THE WEST END

A · B · C · D

1 · 2 · 3 · 4 · 5 · 6

Longford St

York Tce

Baker Street

York Gate

Oldbury Pl

Luxborough St

Nottingham Pl

Devonshire Pl

Marylebone Rd

Park Sq West

Park Square Gardens

Park Sq East

Euston Rd

Conway St

University St

Warren Street

Euston Square

Gower St

Grafton Way

Whitfield St

Tottenham Ct Rd

Gordon St

Huntley St

Torrington Pl

BLOOMSBURY

Taviton St

Tavistock Pl

Woburn Pl

Bedford Way

Woburn Sq

Gower St

Malet St

Montague Pl

Fitzroy Square

Park Cres

Great Portland Street

Chilton St

Baker St

Paddington St

MARYLEBONE

Beaumont St

Devonshire St

Weymouth St

Hallam St

Clipstone St

Howland St

Charlotte St

Goodge St

Whitfield St

Cleveland St

Store St

Store Street

Chenies St

Alfred Pl

Ridgmount St

Gower St

GOODGE STREET

Bedford Ave

Bloomsbury St

Store St

New Oxford St

Bucknall St

British Museum

Dorset St

Manchester St

New Cavendish St

Mansfield St

Hallam St

Duchess St

Great Portland St

FITZROVIA

Foley St

Langham St

Mortimer St

Riding House St

Great Titchfield St

Wells St

Berners St

Newman St

Rathbone Pl

Windmill St

Percy St

Gresse St

Rathbone Pl

Tottenham Court Road

Bedford Sq

Bloomsbury St

Adeline Pl

Tottenham Court Road

SOHO

Sutton Row

Giles High St

New Compton St

Moxon St

Marylebone High St

Aybrook St

Thayer St

Hinde St

Bond Street

James St

Spanish Pl

Manchester Sq

Duke St

Hinde St

Welbeck St

Wimpole St

Harley St

Chandos St

Cavendish Sq

Margaret St

Eastcastle St

Oxford St

Oxford Circus

Great Marlborough St

Noel St

Poland St

Berwick St

Marshall St

Kingly St

Beak St

Broadwick St

Lexington St

Wardour St

Dean St

Frith St

Greek St

Meard St

Old Compton St

Romilly St

Berwick Street Market

Brewer St

Great Windmill St

West St

Lisle St

Leicester Square

Flower Market

Charing Cross Rd

Portman Cl

Portman Sq

Portman St

Orchard St

Edward Mews

Bond Street

North Row

Green St

Lees Pl

North Audley St

Park St

Woods Mws

Upper Brook St

Culross St

Upper Grosvenor St

James St

Marylebone La

Vere St

Henrietta Pl

Brook St

Blenheim St

Dering St

Gilbert St

Binney St

South Molton La

South Molton St

Weighouse St

Brook St

Davies Mws

Grosvenor Mws

New Bond St

Maddox St

Avery Row

Grosvenor St

Oxford St

Conduit St

Savile Row

Old Burlington St

Clifford St

Boyle St

Cork St

Sackville St

Regent St

Warwick St

Glasshouse St

Piccadilly Circus

PICCADILLY CIRCUS

Denman St

Brewer St

Rupert St

Leicester Square

Irving St

Cranbourn St

Orange St

Whitcomb St

Panton St

National Gallery

Nelson's Column

Charing Cross Rd

Park La

Aldford St

South St

MAYFAIR

Grosvenor Sq

Carlos Pl

Mount Row

Adam's Row

Mount St

Farm St

Hill St

Charles St

Hay's Mws

Berkeley Sq

Bruton St

Bourdon St

Grafton St

Dover St

Albemarle St

Old Bond St

Burlington Arc

Vigo St

Bennet St

Arlington St

Duke St

Bury St

King St

Jermyn St

St James's St

St Alban's St

Haymarket

Charles II St

Cockspur St

Trafalgar Square

Leicester Square

Deanery St

South St

Hill St

Queen St

Charles St

Curzon St

Clarges St

Bolton St

Half Moon St

Stratton St

Green Park

Berkeley St

St James's

Ryder St

Pall Mall

ST JAMES'S

Charing Cross Station

Craig's Ct

Hyde Park

Serpentine Rd

South Carriage Dr

Park La

Hamilton Pl

Old Park La

Brick St

Down St

Hertford St

Piccadilly

Green Park

St James's Pl

Cleveland Row

Marlborough Rd

Stable Yard Rd

St James's Park

The Mall

Horse Guards Rd

Horse Guards Parade

Downing

Hyde Park Corner

Hyde Park Corner

Duke of Wellington

Constitution Hill

Buckingham Palace Gardens

Spur Rd

St James's Park Lake

King Charles St

Great George St

Knightsbridge

Wilton Row

Grosvenor Cres

Halkin St

Headfort Pl

Chapel St

Wilton Pl

Wilton St

Wilton Cres

BELGRAVIA

Motcomb St

Lowndes St

Chester St

Grosvenor Pl

Lower Grosvenor Pl

Royal Mews

Buckingham Palace Rd

Bressenden Pl

Eaton La

Allington St

Victoria St

Birdcage Wk

Old Queen St

Queen Anne's Gate

Dartmouth St

Tothill St

St James's Park

Broadway

Petty France

St James's Pl

Caxton St

Buckingham Gate

Catherine Pl

Palace St

Castle La

Howick Pl

Greycoat Pl

Artillery Row

Strutton Ground

Great Peter St

Old Pye St

Victoria St

Tufton St

Great Smith St

Broad Sanctuary

Dean's Yd

Chapel St

Chester Sq

Wilton Mws

Lyall St

Eccleston St

Hobart Pl

Belgrave Pl

Eaton Pl

Eaton La

Eaton Sq

Baker Street

Chiltern St

Dorset St

Blandford St

George St

Montagu Sq

Gloucester Pl

Seymour Pl

See Regent's Park & Camden Town Map pp418-19

See Hyde Park & West London Map pp422-3

See Piccadilly & Soho Map p428

See Earl's Court & South Kensington Map pp436-7

PICCADILLY & SOHO

0 ——————— 200 m
0 ——————— 0.1 mi

A **B** **C** **D**

BLOOMSBURY

1 Langham St

77

137

158
51
13

2 Great Portland St

80 124

134

164 70

84

129

168 94 Great Russell St
140 30 29
Hanway Pl
72 Hanway St 19
152 98 New Oxford Street
99 Tottenham Court Road 3
Falconberg Ct
91 St Giles
7 Soho Sq
Sutton Row

3 Princes St

149 Oxford St 172 57 173 123

102

133 162 59
131 122 Dârblay
68 144 143 117
128
21 2

136 58

161

56

89

Great Marlborough St Poland St

26 93 154
171 159 Manette St
113 151 139 73
49 Bateman
17 25
112 28 14 108 47
53 42 37
44 76 32
71 118 35 79
130 74

SOHO

39 60
119 78
146 23 55 81
104 130 74

4 St George St

132
138 75
83 85
125
145 64

Beak St
Golden Sq
40 65
69

Brewer St
87 82

38
105 100 110
90 92 66 15 27 36
103 11 160
116 106
12 163 Piccadilly Circus
Regent St 150 34
4 97 20 153 6
8 111 170 135
Piccadilly Circus

16 31
24 Lisle St
Gerrard St
36
160
110 Shaftesbury Ave
66
15 27
11 18 86
46 96 165 109
166 67 63 95
43
115 101 61 169

5 Grafton St 1
121 5
142
126 148
157 Royal Arc

54 41 156
33 120
Glasshouse St
Vigo St

Royal Academy of Arts 10

114 155

Piccadilly 141

6 Berkeley St

The Ritz St James's St

147
48

ST JAMES'S

See Covent Garden & Holborn Map p430

428

COVENT GARDEN & HOLBORN

COVENT GARDEN & HOLBORN

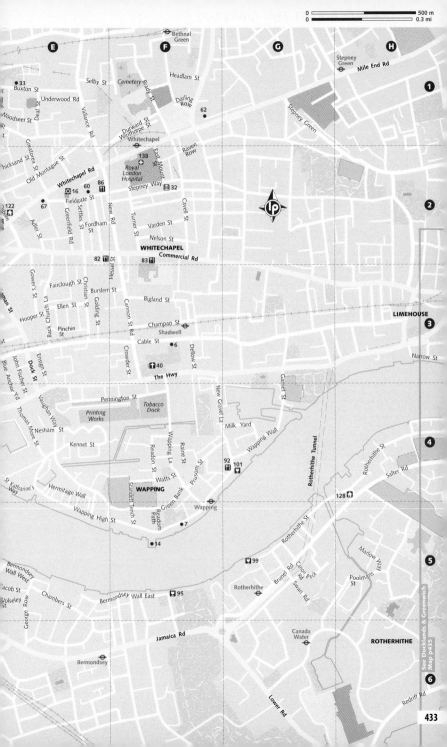

THE CITY & EAST END (pp432-3)

DOCKLANDS & GREENWICH

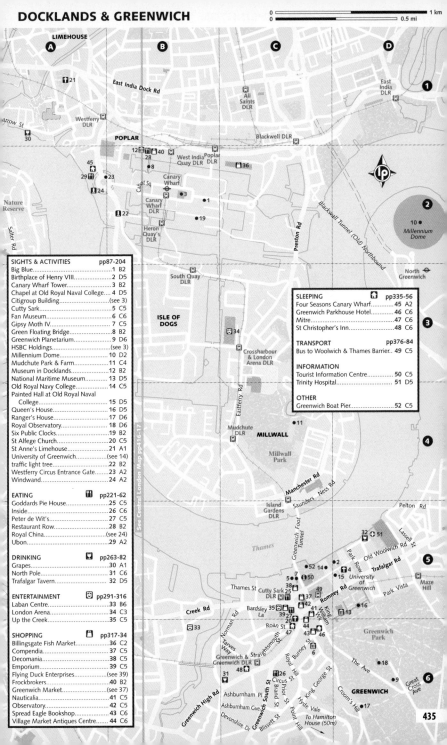

LIMEHOUSE
POPLAR
ISLE OF DOGS
MILLWALL
GREENWICH

East India Dock Rd
Blackwell DLR
Preston Rd
Blackwall Tunnel (Old Northbound)
Eastferry Rd
Manchester Rd
Saunders Ness Rd
Pelton Rd
Old Woolwich Rd
Trafalgar Rd
Park Vista
Maze Hill
Greenwich Park
The Ave
Great Cross Ave
Croom's Hill
Greenwich High Rd
Creek Rd
Norman Rd
Millennium Dome
North Greenwich
Nature Reserve
Millwall Park
Island Gardens DLR
Greenwich Foot Tunnel
Thames
Crossharbour & London Arena DLR

See Central London Map pp416–17

To Hamilton House (50m)

435

A B C D

1 2 3 4 5 6

Kensington (Olympia)

Kensington (Olympia)

Olympia

Oakwood Ct
Ilchester
Melbury Rd
Holland Park Rd
Holland Rd
Warwick Gdns
Warwick Rd
Pembroke Gdns
Pembroke Rd
West Cromwell Rd
Cromwell Cres
Logan Pl
Longridge Rd
Nevern Sq
Earl's Court Rd
Kensington High St
Edwardes Sq
Phillimore Gdns
Phillimore Wk
Wright's La
Allen St
Abingdon Villas
Scarsdale Villas
Pembroke Sq
Stratford Rd
Lexham Gdns
Cromwell Rd
Redfield La
Kenway Rd
Hogarth Rd
Templeton Pl
Trebovir Rd
Penywern Rd
Earl's Ct Gdns
Earl's Ct Sq
Collingham Pl
Collingham Rd
Courtfield Rd
Courtfield Gdns
Collingham Gdns
Harrington
Bramham Gdns
Bolton Gdns
Old Brompton Rd
Redcliffe Gdns
Coleherne Rd
Westgate Tce
Bolton
Pl
The Little Boltons
Harcourt
Tce

High Street Kensington
St Alban's Gve
Stanford Rd
Victoria Rd
Victor
43
105
123
118
114
103
108
72
126
128
19
75
121
46
124
99
59
97

EARL'S COURT
100
Philbeach Gdns
15
120
Eardley Cres
West Kensington
Barons Court
Talgarth Rd
Avonmore Rd
Hammersmith Rd
Edith Rd
Gunterstone Rd

Earl's Court
117
113
110
45
106
21
41
44
18
70
63
68
102

WEST BROMPTON
West Brompton
16
116
Lillie Rd
Ongar Rd
Seagrave Rd
Sedlescombe Rd
Tamworth St
Racton Rd
Anselm Rd
Halford Rd
Brompton Cemetery
Ifield Rd

Walham Gve
Farm La
Dawes Rd
Chelsea Village; Chelsea Football Club; Chelsea World of Sport
77
73
Vanston Pl
Fulham Broadway
Fulham Bdwy
Fulham Rd
92
24
22
Barclay Rd
Effie Rd
Harwood Rd
Waterford Rd
Moore Park Rd
Maxwell Rd
Britannia Rd
Holmead Rd
King's Rd
57
40
Michael Rd
King's Rd
Musgrave Cres
WALHAM GREEN
Eel Brook Common
Novello St
Acre Rd
Basuto Rd
Favart Rd
Crondace Rd
New King's Rd
Wandsworth Bridge Rd
Harwood Tce
Horde
Imperial Rd
1
Parsons Green
Fulham Palace Rd

EARLS COURT & SOUTH KENSINGTON (pp436-7)

RICHMOND

0 _____ 400 m
0 _____ 0.2 mi

Old Deer Park

To Twickenham
St Margaret's
(1 mi)

Twickenham   Rd
Richmond
Richmond
Green

7 🍺 Old Palace La

Cholmondeley
Walk

Thames

Corporation
Island

Willoughby Rd

Richmond Rd

King St   George St

Red Lion St
5 🛏   4 🍴
Water La

Thames Tow Path

To Ham
House
(1.6km)

To
Dysart

The Quadrant

Kew Rd
6 🍺
Richmond
🚉
3 🍴

Sheen Rd
Eton St

Paradise Rd

To Jim
Thompson's
(1.3km)

2 🍴
8 🏨

The Vineyard

Petersham Rd

The Richmond Hill

To Richmond
Park (800m)

SIGHTS & ACTIVITIES		pp87–204
Richmond Palace Remains	1	A2
EATING	🍴	pp221–62
Chez Lindsay	2	B3
Don Fernado's	3	B2
Kozachok	4	B2
DRINKING	🍺	pp263–82
The Old Ship	5	B2
The Orange Tree	6	B1
The White Swan	7	A2
SLEEPING	🏨	pp335–56
Richmond Park Hotel	8	B3

BRIXTON

0 _____ 400 m
0 _____ 0.2 mi

Stockwell Rd

10 🎭

Brixton Rd
3 🍴

Brixton   Station   Rd
Atlantic   Rd

Brixton 🚇
🚇 Brixton

Electric
Ave
Reliance
Arc

Electric La

Market
5 🍴
15 🛍

Coldharbour

Covered
Market

12 🎭

Brighton Tce

13 🎭

2 🍴

9 🍺

8 🛍 14 🛍
1 🍴

7 🍺 6 🍴

Railton Rd

11 🎭   Brixton Hill

Effra Rd

Acre La

Saltoun Rd

Kellett Rd

Porden Rd

4

EATING	🍴	pp221–62
Asmara	1	B2
Bamboula	2	A3
Brixtonian Havana Club	3	B1
Bug Bar	4	B3
Eco	5	B2
Fujiyama	6	B3
DRINKING	🍺	pp263–82
Dogstar	7	B2
Junction	8	B2
Plan B	9	B2
ENTERTAINMENT	🎭	pp291–316
Brixton Academy	10	B1
Fridge	11	A3
MASS	(see 4)	
Ritzy Cinema	12	B3
Substation South	13	A2
SHOPPING	🛍	pp317–34
Granville Arcade	14	C2
Joy	15	B2

439

VICTORIA & BATTERSEA

A   B   C   D

1   2   3   4   5   6

Buckingham Palace Gardens

Chapel St
Grosvenor Pl
Chester St
Wilton St
Upper Belgrave St
Lower Belgrave St
Eaton La
Grosvenor Gdns
Hobart Pl

Royal Mews

Lower Grosvenor

Bressenden Pl

Allington St

Belgrave Sq
W Halkin St
Belgrave Pl
Belgrave Mws
Eccleston Mws

28 Malcomb St
30

See Hyde Park & West London Map pp422–3

Lowndes St

Catherine Pl
Petty France   Tothill St
St James's Park
Buckingham Gate
Caxton St
Broadway

Palace St
Castle La

Broad Sanctuary

Old Pye St
Great Smith St
Monck St
Medway St
Marsham St
Horseferry Rd
Page St

WESTMINSTER

Strutton Ground
Artillery Row
Greycoat Pl
Greencoat Row
Rochester Row
Vincent St

Victoria St
Howick Pl

Ashley Pl
Morpeth Tce
Carlisle Pl
Francis St
Willow Pl
Gillingham St

Vincent Sq
Regency St
Chapter St
Douglas St
Causton St
John Islip St
Herrick St
Erasmus St

Westminster School Playing Field

38
42
48
44
56
57
14
3

35
58
54   59
49
18
17
40
24
53
39
23   46
55
25   19
8
26
36
52   47
32
51
27   20   16
43   22   45
44   9   50
5   29

BELGRAVIA

Eccleston St
Eaton Sq
Chester Sq
Elizabeth St
Ebury Mws
Eccleston Pl
Buckingham Palace Rd
Ebury St
Semley Pl
Cundy St
Ebury Bridge Rd
Ranelagh Grove
Ebury Bridge
Gatliff Rd

Eccleston Bridge

Bridge Pl

Gillingham St
Guildhouse St
Warwick Way
Eccleston Sq
Hugh St
Denbigh St
Clarendon St

Victoria Station

Victoria Coach Station

Elizabeth Bridge

PIMLICO

PIMLICO

Winchester St
Cambridge St
Alderney St
St George's Dr
Sutherland St
Cumberland St
Gloucester St
Charlwood St
Moreton Tce
Moreton Pl
Denbigh St
Lupus St
Tachbrook St

Belgrave Rd

Vauxhall Bridge Rd

Bessborough St

Pimlico

St Georges Sq
Dolphin Sq
Chichester St
Aylesford St

Pimlico Gardens

Clarendon St
Westmoreland Tce
Turpentine La
Peabody Ave
Claverton St
Johnson's St

Churchill Gdns Rd

Grosvenor Rd

Sloane St
Cadogan Pl
Cadogan La
Chesham St
Eaton Mws North
Eaton Mws
Eaton Pl
South Eaton Pl
Chester Row
Eaton Tce
Graham Tce
Bourne St
Holbein Pl
Ellis St
Sloane Tce
Sloane Sq
Cliveden Pl
Lower Sloane St
Sloane Gdns

Sloane Square

SLOANE SQ

Frank's Row
Turk's Row

Royal Hospital Rd

Pimlico Rd
Bloomfield Tce
St Barnabas St

CHELSEA

Chelsea Bridge Rd

Ranelagh Gardens

Chelsea Embankment

4

Chelsea Bridge

Queenstown Rd

Chelsea Bridge

See Earl's Court & South Kensington Map pp436–7

Carriage Dr North
Tennis Courts
Carriage Dr East
Duck Pond
Ladies' Pond
Boating Lake
Carriage Dr South

Children's Zoo

BATTERSEA
Battersea Park

Lurline Gdns
Prince of Wales Dr
Warriner Gdns

BATTERSEA PARK RD

Charlotte Despard Ave

Battersea Power Station
2

Cringle St

NINE ELMS

Nine Elms La
Ponton Rd
Stewarts Rd

Wandsworth

1
Havelock Tce
Battersea Park
21

Queenstown Road

440

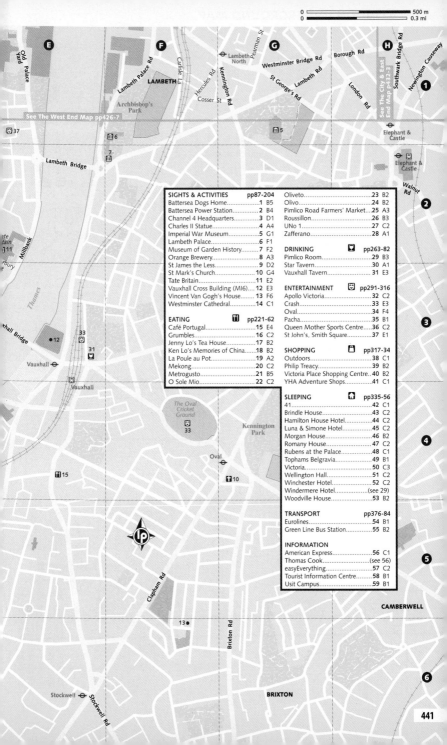

SIGHTS & ACTIVITIES pp87-204	
Battersea Dogs Home	1 B5
Battersea Power Station	2 B4
Channel 4 Headquarters	3 D1
Charles II Statue	4 A4
Imperial War Museum	5 G1
Lambeth Palace	6 F1
Museum of Garden History	7 F2
Orange Brewery	8 A3
St James the Less	9 D2
St Mark's Church	10 G4
Tate Britain	11 E2
Vauxhall Cross Building (MI6)	12 E3
Vincent Van Gogh's House	13 F6
Westminster Cathedral	14 C1

EATING pp221-62	
Café Portugal	15 E4
Grumbles	16 C2
Jenny Lo's Tea House	17 B2
Ken Lo's Memories of China	18 B2
La Poule au Pot	19 A2
Mekong	20 C2
Metrogusto	21 B5
O Sole Mio	22 C2
Oliveto	23 B2
Olivo	24 B2
Pimlico Road Farmers' Market	25 A3
Roussillon	26 B3
UNo 1	27 C2
Zafferano	28 A1

DRINKING pp263-82	
Pimlico Room	29 B3
Star Tavern	30 A1
Vauxhall Tavern	31 E3

ENTERTAINMENT pp291-316	
Apollo Victoria	32 C2
Crash	33 E3
Oval	34 F4
Pacha	35 B1
Queen Mother Sports Centre	36 C2
St John's, Smith Square	37 E1

SHOPPING pp317-34	
Outdoors	38 C1
Philip Treacy	39 B2
Victoria Place Shopping Centre	40 B2
YHA Adventure Shops	41 C1

SLEEPING pp335-56	
41	42 C2
Brindle House	43 C2
Hamilton House Hotel	44 C2
Luna & Simone Hotel	45 C2
Morgan House	46 B2
Romany House	47 C2
Rubens at the Palace	48 C1
Tophams Belgravia	49 B1
Victoria	50 C3
Wellington Hall	51 B2
Winchester Hotel	52 C2
Windermere Hotel	(see 29)
Woodville House	53 B2

TRANSPORT pp376-84	
Eurolines	54 B1
Green Line Bus Station	55 B2

INFORMATION	
American Express	56 C1
Thomas Cook	(see 56)
easyEverything	57 C2
Tourist Information Centre	58 B1
Usit Campus	59 B1

0 — 500 m
0 — 0.3 mi

LONDON UNDERGROUND MAP

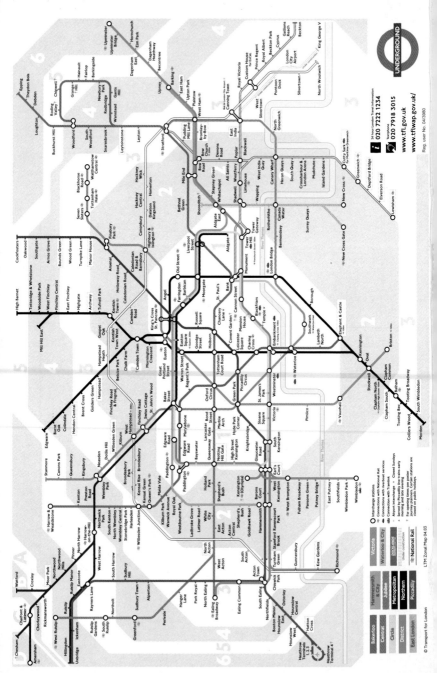